Therapeutic Recreation Practice:
A STRENGTHS APPROACH

Therapeutic Recreation Practice:
A Strengths Approach

by
Lynn Anderson and Linda Heyne

Venture Publishing, Inc.

Copyright © 2012

Venture Publishing, Inc.
1999 Cato Avenue
State College, PA 16801
Phone 814-234-4561; Fax 814-234-1651

No part of the material protected by this copyright notice may be reproduced or utilized in any form or by any means, electronic or mechanical, including photocopying, recording, or by any information storage and retrieval system, without written permission from the copyright owner.

Trademarks: All brand names and product names used in this book are trademarks, registered trademarks, or trade names of their respective holders.

Cover Design: StepUp Communications, Inc.
www.stepupcommunications.com

Library of Congress Catalogue Card Number: 2012951963
ISBN-10: 1-892132-96-6
ISBN-13: 978-1-892132-96-3

Dedication

*To our families,
whose love and encouragement have supported our aspirations
and enabled us to reach our goals and dreams.*

Table of Contents

Foreword: Cynthia Carruthers and Colleen Hood xvii

Preface: Cathy O'Keefe xix

About the Authors xxii

PART I: FOUNDATIONS OF A STRENGTHS-BASED APPROACH TO THERAPEUTIC RECREATION PRACTICE 1

Chapter 1: Introduction to Therapeutic Recreation Practice: A Strengths Approach 3
Introduction to the Strengths Approach 3
Overview of this Book 4
Chapter Structure 5
Chapter Features 5
   1. Compare/Contrast 5
   2. My Cultural Lens 5
   3. Primary Source Support 6
   4. Life Stories 7
Summary 8
Resources 8
References 10

Chapter 2: Paradigm Shifts – A Sea Change in Health and Human Services 11
The Sea Change Before Us 11
A Comparison of the Strengths-Based and Deficits-Based Approaches 12
Biological Support for the Strengths Approach 13
Social and Psychological Support for the Strengths Approach 15
Paradigm Shifts in Services 16
The Ecological Perspective: An Inherent Aspect of the Strengths Approach 19
Current Trends Pushing the Tide of Sea Change 19
Language in the Strengths Perspective 21
The Sea Change Affects People's Quality of Life and Well-Being 22
Summary 22
Resources 25
References 25

Chapter 3: A Sea Change in Therapeutic Recreation 29
A Sea Change in Therapeutic Recreation 29
Therapeutic Recreation in the Strengths Approach   Leisure, Well-Being, and Quality of Life at Our Core 29
   Leisure 30
   Well-Being 31
   Quality of Life 33
   Health and Functional Outcomes 35
Recreation as a Strength and as a Context in Which to Build Strengths 36
Purpose and Definition of Therapeutic Recreation—Why We Exist as a Profession 37
A Brief Review of the Existing Models of Therapeutic Recreation 41
   Continuum Models of Therapeutic Recreation 42

    The Leisure Ability Model 43
    The Health Protection/Health Promotion Model 44
    The Therapeutic Recreation Service Delivery and Outcome Models 45
    The Aristotelian Good Life Model 46
  Pitfalls in the Continuum Approach 47
  Integrated Models of Therapeutic Recreation 48
    The Self-Determination and Enjoyment Enhancement Model 48
    The Optimizing Lifelong Health through Therapeutic Recreation Model 49
    The Ecological Model 50
The Leisure and Well-Being Model as a Theoretical Framework for Strengths-Based Therapeutic
  Recreation Practice 50
  The Ultimate Outcome 51
  Conceptual Basis 51
  Scope of Therapeutic Recreation Services 52
    Enhancing the Leisure Experience 53
    Developing Resources 53
  Role of the Therapeutic Recreation Specialist 54
A Final Note about Therapeutic Recreation Definitions and Models 55
Therapeutic Recreation and the Sea Change 56
Summary 57
Resources 57
References 57

Chapter 4: Introducing the Flourishing through Leisure Model: An Ecological Extension of the Leisure and Well-Being Model 61

Our Definition of Therapeutic Recreation 61
The Flourishing through Leisure Model: An Ecological Extension of the Leisure and Well-Being Model 62
What the Therapeutic Recreation Specialist Does in the Flourishing through Leisure Model 63
  Enhancing the Leisure Experience 65
    Facilitation of Leisure Skills and Knowledge in the Participant 65
    Strengthening Environmental Resources to Enhance Leisure Experiences 68
  Developing Strengths and Resources 68
    Psychological and Emotional Domain 69
    Cognitive Domain 70
    Social Domain 71
    Physical Domain 72
    Spiritual Domain 74
    Summary of Developing Strengths and Resources 75
Outcomes the Participant Experiences in the Flourishing through Leisure Model 76
Summary 77
Resources 78
References 80

Chapter 5: Strengths—At the Heart of Therapeutic Recreation Practice 81

What are Strengths? 81
Internal Strengths 82
  Interests and Preferences 84
  Talents and Abilities 85
  Skills and Competencies 85
  Knowledge 86
  Aspirations and Goals 87
  Character Strengths and Virtues 87

  Virtue One: Wisdom 89
  Virtue Two: Courage 89
  Virtue Three: Humanity 90
  Virtue Four: Justice 90
  Virtue Five: Temperance 91
  Virtue Six: Transcendence 91
External Strengths and Resources 92
 Family Support and Involvement 93
 Social Support and Friendships 93
 Home Resources 94
 Community and Environmental Resources 95
 Opportunities for Participation and Contribution (Inclusive Communities) 96
 High Expectations and Positive Attitudes 97
Play, Recreation, and Leisure as Key Strengths 99
Meaningfulness of Strengths and Application to Therapeutic Recreation Practice 100
Summary 101
Resources 101
References 101

Chapter 6: Theories that Guide Strengths-Based Therapeutic Recreation Practice 107
What is Theory? Why is it Important? 108
Transition to Strengths-Based Theory 108
Part 1: Well-Being and the Individual 109
 Positive Psychology Theories 109
  Happiness 110
  Learned Optimism 111
  Flow 113
  Broaden-and-Build Theory of Positive Emotions 114
 Leisure Coping 116
 Self-Determination 118
 Self-Efficacy 119
Part 2: Well-Being and the Environment 120
 New Theories on Health and Disability 120
  World Health Organization Redefines Disability 120
 A New Theory of Health: Healthy People 2020 123
  Normalization and Social Role Valorization 124
  Social Role Valorization 127
 Social Support 128
  Consequences of a Lack of Close Relationships 129
  Friendship 129
 Community and Community-Building Theory 130
  Community Defined 130
  Social Capital Defined 131
  The Decline of Social Capital 132
  What Makes Community? 132
  Creating Livable Communities 134
  Circle of Courage 135
 Resiliency 136
  Resiliency in Children 137
  Resiliency in Adolescents 137
  Resiliency in Adults 137
Summary 138

Resources 138
References 139

Chapter 7: Principles that Guide Strengths-Based Therapeutic Recreation Practice 145
Principles Defined 145
Principles to Guide Strengths-Based Therapeutic Recreation Practice 145
    Principle 1: Every individual, group, family, and community has strengths...146
    Principle 2: Difficulties are also sources of challenge and opportunity..146
    Principle 3: We do not know the upper limits of a participant's capacity to grow and change—
        only the participant knows..146
    Principle 4: Collaboration (not expert domination) is the basis for our interaction with participants 147
    Principle 5: Every environment is full of resources 148
    Principle 6: Context matters 150
    Principle 7: Hopefulness matters 151
    Principle 8: Strengths can be nurtured—thus, they must be assessed, planned, focused on, and evaluated..........152
Meaningfulness and Application to Therapeutic Recreation Practice..154
Summary 155
Resources 155
References 156

PART II: THE THERAPEUTIC RECREATION PROCESS IN STRENGTHS-BASED PRACTICE 157

Chapter 8: Collaborative Practice in Therapeutic Recreation 159
An Overview of Teams and Collaboration 159
Why is a Team Approach Used in Health and Human Services? 159
Team Members in Health and Human Services 160
    The Participant and Circle of Support as Key Team Members 160
    Other Team Members...164
Team Approaches or Models..165
A Focus on the Transdisciplinary Team Approach 167
Collaboration and Networking as Important Competencies on Teams..169
Advocating for a Strengths Approach on the Team 172
    Language..172
    Focus..172
Summary 173
Resources 175
References 175

Chapter 9: Assessment in Strengths-Based Therapeutic Recreation Practice 181
An Overview and Rationale for Assessment 181
    Builds a Positive Relationship...182
    Establishes a Baseline..182
    Provides the Right Services...182
    Is Solution-Focused 182
    Supports Team Collaboration 182
    Meets Professional Standards of Practice..182
What is Assessment?...182
Principles to Guide Strengths-Based Assessment in Therapeutic Recreation Practice..184
Assessment Basics 186
    Assessment Characteristics 186
        Authentic Assessment 186

  Ecological Assessment...186
  Validity and Credibility 187
  Reliability and Dependability 189
  Fairness and Cultural Relevance 190
  Usability..190
  Standardization 190
  Criterion-Referenced versus Norm-Referenced 190
  Availability..191
 Using Assessment Characteristics to Choose Assessment Tools or Approaches..................................191
The Assessment Process...193
Assessment Techniques or Approaches 195
 Record Review 195
 Interviews..196
  Types of Interviews...196
  Phases of a Typical Interview 196
 Observation 197
 Standardized Assessment Tools and Measurement...201
 Ecological Assessment 201
 Arena Assessments...203
Assessment Focus..203
 Enhanced Leisure Experiences; Internal and External Strengths and Resources 203
 Outcomes of Well-Being and a Flourishing Life..203
Common Team-Based Assessments...205
 International Classification of Functioning, Disability and Health Checklist (ICF)......................205
 Functional Independence Measure (FIM) 207
 Minimum Data Set (MDS) 209
 Global Assessment of Functioning (GAF) 209
 Transdisciplinary Play-Based Assessment (TPBA) 209
 Strengths-Based Interviews 209
A Toolbox of Assessment Resources for Strengths-Based Therapeutic Recreation Practice........................211
 Internal Strengths 213
  Leisure Assessments 213
  Assessment of Leisure Interests, Preferences, and Passions 216
  Functional Assessments..218
  Assessment of Psychological and Emotional Strengths...218
  Assessment of Cognitive Strengths 219
  Assessment of Social Strengths 219
  Assessment of Physical Strengths..219
  Assessment of Spiritual and Psychological Strengths 221
 External Strengths 222
  Assessment of Leisure Resources 222
  Assessment of Functional Resources 222
 Assessment of Global Outcomes of Therapeutic Recreation Services...224
  Happiness and Well-Being...225
  Quality of Life: A Flourishing Life..225
Process for Assessment Selection 226
Final Thoughts on Assessment 226
Summary 228
Resources 229
References 233

Chapter 10: Planning in Strengths-Based Therapeutic Recreation Practice 237
An Introduction to Planning 237
Rationale for Careful and Collaborative Planning 238
- Focuses Attention on the Participant as an Individual 238
- Provides a Systematic Approach to Helping 238
- Assists All Staff in Understanding a Participant's Strengths and Goals 238
- Displays the "Road Map" 238
- Assures the Appropriate Services Based on Assessment Results and Careful Reasoning 238
- Increases the Likelihood of Success 238
- Assists in Documenting Outcomes 238
- Meets Professional Standards of Practice 238
- Empowers the Participant 238
- Inspires the Participant 239

The Link Between Assessment and Planning 239
Principles that Guide Strengths-Based Planning 240
Planning Process 241
- Determine Direction 241
- Determine Actions 244
- Determine Evaluation 244

Role of the Participant, Circle of Support, and Team in Planning 245
Types of Plans 246
- Comprehensive Team-Based Plan 246
- Discipline-Specific Plan 247

Not All Goals Are Created Equal 247
- Intrinsic Goals 249
- Authentic Goals 249
- Approach Goals 250
- Harmonious Goals 250
- Flexible and Appropriate Goals 250
- Activity Goals 250

Objectives 251
- Measurable Objective Key Element #1—Behavior or Action 252
- Measurable Objective Key Element #2—Criterion or Standard 253
- Measurable Objective Key Element #3—Condition 254

Linking Goals to Effective Actions and Strategies 255
Introduction to Activity Analysis as a Part of Planning 258
Documenting the Plan 259
Personal Futures Planning as an Example of the Planning Process in Action 259
Final Thoughts on Planning 265
Summary 266
Resources 266
References 267

Chapter 11: Implementation in Strengths-Based Therapeutic Recreation Practice 273
An Introduction to Implementation 273
General Implementation Principles 276
- Implementation Principle #1: Recreation is at the core of therapeutic recreation services 276
- Implementation Principle #2: The helping relationship is more important than technique 276
- Implementation Principle #3: Contextualized and authentic learning is rich and effective 278
- Implementation Principle #4: Wraparound services are desirable as they are person-centered and sustainable 278

Implementation Principle #5: Activity analysis and activity adaptation are effective tools to support other techniques and to enhance leisure 279
Implementation Principle #6: Advocacy and self-advocacy are important to initiate and sustain change......281
Implementation Principle #6: All interventions require thoughtful planning and delivery to increase effectiveness..281
Introduction to Implementation Strategies 285
Building Leisure Strengths and Resources 285
    Supporting Internal Strengths through Leisure Education 285
        Savoring Leisure 285
        Pursuing Authentic Leisure..285
        Increasing Flow and Leisure Gratifications..285
        Increasing Mindful Leisure 288
        Pursuing Virtuous Leisure...288
        Building Leisure Interests...290
        Building Leisure Knowledge 290
        Building Leisure Skills 291
    Supporting External Leisure Resources 293
Building Psychological and Emotional Strengths and Resources..293
    Supporting Internal Psychological and Emotional Strengths 293
        Cultivating Optimism 293
        Building Portfolios of Positive Emotions 295
        Acting Happy 296
        Enhancing Self-Determination 296
        Building Self-Advocacy...296
        Strengthening Coping Strategies..297
        Identifying Character Strengths and Virtues...297
    Supporting External Psychological and Emotional Resources..298
        Identifying Supporting Individuals and Groups..298
        Identifying or Creating Quiet Spaces in Public Places 298
        Building Positive Accepting Attitudes...298
        Enhancing Natural Cues to Support Learning...298
Building Cognitive Strengths and Resources 298
    Supporting Internal Cognitive Strengths..300
        Avoiding Overthinking 300
        Strengthening Goal Commitment 300
        Remembering or Reminiscing Positive Life Events 301
    Supporting External Cognitive Strengths and Resources 301
        Use of Environmental Cues to Enhance Learning and Orientation 301
Building Social Strengths and Resources 301
    Supporting Internal Social Strengths 301
        Practicing Acts of Kindness...301
        Social Skills Training to Nurture Social Relationships 301
    Supporting Positive Behavior—An In-Depth Look..302
        Assumptions of Positive Behavioral Support..302
        What Do We Mean by "Challenging Behavior"?..302
    Supporting External Social Resources 309
        Enhancing Positive Behavior in the Environment...309
        Enhancing Social Support..309
        Building Friendships 310
    Empowering Families in Leisure 312

    Parent-Professional Partnerships 312
  Enhancing and Building Community..313
    Asset-Based Community Development 313
    Cultural Shifting 315
    Five Commitments that Build Community 317
Building Physical Strengths and Resources 319
  Supporting Internal Physical Strengths 319
    Taking Care of the Body through Physical Activity 319
  Supporting External Physical Resources 320
    Universal Design 320
    Creating and Sustaining Livable Communities...322
Building Spiritual Strengths and Resources 323
  Supporting Internal Spiritual Strengths 323
    Learning to Forgive 324
    Expressing Gratitude 324
    Practicing Religion and Spirituality..324
    Practicing Meditation 324
    Clarifying Values, Goals, and Aspirations (Values Clarification)...325
    Using Character Strengths 325
  Supporting External Spiritual Strengths and Resources 325
    Building and Sustaining a Culture of Hope and High Expectations.......................................325
    Identifying and Supporting Nature-Based Activities 325
    Enhancing Beauty and Aesthetics in the Environment...325
Other Implementation Strategies Commonly Used in Therapeutic Recreation 326
Summary...327
Resources..327
References 332

Chapter 12: Transition and Inclusion in Strengths-Based Therapeutic Recreation Practice 337
Transition and Inclusion: A Common Purpose...337
Transition Services Defined...338
Transition Planning...338
  From Barriers to Solutions..339
  Transition Planning Process..340
  Documenting the Transition or Discharge Plan 340
  Transition Life Stories 341
Inclusion...341
  What is Inclusion? 341
  What Does Inclusion Mean Today? 344
  Rationale for Inclusion...346
  Inclusion as a Therapeutic Intervention 348
    Negative Outcomes of Exclusion 350
    Positive Outcomes of Inclusion 351
  Inclusion and the Therapeutic Recreation Process 352
    Assessment...353
    Planning 355
    Implementation 355
    Evaluation..355
  Quality Indicators of Inclusive Recreation...357
Summary...357
Resources..357
References 358

Chapter 13: Evaluation in Strengths-Based Therapeutic Recreation Practice.. 361
An Introduction to Evaluation 361
Evaluation in Therapeutic Recreation..362
    Formative versus Summative Evaluation...362
    Process versus Outcome Evaluation 365
Empowerment Evaluation in Therapeutic Recreation 365
Evaluating Individual Participant Progress..368
Documentation Basics..368
    What is Documentation?...368
        Referral..369
        Progress Reports or Notes 369
        Discharge Summary or End-of-Service Summary...372
    How Do You Document? 372
        Documentation Organization...372
        Writing Guidelines for Documentation 372
    Streamlining and Improving Documentation 374
        Electronic Records..375
        Checklists, Rating Scales, Flow Sheets, and Other Forms of Documentation 377
    When is Documentation Completed? 377
    Why is Documentation Important?..377
Evaluating Therapeutic Recreation Services or Programs at the Agency Level 380
    Program or Service Evaluation and the Use of Logic Models 381
    Quality Assurance and Performance Improvement Processes 382
Summary...385
Resources..386
References 388

**PART III: PROFESSIONALISM AS A STRENGTHS-BASED THERAPEUTIC
    RECREATION SPECIALIST...389**

Chapter 14: Advocacy in Strengths-Based Therapeutic Recreation Practice... 391
An Introduction to Advocacy...391
What is Advocacy?..392
Self-Advocacy..392
    Building Self-Advocacy 393
Advocating For and With Participants..398
    Individual Level Advocacy...398
    Systems or Community Level Advocacy 399
Advocating for Changes in the Participant's Environment 400
Advocating for a Strengths Approach 402
Advocating for the Profession of Therapeutic Recreation..403
    It Starts with You 403
    Self-Education..403
    Regular Communication with Decision-Makers 405
    Celebrate and Share Successes 405
    Network and Support 405
    Be a Play Expert 405
Balancing Advocacy..407
Summary...407
Resources..409
References 411

Chapter 15: Building Your Strengths as a Therapeutic Recreation Specialist **413**
An Introduction to Professions and Professionalism 413
What Does It Mean to be a Strengths-Based Professional? 414
    Strategy 1: Know and Use Your Strengths and Virtues in Practice 414
    Strategy 2: Know and Use Professional Ethics 417
    Strategy 3: Know and Use the Body of Knowledge 420
    Strategy 4: Know and Use Standards of Practice 424
    Strategy 5: Assure Your Competence to Others 424
    Strategy 6: Continue to Grow as a Professional 426
        Continuing Education 427
        Clinical Supervision 427
        Developing a Peer Supervision Group 430
    Strategy 7: Networking and Professional Support Systems 434
Limits of Professionalization 435
Giving Back to Society and the Profession 435
Being a Strengths-Based Therapeutic Recreation Specialist 437
Summary 438
Resources 438
References 443

Chapter 16: Looking Ahead **447**
An Overview of Looking Ahead 447
    Compare and Contrast: Deficits and Strengths 447
    My Therapeutic Recreation Philosophy 448
    My Definition of Therapeutic Recreation 448
    My Therapeutic Recreation Model of Practice 448
    Recreation as the Foundation of My Work 448
    Assessment of My Personal Strengths and Resources 448
    Myself as a Collaborator 448
    My View of the Therapeutic Recreation Process 448
    My Life Story 448
    Myself as a Strengths-Based Advocate 448
    My Professional Growth and Inspiration 449
    My Top Ten Resources 449
    My Letter from the Future 451
Final Thoughts from the Authors 451
References 451
Worksheets 452

Index 465

Foreword

One of the most fundamental questions you must ask of yourself as a future professional is "What will be the focus of my professional practice?" What you choose as your focus will determine what you see, what you do, and how you judge your effectiveness. When you first meet a client or program participant, will you see the person's problems first or their potential? Very importantly, based on what you first see, how will that focus influence your participants' perceptions of their own capacities and worth? Will you assist participants in their pursuit of a life of happiness, personal growth, and meaning? Will you help build a society where these outcomes are within their reach? Ask yourself also, what are your greatest hopes for your own life? Do have the same hopes for your participants? If you answered yes to these questions, *Therapeutic Recreation Practice: A Strengths Approach* will be an enormous help to you in acquiring the knowledge and skills necessary to build your own strengths-based therapeutic recreation practice.

Focusing on the facilitation of participants' strengths as your primary purpose, rather than the amelioration of problems, represents a paradigm shift, a different way of looking at practice, which is occurring in many professions. Historically, many health and human services professionals focused on the remediation of their participants' problems, believing that problem resolution was the path towards a rich and fulfilling life. True, there have been some individuals who have long argued for a focus on developing human potential. However, it wasn't until the last decade, when a group of prominent psychologists began to challenge psychology's narrow focus on the understanding, prevention, and treatment of illness and suffering, to the exclusion of the understanding and facilitation of optimal human and societal functioning, that a tipping point was reached. Martin Seligman, the leader of this new positive psychology, stated that "the time has finally arrived for a science that seeks to understand positive emotion, build strength and virtue, and provide guideposts for finding what Aristotle called the 'good life'" (2002, p. xi). His work sparked the interest and passion of multitudes of scholars and practitioners and has led to a sea change, a transformation, in the way psychologists understand, examine, and facilitate human strength and well-being.

Over the last decade, positive science research has experienced exponential growth and illuminated clearly the importance of positive emotion and experience, the cultivation and expression of personal strengths and virtues, and the connection of something greater than oneself to happiness and well-being. Of equal importance to positive science is understanding and developing the social systems and infrastructure that support the optimization of human potential. Like an avalanche, this paradigm shift in scholarship and practice has grown and expanded to impact the worlds of education, health care, human services, community development, business, government, and many others. The literature in these various fields is a robust, wonderful resource for therapeutic recreation professionals.

The field of therapeutic recreation has already been impacted by this sea change in health and human services, as well as by the research that emphasizes the centrality of positive emotion, personal growth, and meaning to well-being. While the therapeutic recreation profession has long articulated the value of understanding and appreciating the whole person, including strengths and limitations, our commitment to focus our professional efforts on facilitating the development and expression of participants' strengths and positive experiences has often been divided. However, the positive science literature and research has found its way into our field and is providing great support, direction, and energy to that commitment. Both experienced practitioners and students new to the field are flocking to conference presentations and workshops that articulate the value of positive emotion and experience (as so often embedded in the leisure experience) in helping participants recover, develop, or move toward a more meaningful life. Articles synthesizing research that supports the vital contributions of positive emotion and the cultivation of strengths to well-being are increasingly present in our literature. Paradoxically, positive science is discovering also that the same positive emotions, strengths, and life meanings that contribute to well-being prevent many of the problems that have historically been the focus of therapeutic recreation practice. Therapeutic recreation practitioners and participants alike have been empowered by this new paradigm, providing the impetus for a true transformation of the therapeutic recreation profession.

Therapeutic recreation, with its emphasis on the leisure experience, is ideally situated to use the concepts from positive science to directly impact the quality of life for all members of society regardless of ability or limitation. As Carruthers and Hood (2007) stated:

> The goal of [therapeutic recreation] is to build a positive spiral of emotion and action in clients that energizes and empowers them to take on increasingly greater opportunities and challenges in important, valued life domains successfully, further strengthening their positive beliefs, emotions and capacities. (p. 277)

This book, *Therapeutic Recreation Practice: A Strengths Approach*, formalizes and applies the concepts and empirical research arising from positive science to the practice of therapeutic recreation. Students, as well as practitioners, who immerse themselves in this book will be on the cutting edge of positive change in the articulation and delivery of therapeutic recreation services.

It is an exciting time to be engaged in therapeutic recreation practice. This book invites you to focus your professional effort on the empowerment of clients, to see them as reservoirs of hidden potential, and to help them shape their environments so that they can realize that full potential. As Sharry (2004) so eloquently stated, health and human service professionals "are invited to become detectives of strengths and solutions rather than detectives of pathology and problems, and to honor the client's expertise and capabilities as well as our own" (pp. 8–9). We wish you much joy as you cultivate your capacities in the delivery of strengths-based therapeutic recreation practice. We hope that you find the journey to be meaningful. You are in good hands.

Cynthia Carruthers, Ph.D., CTRS
University of Nevada, Las Vegas

Colleen Deyell Hood, Ph.D., CTRS
Brock University, St. Catharines, Ontario, Canada

References

Carruthers, C., & Hood, C. (2007). Building a life of meaning through therapeutic recreation: The Leisure and Well-Being Model, Part I. *Therapeutic Recreation Journal, 41*(4), 276–297.

Seligman, M. (2002). *Authentic happiness: Using the new positive psychology to realize your potential for lasting fulfillment.* New York: Free Press.

Sharry, J. (2004). *Counseling children, adolescents, and families: A strengths-based approach.* Thousand Oaks, CA: Sage.

Preface

> ## WELCOME TO HOLLAND
> by Emily Perl Kingsley[1]
>
> I am often asked to describe the experience of raising a child with a disability—to try to help people who have not shared that unique experience to understand it, to imagine how it would feel. It's like this...
>
> When you're going to have a baby, it's like planning a fabulous vacation trip—to Italy. You buy a bunch of guidebooks and make your wonderful plans. The Colosseum. The Michelangelo David. The gondolas in Venice. You may learn some handy phrases in Italian. It's all very exciting.
>
> After months of eager anticipation, the day finally arrives. You pack your bags and off you go. Several hours later, the plane lands. The stewardess comes in and says, "Welcome to Holland."
>
> "Holland?!?" you say. "What do you mean Holland?? I signed up for Italy! I'm supposed to be in Italy. All my life I've dreamed of going to Italy."
>
> But there's been a change in the flight plan. They've landed in Holland and there you must stay.
>
> The important thing is that they haven't taken you to a horrible, disgusting, filthy place, full of pestilence, famine, and disease. It's just a different place.
>
> So you must go out and buy new guidebooks. And you must learn a whole new language. And you will meet a whole new group of people you would never have met.
>
> It's just a different place. It's slower-paced than Italy, less flashy than Italy. But after you've been there for a while and you catch your breath, you look around...and you begin to notice that Holland has windmills...and Holland has tulips. Holland even has Rembrandts.
>
> But everyone you know is busy coming and going from Italy...and they're all bragging about what a wonderful time they had there. And for the rest of your life, you will say, "Yes, that's where I was supposed to go. That's what I had planned."
>
> And the pain of that will never, ever, ever, ever go away...because the loss of that dream is a very, very significant loss.
>
> But...if you spend your life mourning the fact that you didn't get to Italy, you may never be free to enjoy the very special, the very lovely things...about Holland.
>
>
>
> Copyright 1987 by Emily Perl Kingsley. All rights reserved.

Most of you who will read this text weren't born when this prose poem was written. You did not witness the pain experienced by families who unwillingly placed their loved ones in institutions for lack of treatment in their communities. You will not know the anguish of parents whose children were prohibited from attending school. Yet among those who faced obstacles were countless individuals whose stories of courage and resilience provided an incubator for this text. The poem selected for the opening page is an artifact of hope, evidence that long before a shift began to occur in the philosophy of treatment by professionals, families were finding their own voices.

The disability rights movement has, for the past 40 years, invited, cajoled, encouraged, and demanded that we recognize the positive force inherent in the energy of change, acknowledging the strengths and capabilities of people with disabilities. That change has healed a social blindness and is now yielding fruit. Much more progress is still needed, but what you can sense in the tentative but loving words of Emily Kingsley is the seed of a deep cultural shift. Each person's life is a gift. The journey through it should be a happy one.

You are about to read a carefully crafted and lovingly prepared text that can teach you to understand the right way of conceptualizing health-related services. Therapeutic recreation, just one of many service disciplines, brings wonderful assets to the table and is the focus of this text. But it is never meant to be seen in isolation, just as leisure is no isolated human need.

By the time you work your way through the ideas and strategies offered by the authors and all the sources they have culled for your benefit, I hope you will feel a sense of anticipation to begin your career of service, as Ms. Kingsley was to get off the plane and discover Holland.

Incidentally, I was happily surprised that she used recreational travel in the analogy about her child. As I read the poem, thoughts of Holland immediately drew me to those romantic windmills and breathtaking natural carpets of colorful tulips. At the same time, I am intellectually aware of the vulnerability of this low country to flooding. We understand its fragility, but we choose to go anyway, to enthusiastically embrace the adventure, to be optimistic and positive.

For those of us with family members who struggle daily to remain healthy, there are challenges, no doubt. On many days the air feels heavy with the mist of acute crises, pain, setbacks, and disappointments. But when the clouds part and we get a good view of the lovely world around us, there is no greater thrill than to be transformed by the journey. You will learn that one of the real treasures of that journey lies in the unique joy nurtured by recreation. Through it, we deepen the bonds of family, create precious memories, discover our interests, and express our talents. Recreation intrinsically moves the positive to the forefront. It transforms every environment and experience into a new and exciting venue.

I am profoundly grateful for the commitment made by the authors to this message and the effort they have made to bring knowledge and understanding to us. Our job now, as students and teachers, is to walk with individuals and families as partners in this transformative journey, recognizing that we will change, too, through the positive experience of that very accompaniment.

Catherine O'Keefe, M.Ed., CTRS
University of South Alabama, Mobile, Alabama

---

[1] Emily Perl Kingsley is a disability activist and the parent of a person with a disability. She has written for *Sesame Street* since 1970 and has won 17 Emmy Awards for her work. She was recently awarded the U.S. Department of Health and Human Services "Secretary's Highest Recognition Award—Entertainment Industry Award" for her work including people with disabilities on *Sesame Street*.

Acknowledgments

We would like to acknowledge the following people who have played a role in the development of this book:

Our mentors and colleagues whose insights and encouragement have inspired our work with the strengths approach in therapeutic recreation

Professionals in the field of therapeutic recreation, many of whom are already using the strengths approach in their practice

Participants in therapeutic recreation services, who have shown us the value of the strengths approach

Last, Katie Caulk (Linda's sister) and Cory Anderson (Lynn's son) for their beautiful artwork throughout the book

About the Authors

Drs. Lynn Anderson, CTRS, CPRP and Linda Heyne, CTRS have worked and studied in the field of therapeutic recreation for over thirty years. During those years, we have seen the field evolve, grow, and change. Involvement in that evolution led to our desire to write this book about a strengths approach in therapeutic recreation.

Dr. Lynn Anderson is a distinguished service professor in the Recreation, Parks, and Leisure Studies Department at the State University of New York at Cortland (SUNY Cortland). She is also the director of the Inclusive Recreation Resource Center, whose mission is to promote and sustain recreation participation by people with disabilities and other differences wherever they choose. Lynn has contributed numerous publications in the field and served in editorial roles with several journals. She has served as director of the Rural Recreation Integration Project, promoting inclusion through training and technical assistance. She also worked with Wilderness Inquiry, an award-winning adventure-based company that provides opportunities for wilderness experiences for people of all abilities. Lynn worked for several years as a therapeutic recreation specialist in a regional medical facility, serving people in psychiatry, addiction, pediatric, and physical rehabilitation programs. Currently, Lynn serves on the board of directors of Greek Peak Adaptive Snowsports, helping all people enjoy the winter environment. Through her work and research, Lynn has used a strengths approach, focusing on the dreams people have, and how strengths and resources can be mobilized to reach those dreams through the recreation experience. She loves to recreate with her husband, Dale, children, Kelly and Cory, and Kelly's husband Adam, pursuing passions like snowboarding, windsurfing, backpacking, kayaking, cross-country skiing, and other outdoor adventures.

Dr. Linda Heyne is a professor in the Department of Recreation and Leisure Studies at Ithaca College in the Finger Lakes region of New York. Along with her commitment to develop and disseminate information about strengths-based therapeutic recreation, her scholarly interests include inclusive recreation, socialization and friendship development between people with and without disabilities, therapeutic recreation in the schools, the Take Back Your Time movement, and an international perspective of the use of recreation for therapeutic purposes. She has authored many publications and delivered numerous presentations on these topics. She has also been an associate editor for the Therapeutic Recreation Journal for many years. Linda founded the inclusive recreation program at the Jewish Community Center of the St. Paul Area, which won several awards for its early inclusionary practices. She is a Fulbright Specialist and a consultant in inclusive practices. She is also a regular faculty member at the International Summer School for Wellbeing at HAMK University in Hämeenlinna, Finland. In her free time, Linda enjoys many leisure pursuits such as hiking, biking, playing music, contra dancing, attending theater, traveling, and being with her friends and family.

Part I

FOUNDATIONS OF A STRENGTHS-BASED APPROACH TO THERAPEUTIC RECREATION PRACTICE

Part I sets the stage for strengths-based practice.
It examines where we've been and where we're going in
therapeutic recreation, recreation, health, and human services.

"Deep in their roots all flowers keep the light."

Theodore Roethke
American poet

The Black-Eyed Susan signifies strength, positivity, and happiness.

Part I Overview

	Chapter 1	*Introduction*	This chapter familiarizes you with the strengths perspective, the need for this book, and the special learning features we use.
	Chapter 2	*Paradigm Shifts—A Sea Change in Health and Human Services*	A large and deep paradigm shift toward strengths is transforming health and human services. We describe it here on several levels—biological, psychological, sociological, and philosophical.
	Chapter 3	*A Sea Change in Therapeutic Recreation*	Therapeutic recreation is a part of the paradigm shift in health and human services. We reinterpret therapeutic recreation as a strengths-based profession.
	Chapter 4	*Introducing the Flourishing through Leisure Model: An Ecological Extension of the Leisure and Well-Being Model*	In this chapter we introduce the Flourishing through Leisure Model: An Ecological Extension of the Leisure and Well-Being Model, based on the Leisure and Well-Being Model originally proposed by Hood and Carruthers (2007)
	Chapter 5	*Strengths—At the Heart of Therapeutic Recreation Practice*	Here you'll learn what we mean by strengths: internal strengths, external strengths, and leisure as a strength to enhance well-being and quality of life.
	Chapter 6	*Theories that Guide Strengths-Based Therapeutic Recreation Practice*	We explain new and long-standing psycho-social theories that support strengths-based practice. Learn the reasons behind what we do in therapeutic recreation and why it is so important and effective.
	Chapter 7	*Principles that Guide Strengths-Based Therapeutic Recreation Practice*	This final foundational chapter distills the previous chapters into principles to guide you in your strengths-based practice.

Chapter 1
INTRODUCTION TO THERAPEUTIC RECREATION PRACTICE: A STRENGTHS APPROACH

The tulip emerges early in the spring—a harbinger of slow, deep change.

"Courage is not the towering oak that sees storms come and go; it is the fragile blossom that opens in the snow."
—*Alice M. Swaim, American author*

OVERVIEW OF CHAPTER 1

- Introduction to the strengths perspective
- Overview of the book content
- Overview of the learning features in the book
- Introduction to critical thinking, cultural competence, and the use of evidence-based practice as part of the competencies needed in therapeutic recreation practice in the 21st century

FOCUS QUESTIONS

- How does this book address a gap in the therapeutic recreation literature? In what ways is the approach different from past practices?
- What is cultural competence, and why is it important to develop?
- What is evidence-based practice, and why is it important?

INTRODUCTION TO THE STRENGTHS APPROACH

We grow up in a culture so ingrained in a certain way of thinking that we rarely are aware of that thought process and how it permeates all we do. In our society, one of those ingrained perspectives is the problem-oriented approach, which we apply to many situations in life. The small body of research that has looked at this issue shows that there is little relationship between being clear on the problem and finding viable solutions, yet we continue to feel we must start with what is wrong, not what is right or what we want to see happen. Imagine a world where we start with strengths, not problems, when we feel a desire to make positive change. Imagine our work if we focus on strengths when we want to increase any indicator of success, whether it be productivity, creativity, or other desired outcomes. Imagine a world where we look at helping other people by starting with their strengths, goals, and aspirations, not their problems. Instead of focusing on what is wrong, imagine a world where we focus on what is aspired to, what is dreamed about, and what is going well.

Slowly, other professions that help people and communities are reorienting themselves to this strengths perspective. New research in brain functioning provides concrete evidence that a positive orientation is far more effective. Therapeutic recreation, as a profession, has often touted itself as focusing on strengths in its practice approach. Yet our literature, though it talks about therapeutic recreation as the strengths profession, ends up in the familiar problem-oriented approach. The focus of assessments is to find needs and problems, the plan is grounded by a list of problems or needs, documentation is problem-oriented, and interventions are designed to address problems or deficits. Even though strengths are used as a tool to help people, they are not the focus of the therapeutic recreation process in most texts in our field.

We hope this book will address this gap in the therapeutic recreation literature. The book is based on the premise that the role of therapeutic recreation is to help people identify goals and aspirations (what they see as possibilities, what they want to have happen), and their accompanying talents, assets, interests, and capacities. We also see therapeutic recreation as identifying family, neighborhood, and community resources to support people in achieving their goals. Using a strengths approach, therapeutic recreation specialists help people link their aspirations to resources and supports, and they help them establish plans to reach their dreams. This approach is grounded in the idea that "goals related to problems" are not necessarily "goals related to solutions" in people's lives. Solutions are what people *want* to have happen, versus problems, which are what people *don't want* to have happen. Our hope is that the book will provide a healthy corrective to the entrenchment of our profession, and our society as a whole, in the ubiquitous problem-oriented approach we use almost without thinking.

Here is a challenge to you! Pay mindful attention over the next week, and see if you can increase your awareness of the extent to which your daily life, the institutions with which you interact (e.g., work, school, the nation, and even the world), are enmeshed in the problem-oriented approach. See if you can identify how often we start with what is wrong to improve a situation. See if you can envision a world where we focus on solutions, aspirations, and dreams to improve a situation! Perhaps the world, the nation, our neighborhoods, and our families could move more quickly to where we want to be if a strengths orientation is followed.

Here is an example, in one community, of the strengths approach at work. In a crime-ridden residential street in one of the worst neighborhoods in this city, someone, during the middle of the night, put green wooden chairs in the front lawn of every house. This person, whoever it was, was using a strengths approach in trying to make this neighborhood a friendlier, safer place. The chair-dropping act inspired many community residents, who came out, talked to each other for the first time in years, and resolved to be out in their yards a lot more. It is hard to be a criminal in a neighborhood when a hundred witnesses are out watching!

OVERVIEW OF THIS BOOK

Therapeutic Recreation Practice: A Strengths Approach is divided into three main sections. In Part 1, we provide you with a foundation of the strengths approach. Chapter 1 *Introduction* provides the framework and strategies for learning used throughout the book. Chapter 2 *Paradigm Shifts* sets the stage for the sweeping changes occurring in recreation, health, education, and human service systems. Social indicators and scientific support for the shift to a strengths-based approach are also presented. Chapter 3 *A Sea Change in Therapeutic Recreation* explores how the shift to a strengths-based ecological approach fits into therapeutic recreation practice, and how therapeutic recreation can flourish as a profession in the paradigm. Chapter 4 *Flourishing through Leisure: An Ecological Extension of the Leisure and Well-Being Model* introduces you to a model of therapeutic recreation practice that is based on the strengths perspective. Chapter 5 *Strengths* provides you with a structure and vocabulary to look closely at and understand strengths relevant to the practice of therapeutic recreation. Chapter 6 *Theories* provides an introduction to theories that guide a strengths perspective and are relevant to therapeutic recreation. Finally, Chapter 7 *Principles* overviews some fundamental guidelines for a strengths-based approach, which emanate from theory and philosophy.

Part 2 is the mainstay of this book. This section looks at the application of the strengths perspective to the therapeutic recreation process: assessment, planning, implementation, and evaluation. In Chapter 8 *Collaborative Practice* we help you understand the importance of collaboration in the therapeutic recreation process, the role of the participant and family in collaboration, and the roles of other professionals with whom you will work in the helping relationship. Chapter 9 *Assessment* provides you with a way to think about and conduct assessment from a strengths perspective to ensure authentic and meaningful practice. Chapter 10 *Planning* examines the link between assessment and planning, and the principles and practice of planning. Chapter 11 *Implementation* provides an overview of common interventions in therapeutic recreation, applied from a strengths perspective. Chapter 12 *Transition and Inclusion* provides a strengths approach to helping participants terminate your services and continue to pursue a meaningful, fully engaged life in their communities. Finally, Chapter 13 *Evaluation* describes the processes you will use in therapeutic recreation to document and evaluate the services you provide.

Part 3 of the book helps you as a professional establish and maintain yourself as a strength-based therapeutic recreation specialist. Chapter 14 *Advocacy* provides a framework and guidelines for advocating the strengths perspective, as well as advocating on behalf of the participants with whom you work. Chapter 15 *Building Your Strengths as a Therapeutic Recreation Specialist* stresses the importance of being well prepared in therapeutic recreation, from credentialing to clinical supervision to continuing education. And last, Chapter 16 *Looking Ahead* helps you put what you learn in this book into the context of your life as a professional in therapeutic recreation.

CHAPTER STRUCTURE

Each chapter in this book is structured to facilitate your learning of important concepts. As you read through each chapter, you will find each of the following sections:

- **Overview**—Provides a brief, bulleted outline of what the chapter will contain
- **Focus questions**—Offers questions that will help focus your reading on important or main points
- **Chapter content**—Divides the content into manageable sections, to help you learn the material more effectively
- **Summary**—Ends each chapter with a summary of the main points
- **Self-assessment of learning**—Asks you questions to help you assess your own understanding of what you read in the chapter, or provides exercises to help you apply the content to your own life
- **Resources**—Lists websites, workbooks, assessment tools, and other resources that help you apply the information in the chapter, or learn the material in more depth
- **References**—Allows further and deeper study in the content areas of the chapter and encourages you to access primary source materials

CHAPTER FEATURES

The chapters in this book also contain four different features to help you understand and apply the strengths approach in therapeutic recreation practice. The consistent use of icons will alert you to the features as you encounter them in each chapter. Each feature is described below.

1. Compare/Contrast

Because we are helping you learn a new way to think about and conceptualize therapeutic recreation practice, we provide frequent opportunities for you to compare and contrast the strengths approach to the commonly used deficits approach, so you may understand the differences more clearly.

The exercise of comparing and contrasting will encourage you to develop your critical thinking skills, essential for therapeutic recreation specialists in the 21st century (O'Neil & PHPC, 1998). Scriven and Paul (2007) define critical thinking as:

> Critical thinking can be seen as having two components: 1) a set of information and belief generating and processing skills, and 2) the habit, based on intellectual commitment, of using those skills to guide behavior. It is thus to be contrasted with: 1) the mere acquisition and retention of information alone, because it involves a particular way in which information is sought and treated; 2) the mere possession of a set of skills, because it involves the continual use of them; and 3) the mere use of those skills ("as an exercise") without acceptance of their results. (para. 5)

Rao, Shafique, Faisal, and Bagais (2006) further define the critical thinking skill of **comparing and contrasting** as the process of looking at similarities and differences to reveal important characteristics of each concept or idea. When we compare and contrast, we are able to see more clearly the important factors within each concept, see patterns, and draw informed conclusions. Comparing and contrasting, because it is often based on at least one concept with which we have familiarity, leads to a deeper understanding of what is being learned and discovered. Each chapter will provide opportunities for you to compare and contrast the strengths and deficits approach to working with people, in the context of the subject matter of that particular chapter.

2. My Cultural Lens

Each chapter in this book will provide you with opportunities to develop your own awareness and competence when working with people from diverse backgrounds. By the year 2050, those groups in the United States now considered minorities will be the majority. The largest growth in these population groups will occur as a result of immigration from another country, and likely another culture (U.S. Census Bureau, 2004). In therapeutic recreation practice, you will work with people from a variety of racial, religious, and cultural backgrounds. In order to be effective in your work in therapeutic recreation, it is imperative to develop cultural competence.

Cultural competence is defined as being able to work effectively with cultures other than your own by using a set of behaviors, attitudes, and policies that are congruent with that culture (Cross, Bazron, Dennis, & Isaacs, 1989). To break this down further, "culture" refers to integrated patterns of human behavior that include the language, thoughts, actions, customs, beliefs, and institutions of racial, ethnic, social, or religious groups. "Competence" implies having the capacity to function effectively as an individual or an organization within the context of the cultural beliefs, practices, and needs presented by people and their communities (American Association of Medical Colleges, 2005; Cross et al., 1989).

To become a culturally competent therapeutic recreation specialist, you must work through stages of development and be aware of where you are in those stages, as well as where your agency is. According to Williams (2001) and King, Sims, and Osher (2007), there are five stages of cultural competence development, along a continuum:

1. *Cultural destructiveness*—This is the most negative stage of the continuum, where attitudes, behaviors, policies, and practices are destructive or harmful to people and their cultures.
2. *Cultural incapacity*—In this stage, the individual or agency does not mean to be destructive to others and their cultures but does not have the capacity or awareness to meet different cultural needs.
3. *Cultural blindness*—At the midpoint of the continuum, the professional or agency provides services with the expressed intent of being unbiased. They function as if the culture makes no difference and all the people are the same. This is sometimes called "color blindness."
4. *Cultural pre-competence*—Individuals and organizations move toward the positive end of the continuum by acknowledging cultural differences and making documented efforts to take them into consideration.
5. *Cultural competence*—At the most positive end of the continuum, competence is indicated by the following practices:
    - acceptance and respect of cultural differences
    - continual expansion of cultural knowledge
    - continued cultural self-assessment
    - attention to the dynamics of cultural differences
    - adoption of culturally relevant service-delivery models to better meet needs

Our intent in each chapter, through the "My Cultural Lens" exercises, is to provide an opportunity for you to begin to develop an awareness of your cultural competency level and to make steps toward developing that level further. Our intent is also to stimulate you to pursue further experiences, training, and education that will develop your cultural competence over your lifetime. Here is your first "My Cultural Lens" exercise (see Figure 1.1).

> ### My Cultural Lens: Meanings of Leisure
>
> Yoshita Iwasaki and colleagues (2007) wrote a compelling reflection on the dominance of Western thought and terminology in global leisure research. They noted that the terms "leisure," "recreation," and "physical activity" do not have equivalent translations in Eastern languages and that the rough translations do not have the same intended meanings as how these terms are used in research studies and in the field. They argue that if we want to understand non-Western ideas of leisure-like phenomena, we should use a "life story" approach. In this approach, we would use prompts like "Tell us about your life" instead of "Tell us about your leisure and recreation." Iwasaki's premise is that in sharing their life story, people will share their leisure-like experiences, but through their own cultural lens.
>
> What is your definition of leisure and recreation? Would you describe your leisure as a part of describing your life story? Would your friends from other cultural backgrounds describe their leisure-like experiences differently than you do? How would they describe them?

Figure 1.1 My Cultural Lens: Meanings of Leisure

3. Primary Source Support

Each chapter will provide you with an opportunity to delve into original research that supports information provided in the chapter. In  a pull-out box, we will provide the primary reference, a summary of the research, and its results. By encouraging you to read and understand research, you will be on the path toward using evidence-based practice in the field of therapeutic recreation.

Evidence-based practice is a competency you will need to be effective in providing therapeutic recreation services (O'Neil & PHPC, 1998; Shank & Coyle, 2002; Stumbo & Peterson, 2004). **Evidence-based practice** is the integration of your individual practice experience with the best available external evidence when you are helping participants make decisions and implement plans for their leisure and well-being. For participants, using evidence-based practices means they can be confident that the therapeutic recreation services they receive meet the guidelines of best practices and are outcome-focused.

Evidence-based practice is based on systematic research results, data collected by your own agency, and judgments made by the participant and you. A key part of evidence-based practice is reading research on an ongoing basis and applying effective interventions from research into your own practice. Thus, the "Primary Source Support" feature is intended to help you not only get comfortable with the journals and research results available to you, but to expose you to new and relevant research findings from a variety of fields that have immediate application to a strengths-based approach in therapeutic recreation. Here is your first "Primary Source Support" feature (see Figure 1.2).

4. Life Stories

"Life Stories" are provided in many chapters to bring key concepts "to life." By hearing the stories of how individuals have used a strengths approach in their lives or how professionals have used the strengths approach in services, the concepts become more real and easier to understand. As authors, we have consciously avoided using the term "case" study or "case" story. A case is often conceptualized as a problem needing to be fixed, or a depersonalized collection of facts about a person. The phrase "life stories," on the other hand, conveys a sense of discovery about the humanness of another person, and what can be learned from her or his story. Some life stories we provide are based on real people we have met or with whom we have worked, while others have been provided to us by therapeutic recreation specialists working in the field, and still others come from current events, published research, or even the popular media. Some are about individual people, and others about agencies or systems.

In sum, the content and structure of this book will help you on the path to developing the competencies and ways of thinking you need to be effective in the therapeutic recreation field. The Pew Health Commission, in a seminal report in 1998, outlined those basic competencies. In Table 1.1, we have provided the list of the 21 competencies identified in exhaustive study and discussion over a 10-year period. Though focused more exclusively on "health care," the competencies have relevance to the delivery of all human services.

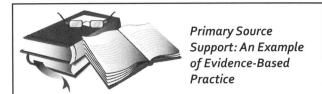

Primary Source Support: An Example of Evidence-Based Practice

Janssen, M. (2004). The effects of leisure education on quality of life in older adults. *Therapeutic Recreation Journal, 39*(3), 275–288.

Janssen (2004), by using an experimental design, studied the effects of a 6-week leisure education program on the perceived quality of life of older adults who resided in residential-style retirement facilities. The theory of quality of life, which guided the research and intervention, states that there is more to life than absence of illness, and that people's perceptions about whether they can enjoy the important possibilities in their lives across multiple domains will determine their sense of life satisfaction and well-being. Leisure is an important life domain that contributes to quality of life. In this study, Janssen facilitated a leisure education program that focused on leisure appreciation, awareness of self in leisure, self-determination in leisure, making decisions regarding leisure participation, knowledge and utilization of leisure resources, and leisure and quality of life. The results of the study showed that those older adults who participated in the leisure education program had higher levels of perceived quality of life (measured with the Quality of Life Profile) than those who did not participate. The older adults who received leisure education from the therapeutic recreation specialist felt they were better able to get out with others, pursue their hobbies, participate in indoor and outdoor recreation activities, and socialize with family and friends. All these factors contributed to a higher quality of life. Janssen provides a strong rationale for the connection between leisure education, self-determination, control, and quality of life.

Figure 1.2 Primary Source Support: An Example of Evidence-Based Practice

Through your active engagement with the material in this book, we hope you will gain a deeper knowledge of how to practice in the therapeutic recreation profession in ways that provide meaningfulness to you and to the people with whom you work. Using a strengths approach—focusing on broadening and building assets in natural settings—will have a profound and positive impact not only on the people with

Table 1.1 Pew Health Commission's Competencies for the 21st Century *(O'Neil & PHPC, 1998)*

1. Embrace a personal ethic of social responsibility and service.
2. Exhibit ethical behavior in all professional activities.
3. Provide evidence-based interventions.
4. Use a broad definition of health (multiple determinants).
5. Apply knowledge of the new sciences (such as brain research).
6. Use critical thinking, reflection, and problem-solving.
7. Understand the role of primary care (sustained partnerships in the context of family and community).
8. Help people and communities promote and protect their health.
9. Adopt a population-wide perspective on services.
10. Improve access to services for all people in a community.
11. Be relationship-centered when providing services for individuals and their families.
12. Provide culturally sensitive services.
13. Partner with communities and support choice and self-determination.
14. Use information and communication technologies effectively and appropriately.
15. Work in teams and across disciplines collaboratively.
16. Ensure services that balance individual, professional, system, and societal needs.
17. Practice leadership—develop partnerships and alliances across systems.
18. Take responsibility for quality—be accountable for your own competence and performance.
19. Help improve the quality of services at all levels—understand and use quality improvement and evaluation processes.
20. Be an advocate for policy that promotes and protects the health of the general public.
21. Continue to learn and grow; mentor and help others learn in your profession.

whom you work, but on yourself as well. Your passion for therapeutic recreation will grow, and you will be capable of doing the good you entered the profession to do. Enjoy your journey!

Summary

The introduction to this book provided you with an overview of the strengths perspective, an overview of the content and structure of the book itself, and an introduction to the learning features in the book. The learning features will help you develop the following areas:

- Critical thinking skills
- Cultural competence
- Habits of evidence-based practice

Resources

The National Center for Cultural Competence
http://www11.georgetown.edu/research/gucchd/nccc

Housed at Georgetown University, the National Center for Cultural Competence is focused on helping agencies and individuals improve cultural competence. The Center works within health care, human service, education, and advocacy systems. On its website, you will find numerous tools and resources to help you assess and improve your own cultural competence.

The Agency for Healthcare Research and Quality
http://www.ahrq.gov

A part of the U.S. Department of Health and Human Services, the Agency for Healthcare Research and Quality has as its mission the improvement of healthcare services for all. The website is a clearinghouse of research results that document evidence-based practice, across populations and settings. New research findings on topics from rural health to disability to health promotion are summarized each month. You can sign up for e-mail alerts, stay on top of cutting-edge research, and download podcasts on a wide variety of topics.

The Handbook of Multicultural Assessment

Published by Jossey-Bass in 2001, *The Handbook of Multicultural Assessment: Clinical, Psychological, and Educational Applications* (2nd ed.) provides a wealth of information on general assessment issues in relation to culture, as well as many tools and techniques to improve your own cultural competence.

The United Nations Cyberschoolbus
http://cyberschoolbus.un.org

The Cyberschoolbus website is a treasure chest of ideas, curricula, initiatives, and resources to promote its mission: global teaching and learning about diversity.

Self-Assessment of Learning

The "Assessing Your Experience with Other Cultural Groups" assessment is provided here to help you along the continuum of cultural competence. Take a moment to complete the self-assessment, and then share it with another student or co-worker. What did you learn about yourself and your environment? Where do you feel you are in your development of cultural competence?

> Assessing Your Experience with Other Cultural Groups
> (Adapted from Fleming & Towey, 2002, pp. 48–49)

People form impressions of others who are from different racial or ethnic groups than their own either by direct interactions or by indirect avenues, such as reading and the media. Interpersonal experiences with people from other cultural groups may exert a powerful influence on your comfort level as you interact with people from backgrounds that differ from your own.

Consider your early life with respect to school, recreation, neighborhood, religion, or other formative experiences. Think about the intensity of those experiences as they related to interactions with other cultural groups and rate them for each life area below.

When you have completed your ratings, add them together—the higher your score, the more direct interactions you have had with people who are different from you. Think of ways you can increase your score right now by increasing your interactions with people from other cultural groups.

Experience	Intensity		
	Limited (1)	Moderate (2)	Extensive (3)
Early school years			
Recreation/leisure			
Neighborhood			
Sports/athletics			
Music, theater, film			
College			
Work			
Travel			
Religion			
TOTAL:			

List specific situations that created uncertainty or discomfort.

_____
_____
_____

List situations that were enjoyable. Include references to food, music, dancing, and other leisure.

_____
_____
_____

REFERENCES

American Association of Medical Colleges. (2005). *Cultural competence education.* Washington, DC: AAMC.

Cross, T., Bazron, B., Dennis, K., & Isaacs, M. (1989). *Towards a culturally competent system of care* (Vol. I). Washington, DC: Georgetown University Child Development Center, CASSP Technical Assistance Center.

Fleming, M., & Towey, K. (2002). *Delivering culturally effective health care to adolescents.* Chicago, IL: American Medical Association.

Iwasaki, Y., Nishino, H., Onda, T., & Bowling, C. (2007). Leisure research in a global world: Time to reverse the Western domination in leisure research? *Leisure Sciences, 29,* 113–117.

Janssen, M. (2004). The effects of leisure education on quality of life in older adults. *Therapeutic Recreation Journal, 39*(3), 275–288.

King, M. A., Sims, A., & Osher, D. (2007). *How is cultural competence integrated into education?* Retrieved from Center for Effective Collaboration and Practice, http://cecp.air.org/cultural/Q_integrated.htm#def

O'Neil, E., & Pew Health Professions Commission (PHPC). (1998). *Recreating health professional practice for a new century.* San Francisco, CA: Pew Health Professions Commission.

Rao, M., Shafique, M., Faisal, K., & Bagais, A. (2006). Infusing critical thinking skill compare and contrast into content of data structures course. Las Vegas, NV: *Proceedings of International Conference on Frontiers in Education: Computer Science and Computer Engineering.* Retrieved from https://eprints.kfupm.edu.sa/14851/

Scriven, M., & Paul, R. (2007). *Defining critical thinking.* Retrieved from http://www.criticalthinking.org/about/centerforCT.cfm

Shank, J., & Coyle, C. (2002). *Therapeutic recreation in health promotion and rehabilitation.* State College, PA: Venture Publishing, Inc.

Stumbo, N., & Peterson, C. (2004). *Therapeutic recreation program design: Principles and procedures* (4th ed.). San Francisco, CA: Pearson.

U.S. Census Bureau. (2004). *U.S. projections by age, sex, race, and Hispanic origin. 2000–2050.* Retrieved from http://www.census.gov/population/www/projections/usinterimproj/

Williams, B. (2001). Accomplishing cross-cultural competence in youth development programs. *Journal of Extension, 39*(6). Retrieved from http://www.joe.org

Chapter 2
Paradigm Shifts: A Sea Change in Health and Human Services

The water lily has deep roots but floats easily on the waves, adapting to the ever-changing water.

"...it doth suffer a sea-change into something rich and strange."

—Ariel in *The Tempest* (William Shakespeare)

OVERVIEW OF CHAPTER 2

- An overview of the sea change in recreation, health, and human services
- A comparison of the strengths-based approach to the deficits-based approach
- Evidence that supports the strengths-based approach
- Paradigm shifts occurring in recreation, health, and human services
- The ecological perspective—an inherent aspect of the strengths approach
- Current trends influencing the sea change
- A new language—ways of communicating in a strengths-based approach

FOCUS QUESTIONS

- What is a sea change, and why is it important to be aware of this change?
- What is meant by the strengths approach? How does it differ from the deficits approach or medical model? How is the ecological perspective inherent in a strengths approach?
- What current research and trends support the shift to a strengths approach in therapeutic recreation and other helping professions?
- What ways of communicating best align with the strengths perspective?

THE SEA CHANGE BEFORE US

A definition of "paradigm":
A philosophical or theoretical framework; an overall concept accepted by most people in an intellectual community

A definition of "paradigm shift":
A change from one way of thinking to another; a transformation driven by agents of change

A definition of "sea change":
A fundamental and profound transformation

As noted above, a sea change is defined as a profound and substantial transformation. As in movements of the ocean, the change may be slow, large, and sometimes imperceptible in the moment. When we are able to take perspective over time, the large and transformative change becomes apparent and its radical nature can surprise us. As Ariel sings in Shakespeare's play, *The Tempest*, where the term was first coined, "... it doth suffer a sea-change into something rich and strange."

Recreation, health, education, and other human services are experiencing such a change. The change is in the paradigm shift from a problem- or deficits-oriented approach, to a strengths- or capability-based approach. Slowly, professions that help people and communities are reorienting themselves to a strengths perspective. The positive psychology movement, the focus on resiliency in youth development, the recovery model in mental health, and the asset-building approach in community coaching are four such examples of this reorientation. New research in brain functioning also provides concrete evidence that a positive orientation is far more effective in creating positive growth and change than is a focus on fixing deficits.

Therapeutic recreation is a profession that intersects all these delivery systems: recreation, health, education, and other human and community services.

It is a profession unique in its breadth of roles and settings and in its long history of focusing on the whole person. The profession is at a place in its development and history in which it can shift its practice and take a leadership role in the profound transformation to a strengths-based approach.

Therapeutic recreation helps people achieve well-being through the leisure experience and an individualized, purposeful process. Therapeutic recreation has often promoted itself as focusing on strengths in its practice approach. Yet, even though strengths may be used as a tool to help people, the development of strengths is seldom the primary focus of the therapeutic recreation process—the reduction of problems and barriers continues to be the focus. This chapter will help you clarify the differences between a strengths approach and the deficits approach that permeates the practice in our profession and many others. We hope you will gain a heightened awareness of the lens through which you view the people we serve in therapeutic recreation and will begin to see new possibilities for your work in the field.

A COMPARISON OF THE STRENGTHS-BASED AND DEFICITS-BASED APPROACHES

What do we mean by each of these approaches, strengths-based versus problem or deficits-based? The **problem-oriented** or **deficits-based approach** has as its main purpose the amelioration of problems through assessment and prescribed interventions. In the problem or deficits approach, we focus our assessments on what is wrong with the person. We develop a problem list, from which emanates goals and interventions. We work with the person, then, to fix the problems we have identified, using interventions focused on those problems. Our focus is on deficits, illness, distress, disability, poor functioning, or other negative states. We may use a person's strengths to help fix the problem, but the nature of the helping relationship is defined by problems.

In the **strengths- or capability-based approach**, the main purpose is to help people reach their goals and aspirations. We focus our attention, and our assessment, on what people want their lives to be like, and what resources and strengths they have or need to get there. Goals and interventions are driven by aspirations identified by the person, and we judge our success in the helping relationship by whether those goals are met. Strengths are the focus of intervention and change; weaknesses or problems are managed and given just enough attention so that they do not interfere with working toward goals. The strengths approach engenders a trusting working relationship, empowers people to take the lead on their own well-being, builds collaboration instead of expert domination, taps into people's personal sources of motivation, and sustains positive change through learning, growth, and capacity-building.

When we compare the strengths-based to the deficits-based perspectives, the differences between the two approaches become clearer. Figure 2.1 provides an opportunity for you to compare and contrast these two broad perspectives in helping professions. When contrasted, it becomes evident that a fundamental shift in thinking must take place to truly implement the strengths approach.

There are many assumptions that underlie both the deficits-based approach and the strengths-based approach to helping others. Contrasting the assumptions that ground the two perspectives further heightens our awareness of which perspective we are using as we interact and work with others (Saleebey, 2006). *Assumptions in the deficits-based approach* include:

- The participant is the pathology or the problem, and the participant needs to be fixed. In the deficits approach, problems or diagnoses take on "master status," which obscures or displaces other relevant information about the person.

- The relationship between the professional helper and the participant is marked by distance, power inequality, control, and manipulation. The professional helper holds the keys to successful recovery or rehabilitation.

- Context is stripped away. Getting clear on the participant's problem entails a reduction and simplification to make it manageable and measurable.

- Since disease, pathology, or disability is assumed to be the cause of the problem, eradicating it automatically becomes the solution. For example, in substance abuse treatment, a focus on alcohol (use or nonuse) is the overriding theme of most interventions.

Assumptions in the strengths-based approach include:

- Participants have aspirations and dreams. They may need help realizing those dreams.

- Professional helpers have strong hopes for participants, and that is shared openly.

Compare/Contrast:
The Deficits Perspective and the Strengths Perspective

From a Deficits Approach ...	To a Strengths Approach
Person is a "case" or a "diagnosis"	Person is unique, with talents and resources
Emphasis is on what is wrong, missing, or abnormal	Emphasis is on strengths, resources, capabilities, and adaptive processes
Intervention is problem-focused	Intervention is possibility-focused
Expert professional interprets the person's story to arrive at a diagnosis	The professional knows the person through the person's interpretation of events and meanings—not through the professional's interpretation
Trauma predicts pathology	Trauma may or may not contribute to strengths or weaknesses of the individual
The professional develops a treatment plan for the individual	Aspirations of the individual, families, and communities are the focus of the work to be done—the plan is developed in collaboration
Professional is the expert concerning the individual's life	Individuals, families, and communities are viewed as the experts
The skills of the professional are the primary resource for the work to be done	Help is focused on getting on with one's life, using the skills and resources of the person
Absence of illness or dysfunction is the goal	Well-being, thriving, and high quality of life are the goals
Medical model is used	Ecological model is used

Figure 2.1 Compare/Contrast: The Deficits Perspective and the Strengths Perspective *(Saleebey, 2006)*

- The relationship between the participant and the helper is marked by collaboration, equality, mutual respect, and confidence in each other's abilities.
- Context matters. The participant is viewed from an ecological perspective, where everything in the environment matters and has the potential to contribute to growth and adaptation.
- Since hopes and dreams are central to the helping process, they lead to solutions.

Utesch (n.d.) asks us:

Is the glass half empty or half full? The glass never changes. The observer has the option to see the glass differently and make a difference in how the glass will be perceived. When people are seen differently by helping professionals, they are given the opportunity to see themselves differently. Unlike glasses of water, people respond to their observers. (p. 7)

Instilling hope and building strengths are key to the effectiveness of the helping relationship, more so than those techniques that are focused only on deficit reduction. Dr. Martin Seligman, in his presidential keynote to the American Psychological Association, stated:

It is possible that building strengths produces a larger improvement for most disorders than the specific damage-healing moves. By working in the medical model and looking solely for the salves to heal wounds, we have misplaced much of our science and much of our training. (1998, p. 1)

Let's take a closer look at some of the science that supports the use of a strengths approach.

Biological Support for the Strengths Approach

What we focus on increases. This fundamental statement summarizes a key finding about cognition and the neurobiology of the brain. By integrating psychology (the study of the human mind and behavior) with neuroscience (the study of the anatomy and physiology of the brain), researchers have learned a great deal about how we think, feel, and act. This knowledge, gained by advances in technology like positron emission tomography (PET scans), functional magnetic resonance imaging (fMRI), and quantitative electroencephalography (QEEG), has given researchers physical evidence to link the brain as a functioning organ with the mind. How we think, feel, act, and perceive can now be physically observed, not just inferred. The integration of mind and body in science has been a fundamental advancement for understanding more deeply the human condition. There are four important breakthroughs from neurobiology and psychology that have relevance to the helping professions: a) change is difficult; b) focus is power; c) expectations shape reality; and d) attention density shapes identity. Rock and Schwartz (2006) have provided an overview of these important findings and their implications for those trying to facilitate positive change. A summary of their overview follows.

The human brain resists change. One thing neuroscience has shown us is that the human brain resists change. Because the brain is the control center for our thoughts, feelings, and actions, its resistance to change has a profound effect on how we live our lives. The brain's innate resistance to change is an important concept for those of us in professions where we focus on helping people change.

There are two main reasons for our resistance to change. First, the area of our brain that takes in new information and compares it to existing information, the working memory or prefrontal cortex, takes a lot of energy to use. This part of the brain can only handle so much information, and it attempts to take that information and "hardwire" it to a less energy-intensive part of the brain, the basal ganglia, where thought can occur without conscious effort. Any activity that becomes repetitive will get pushed to the basal ganglia, become a habit or automatic response, be incorporated into our existing "mental maps," and be much more energy-efficient. Trying to change the hardwired habits stored in our basal ganglia requires a lot of effort and focused attention, feels uncomfortable, and is avoided.

Second, our brain has a strong ability to detect errors—that is, differences between what we expect and what actually happens. When errors are detected, the brain fires off an intense neural response in the part of the brain associated with instinctual responses (the orbital frontal cortex and amygdala). When we try to change a habit or routine behavior (what we expect) with new behavior, these instinctual responses are activated, overpower the parts of the brain associated with more rational thought processes, and take control. This response makes change uncomfortable and stressful, and, when it happens, less higher-order brain functioning is at our disposal. What researchers have learned is that it takes focused, willful effort to make change happen (Schwartz, Stapp, & Beauregard, 2005).

Focus is power. A second fundamental finding for helping professionals is that focus is power. The act of paying attention creates chemical and physical changes in the brain. When we focus our attention on something, like a goal-oriented behavior or an aspiration, that concentration of attention maintains the brain state (i.e., the neural activity) associated with that experience. The new focus keeps the neural circuitry alive and dynamic, and eventually this circuitry becomes not just a chemical link, but a physical structure in our brains. In other words, our brains change as a function of where we put our attention. If we practice or think something everyday, we will literally have a different set of connections in our brain than people who don't practice or think the same thing. We will see the world differently, from a different perspective. And we will hardwire those connections, making them part of our routinized behavior. If we focus on *problems*, we will have hardwired mental maps of problems. If we focus on *desired outcomes*, we will have hardwired mental maps of desired outcomes. What we focus on increases.

Expectations shape reality. Related to the idea that focus is power is the important finding that our expectations and attitudes do, indeed, shape our reality. The idea of *hope*, discussed earlier, has a powerful neurological basis in the brain. Pain research has documented this clearly, showing that an *expectation* of reduced pain is as effective as a dose of morphine (Koyama, McHaffie, Laurienti, & Coghill, 2005). In other words, the old saying, "you get what you expect" actually has a neuroscientific basis. People experience what they expect to experience, whether at an unconscious or conscious level. The mental maps we have developed over time allow us to respond quickly, and sometimes without conscious thinking, to situations and events. The ability of our brains to predict what will happen next has had an evolutionary advantage. Yet, filtering all new experiences through what we already know and expect also creates a disadvantage. When we try to fit new information into our existing mental maps, our expectations are shaping and possibly distorting reality (see Figure 2.2, p. 16).

The effect of expectations on shaping reality has significant implications for using a strengths-based approach, for both the helpers and those seeking help. When helpers expect to see participants as full of potential waiting to be developed, as opposed to the deficits-based approach, where helpers expect to see participants as problems, different solutions or possibilities come into focus. When participants seeking help see their dreams and aspirations, not their problems, become clearer, different levels of possible change can happen.

Hardwired connections, or mental maps, stored in the basal ganglia, are hard to change. They become a part of who we are and how we respond to the world. However, replacing these mental maps can lead to large-scale changes in our behavior. What researchers have learned is that human brains have a great potential to continually grow and change, a potential called neuroplasticity. And this neuroplasticity can be initiated by each of us.

Attention density shapes identity. "Self-directed neuroplasticity" is the neuroscientific term given to the idea that we can change our brain structure by where we focus our attention. If we make the connections ourselves about the change that we want to occur (so-called *aha! moments* that are charged with neural energy), regardless of our genetics or past experiences, we will be more successful in changing how we think and act. Attention density is the amount of attention we give to a particular experience over time. The more we concentrate or focus on a specific idea, the higher the attention density, and the greater the likelihood that the idea will become a part of who we are and how we act. Over time, paying attention to new ideas or ways of thinking allows learning and change to happen and helps us become who we want to be.

Our role as helping professionals becomes one of helping people become clear about what they want and encouraging them (through various approaches) to focus their attention on that idea closely and for a long enough time to make change happen for themselves. Positive feedback and constant, willful attention are keys to creating new mental maps and thus changing our habits and behaviors. Mental maps formed around the problem, or routinized responses we don't want, will still be there, but as more cognitive energy goes into creating solutions and goals, the neural pathways that are entrenched in the problem become like an unused path, and are eventually pruned away, like dead branches on a tree. David Rock (2006) states, "We can leave the problem wiring where it is, and focus wholly and completely on the creation of new wiring. This is just what happens in the brain when we are solutions-focused" (p. 21). If we keep our focus on the neural pathways that are used to think about possibilities, those pathways will become routinized and firmly fixed in the network of mental maps we use to live our daily lives.

This overview gives you a very simplistic picture of how brain functioning supports a strengths approach. If what we focus on increases, as neuroscience tells us, then focusing on possibilities and preferred futures, instead of deficits and problematic pasts, makes sense in creating a life of well-being for the people we want to help. Rock (2006) sums it up like this: "We need to help people focus on solutions instead of problems. We need to give up our desire to find behaviors to fix, and become fascinated with identifying and growing people's strengths, an entirely other discipline" (p. 26). What we focus on increases!

Social and Psychological Support for the Strengths Approach

The breakthroughs in neuroscience complement transformative movements in the social sciences. The growth of positive psychology has especially contributed to the empirical development of the strengths-based approach to helping others. Over 50 years ago, Dr. Donald Clifton asked, "What would happen if we studied what is *right* with people?" (as quoted in Buckingham & Clifton, 2001). They stated:

> Guided by the belief that good is the opposite of bad, mankind [sic] has for centuries pursued its fixation with fault and failing. Doctors have studied disease in order to learn about health. Psychologists have investigated sadness in order to learn about joy. Therapists have looked into causes of divorce in order to learn about happy marriages. And in schools and workplaces around the world, each one of us has been encouraged to identify, analyze, and correct our weaknesses in order to be strong. This advice is well intended, but misguided. Faults and failings deserve study, but they reveal little about strengths. Strengths have their own pattern. (p. 3)

This question led to the study of human strengths in millions of people, through the work of the Gallup Organization. The roots of positive psychology thus firmly planted, the area of study began to flourish with the work of Csíkszentmihályi (1975) on flow and optimal experience, Seligman (1991) on optimism and happiness, Diener et al. (1985) on well-being, Bandura (1977) on self-efficacy, and others. In the 1990s, under Dr. Seligman's leadership, positive psychology began to take shape as a distinct area of study in psychology. According to Seligman (2002) and Peterson (2006), positive psychology has four pillars: the study of (a) positive emotion and experiences, (b) positive traits, (c) positive relationships, and (d) positive and enabling institutions. Positive psychology has helped us understand human goodness and excellence and how to nurture them. In essence, positive institutions facilitate the development and display of positive traits, which facilitate positive subjective experiences (Peterson, 2006). Positive psychology is about studying the "good life," or well-being.

One important outgrowth of positive psychology was the development of the *Handbook of Character Strengths and Virtues* (Peterson & Seligman, 2004). The *Handbook* was developed to carefully classify and describe human strengths, much like the *Diagnostic and Statistical Manual of Mental Disorders (DSM-IV)* was developed to classify and describe human dysfunction. The *Handbook* is described in more depth in Chapter 5 *Strengths*.

Positive psychology has increased our knowledge about important theories of human well-being and quality of life (discussed more fully in Chapter 3 *A Sea Change in Therapeutic Recreation* and Chapter 6 *Theories*). What researchers have learned is that having positive and engaging experiences (including leisure), feeling positive emotions, utilizing strengths, finding meaning and purpose in life, and contributing to positive institutions, whether at work or play, can lead to a life that is satisfying, health-producing, and long (Peterson, 2006; Carruthers & Hood, 2007). Positive psychology has also shown us that we can study and find evidence for the usefulness of different approaches in helping people feel happier and have more fulfilling lives, and that the application of findings of this research has a direct link to physical and emotional health. We now have methods and tools to understand human strengths more clearly. And as a result, the body of knowledge about the positive aspects of human existence is more fully understood. The idea of the "power of positive thinking" now has empirical support beyond the self-help pop culture, and its usefulness can help people change their lives.

Other social science disciplines, such as sociology, philosophy, and economics, have also been influenced by the strengths approach, whether it is through work in resiliency, the capabilities approach (Nussbaum & Sen, 1993), the ecological systems approach, or other

Primary Source Support: "What We Focus on Increases"

McGlone, M., & Aronson, J. (2006). Social identity salience and stereotype threat. *Journal of Applied Developmental Psychology, 27,* 486–493.

McGlone and Aronson (2006) studied the effects of what is called "stereotype threat" on the performance of women on math tests. The common societal stereotype is that women are not as good at math as men. The researchers' basic question was, "What if you prompted people to think about their strengths rather than their stereotypical weaknesses —would that be enough to improve performance in areas where they weren't supposed to do well?" Using an experimental design, the answer they found was yes. Prior to taking tests of spatial reasoning, some subjects were asked unrelated questions that prompted them to think about their gender. Women who were subtly prompted about their gender, in a way unrelated to math performance, did much worse on the test than women who were not prompted and men who were or were not prompted, underscoring how even subtle cues can affect behavior. When the subjects were prompted about their level of academic achievement (a prompt about attending an elite liberal arts college and no prompt about gender) women's scores were much higher, while men's scores stayed the same. The findings highlight how important it is to prompt positive thinking and strengths when working with people and not focus on problems and negative stereotypes. The researchers call this a focus on achievement identity versus ascribed identity.

Though the study did not investigate physiological brain functioning in relation to test-taking and social identity salience, the inference can be made—what we focus on increases!

Figure 2.2 Primary Source Support: What We Focus on Increases

theoretical perspectives. All have combined to provide support for the shift to a strengths perspective.

Paradigm Shifts in Services

Neuroscience and the social sciences provide support for shifting our focus to the positive. There are many examples of the paradigm shift in the services provided by recreation, health, and human service agencies. In areas such as youth development, mental health, developmental disabilities, independent living, and community development, many changes point to a move to the strengths approach in providing services. In the next few pages, we provide some examples to highlight the changes that are happening across systems, service settings, and disciplines.

The developmental asset approach in youth development. Resilience theory addresses the strengths that people and systems demonstrate that enable them to rise above adversity. Based on the theory of resiliency (discussed further in Chapter 6 *Theories*), the asset-building approach to helping youth thrive has become a common framework used in recreation and youth-serving agencies (Witt & Caldwell, 2005). Figure 2.3 gives a schematic overview of the developmental asset-based approach, where the focus of services is on promoting positive behaviors and quality of life to help young people reach their full potential (upper-right-hand quadrant in the figure). The Search Institute in Minneapolis, Minnesota, has articulated well-defined tools for the developmental asset-building approach, focused on both internal and external assets, with a goal of helping young people thrive. The 40 developmental assets are important for therapeutic recreation specialists to use in practice with all people, not just promising youth. At the end of this chapter, we provide an exercise to think about each of the developmental assets and how much they are a part of your own life (see Figure 2.4 for a cultural perspective of developmental assets).

The recovery model in mental health. The recovery model looks at people with chronic mental illness or

> **My Cultural Lens: Unique Strengths, Shared Strengths**
>
> Sesmo and Roehlkepartain (2003), in their study "Unique Strengths, Shared Strengths," asked these questions: "Are developmental assets important for healthy development for young people from *all* racial/ethnic groups, regardless of socioeconomic status? Does the importance of particular categories of assets vary across racial/ethnic groups?"
>
> They found that African American, American Indian, Asian American, Latino/Latina, White, and Multiracial youth **all benefited** similarly from experiencing more of the 40 developmental assets in their lives, regardless of their socioeconomic status. At the same time, the importance of particular categories of assets varied by race/ethnicity, suggesting the need for focused, ongoing dialogue within communities of color about their unique strengths and opportunities for nurturing healthy children and youth.
>
> What kind of dialogue is needed? What unique assets and opportunities exist in your own racial/ethnic group to build strengths? What about groups or communities other than your own?

Figure 2.4 My Cultural Lens: Unique Strengths, Shared Strengths

other mental health issues through a lens of hope and possibility. The recovery model is defined as "a recovery-oriented system of care that identifies and builds upon each individual's assets, strengths, health, and competence, and helps people to achieve a sense of mastery

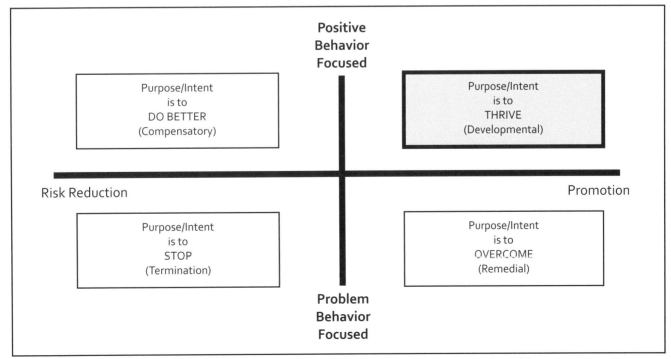

Figure 2.3 Framework for the Developmental Asset Approach in Youth Development *(adapted from Mannes, 2008)*

over their condition while regaining a meaningful, constructive sense of membership in the broader community" (U.S. Department of Health and Human Services Substance Abuse and Mental Health Services, 2005, p. 4). Essentially, the recovery model uses all the core techniques of therapeutic recreation. Ragins (2005) lists those techniques as (a) helping someone form a vision of their own recovery, (b) helping the person set goals, (c) assisting the person in forming emotional connections, (d) treating people with respect, (e) empowering people, (f) giving hope, (g) teaching self-management, (h) facilitating skills training and provide modeling in real settings, (i) building social networks, and (j) fostering community inclusion. In mental health services, the transition from a medical model to a recovery model has helped many people achieve a higher quality of life, despite their disability.

Best Friends Approach in Alzheimer's care. The Best Friends Approach (Bell & Troxel, 2003) is a way of providing support and care to individuals with Alzheimer's and their families. It is an approach based on a positive, optimistic view of individuals with Alzheimer's and their remaining capacities. The Best Friends Approach involves assessing remaining strengths, valuing basic rights, being a good friend, developing meaningful, authentic relationships, and knowing the person's whole life story. In the Best Friends Approach, the context of a person's life, their interests, and their remaining skills become part of the fabric of the daily activities facilitated by helping professionals in a dignified and caring manner. Based on the premise that being a friend means doing things together, the Best Friends Approach lays out what things should be incorporated into daily life with the individual with Alzheimer's (see Table 2.1). The focus on strengths, including friendship, helps maintain well-being.

Circles of Support, MAPS, and PATH in developmental disability services. Three strengths-based approaches used widely in developmental disabilities service settings are Circles, MAPS, and PATH (Falvey, Forest, Pearpoint, & Rosenberg, 2000). A Circle of Support (or Circle of Friends) approach helps to identify and strengthen the relationships in a participant's life, mobilizing that support toward the participant's dreams. MAPS (called either McGill Action Planning System, or Making Action Plans) is a process used by the circle of support to gather information about the participant and use it to develop a plan of action based on listening and dreaming. PATH (Planning Alternative Tomorrows with Hope) is a more sharply focused process that provides a detailed plan of action through eight distinct steps: touching the dream, setting the goal, grounding in the now, identifying people to enroll, recognizing ways to build strengths, charting action for the next few months, planning the next month's work, and committing to the first step. Chapter 9 *Assessment* and Chapter 10 *Planning* will provide more detail on these approaches and how to implement them in therapeutic recreation services.

Table 2.1 The Best Friends Approach in Alzheimer's Care – What Friends Do Together in the Strengths-Based Approach *(adapted from Bell & Troxel, 2003)*

A Best Friend....		
Involves the person in activities and chores	Initiates activities	Ties activities into the person's past skills and interests
Encourages the person to enjoy the simple things in life	Remembers to celebrate special occasions and is sensitive to traditions	Becomes the person's memory
Listens, speaks, and asks questions skillfully and with patience	Speaks using body language and touch	Gently encourages participation in conversations
Gives compliments often	Always offers encouragement	Offers congratulations
Tells jokes and funny stories and uses humor often	Takes advantage of spontaneous fun	Does not talk down to the person
Always works to protect the dignity of the person and helps them save face	Does not assume a supervisory or "bossy" role	Recognizes that learning goes both ways, and much can be learned from the person
Is not overly sensitive	Works at the relationship, and builds trust	Shows affection often

Community-based rehabilitation. According to the World Health Organization (2004), "Community-based rehabilitation (CBR) promotes collaboration among community leaders, people with disabilities, their families, and other concerned citizens to provide equal opportunities for all people with disabilities in the community" (p. 1). Community-based rehabilitation uses a social model of disability, instead of a medical model. In essence, disability is not seen just as a function of impairment, but also a function of the environment in which people live, work, and play. The environment can contribute to disability as much or more than individual functional ability. Community-based rehabilitation focuses on ensuring that people with disabilities have access to basic rehabilitation services in their community, and it equally focuses on building community capacity to include people with disabilities across all domains, from work to school to recreation. In addition, when a person with a disability participates in any rehabilitation or medical services, that person is an equal partner in the process of decision-making about services and outcomes. The Independent Living Movement is closely related to community-based rehabilitation, and both are strengths-based in their approach.

Community coaching in community development. We have given several examples of paradigm shifts in health and human services to a strengths-based approach. But this sea change extends beyond those services and into areas such as community development, education, and even business. One last example we provide is community coaching, in the area of community development. In this asset-building approach, community coaches establish relationships with community leaders and members and work to deepen their understanding of issues by creating opportunities for people to deliberate with one another about their circumstances. They then *reinterpret* these circumstances in ways that open up new possibilities for action and develop strategies and tactics that make creative use of the resources and opportunities that their circumstances afford (Cohen, 2005). Community coaching helps community members discover the assets and capabilities of their community, and helps them capitalize on those strengths. Through community coaching and community asset building, communities can become more inclusive and accessible to people with disabilities and other differences.

Examples abound of the sea change we are experiencing, as society moves from a deficit-oriented approach to a strengths-based approach. We hope the examples we have provided help you understand the significant differences between the two paradigms, and how those differences affect the way services are planned and provided. In Figure 2.5, we provide an overview of themes in service changes that are occurring in the sea change to a strengths approach.

THE ECOLOGICAL PERSPECTIVE: AN INHERENT ASPECT OF THE STRENGTHS APPROACH

A theme you can identify as you read about the characteristics, assumptions, and services of a strengths approach is the importance of the person in their environment. This is called an ecological perspective (Bronfenbrenner, 1979) and is based on the concept of an interdependent system where human beings are reliant on each other and their environments. In this system, the whole is greater than the sum of individual elements or people, due to the interaction and energy of relationships. "Environment" includes the micro, meso, and macro levels—from the home and family, to the neighborhood and community, to the nation and world. The whole includes not only people and their physical environment but also their policies, cultures, and norms.

Howe-Murphy and Charboneau (1987) provided an important contribution to the therapeutic recreation literature with the publication of *Therapeutic Recreation Intervention: An Ecological Perspective*. It is also a major aspect of the Flourishing through Leisure Model, which we introduce in Chapter 4.

The ecological perspective, using a strengths approach, asks therapeutic recreation specialists (and other helping professionals) to not only focus on helping individuals build strengths, but to help communities and systems also build strengths. This approach extends our scope of practice, and situates our profession firmly in the intersection of recreation, health, and human service systems.

CURRENT TRENDS PUSHING THE TIDE OF SEA CHANGE

There are many current and related trends that are part of the underlying paradigm shift to a strengths approach. One positive trend is our changing conception of disability. As noted above, the social model of disability is replacing the medical model. This is partly driven by a change in the way society views disability. Instead of seeing disability as damage, we see **disability**

Figure 2.5 Compare/Contrast: Deficit-Based Services and Strengths-Based Services

as a variation in the human condition. When disability is viewed as a variation in who we are as humans, we shift our "gaze" from one attribute of a person (the disability), which may be interpreted as marginalizing, to the whole person. Dieser and colleagues (2005) call this "gaze" the "observing power," and those who wield it are in positions of control and privilege. When we shift our gaze to the whole person in their environment and accept increased variation in the human condition, we widen the boundaries of what we consider to be part of mainstream culture. This broader and more inclusive view, in turn, empowers people. Dr. Patricia Deegan, a respected self-advocate in the mental health field, stated, "We don't want to be mainstreamed. We say let the mainstream become a wide stream that has room for all of us and leaves no one stranded" (as quoted in Rapp & Goscha, 2006, p. 28).

A related trend to viewing disability as a variation in the human condition is the trend toward **inclusion, contextualized learning, and the ecological approach**. People are receiving fewer and fewer institutionalized services, and more supports in real-life environments, like their own homes, their own communities, and their own friendship circles. The trend to provide services, supports, and learning opportunities in real environments has been called "in situ learning," "in vivo training," and "situational learning." It is an approach that is increasingly prevalent across service settings, from schools to rehabilitation programs. Inclusion and the ecological approach have allowed people to live full lives in their homes and communities, without having to gain "prerequisite skills" in "stepping stone" rehabilitation or therapy programs. This has given momentum to the strengths approach.

Related to inclusion and the ecological perspective is a trend toward **universal access and universal design**. Universal access and design is a movement to design environments, services, and products so they are accessible and usable by a broad range of people. Legislation like the Americans with Disabilities Act has provided impetus to universal design, and this, in turn, has facilitated inclusion. As we have seen people of all abilities working, living, and playing side-by-side in our communities, our perspective has shifted from a deficits to a strengths perspective.

Another major trend that has affected the sea change is a change in the way **medical services** are provided. The medical model and medical professionals have lost the monopoly once held over medical and health knowledge. People are taking a more active role in their own healthcare and have many more resources at their disposal to do so. For example, in a national study, researchers found a "tectonic shift" in the way people get and use health and medical information (Hesse et al., 2005). They found people use the Internet to get medical and health information for themselves and others at a much greater rate than they see a physician for that information. Further, shorter lengths of stay in hospitals are prompting people to find alternative ways to meet their health and rehabilitation needs in community-based programs and services that are not necessarily medical in nature. This, in turn, has prompted service systems, such as parks and recreation, to be more involved in health initiatives.

Parks and recreation have historically been linked to health (Wankel, 1994). Recently, however, the field has become even more involved in healthy-lifestyle promotion through initiatives like the Active Living Network (http://www.activeliving.org), a broad group of organizations that promotes active lifestyles and healthy communities through programs, parks, trails, fitness facilities, and other community resources. In a national study, Godbey and colleagues (1998) found that the majority of parks and recreation agencies, particularly at the local level, were engaged in providing health-promotion services at some level. And another review of more recent research (Ho et al., 2003) showed that trend increasing. Research into the benefits of physical activity on well-being has grown, and benefits extend not just to physical health, but to emotional health as well. John Ratey, a neuroscientist who studies how the brain and body respond to physical activity, explained the connection this way:

> In a way, exercise can be thought of as a psychiatrist's dream treatment. It works on anxiety, on panic disorder, and on stress in general, which has a lot to do with depression. And it generates the release of neurotransmitters—norepinephrine, serotonin, and dopamine—that are very similar to our most important psychiatric medicines. Having a bout of exercise is like taking a little bit of Prozac and a little bit of Ritalin, right where it is supposed to go. (Ratey, 2012)

As health has become "demedicalized," and the health benefits of recreation more researched, participating in parks and recreation opportunities becomes a strengths-based strategy to well-being.

LANGUAGE IN THE STRENGTHS PERSPECTIVE

"Language shapes reality" (Wilkins, 2012, p. 40). The language we use has a powerful effect on ourselves, on others, and on our cultural norms. For this reason, it is important to reflect on the language we use in our everyday and professional interactions and on what it conveys to the people with whom we work. Language reflects our beliefs and values, and we can shape and control it (Wilkins, 2012). How we talk and write about the participants with whom we work in therapeutic recreation can show respect, positivity, and accuracy. Language can instill hopefulness and a sense of possibility, or it can instill a sense of "handicaptivity," damage, and hopelessness (Deegan, 2006).

First and foremost, it is imperative that we use person-first language. In other words, we must always use the disability, disorder, or disease as an adjective only, if it is necessary at all. For example, we would never say, "I am going to meet with the hip replacement in Room 4." Instead, we would say, "I am going to meet the woman with the hip replacement in Room 4." Better yet, we would say, "I am going to meet Janet, the woman in Room 4." When using person-first language, we always use the person first, and then the descriptor, only if it is needed. The disability, disease, or disorder does not define who the person is—it is only one part of that person. Our language needs to reflect this level of sensitivity and accuracy.

Second, our language must be positive, strengths-based, and as free of professional jargon as possible. Let's look at an example to understand how language can convey or frame our expectations. Read through the description of the two girls in Table 2.2. These descriptions are from the work of Mayer Shevin (2003) and his poem "The Language of Us and Them." What do you notice about these two girls?

You may have noticed that these two girls are very much alike! But the language used framed them so differently. Jenny seems the "problem child," Sara the "normal kid"! As you work in therapeutic recreation, it is important to talk about people first, and with respect, positivity, and accuracy. As Carruthers and Hood (2007) stated, "If the language used with

Table 2.2 Meet Jenny and Sara *(adapted from Shevin, 2003)*

Meet Jenny.....	Meet Sara.....
Fixates on animals and lights/motion	Likes cats and playing computer games
Displays attention-seeking behaviors around peers	Likes to make friends
Displays off-task behaviors when fatigued at school	Works hard at school, but likes to take breaks
Is at times non-compliant	Stands up for herself when picked on
Displays self-stimulating behaviors	Has many hobbies that interest and absorb her
Displays poor socialization skills	Chooses her friends wisely
Perseverates	Shows perseverance
Has dependencies on others	Loves people
Runs away	Goes for walks
Has tantrums	Insists on having her way
Disoriented and short attention span	Changes her mind about things at times
Splinter skills	Talented in some areas

clients and others consistently reflects a strengths-based perspective of TR practice, it can transform the profession" (p. 278).

One final note on language. What do we call the people with whom we work in therapeutic recreation? In our practice, and in this book, we have chosen to use the term "participant," since it is action-oriented, engaged, positive, sensitive, and accurate. We have chosen *not* to use the term "patient," since it conveys helplessness, disease, and a strong linkage to the medical, deficit-based model. We have chosen *not* to use the term "client," since this word conveys a lack of expertise and a lack of ability to collaborate with the helper. In fact, a dictionary definition of the word states, "a dependent, one under the protection of another." We have chosen *not* to use the term "consumer," since this word conveys a materialistic, shallow purchase of services, which does not in any way capture the essence of a helping relationship developed in therapeutic recreation.

Other terms used by self-advocates that are empowering include "service user" or "individual with . . . [the disability, disorder, or need]." When you work with participants in agencies and settings, the culture of the setting may determine the language used. If it is not possible for you to change a culture where deficits-based language is used, then using the participant's name, instead of a label, is the best recourse for you to take.

THE SEA CHANGE AFFECTS PEOPLE'S QUALITY OF LIFE AND WELL-BEING

In this chapter, we have provided a broad overview of the changes occurring in recreation, health, and human services in the shift toward a strengths approach. We would like to close with a true story of a young woman who had a dream. Hilary Lister's story (provided in Figure 2.6) could be told through the lens of the deficits approach or the lens of the strengths approach. It is our hope that Hilary's story will bring to life the exciting possibilities that the strengths approach holds for the quality of life and well-being of people with disabilities.

SUMMARY

A sea change is a profound and fundamental change or shift in how we see the world. In recreation, health, and other human services, there is a sea change from a deficits or problem-oriented approach to a strengths or capability approach. The differences between the two approaches are significant and can be seen in not only the assumptions we make about people seeking help, but also in the way we conceptualize and deliver services. There is support for the strengths approach in neuroscience and the social sciences. Several trends underlie the movement toward a strengths approach, including a more positive view of disability and the more prevalent use of the ecological perspective. The language we use in our practice and interaction with people seeking help must align with the strengths approach.

Now that you have read about the strengths movement across health, human, and recreation services, in the next chapter we turn to the profession of therapeutic recreation and how it fits within this sea change.

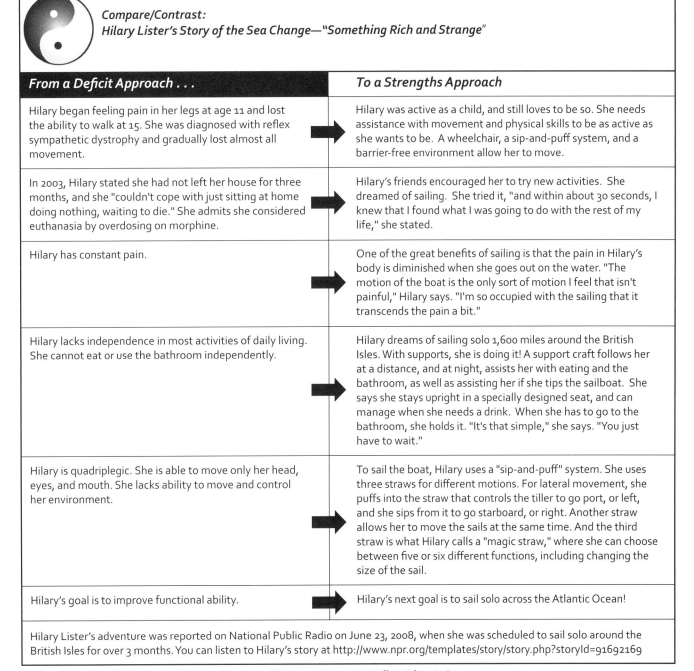

Figure 2.6 Compare/Contrast: Hilary Lister's Story

Self-Assessment of Learning

One of the initiatives we discussed in this chapter, the promotion of developmental assets to strengthen youth and communities, has at its core the identification and nurturing of 40 developmental assets. Below, identify the top 10 developmental assets that are present in your own life, based on the list developed by the Search Institute (2006).

EXTERNAL ASSETS

SUPPORT

1. Family support—Family life provides high levels of love and support.
2. Positive family communication—Young person and her or his parent(s) communicate positively, and young person is willing to seek advice and counsel from parents.
3. Other adult relationships—Young person receives support from three or more non-parent adults.
4. Caring neighborhood—Young person experiences caring neighbors.
5. Caring school climate—School provides a caring, encouraging environment.
6. Parent involvement in schooling—Parent(s) are actively involved in helping young person succeed in school.

EMPOWERMENT

7. Community values youth—Adults in the community value youth.
8. Youth as resources—Young people are given useful roles in the community.
9. Service to others—Young person serves in the community one hour or more per week.
10. Safety—Young person feels safe at home, school, and in the neighborhood.

BOUNDARIES AND EXPECTATIONS

11. Family boundaries—Family has clear rules and consequences and monitors the young person's whereabouts.
12. School boundaries—School provides clear rules and consequences.
13. Neighborhood boundaries—Neighbors take responsibility for monitoring young people's behavior.
14. Adult role models—Parent(s) and other adults model positive, responsible behavior.
15. Positive peer influence—Young person's best friends model responsible behavior.
16. High expectations—Both parent(s) and teachers encourage the young person to do well.

CONSTRUCTIVE USE OF TIME

17. Creative activities—Young person spends three or more hours per week in lessons or practice in music, theater, or other arts.
18. Youth programs—Young person spends three or more hours per week in sports, clubs, or organizations at school and/or in the community.
19. Religious community—Young person spends one or more hours per week in activities in a religious institution.
20. Time at home—Young person is out with friends "with nothing special to do" two or fewer nights per week.

INTERNAL ASSETS

COMMITMENT TO LEARNING

21. Achievement motivation—Young person is motivated to do well in school.
22. School engagement—Young person is actively engaged in learning.
23. Homework—Young person reports doing at least one hour of homework every school day.
24. Bonding to school—Young person cares about her or his school.
25. Reading for Pleasure—Young person reads for pleasure three or more hours per week.

POSITIVE VALUES

26. Caring—Young person places high value on helping other people.
27. Equality and social justice—Young person places high value on promoting equality and reducing hunger and poverty.
28. Integrity—Young person acts on convictions and stands up for her or his beliefs.
29. Honesty—Young person "tells the truth even when it is not easy."
30. Responsibility—Young person accepts and takes personal responsibility.

SOCIAL COMPETENCIES

31. Restraint—Young person believes it is important not to be sexually active or to use alcohol or other drugs.
32. Planning and decision-making—Young person knows how to plan ahead and make choices.
33. Interpersonal competence—Young person has empathy, sensitivity, and friendship skills.
34. Cultural competence—Young person has knowledge of and comfort with people of different cultural/racial/ethnic backgrounds.
35. Resistance skills—Young person can resist negative peer pressure and dangerous situations.
36. Peaceful conflict resolution—Young person seeks to resolve conflict nonviolently.

POSITIVE IDENTITY

37. Personal power—Young person feels he or she has control over "things that happen to me."
38. Self-esteem—Young person reports having a high self-esteem.
39. Sense of purpose—Young person reports that "my life has a purpose."
40. Positive view of personal future—Young person is optimistic about her or his personal future.

Search Institute, 2006

Resources

Resources on Neuroscience

In this chapter, we provided a very brief overview of the neuropsychological support for shifting to a strengths approach in the helping professions. If you want to learn more about the brain, and how it functions, here are some excellent websites:

- Dr. Robert Gabrieli's website at MIT: *http://gablab.mit.edu*
- Dr. Eric Chudler's Neuroscience for Kids website at University of Washington: *http://faculty.washington.edu/chudler/neurok.html*
- National Institute for Health (NIH) website: *http://neuroscience.nih.gov*

Positive Psychology Resources

Excellent websites on positive psychology are:

- The Positive Psychology Center at the University of Pennsylvania: *http://www.ppc.sas.upenn.edu/index.html*
- The Authentic Happiness website, also at the University of Pennsylvania: *http://www.authentichappiness.sas.upenn.edu/default.aspx*
- The Positive Emotions and Psychophysiology Lab at the University of North Carolina at Chapel Hill: *http://www.unc.edu/peplab/barb_fredrickson_page.html*
- The Positive Psychology Laboratory at the University of California, Riverside: *http://www.faculty.ucr.edu/~sonja/ppl.html*

Developmental Assets
http://www.search-institute.org

The Search Institute has excellent resources on developmental assets and resiliency.

References

Bandura, A. (1977). Self-efficacy: Toward a unifying theory of behavioral change. *Psychological Review, 84*, 191–215.

Bell, V., & Troxel, D. (2003). *The Best Friends Approach to Alzheimer's care* (revised). Baltimore, MD: Health Professions.

Bronfenbrenner, U. (1979). *The ecology of human development: Experiments by nature and design.* Cambridge, MA: Harvard University Press.

Buckingham, M., & Clifton, D. (2001). *Now, discover your strengths.* New York, NY: Free Press.

Carruthers, C., & Hood, C. (2007). Building a life of meaning through therapeutic recreation: The Leisure and Well-Being Model, part I. *Therapeutic Recreation Journal, 41*(4), 276–297.

Cohen, K. (2005). Complexity, content, and community coaching: A new method for collective decision-making. *eReview of Tourism Research, Conference Abstracts.* Retrieved from http://ertr.tamu.edu/index.cfm

Csíkszentmihályi, M. (1975). *Beyond boredom and anxiety.* San Francisco, CA: Jossey-Bass.

Deegan, P. (2006). Foreword. In C. Rapp & R. Goscha (Eds.), *The strengths model: Case management with people with psychiatric disabilities* (2nd ed.). New York, NY: Oxford University Press.

Diener, E., Emmons, R. A., Larsen, R. J., & Griffin, S. (1985). The Satisfaction with Life Scale. *Journal of Personality Assessment, 49*, 71–75.

Dieser, R., Hutchinson, S., Fox, K., & Scholl, K. (2005). Achieving awareness in clinical therapeutic recreation practice: Unmasking covert frameworks. In *Philosophy of therapeutic recreation: Ideas and issues* (Vol. III). Ashburn, VA: National Therapeutic Recreation Society.

Falvey, M., Forest, M., Pearpoint, J., & Rosenberg, R. (2000). *All my life's a circle: Using the tools Circles, MAPS, and PATH.* Toronto, ON, Canada: Inclusion.

Godbey, G., Roy, M., Payne, L., & Orsega-Smith, E. (1998). *Final report on the health and park use study.* Ashburn, VA: The National Recreation and Park Association.

Hesse, B., Nelson, D., Kreps, G., Croyle, R., Arora, N., Rimer, B., & Viswanath, K. (2005). The impact of the Internet and its implications for health care providers: Findings from the first health information national trends study. *Archives of Internal Medicine, 165*(12), 2618–2624.

Ho, C., Payne, L., Orsega-Smith, E., & Godbey, G. (2003, April). Parks, recreation, and public health: Parks and recreation improve the physical and mental health of our nation—Research Update. *Parks and Recreation.* Retrieved from http://www.nrpa.org

Hood, C., & Carruthers, C. (2007). Enhancing leisure experiences and developing resources: The Leisure and Well-Being Model, part II. *Therapeutic Recreation Journal, 41*(4), 298–325.

Howe-Murphy, R., & Charboneau, B. (1987). *Therapeutic recreation intervention: An ecological perspective.* Englewood Cliffs, NJ: Prentice-Hall.

Koyama, T., McHaffie, J., Laurienti, P., & Coghill, R. (2005). The subjective experience of pain: Where expectations become reality. *Proceedings of the National Academy of Sciences, 102*(36), 12950–12955.

Mannes, M. (2008). Transforming community systems prevention, treatment, and recovery. Minneapolis, MN: Search Institute. Retrieved from http://www.search-institute.org

McGlone, M., & Aronson, J. (2006). Social identity salience and stereotype threat. *Journal of Applied Developmental Psychology, 27,* 486–493.

Nussbaum, M., & Sen, A. (1993). *The quality of life.* New York, NY: Oxford University Press.

Peterson, C. (2006). *A primer in positive psychology.* New York, NY: Oxford University Press.

Peterson, C., & Seligman, M. (2004). *Character strengths and virtues: A handbook and classification.* New York, NY: Oxford University Press.

Ragins, M. (2005). Training psychosocial rehabilitation psychiatrists. *The Village.* Retrieved from http://www.mhavillage.org/writings.html

Rapp, C., & Goscha, R. (2006). *The strengths model: Case management with people with psychiatric disabilities* (2nd ed.). New York, NY: Oxford University Press.

Ratey, J. (2012). *John Ratey, M.D.* Retrieved from http://www.johnratey.com

Rock, D. (2006). *Quiet leadership.* New York, NY: HarperCollins.

Rock, D., & Schwartz, J. (2006). The neuroscience of leadership. *Strategy + Business, 43*(2), 1–10.

Saleebey, D. (2006). *The strengths perspective in social work practice* (4th ed.). Boston, MA: Pearson Education.

Schwartz, J., Stapp, H., & Beauregard, M. (2005). Quantum physics in neuroscience and psychology: A neurophysical model of mind-brain interaction. *Philosophical Transactions of the Royal Society B, 10,* 1–19.

Search Institute. (2006). *Developmental assets.* Retrieved from http://www.search-institute.org/developmental-assets

Seligman, M. (1991). *Learned optimism.* New York, NY: Alfred A. Knopf.

Seligman, M. (1998). Why therapy works. *APA Monitor, 29*(12), 1–2. Retrieved from http://www.apa.org/monitor/

Seligman, M. (2002). *Authentic happiness: Using the new positive psychology to realize your potential for lasting fulfillment.* New York, NY: Free Press.

Sesmo, A., & Roehlkepartain, E. (2003). Unique strengths, shared strengths: Developmental assets among youth of color. *Insight & Evidence, 1*(2), 1–13.

Shevin, M. (2003). The language of us and them. Retrieved from http://www.shevin.org/articles-harmonica.html

U.S. Department of Health and Human Services Substance Abuse and Mental Health Services.

(2005). Transformation is now. *Mental Health Transformation Trends, 1*(2), 1–6.

Utesch, W. (n.d.). *From a glass half empty to a glass half full: A review of the transition from deficit to strength-based approaches*. Fort Wayne, IN: Foellinger Foundation.

Wankel, L. (1994, April). Health and leisure: Inextricably linked. *Journal of Physical Education, Recreation and Dance*, 28–31.

Wilkins, V. (2012). Communicating humanness: Attitudes and language. *Social Advocacy and System Change Journal, 3*(1), 38–43.

Witt, P., & Caldwell, L. (2005). *Recreation and youth development*. State College, PA: Venture Publishing, Inc.

World Health Organization. (2004). *Joint position paper—Community-based rehabilitation: A strategy for rehabilitation, equalization of opportunities, poverty reduction, and social inclusion of people with disabilities*. Geneva, Switzerland: World Health Organization.

Chapter 3
A Sea Change in Therapeutic Recreation

The daffodil emerges in the snow and is an early sign of change.

"Leisure and the cultivation of human capacities are inextricably interdependent."

—*Margaret Mead, American anthropologist*

Overview of Chapter 3

- How therapeutic recreation fits within the sea change in recreation, health, and human services
- Therapeutic recreation using a strengths approach—leisure, well-being, and quality of life at our core
- Recreation as a strength and as a context to build strengths
- Purpose and definition of therapeutic recreation—why we exist as a profession
- A brief review of the existing models of therapeutic recreation
- The Leisure and Well-Being Model as a theoretical framework that supports the strengths approach

Focus Questions

- What paradigm shifts are occurring in both the philosophy and delivery of therapeutic recreation practice?
- What is the foundation of therapeutic recreation? Why does therapeutic recreation exist?
- What are the conceptual roots of therapeutic recreation?
- How are the conceptual roots evident in our current therapeutic recreation definitions and service models?

A Sea Change in Therapeutic Recreation

Dr. Martin Seligman, the "father of positive psychology," once stated that the three great realms of life are work, love, and play (Seligman, 1998). The profession of therapeutic recreation has throughout its history had a focus on play, recreation, and leisure and a focus on helping people have a better life. We practice in one of the three great realms, that of play. We also work across many service delivery systems and in many paradigms, which can present challenges and opportunities for our field. Having a clear vision of *why therapeutic recreation exists* is important. That clear vision can serve as our guidepost as we help people in many different ways in many different contexts. This chapter is meant to remind you about the purpose of therapeutic recreation, the conceptual roots of the field, and how those roots can shape our current practice. This chapter leaves you with a question: What is your role in the sea change in therapeutic recreation?

Therapeutic Recreation in the Strengths Approach— Leisure, Well-Being, and Quality of Life at Our Core

Imagine you are riding the elevator and, to pass the time, another passenger asks you, "So, what's your line of work?" Or imagine you are at your first team meeting at your agency, and another professional asks, "So, what do you bring to the table at these team meetings? How do you help the participants served at our agency?" As a therapeutic recreation specialist, how will you respond in these situations? How well are you able to define to those outside and inside the field what you do and why?

As authors, we want you to be comfortable and confident in your vision of what therapeutic recreation is and why you do it from a strengths approach.

The core values and concepts on which we base therapeutic recreation practice are a meaningful starting point for developing your vision and definition of the field. We present three core concepts in this section that will help you clarify the meaning and existence of therapeutic recreation: leisure, well-being, and quality of life. Cultural anthropologist Margaret Mead sums up our belief about how important these core concepts are to the work we do in therapeutic recreation: "Leisure and the cultivation of human capacities are inextricably interdependent."

Leisure

Leisure is the focus of study in many fields, from sociology to psychology to public administration. But no field has studied, and thus understands, the phenomenon of leisure as deeply as ours. It is beyond the scope of this book to provide an in-depth discussion of all that we know about leisure, and it is our hope that you will pursue many avenues to learn about leisure and recreation, whether through your formal degree program or through continuing education. But it is important for us to summarize the key elements of a positive leisure experience, and to explain why it is an important aspect of enhanced well-being and quality of life.

Hood and Carruthers (2007) define leisure as "those experiences that are pleasant in expectation, experience, or recollection; intrinsically motivated; optional in nature; autonomous; and engaging. The term leisure thus includes play and recreation activities as well as other less structured meaningful engagements" (p. 300). Sylvester, Voelkl, and Ellis (2001) believe that the defining element of leisure is freedom, both freedom from unnecessary impediments and freedom to do as one chooses. They contend that leisure has two inextricably related dimensions—the subjective side of leisure, an attitude of intrinsic motivation and free choice, and the objective side, an action that occurs in time and space. Without freedom, leisure becomes obligatory activity, and many of the inherent values and identifying attributes of leisure are lost. In O'Keefe's essay, "Let's First Revisit the Meaning of Leisure" (2007), she states, "Leisure comes from the Latin 'licere,' meaning freedom. It is the freedom to become your true self. In this sense, truth is both intensely individual and unique and yet shares so many common elements across the human family that it creates community in the process" (p. 2). Witt and Ellis (2002) conceptualize leisure as a perceived state based on feelings of perceived competence in leisure, perceived control in leisure, satisfaction of needs in leisure, depth of involvement in leisure, and ability to feel playful. Table 3.1 provides a summary of the key characteristics of leisure.

Though many differing theories and concepts of leisure have been proposed, key characteristics are evident. As therapeutic recreation specialists, we can focus on those characteristics that will help enhance the leisure experience and increase the quality of that experience for the participants with whom we work. This work is critical, as the ability to have a satisfying

Table 3.1 Key Characteristics of Leisure

Pleasurable in expectation, experience, or recollection	Positive emotion is experienced in some phase of the leisure experience, which directly affects happiness and the ability to grow and learn.
Engaging	Leisure is absorbing, and attention is focused on the experience at hand.
Competence	Competence denotes the ability to perform the activity at a level that ensures successful engagement; it implies the ability to understand and make decisions, with or without interdependent support.
Intrinsically motivated	Leisure is chosen by the participant (or his or her collective group in a culture with a collectivist orientation that respects all members) for the meaningful qualities the experience holds for the participant, and not necessarily for the external gains that may accrue as a result of participation.
Optional in nature	Optional involves choices—of types of activities, places to do activities, people with whom to do activities, or choosing to do nothing.
Autonomous	Autonomy implies both the ability to freely decide and control one's leisure, as an individual or as a mutually respected member of a collective group, as well as the ability to critically evaluate or reflect on those choices.
Freedom	Freedom is choice made under one's own power, and not the power of another. In collectivist cultures, freedom may be experienced by a group of mutually respected and empowered, interdependent individuals.

life, with full and satisfying leisure involvement, is a keystone to well-being.

Well-Being

Think about your own life. If someone asked you, "What is your level of well-being?," how would you respond? What things would you list or identify as contributing to your own well-being and to the "good life"? Would you be able to identify things you want to increase in your life to improve your sense of well-being?

Philosophers and social scientists have grappled with the notion of well-being throughout recorded history. It has been used interchangeably with health, happiness, and quality of life. It is nebulous and hard to define. Yet well-being is important to our daily existence, and we all know how to define it in some small way when we think of our own lives.

Philosophers have thought critically about theories of well-being, in ancient and contemporary works. Well-being was the focus of Aristotle's work, the *Nicomachean Ethics*, written in 350 B.C. Aristotle used the term *eudaimonia* to describe the idea of well-being or flourishing. In Greek, *eu* means "well" and *daimon* means "spirit." Aristotle argued that **well-being** consists of excellent or virtuous activity, contemplation, and justice, and that an individual's well-being is integrated with the good of others. In other words, well-being is just as much about the excellence of the civic and community institutions that must be in place to foster well-being, as it is about the excellence of an individual. When Aristotle asked, "How is it good to live our lives?," he was also asking, "How is it good to organize our communities?" (Kraut, 2002). Though some philosophers would argue that well-being can only be about an individual's life and how well that life is going for that person, in an ecological perspective, it is difficult to separate individuals from the contexts in which they live.

Martha Nussbaum, a contemporary American philosopher, furthers the idea of well-being and community in her **capabilities approach** (2006). In the capabilities approach, Nussbaum and her colleagues conceptualize well-being as internal (how well one is able to be and to achieve) and external (sources of well-being, such as public action and social policy) (Nussbaum & Sen, 1993). Nussbaum (2006) identifies 10 core capabilities that must be present for the good life, for well-being, and for human dignity. These core capabilities, described in Table 3.2, are what Nussbaum calls the bare minimum of what respect for human dignity requires. Play, or recreation, is one of the fundamental capabilities that a culture or community must support for well-being to flourish and for people to achieve.

Well-being is what is "good for" a person. How do we clarify the notion of "good for"? Nussbaum and Sen (1993) help us get clearer about the relationship between individuals' well-being, their goals, and their capabilities. Figure 3.1 provides a picture of this relationship.

As can be seen in the figure, achieving goals and having choices is related to, but not the same as well-being. People can pursue and achieve goals that

Table 3.2 Nussbaum's Core Capabilities for Well-Being *(Nussbaum, 2006)*

1.	Life	Being able to live to the natural end of a human life
2.	Bodily health	Being able to have good health and adequate nourishment
3.	Bodily integrity	Being secure and safe, without fear of harm as one travels from place to place
4.	Senses, imagination, and thought	Being able to think, reason, and imagine, informed by an adequate education; freedom of expression; freedom to have pleasurable experiences
5.	Emotions	Having opportunities to love and be loved and to experience a broad range of emotions
6.	Practical reason	Being able to form an idea about goodness, and engage in critical reflection on one's life and its direction
7.	Affiliation	Being able to live and engage fully with others, with self-respect and nondiscrimination
8.	Other species	Being able to live in a sustainable and respectful way with the natural world
9.	Play	Being able to enjoy recreational activities, to laugh, and to play
10.	Control over one's environment	Being able to participate in the political process, to have material possessions, and to work in respected employment

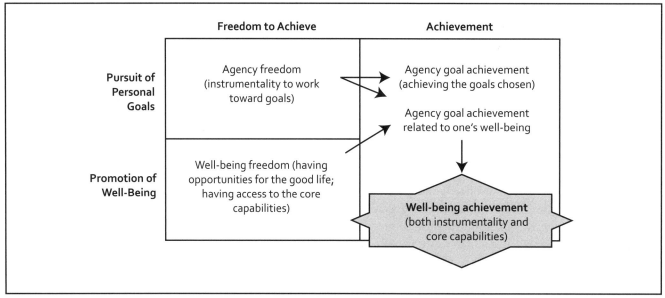

Figure 3.1 Relationship of Capabilities, Goals, and Well-Being

do not contribute to well-being. This can be especially true in the domain of play and leisure, where choice is more free and pleasure may drive choices that do not result in other positive outcomes for an individual, and could even lead to negative outcomes. So achievement of well-being and achievement of goals must both be considered when helping someone have a good life.

People must also have *opportunities*, or the freedom to achieve well-being and goals. Without the freedom to lead different types of lives and pursue different types of goals, well-being is not possible. In the helping professions, such as therapeutic recreation, focusing on well-being achievement (that is, helping people reach goals that increase well-being) and well-being freedom (that is, advocating for and creating opportunities in the environment) can help people have the life that is good for them.

The field of psychology has studied well-being extensively (Diener, 2006; Diener & Lucas, 2000; Lyubomirsky, 2007; Ryan & Deci, 2001). Two traditions in the study of well-being have evolved. One view, the **hedonic view**, equates well-being with pleasure. The goal of life is to experience the maximum amount of pleasure, or experience more positive than negative events. In the second tradition, the **eudaimonic view**, well-being occurs when people's life activities are fully engaging and mesh with deeply held values (Ryan & Deci, 2001).

More recently, a more multidimensional view of well-being has emerged, where both views are integrated. Sometimes called **subjective well-being**, psychologists define well-being as

. . . all the various types of evaluations, both positive and negative, that people make of their lives. It includes reflective cognitive evaluations, such as life satisfaction, interests and engagement, and affective reactions to life events, such as joy and sadness. Thus, subjective well-being is an umbrella term for the different valuations people make regarding their lives, the events happening to them, their bodies and minds, and the circumstances in which they live. (Diener, 2006, p. 399)

Further, psychologists have identified six dimensions of well-being that are related to the good life (Reis, Sheldon, Gable, Roscoe, & Ryan, 2000; Ryff & Singer, 1998):

- Acceptance of oneself
- Positive relations with others
- Autonomy and self-determination
- Environmental mastery and competence
- Purpose in life
- Personal growth

The concept of **happiness** has also been used interchangeably with well-being. Lyubomirsky (2007) describes happiness as "the experience of joy, contentment, or positive well-being, combined with a sense that one's life is good, meaningful, and worthwhile" (p. 32). Seligman (2002) has furthered that definition by coining the term "authentic happiness," which defines positive well-being as coming from the exercise or engagement of our strengths and virtues every day of our lives. Some psychologists have argued that happiness is the pure measure of well-being—it is what has *final value* for a person (Brulde, 2007). Other dimensions of well-being are a means to achieve happiness.

Researchers in therapeutic recreation have also attempted to conceptualize well-being. According to Carruthers and Hood (2007), "Well-being is a state of successful, satisfying, and productive engagement with one's life and the realization of one's full physical, cognitive, and social-emotional potential" (p. 280). Sylvester, Voelkl, and Ellis (2001) have defined well-being as including health and other basic needs, as well as values and attributes that contribute to a life of dignity and worth. These values and attributes include things like autonomy, enjoyment, play, and aesthetic experiences. Widmer and Ellis (1998) feel the terms well-being and happiness are value-laden and, in order to understand them, therapeutic recreation specialists must integrate ethics into practice perspectives. They define "the good life," based on Aristotelian ethics, as being achievable by these actions:

- Seeking only enough in our lives (not more or less than we need to meet our reasonable needs)
- Understanding the difference between real goods (those that help us lead meaningful, purposeful lives) and apparent goods (those that we seek for the sake of happiness, but that don't actually help us find it)
- Choosing right over wrong desires (choosing real goods that help us lead the good life)

Well-being is an important concept for us to understand in therapeutic recreation, whether it is conceptualized through a philosophical, scientific, or practical lens. Well-being is at the heart of therapeutic recreation practice, and many of our efforts focus on helping people achieve that promise through enhanced leisure and development of strengths.

Quality of Life

"Quality of life" and "well-being" have often been used interchangeably. In addition, quality of life has many different meanings, and is used differently in various disciplines. Whereas well-being consistently has a fairly focused meaning, both philosophically and scientifically, quality of life has been construed as narrowly as health in medicine to as broadly as the gross domestic product in economics. In therapeutic recreation, quality of life has often been associated with the profession, from definitional statements to marketing materials. Just what is meant by quality of life?

The dictionary definition of **quality of life** (Free Dictionary, 2008) is twofold. At a personal level, quality of life is defined as the degree of enjoyment and satisfaction experienced in everyday life, including health, personal relationships, the environment, quality of working life, social life, and leisure time. At the community level, quality of life is defined as a set of social indicators such as nutrition, air quality, incidence of disease, crime rates, health care, educational services, and divorce rates.

Researchers have explored and defined quality of life in many different fields, from disability studies to rehabilitation medicine. Schlalock and colleagues (2002), scholars in the field of intellectual disabilities, have defined quality of life as people feeling satisfied with the following core dimensions of their lives:

- Emotional well-being (including psychological well-being)
- Interpersonal relations (including social relationships)
- Material well-being (including employment and economic security)
- Personal development (including personal competence and personal goals)
- Physical well-being (including wellness and recreation/leisure)
- Self-determination (including individual control and decisions)
- Social inclusion (including dignity and worth)
- Rights (including privacy)

The Quality of Life Research Unit, based at the University of Toronto in Canada, has defined quality of life as "the degree to which a person enjoys the important possibilities of his or her life" (Quality of Life Research Unit, 2005, para. 4). Possibilities are the personal and environmental opportunities and limitations people have in their lives, and enjoyment is how much people are able to experience satisfaction in those opportunities, especially those that are important to them. Table 3.3 presents the conceptual framework for the quality-of-life model developed by the University of Toronto. Being, belonging, and becoming are shown as the three major areas of quality of life, and within each of those, subdomains are identified.

Table 3.3 Quality of Life Model from the University of Toronto Quality of Life Research Unit
(The Quality of Life Research Unit, University of Toronto, 2005)

Domains and Sub-Domains of Quality of Life	Definition
Domain: Being	*Who one is*
Physical Being	• Physical health and general physical appearance • Hygiene, grooming, and clothing • Nutrition • Exercise
Psychological Being	• Psychological health and adjustment • Cognitions • Feelings/emotions • Self-esteem, self-concept, and self-control
Spiritual Being	• Personal values • Personal standards of conduct • Spiritual beliefs
Domain: Belonging	*Connections with one's environments*
Physical Belonging	• Home • Workplace/school • Neighborhood • Community
Social Belonging	• Intimate others • Family • Friends • Co-workers • Neighborhood and community
Community belonging	• Adequate income • Health and social services • Employment • Educational programs • Recreational programs • Community events and activities
Domain: Becoming	*Achieving personal goals, hopes, & aspirations*
Practical Becoming	• Domestic activities • Paid work • School and volunteer activities • Seeing to health and social needs
Leisure Becoming	• Activities that promote relaxation and stress reduction
Growth Becoming	• Activities that promote the maintenance and improvement of knowledge and skills • Adapting to change

Diener (2006) and other positive psychologists, as a part of a national indicators study, defined quality of life as:

> the degree to which a person's life is desirable versus undesirable, often with an emphasis on external components, such as environmental factors and income. In contrast to subjective well-being, which is based on subjective experience, quality of life is often expressed as more "objective" and describes the circumstances of a person's life rather than his or her reaction to those circumstances. (p. 401)

The fields of medicine and rehabilitation define quality of life even more narrowly, sometimes calling it "health-related quality of life." Most definitions in medical fields refer to physical, psychological, and social domains of health, which are distinct areas influenced by a person's beliefs, expectations, and perceptions, and thus include both objective and subjective dimensions (Testa & Simonson, 1996). Though health-related quality of life tends to focus on functional status, the medical profession has recognized that it must move beyond functional outcomes as an indicator of quality of life and recognize that every human being has the potential for high quality of life, regardless of disability (Pain, Dunn, & Anderson, 1998).

In therapeutic recreation, quality of life has always played an important role. The National Therapeutic Recreation Society (1996), in its philosophical position statement, delineated quality of life as one of three core values that guide therapeutic recreation practice. The other two values, right to leisure and self-determination, contribute to quality of life and are viewed as an integral component of quality of life. In its *Position Statement on Inclusion*, the National Therapeutic Recreation Society (1997) also identified quality of life as a fundamental concept underlying the profession. Quality of life is further delineated as growth and development across the lifespan, and leisure experiences are identified as a means to enhance competence and self-direction, health and wellness, social connection, and individual choice.

Sylvester, Voelkl, and Ellis (2001) define quality of life as the subjective experience that life is good, meaningful, and satisfying. Leisure plays a central role in experiencing quality of life, especially when a person is undergoing medical treatment or rehabilitation. Sylvester (1987) writes:

> Leisure is the end or goal of therapeutic recreation, and professionals [therapeutic recreation specialists] assist people in various states of health to bring joy, value, and meaning to their lives. Particularly in more restrictive clinical settings, plots of freedom are provided for clients to exercise their own "tillable acreage," assisting them in the progression to environs increasingly suitable to their humanity and happiness. (p. 86)

Health and Functional Outcomes

When someone asks you if you are healthy, what comes to mind? Health is typically thought of as the absence of illness or the general condition of the body. Historically, health was defined as freedom from disease, discomfort, and pain, as well as the ability to function in one's environment (Sylvester, 1987). The word "health" is derived from the old English word *hoelth*, which means a state of being sound, and was generally used to imply a soundness of the body (Üstün & Jakob, 2005).

In 1946, the World Health Organization (2008) defined health as "a state of complete physical, mental and social well-being and not merely the absence of disease or infirmity." This definition extends beyond the traditional paradigm that treats body, mind, and society as separate entities, and it reflects a more holistic understanding of health. However, this expanded definition of health has been criticized for inflating the meaning of health to include happiness and well-being. Sylvester (1987) states, "Health is not the totality of life. Indeed, if health is conceived as *complete* mental, social, and physical well-being, the world is a gigantic waiting room, for no one this side of death is absolutely free of ailments or problems" (p. 78). Üstün and Jakob (2005) state that health is confused with happiness in the definition, and that failure to distinguish health from happiness implies that any disturbance in happiness will be perceived as a health problem. Conversely, people experiencing health problems can also be very happy people.

Health, then, is more rightly defined as a *condition* of well-being, freedom from disease or illness, and a basic and universal human right. Health is a component of quality of life, and one's quality of life can impact health, but it is not synonymous with quality of life. Sylvester states, "Health is a necessary but insufficient condition for happiness, for one can be functionally fit but morally unfulfilled" (p. 79).

Related to the concept of health is **functional ability**. The World Health Organization (2002) defines "functioning" as the ability to meet the demands of the environment through bodily functions, activities, and participation in day-to-day life. Three levels of human functioning exist: (a) the level of the body or body part, (b) the level of the whole person, and (c) the level of the whole person in a social context (this idea will be discussed in more depth in Chapter 6 *Theories*). In medicine and rehabilitation, interventions are often directed at the bodily level and attempt to improve functional limitations in the person. However, functional ability can also be improved by focusing on the environment in which a person lives and changing the social context. These two differing approaches are called the medical model of disability and the social model of disability. The social model of disability aligns closely with the strengths approach, where the focus is on what a person *can* do and wants to achieve in his or her life. Like health, functional ability is a component of life quality and well-being, but it is not synonymous with them. And, likewise, an impairment at the bodily or body-part level does not mean that a person cannot pursue quality leisure experiences necessary to enjoy a high quality of life.

The conceptual roots of therapeutic recreation—leisure, well-being, and quality of life—are complex and rich ideas. The interrelationship between the concepts is strong, and teasing one idea out from the others is difficult. The idea that leisure is superfluous to "the good life" is clearly mistaken. When we work in the strengths approach in therapeutic recreation, leisure takes center stage in our practice. Though health and functional ability are also important to well-being and quality of life, many disciplines assist participants in treatment and rehabilitation. Therapeutic recreation alone has the expertise in leisure, and it alone advocates for and enhances leisure in a participant's life. Using an ecological perspective in a strengths approach, leisure becomes one of the most important areas of participants' lives—one of the great realms. Ed's story, "The Freedom to be Spontaneous," brings to life the concepts of leisure, freedom, functional ability, well-being, quality of life, and the social model of disability (Figure 3.2). Though Ed has lifelong functional impairments, by using a strengths approach and an ecological, social model of disability, Ed is now experiencing more happiness and well-being in his life than ever before.

RECREATION AS A STRENGTH AND AS A CONTEXT IN WHICH TO BUILD STRENGTHS

Leisure, or recreation, is the core of therapeutic recreation practice because of its power to help people feel good about their lives and make the positive changes they want to see in their lives. When people have

Life Story:
The Freedom to be Spontaneous
Adapted from a story by Ed Bartz

"You can't do that Ed!"
"How will you manage on your own?"
"What will happen if you need help?"
"Do you really think this is a good idea?"
"What if a fire breaks out?"

These are just some of the reactions I faced when I decided to become independent of a traditional residential program. To help someone who is unfamiliar with that kind of program, I'll try to give you some background. Over my 43 years, I have lived in many kinds of situations—many of which would be worth forgetting. However, fortunately, people with disabilities have gained so much dignity and respect that being "put away" in an institution is not even thought of anymore. In any case, most recently I lived in my own apartment and shared support staff with seven other people who needed help. While that kind of apartment living is a step up from being in a group residence, it still has some drawbacks. While the agency overseeing my living situation did their best to meet my needs, with a limited ratio of staff to residents, the task was difficult.

Depending on the event or activity, I sometimes need help getting into the community. This requires a lot of planning and the consideration of staff. To give a comparison, let's say you plan to attend a concert. You make plans to have somebody help your ailing mother while you are at the concert, but on that day, the person you're relying on can't make it. You call other friends, but they have commitments of their own. As a result, you end up not being able to go to the concert. This is what it can be like for a group of folks with disabilities that rely on assistance. Staff or volunteers can get sick or have things going on in their own lives and that impacts you.

Since I started using a new service that allows me and my circle of support to manage the use of funds, I have been living a life of true independence. I can choose supports and services, which are in my Person-Centered Plan, and I have complete say in how money is spent to support the services I need. This means taking on more responsibility, but the freedom to be spontaneous is irreplaceable. With my circle of support behind me, I hire people to assist me in living a higher quality of life. My circle consists of people who have known me for many years, and they help me problem-solve and make crucial decisions, and my success is just as important to them as it is to me.

I finally have control over my living environment just like everybody else does and it feels good to have a say in every aspect of my life. I need to be more organized, but I wouldn't give up my new way of life for the world!

Figure 3.2 Life Story: The Freedom to be Spontaneous *(adapted from Self-Advocacy Association of New York State, Inc., 2006)*

interests, preferences, talents, and passions that they pursue, they feel alive, vibrant, strong, and complex as a human being. Their lives are textured and interesting (Pedlar et al., 1999), infused with meaning and purpose. Involvement in high-quality leisure experiences also leads to growth and adaptation. Leisure is a strength; leisure provides a context in which to build strengths.

Carruthers and Hood (2007), Sylvester (2005), and Sylvester, Voelkl, and Ellis (2001) have provided powerful rationales for why leisure, with its inherent characteristics, is necessary for well-being and quality of life, and why it is the center of practice in therapeutic recreation:

- Leisure provides a context for the experience of positive emotions, which are directly linked to health and well-being.
- Leisure contributes to the development of resources and strengths in one's life, from physical to social to cognitive to environmental resources.
- Leisure directly impacts self-development and self-determination, which are essential to well-being.
- Leisure provides opportunities to fully engage in activity and acts as a stimulus to health.
- Leisure directly meets the creative-expressive needs of people and their drive to find meaning and purpose in their lives.
- Leisure provides a natural vehicle to promote inclusion in communities and develop friendship circles, again essential to well-being.
- Leisure can change communities, making communities healthier and more welcoming of differences, including disability and illness.
- Leisure can be pursued by everyone, every day, everywhere—regardless of how ill, or how "broken" one may be. Leisure can infuse well-being in everyone's life everyday, regardless of functional ability.
- People, *all* people, have a fundamental right to leisure.

The strengths approach, where the goals and aspirations of participants drive the therapeutic recreation process, elevates leisure as a powerful force to help participants have the lives they want. The expert is the participant—the therapeutic recreation specialist is the facilitator of increased freedom, autonomy, and enjoyment, and thus well-being. In the strengths approach, the leisure experience is preserved and enhanced, and therapeutic goals are realized through positive collaboration. Read Figure 3.3 to compare and contrast the role of leisure in both the strengths approach and the deficit approach. The recreation roots of the therapeutic recreation profession are clearly more nurturing in the strengths approach.

Purpose and Definition of Therapeutic Recreation: Why We Exist as a Profession

We hope the preceding discussion of leisure, well-being, and quality of life helps you understand the conceptual roots of our field. Those conceptual roots lay the foundation for a succinct definition of therapeutic recreation. Many definitions have been put forth, with varying orientations. A critical analysis of the definitions published in the field, and the assumptions on which those definitions are based, will bring you closer to your own meaning of therapeutic recreation. This sort of analysis will help you clarify which definitions are rooted in a deficit approach and which are firmly planted in a strengths approach. An analysis will also help you clarify which definitions are rooted in "the great realm of life," leisure, and which are rooted in more narrow domains, such as health or functional outcomes.

Therapeutic recreation has been defined by professional organizations, such as the National Therapeutic Recreation Society, the American Therapeutic Recreation Association, and the Canadian Therapeutic Recreation Association, as well as the credentialing body, the National Council for Therapeutic Recreation Certification. In Table 3.4, each of these professional definitions is provided.

Academic researchers in therapeutic recreation have also defined therapeutic recreation in textbooks, research articles, and monographs. Table 3.5 provides some of the most cited academic definitions of therapeutic recreation.

As you read the definitions in both Tables 3.4 and 3.5, ask yourself these questions about each definition:

- What is the **goal** of therapeutic recreation? Remediation or capacity-building? Deficit reduction or building a meaningful life?
- What is the **focus** of therapeutic recreation services or interventions? Functional impairment reduction or enhancement of leisure? Strengths or deficits? Goals and aspirations or problems?

Compare/Contrast:
The Role of Leisure in the Strengths versus the Deficits Approach

Deficits Approach—The Medical Model Perspective	Strengths Approach—A Capabilities Perspective
Health and functional outcomes are a key focus. Because it is not controlled by the "therapist," leisure is diversional and outside the treatment process. The therapist must control and prescribe the intervention for predicted health and functional outcomes to occur. The freedom associated with leisure makes it a difficult tool to use to make prescribed change.	Leisure is a key component of life quality and well-being as it is controlled by the participant, providing important sources for self-determination and utilization of strengths. In the process of building meaningful leisure, well-being is improved across multiple domains.
Participant problems and deficits drive the helping relationship—leisure is reduced to a tool to fix the deficits in a prescribed manner.	Participant aspirations and dreams drive the helping relationship—leisure is often a key part of a participant's personal goals for a meaningful life.
Participant strengths are used as a tool to fix deficits. Strengths are only important in that they can be directed at remediation of weaknesses, which, in the medical model, is the focus of the helping process.	Participant strengths are nurtured and developed to a higher level. Leisure, freely chosen, is an arena and context to build strengths, as well as a strength in itself.
Enhancement of the leisure experience is only useful if it leads to a remediation of deficits on which the helping process is focused. Leisure is a means to an end.	Enhancement of the leisure experience is an important outcome of therapeutic recreation services. It also contributes to improved well-being. Leisure is an end in and of itself, and it is also a means to a higher quality of life.
According to Mobily (1999), "the 'angst' created is evident in the tortuous fit between recreation/leisure (demanded by leisure theory and research) and the health/functional outcomes (necessary for reimbursement of services) evident in most of the models [using a deficits approach]. The difficulties reflect the difference between what has been learned theoretically (about leisure behavior) and the expectations and standards of the audiences the TR profession must play to in reality. Trying to wed therapeutic outcomes to leisure without losing the essence of the leisure experience is 'the struggle.'"	There is a harmonious fit between leisure and the outcomes expected by the audiences the TR profession plays to in a strengths approach. Leisure is closely tied to therapeutic outcomes that build strengths and a life of meaning and well-being. Agencies and professionals using the strengths approach clearly see the need for high-quality leisure experiences as a part of the helping process.

Figure 3.3 Compare/Contrast: The Role of Leisure in the Strengths versus Deficits Approach

- What are the **integral services** provided by therapeutic recreation? Treatment? Enhancement of the leisure experience?
- How are the **participants** receiving therapeutic recreation services conceptualized? As having deficits that need to fixed? Or as having strengths that can be enhanced?
- What is the **ultimate purpose** or outcome from receiving therapeutic recreation services? To reduce illness and disability or to enhance and build leisure, well-being, and life quality?

As you carefully answer each of these questions about each definition in the tables, assumptions and concepts important to our field become clearer. Many of the definitions focus on remediation, often with an ultimate goal of improved health and quality of life. The assumption underlying these definitions is that a participant's functional deficits must be remedied before quality of life is possible. However, some of the definitions (such as Anderson & Heyne, 2012; Hood & Carruthers, 2007; Howe-Murphy & Charboneau, 1987; O'Keefe, n. d.; and Robertson & Long, 2008) focus on building capacity, enhancing leisure experiences, and strengthening self-determination. These definitions assume competence and opportunities for building strengths in participants.

In most of the professional definitions and all of the academic definitions, leisure is integral in some way to services provided by therapeutic recreation specialists. Of all the definitions provided, those by ATRA

Table 3.4 Professional Definitions of Therapeutic Recreation

Professional Group	Definition
American Therapeutic Recreation Association	"Recreational Therapy" means a treatment service designed to restore, remediate and rehabilitate a person's level of functioning and independence in life activities, to promote health and wellness as well as reduce or eliminate the activity limitations and restrictions to participation in life situations caused by an illness or disabling condition. (2009, para. 4)
Canadian Therapeutic Recreation Association (Association Canadienne de Loisir Therapeutique)	Therapeutic recreation is a profession which recognizes leisure, recreation, and play as integral components of quality of life. Service is provided to individuals who have physical, mental, social, or emotional limitations which impact their ability to engage in meaningful leisure experiences. Therapeutic recreation is directed toward functional interventions, leisure education, and participation opportunities. These processes support the goal of assisting the individual to maximize independence in leisure, optimal health, and the highest possible quality of life. (2008, para. 2)
National Council for Therapeutic Recreation Certification	The primary purpose of recreation therapy practice is to improve health and quality of life by reducing impairments of body function and structure, reducing activity limitations, participation restrictions, and environmental barriers of the clients served. The ultimate goal of recreation therapy is to facilitate full and optimal involvement in community life. (2004, para. 1)
National Therapeutic Recreation Society*	Therapeutic recreation uses treatment, education, and recreation services to help people with illnesses, disabilities, and other conditions to develop and use their leisure in ways that enhance their health, functional abilities, independence, and quality of life. (2000, para. 3)

* The National Recreation and Park Association changed its branches, including the National Therapeutic Recreation Society (NTRS), to networks in 2010. Though NTRS is no longer a formal branch, the significant work it produced over its 45-year history remains highly relevant and valid for the field.

and NCTRC are most oriented to a deficit model and do not root therapeutic recreation solidly in leisure theory. In fact, neither definition uses the term "leisure" anywhere in its definition of the field, and its use of the term "recreation therapy" typically applies to therapeutic recreation practice in medical settings.

Most of the definitions have quality of life or well-being as an end goal, yet they provide differing conceptions of therapeutic recreation services to reach that end goal. Some of the definitions focus strongly on health and functional outcomes, while others focus solidly on leisure as the key to well-being that can be most effectively facilitated by therapeutic recreation specialists.

We have challenged you throughout this chapter to formulate your own definition of therapeutic recreation. We hope a careful review of the definitions published in the field will help you in your own formulation of a definition that aligns with your beliefs about the field. As authors, we challenged ourselves to develop a definition of therapeutic recreation, and we would like to share it with you:

> Therapeutic recreation is the purposeful and careful facilitation of quality leisure experiences and the development of personal and environmental strengths, which lead to greater well-being for people who, due to illness, disability, or other life circumstances, need individualized assistance to achieve their goals and dreams.

We have chosen each word in our definition judiciously. *Purposeful facilitation* means that the leisure experiences and strengths that will be enhanced are chosen through the diligent application of authentic assessment and are oriented toward the goals, dreams, and aspirations of the participant. Authentic assessment will be discussed in depth in Chapter 9 of this book. *Careful facilitation* means that the therapeutic recreation specialist uses well-developed facilitation skills in all aspects of service delivery. Unfortunately, especially when the medical model is followed, therapeutic recreation specialists have often delegated facilitation of recreation experiences to aides or assistants, since these experiences are seen as diversional and not a key aspect of the helping process. The facilitation of quality leisure experiences is one of the richest and most powerful therapeutic recreation interventions we have and is a part of our practice that should not be delegated if it is to be effectively executed. We cannot assume that paraprofessionals, who do not have the grounding in leisure theory that a therapeutic recreation specialist has, could facilitate the powerful opportunities found in leisure engagement. A therapeutic recreation specialist who delegates facilitation of leisure or recreation participation to paraprofessionals or direct care staff would be like a dentist who delegates restorative work on teeth to a dental assistant, or a surgeon who delegates surgery to

Table 3.5 Academic Definitions of Therapeutic Recreation

Author(s)	Definition
Anderson and Heyne (2012)	Therapeutic recreation is the purposeful and careful facilitation of quality leisure experiences and the development of personal and environmental strengths, which lead to greater well-being for people who, due to illness, disability, or other life circumstances, need individualized assistance in achieving their goals and dreams. (p. 130)
Austin and Crawford (2001)	Therapeutic recreation is a means, first, to restore oneself or regain stability or equilibrium following a threat to health (health protection), and second, to develop oneself through leisure as a means to self-actualization (health promotion). Therapeutic recreation has the primary goals of restoring health and helping people learn how to use their leisure in optimizing their potential, in order to enjoy as high a quality of life as possible. (p. 9)
Carter, Van Andel, and Robb (2003)	Therapeutic recreation is the specialized application of recreation and experiential activities or interventions that assist in maintaining or improving the health status, functional capabilities, and ultimately, the quality of life of people with special needs. (p. 9)
Dattilo, Kleiber, and Williams (1998)	Therapeutic recreation is the delivery of services designed to support participants in achieving the goals of self-determination and enjoyment and, ultimately, functional improvement. (p. 259)
Hood and Carruthers (2007)	Therapeutic recreation is the facilitation of client well-being through enhancement of positive emotion and the leisure experience, and the development of client resources. (p. 299)
Howe-Murphy and Charboneau (1987)	Therapeutic recreation is a planned process of intervention directed toward specific environmental and/or individual change. The goals of the change process are to maximize the quality of life, enhance leisure functioning of the individual, and promote acceptance of persons with disabilities in the community. (p. 9)
O'Keefe (n.d.)	From *An Essay for Students Interested in Therapeutic Recreation*: Therapeutic recreation is helping people find meaning and personal satisfaction through choices that they make with their leisure. (p. 8)
Robertson and Long (2008)	Therapeutic recreation is the purposeful utilization or enhancement of leisure as a way to maximize a person's overall health, well-being, or quality of life. (p. 4)
Shank and Coyle (2002)	Therapeutic recreation clinical practice is the deliberate and purposeful use of an intervention process aimed at helping people with illnesses and disabilities improve their health and increase their capacity to use play, recreation, and leisure for ongoing health and quality of life. (p. 53)
Stumbo and Peterson (2004)	Therapeutic recreation is a necessary service to help reduce, eliminate, or overcome barriers to leisure. The purpose of therapeutic recreation is to facilitate the development, maintenance, and expression of an appropriate leisure lifestyle for individuals with disabilities and/or illnesses. (p. 18)
Sylvester, Voelkl, and Ellis (2001)	Therapeutic recreation is a service that uses the modalities of activity therapy, education, and recreation to promote the health and well-being of persons who require specialized care because of illness, disability, or social condition. Furthermore, recognizing the potential for leisure for contributing to quality of life of all people, therapeutic recreation facilitates leisure opportunities as an integral component of comprehensive care. (p. 17)
Wilhite and Keller (2000)	Therapeutic recreation is about making a difference in the lives of clients as a result of specific intervention at specific points in time. The primary goal of therapeutic recreation is to enable clients to live in the least restrictive and least costly environment at their highest possible level of independence and quality of life. (p. 7)

the surgical assistant. Just as these professionals would not delegate the skill- and knowledge-laden heart of their practice away to assistants, we in therapeutic recreation should not do the same with the recreation experience. Though other team members can contribute to a "leisure-enriched milieu," the therapeutic recreation specialist has the knowledge and skills to amplify the power of leisure.

Lastly, we chose the words, *people who, due to illness, disability, or other life circumstances, need individualized assistance to achieve their goals and dreams*, to delineate the very unique body of knowledge and focus of services of therapeutic recreation. Our focus

Life Story:
A Recent Immigrant from Russia at JCC

When Emily wanted to be involved in youth programs at the Jewish Community Center, as the inclusion coordinator I was faced with a question that usually presents itself whenever a new child with a disability came to the Center. Should I give an orientation about the person and his or her disability to the peers without disabilities in the program? There were several questions to consider:

- Was an orientation necessary?
- Would an orientation promote socialization or negatively stigmatize the participant with a disability?
- What information should be shared with the group?
- How should the information be shared?
- Who was the best person to share the information?
- Should the participant be present or not?

In mulling over these questions, I routinely consult with the family. In fact, I invariably depend on the family for their input on what information to share, how to share it, and who should share it.

In talking with Emily and her family, Emily's mother volunteered to introduce Emily to the group. So, before the next youth outing, Emily's mother told the teens about Emily's likes and dislikes, favorite leisure activities, and the school she attended. Her mother explained what cerebral palsy was and how it affected Emily's ability to speak and move. Emily's mother showed the teens how to interact with Emily using her communication board and how her wheelchair folded up to fit in a car. Then Emily left with the other teens for a night of pizza and video games. Upon their return, the youth director Jeff was excited about how the evening had gone: "The kids took a while to warm up, but mostly they tried really hard to talk with Emily and sit by her. She was smiling a lot!"

Not long after Emily's orientation, I noticed a teenager hanging out in the teen lounge. His name was Andres, and he and his family had recently emigrated from Russia to St. Paul, where an influx of Russian immigrants was beginning to settle. Andres was still struggling to learn English, and almost every afternoon I found him sitting by himself in the youth lounge watching TV.

One day Andres asked me, "You do talk for me like Emily?" It wasn't until that moment that I saw the connection between including Emily and including someone like Andres who was going through a difficult transition or, as our definition of therapeutic recreation says, an "other life circumstance." Andres, like Emily, was at risk of social isolation and misunderstanding. He needed support to converse with others, make friends, and begin his new life in a new country.

Jeff and I talked with Andres and planned what to do so he could feel more welcomed at the Center. Rather than hold a formal orientation, we decided an informal approach would be more natural and less intrusive. Jeff usually chaperoned the youth outings, and he took it upon himself to facilitate interaction between Andres and the other teens as opportunities arose spontaneously. Jeff encouraged the group to tell Andres words in English while he spoke the words in Russian. Jeff facilitated conversation about events that were happening in the teens' lives and other common concerns. Jeff also made sure Andres had opportunities to state his preferences and take turns, and that he was able to interact with others.

Over time, Andres grew more confident, and his ability to speak English improved. Soon he became involved in other teen social activities such as sports, theater, and summer camp. It was exciting to see how therapeutic recreation can be applied to support someone who needs a little extra help to feel a part of the community.

Figure 3.4 Life Story: A Recent Immigrant from Russia at JCC

on leisure, strengths, aspirations, and environmental context distinguishes us from other health professionals. Our expertise in disability (and other differences), our use of the individualized approach using a systematic process, and our helping skills differentiate us from general recreation specialists. Our unique blend of knowledge and skills is important in helping participants with varying abilities that may need individualized assistance to achieve well-being (see Figure 3.4).

A Brief Review of the Existing Models of Therapeutic Recreation

We hope you are now clearer on the conceptual roots of therapeutic recreation, and how those roots are evident or not in the various definitions of our profession. It is beyond the intent of this chapter to review the history of our profession and how it came to its current status. What is *new* to the story of therapeutic recreation is the significant sea change occurring in the helping professions, with the fundamental and deep shift to a strengths approach.

***Primary Source Support*: Critical Theory and Therapeutic Recreation**

Sylvester, C. (1995, October). *Critical theory and therapeutic recreation: Breaking new ground*. Paper presented at the Symposium on Leisure Research, National Recreation and Park Association, San Antonio, TX.

Critical inquiry is a form of research that looks carefully and intentionally at social phenomena, power structures, and social justice. In general, critical inquiry asks: What are we doing now? How did it come to be this way? Whose interests are or are not being served by the way things are now? What information do we have that brings the issues to light? Is this the way we want things? What are we going to do about it?

Dr. Charles Sylvester conducted a critical inquiry study that focused on the social need for therapeutic recreation and aspects of the field that undermine its normative commitments as a helping profession. Dr. Sylvester reviewed the literature in therapeutic recreation and, based on that review, defined our normative commitments as freedom, autonomy, and self-determination. He found the literature overwhelmingly supported therapeutic recreation's commitment to these three defining characteristics. He then searched for aspects of the therapeutic recreation field that undermined the goals of freedom, autonomy, and self-determination. Sylvester found many examples in the professional literature where the three goals of therapeutic recreation were subverted by actions of professionals in the field. He cites concrete examples of this subversion. These include such things as "health care" evolving to a "health care industry" where only cost-effective services are desired, as dictated by third-party payers like insurance companies. Another example Sylvester cites is the practice of "prioritizing patients" to provide therapeutic recreation services only to those who will show efficient outcomes in a cost-effective manner, regardless of social need. He illuminates the tyranny of the medical model in therapeutic recreation, citing documents where leisure (and its inherent characteristics of freedom, autonomy, and self-determination) is marginalized as diversional, and only prescribed activity that is valued by third-party payers is promoted. In conclusion, Sylvester contends that, "instead of conforming to the ideology of the health care 'industry,' therapeutic recreation should become the point of resistance, pressing for reform that respects human values despite the 'cost'" (p. 6). Using critical inquiry, implicit and subtle value orientations in the field are illuminated and scrutinized, and the fundamental question, "Who benefits by this value orientation?" is addressed in open dialogue.

Figure 3.5 Primary Source Support: Critical Theory and Therapeutic Recreation

Many of the divergent definitions of therapeutic recreation are as much a function of the context in which they evolved as they are about the conceptual roots of the field. The tyranny of the medical model across not only health-related professions, but in all human services, contributed to this confusion in our profession. Under the medical model, the pressure to show functional or health outcomes, at the expense of the leisure experience, has tended to distort the true nature of our field. But the paradigm shift to a strengths approach will be a healthy corrective to our practice perspective. In addition, as therapeutic recreation shifts its practice arena from medical facilities to more community-based services, the corrective to a strengths approach will be even more necessary (see Figure 3.5).

To help you understand the influence of the medical model, and the evolution of our field, we will very briefly provide an overview of therapeutic recreation service models that have influenced practice through the last several decades. A service model is basically a graphic representation that captures the purpose and scope of practice. In therapeutic recreation, these models can be categorized as basically *continuum models* or *integrated models*. We will first look at the continuum models.

Continuum Models of Therapeutic Recreation

The continuum models we overview in this section all share the characteristic that the participants we serve must work through a continuum from less functional and unhealthy to more functional and healthy. In other words, the deficits of the participants place them somewhere along a continuum, and they will progress to higher levels within that continuum based on remediation of problems they have, and they will receive differing intensive services depending on their level of functioning. Fundamental to all these models is the idea that the participant has deficits that must be fixed in order to move toward health and quality of life. Typically, the change must happen in the person.

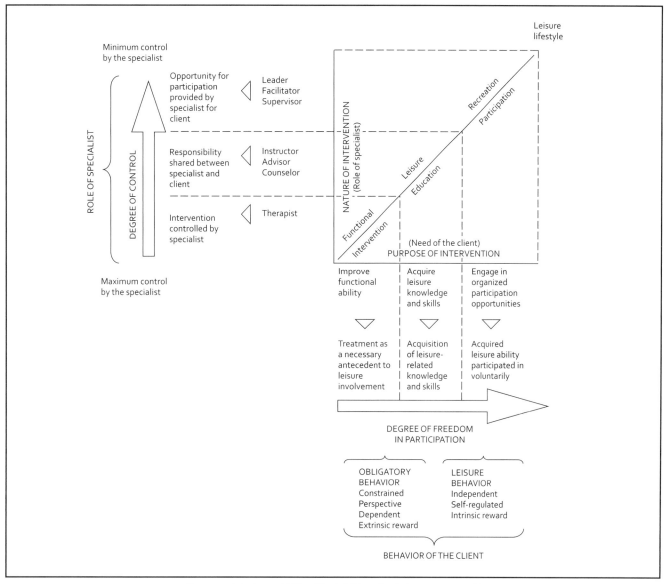

Figure 3.6 Leisure Ability Model *(Stumbo & Peterson, 1998)*

The Leisure Ability Model

One of the oldest and perhaps the most widely used model in therapeutic recreation is the Leisure Ability Model (Gunn & Peterson, 1978; Stumbo & Peterson, 2004), shown in Figure 3.6. The ultimate goal of this model is independent and satisfying leisure functioning. Its conceptual basis is leisure, and its theoretical foundations are rooted in ideas of self-determination, control, and choice.

The Leisure Ability Model identifies three areas of service: functional intervention, leisure education, and recreation participation. **Functional intervention** is considered a "prerequisite" service based on participant deficits, and it prepares the participant for future leisure participation (Stumbo & Peterson, 2004). According to the model, in the functional intervention service area, the "intervention is mostly controlled by the specialist" who "must be able to assess accurately the client's functional deficits, create and implement specific interventions to improve those deficits, and evaluate the client outcomes achieved" (p. 46). The targeted change must happen in the participant and, when and if that happens, then the participant gains more control.

The next level of service area is **leisure education**, where the focus is on helping the participant develop the knowledge, skills, and attitudes necessary for successful leisure involvement. Again, the model assumes the participant is lacking the necessary competencies for leisure. In the Leisure Ability Model, leisure education consists of four areas: leisure awareness, social interaction skills, leisure resources, and leisure activity skills. In this service area, the control is more evenly shared between the therapeutic recreation specialist, who acts as an educator, and the participant, who has more freedom of choice in the process.

The last area of service identified in the Leisure Ability Model is **recreation participation**. In this service area, the focus is on facilitating participation in fun, enjoyable, freely chosen recreation activities. The other two service areas, functional intervention and leisure education, are seen as prerequisite and developmental to recreation participation. In the recreation participation service area, the role of the therapeutic recreation specialist is that of leader, facilitator, and supervisor. The participant has the most control over the recreation experience, and the therapeutic recreation specialist leads or supervises the activity, maintaining safety.

Overall, the Leisure Ability Model is primarily focused on the value of leisure in quality of life. However, the level of control the therapeutic recreation specialist is able to exert over the participant can compromise the leisure experience, as does the focus on deficit reduction as the criterion to "graduate" to recreation participation. This model does have the potential to be strengths-based, if functional intervention were conceptualized according to a social model of disability, as defined by the World Health Organization.

The Health Protection/Health Promotion Model

The Health Protection/Health Promotion Model has as its ultimate outcome health promotion as a component of quality of life (Austin, 1998). As seen in Figure 3.7, its conceptual basis is health, and its theoretical foundations are rooted in ideas of wellness, stabilization/actualization, and a humanistic perspective, where humans are viewed as self-directed and self-developing. The Health Protection/Health Promotion Model delineates three areas of therapeutic recreation services: prescriptive activities, recreation, and leisure. Like the Leisure Ability Model, this model is based on a continuum of control and functional status. As the participant becomes healthier, he or she gains more control over his or her life and more likelihood of experiencing leisure.

In the **prescriptive activities** service area, the focus is on helping participants restore or regain stability to their health using activity as a tool. The participant has little control over the process, and the therapeutic recreation specialist has the role of therapist. Once stabilized using prescriptive activity, the participant is ready to move to the recreation component of treatment.

In the **recreation component** of the Health Protection/Health Promotion Model, participants engage in intrinsically motivated, freely chosen activities, with a focus on increased health stabilization and restoration. The role of the therapeutic recreation specialist is to assist in the selection of and participation in recreation activities that promote health improvement. Control is shared by the therapeutic recreation specialist and the participant.

In the **leisure component** of the model, the focus is less on restoration and more on growth and self-actualization. The participant has freedom of choice in his or her leisure and controls how that leisure is experienced. The role of the therapeutic recreation specialist is minimal, as leisure is experienced as optimal health in favorable environments. Theoretically, according to the model, those who enjoy peak health will experience self-actualization.

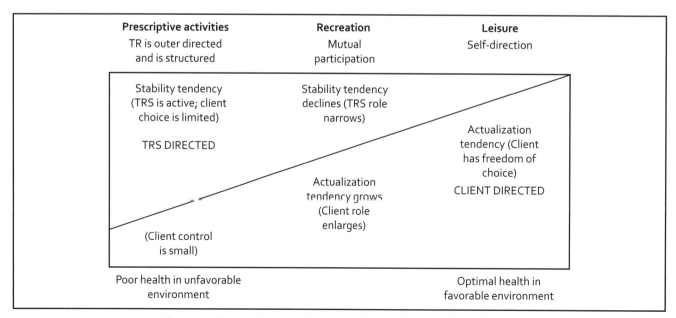

Figure 3.7 The Health Protection/Health Promotion Model *(Austin, 1998)*

The model is based on a continuum approach, and the participant must stabilize and protect her health before she is able to experience leisure. The participant must change, with assistance from the therapeutic recreation specialist, in order to reach the leisure component of the model, where self-actualization can occur.

The Therapeutic Recreation Service Delivery and Outcome Models

The TR Service Delivery and TR Outcome Models were proposed by Van Andel (1998) to delineate outcomes from therapeutic recreation services and service components of practice. Shown in Figure 3.8, the two models work in concert with each other and have as their ultimate goal quality of life, as defined by health status and functional capacity (Carter, Van Andel, & Robb, 2003).

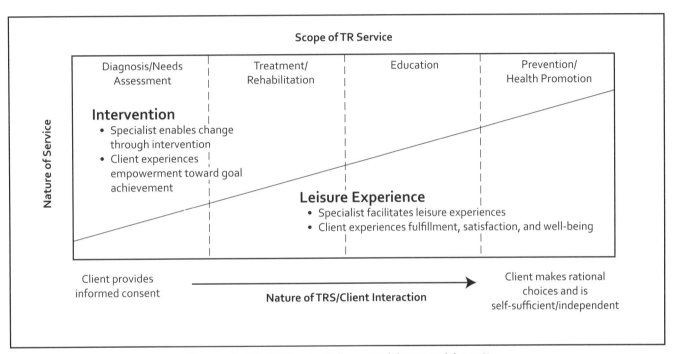

Figure 3.8a The TR Service Delivery Model *(Van Andel, 1998)*

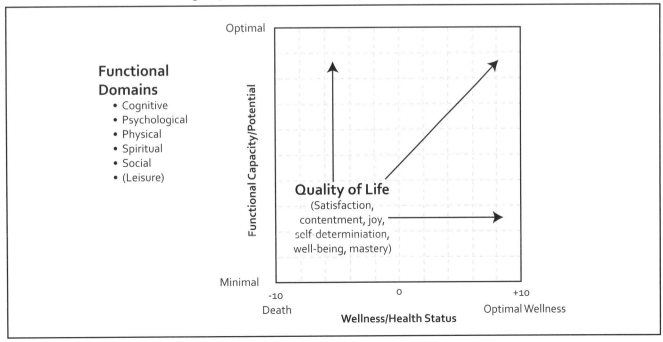

Figure 3.8b The TR Outcome Model *(Van Andel, 1998)*

The **Outcome Model** is a continuum model based on concepts of health status (from death to optimal wellness) and functional capacity (from minimal to optimal) in the areas of mental, emotional, physical, spiritual, and social functioning. Leisure is also identified as an area of functional capacity. For the third concept of the model, quality of life, the continuum moves from low to high and is an interaction of health and functional capacities. Thus, if a participant has minimal functional capacities and poor health, her or his quality of life is low.

The **Service Delivery Model** is comprised of four therapeutic recreation service areas: diagnosis/needs assessment, treatment/rehabilitation, education, and prevention/health promotion (the ultimate outcome and conceptual basis for these four areas are described in the Outcome Model). This model is again based on a continuum with more choice (consent) for the participant as he or she moves through the service components, and more participation in the leisure experience (as participation in the intervention lessens).

In the **diagnosis/assessment component** of the model, the focus is on determining the strengths, limitations, and abilities of the participant in achieving goals. The **treatment/rehabilitation component** focuses on remediation of deficits in health or functional limitations in the participant. In the **education component**, the therapeutic recreation specialist focuses on assisting the participant in developing skills, attitudes, and values that will allow him or her to function in society, improve health, and achieve a higher quality of life. Lastly, the **prevention/health promotion** component focuses on attitudes and behaviors that protect or promote healthy lifestyles. Throughout the service components, the role of the therapeutic recreation specialist is to facilitate leisure experiences and enable change through specific interventions.

Both models, the Outcome Model and the Service Delivery Model, assume a continuum approach, where the participant must reduce deficits to move toward a higher quality of life. There is variability in the focus of services, depending on setting, where the emphasis can be placed more strongly on leisure experiences or intervention services.

The Aristotelian Good Life Model

This model was developed by Widmer and Ellis (1998), and is based on Aristotelian ethics and values (see Figure 3.9). The ultimate goal of services, as conceptualized by the Aristotelian Good Life Model, is attainment of happiness and the good life. The conceptual basis of this model was described in the section

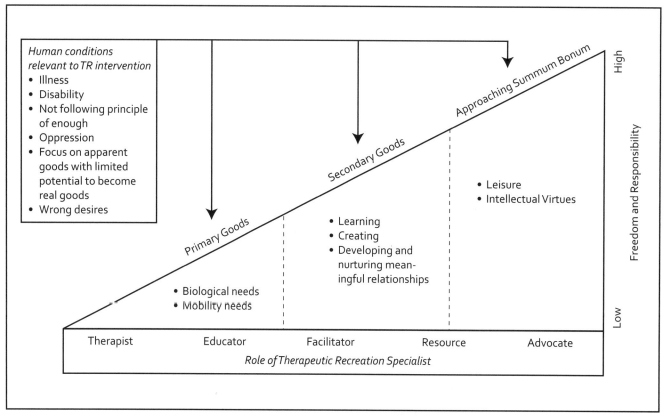

Figure 3.9 The Aristotelian Good Life Model *(Widmer & Ellis, 1998)*

on well-being in this chapter. In essence, the model is rooted in theories of human happiness, both classical and contemporary.

The model is based on a continuum of the concept of "the good life," with the participant gaining more freedom and responsibility as he or she is able to attain the elements necessary for the good life. The hierarchical elements are primary goods, secondary goods, and "summum bonum" (conceptualized in the model as leisure and intellectual virtues). **Primary goods** are biological needs and functional abilities. **Secondary goods** are learning, creativity, and development of relationships. **Summum bonum**, or leisure and intellectual virtues, are the final element. As participants overcome deficits, freedom increases, and they move along the continuum toward happiness.

The role of the therapeutic recreation specialist is determined by the functioning of the participant, ranging from therapist (with more control) to educator, facilitator, resource, and, finally, advocate (where the participant has freedom and responsibility).

Like the other continuum models, the progression of a participant to higher levels of freedom is contingent on change in the participant, and a reduction of deficits (in this model, called afflictions and oppression). The model makes the assumption that happiness, the ultimate outcome, comes to those who are able to overcome affliction and oppression (such as disability and illness) and is not available to those who have not mastered them.

Pitfalls in the Continuum Approach

The continuum approach, though intuitively attractive, has several pitfalls that we want to make explicit to truly understand the limitations of this approach in conceptualizing therapeutic recreation services. Taylor (2004) described one major pitfall as a "readiness" assumption, where participants get "caught in the continuum" because they are unable to "earn" their readiness to move to the next level of services and, consequently, the next level of control in their own lives. In most of the models described above, participants do not "graduate" to the next level of control until they have reached a certain level of functioning. The vicious cycle of lack of self-determination leads to further entrapment in the continuum, leading to further erosion of freedom and self-determination. Taylor (2004) emphasizes the irony of this trap, as the most restrictive services do not prepare people for self-determined community living that is needed for a high quality of life.

The continuum models also assume that more intensive and skilled services need to be provided by the therapeutic recreation specialist in the area of the continuum where the participant lacks control (functional intervention, treatment, prescriptive activities), often in institution-based settings like hospitals or treatment facilities. The reductionist approach to treating functional deficits may in fact be easier to facilitate and require less skill on the part of the therapeutic recreation specialist because environments are controlled and the focus is on a small part of the person. In the controlled, clinical setting, the therapeutic recreation specialist does not need to manage the natural cues and natural consequences that are rich in less controlled settings such as inclusion-based services or community reintegration. To facilitate high quality leisure experiences in natural contexts takes very careful and skillful facilitation on the part of the therapeutic recreation specialist. And the natural cues and consequences prevalent in less controlled settings are powerful signals to help participants grow and learn; their absence in the controlled setting reduces the therapeutic value of that setting.

Another pitfall of the continuum models is the idea that the professional has the "control of control." In other words, it is the therapeutic recreation specialist who decides when the participant is ready for more control in his or her life. The primacy of the professional, the inequality of power, and the message that the professional knows better than the participant about his or her life are disempowering. The continuum approach legitimizes this professional approach.

Lastly, the continuum approach makes the assumption that change must happen *in* the participant in order to move up the continuum toward more freedom. The approach lacks attention to the environmental changes, supports, and accommodations that may need to take place for a participant to achieve quality of life.

Some have argued that the continuum is fluid, and a participant can be in different places along the continuum at the same time. The logic of this argument is hard to defend, as it seems implausible that a participant can have self-control to participate in a recreation experience, then lose control when she goes to her "activity therapy group" later that day. Though it may be nice to think that participants can have a diversity of services requiring more or less self-control to help them reach their goals, the reality is that the continuum approach may restrict them to the "readiness model" and a fixed point on the continuum, based on their current level of functioning as assessed by the professional.

It is important to think about the continuum models in the context of time and evolution of our field. Most of these models were proposed when the deficit approach was the dominant paradigm, and they gave much-needed direction to practice. These models integrated what we knew at the time about how to help humans achieve a better life. They laid the foundation for the field to move forward, and bring us to the point where we can integrate a strengths approach.

Integrated Models of Therapeutic Recreation

Integrated models of therapeutic recreation share a cyclical rather than a continuum approach to therapeutic recreation service.

The Self-Determination and Enjoyment Enhancement Model

The Self-Determination and Enjoyment Enhancement Model (Dattilo, Kleiber, & Williams, 1998) is a departure from the continuum/control models described above. As shown in Figure 3.10, the ultimate outcome in this model is the cultivation of enjoyment and functional improvement, which are allegedly strongly related. The conceptual foundations of the Self-Determination and Enjoyment Enhancement Model are theories of self-determination, the role of enjoyment in well-being and personal growth, flow, and intrinsic motivation. The model makes the assumption that enjoyment and functional improvement lead to greater self-determination, which leads to greater challenges and, in turn, to greater self-determination, and so on. This self-reinforcing cycle of growth is facilitated by the therapeutic recreation specialist through a variety of approaches. The Self-Determination and Enjoyment Enhancement Model has six components, with related roles for the therapeutic recreation specialist: self-determination, intrinsic motivation, perception of manageable challenge, and investment of attention, with the outcomes of enjoyment and functional improvement.

One component of the model is **self-determination**. This area of the model focuses on assisting participants in becoming the primary causal agents in their own lives, making choices and decisions of their own accord. The role of the therapeutic recreation specialist is to assist participants in developing the skills and confidence to make decisions, communicate preferences, set goals, and increase self-awareness. Self-determination is integral to enjoyment and intrinsic motivation.

Another component is **intrinsic motivation**. Participants who experience intrinsic motivation will seek challenges that allow them to use their competencies, leading to enjoyment. Intrinsic motivation is fundamental to self-determination. The role of the

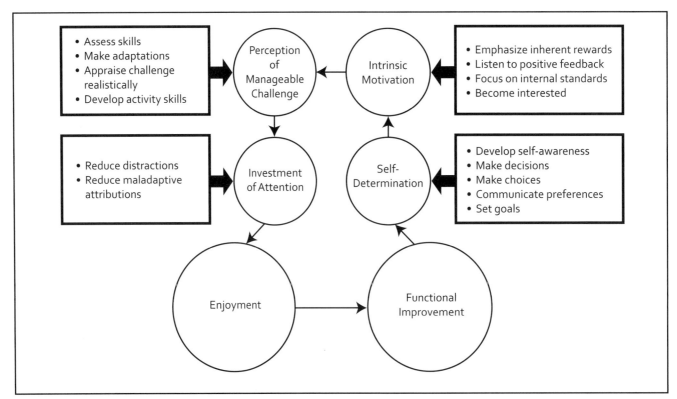

Figure 3.10 The Self-Determination and Enjoyment Enhancement Model *(Dattilo, Kleiber, & Williams, 1998)*

therapeutic recreation specialist is to assist in exploring preferences and interests, emphasize inherent rewards, reinforce positive feedback that naturally occurs in the experience, and keep the focus on internal standards.

Perception of manageable challenge is a third component of the Self-Determination and Enjoyment Enhancement Model. The psychological state that occurs when participants feel that their skills and abilities match the challenge of the activity is called *flow*. The role of the therapeutic recreation specialist in this component is to help assess skills, make adaptations based on skill and challenge, and help build those skills. In the flow state, participants feel a merging of action and awareness, which leads to the fourth model component, **investment of attention**. When participants are involved in an activity in a state of flow, they are focused and feel a strong sense of control. Goals are clear, feedback is relevant, and challenge and skills are in balance. Investment of attention is facilitated by the therapeutic recreation specialist through reducing distractions in the environment and helping participants develop accurate perceptions about their success or failure in an activity.

The last two components of the model, **enjoyment** and **functional improvement**, are the outcomes of therapeutic recreation service. They are reinforcing in that, when experienced, they in turn increase the level of the other components in the model (self-determination, intrinsic motivation, perception of manageable challenges, and investment of attention). The strength of this model lies in its cyclical nature, its focus on enjoyment, the facilitative role of the therapeutic recreation specialist, the transference of control to the participant, and its strong theoretical foundation. When first proposed in 1999, the model was criticized for the lack of empirical research validating the link between enjoyment and functional improvement. Since that time, a large and rigorous body of research has substantiated this link (Fredrickson, 2009; Lyubomirsky, 2007).

The Optimizing Lifelong Health through Therapeutic Recreation Model

The ultimate outcomes of the Optimizing Lifelong Health through Therapeutic Recreation Model are health enhancement and a healthy leisure lifestyle (Wilhite, Keller, & Caldwell, 1999; see Figure 3.11). The conceptual basis of the model is grounded in developmental theory and successful aging through selective optimization. Participants make informed decisions to accommodate changes in their functional abilities in order to remain involved in valued leisure activities, either independently or in an interdependent manner. The elements of the model include selection (of activities and goals), optimization (of personal and environmental resources), compensation

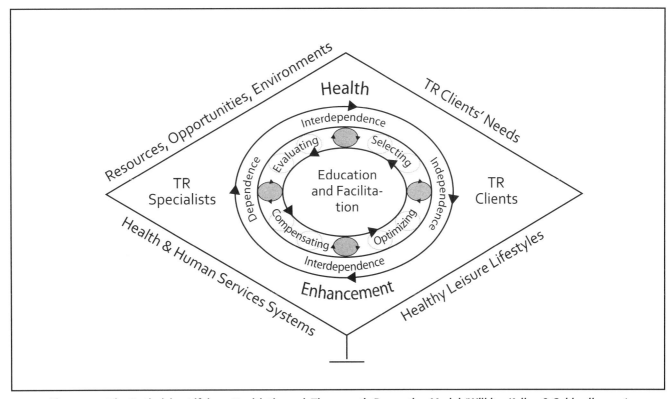

Figure 3.11 The Optimizing Lifelong Health through Therapeutic Recreation Model *(Wilhite, Keller, & Caldwell, 1999)*

(for impaired abilities), and evaluation (for effectiveness in promoting a valued leisure lifestyle). The therapeutic recreation specialist, as an educator and a facilitator, focuses on what the participant can do in her or his environment and helps to adapt or modify for any impaired abilities.

The Optimizing Lifelong Health through Therapeutic Recreation Model is a cyclical model that focuses on the abilities of participants in their environment. Through continued involvement in leisure, regardless of impairment, participants are able to maintain or enhance their health.

The Ecological Model

In 1987, Howe-Murphy and Charboneau published a seminal textbook, *Therapeutic Recreation Intervention: An Ecological Perspective.* In that text, they provided a preliminary outline of a model for therapeutic recreation, based on the ecological perspective. As can be seen in Figure 3.12, therapeutic recreation is concerned with the individual, the environment, and their process of interaction. The model is based on a theory of human ecology and social systems, with its varying levels (from the individual to the family, community, and world), inputs, interactions, energy, and outcomes.

The conceptual basis of the Ecological Model is one of capability, growth, and creative adaptation through the leisure experience. The model also delineates the role of the therapeutic recreation specialist, focusing on assessment, planning, implementation, and evaluation at the individual and environmental level. Although not fully developed, the model is important to present in this text, since it has tremendous potential for further development in the field.

THE LEISURE AND WELL-BEING MODEL AS A THEORETICAL FRAMEWORK FOR STRENGTHS-BASED THERAPEUTIC RECREATION PRACTICE

The Leisure and Well-Being Model was developed by Hood and Carruthers (Carruthers & Hood, 2007; Hood & Carruthers, 2007) in order to capture the conceptual roots of leisure and well-being from a strengths approach, and to use it as the guiding framework for therapeutic recreation practice. We will look in depth at this model (and propose our own extensions to the model in Chapter 4), as it holds great promise to guide you in the practice of strengths-based therapeutic recreation.

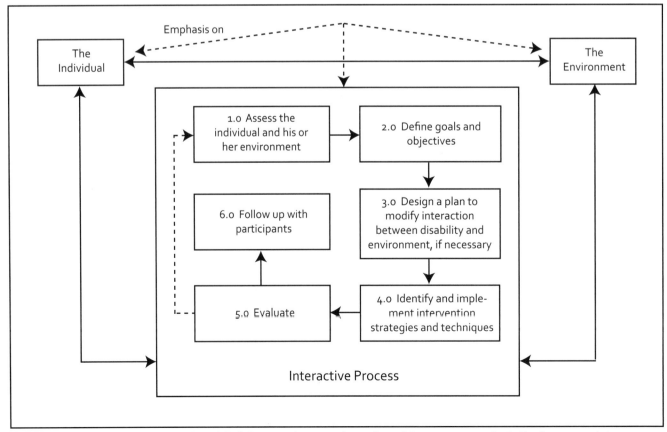

Figure 3.12 The Ecological Model of Therapeutic Recreation *(adapted from Howe-Murphy & Charboneau, 1987)*

The Ultimate Outcome

The Leisure and Well-Being Model has well-being as its ultimate, or distal, outcome (see Figure 3.13). As noted earlier, Carruthers and Hood (2007) describe well-being as "a state of successful, satisfying, and productive engagement with one's life and the realization of one's full physical, cognitive, and social-emotional potential" (p. 280). Immediate (or proximal) goals in the Leisure and Well-Being Model are enhanced leisure experiences and strengthened resources. These, in turn, contribute to increased well-being.

Conceptual Basis

The Leisure and Well-Being Model is based on the concepts of leisure, a strengths-based focus on resource development, and well-being. Carruthers and Hood (2007) clearly identify how these three theoretical perspectives converge to provide a solid rationale for the model.

Well-being is developed in asset-rich environments, where participants have opportunities to acquire resources that help them to flourish. Leisure and therapeutic recreation services provide resource-development opportunities. Well-being can also develop in response

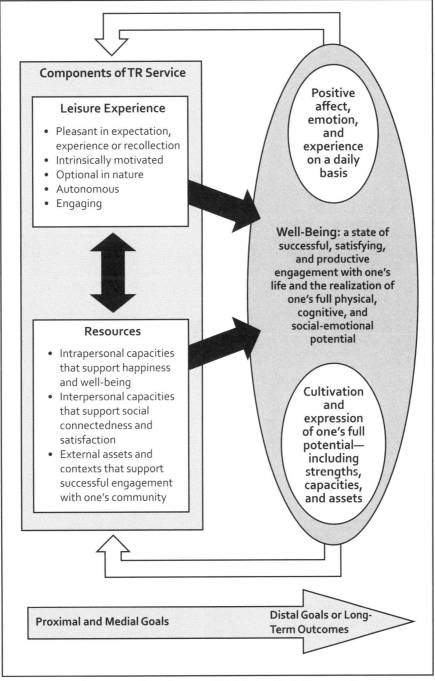

Figure 3.13 The Leisure and Well-Being Model (part one)
(from Carruthers & Hood, 2007)

to adversity or turning points (positive or negative), where a deeper meaning and purpose in life may develop. Therapeutic recreation can help guide that discovery and use leisure to help participants develop that meaning.

Leisure has a central role in well-being in that it evokes positive emotion, essential for well-being, and provides opportunities for self-determination and expression of one's strengths, also essential for well-being. Carruthers and Hood (2007) provide a sound conceptual basis for the contribution of leisure to well-being. In addition, leisure enhances a participant's resources, which are essential for well-being. The interdependence of these two concepts, and the role they play in facilitating well-being, form the solid theoretical base for the Leisure and Well-Being Model.

Scope of Therapeutic Recreation Services

The Leisure and Well-Being Model delineates two main areas of service for therapeutic recreation: enhancing leisure experiences and developing resources (see Figure 3.14). These two service components are

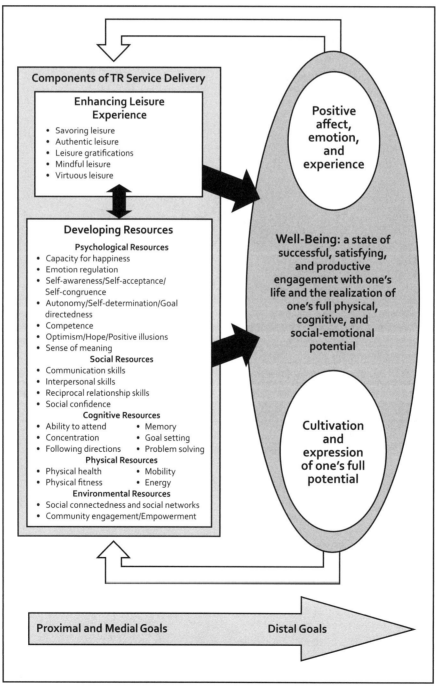

Figure 3.14 The Leisure and Well-Being Model (part two)
(from Carruthers & Hood, 2007)

cyclical and reinforcing of each other. As the therapeutic recreation specialist works to enhance leisure experiences of participants, their resources are strengthened. As participants' resources are strengthened, leisure is enhanced. This reciprocal relationship in turn strengthens participant well-being. Each service component is comprised of several purposefully identified foci, based on a large body of empirical research.

Enhancing the Leisure Experience

The Leisure and Well-Being Model is based on the premise that the type and quality of a participant's leisure experience has a major effect on well-being. Both "doing" leisure and enhancing the quality of that "doing" are important to promoting strengths development and well-being. Based on research, five ways to cultivate quality in leisure experiences are delineated in this part of the model: savoring leisure, authentic leisure, leisure gratifications, mindful leisure, and virtuous leisure.

Savoring leisure is defined as consciously paying attention to the positive aspects of leisure involvement, including positive emotions, and purposefully seeking leisure activities that create positive emotions (Hood & Carruthers, 2007). Since leisure is an area of one's life where choice is abundant, and because that choice is driven by preferences and interests, it is a rich context to seek opportunities that lend themselves to savoring. Savoring has been found to be a powerful strategy to increase well-being and other resources in one's life, such as positive self-evaluation, self-efficacy, improved social relationships, improved immune system functioning, and more (Lyubomirsky, 2007).

Facilitating **authentic leisure** is defined as the purposive selection of leisure involvement that reflects essential aspects of the self (Carruthers & Hood, 2007). Authentic leisure involves increasing self-awareness of interests, preferences, values, beliefs, feelings, and thoughts, and choosing carefully leisure involvement that allows for the full expression of those essential aspects. Carruthers and Hood (2007) identify authentic leisure as involvement in leisure activities that "feel right" and relate directly to resource development. Additionally, building authentic leisure around strengths and capabilities, rather than around remediation of weaknesses or deficits, is more powerful in impacting improved well-being (Seligman, 2002).

Leisure gratifications is defined as leisure experiences that are optimally engaging and challenging, require sustained effort and commitment, and lead to the development of strengths and personal attributes that are meaningful and rewarding for the individual.

Flow, also discussed in Chapter 6 *Theories*, provides a conceptual framework for leisure gratifications.

Mindful leisure is defined as being fully immersed in the moments of the current leisure experience using one's full attention and awareness to enhance the present moment during the experience. Mindful leisure implies full attention to the current experience—all its sights, sounds, smells, feelings and the like—and a total disengagement from thoughts, feelings, or concerns about other things in one's life. When a person is mindful during leisure, the experience is enhanced or amplified, and more beneficial to the individual in many ways (Seligman, 2002).

Virtuous leisure is defined as using one's strengths and leisure interests in the service of something larger than oneself. Virtuous leisure can include volunteering, participating in community or environmental organizations and activities, among other enterprises. It can also include informal leisure, like reading to an elderly neighbor or doing random acts of kindness. Virtuous leisure provides a sense of accomplishment and a feeling of contributing to the good in the world.

Savoring leisure, authentic leisure, leisure gratifications, mindful leisure, and virtuous leisure all enhance the leisure experience, and lead to increased well-being. They also help participants develop resources, which may also be perceived as strengths.

Developing Resources

The second area of therapeutic-recreation focus in the Leisure and Well-Being Model is developing resources. According to the model, resources include psychological, social, cognitive, physical, and environmental resources. Enhancing leisure experiences will contribute to the development of resources, but resources can also be enhanced through psycho-educational interventions, the helping relationship, and advocacy. Hood and Carruthers (2007) identify resources within each category, based on what is most amenable to therapeutic recreation services, what resources are key to well-being and leisure, and what resources are related to each other.

Psychological resources, those that help us think, feel, and reason, include capacity for happiness, emotion regulation, self-awareness, autonomy/goal directedness, competence, optimism, and a sense of meaning in one's life. Each of these resources, when further developed through leisure or other interventions, contribute to well-being and mental health.

Cognitive resources, those that help us learn and process information, include the ability to pay attention, to concentrate, to follow directions, to solve problems, to remember, and to set goals. Cognitive resources are developed further during leisure experiences, and they can enhance those experiences.

Social resources, those that help us relate to others and form social connections, include communication skills, interpersonal skills, reciprocal-relationship skills, and social confidence. Social resources are strengthened during leisure, due to its social and voluntary nature, and leisure is enhanced through effective social relationships.

Physical resources, those that help us use our bodies to move and function in our environment, include physical health, physical fitness, mobility, and energy or vitality. Physical resources are strengthened through leisure experiences when those experiences include physical activity. Physical resources enhance leisure experiences through the joy of movement, effective mastery over the environment, and development of skill and competence. In addition, a large body of research shows that physical activity affects our psychological resources in a positive way as well.

Hood and Carruthers (2007) identify these four areas of resources (psychological, cognitive, social, and physical) as being about the individual. They then define **environmental resources** as those that are outside the individual, and include social connectedness/social networks, community engagement, and empowerment. Environmental resources impact the leisure experience and, in turn, are strengthened by leisure involvement and inclusion (see Figure 3.15).

In sum, enhancing the leisure experience and developing resources, the two areas of therapeutic recreation intervention in the Leisure and Well-Being Model, are reciprocally reinforcing, and when optimally facilitated, contribute to well-being. The therapeutic recreation specialist focuses on a participant's strengths, interests, preferences, and abilities to develop resources and enhance leisure.

Role of the Therapeutic Recreation Specialist

The Leisure and Well-Being Model uses a strengths-based approach. Though not explicitly stated in the model, we deduce that the therapeutic recreation specialist is a leisure educator, leisure counselor, advocate, facilitator, skills trainer, and coach. The therapeutic recreation specialist uses empirically tested approaches

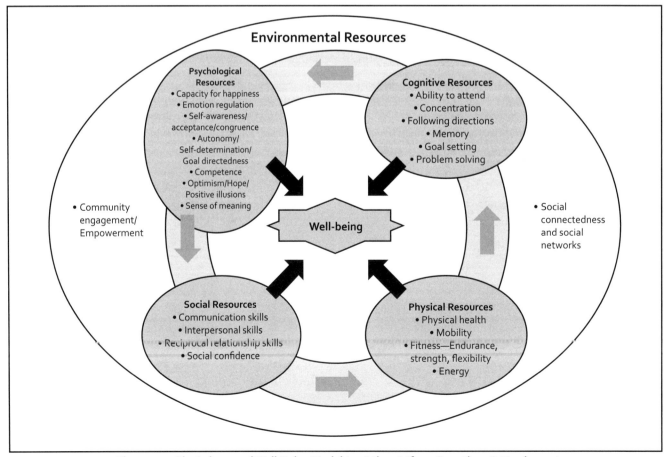

Figure 3.15 The Leisure and Well-Being Model (part three) *(from Carruthers & Hood, 2007)*

to assist participants in engaging in "smart leisure" (Lyubomirsky, 2007) that maximizes the leisure experience. The therapeutic recreation specialist advocates for participants across health, human, and recreation service delivery systems to maximize environmental resources that are necessary for well-being. Though the therapeutic recreation specialist may at times need to work in the deficit model (e.g., in acute medical settings), the focus is primarily on the strengths and capacities of the individual and on assisting him or her to develop them to their full potential.

Enhancing leisure experiences and developing resources can be directly addressed by skilled, well-educated therapeutic recreation specialists who have a deep knowledge of leisure and the systems in which leisure is typically delivered. In Chapter 11 *Implementation* we will look more in-depth at some effective strategies therapeutic recreation specialists can use to facilitate enhancement of the leisure experience and the development of strengths, or resources.

To close this discussion of therapeutic recreation models, we would like you to consider the cultural implications of each model (see Figure 3.16). We would also like to acknowledge that more models continue to emerge in the field (e.g., Heintzman, 2008) that we do not have the space to review. Lastly, we would like to offer an extension to the Leisure and Well-Being Model proposed by Drs. Hood and Carruthers, to ground it more solidly in an ecological perspective. The current Leisure and Well-Being Model has a strong focus on the individual. Our revision of the model situates the participant more firmly in his or her environment, and extends therapeutic recreation practice to more explicitly include environmental approaches as well as approaches with the individual participant. Embedding the individual in the environment is a hallmark of the positive psychology movement, where "positive institutions" is one of the pillars supporting the good life, and necessary for the ecological perspective. In Chapter 4 we present *Flourishing through Leisure: An Ecological Extension of the Leisure and Well-Being Model*.

A Final Note about Therapeutic Recreation Definitions and Models

Perhaps you noticed, as we reviewed all the various models and definitions of therapeutic recreation, that we do not use the term "recreational therapy" and rarely use the word "therapy" in our conceptualization of the field. We also do not use the term that is found frequently in professional literature, "RT/TR," as if "recreational therapy" and "therapeutic recreation" could be

My Cultural Lens:
Looking at Models from a Multi-Cultural Framework

Dieser (2002) and Dieser and Peregoy (1999) have provided useful critiques of the numerous therapeutic recreation service models from a multicultural framework. They ask us to be aware of the cultural lens that may bias assumptions we may make and ask us to make those assumptions explicit. This allows us to decide if a particular model is appropriate to use with the participants with whom we are working and any adaptations are needed to address cultural differences. For example, in several of the models, self-determination, autonomy, freedom, independence, and choice are key variables related to leisure, health, and well-being. Yet Dieser tells us that these goals are individualistically oriented, and cultures that value a collective identity, such as First Nation people, may not aspire to achieving goals that are more individualistic. Instead, they may value goals of belongingness, and be willing to subordinate their personal goals, if they have any, for the goals of the collective group. Dieser asks us to look at each therapeutic recreation service model and ask these questions:

- Is there an assumption that there is a single measure of normal behavior, regardless of cultural differences that may exist?
- Is there an assumption that individuals or collectives of people are the basic building block of society?
- Is there an assumption that the context matters in understanding key concepts?
- Is there an assumption that independence is desirable and dependence is undesirable?
- Is there an assumption that people are helped more by formal interventions and therapy than by naturally occurring, culturally appropriate support systems?
- Does the model depend on linear thinking, or on circular thinking and intuitive reasoning?

Talk through each model with a classmate or colleague and answer the questions. Then read the critiques offered by Dieser and Peregoy in the *Therapeutic Recreation Journal* to compare your observations. This exercise should help you use the therapeutic recreation service models in a culturally sensitive manner.

Figure 3.16 My Cultural Lens:
Looking at Models from a Multi-Cultural Framework

used interchangeably. We have purposely and carefully used the terms we have chosen. "Recreational therapy," which is predominantly used in medically oriented facilities, does not capture the breadth of our field. "Therapy" comes from the Greek word *therapeia*, which means to be of service to or to attend to. However, its modern meaning is "to take care of, to treat using medication or remedial training." The word "therapy" implies an unequal relationship based on sickness, deficits, and remediation. The word "therapeutic," on the other hand, implies the art or science of healing, of helping to return to wholeness. "Therapeutic recreation" is a broader, more inclusive term that includes all aspects of service provision in our field, from advocacy to therapy, education, and facilitation. The term "therapeutic recreation" embraces recreation for its inherent qualities to help people have a life of well-being.

Some in the field have suggested that we drop the word "therapeutic" from our professional title (Mobily, 1999; Sylvester, 2006), since recreation is, in and of itself, beneficial and an effective change agent. The word "therapeutic," they argue, is tantamount to the word "recreation." We would argue that "therapeutic recreation," as the title of our profession, makes explicit the unique knowledge, skills, and competencies that we learn and practice. Professionals in recreation share some of those knowledge areas and competencies, and professionals in other helping professions like social work, counseling, or occupational therapy, share a different subset of those knowledge areas and skills. But therapeutic recreation is unique in the combination of subsets of knowledge and skills we can use to help people have a life of well-being. Neither the general recreator, nor the activity therapist, has the singularly effective professional education that the therapeutic recreation specialist has. No other profession has the focus we have on the purposeful and careful facilitation of quality leisure experiences and the development of personal and environmental strengths, which lead to greater well-being for people who, due to illness, disability, or other life circumstances, need individualized assistance to achieve their goals and dreams.

The title of our professional role, therapeutic recreation specialist, captures the breadth and richness of the important and unique work we do in therapeutic recreation. In the field, however, you will find many different job titles across a wide variety of settings and systems in which we work. Table 3.6 gives a listing of some of the possible job titles you will find in therapeutic recreation. Though our job titles may change depending on agencies and settings, we are all therapeutic recreation specialists. As Dr. Nancy Navar stated at a therapeutic recreation conference, "We are one profession, many roles" (personal communication, TREC Conference, 2005).

THERAPEUTIC RECREATION AND THE SEA CHANGE

The sea change to a strengths approach is happening on a slow and grand scale across many systems, including health and human services. Therapeutic recreation, with its conceptual roots firmly planted in freedom, leisure, and self-determination—key aspects of well-being and a high quality of life—is in a unique and exciting position. We are poised to "take the rudder" and steer our profession, and others affiliated with us, into the new paradigm. In the strengths approach, leisure is valued as one of the great realms of life that can be enhanced. Improved well-being is holistic and inclusive, and health and functional ability are just one component out of many. In fact, by building on people's intrinsic goals and dreams using their strengths, passions, and

Table 3.6 Job Titles of a Therapeutic Recreation Specialist

Therapeutic recreation specialists work in many settings and many systems. Job titles tend to vary by setting, but all fall under the umbrella title in the profession, *Therapeutic Recreation Specialist*.*

Sample Job Titles		
• Activity Director	• Activity Specialist	• Activity Therapist
• Adaptive Recreation Specialist	• Case Manager	• Clinical Rehabilitation Manager
• Diversional Therapist (in Australia)	• Experiential therapist	• Inclusion Coordinator
• Inclusion Specialist	• Life Enrichment Coordinator	• Recreation Leader
• Recreation Therapist	• Recreational Therapist (job title used by the U.S. Department of Labor)	• Rehabilitation Therapist
• Therapeutic Recreation Coordinator	• Therapeutic Recreation Director	• Therapeutic Recreation Program Leader
• Therapeutic Recreation Specialist	• Therapeutic Recreationalist	• Treatment Team Leader
	• Wilderness Therapist	

Therapeutic Recreation—One Profession, Many Roles

*Certified therapeutic recreation specialist should not be used as a job title, and is only used by an individual practitioner if nationally certified by the National Council for Therapeutic Recreation. See http://www.nctrc.org/employerinfo.htm for more information. (NCTRC, 2012)

interests, health and functional ability often improve concomitantly, without a sole focus on those areas. Therapeutic recreation specialists are natural leaders in the strengths approach, and leisure is a natural arena to build strengths.

We end this chapter with a question for you. What is your role in the sea change in therapeutic recreation? Where will you focus your practice? How will you facilitate a better life with the participants with whom you work? When your fellow team members ask you what you bring to the table, what will you say? How will you mesh your values about freedom, leisure, and self-determination with the pressures of systems undergoing slow change? These are all important questions that are worthy of reflection and deep thought. The answers you give will determine your own quality of life as a therapeutic recreation specialist.

Summary

This chapter provided you with the conceptual foundations of therapeutic recreation—leisure, well-being, and quality of life—and a rationale for the centrality of the leisure experience for therapeutic recreation practice. We provided several professional and academic definitions of therapeutic recreation, as well as our own definition, and overviewed several existing therapeutic recreation service models. The Leisure and Well-Being Model was discussed in depth. Lastly, we clarified the words and title used to describe our profession, and the many job titles you will encounter in the field. In the *Self-Assessment of Learning*, we leave you with several reflective questions about your own philosophy and definition of the rich, diverse, and exciting field of therapeutic recreation.

Resources

The Quality of Life Research Unit at the University of Toronto
http://www.utoronto.ca/qol

The Quality of Life Research Unit has developed an online resource center on quality of life, as well as a sophisticated online assessment tool for quality of life.

Therapeutic Recreation: Purpose, Passion, Progress
http://recreationtherapy.com/TR.Purpose-Passion-Progress.pdf

Published by the National Recreation and Park Association (National Therapeutic Recreation Society),

Self-Assessment of Learning

- Review the professional and academic definitions of therapeutic recreation. Write your own definition of therapeutic recreation. Craft your definition, imagining yourself on an elevator, describing to a stranger what you do in therapeutic recreation.

- Over the next week, share your definition of therapeutic recreation with participants who receive therapeutic recreation services, with colleagues or classmates, and with other team members at your agency or students on your campus. After sharing your definition with several others, rewrite it to improve it.

- Write a letter or e-mail to a relative, telling them about your chosen field, therapeutic recreation. Share your letter with colleagues or classmates before you send it.

this colorful and attractive 12-page brochure wonderfully explains what therapeutic recreation is, what types of roles, settings, and approaches we use, and how we are educated. The brochure is available from the National Recreation and Park Association.

I am Your TR
http://www.cortland.edu/rec/I%20am%20Your%20TR%20booklet.pdf

Written by Dr. Lynn Anderson and her students in therapeutic recreation at SUNY Cortland, and published by the New York State Therapeutic Recreation Association, this 25-page booklet features several practicing therapeutic recreation specialists across a broad range of service settings and systems, from home health to advocacy to inpatient rehabilitation. The brochure is available for downloading at the website.

References

American Therapeutic Recreation Association. (2009). *Definition statement*. Retrieved from http://atra-online.com

Anderson, L., & Heyne, L. (2012). Flourishing through leisure: An ecological extension of the Leisure and Well-Being Model in therapeutic recreation strengths based practice. *Therapeutic Recreation Journal, 46*(2), 129–152.

Aristotle. (trans. 2000). *The Nicomachean Ethics by Aristotle* (W. Ross, Trans.). Internet Classics Archive. Retrieved from http://classics.mit.edu

Austin, D. (1998). The Health Protection/Health Promotion Model. *Therapeutic Recreation Journal, 32*(2), 109–117.

Austin, D., & Crawford, M. (2001). *Therapeutic recreation: An introduction* (3rd ed.). Needham Heights, MA: Allyn & Bacon.

Brulde, B. (2007). Happiness and the good life: Introduction and conceptual framework. *Journal of Happiness Studies, 8*, 1–14.

Canadian Therapeutic Recreation Association (Association Canadienne de Loisir Thérapeutique). (2008). *Philosophy*. Retrieved from http://www.canadian-tr.org

Carruthers, C., & Hood, C. (2007). Building a life of meaning through therapeutic recreation: The Leisure and Well-Being Model, part I. *Therapeutic Recreation Journal, 41*(4), 276–297.

Carter, M., Van Andel, G., & Robb, G. (2003). *Therapeutic recreation: A practical approach* (3rd ed.). Prospect Heights, IL: Waveland.

Dattilo, J., Kleiber, D., & Williams, R. (1998). Self-determination and enjoyment enhancement: A psychologically-based service delivery model for therapeutic recreation. *Therapeutic Recreation Journal, 32*(4), 258–271.

Diener, E. (2006). Guidelines for national indicators of subjective well-being and ill-being. *Journal of Happiness Studies, 7*, 397–404.

Diener, E., & Lucas, R. E. (2000). Subjective emotional well-being. In M. Lewis & M. Haviland (Eds.), *Handbook of emotions* (pp. 325–337). New York, NY: Guildford.

Dieser, R. (2002). A cross-cultural critique of newer therapeutic recreation practice models: The Self-Determination and Enjoyment Enhancement Model, Aristotelian Good Life Model, and the Optimizing Lifelong Health Through Therapeutic Recreation Model. *Therapeutic Recreation Journal, 41*(4), 352–368.

Dieser, R., & Peregoy, J. (1999). A multi-cultural critique of three therapeutic recreation service models. *Annual in Therapeutic Recreation, 8*, 56–69.

Fredrickson, B. L. (2009). *Positivity: Groundbreaking research reveals how to embrace the hidden strength of positive emotions, overcome negativity, and think.* New York, NY: Crown.

Free Dictionary (2008). *Quality of life definition*. Retrieved from http://www.thefreedictionary.com

Gunn, S., & Peterson, C. (1978). *Therapeutic recreation program design: Principles and procedures* (1st ed.). Englewood Cliffs, NJ: Prentice-Hall.

Heintzman, P. (2008). Leisure-spirited coping: A model for therapeutic recreation and leisure services. *Therapeutic Recreation Journal, 42*(1), 56–73.

Hood, C., & Carruthers, C. (2007). Enhancing leisure experience and developing resources: The Leisure and Well-Being Model, part II. *Therapeutic Recreation Journal, 41*(4), 298–325.

Howe-Murphy, R., & Charboneau, B. (1987). *Therapeutic recreation intervention: An ecological perspective*. Englewood Cliffs, NJ: Prentice-Hall.

Kraut, R. (2002). *Aristotle: Political philosophy*. New York, NY: Oxford University Press.

Lyubomirsky, S. (2007). *The how of happiness*. New York, NY: Penguin.

Mobily, K. (1999). New horizons in models of practice in therapeutic recreation. *Therapeutic Recreation Journal, 33*(3), 174–194.

National Council for Therapeutic Recreation Certification. (2004). *Scope of practice for the practice of recreation therapy*. Retrieved from http://www.nctrc.org

National Therapeutic Recreation Society. (1996). *NTRS philosophical position statement*. Retrieved from http://www.nrpa.org

National Therapeutic Recreation Society. (1997). *NTRS position statement on inclusion*. Retrieved from http://www.nrpa.org

National Therapeutic Recreation Society. (2004). *NTRS standards of practice.* Retrieved from http://www.nrpa.org

Nussbaum, M. (2006). *Frontiers of justice: Disability, nationality, species membership.* Cambridge, MA: Harvard University Press.

Nussbaum, M., & Sen, A. (1993). *The quality of life.* New York, NY: Oxford University Press.

O'Keefe, C. (2007). *Let's first revisit the meaning of leisure.* Handout given at the 57th Annual Metcalf Endowed Keynote Speech, Cortland Recreation Conference, SUNY Cortland, NY.

O'Keefe, C. (n.d.). *An essay for students interested in therapeutic recreation.* Retrieved from http://www.nrpa.org

Pain, K., Dunn, M., & Anderson, G. (1998). Quality of life: What does it mean in rehabilitation? *Journal of Rehabilitation, 64*(2), 5–11.

Pedlar, A., Haworth, L., Hutchinson, P., Taylor, A., & Dunn, P. (1999). *A textured life: Empowerment and adults with developmental disabilities.* Waterloo, ON, Canada: Wilfrid Laurier University Press.

Quality of Life Research Unit. (2005). *The Quality of Life Model.* Retrieved from http://www.utoronto.ca/qol/concepts.htm

Reis, H., Sheldon, K., Gable, S., Roscoe, J., & Ryan, R. (2000). Daily well-being: The role of autonomy, competence, and relatedness. *Personality and Social Psychology Bulletin, 26*(4), 419–435.

Robertson, T., & Long, T. (2008). *Foundations of therapeutic recreation: Perceptions, philosophies, and practices for the 21st century.* Champaign, IL: Human Kinetics.

Ryan, R., & Deci, E. (2001). On happiness and human potentials: A review of research on hedonic and eudaimonic well-being. *Annual Review of Psychology, 52,* 141–166.

Ryff, C., & Singer, B. (1998). The contours of positive mental health. *Psychological Inquiry, 9,* 1–28.

Schlalock, R., Brown, I., Brown, R., Cummins, R., Felce, D., Matikka, L., Keither, K., & Parmenter, T. (2002). Quality of life: Its conceptualization, measurement and application. A consensus document. *Mental Retardation, 40,* 457–470.

Self-Advocacy Association of New York State, Inc. (2006). *Making it happen. Stories of self-determination.* Albany, NY: SANYS and NYSDDPC.

Seligman, M. (1998, August). Work, love and play. President's Column. *APA Monitor, 29*(8), 1–2.

Seligman, M. (2002). *Authentic happiness: Using the new positive psychology to realize your full potential for lasting fulfillment.* New York, NY: Free Press.

Shank, J., & Coyle, C. (2002). *Therapeutic recreation in health promotion and rehabilitation.* State College, PA: Venture Publishing, Inc.

Stumbo, N., & Peterson, C. (1998). The Leisureability Model. *Therapeutic Recreation Journal, 32*(2), 82–96.

Stumbo, N., & Peterson, C. (2004). *Therapeutic recreation program design: Principles and procedures* (4th ed.). San Francisco, CA: Pearson Education.

Sylvester, C. (1987). Therapeutic recreation and the end of leisure. In C. Sylvester (Ed.), *Philosophy of therapeutic recreation: Ideas and issues* (pp. 76–89). Ashburn, VA: National Recreation and Park Association.

Sylvester, C. (1995, October). *Critical theory and therapeutic recreation: Breaking new ground.* Paper presented at the Symposium on Leisure Research, National Recreation and Park Association, San Antonio, TX.

Sylvester, C. (Ed.). (2005). *Philosophy of therapeutic recreation: Ideas and issues* (Vol. III). Ashburn, VA: National Recreation and Park Association.

Sylvester, C. (2006). With leisure and recreation for all: Preserving and promoting a worthy pledge. *Purpose, passion, progress: Celebrating 40 years of NTRS.* Ashburn, VA: National Recreation and Park Association.

Sylvester, C., Voelkl, J., & Ellis, G. (2001). *Therapeutic recreation programming: Theory and practice.* State College, PA: Venture Publishing, Inc.

Taylor, S. (2004). Caught in the continuum: A critical analysis of the least restrictive environment. *Research & Practice for Persons with Severe Disabilities, 29*(4), 218–230.

Testa, M., & Simonson, D. (1996). Assessment of quality of life outcomes. *The New England Journal of Medicine, 334*, 835–840.

Üstün B., & Jakob, R. (2005). Calling a spade a spade: Meaningful definitions of health conditions. *Bulletin of the World Health Organization, 83*, 802. Retrieved from http://www.who.int/bulletin/bulletin_board/83/ustun11051/en/

Van Andel, G. (1998). TR Service Delivery and Outcome Models. *Therapeutic Recreation Journal, 32*(3), 180–193.

Widmer, M., & Ellis, G. (1998). The Aristotelian Good Life Model: Integration of values into therapeutic recreation service delivery. *Therapeutic Recreation Journal, 32*(4), 290–302.

Wilhite, B., & Keller, J. (2000). *Therapeutic recreation: Cases and exercises* (2nd ed.). State College, PA: Venture Publishing, Inc.

Wilhite, B., Keller, J., & Caldwell, L. (1999). Optimizing lifelong health and well-being: A health enhancing model of therapeutic recreation. *Therapeutic Recreation Journal, 33*(2), 98–108.

Witt, P., & Ellis, G. (2002). *Leisure Diagnostic Battery.* State College, PA: Venture Publishing, Inc.

World Health Organization. (2002). *Toward a common language for functioning, disability, and health: ICF.* Retrieved from http://www.who.int/classifications/icf/training/icfbeginnersguide.pdf

World Health Organization. (2008). *About the World Health Organization.* Retrieved from http://www.who.int/about/governance/en/index.html

Chapter 4
INTRODUCING THE FLOURISHING THROUGH LEISURE MODEL: AN ECOLOGICAL EXTENSION OF THE LEISURE AND WELL-BEING MODEL

The golden currant is a highly adaptable plant that provides many benefits, from its beautiful blooms to abundant fruit. It provides sustenance to many living beings and has been used to create art by native peoples.

"Far away there in the sunshine are my highest aspirations. I may not reach them, but I can look up and see their beauty, believe in them, and try to follow where they lead."

—Louisa May Alcott, American author

OVERVIEW OF CHAPTER 4

- A review of our definition of therapeutic recreation
- Overview of the Flourishing through Leisure Model: An Ecological Extension of the Leisure and Well-Being Model

FOCUS QUESTIONS

- Why is an ecological approach important to therapeutic recreation practice?
- In the Flourishing through Leisure Model, what areas of practice focus on the participant?
- What areas of practice focus on the environment of the participant?
- What outcomes does the participant achieve in the Flourishing through Leisure Model?

Remember our challenge to you to be able to describe your profession clearly and succinctly to a stranger on the elevator? Or to other team members at your agency? We hope this chapter will help you become even more clear and confident in your conceptualization of therapeutic recreation. We start this chapter with a review of our definition of therapeutic recreation. We then introduce you to the Flourishing through Leisure Model. Our definition and our extension of the Leisure and Well-Being Model align with the assumptions of a strengths-based and ecological approach in therapeutic recreation practice.

OUR DEFINITION OF THERAPEUTIC RECREATION

Recall in Chapter 3 that we presented many definitions of therapeutic recreation, from both researchers and professional groups. We used those definitions, as well as theory and philosophy, to develop our own definition of the field of therapeutic recreation. Our definition is as follows:

> Therapeutic recreation is the purposeful and careful facilitation of quality leisure experiences and the development of personal and environmental strengths, which lead to greater well-being for people who, due to illness, disability, or other life circumstances, need individualized assistance to achieve their goals and dreams.

Remember that we have chosen each word in our definition carefully.

- *Purposeful facilitation* means that the leisure experiences and strengths that will be enhanced are chosen through the diligent application of individualized assessment, and are oriented toward the goals, dreams, and aspirations of the participant.
- *Careful facilitation* means that the therapeutic recreation specialist uses an individualized plan, created with the participant, and well-developed facilitation skills in all aspects of service delivery, tailored to the unique situation of each individual.
- *Quality leisure experiences* means participants find meaning, enjoyment, and growth in their leisure pursuits by exercising effortful skill in concert with stimulating challenges, using their strengths.

- *Personal strengths and environmental resources* means that we focus on those things that participants do well, that have meaning for them, and that give them hope. It means we focus on the context and environment of participants, and the strengths and resources in that environment.

- *People who, due to illness, disability, or other life circumstances, need individualized assistance to achieve their goals and dreams* delineates the very unique body of knowledge and focus of therapeutic recreation services.

  - Our expertise in leisure, strengths, aspirations, and environmental context differentiates what we do from other health and human service professionals, who tend to focus on deficits in isolated settings and have little focus on or expertise about leisure, one of the three great realms of life.

  - Our expertise in disability, use of an individualized approach using a systematic process, and skills and knowledge in forming a helping relationship differentiate us from general recreation specialists, who tend to focus on groups of people using management skills and do not have the depth of preparation in the helping relationship.

  - Our unique blend of knowledge and skills about leisure, disability, and the helping relationship is important for participants with all types of differences that may need individualized assistance to achieve well-being through leisure (see Figure 4.1).

In this chapter, we provide the conceptual framework for our definition of therapeutic recreation. The Flourishing through Leisure Model is an extension of the Leisure and Well-Being Model (LWM) developed by Drs. Carruthers and Hood (which we described in depth in the previous chapter). The Flourishing through Leisure Model grounds therapeutic recreation practice more solidly in an ecological perspective. The Leisure and Well-Being Model developed by Drs. Carruthers and Hood has a strong focus on the individual. Our expansion of the model situates the participant more firmly in his or her environment. The broadening of the model extends therapeutic recreation practice to more explicitly include environmental approaches, as well as approaches that only focus on the individual participant. Embedding the individual in the environment is a hallmark of the positive science movement, where "positive institutions" is one of the pillars supporting the good life, and is inherent in the ecological perspective.

THE FLOURISHING THROUGH LEISURE MODEL: AN ECOLOGICAL EXTENSION OF THE LEISURE AND WELL-BEING MODEL

The Flourishing through Leisure Model is grounded on a social model of disability, as recommended by the World Health Organization (2002) in its International Classification of Functioning, Disability and Health (ICF). The ICF, which will be discussed in detail in the next two chapters (*Strengths* and *Theories*), clearly lays the groundwork for professionals, including therapeutic

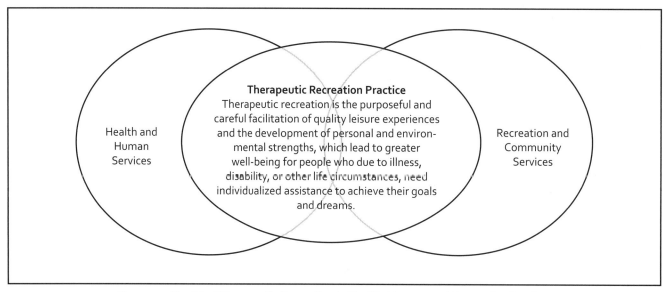

Figure 4.1 The Fit of Therapeutic Recreation in Health, Human, and Recreation Services

recreation specialists, to focus equally on environmental changes and changes within an individual with a disability See Figure 4.2 to learn more about the Social Model of Disability.

In Figure 4.3 (p. 64), we offer the Flourishing through Leisure Model: An Ecological Extension of the Leisure and Well-Being Model. The Flourishing through Leisure Model situates the **person in the environment**, and explicitly makes environmental interventions a part of therapeutic recreation practice. We have expanded both the components of therapeutic recreation practice and the outcomes of our services, based on an ecological approach and a social model of disability.

Under "What the Therapeutic Recreation Specialist Does" on the left side of the model, we have delineated two distinct foci: personal strengths and environmental resources. In addition to the goals, dreams, and aspirations of participants, these two focus areas steer the services provided by therapeutic recreation specialists. On the far left of the model, the therapeutic recreation specialist helps participants enhance their leisure and build their strengths in pursuit of their goals, much like the LWM does, with a focus on the individual.

On the right half of "What the Therapeutic Recreation Specialist Does," therapeutic recreation specialists help to make changes to the environment that will support participants in achieving their dreams, goals, and aspirations.

On the far-right side of the Flourishing through Leisure Model, the outcomes experienced by participants are pictured. The outcomes of our services are well-being in leisure and in the psychological/emotional, cognitive, social, physical, and spiritual aspects of participants' lives. Well-being, where one experiences productive, satisfying, and successful engagement with one's life in a resource-rich environment, leads to a flourishing life. Let's look at each component of the Flourishing through Leisure Model in detail.

What the Therapeutic Recreation Specialist Does in the Flourishing through Leisure Model

The Flourishing through Leisure Model allows for a wide variety of therapeutic recreation interventions and approaches to facilitate desired change. The focus is on the individual in his or her environment. The model

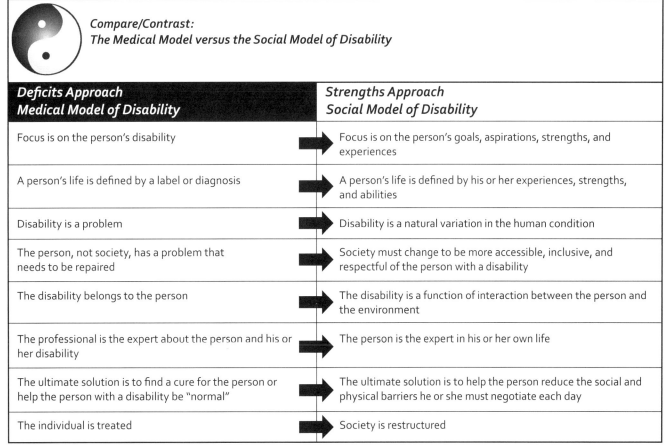

Figure 4.2 Compare/Contrast: The Medical Model versus the Social Model of Disability

64 • Therapeutic Recreation Practice: A Strengths Approach

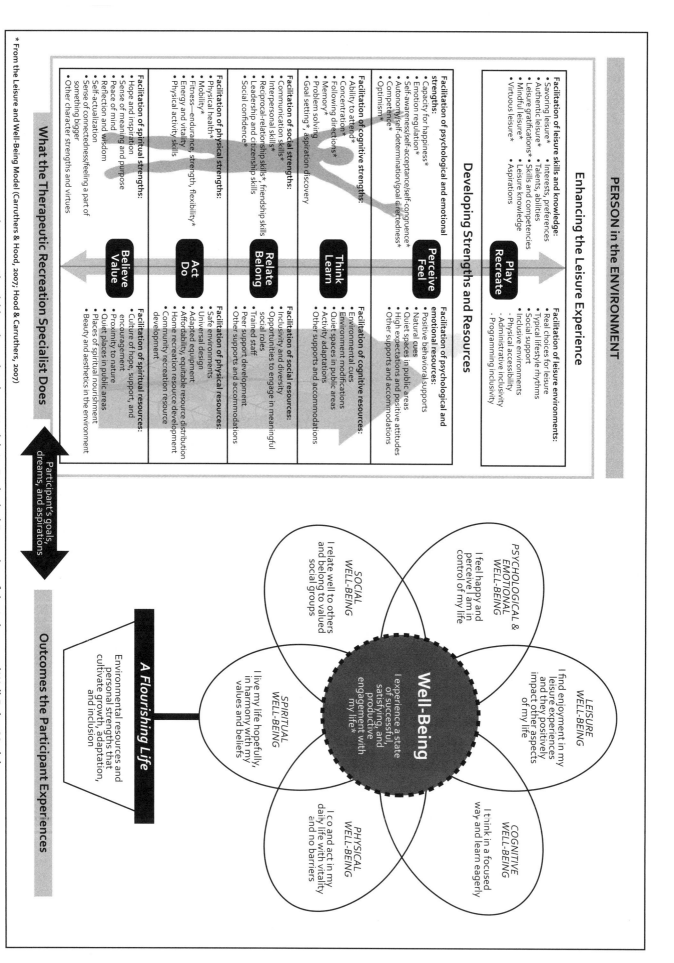

Figure 4.3 Flourishing through Leisure Model: An Ecological Extension of the Leisure and Well-Being Model (Carruthers & Hood, 2007; Hood & Carruthers, 2007)

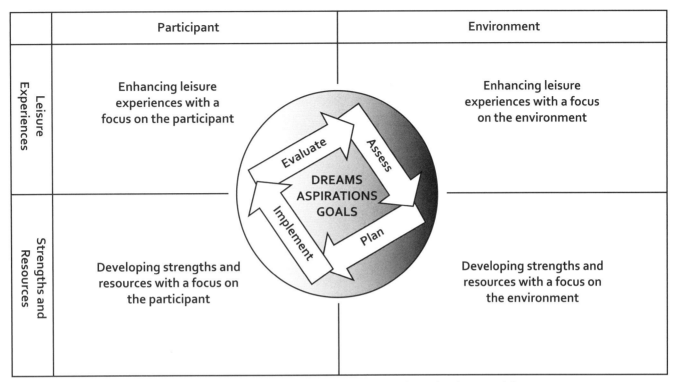

Figure 4.4 A Simplified Look at the Flourishing through Leisure Model

also targets participants' leisure experiences, and building strengths and resources, both within the participant and in the environment. The four focal areas of the Flourishing through Leisure Model are depicted in a simplified way in Figure 4.4. Driving services are the goals, dreams, and aspirations of participants and their circles of support. Helping to design services is the interactive therapeutic recreation process.

Enhancing the Leisure Experience

Therapeutic recreation specialists help participants enhance their leisure experiences in two main ways: facilitating participants' leisure skills and knowledge, and facilitating environments to support the leisure experience. In Figure 4.5, we provide the section of the Flourishing through Leisure Model that addresses enhancing leisure experiences. It is important to note that when leisure experiences are enriched, other strengths and resources develop as well, as shown by the interactive arrow in the model.

Facilitation of Leisure Skills and Knowledge in the Participant

Therapeutic recreation has traditionally included assisting participants in building their knowledge and skills in leisure, in order to experience increased leisure and life satisfaction. In the Flourishing through Leisure Model, leisure is enhanced by the important skills and knowledge delineated by Drs. Hood and Carruthers in the Leisure and Well-Being Model: savoring, authentic leisure, leisure gratification, mindful leisure, and virtuous leisure.

Remember that **savoring leisure** is consciously paying attention to the positive aspects of leisure involvement, including positive emotions, and purposefully seeking leisure activities that create positive emotions. Therapeutic recreation specialists can use many approaches to help participants more consciously savor their experiences in leisure. For example, one strategy is to give participants a homework assignment to make savoring a habit. A recent study asked participants to take a few minutes each day to savor and relish a moment they would usually rush through, and to focus on the pleasure they experienced in those moments. They then wrote down what they experienced in comparison to times they usually rushed through things, and reported feeling significant increases in happiness and a reduction in depression (Seligman, Rashid, & Parks, 2006). Savoring is a skill that can be taught in traditional leisure education, or in situ during leisure experiences. In Chapter 11 *Implementation* we will share more strategies focused on savoring.

Authentic leisure is the purposive selection of leisure involvement that reflects essential aspects of the self. Authentic leisure can be facilitated by supporting participants to clarify or discover their strengths, and then to use those strengths to pursue interests and

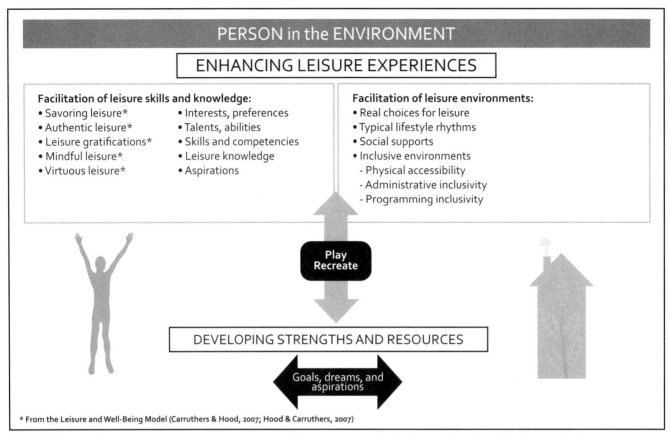

Figure 4.5 The "Enhancing Leisure Experiences" Section of the Flourishing through Leisure Model

preferences. For example, we may help a participant discover that his or her character strength is kindness and generosity. We can then assist that participant in exploring leisure interests where generosity is fundamental to participation, such as volunteering. In Chapter 9 *Assessment* we share assessment tools that enable participants to learn more about their own strengths and interests.

Leisure gratifications are leisure experiences that optimally engage and challenge the participant, require sustained effort and commitment, and lead to the development of strengths and personal attributes that are meaningful and rewarding. We can facilitate flow-like experiences by helping participants manage challenges and build skills, and thus enhance leisure. We talk more about flow in Chapter 6 *Theories* and how to facilitate it in Chapter 11 *Implementation*.

Mindful leisure is being fully immersed in the moment of the current leisure experience and using your full attention and awareness to enrich the present moment. It is akin to meditation, but it is a purposeful way of thinking during activity. It is different from savoring in that there is no attempt to relish the moment or look for pleasure. Instead, mindfulness is directing your full attention to the moment and being fully immersed by every sight, sound, smell, touch, and taste associated with that experience. Mindful leisure allows for full attention to the here and now, with no rumination about the past or the future (see Figure 4.6).

Virtuous leisure is using one's strengths and leisure interests in the service of something larger than oneself. Virtuous leisure is sharing yourself with others through leisure experiences, whether it be volunteering, helping a neighbor, or sharing skills and talents with family members. Virtuous leisure provides a sense of meaning and contribution. Therapeutic recreation specialists can help participants discover opportunities to share their strengths and talents through leisure education or as part of the therapeutic milieu, where participants help other participants learn new leisure skills.

Development of interests, preferences, talents, abilities, skills, and competencies is an area we have added to the Flourishing through Leisure Model. These are more traditional leisure education areas, and well-defined interventions and approaches are available to therapeutic recreation specialists to help participants develop in these areas (Dattilo, 2008; Stumbo, 1997, 1998, 2002a, 2002b). We can assist participants in clarifying interests and talents, as well as building skills and competencies in leisure.

Life Story:
Using Mindfulness in Leisure Education
By Brandon Cruz

Brandon Cruz developed a leisure education program centered on mindfulness as a part of his graduate work at the State University of New York at Cortland. He was working with children and adolescents who were participating in a community-based mental health program. Here he describes briefly what he did, and how the participants responded to the approach.

In Mindfulness-Based Therapeutic Recreation programs, mindful leisure and recreation experiences are promoted through the facilitation of various mindfulness techniques and practices. Often, such programs resemble informal guided meditations, in which the facilitator steadily reminds the participants to bring their attention to the present moment and the sensory experience while maintaining a nonjudgmental attitude. One of my favorite experiences facilitating a mindful leisure activity took place in the Adirondack Mountains of New York after an overnight stay in the wilderness. The group consisted of seven boys, ages ranging from 9 to 14 years. We had just completed a 2-mile hike with heavy packs, across a slippery, rocky trail through a dense, wet forest. Upon returning to the trailhead, the kids were tired, wet, and hungry. Irritability levels were high and personality conflicts were beginning to emerge. A perfect time for a mindfulness activity, which at this point, the kids were somewhat accustomed to. So it began.

> All right everyone, time for a mindfulness activity. This is a silent activity and your participation is required. These are the rules: First, everyone must remain silent for the complete 10 minutes of the activity. Second, during this time you will be encouraged to bring your attention to all you notice in the present moment. Sights, sounds, tastes, smells, thoughts, emotions, feelings and whatever else may come into your awareness. The idea is to notice everything and allow everything to be exactly as it is. Not judging anything, simply observing and allowing and being present. Third, for this activity you may remain seated where you are, you may close your eyes if you like, or you may move or walk around the near area. It is your choice. However, you must stay in sight. Any questions, comments, or concerns? No? O.K. The time begins . . . now.

At first, while I was explaining the rules of the activity, some kids remained seated in the vans where they had already "claimed" their seats. Some had their eyes closed and appeared to be taking this time just to relax. Some were finishing repacking their bags, and others were simply just wandering around taking in their surroundings and listening to the instructions for the activity. What eventually began to happen was very interesting.

After realizing they were free to move around, a silent adventure began to take place. All individuals were quickly paying attention to what each other was doing and where people might be going. Soon, a very cohesive group formed and headed to a nearby brook to explore. During this time, I would subtly remind them of the intention of the activity, gently bringing their attention to different aspects of the environment and themselves. "Notice the sound of the plane passing over head. Notice the sound of the brook. The sound of the wind in the leaves and branches of the trees. Notice the light on the water. The feeling of the rocks beneath your feet. Notice how much there is to explore within the space very close to you." And so on.

At the end of this activity, the energy of the group was much more calm and relaxed. The kids seemed much more reflective, insightful, and at peace. They seemed more mindful and better able to pay attention. Any conflicts that existed before the activity had dissolved and were let go. Afterwards, we all enjoyed a spectacular drive to our next destination and activity, which at this point the kids were demonstrating they would be able to participate in safely. Cliff jumping on the Ausable River!

Figure 4.6 Life Story: Using Mindfulness in Leisure Education

Increased leisure knowledge and awareness for participants is another area that can be facilitated by therapeutic recreation. Knowing more about leisure, and about one's attitudes and values toward leisure, enables participants to make better choices and decisions for enjoyable experiences (Stumbo & Peterson, 2004).

Clarification or discovery of aspirations for leisure is another area we can facilitate in therapeutic recreation. Most people, when they are asked what they most want in life, will have leisure experiences as a part of their response. Doing fun things with family and friends, experiencing enjoyment and health, traveling, having a stimulating and enjoyable hobby, contributing to the community through clubs and groups, and other leisure activities—these are typical responses when people are asked about their goals or dreams. We can help participants clarify their goals for leisure, which will directly impact their well-being. We discuss this idea more in Chapter 9 *Assessment* and Chapter 11 *Implementation*.

Though these areas we have added to the Flourishing through Leisure Model could be addressed in authentic leisure and virtuous leisure, we want to make them explicit in the practice of therapeutic recreation. Helping participants clarify their interests, preferences, talents, and aspirations is at the heart of strengths-based therapeutic recreation practice. Helping participants develop awareness of leisure, and build knowledge, skills, and competencies supports the development of their interests and talents and helps them reach their aspirations. We explore each of these areas more fully in Chapter 5 *Strengths*.

Strengthening Environmental Resources to Enhance Leisure Experiences

Often, change must happen in the environment for a participant to fully experience leisure. One specific area to focus on is the **facilitation of real choices for leisure**, where the therapeutic recreation specialist advocates for home and community recreation resources and opportunities that are accessible to participants, regardless of their life situation. Often, especially when participants live in institutional settings, imposed choices for leisure, instead of real ones, exist. Only narrow choices that are convenient are offered. In the Flourishing through Leisure Model, the therapeutic recreation specialist would ensure *real* leisure choices. For example, participants with developmental disabilities who live in a group-home setting would have several choices for their leisure that day, based on their interests and talents, instead of only two choices such as going to the grocery store or the shopping mall, neither of which may interest them or develop their talents. Facilitation of real choices for leisure puts the therapeutic recreation specialist in the role of advocate, networker, and resource/community developer.

Facilitation of typical lifestyle rhythms is another area of ecologically based therapeutic recreation practice. Often, institutional rhythms are followed in health and human service settings. In the Flourishing through Leisure Model, the therapeutic recreation specialist would ensure typical lifestyle rhythms. For example, in a long-term care facility, residents would sleep until they want to get up, eat when they are hungry, recreate when they choose, and other rhythms that allow continuity from their life before institutionalization, instead of following regimented routines. Therapeutic recreation services, tailored to the self-determined rhythms of participants' lives, often take the form of supports, accommodations, and environmental enhancements to home and community leisure.

Facilitation of social supports is another specific area of environmental enhancement for leisure in the Flourishing through Leisure Model. Therapeutic recreation specialists take an active role in exploring social networks in preferred leisure settings, helping participants make connections with others, building bridges to relationships, and fading out their involvement as natural friendships form or group membership is solidified. Often this approach entails educating others about disability and the supports participants need to be included. For example, a therapeutic recreation specialist may assist a participant with a chronic mental illness in joining an art club, provide transportation to initial club events, and observe the kinds of social networks in place at the events. Through observation, the therapeutic recreation specialist identifies other participants who appear interested and friendly, and helps nurture those relationships with the participant. The therapeutic recreation specialist, with the permission of the participant, shares information with other club members so they know how to assist the participant with the disability in fully participating, whether it is through understanding what behavioral supports are needed, or offering assistance with transportation.

Lastly, in order to enhance leisure environments for the participants we serve, therapeutic recreation specialists can **facilitate inclusive environments—physically, administratively, and programmatically**. Therapeutic recreation specialists provide technical assistance and advocacy to help make recreation agencies and settings more physically accessible. Therapeutic recreation specialists assist agencies in being more socially inclusive, whether in programming or administrative practices, again through advocacy, technical assistance, and staff or peer training. Many of the interventions introduced here are described in more detail in the rest of this book, particularly in Chapter 11 *Implementation* and Chapter 12 *Transition and Inclusion*.

Developing Strengths and Resources

Therapeutic recreation specialists help participants build or use their own strengths and resources both through enhancing their leisure experiences and through other approaches, when needed. As can be seen in the left side of the model in Figure 4.3, the Flourishing through Leisure Model focuses on services to build strengths in the participant and resources in the environment across five life domains: (a) psychological/emotional, (b) cognitive, (c) social, (d) physical, and (e) spiritual.

Psychological and Emotional Domain

Facilitation of Psychological and Emotional Strengths in the Person

Psychological and emotional strengths are those that help us perceive the world around us, and feel and regulate a range of emotions. Figure 4.7 shows the part of the Flourishing through Leisure Model that focuses on some of the psychological and emotional strengths of the participant that can be facilitated by a therapeutic recreation specialist through leisure experiences and many other approaches. These strengths include capacity for happiness, emotion regulation, self-awareness, self-acceptance and self-congruence, a sense of autonomy and goal-directedness, competence, and optimism. Drs. Hood and Carruthers identified these particular strengths in the Leisure and Well-Being Model as those that are especially amenable to therapeutic recreation intervention and are key to well-being. In Chapter 6 *Theories* and Chapter 11 *Implementation* we look at how to facilitate optimism, autonomy/self-determination, and increased happiness. Interventions can include leisure education and psycho-educational interventions such as relaxation training, guided imagery, pet therapy, therapeutic use of creative arts, anger management, therapeutic adventure activities, medical play, therapeutic use of play, and more.

Facilitation of Resources in the Environment to Help Build Psychological and Emotional Strengths

In order to enhance resources in the environment to help participants build their psychological and emotional strengths, therapeutic recreation interventions can include the following approaches.

Facilitation of positive behavioral supports is an approach that is helpful to participants who need assistance in communicating effectively or regulating emotions. Positive behavioral supports assist participants in being fully included in spite of challenges they may experience at a certain point in time. Positive behavioral support is based on the premise that all behavior is a form of communication and that we must learn to listen more carefully to participants who are communicating an important need to us through their behavior. We talk about positive behavioral supports in depth in Chapter 11 *Implementation*.

Natural cues and consequences can help participants learn effectively, adapt more flexibly, and generalize learning across many functional environments. When participating in leisure experiences in typical settings, therapeutic recreation specialists can enhance cues and consequences to heighten learning and growth, through activity analysis and adaptation, through careful activity leadership, through hierarchical prompts, and through debriefing and other reflection exercises.

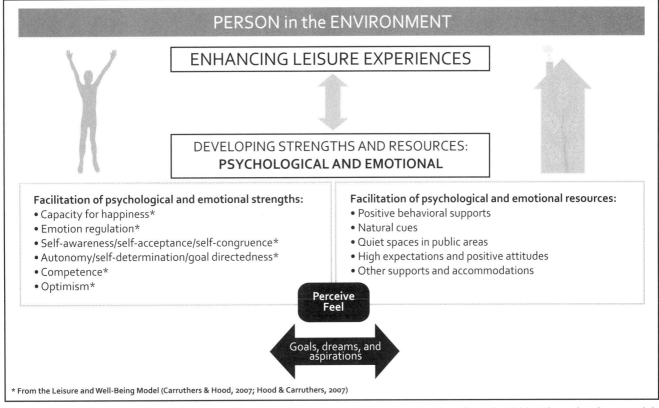

Figure 4.7 The "Developing Psychological and Emotional Strengths and Resources" Section of the Flourishing through Leisure Model

Quiet spaces in public areas allow participants a place to regroup, reduce anxiety, or relax temporarily during activities and programs. Therapeutic recreation specialists can ensure these spaces are available through environmental assessment, educating community service agencies about the need for such spaces, providing technical assistance to create spaces, and advocating for spaces when needed.

Communication of high expectations and positive attitudes on the part of others toward the participant with a disability is an area where we as therapeutic recreation specialists can make a significant difference. First, we can model high expectations. We can structure activities to promote the development of positive attitudes, using best practices in inclusion and cooperative activities. We can do many activities to help change negative attitudes, from disability awareness training, to peer orientations, to creating leadership positions for people with disabilities.

Other supports and accommodations may be needed by participants to develop and use their psychological and emotional strengths fully. The list of interventions provided here are commonly used and effective approaches, but there are many others available to help enrich the environment for the participant.

Cognitive Domain

Facilitation of Cognitive Strengths in the Person

Cognitive strengths are those that help us think and learn. Cognitive strengths include the ability to attend, ability to concentrate, ability to follow directions, memory, problem-solving skills, and goal-setting and aspiration-discovery. Figure 4.8 shows the part of the Flourishing through Leisure Model that focuses on some of the cognitive strengths of the participant that can be facilitated by the therapeutic recreation specialist through leisure experiences and many other approaches. Drs. Carruthers and Hood, in the Leisure and Well-Being Model, provide empirical support for the role of leisure experiences in building cognitive resources. In addition, therapeutic recreation specialists can use approaches such as reminiscing, remotivation, sensory stimulation, problem-solving groups, cognitive retraining, adapted activities, and more.

Facilitation of Resources in the Environment to Help Build Cognitive Strengths

In order to enhance resources in the environment and help participants build their cognitive strengths,

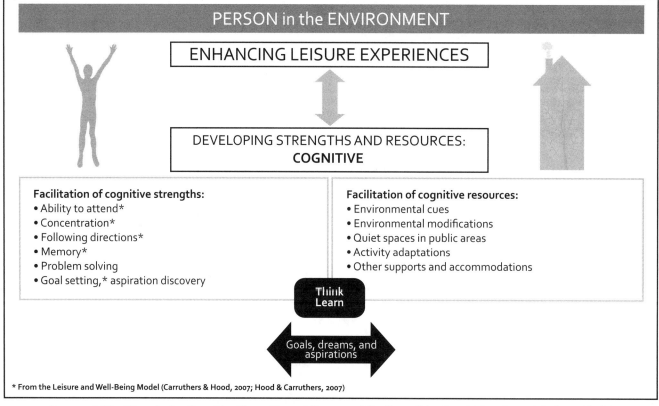

Figure 4.8 The "Developing Cognitive Strengths and Resources" Section of the Flourishing through Leisure Model

therapeutic recreation interventions can range from creating a relevant context in an institutional setting to adapting equipment. We describe some common approaches here.

Facilitation of environmental cues and prompts, such as activity calendars and holiday decorations in residential environments, or picture-cue books in activity programs, is an effective environmental approach to help participants build cognitive strengths. Even the color schemes of rooms and buildings can make a difference in cognitive response, and should be chosen carefully (e.g., blues are cooler and more relaxing, reds are warmer and more stimulating). In addition, having numerous resources available for cognitive stimulation in residential or institutional settings is imperative. Books, music, puzzles, word games, and the like will help participants easily access leisure experiences that promote stimulating and novel involvement that supports cognitive development.

Environmental modifications can be made by the therapeutic recreation specialist to assist participants in thinking and learning more easily. Some examples of environmental modifications include providing clear, contrasting paint schemes in facilities, with pictorial and large-print room numbers to help participants navigate a facility. De-cluttering hallways and paths of travel can reduce distraction. Reducing noise level and background noise can help participants focus better. Providing numerous pictorial prompts in the environment can help with memory. These are just some examples of the numerous ways environments can be modified to support cognitive abilities.

Quiet spaces in public areas is an approach described earlier under psychological/emotional strengths development. Participants may also need quiet spaces to provide support for needs in the cognitive domain. A quiet space allows participants to reduce the amount of stimuli and integrate sensory input more coherently. This is especially true for participants with autism, who may have a heightened sensory input system, and will need a quiet space during activities or programs to reduce the amount of stimuli to the senses and allow sensory reintegration before rejoining an activity.

Activity and equipment adaptations encourage participants of varying levels of cognitive functioning to fully participate in leisure experiences. By slowing down an activity, breaking it into smaller steps, reducing the amount of complicated rules, and taking similar measures, one will facilitate fuller participation.

Other supports and accommodations may be needed by participants to fully develop and use their cognitive strengths. The list of interventions provided here are commonly used and effective approaches, but many more are available to help enrich the environment for the participant. Often, therapeutic recreation specialists will need to provide advocacy and technical assistance to ensure that people with disabilities have the enriched environments they need to flourish.

Social Domain

Facilitation of Social Strengths in the Person

Social strengths are those that help us relate to others and belong to valued social groups. The facilitation of social strengths in the participant and the development of social resources in the environment are shown in Figure 4.9 (see p. 72).

Social strengths that can be facilitated by therapeutic recreation, through the leisure experience and other approaches, include communication skills, interpersonal skills, friendship skills, leadership and citizenship skills, and social confidence. Including friendship, leadership, and citizenship skills is important to help participants develop meaningful and socially valued connections with others, and acknowledges that people of all abilities can contribute to our communities and society.

Social strengths can be facilitated exceptionally well through leisure experiences. In addition, we can use approaches such as leisure education, social skills training, assertiveness training, leadership development, activity-based self-esteem groups, animal-facilitated therapy, horticulture therapy, therapeutic use of humor, and other psycho-educational interventions.

Facilitation of Resources in the Environment to Help Build Social Strengths

In order to enhance resources in the environment to help participants build their social strengths, therapeutic recreation interventions can include a variety of strategies that focus on education, advocacy, and community building.

Fostering inclusivity and diversity is a continual approach that helps agencies, community groups, and programs become more welcoming of all people. In Chapter 12 *Transition and Inclusion* we will look more in-depth at how to help communities become more physically, administratively, and programmatically inclusive.

Opportunities to engage in meaningful social roles can be facilitated through networking, community-building, and program development. People with disabilities have much to offer in terms of skills, knowledge, and competency. Helping participants find their niche in their communities, and helping that niche become inclusive and welcoming, is an important therapeutic approach.

Training agency and program staff so they understand disability and inclusion is an important strategy for building social resources. As a therapeutic recreation specialist, you have a unique body of knowledge in disability and the leisure experience that makes you especially capable of providing staff training to a wide variety of groups and agencies. By training staff, the environment is enhanced for social development.

Development of peer and natural supports is another important strategy focused on building social resources in the environment. Helping a participant connect, be welcomed, and then belong for the long-term takes effort. Therapeutic recreation specialists can help build social networks, peer support, and other naturally occurring social supports through a variety of strategies. We discuss these approaches in more depth in Chapter 11 *Implementation*.

Participants may need other supports and accommodations in order to fully develop and use their social strengths. The interventions listed here are commonly used and effective approaches. Often, therapeutic recreation specialists will need to provide education, advocacy, and technical assistance to ensure that people with disabilities have enriched environments to use or build social strengths.

Physical Domain

Facilitation of Physical Strengths in the Person

Physical strengths are those that help us "act" and "do" with no barriers. Physical strengths help us experience functional physical abilities and health. Figure 4.10 shows the section of the Flourishing through Leisure Model that focuses on physical strengths and resources.

Physical strengths that can be facilitated by therapeutic recreation through leisure and other approaches include physical health; mobility; fitness, including endurance, strength, and flexibility; energy and vitality; and physical activity skills in the context of leisure. Leisure is a natural medium through which to build physical strengths. Many leisure activities involve physical effort and movement, which contribute to physical fitness. In addition, participants are typically more motivated to consistently engage in physical activity if it aligns with their interests and preferences and is enjoyable. Other typical approaches used by therapeutic recreation to build physical strength include exercise groups, tai chi, yoga, equine-assisted therapy, aquatic therapy, wellness education groups, adapted sports and games, and the like. We look more closely at physical activity in Chapter 11 *Implementation*, as it has been found to be one of the more effective strategies to build happiness and well-being.

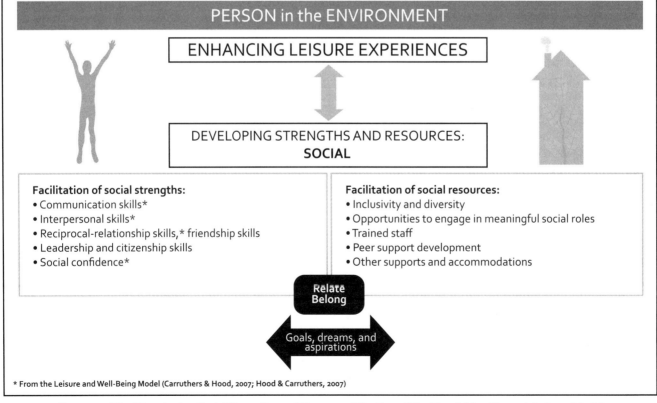

Figure 4.9 The "Developing Social Strengths and Resources" Section of the Flourishing through Leisure Model

Facilitation of Resources in the Environment to Help Build Physical Strengths

In order to enhance resources in the environment to help participants build their physical strengths, therapeutic recreation interventions can include many differing approaches. Some of the more common approaches are provided below.

Facilitation of safe environments for physical activity is an important intervention for therapeutic recreation. Safe environments encompass not only indoor facilities, but outdoor spaces as well. Safe places to walk, bike, play, and run, such as trails, playgrounds, and parks that are easily accessible to where participants reside, are important. Therapeutic recreation specialists are involved in community planning, park planning, and other initiatives to ensure safe recreational environments.

Universal design is a planning concept that holds that all environments, both built and natural, should be designed so that they can be accessed by all people, regardless of size, shape, or ability. Therapeutic recreation specialists have expertise in accessibility and universal design, and they provide advocacy, technical assistance, and staff training to ensure participants can access environments for leisure experiences.

Adapted equipment and activities is a strategy that allows participants to pursue the leisure experiences of their choice, regardless of ability. A wealth of adaptive equipment exists, or can be created from scratch, to bridge the gap between what the participant can do, and what the activity or environment demands. Equipment can range from all-terrain wheelchairs, to grasping cuffs, to large-print playing cards. Often, therapeutic recreation specialists develop adaptive equipment or provide technical assistance for other recreation providers so that participants can fully participate in programs and services.

Affordability and equitable resource distribution is an area of focus for therapeutic recreation specialists in helping participants pursue leisure experiences. Therapeutic recreation specialists assist in securing scholarships or reduced fees, if needed, or in advocating for sliding fee scales or increased service provision in neighborhoods. Networking and advocacy are key skills used by therapeutic recreation specialists to help participants pursue their goals for leisure and well-being.

Home and community recreation resource development is an important task for therapeutic recreation specialists to help participants sustain quality leisure experiences in their lives. Resource development can range from serving on advisory boards of community agencies, to advocacy, to leisure education.

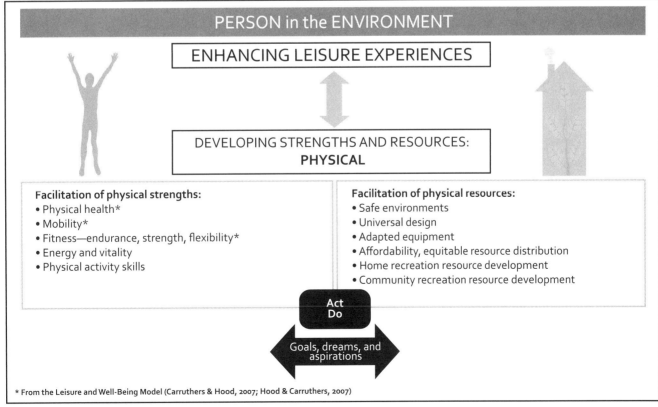

Figure 4.10 The "Developing Physical Strengths and Resources" Section of the Flourishing through Leisure Model

Spiritual Domain

Facilitation of Spiritual Strengths in the Person

Spirituality is defined as having strong and coherent beliefs about the higher purpose and meaning of life (Seligman, 2002). It is the search for meaning in life through something that is larger than the individual self (Lyubomirsky, 2007). Saleebey (2006) identifies three core assertions about spirituality: (a) it incorporates yet transcends the biological, social, psychological, political, and cultural aspects of a person; (b) it reflects our struggle to find meaning and purpose beyond our own concerns; and (c) it is the essence that joins us with greater complexities in life and inspires reverence. Spirituality is an important aspect of the person and the environment, and an area where therapeutic recreation specialists can facilitate greater strengths. Figure 4.11 shows the spiritual section of the Flourishing through Leisure Model.

In this area, we delineated specific strengths as having hope and inspiration, a sense of meaning and purpose (moved from psychological resources in the original Leisure and Well-Being Model), peace of mind, a sense of connectedness (through which one feels a part of something larger than oneself, and a kinship to the other people, plants, and animals on earth), reflection and wisdom, self-actualization, and other character strengths and virtues (which will be introduced in Chapter 5 *Strengths*). Spiritual strengths can be fostered through authentic and virtuous leisure. In addition, therapeutic recreation specialists use interventions such as values clarification, meditation, reminiscence, life review, journaling, yoga, tai chi, religious traditions and rituals, and other approaches.

Facilitation of Spiritual Resources in the Environment

In order to enhance resources in the environment to help participants build their spiritual strengths, therapeutic recreation interventions can include many activities that provide a place and space for spiritual activities.

Facilitation of proximity to nature is a very important area for therapeutic recreation specialists. Increasingly the research shows how important being in nature is to our mental and physical health, as well as to our spirit (see Figure 4.12).

Communities of worship/meditation are often facilitated by therapeutic recreation specialists in collaboration with other team members. Participants' leisure experiences frequently revolve around a valued social group related to religion or spirituality, especially in some cultures. Facilitating access and social inclusion in those communities is an important role for therapeutic recreation.

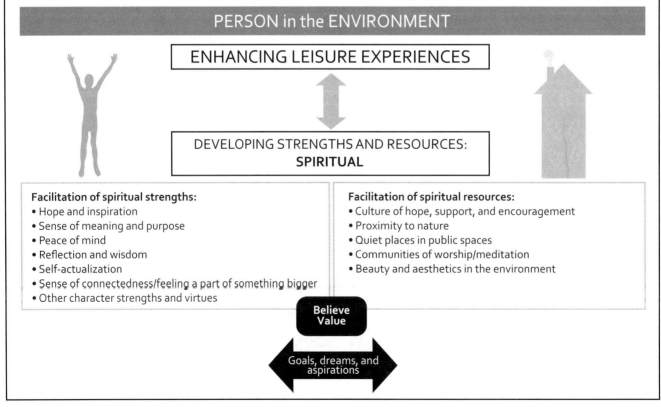

Figure 4.11 The "Developing Spiritual Strengths and Resources" Section of the Flourishing through Leisure Model

Primary Source Support: A Dose of Nature

Taylor, F., & Kuo, F. (2009). Children with attention deficits concentrate better after a walk in the park. *Journal of Attention Disorders, 12*(5), 402–409.

In the general population, attention is reliably enhanced after exposure to certain physical environments, particularly natural environments. This study examined the impacts of environments on attention in children with Attention Deficit Hyperactivity Disorder (ADHD). Taylor and Kuo took children on walks in three different settings—one especially "green" and two less "green"—and kept everything about the walks as similar as possible. They found that after the walk in the park, children generally concentrated better than they did after a walk in the downtown area or the neighborhood area. The greenest space was best at improving attention after exposure.

What this particular study tells us is that the physical environment matters. The researchers didn't know what it was about the park, exactly—the greenness or lack of buildings—that seemed to improve attention, but what the study did find is that even though everything else was the same (who the child was with, the levels of noise, the length of time, the time of day, whether the child was on medication), if they just changed the environment to a "green park," they saw a measurable improvement in children's ability to concentrate.

The researchers concluded that the benefits of a dose of nature don't apply just to children with ADHD. "We're all on a continuum of attention so this study has implications for all of us," said Taylor, one of the researchers. "ADHD is just at the far end of attention functioning, but there're plenty of us who fall somewhere close to that end of the continuum, and we all experience times when we're mentally fatigued—times when we're less able to focus and do tasks and get easily distracted. The evidence suggests that natural settings can benefit everyone, even children (and adults) who have not been diagnosed with ADHD."

Figure 4.12 Primary Source Support: A Dose of Nature

Beauty and aesthetics in the environment is another area of focus for therapeutic recreation. In institutional settings, assisting participants in creating a milieu that is aesthetically pleasing and inviting is particularly important in sending a message of respect and hope. Leisure activities that are creative and expressive can often enrich environments, whether through participants' artwork, music, or plants and animals. Therapeutic recreation is in a unique position to facilitate a beautiful and aesthetically pleasing environment that helps build a stronger sense of peace and spirituality.

Cultures of hope, support, and encouragement can be facilitated by all team members, but therapeutic recreation specialists have more opportunities to provide this important environmental resource. Assisting people in pursuing their leisure goals provides the kind of hope and support needed to begin to see that there is meaning and joy in their lives. It is often said of therapeutic recreation that, after other team members have helped them walk, we give them somewhere they want to walk to and someone with whom they want to walk.

Quiet places in public spaces is again an important resource to advocate for, in order to facilitate the development of spiritual strengths. Reflection, contemplation, and other activities that help sustain spirituality need a quiet, non-distracting, and soothing place to happen.

Summary of Developing Strengths and Resources

In sum, we have conceptualized the areas of strengths development for the participant and resource development in the environment as:

- Perceiving and feeling (psychological strengths)
- Thinking and learning (cognitive strengths)
- Relating and belonging (social strengths)
- Acting and doing (physical strengths)
- Believing and valuing (spiritual strengths).

For each of these areas of strength, both the person and the environment can be enhanced and developed. Enhancing leisure experiences and developing strengths and resources (the targets of therapeutic recreation intervention) are reciprocally reinforcing, and when optimally facilitated in the person and his or her environment, contribute to well-being.

Based on the Leisure and Well-Being Model developed by Drs. Hood and Carruthers, the Flourishing through Leisure Model: An Ecological Extension of the Leisure and Well-Being Model makes explicit all the truly effective work we do as therapeutic recreation specialists in the communities and other contexts of participants' lives.

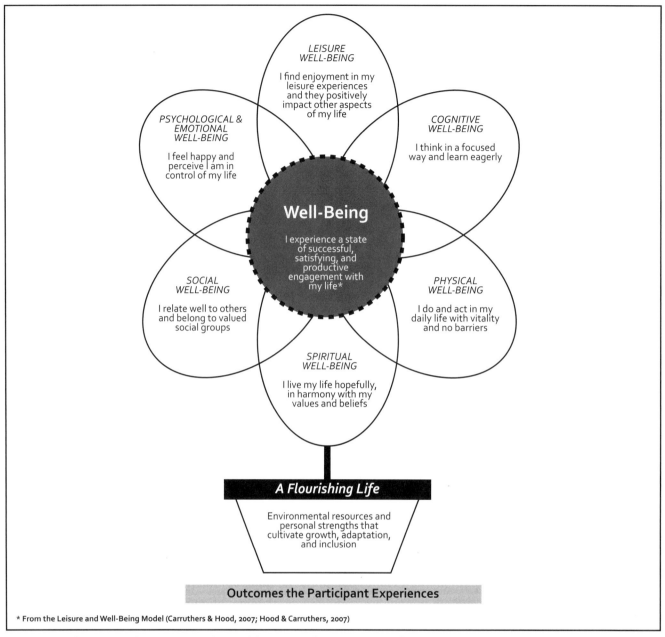

Figure 4.13 The "Outcomes the Participant Experiences" Section of the Flourishing through Leisure Model

OUTCOMES THE PARTICIPANT EXPERIENCES IN THE FLOURISHING THROUGH LEISURE MODEL

In the Flourishing through Leisure Model, the outcome of therapeutic recreation services is enhanced well-being in asset-rich environments, where participants' goals, dreams, and aspirations have been furthered. Enhanced leisure and development of strengths across any of the five domains are the components that contribute to well-being, and are also important outcomes of therapeutic recreation practice. These six areas, as shown in Figure 4.13, all interrelate and form the basis of overall well-being and a flourishing life:

- Leisure well-being, where participants find enjoyment and pleasure in their leisure experiences (which also impact positively on other aspects of their lives), savor leisure experiences, and feel that they use their strengths in leisure

- Psychological and emotional well-being, where participants feel happy and perceive control in their lives

- Cognitive well-being, where participants think in a focused way and eagerly learn

- Social well-being, where participants relate well to others and belong to valued social groups

- Physical well-being, where participants do and act in their daily lives with vitality and without barriers
- Spiritual well-being, where participants live their lives in a hopeful manner, in harmony with their values and beliefs

It isn't necessary for participants to be "strong" or high-functioning in every aspect of well-being. For example, a participant can experience overall well-being even if he or she physically cannot do certain activities due to a functional impairment or difference, such as a spinal cord injury.

We used the metaphor of a golden currant flower to introduce this chapter. A golden currant is a highly adaptable, useful, and vigorous flower, with desirable fruit. In fact, many Native American tribes used the golden currant to make one of their foods that sustained them, pemmican. The golden currant has variability in its form in nature. It can have five or six petals and still be "whole." This is much like our model, where someone may be lacking in an area of well-being, but still have a good life, and still enjoy the fruits of leisure to sustain them in a high quality of life (see Figure 4.14).

The Flourishing through Leisure Model assumes strengths are everywhere, in people and environments. The left side of the model, "What the Therapeutic Recreation Specialist Does," provides approaches that draw out and amplify those strengths and resources. Using the metaphor of the flower, and a flourishing life, the left side of the model would be akin to a bag of fertilizer, or plant food. It boosts those naturally occurring strengths and helps them grow.

Summary

In this chapter, we provided a brief review of our definition of therapeutic recreation. We then presented the Flourishing through Leisure Model: An Ecological Extension of the Leisure and Well-Being Model, based on the Leisure and Well-Being Model developed by Drs. Hood and Carruthers. The Flourishing through Leisure Model moves therapeutic recreation practice to an ecological approach and focuses our practice not just on individuals, but on environments and contexts as well. The Flourishing through Leisure Model, like the original Leisure and Well-Being Model, identifies two main areas of focus for therapeutic recreation practice: enhancing the leisure experience and developing strengths and resources. In both areas, we focus on the individual *and* the environment. Strengths are further defined as psychological/emotional, cognitive, social, physical, and spiritual, and they can be developed in the individual and the environment. The outcome of therapeutic recreation practice is a flourishing life and well-being across several domains in enriched environments. The entire process is driven by the goals, dreams, and aspirations of the participant (see p. 78 for Table 4.1 and Figure 4.15). See Figure 4.16 (p. 79) for an example of the Flourishing through Leisure Model in practice.

In the next three chapters, we will explore in much more depth what strengths are, what theories underlie the development of strengths and well-being, and what principles guide therapeutic recreation

Primary Source Support: The Red Hat Society and Well-Being

Son, J., Kersetter, D., Yarnal, C., & Baker, B. (2007). Promoting older women's health and well-being through social leisure environments: What we have learned from the Red Hat Society. *Journal of Women and Aging, 19*(3/4), 89–104.

The Red Hat Society is an organization founded by women for women, to promote playfulness and positive social relationships. There are over a million members across the world. Women over 50 years wear red hats to organizational functions, while women under 50 wear pink ones. The red hats are a symbol of the fun, verve, humor, and "élan" or joy of spirit that the Society has as its mission. The motto of the Red Hat Society is "We celebrate life at every age." Activities of the society range from traveling to going out to tea to "doing exactly what we wish to do."

Son and colleagues surveyed over 1,600 women in the Red Hat Society to determine how membership contributed to their health and well-being. The women reported that their lives were changed and enriched by their involvement with the Red Hat Society. The main benefits they reported were the creation of happy moments, support in responding to transitions and negative events in their lives, and an enhancement of the self. The researchers concluded that being involved in the social leisure environment of the Red Hat Society provided social support and coping, transformative leisure processes, social identity formation, and enhanced well-being. They conclude by strongly recommending that doctors and therapeutic recreation specialists should encourage and support participation in the Red Hat Society!

Figure 4.14 Primary Source Support: The Red Hat Society and Well-Being

Table 4.1 The Heart of the Flourishing through Leisure Model

Several themes flow through the Flourishing through Leisure Model, which represent the essence of the model:

- The participant is at the center of therapeutic recreation services.

- The participant's goals, dreams, and aspirations drive the therapeutic recreation process.

- The participant is seen within the rich contexts of the environments in which she or he participates.

- The therapeutic recreation specialist considers all aspects of the participant holistically—psychological, emotional, social, cognitive, physical, spiritual, as well as leisure.

- Both the participant's individual strengths and the environmental resources are taken into account during assessment and planning.

- The participant's environmental strengths and resources are like the fertilizer that nourishes the soil, from which personal strengths and a flourishing life grow.

- Therapeutic recreation services are outcomes-based and reflect the multidimensionality of human well-being and quality of life.

practice, as framed by the Flourishing through Leisure Model: An Ecological Extension of the Leisure and Well-Being Model.

In closing, we as authors want to recognize the enormous contribution Drs. Cynthia Carruthers and Colleen Hood have made to the profession of therapeutic recreation in their development of the Leisure and Well-Being Model. The model provided us, as authors, a rigorous and well-conceptualized foundation to broaden and expand our ideas on strengths-based and ecological principles for therapeutic recreation practice. Drs. Hood and Carruthers have made a unique and lasting contribution to the field of therapeutic recreation, and we sincerely thank them for helping to move therapeutic recreation toward strengths-based practice in the sea change we are experiencing in health and human services.

Resources

The Well-Being Index
http://www.well-beingindex.com

In an inspirationally bold initiative, the Gallup Organization and Healthwise have undertaken an ambitious project to measure the daily well-being of people in the U.S. for 25 years. The *Well-Being Index*, which measures aspects of well-being (which align with the Flourishing through Leisure Model), is administered daily to 1,000 randomly sampled U.S. citizens. From the information collected, you can track how Americans fare in their level of well-being, from "suffering" to "struggling" to "thriving." The U.S. Well-Being Index is charted in real time at the website.

The Science Network
http://thesciencenetwork.org/programs/beyond-belief-candles-in-the-dark/panel-human-flourishing-eudaimonics

The Science Network is dedicated to using science as "a candle in the dark." The Network makes programs about science and stimulates national dialogue on important topics. Recently, the Science Network created a series on well-being and human flourishing. You can watch some of the greatest scientists and philosophers of our time share their research and reflections in this important area.

My Cultural Lens: Cross-Cultural Variations in Well-Being

Uchida and colleagues (2004) looked at cross-cultural variations in happiness and subjective well-being. They found cultural variations in the meaning of happiness, motivators underlying happiness, and predictors of happiness. In North American cultures, happiness tended to be defined by personal achievement. Motivators tended to be experiencing positive affect. Happiness was best predicted by self-esteem. In East Asian cultures, happiness tended to be defined by interpersonal connectedness. Motivators tended to be experiencing a balance of positive and negative affect. And happiness was best predicted by social relationships. How do these cross-cultural variations affect how you practice therapeutic recreation? Though our ultimate outcome is enhanced well-being for the participants with whom we work, how might we change the approaches and focus we use with individuals, based on their cultural context?

Figure 4.15 My Cultural Lens: Cross-Cultural Variations in Well-Being

Life Story:
Joanna as a Person in Her Environment

Becca, a therapeutic recreation specialist who worked for a community inclusion cooperative, was asked to work with a young girl named Joanna, who happened to have Down syndrome. Joanna's family had several dreams for her, mostly centered on making friends, being healthy, and succeeding at her life in whatever she chose to do. Joanna had one dream—to be a gymnast! Working with the family, the local park district who offered gymnastics, and the IEP (Individualized Education Plan) team, Becca helped Joanna and her family along the path to their aspirations.

First, Becca spent time with Joanna to learn more about her abilities and strengths. She found Joanna to be fun-loving, personable, and spontaneous. When she was given extra time, Joanna could communicate with those around her. Physically, Joanna would benefit from additional physical activity in her life, and her family physician cleared her for participation in gymnastics. Joanna did need help in learning some new social skills to help her succeed in the gymnastics program. Mostly, she needed to learn to wait her turn and be patient, both skills needed to function successfully in the program.

Becca spent time at the gymnastics program to understand what supports or accommodations might be needed to help Joanna be a gymnast. She noted that the program was structured by ability level, not age, and small groups of girls rotated around the gym together. The beginners group that Joanna would join had girls her own age in it, as well as some younger children. Becca also noted that a fair amount of time was spent waiting in line for turns on the equipment. The girls in line were mostly left to their own devices as the program staff focused on the one or two girls whose turn it was on the equipment. Becca identified this as an area where changes would be needed for Joanna to be successful.

Prior to Joanna joining the gymnastics program, and with the help of Joanna's mom, Becca met with the staff and the girls in Joanna's new class. Becca facilitated a peer orientation, where she shared information about Joanna. Becca shared the things Joanna loved—pizza, sleepovers, Hannah Montana, riding a bike, and more—the same kinds of things they loved. She also shared that Joanna needed a little more time to communicate and asked the girls to be sure to slow down and give her that time and always ask her to repeat things they didn't understand. Becca shared that standing in line was a challenge for Joanna, like it was for many of them. She asked the girls to come up with ways they could help make standing in line go better, and to share those ideas with her and the gymnastics staff.

Becca brought Joanna to the gymnastics program the first day to meet the girls and to watch how the program worked. Becca explained to Joanna how the rotations work, and how the girls need to stand in line and wait their turn. Joanna watched excitedly and practiced standing in place quietly and patiently. The next class period, Joanna joined her group fully, with support from Becca, who rotated around with her, and only intervened when needed. The girls in Joanna's group came up with the solution to play string games, or "cat's cradle" with Joanna, while waiting in line. Soon all the girls in the gym were coming to class with their piece of yarn. "Cat's cradle" became the rage in the program, and all the children were much more content to wait their turn! Joanna soon became a full member of her team. She learned to wait patiently, and her behavior was reinforced by the activities she loved to do—gymnastics and playing with other children. She gained in physical fitness as she progressed in the program, and made friends with the other girls.

Becca faded out of being present at the gymnastics program very quickly, and monitored how things progressed with Joanna over time. Because Becca was able to foster natural supports by having the other girls in the program help with Joanna's behavior differences, the transition to full participation went well. Becca met with Joanna's parents and the gymnastics staff to discuss the next steps. Joanna's parents were so happy with how well she was doing in the program. They talked about how Joanna had learned to wait more patiently in other aspects of her life, and how the other girls on the team had invited Joanna to sleepovers and other fun events. They also shared that Joanna had lost excess weight and had more energy. The gymnastics staff members were especially surprised at how successful the girls' ideas were for making standing in line an enriched time, with small games and activities. By changing the program structure, all the girls benefited, not just Joanna.

Becca used an ecological, strengths-based approach to help Joanna and her circle of support reach her dreams and aspirations. Becca focused on helping build Joanna's strengths and interests and changing the environment to be more supportive and enriching. Joanna's life story is a nice example of the Flourishing through Leisure Model in action.

Figure 4.16. Life Story: Joanna as a Person in her Environment

Self-Assessment of Learning

- Using the Flourishing through Leisure Model: An Ecological Extension of the Leisure and Well-Being Model as a framework, identify your own leisure, psychological/emotional, cognitive, social, and spiritual strengths, and brainstorm how they may be further strengthened through enhancement of resources in your home, community, and other environments.

- Consider a participant with whom you work or volunteer. How does the Flourishing through Leisure Model apply to his or her life? What are the participant's strengths and potential environmental resources? How can you enhance their leisure experiences and environment?

Clay Dyer, the Most Inspirational Fisherman Ever
http://sportsvideo2.magnify.net/video/Clay-Dyer-The-Most-Inspiratio

On the website provided, you can view a 9-minute video about Clay Dyer. Clay is a pro bass fisherman. He also happens to have a significant disability. But Clay is not defined by his impairment; he is known for his dreams, skills, talents, character strengths, and supportive contexts. Clay Dyer's life encapsulates the essence of the Flourishing through Leisure Model, as he aspires to become a pro champion.

References

Carruthers, C., & Hood, C. (2007). Building a life of meaning through therapeutic recreation: The Leisure and Well-Being Model, part I. *Therapeutic Recreation Journal, 41*(4), 276–297.

Dattilo, J. (2008). *Leisure education program planning: A systematic approach* (3rd ed.). State College, PA: Venture Publishing, Inc.

Hood, C., & Carruthers, C. (2007). Enhancing leisure experience and developing resources: The Leisure and Well-Being Model, part II. *Therapeutic Recreation Journal, 41*(4), 298–325.

Lyubomirsky, S. (2007). *The how of happiness.* New York, NY: Penguin.

Saleebey, D. (2006). *The strengths perspective in social work practice* (4th ed.). Boston, MA: Allyn & Bacon.

Seligman, M. (2002). *Authentic happiness: Using the new positive psychology to realize your full potential for lasting fulfillment.* New York, NY: Free Press.

Seligman, M., Rashid, T., & Parks, A. (2006). Positive psychotherapy. *American Psychologist, 61,* 774–778.

Son, J., Kersetter, D., Yarnal, C., & Baker, B. (2007). Promoting older women's health and well-being through social leisure environments: What we have learned from the Red Hat Society. *Journal of Women and Aging, 19*(3/4), 89–104.

Stumbo, N. (1997). *Leisure education III: More goal-oriented activities.* State College, PA: Venture Publishing, Inc.

Stumbo, N. (1998). *Leisure education IV: Activities for individuals with substance addictions.* State College, PA: Venture Publishing, Inc.

Stumbo, N. (2002a). *Leisure education I: A manual of activities and resources* (2nd ed.). State College, PA: Venture Publishing, Inc.

Stumbo, N. (2002b). *Leisure education II: A manual of activities and resources* (2nd ed.). State College, PA: Venture Publishing, Inc.

Stumbo, N., & Peterson, C. (2004). *Therapeutic recreation program design: Principles and procedures* (4th ed.). San Francisco, CA: Pearson.

Taylor, F., & Kuo, F. (2009). Children with attention deficits concentrate better after a walk in the park. *Journal of Attention Disorders, 12*(5), 402–409.

Uchida, Y., Norasakkunkit, V., & Kitayama, S. (2004). Cultural constructions of happiness: Theory and empirical evidence. *Journal of Happiness Studies, 5,* 223–239.

World Health Organization. (2002). Toward a common language for functioning, disability, and health: ICF. Retrieved from http://www.who.int/classifications/icf/training/icfbeginnersguide.pdf

Chapter 5
Strengths—At the Heart of Therapeutic Recreation Practice

The Jack-in-the-Pulpit is a strong, bold flower with high variability.

"When I use my strength in the service of my vision it makes no difference whether or not I am afraid."

—Audre Lorde, American poet, teacher, and activist

Overview of Chapter 5

- An overview of strengths and related concepts
- An encyclopedia of strengths
  - Internal strengths
  - External strengths and resources
- Recreation and leisure as key strengths and opportunities to build other strengths
- Meaningfulness of strengths and application to therapeutic recreation practice

Focus Questions

- What do strengths mean for the people we serve in therapeutic recreation? Why are strengths at the heart of therapeutic recreation practice, guiding what we do?
- What internal strengths do people have? Why are these strengths important to people's well-being, and to their goals and aspirations?
- What external strengths and resources are important in the context of people's lives? Why do these strengths matter in therapeutic recreation practice?
- What roles do play, recreation, and leisure have in adding strength to a person's life?

What are Strengths?

A definition of "strength"
The quality or state of being strong; vigor; power of resistance; vigor of action; a strong or valuable attribute; a source of power or encouragement; sustenance

Synonyms of "strength"
Hardiness, sturdiness, vigor, power, mighty, the good part of, endurance, stalwart, sound, capable, potent, effective, durable, permanent, persistent

Synonyms of "problem"
Trouble, difficulty, deficiency, weakness, a lack of, disrepair

Strengths are at the heart of therapeutic recreation practice. When we as therapeutic recreation specialists focus our attention on what people hope for or what they want to see happen in their lives, what they are good at, what is supportive in their environment, and what they value, we are best able to help them achieve their goals and aspirations. We are able to help them improve their well-being and quality of life. In order to systematically and carefully focus on strengths, we must have a clear and deliberate understanding of what those strengths are.

This chapter will look closely at strengths and provide an encyclopedic overview using an ecological approach—that is, an approach that considers the person *and* the environments in which she or he lives, works, and plays. Using an ecological approach, strengths can be conceptualized as being internal and external. Internal strengths include interests and preferences, talents and abilities, skills and competencies, knowledge, aspirations and goals, and character strengths and virtues. External strengths include family support, social support and friendships, community resources, home resources, opportunities for participation and contribution, and high expectations. Leisure and recreation are also key factors in people's well-being, as well as an avenue to build other strengths. Figure 5.1 provides a visual representation of the internal and external strengths that will be described in this chapter. While internal and external strengths are presented as two distinct spheres, a very dynamic and complex relationship actually exists between them, as suggested by the dotted line that separates the two circles. This permeable dotted line implies a symbiotic interplay between the two kinds of strengths: internal strengths can be directed toward building external environmental supports; environmental supports can strengthen and nurture internal strengths.

The strengths-based approach is different than the problem-oriented, or deficits approach, which is often used in health and human service professions (see Figure 5.2). In a strengths-based approach, the people with whom we work in therapeutic recreation are viewed as having potential that is waiting to be developed, not problems that need to be fixed. Strengths are the center of attention of our practice, not merely tools to fix problems. Our work focuses on building and developing strengths, not merely easing problems. Keep this philosophical difference in mind as you learn more deeply about strengths. Focusing your attention in this way will help you create the mental maps needed to practice therapeutic recreation from a strengths perspective.

This chapter will focus on strengths, but it is first helpful to clarify related concepts. Other similar terms used in recreation, health, and human services include "resources," "assets," "protective factors," and "capabilities."

Strengths, in general, can be defined as the qualities or states of being strong, as having the capacity for exertion or endurance. When talking about people, strengths include desirable personal qualities and characteristics, talents and skills, environment, interests, and aspirations (Rapp & Goscha, 2006). A strength is the ability to consistently produce a positive outcome, and is composed of skills, knowledge, and talent (Buckingham & Clifton, 2001).

Resources can be defined as a source of supply or support, an available means, and a natural feature or phenomenon that enhances the quality of human life. Resources are reserves, both internal and external, that people can draw upon when they need them in their lives (Hood & Carruthers, 2007). Carruthers and Hood used the term "resources" in their Leisure Well-Being Model, discussed in Chapter 3, as they felt that the term was closely tied to the theoretical construct of well-being and because resources are amenable to development through therapeutic recreation intervention.

Assets are defined as advantages or resources. This term is broadly used in the youth development and community development fields. In youth development, external assets are relationships, activities, and structures that create a positive environment for people through support, empowerment, boundaries and expectations, and constructive use of time. Internal assets are values, skills, and beliefs that people need to fully engage with and function in the world around them as a result of a commitment to learning, positive values, social competencies, and a positive identity (Mannes, 2008).

Protective factors are discussed in the child and youth development field. They are the qualities of a person or context or their interaction that predicts positive outcomes, particularly in situations of risk or adversity (Wright & Masten, 2004).

Capabilities, in general, can be defined as the possession of attributes (such as physical or mental power) required for performance or accomplishment. Capabilities are the abilities to take effective and appropriate actions to live effectively with others (Staron, Jasinksi, & Weatherley, 2006).

We have chosen to use the term "strengths" in our work, as we view strengths as resources that have been capitalized on and developed more fully. Strengths are "actualized resources" that are part of the fabric of well-being of a person's life. Use of the term "strengths" aligns well with therapeutic recreation practice, as we have historically defined ourselves as the "strengths profession." Also, the word "strengths" has an inspiring appeal—helping people build strengths is a noble calling! However, the term you will use in practice may vary by the setting in which you provide therapeutic recreation services. The important principle to remember, regardless of the terminology used, is to focus on those aspects of people and their environments that are positive, and that will help them experience well-being and quality of life.

The remainder of this chapter will provide you with a clear understanding of the strengths you can help people build to create a life of meaning and quality.

INTERNAL STRENGTHS

Internal strengths belong to the person. They are the characteristics, attributes, and behaviors that make up the person. Though not an exhaustive list, internal strengths include interests and preferences, talents and abilities, skills and competencies, knowledge, aspirations and goals, and character strengths and virtues.

Chapter 5–Strengths—At the Heart of Therapeutic Recreation Practice • 83

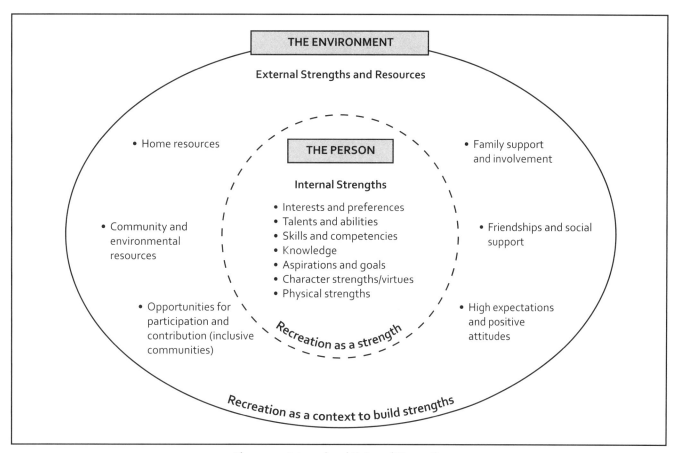

Figure 5.1 Internal and External Strengths

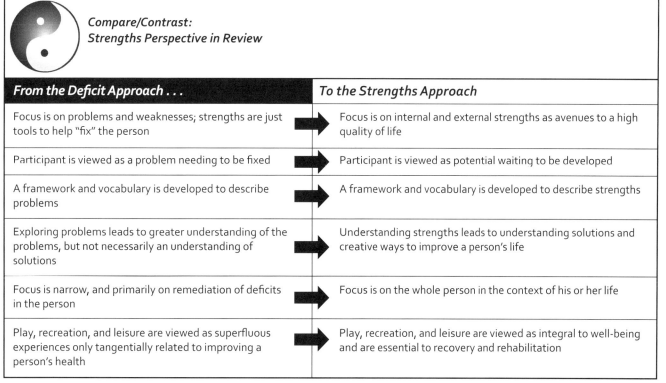

Figure 5.2 Compare/Contrast: Strengths Perspective in Review

Table 5.1 Forms of Recreation Interests and Preferences

Witt & Ellis (2002)
(from the Leisure Diagnostic Battery)

Recreation Activity Domains
- Outdoor/nature
- Music/dance/drama
- Sports
- Arts/crafts/hobbies
- Mental linguistic

Style Domains
- Individual/group
- Risk/non-risk
- Active/passive

World Health Organization (2003)
(from the International Classification of Functioning)

Recreation and Leisure Classifications
- Play
- Sports
- Arts and culture
- Crafts
- Hobbies
- Socializing
- Other recreation and leisure not specified

Community Life Classifications
- Informal associations
- Formal associations
- Ceremonies
- Other community life not specified

Edginton, DeGraaf, Dieser, & Edginton (2006)

Recreation Activity Categories
- Sports
- Outdoor recreation
- Performing arts (dance, drama, music)
- Arts
- New arts (use of technology)
- Travel and tourism
- Crafts
- Literary
- Self-improvement
- Hobbies
- Social recreation
- Voluntary services

Nall Schenk (2002)
(from the Leisurescope Plus)

Recreation Categories
- Games
- Sports
- Nature
- Collection
- Crafts
- Art and music
- Entertainment
- Volunteerism
- Social affiliation
- Adventure

Caldwell (2004)
(from TimeWise)

Categories of Recreation Activities
- Sports
- Exercise
- Creative activities
- Performance arts
- Music
- Outdoor interests

Benefits of Participation
- Physical
- Social
- Mental
- Future
- Psychological
- Spiritual
- Natural
- Creative
- Community

Beard & Ragheb (2002)
(from the Leisure Interest Measure)

Leisure Activity Domains
- Physical
- Outdoor
- Mechanical
- Artistic
- Service
- Social
- Cultural
- Reading

Interests and Preferences

Interests are a feeling of having your attention and curiosity particularly engaged by something. **Preferences** are things that are liked more than others, things that are set or held above others. Preferences drive your choices or selections (Lichtenstein & Slovic, 2006; Peterson, 2006). Taken together, interests and preferences help us choose those things we want to include in our lives for enrichment and satisfaction. When we engage in activities and experiences that hold our attention and that we value, we feel self-determined and motivated. We learn more, feel happier, and persevere longer when we pursue our interests and preferences. Interests are often maintained over time and are an expression of our personality (Kolanowski, Buettner, Costa, & Litaker, 2001; Lopez & Snyder, 2003). See Figure 5.3 for a cultural perspective of interests and preferences.

All people have a breadth and depth of interests and preferences—some we are born into through our family and culture; others we build through experiences in our lives. Some of these interests become passions for

My Cultural Lens: Formation of Interests and Preferences

Heejung and Sherman (2007) found that there are cultural differences in how preferences are formed between Americans and Asians. Where self-expression is valued and a part of preference formation in the United States, it is not given such a cultural emphasis in East Asia. How do you think your culture has influenced your preferences and interests? How has family or geography affected your preferences and interests? Ask your friends or acquaintances from other cultures how they feel their preferences are the same or different than yours.

Figure 5.3 My Cultural Lens: Formation of Interests and Preferences

us. **Passion** is "what compels us to pursue and devote ourselves to certain goals and activities, and is one of the strongest expressions of our desires" (McGill, 1996, p. 9). Vallerand and colleagues (2008) define passion as a strong inclination toward an activity that individuals like or love, that they find important, and in which they invest time and energy. The passion becomes a part of a person's identity, and can even become a central feature of self-identity. We may define ourselves, for example, as a windsurfer, or as a cyclist. Preferences or passions for recreation experiences are an outcome of many factors, such as gender, age, race, friends, environmental opportunities, socioeconomic status, culture, and ability (Raymore, 2002).

Forms of recreation activities and styles of participation have been categorized in many ways, all of which provide a framework or vocabulary to focus on when discussing interests and preferences with participants. Table 5.1 presents examples of ways recreation interests and preferences have been conceptualized. Leisure interest assessment tools, developed to help people increase awareness of their preferences, will be discussed in greater depth in Chapter 9 *Assessment*. These examples are provided here to help you begin to create your own vocabulary to focus on and discuss interests and preferences as key strengths in the people we serve in therapeutic recreation.

Talents and Abilities

Talents are the special, often creative, natural abilities or aptitudes that people have. Talents are those innate abilities that we are born with and which we may or may not develop to their full potential (Moon, 2003; Papierno, Ceci, Makel, & Williams, 2005; Seligman, 2002). A talent is something like perfect pitch or lightning speed. We can be surprised sometimes by people's talents. If a talent has lain dormant, it can even surprise the person who possesses it once it is rediscovered and used again (Saleebey, 2006).

In recreation, people can utilize their talents in many ways, from music to athleticism to leadership. Recreation provides an avenue to help people fully develop talents they possess and may not have an opportunity to use in other life domains. Recreation may also provide an avenue for a talent to be used in a meaningful way that improves social standing. For example, an individual with autism and mathematical talent can participate fully and excel in a math Olympics team in his community.

Abilities are shown when people differ in their performance of a behavior for which there is some objective or external standard (Peterson, 2006). One well-known way to think about abilities is the theory of multiple intelligences (Gardner, 1993). Multiple intelligence theory states that people have a plurality of abilities, and that there are eight (or nine) main types of abilities or intelligences. People have all these abilities but in varying degrees and varying combinations, making each of us unique. Table 5.2 shows the multiple intelligences or basic abilities. Knowing a person's natural abilities can help build other strengths in that person's life. For example, a person who has high interpersonal abilities may find it rewarding to develop leadership skills in a volunteer organization in her community.

Skills and Competencies

A **skill** is the ability to do something well, arising from talent, training, and practice. **Competency** is the possession of required skills, knowledge, experience, or capacity for a particular task or activity. Level of competency in a skill can be internal or external. Internal, or inherent, aspects of the activity can dictate a certain level of competence in a skill in order to successfully participate. For example, you must have basic skills in running and kicking a ball in order to play soccer. External competencies include standards or eligibility requirements, set by some external group. For example, in order to participate on the traveling soccer team, you must possess a certain level of soccer skills. A person's skill level or competence changes through practice and repetition. When people are able to match the challenge of the activity with their skill level, they are better able to enjoy and be absorbed by those activities, a state called *flow* (Csíkszentmihályi, 1990), discussed in more detail in Chapter 6 *Theories*.

Table 5.2 Multiple Intelligences—Our Natural Abilities *(Gardner, 2005)*

Intelligence	Description
Linguistic	The ability to express one's self in language, and understand how others communicate using words
Logical-Mathematical	The ability to detect patterns, think logically, reason deductively, and carry out mathematical operations
Musical	The ability to recognize and compose musical pitches, tones, rhythms, and patterns, and to use them for performance or composition
Spatial	The ability to recognize and manipulate the patterns of wide and confined spaces, as in navigation or sculpting
Bodily-Kinesthetic	The ability to use one's body to solve problems, make things, or perform
Interpersonal	The ability to understand other people—how they think, feel, and act
Intrapersonal	The ability to understand one's self—how one thinks, feels, and acts, and use that information to regulate one's own life
Naturalistic	The ability to demonstrate expertise in recognition and classification of the numerous species—the flora and fauna—of her or his environment
Existential*	This ability is the "intelligence of big questions." When children ask about the size of the universe, and when adults ponder death, love, conflict, the meaning of life, or the future of the planet, they are engaging with existential issues.

*This intelligence is still being researched, and has not yet been formally identified as one of the multiple intelligences.

People can possess skills and competencies across all the domains of life, from work to leisure to interpersonal relationships. One simplistic way to conceptualize skills in therapeutic recreation is to categorize them according to physical, cognitive, social, emotional, spiritual, daily living, and recreation domains. Recreation, though it has specific skills associated with it (depending on the activity), also uses and develops skills in all other domains. When you enable people to pursue their dreams and goals for recreation and well-being, you also help them build skills in broad areas of their lives. Table 5.3 provides a snapshot of various skills across these domains (Hood & Carruthers, 2007; Shank & Coyle, 2002; Stumbo & Peterson, 2004; World Health Organization, 2003), as we introduced in the Flourishing through Leisure Model.

Related to the meaning of skills and competencies, the World Health Organization has developed specialized definitions for the terms **performance** and **capacity** that are used with the International Classification of Functioning, Disability and Health (Porter & VanPuymbroeck, 2007). Performance is defined as the level at which a person can do an activity in his or her real-life environment. Capacity is the level at which a person can do an activity in a standardized environment, like a clinic area or hospital room.

Knowledge

Knowledge is defined as an acquaintance with facts, truths, or principles. Knowledge means having a clear and certain understanding of a topic or subject area. People can have knowledge in many different topics or subjects. Because it takes effort to learn and retain knowledge, those subject areas in which people show a depth of understanding reveal their preferences and interests.

Knowledge can be gained through educational experiences or distilled from life experiences (Saleebey, 2006). Knowledge can be intellectual or practical. It can focus on the world around us; it can focus on ourselves. The depth of knowledge many people develop throughout their lives can be surprising.

In therapeutic recreation, we are especially concerned with the knowledge people have about recreation and leisure, and how it may be used to enhance their well-being. According to the Leisure Ability Model, knowledge of leisure can be categorized as leisure knowledge, self-awareness in leisure, leisure and play attitudes, and related participatory- and decision-making skills (Stumbo & Peterson, 2004). According to the Leisure Well-Being Model and the Flourishing through Leisure Model, knowledge of ways to enhance leisure can include savoring, authenticity, gratification, mindful leisure, and virtuous

Table 5.3 **Examples of Skills and Competencies across Domains** *(Anderson & Heyne, 2012; Hood & Carruthers, 2007; Shank & Coyle, 2002; Stumbo & Peterson, 2004; World Health Organization, 2003)*

Physical Domain
- Movement/mobility skills
- Fitness (strength, cardiovascular and muscular endurance, flexibility); energy
- Balance
- Fine and gross motor skills
- Kinesthetic awareness skills
- Visual and auditory skills

Social Domain
- Communication skills
- Relationship-building and friendship skills
- Self-presentation skills
- Group participation skills
- Basic and complex interpersonal skills
- Cultural competence
- Social confidence
- Leadership and citizenship skills

Spiritual Skills
- Sense of meaning
- Reflection skills
- Development of character strengths and virtues

Recreation Skills
- Formal activity skills (see categories in Table 5.1)
- Informal activity skills (e.g., shopping, computer and Internet activities)

Cognitive Domain
- Attention/concentration
- Following directions
- Memory
- Decision-making skills
- Goal-setting skills; aspiration identification
- Problem-solving skills
- Language skills
- Math skills

Emotional and Psychological Domain
- Emotional regulation
- Coping skills
- Enjoyment; capacity for happiness
- Mindfulness
- Optimism
- Self-awareness
- Autonomy; self-determination; goal-directedness

Daily Living Skills
- Self-care skills
- Transportation
- Money handling skills
- Meal and diet planning
- Time management skills
- Leisure planning skills

leisure (Hood & Carruthers, 2007). These knowledge areas are summarized in Table 5.4.

Aspirations and Goals

An **aspiration** is a strong desire, longing, or hope. Aspirations are the dreams and visions we have about our own lives. A **goal** is the result or achievement toward which effort is directed. Simply put, a goal is an aim or an end. Taken together, aspirations and goals are among the greatest strengths we have to mobilize our personal and situational resources to change in ways we view as positive. Aspirations and goals must be nurtured through genuine respect and interest (Saleebey, 2006). They must be the starting point for a helping relationship. Weick, Kreider, and Chamberlain (2006) call the power of aspirations the "fuel for making change" (p. 118). Linking the aspirations and goals of participants with their other strengths is key in assisting people to achieve positive outcomes in their lives through leisure.

It is important to note, however, that some types of aspirations are more positively associated with quality of life and well-being than others. Researchers have classified aspirations as extrinsic (such as pursuing wealth, fame, and image) and intrinsic (such as developing meaningful relationships, personal growth, and community contribution) (Kasser & Ryan, 1996; Ryan et al., 1999). Intrinsic aspirations are those that are positively associated with well-being, and those that can be best nurtured through leisure.

Character Strengths and Virtues

Character strengths and virtues are the positive traits that define who we are as human beings. Peterson and Seligman (2004) stated, "We believe that character strengths are the bedrock of the human condition and that strength-congruent activity represents an important route to the psychological good life" (p. 4). When people are able to exercise their character strengths, they will experience higher levels of well-being (Rath, 2006). Recreation and leisure are ideal arenas for people to employ their strengths, due to the level of choice people have to express themselves.

In their study of character strengths and virtues, psychologists Peterson and Seligman (2004), with a

Table 5.4 Leisure-Related Knowledge Areas

Leisure Ability Model (Stumbo & Peterson, 2004)	
Knowledge of Leisure Concepts • Concepts of leisure • Benefits of leisure • Forms and contexts of leisure • Balance in work and leisure • Personal responsibility for leisure • Leisure resources in home and community *Knowledge of Leisure and Play Attitudes* • Societal attitudes about leisure • Personal beliefs and values about leisure • Attitudes toward leisure and personal satisfaction with lifestyle	*Knowledge of Self in Leisure* • Current leisure involvement and satisfaction • Past leisure and play involvement • Goal areas for leisure • Personal resources for leisure *Knowledge of Related Participation Skill Areas* • Leisure planning skills • Leisure decision-making skills • Problem-solving skills • Coping skills
Flourishing through Leisure Model: An Ecological Extension of the Leisure and Well-Being Model (Anderson & Heyne, 2012) and the Leisure Well-Being Model (Hood & Carruthers, 2007)	
Knowledge of Savoring Leisure (paying attention to the positive aspects and emotions of the leisure experience) • Purposeful and conscious attention to the positive aspects of an experience • Increasing the number of opportunities to experience pleasure daily • Active (versus passive) engagement to maximize positive experience and emotion *Knowledge of Leisure Gratifications* (optimally challenging, meaningful, and sustained leisure) • Selection and modification of leisure experiences to be optimally enjoyable • Self-monitoring of skills and challenges *Knowledge of Virtuous Leisure* (building leisure around one's strengths) • Self-awareness of character strengths and virtues • Awareness of contexts and opportunities to use character strengths • Awareness of opportunities to provide service to others through one's leisure	*Knowledge of Authentic Leisure* (leisure experiences that help to know one's self and express one's self) • Discovery of personal interests, strengths, and assets • Opportunities and contexts for expression of personal interests, strengths, and assets *Knowledge of Mindful Leisure* (full and present engagement in the leisure experience) • Slowing thoughts and focusing attention through various techniques (deep breathing, meditation, etc.) • Focus on the present through various techniques (thought stopping, etc.) • Attention to the selection of leisure experiences that are meaningful and optimally challenging

team of respected experts from philosophy, anthropology, sociology, religious studies, youth development, and other fields, undertook an exhaustive review of literature to learn about character strengths and virtues valued across cultures and throughout history. From this study, the research team identified six core virtues, the "high six" (Peterson & Seligman, 2004, p. 36). They also distinguished 24 character strengths, using a carefully crafted classification system to describe and define them. The result of this exhaustive study and thoughtful classification was the publication of an 800-page volume, *Character Strengths and Virtues: A Handbook and Classification*. Peterson and Seligman (2004) describe the handbook as "a manual of the sanities" (p. 1), as opposed to the *Diagnostic and Statistical Manual of Mental Disorders* (*DSM*) (American Psychiatric Association, 2000), which is a catalog or classification system of problems, disorders, and "insanities." Whereas the *DSM* focuses on understanding psychological illnesses, the *Handbook* focuses on understanding psychological health.

Virtues are the six core characteristics valued across culture and time, which Peterson and Seligman identify as wisdom, courage, humanity, justice, temperance, and transcendence. Character strengths are the processes or pathways that lead to the broad virtues and allow people who exercise their strengths to live a life where virtues can be displayed. To be included in the *Handbook*, character strengths had to meet several criteria, as listed in Table 5.5.

Next, we describe each of the six core virtues and the character strengths that comprise each virtue. For detailed descriptions of how each of the character strengths meets the criteria listed in Table 5.5, and the supporting evidence used to identify each virtue and character strength, we recommend reading the *Handbook* itself.

Virtue One: Wisdom

Wisdom is comprised of the cognitive strengths, often hard won, that help you gain and use knowledge about the world in a way that enriches those around you (Peterson & Seligman, 2004). Wisdom is more than intelligence and knowledge. Wisdom means you know how to apply that knowledge, using reflective judgment, in ways that lead to good for others as well as yourself.

The strengths that lead to wisdom are curiosity, love of learning, judgment, ingenuity, and perspective. According to Seligman (2002), these strengths range developmentally from the most basic to the most mature. Recreation provides an ideal context to use these strengths, whether through formal classes and activities, or informal recreation activities that involve exploration, adventure, and perspective-taking.

Curiosity

Curiosity is an openness and eagerness to learn about and experience the world around you. A person with this strength takes an interest in experiences and ideas, and loves exploration and discovery for its own sake. A curious person thrives on ambiguity and the mysteries held by it. Curiosity entails openness and flexibility in new situations or settings.

Table 5.5 Criteria that Define Character Strengths
(Peterson & Seligman, 2004; Seligman, 2002)

- Leads to fulfillment when exercised
- Is morally valued
- Does not diminish others when exercised
- Has a non-felicitous or negative opposite
- Has generalizability across situations, and is stable across time
- Is distinct from other strengths
- Is role-modeled in one's culture
- Begins to express itself early in life
- Can be completely lacking in a person
- Is nurtured by society through institutions and rituals

Love of Learning

Love of learning is a strength centered on acquiring new skills, knowledge, or ideas, and doing so for its own value. A person with this strength will seek out both formal and informal ways to learn new things, whether it is taking classes, going to museums, or reading all the interpretive signs on a self-guided nature trail. A person who loves to learn will continually seek avenues to add to their knowledge and master new skills, with no external incentive to do so.

Judgment

Judgment involves being open-minded and thinking critically. If you have this strength, you think things through and examine them from all sides. You look for evidence that supports and refutes your beliefs, and use that evidence to come to sound conclusions. You may change your conclusions based on new evidence presented to you. People with judgment weigh all evidence and do not jump to conclusions. They do not confuse their wants and needs with the facts the world presents.

Ingenuity

Ingenuity is being creative and finding original, productive ways of doing things. If you are high in this strength, you often think of novel ways to achieve a goal or develop a plan. Seligman (2002) also calls this strength "street smart" or practical common sense (p. 143). People with this strength often operate in unconventional ways yet meet their goals.

Perspective

Perspective is the most developmentally mature strength that comprises wisdom. Perspective means that you are able to step outside your self-centeredness and look at the world in a way that makes sense to others as much as it does to you. People with this strength are sought after for their advice and views. They can see the "big picture" and can help others see their place in that picture. If perspective is a strength of yours, you have a knack for seeing your way through some of life's toughest problems and landing on your feet.

Virtue Two: Courage

Courage is a virtue, valued across time and culture, which forms legends and defines heroes. Yet, simply defined, courage is a willingness to take on something worthy when the outcome is uncertain and adversity is likely. The path to courage is through the strengths of valor, perseverance, integrity, and vitality.

Valor

Valor includes physical, social, and emotional bravery. People who have valor will face a danger, even in the presence of fear, threat, pain, or difficulty. They will maintain their stance when they feel their position is right or moral, even if that stance is unpopular or even dangerous. People with valor or bravery stay the course, even in the face of opposition. Many disability- and civil-rights leaders, such as Ed Roberts (O'Hara, 2000), Martin Luther King, Jr., or Christopher Reeve, are examples of courageous people who showed the strength of valor.

Perseverance

Perseverance is diligence in completing what you start. A person with perseverance approaches tasks with a positive attitude and cheerfully persists until they are completed. If you have this strength, you are industrious, flexible, and goal-oriented, but not a perfectionist. You are intrinsically motivated to persist in your actions, even if obstacles get in your way. However, perseverance is seen as a strength only in its positive expression, unlike stubbornness or inflexibility, and it requires judgment as well as diligence.

Integrity

If you present yourself in a genuine, authentic way and take responsibility for your actions and words, then you have integrity. People with integrity live their lives in an honest, sincere way. They reveal their intentions and commitments and do not "play games" with others. When they make a promise to you, they keep it.

Vitality or Zest

Vitality is comprised of both physical and psychological aspects. If you are high in this strength, you approach life with vigor and enthusiasm. You feel alive and fully engaged, both psychologically and physically. You have a high level of energy that is positive and focused in meaningful ways. People who have zest are thought of as bright-eyed and eager. They use their energy toward worthy activities in a whole-hearted manner, even in times of adversity or hardship. Vitality is expressed during the total absorption one feels in a state of flow.

Virtue Three: Humanity

The virtue of humanity is comprised of the strengths of social intelligence, loving, and kindness. Humanity is a virtue most often expressed in one-to-one caring relationships with other people, including family, friends, acquaintances, and even strangers.

Kindness

Kindness is expressed through generosity toward others, compassion, and nurturance. People who have this strength are thought of as nice and as caring about others. If you are high in this strength, you like to do favors and good deeds for others, with no expectation of anything in return. At the core of this strength is embracing the worth of another person.

Loving

Loving is valuing and maintaining close and intimate reciprocal relationships. People high in this strength value romantic relationships, family ties, friendships, and the bonds with coworkers, teammates, and other people with whom they have reciprocal contact. Loving is characterized by positive feelings toward others and a commitment to them.

Social Intelligence

Social intelligence is being aware of what others are feeling, as well as how you feel. It also entails regulating one's emotions. People with this strength are sometimes called intuitive when it comes to interacting with others. They are sensitive to the moods and motives of others, and use that sensitivity to facilitate good social interaction or positive social outcomes.

Virtue Four: Justice

Justice is a virtue focused on relationships within society. While humanity focuses on one-to-one relationships, justice focuses on broader, societal relationships. Justice is expressed in groups and communities of people through the exercise of citizenship, fairness, and leadership.

Citizenship

The strength of citizenship can be characterized by social responsibility, loyalty, and teamwork. People high in this strength feel a sense of obligation to the common good and can move beyond their own interests to serve those of the group. If you have this strength, you work well in groups. You always do your part, not because of some external force, but because it is the right thing to do.

Fairness

Fairness is expressed through giving everyone a chance. If you are high in this strength, you do not let your personal feelings bias how you treat others. You want to see people treated equally and equitably. People with this strength believe the same rules should apply to everyone in similar situations.

Leadership

Leadership is the most mature strength in the virtue of justice. To be fully expressed, leadership relies on fairness and citizenship. People who have strength in leadership are able to help groups meet their goals, while attending to relationships in the group. If you have this strength, you are able to organize the activities of a group while keeping relationships positive and productive.

Virtue Five: Temperance

Temperance is comprised of the strengths of self-control, prudence, humility, and forgiveness. Temperance is characterized by being able to satisfy needs in the right place and at the right time, and never at the expense of other people. Temperance means avoiding excess of all types.

Self-Control or Self-Regulation

The strength of self-control is defined as being able to exert control over your thoughts, behaviors, and actions in order to pursue goals or live up to standards. Self-control involves both initiation of a response (e.g., going for a run) or inhibition of a response (e.g., doing without dessert). People who have high self-control are able to exercise discipline and control their thoughts, emotions, and behaviors. If you have this strength, you are able to set a goal or standard, then monitor your progress toward it as you change. You continually make decisions to do something positive even in the face of temptation to do otherwise.

Prudence

If you are careful about the choices you make, or the words you use, you are exercising the strength of prudence. Prudence is characterized by an orientation to the future, weighing choices and consequences, and choosing actions that lead to long-term goals. People who are prudent are reflective, deliberate, and practical. They weigh the costs, risks, and benefits of a course of action, and choose that which best takes them on the path to their long-term vision.

Humility

Humility is characterized by modesty, an accurate assessment of your abilities, an ease in admitting your mistakes, and an ability to keep your accomplishments in perspective. People who have humility are not focused on themselves, even though they may be accomplishing great things. If you have the strength of humility, you are not motivated by extrinsic forces and do not need praise to stay focused on tasks and activities in your life. You appreciate what others do, and do not see yourself as any more special than anyone else.

Forgiveness

Forgiveness, also referred to as mercy, is defined as being tolerant of those who have offended you and accepting the faults of others. If you have this strength, you are able to be positive, compassionate, and peaceful toward someone who has hurt you, and you do not feel anger toward or the need to avoid that person. You do not condone, excuse, rationalize, or forget the hurt—you forgive it. You have a high level of empathy and are willing to give people a second chance.

Virtue Six: Transcendence

Transcendence, the last of the six core virtues, is made up of the strengths of appreciation of beauty, gratitude, hope, spirituality, and humor. Transcendence is comprised of strengths that connect people to something larger and more permanent than themselves. These connections help people find meaning and purpose in their individual lives.

Appreciation of Beauty

This strength is embodied by the phrase, "stop and smell the roses." People with this strength appreciate beauty, excellence, and skill across life's domains, in both the physical and social worlds. If you have this strength, you find, recognize, and take pleasure in the goodness in the world, such as art, music, nature, sport, or high moral behavior. You often experience awe and wonder and feel uplifted by beauty, talent, or goodness. Mindfulness and savoring are cognitive activities that are used as this strength is exercised.

Gratitude

Gratitude is characterized by being aware of and thankful for the good things in life. If you have this strength, you feel grateful and appreciative, and express your gratitude to others. You do not take things for granted in your life. You feel a sense of gratefulness toward others and toward something larger than yourself, such as a god or higher power. Exercising the strength of gratitude evokes positive emotions like joy and brings purpose and meaning to people's lives.

Hope

Hope can also be described as optimism and future-mindedness. If you have this strength, you expect the best in your future and you plan your life toward that end. Despite challenges and setbacks, people strong in hope feel good about their futures, and stay focused on their goals. They see the "glass half full, not half empty" and believe good will prevail over bad. When people have hope, they are able to endure hard times and feel things will always get better.

Spirituality

The strength, spirituality, is defined as having a strong sense of or belief in a higher purpose. People high in this strength have clear, well-articulated beliefs about their place in the universe and how that outlook affects their daily lives. Those beliefs not only shape action, they provide comfort. Spirituality can also be described as faith, sense of purpose, and religiousness. At the core of spirituality is transcendence from daily life.

Humor

Humor, or playfulness, can be defined in three ways. Humor is the ability to see the light side of things, even during adversity. It is also the recognition and enjoyment of incongruities. Lastly, it is the ability to make people smile or laugh. Playfulness is the ability to be spontaneous and enjoy the moment. If you have this strength, you can make people laugh or smile, and you can find the humor in situations as well. You enjoy being playful and funny and like to laugh and tease.

Table 5.6 summarizes the six core virtues and 24 character strengths. It is interesting to note that research has found five of these strengths to be most highly related to well-being and life satisfaction: gratitude, optimism, zest, curiosity, and the ability to love and be loved (Dean, 2002). These virtues and strengths are an important part of what therapeutic recreation specialists need to know about the participants with whom they work. Character strengths and virtues can be nurtured and grown, like all other strengths, and they must be carefully assessed and purposefully addressed in therapeutic recreation practice. To enhance the leisure experience, people need to understand their strengths and to seek opportunities and experiences where they can use their strengths. As therapeutic recreation specialists, we can facilitate this process tremendously through our practice. See Figure 5.4 to think critically about character strengths and virtues from a cultural perspective.

EXTERNAL STRENGTHS AND RESOURCES

When using a strengths-based, ecological approach to therapeutic recreation, we must understand people in the context of the environments in which they

Table 5.6 Six Core Virtues and 24 Character Strengths
(Peterson & Seligman, 2004)

Wisdom	Courage
• Curiosity	• Valor
• Love of learning	• Perseverance
• Judgment	• Integrity
• Ingenuity	• Zest and vitality
• Perspective	
Humanity	**Justice**
• Kindness	• Citizenship
• Loving	• Fairness
• Social intelligence	• Leadership
Temperance	**Transcendence**
• Self-control	• Appreciation of beauty
• Prudence	• Gratitude
• Humility	• Hope
• Forgiveness	• Spirituality
	• Humor

live and play. The World Health Organization has recognized the importance of the environment in its conceptualization of the International Classification of Functioning, Disability and Health (ICF) (2003). The ICF looks not only at how a person functions, it considers the "environmental factors" in which that functioning occurs. In a strengths-based approach, your role as a therapeutic recreation specialist is to find and use the strengths in an environment, not to focus on what is wrong with that environment.

All environments have resources that can be capitalized on to build internal and external strengths. External strengths can include family support, social support and friendships, community resources, home resources, opportunities for participation and contribution, high expectations, and positive attitudes.

My Cultural Lens: Character Strengths and Virtues Across Cultures?

Dieser (2005) stated that the character strengths and virtues identified by Seligman (2002), and later classified by Peterson and Seligman (2004), are embedded in a White Euro-North American individualistic value system and do not focus enough on cross-cultural differences, where individualism is not valued. How do the character strengths and virtues align with the values held by your culture? How about the cultures of others you know, cultures different from your own? Seek out a classmate, colleague, or friend from a different culture than your own, and discuss the character strengths and virtues through each of your cultural lenses.

Figure 5.4 My Cultural Lens: Character Strengths and Virtues Across Cultures?

Family Support and Involvement

Merriam-Webster (2010) defines "family" generally as "a group of persons who form a household." Families have become increasingly diverse—no longer is there any one family form, especially not the "two heterosexual parents, one income with children structure" (Kelly & Freysinger, 2000). Families who have a member with a disability or illness are just as diverse, and maybe more so. Families are typically considered to be people who are related to each other, but families can also be people with whom you live and share your daily life. Whatever its form, families are an interdependent social unit that exerts a powerful social force upon its members. This may be even truer for families who experience disability (Howe-Murphy & Charboneau, 1987; Pedlar, Haworth, Hutchinson, Taylor, & Dunn, 1999).

Families can be conceptualized as having varying degrees of cohesiveness and varying levels of adaptability (Olson, Sprenkle, & Russell, 1979; Zabriskie & McCormick, 2003). Families serve many functions in a person's life. They are typically the primary source of nurturance, socialization, and enculturation for children. Families are instrumental in forming our values, our interests, and our talents.

Leisure is an important aspect of family life (Kelly, 1999; Zabriskie & McCormick, 2003). Families provide opportunities for "core" patterns of leisure, which includes participation that is familiar, stable, and consistent. Core patterns of leisure include common, everyday, low-cost, relatively accessible, and often home-based activities that many families do frequently. These activities might include riding bikes, playing cards, or watching movies. Families also provide opportunities for "balance" patterns of leisure, which are activities that are generally less common, less frequent, more out of the ordinary, and usually not home-based, thus providing novel experiences (Zabriskie & McCormick, 2003). Balance activities might include visiting an amusement park, camping, or going to an art museum or a professional sporting event in a big city. Thus, the family is our primary resource for leisure education and expression of a leisure lifestyle.

Besides providing daily opportunities to learn and participate in a variety of leisure experiences, families have resources and social connections. Every family member comes with his or her own set of strengths—interests, skills, talents—that can be shared with other family members. Family members often have relationships outside of the context of the family, whether they are with friends, teammates, or as members of groups to which they belong. These are relationships that can be shared and extended to other family members. Lastly, family members often become lifelong friends and share leisure across the lifespan.

Research has shown that, if families provide essential protective factors in the home, family members will flourish (Benard, 2006). These protective factors are caring relationships, high expectation messages, and opportunities for participation and contribution. Leisure and recreation provide an arena for all of these protective factors to be exercised in the family (Zabriskie & Heyne, 2003).

Because families have such a powerful influence, even into adulthood, on the leisure and quality of life of people we serve in therapeutic recreation, we need to understand what strengths a family possesses. We need to explore how we can collaborate with families to help participants realize their aspirations and dreams. Often, those dreams focus on leisure and relationships. We need to conceptualize people with disabilities as family members differently than we have in the deficit-based approach to service. Hutchinson and McGill (1992) provided a framework for transitioning our thinking about people with disabilities as family members, illustrated in Figure 5.5 (see p. 94).

Social Support and Friendships

Friendship and social support generated through leisure have consistently been identified in the research literature as key to well-being and quality of life (Coleman & Iso-Ahola; Hood & Carruthers, 2007). Our sense of well-being is intricately tied to feelings of belonging and connectedness with others (Hutchinson & McGill, 1992). Social support and friendships are important external strengths that can be built on in the therapeutic recreation process (Heyne, Schleien, & McAvoy, 2003).

Social support is comprised of freely chosen networks of people that provide assistance and resources to meet goals (Hutchinson & McGill, 1992). Social support has been conceptualized in four ways: instrumental, emotional, informational, and appraisal support (Orsega-Smith et al., 2007; Peterson, 2006).

- **Instrumental support** includes helping to garner tangible or physical assistance for somconc, such as transportation.
- **Emotional support** is interpersonal in nature, such as checking up on someone or encouraging them.
- **Informational support** is sharing information, such as opportunities for leisure in the community.

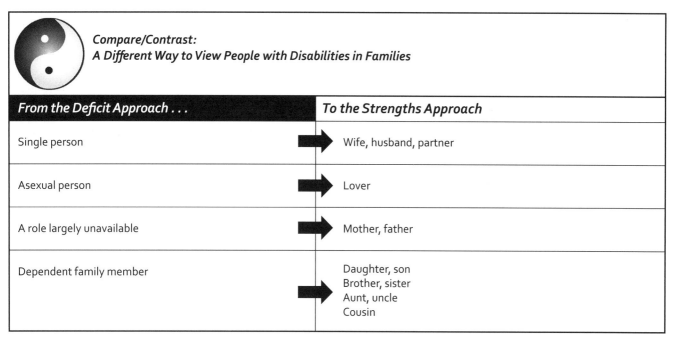

Figure 5.5 Compare/Contrast: A Different Way to View People with Disabilities in Families *(Hutchinson & McGill, 1992)*

- **Appraisal support** is giving feedback or reinforcement that helps a person meet her or his goals.

Social support networks can include family, friends, neighbors, acquaintances, and formal and informal community groups, all of whom provide different support in different ways. Table 5.7 lists the types of connections people can have in their lives to provide social support. For social support to be an asset in developing or maintaining well-being, it needs to be freely chosen and not obligatory (Coleman & Iso-Ahola, 1993). This notion makes recreation and leisure involvement very important in developing social support, as self-determination is often exercised in choosing enduring involvement. It is also important to remember that social support is something we *do*, not something we *have* (Taylor, Sylvestre, & Botschner, 1998), and that part of our role in therapeutic recreation is to enable people to both give and receive social support.

Friendship is perhaps one of the greatest strengths you can facilitate as a therapeutic recreation specialist (Heyne, Schleien, & McAvoy, 1993). Quality friendships are one of the strongest indicators of well-being in our lives. Friendship is defined as those relationships where liking is coupled with a mutual perception of similarity and expectations of reciprocity and parity (Peterson, 2006). Pedlar et al. (1999) made this observation about friendships in the lives of people with disabilities:

True friendships tend to occur when people feel valued and appreciated for who they are as people, when they feel they are "givers" as well as "receivers," and when they share information and feelings openly. Friendships are seen as critical resources for people with disabilities in part because they represent windows of opportunity for expanding one's social circle beyond the confines of the disability service system, offering vitality and texture to people's lives. (p. 119)

Having deep, quality friendships is more important than having a breadth of friendships (Rath, 2006). These kinds of friendships measurably improve our satisfaction with life and without them our quality of life would decrease. Friends improve our lives in many different ways, every friend playing different and valued roles. Table 5.8 (p. 96) outlines the unique roles that friends play in our lives, based on research by the Gallup Organization (Rath, 2006). We provide this information to help you develop a common vocabulary to talk about friendships with participants, as you support them in assessing and building this strength in their lives. See Figure 5.6 on the cultural differences in the meaning of friends.

Home Resources

Every home environment, regardless of socioeconomic status, has potential resources that can be used to help

Table 5.7 Ways People Relate and Connect to Form Social Networks and Social Support
(Amado, Conklin, & Wells, 1990; Heyne & Schleien, 1997; Peterson, 2006; Rybak & McAndrew, 2006; Schleien, Green, & Stone, 1999)

Being part of a family	Relationships that have an active connection with family life
Having a partner	A relationship that involves intimacy, positive emotion, reciprocated exclusiveness, and a long-term commitment
Friendship	Relationships that are freely chosen, mutual, reciprocal, consistent, and enduring. They have a positive affective tie, a sense of closeness, and a sharing of experiences. "Best friends" are those friendships that are more intense and close than other friendships.
Acquaintance	Relationships with others, but not particularly close; recent, relatively brief interactions; distinguished from friendship by the intensity and mutual commitment of the relationship
Membership	Relationships related to being a member of a club, group, or association
Being a neighbor	Relationships with those living near someone (next door, down the street, down the road, etc.)
Knowing or being known in a neighborhood	Using the resources of the neighborhood and recognizing and being recognized by others who use them too
Keeping in touch; social network	Relationships related to belonging to social worlds; keeping in touch and current with the trends and movements that are a part of that special interest or social world (may be electronic-based as well)
Paid professionals and volunteers	Relationships that are maintained as a service to a person, such as a personal care attendant, a "leisure buddy," or staff at a group home

people achieve their goals for a satisfying life. Home resources include physical assets for recreation and leisure involvement in formal and informal activities. Figure 5.7 (see p. 97) lists common and potential resources that may be found in a participant's home environment.

Home resources also include social support resources, such as siblings, extended family members, and neighbors, already discussed under the strengths of family and social support. Home resources will vary greatly depending on culture, geographic location, socioeconomic status, and family structure.

Community and Environmental Resources

Community resources are those physical and environmental resources for recreation and socialization outside of the home environment. They range from resources in the neighborhood to resources in the world. Community resources, the physical assets available to us for our recreation and well-being, are an important part of the fabric of strengths that we can help people build in their lives. In our work as therapeutic recreation specialists, using the ecological perspective, our focus is as much on building community resources for recreation as it is on helping the individual participant grow and change (Howe-Murphy & Charboneau, 1987). This work with community resources may involve basic

My Cultural Lens: Cultural Differences in the Meaning of Friends

Rybak and McAndrew (2006) studied differences in how friendship is defined in different cultures. In reviewing other research, and in their own study, they found there is a difference in the ease in which people label someone as a friend. People in North America are much more comfortable calling another person a friend, whereas people in other cultures, such as China, Japan, Korea, or Poland, are less likely to use the term unless a higher degree of intimacy is present in the relationship. In fact, in one study, people in China counted only 7% of the people in their social network as friends, whereas people in North America counted 68% as friends! In cultures where kinships/family is the strongest tie, friendship is less salient. Amado, Conklin, and Wells (1990) reported that people with developmental disabilities may use the term "friend" loosely, and may have difficulty differentiating casual acquaintances and service providers from friends. Anderson, Schleien, and Green (1993) found that people with developmental disabilities involved in "leisure buddy" volunteer programs were confused when their volunteer "friends" finished their service commitment and were no longer a part of their lives. How do you think your culture and your social environment affect how you define friendship? Discuss the idea of friendship with others in your social network and compare differences depending on culture, family, and social networks.

Figure 5.6 My Cultural Lens: Cultural Differences in the Meaning of Friends

Table 5.8 Roles Friendships Play in People's Lives *(Rath, 2006)*

Friendship Role	Definition
Builder	Friends who motivate, push, and serve as a catalyst for personal growth
Champion	Friends who provide praise, loyalty, and advocacy
Collaborator	Friends who actively share similar interests and passions
Companion	Friends who are truly supportive, openly share and understand feelings, and are "always there"
Connector	Friends who are bridge-builders to other relationships, and who know many other people
Energizer	Friends who are fun, and know how to boost others' moods through their words and actions
Mind-opener	Friends who introduce others to new ideas, opportunities, cultures, and innovations
Navigator	Friends who give advice and help with decision-making in important life events

skills and knowledge you gain in becoming a professional in the recreation field, as well as advocacy and community-building skills. Table 5.9 (see p. 98) lists several different ways you can think about, or classify, the physical assets or resources available to people for recreation involvement outside the home.

Opportunities for Participation and Contribution (Inclusive Communities)

Communities differ in the opportunities they provide for involvement. Putman (2000) documented the decline of civic or social life in communities, where clubs, leagues, and other social or voluntary groups were experiencing a significant drop in participation. However, Florida (2002) described a new form of community that is developing, where the social structure is looser, casual, yet just as social. Whatever form a community takes, whether the culture is more focused on formal organizations or informal, loose social groups, there is an opportunity for the people with whom we work to find a place to be included and supported.

Inclusive communities that foster strengths in their members share these characteristics:

- Openness to diverse people and ideas
- Easily accessed networking systems
- Opportunities for meaningful contribution through formal or informal social networks
- Responsive leadership
- Meaningful participation in community decision-making
- Awareness of sense of place and the resources embedded in that place
- Opportunities for optimal well-being (Hutchinson & McGill, 1992)

Inclusive communities are founded on valued recognition for individuals and groups, opportunities for nurturance of talents and skills, the right and necessary supports for full engagement, physical proximity, and material well-being (Freiler, 2003). Inclusive Cities Canada (2007) describe how these characteristics would look in practical terms:

> Practical expressions of inclusion are universal access to meaningful opportunities in education, the arts, culture, and recreation; relevant health services and school curricula adapted to specific needs and strengths; family support services and respite; safe streets and parks, and responsive governance on all levels.

As therapeutic recreation specialists, we have a large and important responsibility to facilitate inclusion for all people in their communities in the recreation activities of their choice, whether that is a part of organized groups and activities or informal social networks, and to learn and use strategies that can build this important strength (Anderson & Kress, 2003). We must conceptualize our practice not just as "community-based," that is, a place we may provide therapeutic recreation services, but as "community-built," where one aspect of our services is developing the strengths of a community for the benefit of those we serve. When communities are inclusive and provide multiple opportunities for meaningful contributions by all community members, high expectations for people's potential occur naturally, which leads to the next important strength we can help people build. You

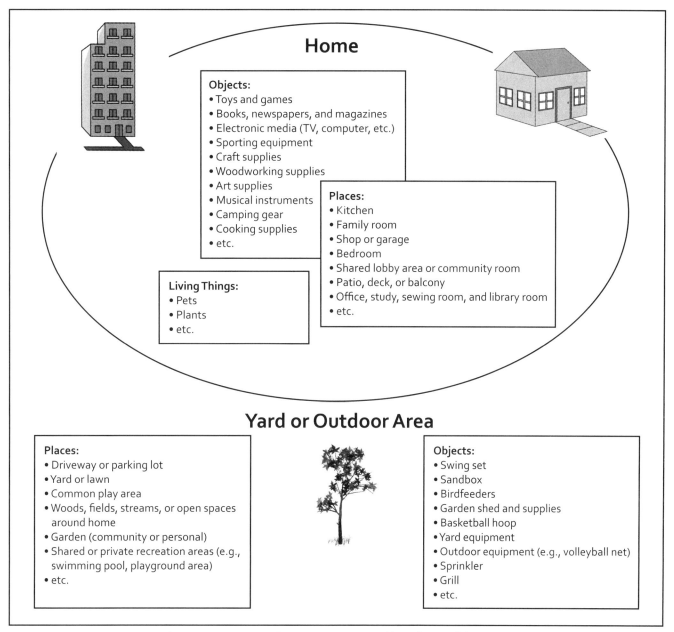

Figure 5.7 Common Leisure Resources Found in and around the Home

will read about inclusion in more detail in Chapter 12 *Transition and Inclusion*.

High Expectations and Positive Attitudes

> When I was a child, my mother said to me, "If you become a soldier, you will be a general. If you become a monk, you will end up the pope." Instead, I became a painter, and wound up as Picasso.
>
> —*Pablo Picasso*

High expectations are those attitudes that surround people in their environments and influence their aspirations and quality of life. As therapeutic recreation specialists, we must send a strong message that we expect people to do well and prevail through whatever difficulty brought them to us for services. This message of high expectations translates into hope and a focus on possibilities.

Research repeatedly shows that hope and high expectations are powerful in helping people thrive. Table 5.10 (see p. 99) shows the results of research, using a meta-analysis of many studies that highlight the common factors that help people change and grow. Hope and high expectations are a significant part of positive change.

When the social supports that surround us have high expectations, this in turn leads to greater opportunities and choices. In other words, if others

Table 5.9 Different Ways to Classify Community/Environmental Resources for Recreation and Leisure

World Health Organization (2003)
(relevant resources for recreation classified under *Environmental Factors: Services, Systems, and Policies*)
- Communication services (e.g., Internet)
- Transportation services (e.g., public transportation)
- Associations and organizational services (e.g., clubs, groups, sporting, cultural, religious)
- Media services (e.g., television, radio, newspapers)
- Social support services (e.g., those aimed at specific needs in the community like aging or disability)
- Health services (e.g., those aimed at health promotion and disease prevention)
- Education and training services (e.g., classes and programs to learn new skills)

Russell (2005)
Commercial, private nonprofit, and public agencies that offer:
- Sports and games
- Cultural arts
- Outdoor recreation
- Travel
- Hobbies
- Social recreation

Search Institute (Mannes, 2008)
(external assets related to recreation and constructive use of time)
- Creative activities
- Youth programs
- Religious community
- Time at home

Edginton, DeGraaf, Dieser, & Edginton (2006)
- Local government resources (e.g., parks, programs, school-based activities)
- State government resources (e.g., parks, programs, tourism)
- Federal government resources (e.g., national parks, national forests, arts)
- Non-profit resources (e.g., nature centers, Boys & Girls Clubs, YM/WCAs, Scouts, camps)
- Commercial resources (e.g., entertainment, sports, fitness, special events, and programs)

Wilkins & Murphy (2000)
- Leisure resources within my reach
- Leisure resources in my home
- Leisure resources in my local community and my part of the state
- Leisure resources in my state, and my part of the country
- Leisure resources in my country and beyond
- Equipment and facilities
- Cost

Stumbo & Peterson (2004)
- Community resources (e.g., agencies, commercial enterprises, places, and facilities)
- State and national resources (e.g., travel)

believe we are capable, we are offered more chances to try and do things in our lives than if they believe we cannot accomplish positive outcomes. The World Health Organization (2003) recognizes that the attitudes that surround us are an important environmental factor, as shown in the ICF:

> Attitudes are the observable consequences of customs, practices, ideologies, values, norms, factual beliefs and religious beliefs. These attitudes influence individual behaviour and social life at all levels, from interpersonal relationships and community associations to political, economic and legal structures; for example, individual or societal attitudes about a person's trustworthiness and value as a human being that may motivate positive, honorific practices or negative and discriminatory practices (e.g., stigmatizing, stereotyping and marginalizing or neglect of the person). (2003, para 4)

The ICF asks us to look at attitudes and expectations at several levels in the environment, from attitudes of family and friends, to attitudes of community members, to social norms (see Table 5.11). These outlooks all affect a person's ability to expect to have a high quality of life.

Part of our role as therapeutic recreation specialists is to communicate respect, high positive regard, and a sense of belief in the goals and aspirations of those with whom we work. Our role is also to help improve community attitudes toward disability and foster inclusion. By increasing expectations in people's environments, we will help them have greater opportunities for leisure and quality of life.

Table 5.10 Common Factors that Facilitate Growth and Change in the Helping Relationship

Common Factor (listed from most powerful to least powerful change agent)	Description of Factor
• Client factors (40% of therapeutic change)	Strengths, assets, and resources of the individual, the family, and the environment "It is important to remember that the purpose [of therapies] is not to identify what clients need, but what they already have that can be put to use in reaching their goals." (Duncan, Miller, & Sparks, 2003, p. 115)
• Relationship factors (30% of therapeutic change)	The therapeutic alliance between collaborating helpers and those seeking help "The collaborative helping relationship is purposeful, reciprocal, friendly, trusting, and empowering." (Saleebey, 2006, p. 80)
• Hope, positive expectations, and placebo factors (15% of therapeutic change)	The expectation that individuals will improve and change for the positive "You should never underestimate the sway of hope, the belief that things can improve. Such a prospect is vital to those individuals and groups who struggle against the tide of low expectations, little opportunity, belittled self-esteem, and thwarted justice." (Saleebey, 2006, p. 80)
• Interventions, techniques, and methods factors (15% of therapeutic change)	The methods, techniques, and interventions used by helpers to facilitate positive change for those seeking help "Their [techniques'] principal contribution to therapy comes about by enhancing the potency of the other common factors—client, relationship, and hope." (Duncan, Miller, & Sparks, 2003, p. 116)

PLAY, RECREATION, AND LEISURE AS KEY STRENGTHS

In this chapter, we have examined internal and external strengths that all people may potentially have. Cutting across these strengths is the powerful life area of leisure, play, and recreation. Because it is freely chosen, intrinsically motivated, and driven by interests, preferences, and talents, recreation has the potential to provide many benefits.

Table 5.11 Environmental Attitudes and Expectations in the WHO ICF

Environmental attitudes and expectations of the following individuals all influence a person's ability to experience well-being and a high quality of life:

- Immediate family members
- Extended family members
- Friends
- Acquaintances, peers, colleagues, neighbors, and community members
- People in positions of authority
- People in subordinate positions
- Personal care providers and personal assistants
- Strangers
- Health professionals
- Health-related professionals
- Societal attitudes
- Social norms, practices, and ideologies

Possessing recreation interests and quality leisure experiences is a strength in and of itself. But, in addition, recreation and leisure can build other strengths, and provide a context to improve our well-being. Through leisure and recreation, people are able to experience enjoyment and positive emotions, which in turn lead to other benefits. Dr. Barbara Fredrickson (2003) has fully developed this idea in the Broaden-and-Build Theory (see Figure 5.8, p. 100). Hood and Carruthers have fully conceptualized the connection between leisure and well-being in the Leisure and Well-Being Model (Carruthers & Hood, 2007; Hood & Carruthers, 2007), as described in Chapter 3. We have furthered that model with the Flourishing through Leisure Model: An Ecological Extension of the Leisure and Well-Being Model, as introduced in Chapter 4.

Our field has historically embraced the idea of the benefits of recreation and leisure and has produced numerous publications and materials that show the connection between participation in meaningful recreation and positive outcomes for the individual, the community, and the environment. Table 5.12 (see p. 102) shows the most available publications in the area of leisure and recreation benefits, as well as therapeutic recreation benefits.

Meaningfulness of Strengths and Application to Therapeutic Recreation Practice

This chapter has provided a vocabulary and encyclopedia for strengths. Strengths, whether internal or external, are at the heart of practice in therapeutic recreation, due to the nature of our profession. Therapeutic recreation is focused on facilitating play, recreation, and leisure for all people, regardless of illness or disability, to improve well-being and quality of life. Recreation and leisure are key strengths in people's lives, and the arena to develop other strengths further. Recreation interests, skills, and talents are strengths that build other strengths, which in turn build wellness and a high quality of life. Recreation and leisure are a part of most people's vision of a "good life."

Primary Source Support:

Dr. Barbara Fredrickson and the "Broaden-and-Build Theory of Positive Emotions"

Dr. Barbara Fredrickson is the director of the Positive Emotions and Psychophysiology Laboratory at the University of North Carolina at Chapel Hill. According to Dr. Fredrickson,

> Our purpose is to understand and to share the full significance of positive emotions. We have three core ideals:
> - To do high-quality science,
> - To answer questions that matter to humanity, and
> - To have fun and feel good about doing it.
>
> Our goal is to uncover the universal recipe for human flourishing and to give this recipe as a gift to the world. Our science to date tells us that genuine positive emotions may in fact be the single most important active ingredient in this recipe for flourishing. When this ingredient is lacking, or in poor supply—people get stuck. They lose their freedom of choice. They become stagnant and painfully predictable. But when this ingredient is in ample supply—people take off. They become generative, creative, resilient, ripe with possibility, and beautifully unpredictable. Our research team is working to show how it is that being moved by positive emotions can move you forward, and not only lift you to your higher ground, but also create a world that is worth giving to our children. (www.unc.edu/peplab/purpose.html)

Dr. Fredrickson developed the Broaden-and-Build Theory of Positive Emotions to explain how positive emotions were important. According to the theory, positive emotions expand cognition and behavioral tendencies. Positive emotions increase the number of potential behavioral options. The expanded cognitive flexibility evident during positive emotional states results in resource- or strength-building that is useful over time. Even though a positive emotional state is only momentary, the benefits last in the form of traits, social bonds, and abilities that endure into the future. The implication of this theory is that positive emotions have inherent value to human growth and development and cultivation of positive emotions will help people lead fuller lives. Recreation, play, and leisure are key life venues in which we experience positive emotions. Thus, according to the Broaden-and-Build Theory, recreation is an area of our lives that is not only worthy in its own right, but helps us function better across all other areas of our lives. Recreation, play, and leisure can help people stay "unstuck."

The Broaden-and-Build Theory is discussed in more depth in Chapter 6 *Theories*. You can also learn more about Dr. Fredrickson and the research that supports the Broaden-and-Build Theory by visiting the Positive Emotions and Psychophysiology Laboratory website at http://www.unc.edu/peplab/home.html.

Figure 5.8 Primary Source Support: Broaden and Build Theory

Summary

Strengths are at the heart of therapeutic recreation practice. Strengths can be thought of as internal to individuals, and external, occurring in their environment and context. Internal strengths include:

- Interests and preferences
- Talents and abilities
- Skills and competencies
- Knowledge
- Aspirations and goals
- Character strengths and virtues

External strengths and resources include:

- Family support and involvement
- Social support and friendships
- Home resources
- Community resources
- Opportunities for meaningful participation
- High expectations and positive attitudes in the environment

Recreation and leisure are key strengths, both internal and external to the person. Recreation and leisure provide many benefits to individuals and communities. Recreation and leisure provide an arena for other strengths to be fully developed and exercised. Recreation and leisure, the focus of therapeutic recreation practice, are, as Davidson and colleagues (2006) state, the "stuff" and "foundation" for positive change for a high quality of life.

Resources

Authentic Happiness Coaching Newsletters
http://www.authentichappiness.sas.upenn.edu/newletters.aspx

These newsletters give a "Reader's Digest" overview of select character strengths and virtues. Past issues can be accessed online.

Character Strengths and Virtues: A Handbook and Classification
http://www.viastrengths.org

This handbook, by Christopher Peterson and Martin Seligman (2004), provides a comprehensive classification of the 24 character strengths. Each strength is described in depth, with supporting research and specific tools to assess each area. Published by Oxford University Press and the American Psychological Association, this is a valuable resource for therapeutic recreation specialists to own and use in practice.

International Classification of Functioning, Disability and Health
http://www.who.int/classifications/icf/en

The World Health Organization's website has a wealth of information on which to learn and understand the new ICF. You can download the "Beginner's Guide" to the ICF, explore the online taxonomy used in the ICF, or download the checklist itself.

References

Amado, A., Conklin, F., & Wells, J. (1990). *Friends: A manual for connecting persons with disabilities and community members.* St. Paul, MN: Human Services Research and Development Center.

American Psychiatric Association. (2000). *Diagnostic and Statistical Manual of Mental Disorders, Fourth Edition, Text Revision (DSM-IV-TR®).* Arlington, VA: American Psychiatric Association.

Anderson, L., & Heyne, L. (2012). Flourishing through Leisure: An Ecological Extension of the Leisure and Well-Being Model in therapeutic recreation strengths-based practice. *Therapeutic Recreation Journal, 46*(2), 129–152.

Anderson, L., & Kress, C. (2003). *Inclusion: Strategies for including people with disabilities in parks and recreation opportunities.* State College, PA: Venture Publishing, Inc.

Anderson, L., Schleien, S., & Green, F. (1993). Educating for social responsibility: The effectiveness and ethics of a community service project with persons with disabilities. *Schole, 8*, 17–35.

Beard, J., & Ragheb, M. (2002). Leisure interest measure. In J. Burlingame & T. Blaschko (Eds.), *Assessment tools for recreational therapy and related fields* (3rd ed.). Ravensdale, WA: Idyll Arbor.

Benard, B. (2006). Using strengths-based practice to tap the resilience of families. In D. Saleebey (Ed.),

Table 5.12 Common Ways to Conceptualize Benefits of Recreation in the Field

National Recreation and Park Association
(O'Sullivan, 1999)

- Personal benefits
- Social benefits
- Economic benefits
- Environmental benefits

National Therapeutic Recreation Society
(Broida, 2000)

- Physical benefits
- Social benefits
- Psychological/emotional benefits
- Cognitive benefits
- Expressive benefits
- Leisure and recreation development
- Benefits to the profession/staff
- Benefits to caregivers/parents/family

Benefits of Therapeutic Recreation: A Consensus View
(Coyle, Kinney, Riley, & Shank, 1991)

- Physical health and health maintenance
- Cognitive functioning
- Psychosocial health
- Growth and development
- Personal and life satisfaction
- Societal and health care systems benefits

Benefits Catalogue, Canadian Recreation and Park Association
(1997)

- Recreation is essential to personal health
- Recreation is key to balanced human development
- Recreation is essential to quality of life
- Recreation reduces self-destructive and anti-social behavior
- Recreation builds strong families and healthy communities
- Recreation reduces health care, social service, and police/justice costs
- Recreation and parks are significant economic generators in the community
- Parks, open space, and natural areas are essential to ecological survival

Benefits of Leisure
(Driver, Brown, & Peterson, 1991)

- Physiological and psycho-physiological benefits
- Psychological benefits
- Social benefits
- Economic benefits
- Environmental benefits

Self-Assessment of Learning

- Discuss these questions with your classmates or colleagues:
    1. Why is it important to have a clear conceptual understanding of what is meant by "strengths"?
    2. What are some types of internal strengths that you and others possess?
    3. What are some types of external strengths that can exist in the context of our environments?
    4. How are leisure and recreation key aspects of well-being?
    5. What is meant by the idea that recreation is both a strength in and of itself and a pathway to build other strengths?

- Take time now to get clearer on your own strengths. Visit this website to complete the *Values in Action (VIA) Inventory of Strengths* at http://www.viastrengths.org. According to Peterson and Seligman (2004), authors of the *VIA*,

    The **VIA Inventory of Strengths** is a 240-item self-report questionnaire that is intended for use by adults. It measures the degree to which respondents endorse each of the 24 strengths of character in the VIA Classification. It takes approximately 30 minutes to complete. A report is immediately generated indicating 5 top strengths, a description of each, and a comparison of your scores to others who have taken the test. (para. 2)

The strengths perspective in social work practice (4th ed.). Boston, MA: Allyn & Bacon.

Broida, J. (2000). *Therapeutic recreation – The benefits are endless training and resource guide.* Ashburn, VA: National Recreation and Park Association.

Buckingham, M., & Clifton, D. (2001). *Now, discover your strengths.* New York, NY: Free Press.

Caldwell, L. (2004). *TimeWise: Taking charge of leisure time.* Scotts Valley, CA: ETR Associates.

Canadian Recreation and Park Association. (1997). *The benefits catalogue.* Ottawa, ON, Canada: CRPA.

Carruthers, C., & Hood, C. (2007). Building a life of meaning through therapeutic recreation: The Leisure and Well-Being Model, part I. *Therapeutic Recreation Journal, 41*(4), 276–297.

Coleman, D., & Iso-Ahola, S. (1993). Leisure and health: The role of social support and self-determination. *Journal of Leisure Research, 25*(2), 111–128.

Coyle, C., Kinney, T., Riley, B., & Shank, J. (1991). *Benefits of therapeutic recreation: A consensus view.* Washington, DC: National Institute on Disability and Rehabilitation Research.

Csíkszentmihályi, M. (1990). *Flow: The psychology of optimal experience.* New York, NY: HarperCollins.

Davidson, G., Shahar, L., Stacheli Lawless, M., Sells, D., & Tondora, J. (2006). Play, pleasure, and other positive life events: Factors in recovery from mental illness? *Psychiatry, 69*(2), 151–163.

Dean, B. (2002). Five key strengths. *Authentic Happiness Newsletter, 2*(7). Retrieved from http://viacharacter.org

Dieser, R. (2005). A book review: Authentic happiness. *Therapeutic Recreation Journal, 39*(3), 241–247.

Driver, B., Brown, P., & Peterson, G. (1991). *The benefits of leisure.* State College, PA: Venture Publishing, Inc.

Duncan, B., Miller, S., & Sparks, J. (2003). Interactional and solution-focused brief therapies: Evolving concepts of change. In T. Sexton, G. Weeks, & M. Robbins (Eds.), *Handbook of family therapy: The science and practice of working with families and couples.* New York, NY: Brunner-Routledge.

Edginton, C., DeGraaf, D., Dieser, R., & Edginton, S. (2006). *Leisure and life satisfaction: Foundational perspectives* (4th ed.). New York, NY: McGraw Hill.

Florida, R. (2002). *The rise of the creative class.* New York, NY: Basic.

Fredrickson, B. L. (2003). The value of positive emotions. *American Scientist, 91,* 330–335.

Freiler, C. (2003). From risk to human development: Social inclusion as a focus of individual and collective well-being. *Perception, 26,* 1–2. Retrieved from http://www.ccsd.ca/perception/2612/index.htm

Gardner, H. (1993). *Frames of mind: The theory of multiple intelligences.* New York, NY: Basic.

Gardner, H. (2005, May). *Multiple lenses on the mind.* Paper presented at the ExpoGestian Conference, Bogota, Colombia. Retrieved from http://pzweb.harvard.edu/PIs/MultipleLensMay2005.pdf

Green, F., & Heyne, L. (1997). Friendships. In S. Schleien, M. Ray, & F. Green (Eds.), *Community recreation and people with disabilities* (2nd ed., pp. 129–150). Baltimore, MD: Brookes.

Heejung, K., & Sherman, D. (2007). "Express yourself": Culture and the effect of self-expression on choice. *Journal of Personality and Social Psychology, 92*(1), 1–11.

Heyne, L., & Schleien, S. (1997). Teaming up with parents to support inclusive recreation. *Parks and Recreation, 32*(5), 76–81.

Heyne, L., Schleien, S., & McAvoy, L. (1993). *Making friends: Using recreation activities to promote friendship between children with and without disabilities.* Minneapolis, MN: Institute on Commmunity Integration, University of Minnesota.

Heyne, L., Schleien, S., & McAvoy, L. (2003). Ideas for encouraging children's friendships through recreation. *Impact, 16*(2), 10–11, 34.

Hood, C., & Carruthers, C. (2007). Enhancing leisure experience and developing resources: The Leisure and Well-Being Model, part II. *Therapeutic Recreation Journal, 41*(4), 298–325.

Howe-Murphy, R., & Charboneau, B. (1987). *Therapeutic recreation intervention: An ecological perspective.* Englewood Cliffs, NJ: Prentice-Hall.

Hutchinson, P., & McGill, J. (1992). *Leisure, integration, and community.* Toronto, ON, Canada: Leisurability Publications.

Inclusive Cities Canada. (2007). *Current developments.* Retrieved from http://www.inclusivecities.ca/index.html

Kasser, T., & Ryan, R. (1996). Further examining the American dream: Differential correlates of intrinsic and extrinsic goals. *Personality and Social Psychology Bulletin, 22,* 280–287.

Kelly, J. (1999). Leisure and society: A dialectical analysis. In E. Jackson & T. Burton (Eds.), *Leisure studies: Prospects for the twenty-first century.* State College, PA: Venture Publishing, Inc.

Kelly, J., & Freysinger, V. (2000). *21st century leisure: Current issues.* Needham Heights, MA: Allyn & Bacon.

Kolanowski, A., Buettner, L., Costa, P., & Litaker, J. (2001). Capturing interests: Therapeutic recreation activities for persons with dementia. *Therapeutic Recreation Journal, 35*(3), 220–235.

Lichtenstein, S., & Slovic, P. (2006). *The construction of preferences.* New York, NY: Cambridge University Press.

Lopez, S., & Snyder, C. (2003). *Positive psychological assessment: A handbook of models and measures.* Washington, DC: American Psychological Association.

Mannes, M. (2008). *Transforming what we see and do in human services.* Minneapolis, MN: Search Institute. Retrieved from http://www.search-institute.org/downloads/

McGill, J. (1996). *Developing leisure identities.* Toronto, ON, Canada: Leisurability.

Merriam-Webster Online Dictionary. (2010). Family. Retrieved from http://www.merriam-webster.com/dictionary/family

Moon, S. (2003). Personal talent. *High Ability Studies, 14*(1), 5–21.

Nall Schenk, C. (2002). Leisurescope Plus. In J. Burlingame & T. Blaschko (Eds.), *Assessment tools for recreational therapy and related fields.* Ravensdale, WA: Idyll Arbor.

O'Hara, S. (2000). The disability rights and independent living movement. *Bene Legere, 55.* Retrieved from http://www.lib.berkeley.edu/give/bene55/disability.html

O'Sullivan, E. (1999). Setting a course for change: The benefits movement. Ashburn, VA: National Recreation and Park Association.

Olson, D., Sprenkle, D., & Russell, C. (1979). Circumplex model of marital and family systems: Cohesion and adaptability dimensions, family types, and clinical applications. *Family Processes, 18*(1), 3–27.

Orsega-Smith, E., Payne, L., Mowen, A., Ho, C., & Godbey, G. (2007). The role of social support and self-efficacy in shaping the leisure time physical activity of older adults. *Journal of Leisure Research, 39*(4), 705–727.

Papierno, P., Ceci, S., Makel, M., & Williams, W. (2005). The nature and nurture of talent: A bioecological perspective on the ontogeny of exceptional abilities. *Journal for the Education of the Gifted, 28*(3–4), 312–332.

Pedlar, A., Haworth, L., Hutchinson, P., Taylor, A., & Dunn, P. (1999). *A textured life: Empowerment and adults with developmental disabilities.* Waterloo, ON, Canada: Wilfrid Laurier University Press.

Peterson, C. (2006). *A primer in positive psychology.* New York, NY: Oxford University Press.

Peterson, C., & Seligman, M. (2004). *Character strengths and virtues: A handbook and classification.* New York, NY: Oxford University Press.

Porter, H., & VanPuymbroeck, M. (2007). Utilization of the International Classification of Functioning, Disability and Health within therapeutic recreation practice. *Therapeutic Recreation Journal, 41*(1), 47–60.

Putman, R. (2000). *Bowling alone: The collapse and revival of American community*. New York, NY: Simon and Schuster.

Rapp, C., & Goscha, R. (2006). *The strengths model: Case management with people with psychiatric disabilities*. New York, NY: Oxford University Press.

Rath, T. (2006). *Vital friends*. New York, NY: Gallup.

Raymore, L. (2002). Facilitators to leisure. *Journal of Leisure Research, 34*(1), 37–51.

Russell, R. (2005). *Pastimes: The context of contemporary leisure* (3rd ed.). Champaign, IL: Sagamore.

Ryan, R., Chirkov, V., Little, T., Sheldon, K., Timoshina, E., & Deci, E. (1999). The American Dream in Russia: Extrinsic aspirations and well-being in two cultures. *Personality and Social Psychology Bulletin, 25*, 1509–1524.

Rybak, A., & McAndrew, F. (2006). How do we decide whom our friends are? Defining levels of friendship in Poland and the United States. *Journal of Social Psychology, 146*(2), 147–163.

Saleebey, D. (2006). *The strengths perspective in social work practice* (4th ed.). Boston, MA: Allyn & Bacon.

Schleien, S., Green, F., & Stone, C. (1999). Making friends within inclusive community recreation programs. *Journal of Leisurability, 26*(3), 33–43.

Seligman, M. (2002). *Authentic happiness: Using the new positive psychology to realize your full potential for lasting fulfillment*. New York, NY: Free Press.

Shank, J., & Coyle, C. (2002). *Therapeutic recreation in health promotion and rehabilitation*. State College, PA: Venture Publishing, Inc.

Staron, M., Jasinski, M., & Weatherley, R. (2006). *Life-based learning: A strengths-based approach for capability development in vocational and technical education*. Darlinghurst, Australia: Department of Education, Science, and Training.

Stumbo, N., & Peterson, C. (2004). *Therapeutic recreation program design: Principles and procedures* (4th ed.). San Francisco, CA: Pearson.

Taylor, A., Sylvestre, J., & Botschner, J. (1998). Social support is something you do, not something you provide: Implications for linking formal and informal support. *Journal of Leisurability, 25*(4), 3–13.

Vallerand, G., Mageau, G., Elliot, A., Dumais, A., Demers, M., & Rousseau, F. (2008). Passion and performance attainment in sport. *Psychology of Sport and Exercise, 9*, 373–392.

Weick, A., Kreider, J., & Chamberlain, R. (2006). Solving problems from a strengths perspective. In D. Saleebey (Ed.), *The strengths perspective in social work practice* (4th ed.). Boston, MA: Allyn & Bacon.

Wilkins, V., & Murphy, K. (2000). *Leisure education: The power of games*. Unpublished manuscript.

Witt, P., & Ellis, G. (2002). *Leisure diagnostic battery*. State College, PA: Venture Publishing, Inc.

World Health Organization. (2003). *International Classification of Functioning, Disability and Health Version 2.1a*. Retrieved from http://www.who.int/classifications/icf/site/checklist/icf-checklist.pdf

Wright, M., & Masten, A. (2004). Resilience processes and development: Fostering positive adaptation following childhood adversity. In S. Goldstein & R. Brooks (Eds.), *Handbook of resilience in children*. New York, NY: Plenum.

Zabriskie, R., & Heyne, L. (2003). Introduction to the special issue on the family: A refocus on family. *Therapeutic Recreation Journal, 37*(1), 15–17.

Zabriskie, R., & McCormick, B. (2003). Parent and child perspectives of family leisure involvement and satisfaction with family life. *Journal of Leisure Research, 35*(2), 163–189.

Chapter 6
THEORIES THAT GUIDE STRENGTHS-BASED THERAPEUTIC RECREATION PRACTICE

The coneflower has a clear center with many seeds.

"Creating a new theory is not like destroying an old barn and erecting a skyscraper in its place. It is rather like climbing a mountain, gaining new and wider views, discovering unexpected connections between our starting points and its rich environment."

—*Albert Einstein*

OVERVIEW OF CHAPTER 6

- What is theory? Why is it important?
- Transition to strengths-based theory
- Part 1: Well-being and the individual
  - Positive psychology theories
    - Happiness
    - Learned optimism
    - Flow
    - Broaden-and-build theory of positive emotions
  - Leisure coping
  - Self-determination
  - Self-efficacy
- Part 2: Well-being and the environment
  - New theories of health and disability
    - World Health Organization redefines disability
    - Healthy People 2020
  - Normalization and social role valorization
  - Social support and friendships
- Community and community building theory
  - Social capital
  - What makes community?
  - Creating Livable Communities
  - Circle of Courage
- Resiliency

FOCUS QUESTIONS

- What is a theory?
- Why is theory important in therapeutic recreation practice?
- What strengths-based theories support an individual's sense of well-being?
- What strengths-based theories take into account the contextual, environmental factors that influence an individual's well-being?
- What are the implications of strength-based theories for therapeutic recreation practice?

What is Theory? Why is it Important?

A definition of "theory":
(a) the analysis of a set of facts in their relation to one another
(b) a belief, policy, or procedure proposed or followed as the basis of action
(c) a plausible or scientifically acceptable general principle or body of principles offered to explain phenomena

In the previous chapters we have taken you through the sea change in health and human services and, specifically, in therapeutic recreation. We have presented the Flourishing through Leisure Model, an ecological approach to the Leisure and Well-Being Model. And we have featured internal and external strengths as reliable avenues to develop well-being and quality of life. Now we turn to the theories that, like underlying currents, propelled this sea change toward strengths-based practice. But, first, let's answer, "What is theory?" and "Why is it important?"

As the dictionary definition above indicates, theory offers plausible, scientifically acceptable explanations for phenomena and how various components of phenomena interact (Caldwell, 2000; Devine & Wilhite, 1999; Hood & Carruthers, 2002; Shank & Coyle, 2002). The following rationale for the importance of drawing from theory to guide therapeutic recreation practice is offered by Shank and Coyle (2002):

> A *theory* serves multiple functions. It provides a framework that combines, organizes, and synthesizes concepts that form a body of knowledge. This theoretical framework gives meaning to observed facts and provides a logical basis for explaining and predicting a phenomena, such as human behavior and experiences (Wiersma, 1991). Theories also provide a basis for developing and testing new knowledge, which is critical to advancing clinical practice in the health professions. Furthermore, theories provided a conceptual base from which to plan interventions that promote lifestyle change. For these reasons, understanding theoretical foundations that guide TR practice is critical. (p. 63)

Leonardo da Vinci—Renaissance artist, architect, inventor, and philosopher—also gives us some vivid imagery to illustrate the importance of theory for practice:

> Those who are enamoured [*sic*] of practice without science are like a pilot who boards a ship without rudder or compass and never has any certainty of where he is going. Practice should always be based upon a sound knowledge of theory. (qtd. in Space and Motion, 2010, p. 1)

To extend da Vinci's analogy further, a therapeutic recreation specialist is like a pilot who, with the participant at the helm, aims the needle of the compass toward the participant's goals and dreams, and follows the map and undercurrents to track progress safely to its destination.

Therapeutic recreation is a profession largely rooted in the disciplines of psychology and sociology, and therapeutic recreation specialists have traditionally drawn from psycho-social theory to guide their practice. In this text, we continue this tradition by drawing from the strengths-based theories in psychology and sociology that give us a new framework for understanding and facilitating change in human behavior. We hope you will be as excited about the theories presented in this chapter as we are, and that you will be inspired to think imaginatively about how you can use strengths-based theory in your own practice. Like the coneflower on the frontispiece of this chapter, with its clear center and many seeds, theory provides clarity of focus that can lead to numerous beneficial outcomes for the participants with whom we work.

Transition to Strengths-Based Theory

In this chapter we continue the thematic thread of this book—that is, the transition from a deficits model of theory and practice to one that is oriented around strengths. We focus here on theory that supports human flourishing, well-being, and quality of life. To give you a sense of how theory has evolved in recent years, see Figure 6.1. Here you will find assumptions that underlie deficits-based theory alongside the fundamentally disparate assumptions that ground strengths-based theory. The left column of Figure 6.1 captures the corrective approach of theories that are built upon people's problems and deficiencies, as fixed by the professional.

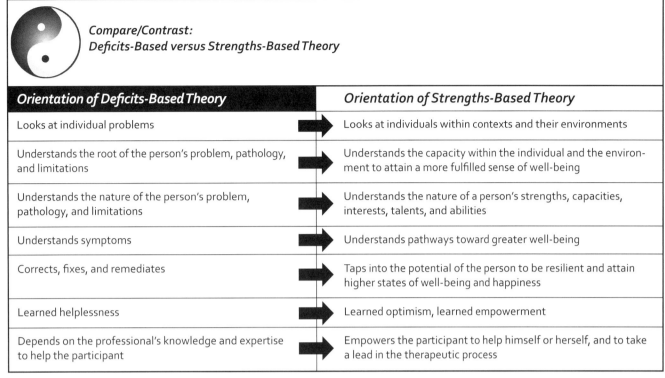

Figure 6.1 Compare/Contrast: Deficits-Based versus Strengths-Based Theory

In contrast, the right column characterizes theories that capitalize on people's potentiality within the natural supports of their environments, and empower people to lead with their strengths to achieve a greater sense of well-being.

To help organize your thinking about the strengths-oriented theories in this chapter, we separate them into two sections. Part 1: *Well-Being and the Individual* describes theories that relate to supporting well-being *within the individual*. While some of these theories consider how environmental factors shape well-being, their primary focus is well-being within the person. Part 2: *Well-Being and the Environment* looks at theories that pertain to *contextual* factors that can elevate an individual's sense of well-being.

PART 1:
WELL-BEING AND THE INDIVIDUAL

This portion of the chapter discusses strengths-oriented theories that apply to well-being within the individual. We include pertinent theory from the study of positive psychology, as well as the theories of leisure coping, self-determination, and self-efficacy.

Positive Psychology Theories

> I believe that psychology should be about more than repairing what is wrong. It should also be about identifying and nurturing what is good.
>
> —*Martin Seligman (2003, p. xi)*

When Martin Seligman became president of the American Psychological Association in 1998, he initiated a radical shift in the organization's direction. He noted that, for many years, psychologists had focused on what ails us—anxiety, depression, obsession, compulsion, neurosis. This lopsided point of reference prompted him to call his profession "half-baked." Seligman acknowledged that psychologists knew a great deal about the sources of suffering, yet he wondered, "What are the enabling conditions that make human beings flourish?" (Wallis, 2004, p. 1). His simple query spawned an explosion of research to scientifically test what makes people happy. This explosion became known as the field of positive psychology and Seligman was dubbed its founder.

What is positive psychology? Seligman (2009) describes it as "the scientific study of the strengths and virtues that enable individuals and communities to thrive" (p. 1). He says positive psychology "is founded on the belief that people want to lead meaningful and fulfilling lives, to cultivate what is best within themselves, and to enhance their experiences of love, work, and play" (p. 1). Similarly, O'Hanlon (2008) defines positive psychology as "research evidence about what works in human life; what makes people happier; what gives their lives a sense of satisfaction and meaning" (slide 2). Others simply call positive psychology "the scientific study of optimal human functioning" (Sheldon, Fredrickson, Rathunde, Csíkszentmihályi, & Haidt, 2000, p. 1).

This new sphere of research focuses on four main areas of scientific inquiry (Peterson, 2006; Peterson & Park, 2009):

1. *Positive emotion and experiences*: The study of positive emotions such as hope, love, trust, enjoyment, and confidence examines positive feelings about the past, happiness in the present, and hopefulness for the future. Cultivating positive emotion enriches our lives from day to day and prepares us to weather the trying times.

2. *Positive individual traits*: Positive psychologists believe we must do more than heal emotional disturbance; we must also cultivate positive traits that can help buffer against discouragement and strengthen resiliency. These traits include *abilities* such as intelligence or musicianship, along with *character strengths and virtues*, which you read about in Chapter 5 *Strengths*. You will recall that character strengths and virtues include the individual human capacities for love, courage, compassion, resilience, integrity, curiosity, self-control, and wisdom, among several others.

3. *Positive relationships*: Research findings in positive psychology contend that good relationships with other people are vital for individual happiness. Through socialization, people find pleasure and ways to savor the good things that happen in their lives.

4. *Positive and enabling institutions*: Research on positive institutions centers upon understanding the strengths that improve our communities. Some of these strengths include justice, tolerance, leadership, democracy, teamwork, and responsibility, to name a few.

In the following sections we describe four theories that capture some of the recent findings of positive psychology research: happiness, learned optimism, flow, and the broaden-and-build theory of positive emotions.

Happiness

> Happiness is the meaning and the purpose of life, the whole aim and end of human existence.
>
> —*Aristotle, 384–322 B.C.*

The roots of the current discussion on the nature of happiness are found in Greek philosophy and ethics. Aristotle has handed down to us the concept of the "good life," or *eudiamonia*, a theory we introduced you to in Chapter 3 *A Sea Change in Therapeutic Recreation*. In that chapter, eudiamonia was defined as "well spirit." It may also sometimes be translated as "flourishing" or "living well and doing well."

Aristotle's and Seligman's understandings of the concept of happiness are very congruent. Similar to Aristotle, Seligman believes "authentic happiness comes from identifying and cultivating your most fundamental strengths and using them in work, love, play, and parenting" (2002, p. xiii). His research encourages us to develop character by exercising our strengths and virtues. Seligman concludes, much like Aristotle, that active and virtuous engagement with life through the use of our strengths and talents is the ideal pathway to finding meaning and happiness in life.

One of the most noteworthy findings in positive psychology is the discovery of what determines human happiness. Investigators have found that we can control more of our happiness than we ever thought possible (Fredrickson, 2009; Lyubomirsky, 2008; Seligman, 2002). Seligman (2002) has shown that approximately one-half of our happiness—our happiness "set point"—is determined genetically. We may experience tremendous joy or plumb the depths of sorrow, but we will eventually return to our personal baseline of happiness. Every person's set point is individually determined, and it is only a starting point upon which to build further happiness.

In recent years, Lyubomirsky (2008) has extended scientific knowledge related to our potential to experience happiness. Remember from Chapter 3 that she defined happiness as "the experience of joy, contentment, or positive well-being, combined with a sense that one's life is good, meaningful, and worthwhile" (p. 32). Happiness, she says, lies on a continuum, similar to height or temperature. Our level of happiness may be extremely low, extremely high, or anywhere in between.

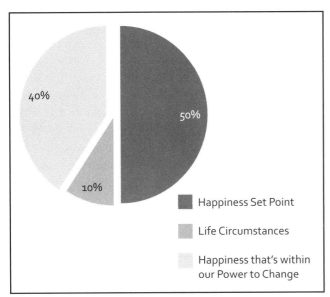

Figure 6.2 Pie of Happiness—What Determines Happiness? *(adapted from Lyubomirsky, 2008)*

It also fluctuates depending on our situation and our intentional efforts to increase our happiness.

Lyubomirsky agrees with Seligman that one's happiness set point comprises roughly half of one's total capacity for happiness (see Figure 6.2). Through her research, Lyubomirsky has found that another 10% of the "pie of happiness" is made up of life circumstances—factors such as where we live, how much money we make, the state of our health, and whether we're single or partnered. The remaining 40% of the "pie of happiness" is within our control to intentionally enhance. The implications of this finding are potentially life-changing—not only for us as therapeutic recreation professionals but also for our participants.

So, what are the secret ingredients that make up this 40% of happiness that is within our power to influence? According to Lyubomirsky, it is our behavior and our thoughts. What we *do* and what we *think* from day to day has a tremendous impact on how much happiness we feel. Lyubomirsky purports that, if we learn what typically makes people happy, we can duplicate some of those thought and behavior patterns to elevate our own sense of well-being. By systematically observing and comparing very happy people and very unhappy people, Lyubomirsky and other researchers have gained insight into the thoughts and behaviors of the happiest individuals (see Figure 6.3).

Lyubomirsky (2008) has found that adopting even one new pattern of thinking or behaving in Figure 6.3 will bring a sizeable degree of well-being and meaning to one's life. For increased happiness to be lasting, however, Lyubomirsky cautions that considerable effort and commitment is required on a daily basis. She contends, however, that there is no other work in life more worthwhile.

Lyubomirsky's research on happiness goes beyond theory to the development of "happiness activities" that have been proven to increase happiness among her research participants (2008). She offers several happiness-producing activities that address thoughts and behaviors similar to those in Figure 6.3. When practiced regularly, these activities can help harness the 40% of potential happiness within your power to develop. You will learn more about these happiness activities in Chapter 11 *Implementation*.

Learned Optimism

Positive psychologists have discovered that we actually have a *choice* about whether our outlook is bright or gloomy. Many of us presume that a person is either fortunate enough to be born optimistic or hapless enough to be born pessimistic—that optimism and pessimism are innate characteristics. There may be some truth to this, however positive psychologists have discovered that, even if our "set point" for happiness is low (see previous section), we don't need to resign ourselves to pessimistic thinking. In fact scientists tell

---

Sonja Lyubomirsky

Thinking and Behavior Patterns of Happy People

Sonja Lyubomirsky (2008) concludes that happy people tend to think and act in the following ways:

- A large part of their attention is devoted to nurturing and enjoying relationships with family and friends.
- They are grateful for all that they have and are comfortable expressing such gratitude.
- When others need help, they are often the first to offer assistance.
- They practice optimism when imagining their future.
- They try to live in the present and savor life's pleasures.
- They exercise weekly and sometimes daily.
- They have lifelong goals and ambitions to which they are deeply committed.
- When faced with adversity, they cope with poise and inner strength.

Figure 6.3 Thinking and Behavior Patterns of Happy People

us that optimism can be *learned*. That is, we can develop a brighter outlook by acquiring new cognitive skills that research has proven will shift habitual pessimism toward optimism. A positive viewpoint brings many rewards. For instance, intentionally choosing to look at a difficult situation from a hopeful perspective can turn a distressing situation completely around. What an empowering concept this is to pass on to our participants! In his book, *Learned Optimism*, Martin Seligman (1991) discusses pessimism and optimism as two very different ways of looking at the world. The Compare/Contrast feature in Figure 6.4 juxtaposes these viewpoints side by side.

Seligman believes an optimistic outlook is indispensable for grappling with adversity in life: "Our thoughts are not merely reactions to events; they change what ensues" (p. 7). Researchers in positive psychology have discovered that our thoughts influence our feelings, which influence our behavior—a dynamic that can become deeply ingrained in us as habitual reactions. Fortunately, positive psychologists have also discovered that we have the power to *control* our thoughts, thus our feelings, and likewise our behavior. Figure 6.4 shows just how pervasively our attitude affects who we are and what we do. Our outlook affects how we feel, how we act, our relationships with others, our confidence, our health, and our energy.

Seligman derived his theory of learned optimism from an earlier theory he developed in the mid-1970s called *learned helplessness*. This theory holds that, when we perceive there is nothing we can do to affect the outcome of a situation, we give up trying (Seligman, 1975, 1991). We believe we have no personal control over the situation and develop a quitting response. Seligman reasoned that, if we can learn to be helpless, we can also unlearn helplessness. Beyond that, we can learn to be optimistic by strengthening our sense of empowerment and self-determination.

Seligman (2002) closely examines the two distinct thought processes of optimistic and pessimistic people. Optimistic people, he says, are those "who make *permanent* and *universal* explanations for good events, as well as *temporary* and *specific* explanations for bad events" (p. 93). The optimist usually sees the permanent causes of good events as originating from his or her personal traits and abilities, which may include working diligently, showing compassion, or a well-timed sense of humor. The optimist tends to see the positivity of the good event as spilling over to enhance everything in his or her life. When unfortunate events occur, the optimist gives rational situation-specific

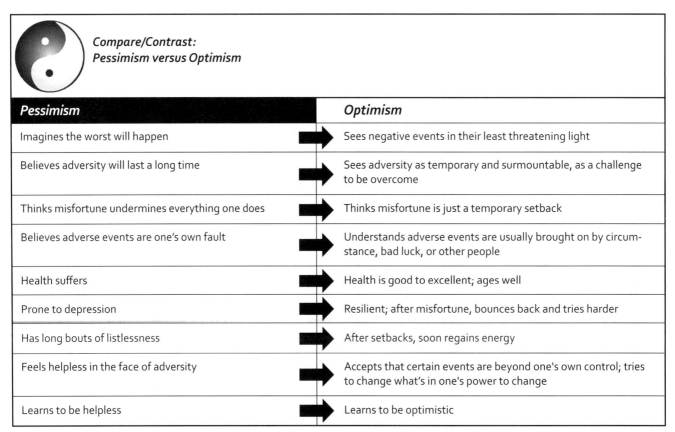

Figure 6.4 Compare/Contrast: Pessimism versus Optimism *(adapted from Seligman, 1991)*

explanations for them, containing negativity to one specific occurrence instead of letting it contaminate other life areas. This outlook helps optimists "bounce back" from setbacks and, when they experience success, to get "on a roll." Pessimistic people show opposite tendencies. They "make temporary and specific explanations for success, and permanent and universal explanations for setbacks" (p. 93). Thus, success for the pessimist is short-lived, and setbacks are attributed to all-encompassing personal shortcomings. This outlook often signals learned helplessness.

Seligman (1991) informs us that learning optimism is more than the power of positive thinking and positive self-talk. It is "what you think when you fail, using the power of 'non-negative thinking.' Changing the central things you say to yourself when you experience the setbacks that life deals all of us is the central skill of optimism" (p. 15). In Chapter 11 *Implementation* you will read about one of the techniques for boosting optimism so you can experience the benefits of learned optimism for yourself and for your participants.

Flow

Mihalyi Csíkszentmihályi (pronounced cheeks-sent-me-high), a professor of psychology and education at the University of Chicago for many years, came to his theory of "flow" by first reflecting on the nature of happiness. Csíkszentmihályi (1990) reasoned that happiness is not something that happens by chance; it is not random. Nor does happiness depend on external events; it depends more on how we *interpret* those events. Csíkszentmihályi believes we each need to cultivate happiness within ourselves, yet he cautions that, paradoxically, happiness cannot be pursued directly. He quotes Viktor Frankl (1959), the Austrian psychologist, from his classic book, *Man's Search for Meaning*: "[Happiness] cannot be pursued; it must *ensue*... as the unintended side-effect of one's personal dedication to a course greater than oneself" (Csíkszentmihályi, 1990, p. 2). Csíkszentmihályi's insights into happiness sent him on a path to extrapolate a notion very close in meaning to happiness—the concept of optimal experience, or "flow."

Csíkszentmihályi (1997) sees flow as those "exceptional moments" (p. 29) in which we feel very much alive and in the moment—alert, focused, in control. We are wholly engaged with life and feel, as athletes sometimes say, "in the zone." The times we experience flow often stand out as the most enjoyable of life's memories. In Figure 6.5 you will find the conditions that are typically present when flow is experienced, such as losing track of time, intense engagement, personal growth, and a sense of mastery.

As Figure 6.6 illustrates, matching a person's skill level with the appropriate level of challenge is central to the flow experience. If the task is too simple, the participant is likely to lose interest or become bored. If the activity is too difficult, the participant may become frustrated or anxious. Somewhere along the fine line between these two levels of difficulty lies a "flow channel" in which the person stretches his or her skills to meet the challenge of the activity. Csíkszentmihályi (1997) describes the skill-challenge dynamic in this way: "when high challenges are matched with high

---

Conditions of the Flow Experience

Mihalyi Csíkszentmihályi (1990, 1997) describes "flow" as experiencing those exceptional moments when one is in control, focused, and entirely engaged in an activity. When you are in a state of flow, Csíkszentmihályi says the following conditions exist:

Mihalyi Csíkszentmihályi

- Your attention is so intensely focused that you are not distracted by irrelevant thoughts or feelings.
- You feel strong and in control. You are functioning at your optimal level of challenge, at the peak of your abilities. The task in which you are engaged is neither too simple nor too complex for your abilities.
- The task is goal-directed and, through it, you continue to build skills. You feel a sense of mastery.
- The task provides instantaneous feedback. You are able to judge immediately how well you are doing.
- You have a sense of timelessness. Hours may seem like minutes.
- You are so absorbed in the task that self-consciousness disappears.
- Your state of consciousness feels "harmoniously ordered."
- You perceive the task as something worth doing for its own sake. You expect nothing in return for your effort.
- From the state of flow springs a sense of personal growth, derived from a direct link with intangible forces such as creativity, joy, discovery, or transcendence.

Figure 6.5 Conditions of the Flow Experience

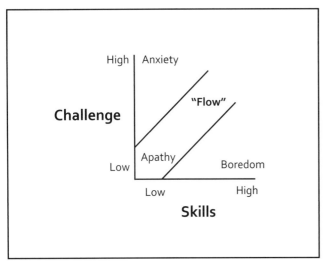

Figure 6.6 The Flow Channel

skills, then the deep involvement that sets flow apart from ordinary life is likely to occur" (p. 30). Figure 6.6 diagrams Csíkszentmihályi's conception of the balance between skill and challenge that produces the flow experience.

Csíkszentmihályi (1997) maintains that flow doesn't need to be a rare occurrence, and that we actually have the power to cultivate flow experiences within ourselves. He adds that the best moments in life are not necessarily the times we are passively relaxing; rather "the best moments usually occur when a person's body or mind is stretched to its limits in a voluntary effort to accomplish something difficult and worthwhile. Optimal experience is thus something we *make* happen" (p. 3).

But how exactly can we cultivate flow within ourselves? Csíkszentmihályi (1990) suggests we can access flow by achieving a kind of control over our inner lives. We need to arrange our consciousness to be harmonious so we can enlarge our capacity to manage our thoughts and feelings, block out irrelevant thoughts and feelings, and enter more readily into a state of flow. Along these same lines, Csíkszentmihályi explores why some people buckle under stress while others engage with stress in a way that allows them to rise to the demands of the occasion, to rebound, and to thrive:

> Why are some people weakened by stress, while others gain strength from it? Basically the answer is simple: those who know how to transform a hopeless situation into a new flow activity that can be controlled will be able to enjoy themselves, and emerge stronger from the ordeal. (p. 203)

Csíkszentmihályi recommends a disciplined process whereby we can increase the experience of flow in our lives. You will learn about this technique in Chapter 11 *Implementation*.

The theory of flow applies widely to the field of recreation, park, and leisure studies—and, when used intentionally with participants, to therapeutic recreation practice (see Figure 6.7). In fact, Csíkszentmihályi (1990) recognizes that most flow states result from engagement in recreation and leisure activities. He cites sports, games, art, and hobbies as consistent sources of flow, and specifically names the activities of making music, rock climbing, dancing, sailing, and chess as flow-producing. A person may achieve flow through work and other non-leisure activities too. Csíkszentmihályi encourages us to cultivate flow in these situations as well, yet leisure is recognized as the most potent milieu to experience joyful states of flow. Thus, using flow as a therapeutic recreation strengths-based practice has tremendous potential to effect positive change and personal growth within our participants.

Broaden-and-Build Theory of Positive Emotions

Similar to flow theory, Barbara Fredrickson's broaden-and-build theory of positive emotions acknowledges the importance of enjoyment and positive emotion for experiencing happiness. You will remember from Chapter 5 *Strengths* that Fredrickson developed the broaden-and-build theory to explain the value of positive emotions (see Figure 5.7). In this chapter we describe her theory in greater detail.

Fredrickson (2001, 2005, 2009) sees positive emotions, such as joy, interest, contentment, love, pride, and anticipation, as central to human flourishing. A flourishing life, she says, is "to live within an optimal range of human functioning, one that connotes goodness, generativity, growth, and resilience" (2005, p. 678). The broaden-and-build theory asserts that positive emotions "broaden" our outlooks and "build" resources over time that add value to our lives and help us flourish.

The broaden-and-build theory suggests two core truths about positive emotions (Fredrickson, 2009). First, unlike negative emotions, which tend to narrow and constrict our outlook, positive emotions "open our hearts and our minds, making us more receptive and creative" (p. 21). For example, playing ball with a dog, marveling at a child's first steps, laughing with a friend you haven't seen for a long time—these kinds of experiences open us to a sense of possibility and to novel ways of looking at the world. This phenomenon is what Fredrickson calls the "broadening" aspect of the broaden-and-build theory. The momentary positive emotion we experience impels us to broaden our experience by playing, exploring, creating, envisioning

Primary Source Support:

Cultivating Flow with People with Dementia

Allan, K. (2008). Positive psychology: Using strengths and experiencing flow. *Journal of Dementia Care, 16*(6), 24–26.

Kate Allan works with people with dementia in the United Kingdom. Recently she has steeped herself in the positive psychology literature, and now she is experimenting with how to apply it in her practice. Allan questions the emphasis the world places on "intellectual prowess"—a bias that often overlooks the character strengths and virtues that people with dementia possess:

> The value we ascribe to cognitive sophistication is one of the reasons that people with dementia are so marginalized in our society. Imagine how different it would be if we were to take, say, loving and allowing oneself to be loved, playfulness and humor or gratitude as seriously as being able to find words, remember facts or solve a problem? (p. 24)

Allan values the full spectrum of character strengths and virtues in her work with people with dementia. She has noticed how people with dementia appear to have the ability to experience flow and how, during those times, they exhibit their unique character strengths and virtues. She tells of a woman who, upon discovering watercolor painting, exclaimed, "I don't know why so many things are so hard now and this is so easy!" Allan believes the woman was experiencing flow. Allan also recounts a colleague's description of a man intensely involved in painting a wall:

> Engrossed in the task, he worked under minimal direction for days, recoating the area. Watching him, no one would have believed this man experienced memory problems and other health issues—he was so energetically and proudly engaged in constructive work. (p. 25)

She suggests that flow opportunities could arise from the person's previous interests or from a new activity. And activities could be creative, artistic, domestic, or physical, depending on the person's preference.

Beyond helping people with dementia experience the joyous feelings associated with flow, Allan believes flow has the potential to augment their cognitive function. Consider this story of two women with dementia who became involved in a creative task together:

> Neither required much guidance as they became absorbed in the challenge. They were totally occupied with the task, showing increased concentration and improved communication skills throughout the sessions. Noticeably, word finding and fluency seemed to improve as they were under no direct pressure to converse or give opinions. Conversation was spontaneous and humour followed. (p. 25)

While more research needs to be done in this area, experiencing flow shows great promise for balancing the deteriorating trend usually associated with dementia. Allan's work shows the potential of flow to engage people with dementia and actually strengthen their capabilities and ability to enjoy life!

Figure 6.7 Primary Source Support: Cultivating Flow with People with Dementia

a new direction, and expanding our everyday limits (Fredrickson, 2001).

The second core truth of positive emotion is that "positivity transforms us for the better" (2009, p. 24). Fredrickson continues, "By opening our hearts and minds, positive emotions allow us to discover and build new skills, new ties, new knowledge, and new ways of being." A passionate interest in wilderness preservation, for example, may lead someone to invent products that use only renewable resources. A pleasant conversation with a stranger from another country may lead to a life-long friendship. Perhaps you can think of an incident in your life where a single positive, seemingly chance event inspired you to move in an entirely new direction and catapulted you to a completely different place and mindset. Thus, we "build" on the initial positive emotion we experience, and tap into intellectual, psychological, social, and physical resources that expand our capacities and strengthen us over time.

Fredrickson tells us that positive emotions are worth cultivating for two reasons (2001, 2005, 2009). First, they may be enjoyed as *ends* in themselves, as pleasurable experiences in the present moment (the "broadening" aspect of the theory). Secondly, positive emotions may also serve as the *means* to tap into resources that lead to our psychological growth and improved well-being over time (the "build" aspect of the theory). Similarly, consider how leisure satisfies these two purposes. A recreational activity may be enjoyed as an end in itself, for the pleasure it gives us in the moment; it may also be a catalyst for building personal satisfaction and a flourishing life over time.

Fredrickson (2009) also explores how negative and positive emotions impact people differently. A negative emotion such as fear, for example, usually triggers an urgent "fight-or-flight" reaction—vital for immediate survival but not especially useful for improving future resiliency. By contrast, positive emotions open our minds to consider various options for how we can choose to behave. Positive emotions allow us to build upon our resources to create a more enduring form of survival that enhances well-being overall. As Fredrickson puts it, positive emotion enables us to "live longer, live stronger" (p. 25).

If we wish to transform our lives for the better—to "live longer and stronger"—Fredrickson (2009) suggests we sow the seeds of positive emotion plentifully throughout our lives. In fact, based on her research, Fredrickson advises us to regularly experience a *positivity ratio* of three positive emotions to every negative emotion. That is, for every "heart wrenching negative emotional experience we endure, we experience at least three heartfelt positive emotional experiences that [can] uplift" (p. 32). The three-to-one positivity ratio is necessary for producing the transformative effect of living "longer and stronger." In fact, the positivity ratio is the "tipping point" that predicts whether a person will flourish or languish. (To calculate your positivity ratio, divide the number of positive emotions you experience by the number of your negative emotions during any given time period.)

The purpose of elevating your positivity ratio to three-to-one is not solely to be happier, though Fredrickson says you will be. The larger intention is to be *engaged* in life—with your family, your friends, your work, your community. You will feel good, yes; you will also be *doing* good. Your sense of purpose will transcend self-interest and what you do in your day, large or small, will profit the world for the better. As Desmond Tutu, South African cleric and activist, says, "Do your little bit of good where you are; it's those little bits of good put together that overwhelm the world."

The broaden-and-build theory holds tremendous promise for us who work in the field of therapeutic recreation. As you read in Chapter 3 *A Sea Change in Therapeutic Recreation*, people engage in leisure and recreation, by definition, for purposes of enjoyment and well-being—that is, to experience positive emotion and positive growth. Through leisure participation, a participant has numerous opportunities to experience the "broadening" influence of positive emotion, which can then be intentionally "built" upon to fulfill the person's goals, dreams, and aspirations.

Leisure Coping

Coping implies that a person is suffering in some way, yet coping is also a pathway to one's truer, stronger self. Psychosocial theories of coping are relevant to therapeutic recreation strengths-based practice, and several researchers in our field have noted its value (Hood & Carruthers, 2002; Hutchinson, Loy, Kleiber, & Dattilo, 2003; Iwasaki & Mannell, 2000). In this section we focus on the work of Hood and Carruthers, who provide us with a synthesis of the literature on coping and its application to therapeutic recreation practice.

Hood and Carruthers (2002) are particularly strong proponents of drawing from theory to promote effective coping in participants who receive therapeutic recreation services. They cite the definition of coping by two well-known theorists in the area, Lazarus and Folkman (1984): "constantly changing cognitive and behavioral efforts to manage specific external and/or internal demands that are appraised as taxing or exceeding the resources of the person" (p. 41). Hood and Carruthers encourage us to integrate the four stages of coping developed by Lazarus and Folkman into the design of therapeutic recreation interventions (see Table 6.1).

In their synthesis of the coping literature, Hood and Carruthers (2002) note two general approaches to coping: (a) reducing or eliminating the negative demands of the situation and (b) increasing one's positive resources. Developing skills and abilities in both these areas, they say, are important components to include in any coping skills intervention in therapeutic recreation. More attention has been given to the first area of "reducing the negative" than the second, "increasing the positive," which will come as no surprise to you considering the past emphasis placed on deficits.

Hood and Carruthers highlight two coping strategies aimed at mitigating the negative demands of a situation, as put forth by Lazarus and Folkman (1984): (a) problem-focused coping, and (b) emotion-focused coping. In problem-focused coping, the participant attempts to manage or alter the problem, either by focusing on something in the external environment or something within oneself. Problem-focused coping strategies include basic problem solving, adjusting personal motivations, and enhancing skills related to the problem. In emotion-focused coping, the person adjusts his or her emotional response to the situation. The person may reappraise the importance of the problem,

Chapter 6–Theories that Guide Strengths-Based Therapeutic Recreation Practice • 117

Table 6.1 Four Stages of Coping *(adapted from Lazarus & Folkman, 1984)*

Four Stages of Coping

Lazarus and Folkman (1984), scholars in the area of coping theory, have identified four stages to the coping process:

STAGE 1: Appraisal
The person determines the meaning of an event or situation and the implications for his or her well-being. Both the demands and stressors of the situation as well as the person's resources to address them are appraised.

STAGE 2: Assessment of coping resources
From among the coping resources available to the person, he or she selects a strategy that is likely to be the most effective. Resources may include health, energy, problem solving skills, social support, material resources, or a positive belief system that includes hope and high self-esteem.

STAGE 3: Applying the coping strategy
The individual undertakes the selected coping strategy.

STAGE 4: Evaluation
The person evaluates the effectiveness of the coping strategy to alleviate the stressor and to manage his or her responses to the situation.

seek distractions, avoid the problem, or accept the situation. The literature notes that this approach is often adopted when a person feels he or she has little or no control over the situation.

Along with these methods of coping, Hood and Carruthers (2002) review recent strategies to increase *positive resources* that strengthen one's resilience and ability to cope. Positive resources, they suggest, may be physical, psychological, or social. They may also include high self-esteem and the ability to change one's thought-patterns, to relax, and to divert one's attention toward more positive engagement. These kinds of coping strategies that draw on positive resources are explained more fully in Table 6.2. As you can see from the table, there is a direct link between leisure and the ability to cope with stressful situations. Hood and

Table 6.2 Strengthen Coping Skills by Increasing Positive Resources *(adapted from Hood & Carruthers, 2002)*

Hood and Carruthers (2002) have identified a variety of ways we can cope more effectively by increasing our positive resources. As you can see from the list below, potential resources for coping are plentiful and exist in many areas of life.

Physical Resources: Physical resources include positive traits such as health, fitness, and energy. While physical resources can help alleviate stressful situations, Lazarus and Folkman (1984) suggest they are not necessarily required for successful coping. For example, they cite the many people with physically limiting disabilities who are able to cope effectively without possessing these kinds of physical resources.

Psychological Resources: Researchers have identified several psychological resources that can improve our ability to cope. For instance, personality strengths such as self-esteem and mastery can act as barriers to stress. A positive belief system—one that includes hope, self-efficacy, and a perception of control—supports our resiliency and thus our ability to cope. Self-determination and decision-making, skills that are closely linked to leisure participation are also tied to effective coping. Another valuable psychological resource is changing our self-talk to positive self-appraisals geared to improve our motivation and enhance our emotions.

Social Resources: Companionship, friendship, intimate relationships, and other kinds of social support are vital for well-being and, thus, for coping. Hood and Carruthers (2002) summarize the value of leisure for cultivating human relationship: "Leisure is often seen as an ideal context in which to develop social skills and to nurture the social relationships needed for both expressive and instrumental social support" (p. 150).

Lifestyle Resources: Leisure, enjoyment, community involvement, and civic participation are all positive resources that build coping skills. Lazarus and Folkman have identified the ability to distract oneself from a problematic situation as an important coping strategy. It is usually not enough to distract oneself, however. One also needs to engage in meaningful and absorbing activity. Leisure gives us this outlet. It allows us to relax, to recuperate, to disengage from stressful situations, and to involve ourselves in activity that is optimally challenging and rewarding.

Carruthers conclude that using coping theory as a basis for therapeutic recreation intervention has the potential to produce manifold benefits not only for participants but for practitioners as well.

Self-Determination

Self-determination is seen as a basic human right for all people, including those with disabilities. A self-determined life can result in many personal benefits. When we perceive we are in control of our lives, we have a greater sense of motivation, competency, and autonomy. We are more aware of our values, beliefs, and preferences, and this self-awareness enables us to participate more fully in life, including leisure, in an independent and interdependent fashion. If we are self-determined, we are more apt to take responsibility for the choices we make and to regulate our own behavior. As our lives take shape according to our personal visions, self-worth and self-advocacy are strengthened, and the quality of our lives enhanced (Institute on Community Integration, 2002).

Wehmeyer and Berkobien (1991) define a self-determined person as someone who acts as the causal agent or force in his or her life, without excessive external influence. Self-determination involves a variety of skills and sensibilities that are tied to the complex process of maturation into adulthood. These skills and sensibilities include self-awareness, intrinsic motivation, making choices and decisions, self-regulation, and self-advocacy (Bullock & Mahon, 1997; Dattilo, 2008; Ryan & Deci, 2000; Wehmeyer & Berkobien, 1991).

Self-determination implies two things: first, an individual is in charge of his or her life and, second, the person is able to make his or her own decisions. According to Wehmeyer and Berkobien (1991), self-determination has three dimensions: (a) autonomy, (b) self-actualization, and (c) self-regulation. *Autonomy*, a complex concept in its own right, is defined as an individual acting on his or her own behalf, in accordance with his or her priorities and values. Actions that are autonomous imply an ability to function, to a large degree, independently. *Self-actualization* means an individual builds upon his or her unique capacities and talents to the extent that they are fully developed and used. *Self-regulation* refers to an individual's ability to control his or her behavior. The individual takes responsibility for monitoring personal behaviors and impulses so he or she has a positive impact on self and others.

Additionally, Wehmeyer and Berkobien (1991) propose that three assumptions underlie the concept of self-determination. First, the individual is *self-aware*. The person knows basically who he or she is, and understands his or her capabilities and limitations. Second, the individual is *self-confident*—that is, he or she is able to make decisions and follow through on them. The third assumption is that the person is able to act as a *self-advocate*, which requires sufficient communication and assertiveness skills.

The American Institute for Research (1993), as cited by Bullock, Mahon, and Killingsworth (2010), describes a six-step process whereby a person becomes self-determined. Table 6.3 outlines this process, showing how a participant can set direction for his or her life, take action to accomplish personal goals and objectives, evaluate outcomes, and make adjustments to accomplish goals more effectively in the future.

Self-determination is largely viewed as an individual issue, yet Ryan and Deci (2000) emphasize that self-determination is also a function of environment. They define self-determination theory as "an approach to human motivation and personality that . . . highlights the importance of humans' evolved inner resources for personality development and behavioral self-regulation" (p. 68). Ryan and Deci say individuals have three basic needs related to self-determination: competence, relatedness, and autonomy. The degree to which these three needs are met and a person flourishes (i.e., becomes self-determined) depends on how supportive the conditions are in her or his environment. In unsupportive environments people tend to grow passive, apathetic, alienated, and irresponsible. By contrast, supportive environments encourage people to become intrinsically motivated, curious, vital, active, and responsible—in effect, self-determined.

According to Ryan and Deci (2000), the presence of intrinsic motivation is essential to cultivating personal growth and self-determination. Given that leisure provides individuals with opportunities to participate in

Table 6.3 Self-Determination Process

Bullock et al. (2010, p. 66) report six steps to the self-determination process, as identified by the American Institute for Research (1993):

1. Identify and express your needs, interests, and abilities.
2. Set expectations and goals to meet your needs and interests.
3. Make choices and plans to meet your goals and expectations.
4. Take action to complete your plans.
5. Evaluate the results of your actions.
6. Adjust your plans and actions, if necessary, to meet your goals more effectively.

Perceived self-efficacy is people's beliefs in their capabilities to perform in ways that give them control over events that affect their lives. Efficacy beliefs form the foundation of human agency. Unless people believe that they can produce results by their actions, they have little incentive to act.
(Bandura, 2000, p. 212)

Albert Bandura

Figure 6.8 Definition of Self-Efficacy

intrinsically motivated activities, therapeutic recreation specialists have a unique opportunity to build self-determination through leisure by assessing participants' preferred leisure activities. Further, Ryan and Deci have found that "choice, acknowledgement of feelings, and opportunities for self-direction" (p. 70) augment intrinsic motivation. Each of these elements can easily be facilitated through therapeutic recreation planning and programming, thus strengthening the likelihood that self-determination will develop.

Dattilo (2008) is a strong proponent of leisure participation to foster self-determination within people with developmental disabilities. When participants choose *their* preferred leisure activities, he says, they are already beginning to build self-determination. Leisure also gives participants opportunities to experience the freedoms of self-expression, creativity, and enjoyment—all aspects related to self-determination. In Chapter 11 *Implementation* we will give you several other ways therapeutic recreation specialists can enhance self-determination through recreation participation.

Self-Efficacy

When Albert Bandura was a young psychology professor at Stanford University in 1977, he introduced a concept closely linked to the theory of self-determination: self-efficacy. Since that time, hundreds of scholars have used Bandura's theory of self-efficacy as the basis for research with many kinds of people in many different situations. Bandura's widely used definition of self-efficacy appears in Figure 6.8.

Building on Bandura's theory, Maddux (2002) observes that self-efficacy is not concerned with one's beliefs about performing isolated or trivial tasks. Rather, it focuses on one's belief in one's ability to coordinate and complete complex skills in challenging situations. Additionally, self-efficacy does not focus on what one *will* do; it focuses on what one *can* do. How can we develop a healthy and realistic sense of self-efficacy?

Bandura (1977, 1994, 2000) gives us four pathways to self-efficacy:

1. *Mastery experiences*: Experiencing a sense of mastery is the most effective way to create self-efficacy. When we experience success, our personal sense of capability, or efficacy, grows—just as our sense of efficacy diminishes when we experience failure. If we come by success too easily without first putting forth a sustained effort, we are likely to become discouraged quickly when experiencing failure. Conversely, when we do well in situations that challenge us and require sustained effort, our perceptions of efficacy strengthen. By persevering over time to fulfill our aim, we can gradually build confidence in our capabilities.

2. *Social modeling*: A second way to strengthen our beliefs of self-efficacy is by observing people similar to us performing the skills or activities we wish to master. The more that the people we observe appear to be similar to us, the stronger their influence over our sense of self-efficacy will be. When we see them succeed, we believe we can succeed too. Observing a competent model can teach us the knowledge, attitudes, and behaviors required by an activity, as well as the strategies to navigate environmental demands. Competent models also provide a standard by which to judge our own capabilities.

3. *Social persuasion*: A third way we can develop self-efficacy is through persuasion from others. When others convince us that we possess the qualities and characteristics to master an activity, self-doubt diminishes and self-efficacy rises. Social persuasion helps us to try harder, to

persevere, and to acquire new skills. The persuasion we receive needs to accurately reflect our abilities, however. If we're told we're performing well when we aren't, we will eventually learn our performance is inadequate and become discouraged. Bandura has found that, unfortunately, it is much easier to undermine someone's self-efficacy through social persuasion than it is to boost it. Bandura (1994) recommends the following approach as the most effective way to encourage self-efficacy in others:

> Successful efficacy builders do more than convey positive appraisals. In addition to raising people's beliefs in their capabilities, they structure situations for them in ways that bring success and avoid placing people in situations prematurely where they are likely to fail often. They measure success in terms of self-improvement rather than by triumphs over others. (pp. 2–3)

The theory of self-efficacy relates primarily to *individual* well-being but, as you can see from this quote, a receptive and supportive *environment* also influences self-perceptions of capability. Thus, it is critical that we, as therapeutic recreation specialists, consider situational contexts in their entirety when planning how to best meet participants' goals and cultivate their perceptions of self-efficacy.

4. ***Physical and emotional states***: How we feel, physically and emotionally, also influences our perceptions of self-efficacy. Stress reactions may cause us to feel vulnerable to performing poorly, and physical ailments and fatigue may be seen as an overall decline in physical health. When we feel physically strong, however, self-efficacy can soar. Mood also affects how we judge self-efficacy. Positive moods enhance our sense of self-efficacy, while gloomy moods weaken it. Thus, the fourth way to raise perceptions of self-efficacy includes three tactics aimed at improving our emotional well-being: (a) learn to cope with stress in ways that reduce negative reactions; (b) build positive emotions; and (c) reduce or eliminate false interpretations of our capabilities.

How might we, as therapeutic recreation specialists, intentionally apply Bandura's theory of self-efficacy in our practice? There are several ways. We can nurture participants' sense of mastery by presenting opportunities for them to learn and excel at their chosen recreation and leisure activities. During the assessment process, we can collect information about how the participant learns best, then structure environments to support their optimal learning. We can provide examples of people like themselves who have accomplished the recreation goals to which they aspire. We can also give participants positive feedback when they are meeting their leisure goals and performing leisure skills correctly. These are just a few of the ways that therapeutic recreation specialists can increase a participant's sense of self-efficacy. Drawing from your personal and professional experiences, what other ways can you think of?

To summarize, in Part 1 of this chapter we presented theories that relate to well-being *within the individual*. We now turn our attention to theories that explain how factors in the *environment* can be used to enhance an individual's well-being.

PART 2:
WELL-BEING AND THE ENVIRONMENT

Some of the theories presented in Part 1, which focus on well-being within the individual, also refer to the important ways environmental factors influence human development and flourishing (Bandura, 1977, 1994; Fredrickson, 2009; Ryan & Deci, 2000). Indeed, our interaction with people and resources in the environment is a continual process and has a direct, if not always conscious, impact on our well-being. In Part 2 we share some exciting developments in current thinking about how the environment expressly influences individual well-being. Specifically, we discuss constructs related to health, disability, rights of people with disabilities, social support, community, and resiliency.

New Theories on Health and Disability

World Health Organization Redefines Disability

To appreciate the scope of the shift from a deficits orientation to a strengths orientation in health and human services, we need only look at the recent work of the World Health Organization (WHO) and its formulation of a new definition of disability. In this section we will answer the following questions: What organization sponsors WHO and what is its charge? How has WHO redefined the nature of disability? What unique role

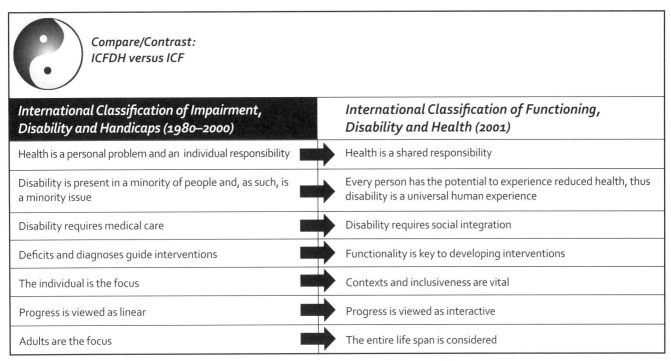

Figure 6.9 Compare/Contrast: ICFDH versus ICF

does recreation and leisure play in the new interpretation of disability? And what implications does this new understanding of disability have for strengths-based therapeutic recreation practice?

World Health Organization

Ever since the United Nations established the WHO in 1948, it has influenced how disability is viewed worldwide. As a global health organization, the WHO pursues a six-point agenda:

- to promote socioeconomic development and reduce poverty;
- to promote health security in the face of epidemic diseases;
- to strengthen health resources and systems;
- to harness research, evidence, and information;
- to enhance partnerships; and
- to improve performance of health organizations through results-oriented management.

This agenda applies to all levels of healthcare—regional, national, and international (WHO, 2012). From this global and inclusive perspective, the WHO developed a new theory of disability, that is, a new way of thinking about disability and health in relation to society.

International Classification of Functioning, Disability and Health

In 2001, the WHO developed a systematic framework for measuring health and disability: the International Classification of Functioning, Disability and Health (ICF). The original name of this classification in 1980 was the International Classification of Impairment, Disability and Handicaps (ICIDH). The name change alone speaks volumes about WHO's shift in perception from a deficits-orientation to a health and functionality orientation. Other key philosophical distinctions between the ICIDH and the new, improved ICF appear in the Compare/Contrast feature in Figure 6.9.

The ICF model, which we introduced in Chapter 5 *Strengths*, appears in Figure 6.10 (p. 122). The ICF provides a framework for looking at disability and health in a way that is scientific, evidence-based, and transcultural. Further, the document that accompanies the model provides a systematic and standardized coding scheme for health information systems. As such, the ICF offers a common language and method for health education and research to be conducted, shared, and compared across nations.

As you can see from Figure 6.10, the ICF is conceptualized at three levels: (a) body function and structures, (b) the whole person, and (c) social and environmental contexts. Health domains and conditions are described from the perspective of the body, the individual, and society. Across all three dimensions, two main areas are featured: "body function and structures" and "activities and participation" (WHO, 2001), which are described below:

- **Body function and structures** refer to physical functioning related to cognition, speech, the senses, cardiovascular health, digestion, reproduction, neuromusculoskeletal health, and related systems.
- **Activities and participation** address a person's capacity and performance in areas such as learning and applying knowledge, communication, interpersonal interactions, movement, self-care, domestic living, as well as community, social, and civic life.

Because participants with disabilities live within the contexts of social and physical environments, and relate to the world from the perspective of personal identity, these facets are also integrated into the model. Thus, the ICF presents a holistic picture of the person and the world within which he or she lives. Environmental aspects that are considered include physical, social, and attitudinal factors, as reflected in the following kinds of questions: What personal support and assistance does the person have? What social attitudes exist among neighbors and social circles? What physical barriers exist? What is the physical climate and terrain like where the person lives?

As you might expect, the ways in which personal factors influence a person's health vary widely across culture and social group. The variance is so great, in fact, that the ICF doesn't even attempt to classify them. Personal factors are taken into account through individualized assessments, where information may be recorded on an ICF Checklist. Personal information includes characteristics such as age, gender, lifestyle, education, race/ethnicity, religion, sexual orientation, and assets (WHO, 2003).

Role of Recreation and Leisure in the ICF

One of the most exciting new developments in the ICF for the field of therapeutic recreation is the prominence given to recreation and leisure. In one chapter of the ICF, *Community, Social and Civic Life*, a definition of recreation and leisure appears under the section *Activities and Participation* (see Table 6.5). Definitions are also provided for distinct categories of recreation and leisure such as play, sports, arts and culture, crafts, hobbies, and socializing (see Figure 6.11).

How does the new social understanding of disability constructed by the ICF support strengths-based practice in therapeutic recreation? WHO's new interpretations of health and disability encourage therapeutic recreation specialists, as well as other health and human service professionals, to view participants in ways that are multidimensional and holistic. Emphasizing functionality and an individual's capacity to participate in recreational activity inherently builds on people's

Table 6.5 ICF Definition of Recreation and Leisure

ICF Definition of Recreation and Leisure
Engaging in any form of play, recreational or leisure activity, such as informal or organized play and sports; programs of physical fitness, relaxation, amusement or diversion; going to art galleries, museums, cinemas or theatres; engaging in crafts or hobbies, reading for enjoyment, playing musical instruments; sightseeing, tourism and traveling for pleasure (WHO, 2001).

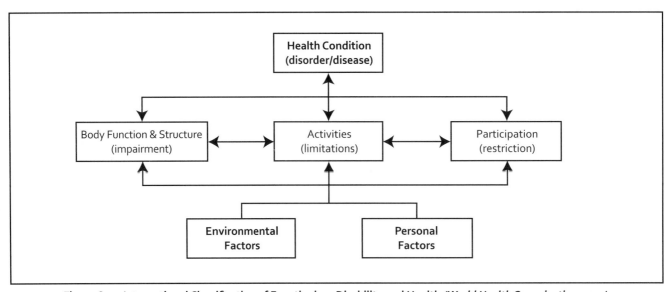

Figure 6.10 International Classification of Functioning, Disability and Health *(World Health Organization, 2003)*

My Cultural Lens: ICF Definition of Recreation and Leisure

The International Classification of Functioning, Disability and Health (ICF) has categorized recreation and leisure into distinct categories: play, sports, arts and culture, crafts, hobbies, and socializing. Excluded from this definition of recreation and leisure are the following activities:

"riding animals for transportation, remunerative and nonremunerative work, religion and spirituality, political life and citizenship."

Depending on your culture, you might argue that some of the excluded activities could actually be considered recreation and leisure, if they are freely chosen during unobligated time and produce feelings of enjoyment. For the sake of developing a definition that is relevant across many nationalities, however, the architects of the ICF settled on the above definition as the most consistent across diverse cultures.

Do you think the activities excluded from the ICF qualify as recreation and leisure? Why or why not? Talk with someone from a culture other than your own and ask what she or he thinks. What cultural perceptions influence how recreation and leisure are viewed?

Figure 6.11 My Cultural Lens: ICF Definition of Recreation and Leisure

potential. Furthermore, therapeutic recreation assessments and program planning can tap into participants' personal attributes that reflect their talents, strengths, preferences, and aptitudes. The ICF also offers us several classifications of activities to incorporate into assessment, planning, implementation, and evaluation processes. Additionally, because of the importance WHO places on recreation and leisure in people's lives, therapeutic recreation specialists can use the ICF to justify the value of the profession to colleagues, participants, community members, and prospective funders. With this global backing, therapeutic recreation has the potential to effect positive change for participants around the world!

A New Theory of Health: Healthy People 2020

As WHO has set the stage worldwide for a new definition of disability, the United States has adopted a new national health agenda. This initiative, called Healthy People, originated with the U.S. Surgeon General's report in 1979, which laid the groundwork for a mission that focuses on health, longevity, and prevention (Healthy People, 2012; Howard, Russoniello, & Rogers, 2004; Shank & Coyle, 2002). The Healthy People agenda is revised every 10 years, using a lengthy and systematic process of scientific inquiry, input from state and national organizations, and public comment.

Healthy People 2020 envisions "a society in which all people live long, healthy lives" (Healthy People, 2012, p. 1). Whereas previous Healthy People initiatives focused mostly on health determinants and interventions at the individual level, Healthy People 2020 more fully assumes a strengths approach by emphasizing the interrelationships of organizational, social, environmental, and policy factors in determining health. This new orientation takes into account social and economic factors, natural and built environments, and policies and programs. In doing so, Health People 2020 embraces both internal and external strengths.

Four overarching goals guide Healthy People 2020 (Healthy People, 2012):

- Attain high-quality, longer lives free of preventable disease, disability, injury, and premature death
- Achieve health equity, eliminate disparities, and improve the health of all groups
- Create social and physical environments that promote good health for all
- Promote quality of life, healthy development, and healthy behaviors across all life stages (p. 1)

The primary aim of the current rendition of Healthy People is to set priority objectives and research-based benchmarks related to health promotion and disease prevention for the nation through the year 2020. These objectives serve as a strategic roadmap to encourage collaboration, measurement, and tracking by diverse individuals and communities as they design programs and environments to support opportunities for all people to enjoy health. Healthy People 2020 objectives address 42 focus areas, from education and community-based programs to social determinants of health. They also provide up-to-date statistics and resources for specific health concerns such as dementia, heart disease, and substance abuse. Additionally, Leading Health Indicators are identified which represent the nation's most pressing concerns (see Table 6.6, p. 124).

Besides its orientation toward internal and external strengths, Healthy People 2020 is particularly important to therapeutic recreation practice because

Table 6.6 Healthy People 2020: Leading Health Indicators *(adapted from* Healthy People, 2012*)*

1. Access to Health Services
   - Increase the proportion of persons with medical insurance
   - Increase the proportion of persons with a usual primary care provider
2. Clinical Preventive Services
   - Increase the proportion of adults who receive a colorectal cancer screening
   - Increase the proportion of adults with hypertension whose blood pressure is under control
   - Reduce the proportion of the diabetic population with an A1c value greater than 9 percent
   - Increase the proportion of children aged 19 to 35 months who receive the recommended doses of DTaP, polio, MMR, Hib, hepatitis B, varicella, and PCV vaccines
3. Environmental Quality
   - Reduce the number of days the Air Quality Index exceeds 100
   - Reduce the proportion of children aged 3 to 11 years exposed to secondhand smoke
4. Injury and Violence
   - Reduce fatal injuries
   - Reduce homicides
5. Maternal, Infant, and Child Health
   - Reduce the rate of all infant deaths
   - Reduce the total amount of preterm births
6. Mental Health
   - Reduce the suicide rate
   - Reduce the proportion of adolescents aged 12 to 17 years who experience major depressive episode
7. Nutrition, Physical Activity, and Obesity
   - Increase the proportion of adults who meet the objectives for aerobic physical activity and for muscle-strengthening activity
   - Reduce the proportion of children, adolescents, and adults who are considered obese
   - Increase the contribution of total vegetables to the diets of the population aged 2 years and older
8. Oral Health
   - Increase the proportion of children, adolescents, and adults who used the oral health care system in the past 12 months
9. Reproductive and Sexual Health
   - Increase the proportion of sexually experienced females aged 15 to 44 years who received reproductive health services in the past 12 months
   - Increase the proportion of persons living with HIV who know their serostatus
10. Social Determinants
    - Increase the proportion of students who graduate with a regular diploma after starting 9th grade
11. Substance Abuse
    - Reduce the proportion of adolescents reporting use of alcohol or any illicit drugs during the past 30 days
    - Reduce the proportion of adults who engaged in binge drinking during the past 30 days
12. Tobacco
    - Reduce cigarette smoking by adults and adolescents

of its emphasis on health and prevention, key concepts in our field. Further, by accessing the Healthy People 2020 website, therapeutic recreation specialists and agencies may partner with colleagues in other disciplines throughout the country to address any number of health concerns.

The new orientation to health and disability established by WHO and Healthy People has set the stage for understanding the two social theories that follow, Normalization and Social Role Valorization. These two theories have served as a catalyst for improving quality of life for people with disabilities in North America and beyond.

Normalization and Social Role Valorization

In the 1960s, two human services pioneers, Bengt Nirje and Wolf Wolfensberger, independently formulated a revolutionary new concept related to how people with disabilities live in society. The implications of this theory, known as the *Normalization* principle, are so far-reaching that it has entirely transformed the way service providers around the world view the lives of people with disabilities and their roles in society (Cocks, 2001; Flynn & Lemay, 1999). Normalization, contrary to what the name might suggest, does not aim to "make people normal." Rather, it acknowledges the rights of people with disabilities to live their lives as ordinary citizens within their culture and community—a radical notion that remains important and relevant today.

> **Life Story:**
> **How Bengt Nirje Formulated the Normalization Principle**
>
>
>
> As a young man in Sweden, Bengt Nirje studied philosophy, literature, cultural anthropology, and ethics, which laid a broad-based, interdisciplinary groundwork for the development of his theory on Normalization. While stationed as Ombudsman of Swedish social services, Nirje traveled around the country visiting people with developmental disabilities in a variety of living situations, including both institutionalized and family settings. Later, while working for the Swedish Red Cross, Nirje was sent to improve the morale of refugees from the Hungarian Revolution of 1956 who were living in Austrian refugee camps (Gray, 2001; Nirje, 1999a; Wikipedia, 2005). In both instances, Nirje observed the limiting and psychologically damaging effects of institutionalization.
>
> Through his experiences in Sweden and Austria, Nirje came to the conclusion that "normal conditions led to normal outcomes whereas abnormal conditions led to abnormal outcomes" (Diligio, 2005, p. 3). To Nirje, "normal" meant growing up within one's family and living as an active member of the community; "abnormal" meant living a regimented life within an institution where choice was limited and conditions substandard. It is from this line of reasoning that the term Normalization was coined.
>
> *Bengt Nirje*
>
> Nirje's formulation of Normalization was also influenced by developments in the field of recreation (Nirje, 1999a). In 1963, while Nirje was traveling in the United States, he met Elliott Avedon, a pioneer in the profession of therapeutic recreation and a professor at Columbia University in New York City. At that time, no one in Sweden had ever heard of recreation as a field of study. Later, when Avedon visited Nirje in Stockholm, Avedon shared a book he had written on social-skills training for participants with intellectual disabilities in the context of recreation programming. Nirje applied Avedon's concepts to his own work with social clubs in Sweden, encouraging participants with developmental disabilities to make their own decisions and to follow through on their choices.
>
> As you can see, Nirje drew from several sources and experiences to formulate the principle of Normalization. His interdisciplinary studies, work experiences, personal encounters with people with disabilities, and conversations with colleagues in Scandinavia and North America all contributed to his conceptualization of the theory. The universal themes of the principle are human rights, independence, self-determination, cultural relevance, and the value of typical, everyday conditions and routines for individuals with disabilities (Nirje, 1999a).

Figure 6.12 Life Story: How Bengt Nirje Formulated the Normalization Principle

Nirje's Theory of Normalization

Bengt Nirje, a native of Sweden, is generally regarded as the first person to formulate a coherent definition of the Normalization principle as we understand it today (Flynn & Lemay, 1999; Wolfensberger, 1983). His studies and a variety of professional experiences led him to formulate the principle, which you can read about in the Life Story in Figure 6.12.

Nirje first defined Normalization in various papers written between 1967 and 1972, which he expanded upon in subsequent publications (Nirje, 1992, 1993, 1999a, 1999b). His definition of Normalization, which appears below, emphasizes the rights of people with disabilities to experience and share in the patterns and conditions of everyday life within one's culture:

> The normalization principle means that you act right when you make available to all persons with intellectual or other impairments those patterns of life and conditions of everyday living that are as close as possible, or indeed the same as, the regular circumstances and ways of life of their communities and culture. (Nirje, 1999a, p. 17)

Nirje's definition identifies eight elements of culturally normative patterns and conditions of everyday life (see Table 6.7). These eight patterns are intrinsically tied to the cultural norms of one's community, yet Nirje emphasizes that a person is not necessarily *bound* by these norms. The individual has the right to *choose* the degree to which she or he will, or will not, conform to cultural expectations. Thus, the principle allows for self-determination and individuality within the context of cultural norms.

Table 6.7 Culturally Normative Patterns *(Nirje, 1999a)*

1. A normal rhythm of the day
2. A normal rhythm of the week
3. A normal rhythm of the year
4. The normal experiences of the life cycle
5. Normal respect for the individual and the right to self-determination
6. The normal sexual patterns of their culture
7. The normal economic patterns and rights of their society
8. The normal environmental patterns and standards in their community

Table 6.8 Normalization by Bengt Nirje (1999b)

Normalization means . . . a normal rhythm of the day.
You get out of bed in the morning . . .
You get dressed,
And leave the house for school or work,
You don't stay home;
In the morning you anticipate events,
In the evening you think back on what you have accomplished;
The day is not a monotonous 24 hours with every minute endless.
You eat at normal times of the day and in a normal fashion;
Not just with a spoon, unless you are an infant;
Not in bed, but at a table;
Not early in the afternoon for the convenience of the staff.

Normalization means . . . a normal rhythm of the week.
You live in one place,
Go to work in another,
And participate in leisure activities in yet another.
You anticipate leisure activities on weekends,
And look forward to getting back to school
Or work on Monday.

Normalization means . . . a normal rhythm of the year.
A vacation to break routines of the year.
Seasonal changes bring with them a variety
Of types of food, work, cultural events, sports,
Leisure activities.
Just think . . . We thrive on these seasonal changes!

Normalization means . . . normal developmental experiences of the life cycle:
In childhood, children, but not adults, go to summer camps.
In adolescence one is interested in grooming, hairstyles,
Music, boyfriends, and girlfriends.
In adulthood, life is filled with work and responsibilities.
In old age, one had memories to look back on, and can
Enjoy the wisdom of experience.

Normalization means . . . having a range of choices,
Wishes, and desires respected and considered.
Adults have the freedom to decide
Where they would like to live,
What kind of job they would like to have, and can best perform.
Whether they would prefer to go bowling with a group,
Instead of staying home to watch television.

Normalization means . . . living in a world made of two sexes.
Children and adults both develop relationships with
Members of the opposite sex.
Teenagers become interested in having
Boyfriends and girlfriends.
Adults may fall in love, and decide to marry.

Normalization means . . . the right to normal economic standards.
All of us have basic financial privileges, and responsibilities,
Are able to take advantage of
Compensatory economic security means,
Such as child allowances, old age pensions, and
Minimum wage regulations.
We should have money to decide how to spend,
On personal luxuries, or necessities.

Normalization means . . . living in normal housing in a normal neighbourhood.
Not in a large facility with 20, 50, or 100 other people
Because you are retarded [sic],
And not isolated from the rest of the community.
Normal locations and normal size homes will give residents
Better opportunities for successful integration
With their communities.

In the composition in Table 6.8, Nirje expands upon these eight cultural elements in language that is both simple and profound, which continues to resonate powerfully today. Notice the frequent references to recreation and leisure as important life areas that contribute to well-being through normalization.

Wolfensberger's Theory of Normalization

Wolf Wolfensberger was instrumental in expanding the influence of the concept of Normalization throughout the United States, and most people in North America associate the theory with him (Bullock et al., 2010). Wolfensberger developed his view of Normalization largely from observing trends in human services in the United States (Wolfensberger, 1999). He grew to reject the centralized and institutionalized services of the day in favor of services that were person-centered—in his words, "normalized, diversified, dispersed, and citizen-controlled" (p. 55). He also opposed applying the medical model to the concept of Normalization and saw disability as a civil rights issue, not as a medical or social charity issue. Wolfensberger's widely quoted definition appears in Figure 6.13 (also see Figure 6.14, p. 128).

While the Normalization principle has endured as perhaps the most influential theory related to community-based services for individuals with disabilities, it has not gone unchallenged. In the next section, you will learn about some of the debate surrounding Wolfensberger's theory as well as the evolution of the Normalization principle into a new theory called *Social Role Valorization*.

Social Role Valorization

As service providers began to apply Wolfensberger's formulation of the Normalization principle to the design and evaluation of services, criticism flared (Bullock et al., 2010). Perrin and Nirje (1985) believed Wolfensberger's principle undercut the values of the original definition, which was built upon equal rights, freedom of choice, and a right to self-determination. As evidence, they objected strongly when Wolfensberger recommended "normalizing" people through "eliciting, shaping, and maintaining normative skills and habits" (Wolfensberger, 1972, p. 32) and when he went so far as to propose that "Normalization measures can be *offered* in some circumstances and *imposed* in others" (Wolfensberger, 1983, p. 28).

Critics also disliked the use of the word "normal" in the term "Normalization." Language is a powerful tool to convey ideas or prejudices, and the word "normal" tends to imply that, if one is not "normal," one must be "abnormal." It is impossible, as Bullock et al. (2010) point out, to define how a normal person looks or behaves. Even Wolfensberger (1983) was dissatisfied with the term "Normalization." He thought too many meanings had been attached to the word and people assumed they knew what the term meant when they didn't. Because the term Normalization had gained momentum and widespread recognition, however, Wolfensberger retained it for many years. Today, most people prefer to avoid the negative nuances of the word "normal" by using more neutral, less stigmatizing words such as "typical," "usual," "regular," "common," or "everyday."

Due in part to the criticism Wolfensberger received and in part to the evolution of his own thinking on the theory of Normalization, in 1983 he proposed a new, related concept called *Social Role Valorization*. This concept, which has become a theory in its own right, emphasizes the importance of valued social roles for people with disabilities to increase their social status and acceptance in society. In his new theory, Wolfensberger (1983) reasoned that people who are devalued by society are apt to be treated poorly, and prolonged poor treatment can result in segregation, isolation, and devalued social roles. These kinds of outcomes beget low expectations from others and continued devaluation, which further prompt devalued

Normalization is "the utilization of means which are as culturally normative as possible, in order to establish or maintain personal behaviors or characteristics which are as culturally normative as possible."

(Wolfensberger, 1972, p. 28)

Figure 6.13 Wolfensberger's Definition of Normalization

Primary Source Support:

Erving Goffman on Stigma and Social Identity

"Stigma is a process by which the reaction of others spoils normal identity."
Erving Goffman, 1922–1982

When Wolf Wolfensberger conceptualized his theory of Normalization, he drew inspiration from readings on social stigma, mass prejudice, and societal changes in attitude. He was particularly moved by the writing of sociologist Erving Goffman, who is best known for his books from the early 1960s, *Asylums: Essays on the Social Situation of Mental Patients and Other Inmates* (1961) and *Stigma: Notes on the Management of Spoiled Identity* (1963). These classic works explore the concepts of self and society, social devaluation, deviance, stigma, and the mechanisms of institutions that perpetuate social stigmatization.

In *Stigma*, Goffman defines stigma as "an attribute that is deeply discrediting within a particular social interaction" (p. 3). He proposes that stigma results from any of the following three circumstances:

(a) physical characteristics;
(b) perceived "blemishes of individual character"; or
(c) tribal stigma traced through lineages of race, nation, and religion.

The stigmatization of people with intellectual disabilities, Goffman believes, arises from the first two circumstances. Goffman's examination of these themes not only shaped Wolfensberger's formulation of the Normalization principle, it grounded subsequent theorizing on stigma, stereotype, and prejudice across many disciplines, and prepared the consciousness of social reformers to accept the underlying values of the Normalization principle.

Your college or university library probably carries a well-worn copy of Goffman's *Stigma*. Check it out for a fascinating exploration of the concepts of social identity and "otherness" that reach beyond the issues of people with disabilities to anyone who varies from a majority population in some way.

Figure 6.14 Primary Source Support: Erving Goffman on Stigma and Social Identity

persons to act in stigmatizing ways. Thus, the cycle of stigmatization and separation perpetuates itself. To break this cycle, Wolfensberger proposed that service providers need to work to enhance the social value of people with disabilities.

Wolfensberger proposed two approaches to provide people with roles and life conditions that are socially valued: (a) enhance the person's *social image or value* as perceived by others; and (b) enhance the person's *competencies and skills*. Wolfensberger reasoned that, as a person gains competencies, she or he acquires enhanced social standing. Similarly, as a person gains value in society, she or he tends to acquire experiences and life conditions that enlarge and sustain her or his personal competencies.

What important lessons can therapeutic recreation specialists draw from the theories of Normalization and Social Role Valorization? Guidelines for therapeutic recreation practice based on these two theories appear in Table 6.9. Similar practice guidelines, which were incorporated into human services across many disciplines, fueled the inclusion movement that ignited some 15 years later (you'll read more about inclusion in Chapter 12 *Transition and Inclusion*). This is an excellent example of how theory can inform practice and shift human services to create the necessary change to realize social justice!

Social Support

In Chapter 5 *Strengths* we discussed the value of social support and friendship for well-being and quality of life. We described social support as freely chosen networks of people that provide assistance and resources to meet our goals (Hutchinson & McGill, 1992). Four kinds of social support were identified: instrumental, emotional, informational, and appraisal (Peterson, 2006; Orsega-Smith et al., 2007). We also presented the various ways we relate to and connect with other people—for example, as a family member, a partner, a friend, or a neighbor. Additionally, we discussed the importance of friendship and the roles it plays in adult lives.

Table 6.9 Implications of Normalization and Social Role Valorization for Therapeutic Recreation Practice

> The following guidelines for therapeutic recreation practice are based on the values and principles that underlie the theories of Normalization and Social Role Valorization:
>
> 1. Provide participants opportunities for participation in a full range of leisure activities
> 2. Offer participants with disabilities the same opportunities for leisure and recreation that are available to and valued by their same-age peers without disabilities
> 3. Provide leisure experiences that are culturally normative
> 4. Give participants with disabilities the opportunity to exercise their right to choose their own activities, with whom they will participate, where they will participate, and whether or not they will participate.
> 5. Structure activities to encourage social interaction and promote friendships
> 6. Provide opportunities for participants to build skills, to gain confidence, and to grow personally
> 7. Provide roles within recreation activities that are socially valued
> 8. Advocate for architectural and programmatic accessibility of recreation programs and facilities
> 9. Use Person First language, which focuses holistically on people's attributes and capabilities, apart from any disability they may happen to have

In this chapter, we report what experts say happens when we don't have close social ties, and we'll expand on the notion of friendship by looking at children's social relationships. In Chapter 11 *Implementation* we'll continue this discussion and introduce you to some practical approaches to cultivate social relationships and friendships.

Consequences of a Lack of Close Relationships

In this book, we intentionally focus on strengths; however, when discussing relationships, it is necessary to acknowledge the disconcerting reality that many people with disabilities have very limited social relationships and networks. Amado (1990) maintains that people with disabilities tend to have far fewer relationships than people without disabilities, and their relationships occur in far fewer areas of life. Relationships for people with disabilities are typically limited to three groups of people: (a) family members, (b) other people with disabilities, and (c) people who are paid to interact with them, such as teachers, recreation staff, social workers, and healthcare providers.

A lack of close relationships can affect our health and longevity dramatically. In a meta-analysis of studies that controlled for factors such as physical health, socioeconomic status, smoking, alcohol, exercise, obesity, race, life satisfaction, and health care, individuals with few or weak social ties were found to be twice as likely to die as those with strong ties (House, Umberson, & Landis, 1988). Similarly, it has been suggested that social isolation is responsible for as many deaths each year as smoking (Condeluci, 2002).

Condeluci (2002) makes these observations about the social relationships of many people with disabilities in our society:

> We know that people with disabilities still are separated from the greater community and mostly involved in special programs and services designed for them. In these realities, the major outlet for social capital is found only within the borders of the special programs. To this extent then, the relationships that constitute the social capital of many people with disabilities are other people with disabilities. The narrowness of this reality leaves a significant void. (p. 13)

As this quotation shows, our society needs to build communities that are accepting and inclusive. We address this need in the following section on community building, as well as in Chapter 11 *Implementation*.

Friendship

> Friendship is a heart-flooding feeling
> that can happen to any two people who
> are caught up in the act of being themselves
> and who like what they see.
> The feeling is deeper than companionship;
> one can hire a companion.
> It is more than affection;
> affection can be as false as a stage kiss.
> It is never one-sided.
> It elevates biology into full humanity.
> *Letty Pogrebin* (1987, p. 35)

In a study at an inclusive elementary school, relationships of students with and without disabilities were followed over a 2-year period (Heyne, Schleien, & McAvoy, 1993). The study investigated the nature of relationships and friendships between children with and without disabilities, barriers to friendship, and strategies to promote social relationships and friendships. Throughout the 2 years, the children were individually

---

Children Talk about Friendship

In a study on friendships between elementary-age children with and without disabilities who played together in inclusive recreational activities, students were interviewed about their relationships. Their answers to two of the questions appear below.

Who is a friend? A friend is someone . . .

Responses by children with disabilities:
   To eat lunch with • Who sits down with me • To play with • Who calls me on the telephone • Who is nice to me

Responses by children without disabilities:
   To have fun with • Who smiles at you • That you like and they like you back • Who says, "Hi!" • Who plays with you • Who doesn't act snotty • Who, like when you're in math class and you are stuck on a problem, they help you • Who never teases you • You've known for a long time • Who cares about you • Who doesn't boss you around, who doesn't say things like, "No, no, no, you can't do that!"

What have you learned from your friend?

Responses by children with disabilities:
   I've learned to play some new games • I learned to go upstairs and downstairs at Emily's house • Anthony will help me on the bus • I learned to play with them

Responses by children without disabilities:
   I learned that you can still be friends, even if someone has a disability • I learned that she can be a friend to me • I've learned some new games • I've learned how to be Aaron's friend • He's not real different. Maybe he looks different, but he's just like everyone else • Even if you have a disability, you are still a person, a human being. You're not an alien from Mars or anything like that! • There's no law against being a friend to someone with a disability • You can make all sorts of friends with all sorts of people • She is a normal kid, just like me

The children's responses in the interviews also revealed the reciprocal nature of the children's relationships. For example, if a student with a disability identified a peer without a disability as a "best friend," the peer also identified the student with a disability as a "best friend." Similarly, if a student with a disability identified a peer with a disability as "just a classmate," the peer identified the student with a disability in the same way. When given the opportunity to develop naturally in inclusive recreation settings, the children's relationships appeared to also develop mutually, with some relationships remaining distant and others becoming close.

Figure 6.15 Children Talk About Friendship *(Heyne, Schleien, & McAvoy, 1993)*

interviewed about their relationships and their perceptions of friendship. You can read some of the children's answers, in their own words, in Figure 6.15.

Community and Community-Building Theory

> If we are to achieve a richer culture,
> rich in contrasting values,
> we must recognize the whole gamut of
> human potentialities,
> and so weave a less arbitrary social fabric,
> one in which each diverse human gift
> will find a fitting place.
> *Margaret Mead*

We all need community. We all need relationships and places where we can connect with others and where, as the theme song for the classic sit-com *Cheers* says, "everyone knows your name." Social scientists have thought deeply on the subject of how community is built—including Martin Brokenleg, Al Condeluci, John McKnight, John O'Brien, Connie Lyle O'Brien, Mary O'Connell, and Robert Putnam, to name a few. In this section, we feature their thinking on this topic. As you read their insights, ask yourself, "What themes emerge from their diverse philosophies?"

Community Defined

First, what do we mean by "community"? Condeluci (2002) points to the Latin roots of the word. *Community* derives from *com* meaning "with" and *unity*, which means "togetherness" and "connectedness." Condeluci says,

> Community is a network of people who regularly come together for some common cause or celebration. A community is not necessarily geographic, although geography can define certain communities. To come to an

understanding of community is to appreciate that community really is based on the relationships that form, not on the space.... The notion of being "with unity" is a good way to think about the concept of community. When people come together for the sake of a unified position or theme, you have community. (p. 11)

Others echo Condeluci's view that community is relationship-based. McKnight (1988) defines community as a collective association that is driven by a common goal. O'Brien and Lyle O'Brien (1996) see community building as "the intentional creation of relationships and social structures that extend the possibilities for shared identity and common action among people outside usual patterns of economics and administrative interaction" (p. 76). Mary O'Connell (1988) offers this definition related to individuals with disabilities: "Community . . . is no different for people with disabilities than for any of the rest of us. It's the free space where people think for themselves, dream their dreams, and come together to create and celebrate their common humanity" (p. 31).

Another way to look at community is to understand how it is influenced by human services systems. Do human services support or stymie community? O'Brien (1986) observes, "We can promote a sense of community if we develop the competence to overcome our habits of segregation, professionalization, and bureaucratization on even the smallest scale. Discovering community means testing the everyday assumptions of the service world through action and reflection." In this same vein, McKnight (1987) compares the differing ways that human services and communities operate (see Figure 6.16).

Among these definitions and insights on community, what common themes do you find? Community can be a hard concept to pinpoint, and we hope the thoughts of these social scientists have brought you closer to an understanding of this important facet of strengths-based practice.

Social Capital Defined

Another concept you should know about, which is closely tied to the notion of community, is *social capital*. This term has arisen as social scientists have grappled with the changing character of American society.

Putnam (2001), author of the best-selling book, *Bowling Alone: The Collapse and Revival of American Community*, defines social capital as "referring to connections among individuals—social networks and the norms of reciprocity and trustworthiness that arise from them" (p. 19). Condeluci (2002) refers to social capital as

the connections and relationships that develop around community and the value these relationships hold for the members. Like physical capital (the tools used by communities), or human capital (the people power brought to a situation), "social capital" is the value brought on by the relationships. (p. 12)

Condeluci notes that some people view social capital as similar to currency. For example, if Beth has a great sense of humor and knows how to make people laugh, she will be a popular person to invite to parties—she is strong in social capital. The "social currency" she exchanges is infectious and multiplies when she is around others.

Condeluci (2002, p. 13) also highlights the ways in which social capital is essential for building community. He says social capital:

- Allows citizens to resolve collective problems more easily
- Widens our awareness of the many ways we are linked

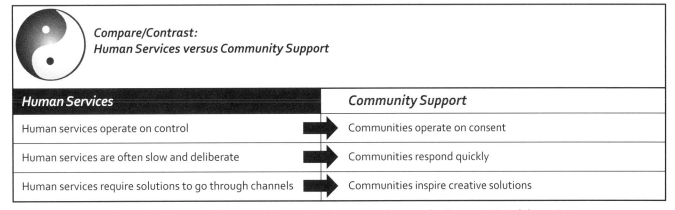

Figure 6.16 Compare/Contrast: Human Services versus Community Support *(McKnight, 1987)*

- Lessens pugnaciousness, or the tendency to fight or be aggressive
- Increases tolerance
- Greases the wheels that allow communities to advance more smoothly
- Enhances psychological processes and, as a result, biological processes

Condeluci points out that this last phrase has prompted Putnam (2001) to exclaim: "If you belong to no groups, but decide to join one, you cut your risk of dying over the next year in half!" In short, the term *social capital* highlights the many ways in which our lives are made more productive, healthy, and meaningful through social connections.

The Decline of Social Capital

In *Bowling Alone: The Collapse and Revival of American Community*, Putnam (2001) documents the steady decline of a sense of community in American society—that is, in the decline of social capital. Through extensive research, Putnam shows how, since the 1960s, people have grown less connected with each other and less inclined to participate in civic affairs than Americans in the first third of the 20th century. He says people have begun to "join less, trust less, give less, vote less, and schmooze less" (Putnam & Feldstein, 2004, p. 4). Even though people may bowl more than ever, they often bowl alone, not in leagues like they used to do. Putnam believes this phenomenon is representative of a larger trend of civic disengagement and alienation in America. Here are some of the statistics he presents:

- From 1974 to 1994, 42% fewer people worked for a political party, 39% fewer served on a civic committee, and 35% fewer attended a public meeting.
- Church attendance was 46% in 1960 and 36% in 1999.
- Trade association membership declined from 70% in 1960 to 40% in 1999.
- Playing cards with friends fell from 16 times a year in 1975 to 8 times in 1999.
- In 1960, 82% of bowlers played in leagues; in 1999, 21% played in leagues.

Similarly, other social scientists have concluded that most of the indicators of community have been on the decline since the 1960s. Condeluci (2002) reports that Putnam sees the following four trends as responsible for the general decline of community, presented here in order of importance:

1. Replacement of civic-minded generation with less involved children and grandchildren
2. Electronic entertainment, especially television
3. Time and money pressures—particularly the stresses on two-career families
4. A trend toward suburbanization, commuting, and urban sprawl

Yet, out of the crumbling of community has emerged the realization that new forms of community and social ties can be created. Condeluci believes people have begun to recognize that a medical-model approach to human "services" hampers community more than promotes it. From this realization has arisen a new strengths orientation to community building. This shift in orientation is reflected in the two Compare/Contrast features in Figures 6.17 and 6.18.

What Makes Community?

Condeluci (2002) has examined the elements that make up community, which are summarized below. As you read about each of these elements, ask yourself, "How well do these elements fit with the communities I know?"

Common theme. Communities form around a common, unifying theme. The theme is the essence of the group, its *raison d'être*. A common theme may be family, spirituality, work, age, neighborhood, ethnicity, sexual orientation, or any number of common interests, particularly leisure interests. People's passions create community.

Membership. Those who rally around a common idea or passion are the members of that community. There are various avenues to membership and, depending on the intent of the community, membership may be formal or informal. For example, you are born into your family's membership. If you pay dues and fill out some paperwork, you can formally belong to a health club. If you love to hike, your passion for that leisure pursuit may be all that is required for membership in an informal hiking club.

Rituals. When people come together regularly around a particular theme or mutual interest, rituals develop. "Ritual is a deep-rooted behavior that the community holds as important," says Condeluci (p. 20).

Figure 6.17 Compare/Contrast: Medical Approach versus Community Approach to Disability *(Condeluci, 2002)*

Behaviors may become so much a part of a community that people no longer notice them—that is, until they are ignored. To grasp what is meant by ritual, think about the rituals around your family holidays, at a house of worship, or in one of your social recreation groups.

Patterns. Condeluci writes, "The patterns of a culture refer to the movements and territory of the members of the community" (p. 23). He maintains that humans are territorial creatures and, if you disagree with him, he suggests you think how you feel when someone sits, uninvited, in your usual place. Observing patterns can help you spot the social connectors as well as the important "gatekeepers" (described below). An example of a pattern is spreading out your sticky mat in the same spot every week in a yoga class, or sitting in the same pew at church. Do you usually seat yourself in the same chair in the classroom? This is also an example

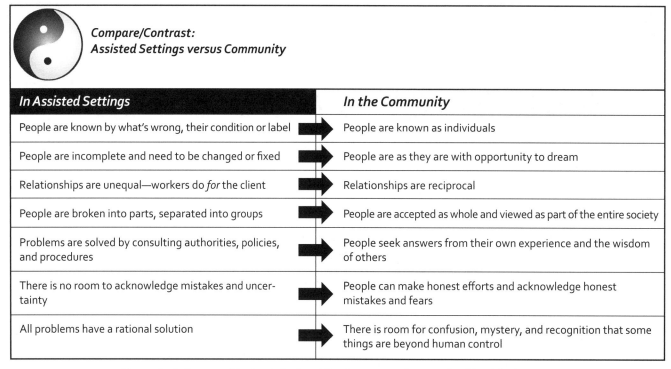

Figure 6.18 Compare/Contrast: Assisted Settings versus Community *(Condeluci, 1995)*

of patterns. It is natural to develop these patterns because we all need to find our space and comfort level in physical and group environments.

Jargon. Condeluci defines jargon as "the words, phrases or lexicon the culture uses to discuss, debate or celebrate the common theme. All communities . . . establish words that have meaning only to them" (p. 24). Jargon may be established by a family, club, profession, or groups that use "hip" or "in" language. Jargon signals who is a member of the community and who is an imposter.

Memory. Communities have a collective memory that archives the history and legacy of the group. Community memory helps members retain a collective culture and pass it on to future group members. Memory may be built through photos, stories, folklore, rituals, patterns, and jargon. Many people who want to be remembered for their contributions invest in a community for the sake of adding to its history as well as to be included in the community history. The most important role that memory can play in a community is to contribute to the evolution of wisdom and shared meaning.

Gatekeepers. A gatekeeper is "an indigenous member of the culture, or someone already included and accepted in the culture, who has some formal or informal influence within the culture" (p. 27). A gatekeeper's influence on the culture may be positive or negative. Gatekeepers may use their power to support or reject an idea, a person, or a product.

Creating Livable Communities

A fascinating illustration of building community is the concept of Creating Livable Communities. This initiative, born of necessity, is a joint endeavor of the National Council of Disability (NCD) and the American Association of Retired Persons (AARP). Both organizations found that their constituents, people with disabilities and elders, share common concerns:

> The disability community and the aging network have much in common. By 2030, one in five people in the United States will be over the age of 65. Currently, more than 4.7 million Americans aged 65 years or older have a sensory disability involving sight or hearing, and more than 6.7 million have difficulty going outside the home. Thus, it makes sense for the disability community and aging community to work together, align goals, and share resources to address the challenges ahead. (National Council on Disability, 2007, p. 5)

Recognition of these common concerns has prompted the two groups to develop shared goals: to foster independence, choice, and control over one's life. Among their shared goals are the following objectives:

- To have affordable, appropriate, and accessible housing
- To ensure accessible, affordable, reliable, and safe transportation
- To enhance inclusiveness and accessibility of physical environments
- To ensure access to key health and supportive services
- To encourage participation in civic, cultural, social, and recreational activities

John Rother, of AARP, sums up the spirit of the joint AARP and NCD agenda in these words:

> We believe that the quality of our lives is a function of the communities we live in. Appropriate housing, transportation options, and ways to be engaged with fellow members of the community are all part of living in a vital community. They are all things that need to be nourished and encouraged by policy in both the public and private sectors. (NCD, 2007, p. 13)

In Chapter 11 *Implementation* we'll continue our discussion of this powerful collaboration and present the strategies that AARP and NCD have proposed to realize their joint agenda.

Circle of Courage

We end this discussion on community building with a model developed by Brendtro, Brokenleg, and Van Bockern (2002) called the Circle of Courage. Many

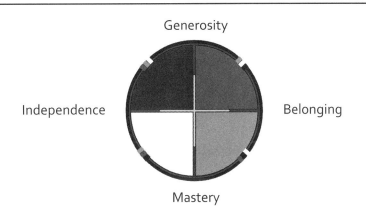

Belonging
In American Indian tribal cultures, significance is nurtured in communities of belonging. Lakota anthropologist Ella Deloria described the core values of belonging in these simple words: "Be related, somehow, to everyone you know." Treating others as kin forges powerful social bonds that draw all into relationships of respect.... Throughout history the tribe, not the nuclear family, always ensured the survival of the culture. Even if parents died or were not responsible, the tribe was always there to nourish the next generation.

Mastery
Competence in traditional cultures is ensured by guaranteed opportunity for mastery. Children are taught to carefully observe and listen to those with more experience. A person with greater ability is seen as a model for learning, not as a rival. Each person strives for mastery for personal growth, not to be superior to someone else. Humans have an innate drive to become competent and solve problems. With success in surmounting challenges, the desire to achieve is strengthened.

Independence
Power in Western culture is based on dominance, but in tribal traditions power means respecting the right to independence. In contrast to obedience models of discipline, Native teaching is designed to build respect and teach inner discipline. From earliest childhood, children are encouraged to make decisions, solve problems, and show personal responsibility. Adults model, nurture, teach values, and give feedback, but children are given abundant opportunities to make choices without coercion.

Generosity
Finally, virtue is reflected in the pre-eminent value of generosity. The central goal in child-rearing is to teach the importance of being generous and unselfish. In the words of a Lakota Elder, "You should be able to give away your most cherished possession without your heart beating faster." In helping others, youth create their own proof of worthiness: they make a positive contribution to another human life.

Figure 6.19 Circle of Courage *(Text Source Quoted from: Reclaiming Youth International, 2012)*

schools and classrooms have adopted this model, which draws from Native American philosophies that emphasize the importance of youth education and youth development in creating communities of inclusion and acceptance. As shown in Figure 6.19, there are four aspects to the Circle of Courage, which are based on the universal growth needs of all children: belonging, mastery, independence, and generosity. The four quadrants represent the four directions: north, south, east, and west. The number four is considered sacred in Native American cultures: A person is seen as standing in the middle of a circle with four directions from which to choose.

Resiliency

You first learned about the concept of resiliency in Chapter 5 where we provided an overview of strengths. In this chapter we provide recent theories on resiliency and the protective factors that enhance one's ability to cope with adversity. We examine resiliency across three age groups: children, youth, and adults.

Ryff and Singer (2003) define resilience as "the capacity to prevail in the face of adversity" and, more poetically, as "flourishing under fire" (p. 16). They view resiliency as the power to derive strength from hardship and suffering:

> [Resilience] draws on the negative in human experience by articulating the many ways in which life can be hard, but it also emphasizes the positive in describing how some, despite (or because of) their travail, are able to love, work, play—in short, embrace life. (p. 16)

Similarly, Tugade and Fredrickson (2004) refer to psychological resilience as "effective coping and adaptation although faced with loss, hardship, or adversity" (p. 320). They liken resilience to elasticity in metals: "cast iron is hard, brittle, and breaks easily (not resilient), whereas wrought iron is soft, malleable, and bends without breaking (resilient)" (p. 320). This metaphor reflects psychological resilience as a person learns to recover from negative emotional experiences, adapt to stressful situations, and derive meaning from distressing experiences.

Early research on resilience during the 1980s and 1990s studied how children's development was affected by living under adverse conditions (Ryff & Singer, 2003). This research documented that children, despite enduring chronic poverty and negative family situations, often became competent and well-adjusted adults. They managed to thrive despite poverty, parental psychopathology, inadequate caregiving, parental divorce, and the trauma of war. Out of these studies grew an interest in strengths-based *protective factors* that help people resist stressors and flourish in spite of them.

Protective factors derive from personal, family, and institutional strengths and serve as a kind of "safety net" to keep psychological well-being intact. Werner (1995) sees protective factors as the mechanisms that help regulate our reactions to stress so we can successfully adapt to unfavorable situations. They keep us from succumbing to negative functioning such as poor physical or mental health, behavior disorders, or affective disorders.

In her review of resiliency literature, Polk (1997) synthesizes the following four patterns of individual resilience, which include a variety of protective factors:

1. *Dispositional Pattern*: A person's self-perception and physical psychosocial attributes serve as protective factors against life's stressors. These attributes include a sense of self-worth, autonomy, and self-reliance, as well as good physical health and appearance.

2. *Relational Pattern*: Relationships are also a source of resilience. Relational patterns include one's role in society as well as the breadth of relationships people experience—from intimate relationships to social relationships within the broader society.

3. *Situational Pattern*: Situational patterns of resilience are reflected in the individual's ability to interact constructively with stressful situations. Protective situational factors include the individual's ability to realistically evaluate the situation, to problem-solve, and to take action as needed to affect a positive outcome.

4. *Philosophical Pattern*: An individual's worldview can also support resilience. A person will prove hardier if she or he believes life has a purpose, personal development is important, and positive meaning can be derived from all experiences.

The literature on both childhood and adult resilience emphasizes the need to articulate *positive outcomes* to challenge, not solely the *absence of negative effects* such as mental or physical illness (Ryff & Singer, 2003). The remainder of this section highlights recent findings on resiliency across the lifespan—in children, adolescents, and adults.

Resiliency in Children

Results from a number of studies on childhood resiliency document the ways in which children can rise above their circumstances (DuPlessis VanBreda, 2001). The protective factors that children draw from appear in Figure 6.20.

DuPlessis VanBreda notes that most of the child development research has been deficits-oriented, hypothesizing that certain risk factors predict disturbances later in life. The numerous proven protective factors in Figure 6.20 refute this assertion. Clearly, children have many internal and external resources to support their growth into healthy, well-adjusted adults.

Resiliency in Adolescents

An excellent resource that identifies protective factors for adolescents is the *40 Developmental Assets for Adolescents* developed by the Search Institute (2006), which you read about in Chapter 2 *Paradigm Shifts*. This indispensible guide divides protective factors for adolescents into two categories: internal assets and external assets. Internal assets, much like the internal strengths discussed in Chapter 5 *Strengths*, consist of a commitment to learning, positive values, social competencies, and a positive identity. External assets, similar to the external strengths also discussed in Chapter 5, include (a) support from family, community members, neighborhoods, and schools; (b) sources of empowerment; (c) respect for boundaries and expectations; and (d) the constructive use of time, including leisure time. See p. 24 for all 40 of these strengths-based "building blocks of healthy development." At the end of this chapter, the *Resources* section provides the Web address for the Search Institute, which identifies many excellent resources on asset-building.

Resiliency in Adults

Two lines of inquiry have guided research on resiliency in adults (Ryff & Singer, 2003). The first area seeks to understand the ability some people have to continue to grow as a human being despite the presence of risk factors. The second area of research focuses on adult recovery from trauma. Let's start by looking more closely at the first area.

Researchers who study the ability to grow and flourish despite risk factors are particularly interested in how people successfully negotiate the challenges of aging. Studies show that resilience in aging occurs in two ways. First, resiliency results from an individual's willingness and capacity to grow and change as a person. And, second, resiliency is a function of one's ability to adapt and perform effectively in various areas

---

Resiliency Factors in Children

In a synthesis of longitudinal studies on resilience in children, DuPlessis VanBreda (2001) found that the following factors help children rebound from adverse situations:

- A personality that is socially open, cooperative, engaging, and likeable
- Early bonding with a mother or other consistent caregiver
- A variety of alternative caregivers who serve as positive identification models
- No separations from the primary caregiver during the first year of life
- Mother or caregiver has steady employment outside the home
- Being born female or first-born
- Required to help with household chores and activities
- Attends good schools with high standards, teacher feedback, praise for good work, and extramural activities; students have positions of trust and responsibility
- Enjoys school
- Has high self-esteem and self-efficacy
- Has strong internal locus of control
- Possesses flexible coping skills
- Has good impulse control
- Has high energy
- Maintains special interests and hobbies
- Is autonomous and independent
- Parental supervision is strict
- Able to ask for help when need it

Figure 6.20 Resiliency Factors in Children *(adapted from DuPlessis VanBreda, 2001)*

of life, such as adjusting to changes in physical and psychological health, at work, in social situations, and in world events.

Ryff and Singer (2003) view resiliency in aging as both an *outcome* and a dynamic *process*. They define resilience as the "maintenance, recovery, or improvement in mental or physical health following challenge" (p. 20). Ryff and Singer shun the traditional view that absence of illness is enough to determine health (for example, *not* being depressed, anxious, or physically ill). Instead, they favor the multidimensional model of psychological well-being which emphasizes the following kinds of resiliency-oriented characteristics: "positive self-regard, quality ties to others, capacity to manage one's surrounding environment, having purpose and meaningful engagement, and continued growth and development" (pp. 20–21). Ryff and Singer acknowledge that aging can be replete with challenges. A person may experience acute health events, become widowed, have difficulty in retirement, or feel forced to move from a long-time residence. The key to resiliency, they say, is not in evading the naturally occurring challenges of aging, but in *engaging* with difficult events and situations in ways that allow a person to effectively maintain equilibrium and well-being.

In the second line of resiliency research with adults, investigators seek to understand successful recovery from trauma. They have begun to uncover how people who experience trauma can also experience a sense of transformation, rebirth, and renewal. Instead of studying Posttraumatic Stress Disorder (PTSD) and all the negative implications of trauma, researchers are changing their terminology and orientation to focus on Posttraumatic Growth (PTG) and the positive outcomes that often follow suffering. This orientation is very much in line with one of the principles of strengths-based practice provided in Chapter 7: difficulties are also sources of challenge and opportunity. Ryff and Singer (2003) report on how PTG can result in significant beneficial change within a person's cognitive and emotional life, which can lead to positive behavioral changes:

> Researchers in this area see PTG as related to constructs of resilience, sense of coherence, hardiness, stress inoculation, toughening, but their emphasis is on refining formulations of the types of growth that can follow crises: perceiving of oneself as survivor rather than victim; increased self-reliance and self-efficacy; heightened awareness of one's own vulnerability and mortality; improvement in ties to others—greater disclosure and emotional expressiveness, more compassion and capacity to give to others; clearer philosophy in life—renewed sense of priorities and appreciation of life, deeper sense of meaning and spirituality. (p. 24)

Ryff and Singer conclude that the emergent literature on growth through trauma underscores the many ways our lives can ultimately be enhanced by adverse situations—in our self-evaluations, our relationships with others, our life philosophy, and our spirituality. Thus, it is extremely important for us to remind our participants (and ourselves) of the benefits that can arise from difficulty. We now know that from out of adversity renewal, hope, a redefinition of self, and a new outlook on life can emerge.

SUMMARY

In this chapter we presented some exciting, thought-provoking theories that support strengths-based practice in therapeutic recreation. We described theories that apply to well-being within the individual, and others that show the many ways that environmental factors can influence our well-being. As you read the next chapter on principles that guide strengths-based practice, recall the theories that underlie them. Moreover, as you read Part 2 of this book on the therapeutic recreation process, consider how these theories lay the foundation for strengths-based practice. It is truly an inspiring time to be working in the field of therapeutic recreation, where current theory matches the spirit of our field so well!

RESOURCES

Authentic Happiness
http://www.authentichappiness.sas.upenn.edu

The Authentic Happiness website features the work of Dr. Martin Seligman, Director of the Positive Psychology Center at the University of Pennsylvania. Online questionnaires are available that measure authentic happiness variables such as optimism, happiness, attachment, strengths, virtues, and life satisfaction, among several others. You will also find positive psychology publications and videos, authentic happiness newsletters, and information about organizational resources. You can even sign up to be one of Dr. Seligman's research participants!

Self-Assessment of Learning

- In this chapter you read about Barbara Fredrickson's broaden-and-build theory (2009), in which she explains the value of positive emotion. To review, Fredrickson says that positive emotions, such as joy, interest, playfulness, and love, "broaden" our hearts and minds, and make us feel creative and receptive to new information and experiences. Think about a time when you experienced a positive emotion that made you feel keenly alive. Relive that moment, letting your positive emotion awaken. Describe your experience. What did you feel inside? What sensations do you recall as a result of those feelings? What did you do or feel like doing? Did your experience confirm Fredrickson's broaden-and-build view of positive emotion?

- How might the individual strengths-based theories in this chapter relate to your work in therapeutic recreation? How might the environmental strengths-based theories be applied? Think of specific examples.

Dr. Barbara Fredrickson

Healthy People
http://www.healthypeople.gov

This is the official website for the United States national health agenda. It offers publications about health and disease prevention, data on the 10 leading health indicators, and a link to http://www.healthfinder.gov, which gives reliable health information from the U.S. Department of Health and Human Services. The website links individuals and organizations together to discuss and work on particular health issues.

Positive Emotions and Psychophysiology Laboratory
http://www.unc.edu/peplab

Dr. Barbara Fredrickson, founder of the broaden-and-build theory of positive emotions, directs this laboratory at the University of North Carolina, Chapel Hill. She and her assistants study how positive emotion influences the ways in which people think and act, including the physiological responses that result from positive emotion. The website includes synopses of the theories that Dr. Fredrickson's group are testing, a listing of their publications, and links to positive psychology organizations and journals.

Resilience Theory: A Literature Review
http://www.vanbreda.org/adrian/resilience.htm

Adrian DuPlessis VanBreda (2001) has uploaded an in-depth literature review of resiliency theory that includes nearly 500 references. The review addresses resiliency in individuals, families, and communities, and looks at resiliency theory related to policy, social work, and cross-cultural implications.

Search Institute
http://www.search-institute.org

The mission of this Minneapolis-based organization is "to provide leadership, knowledge, and resources to promote healthy children, youth, and communities." Resources include developmental assets for children and adolescents, publications on youth empowerment and asset building, action strategies for engaging communities, and blogs intended for parents and educators.

World Health Organization
http://www.who.int/en

The World Health Organization website describes its global agenda, role, governance, history, publications, programs, and projects. International data and reports on the current status of dozens of health conditions and initiatives are provided.

References

Allan, K. (2008). Positive psychology: Using strengths and experiencing flow. *Journal of Dementia Care, 16*(6), 24–26.

Amado, A. N. (1993). *Friendships and community connections between people with and without developmental disabilities.* Baltimore, MD: Paul H. Brookes.

American Institute for Research. (1993). *Self-determination assessment.* Washington, DC: Author.

Bandura, A. (1977). Self-efficacy: Toward a unifying theory of behavioral change. *Psychological Review, 84,* 191–215.

Bandura, A. (1994). Self-efficacy. In V. S. Ramachandran (Ed.), *Encyclopedia of human behavior* (Vol. 4, pp. 71–81). New York, NY: Academic.

Bandura, A. (2000). Self-efficacy. In *Encyclopedia of Psychology* (Vol. 8, pp. 212–213). Washington, DC: American Psychological Association.

Brendtro, L. K., Brokenleg, M., & Van Bockern, S. (2002). *Reclaiming youth at risk: Our hope for the future.* Bloomington, IN: National Education Service.

Bullock, C. C., Mahon, M. J., & Killingsworth (2010). *Introduction to recreation services for people with disabilities: A person–centered approach* (3rd ed.). Champaign, IL: Sagamore.

Caldwell, L. (2000). The role of theory in TR: A practical approach. In N. Stumbo (Ed.), *Professional issues in therapeutic recreation: On competence and outcomes* (pp. 349–364). Champaign, IL: Sagamore.

Carruthers, C., & Hood, C. (2007). Building a life of meaning through therapeutic recreation: The Leisure and Well–Being Model, Part I. *Therapeutic Recreation Journal, 41*(4), 276–297.

Cocks, E. (2001). Normalisation and social role valorization: Guidance for human service development. *Hong Kong Journal of Psychiatry, 11*(1), 12–16.

Condeluci, A. (1995). *Interdependence: The route to community.* Winter Park, FL: G. R. Press.

Condeluci, A. (2002). *Cultural shifting: Community leadership and change.* St. Augustine, FL: Training Resources Network.

Csíkszentmihályi, M. (1990). *Flow: The psychology of optimal experience.* New York, NY: Harper and Row.

Csíkszentmihályi, M. (1997). *Finding Flow: The psychology of engagement with everyday life.* New York, NY: HarperCollins.

Dattilo, J. (2008). *Leisure education program planning: A systematic approach* (3rd ed.). State College, PA: Venture Publishing, Inc.

Devine, M. A., & Wilhite, B. (1999). Theory application in therapeutic recreation practice and research. *Therapeutic Recreation Journal, 33*(1), 29–45.

Diligio. (2005, January 17). The origins of Normalization [Electronic version]. Retrieved April 14, 2005, from http://www.diligio.com/nirje.htm

DuPlessis VanBreda, A. (2001). *Resiliency theory: A literature review.* Pretoria, South Africa: South African Military Health Service. Retrieved from http://www.vanbreda.org/adrian/resilience/resilience7.pdf

Flynn, R. J., & Lemay, R. A. (Eds.). (1999). *A quarter–century of normalization and social role valorization: Evolution and impact.* Ottawa, ON, Canada: University of Ottawa Press.

Frankl, V. (1959). *Man's search for meaning.* Boston, MA: Beacon.

Fredrickson, B. L. (2001). The role of positive emotions in positive psychology: The broaden-and-build theory of positive emotions. *American Psychologist, 56*(3), 218–226.

Fredrickson, B. L. (2005). Positive affect and the complex dynamics of human flourishing. *American Psychologist, 60*(7), 678–686.

Fredrickson, B. L. (2009). *Positivity: Groundbreaking research reveals how to embrace the hidden strength of positive emotions, overcome negativity, and thrive.* New York, NY: Crown.

Freidson, E. (1983). Celebrating Erving Goffman, *Contemporary Sociology, 12*(4), 359–362.

Goffman, E. (1961). *Asylums: Essays on the social situation of mental patients and other inmates.* Garden City, NY: Doubleday Anchor.

Goffman, E. (1963). *Stigma. Notes on the management of spoiled identity.* Englewood Cliffs, NJ: Prentice-Hall.

Gray, B. (2001). Book review [Review of the book *A quarter–century of normalization and social role valorization: Evolution and impact*]. *The British Journal of Developmental Disabilities, 47*(93), 113–117.

Healthy People. (2012). *Healthy People 2020.* Washington, DC: Author. Retrieved from http://www.healthypeople.gov

Heyne, L., Schleien, S. J., & McAvoy, L. (1993). *Making friends: Using recreation activities to promote friendship between children with and without disabilities.* Minneapolis, MN: Institute on Community Integration, University of Minnesota.

Hood, C., & Carruthers, C. (2002). Coping skills theory as an underlying framework for therapeutic recreation services. *Therapeutic Recreation Journal, 36*(2), 137–153.

House, J. S., Umberson, D., & Landis, K. R. (1988). Structures and processes of social support. *Annual Review of Sociology, 14*, 293–318.

Howard, D., Russoniello, C., & Rogers, D. (2004). Healthy People 2010 and therapeutic recreation: Professional opportunities to promote public health. *Therapeutic Recreation Journal, 38*(2), 116–132.

Hutchinson, P., & McGill, J. (1992). *Leisure, integration, and community.* Toronto, ON, Canada: Leisurability.

Hutchinson, S. L., Loy, D. P., Kleiber, D. A., & Dattilo, J. (2003). Leisure as a coping resource: Variations in coping with traumatic injury and illness. *Leisure Sciences, 25*(2), 143–161.

Institute on Community Integration. (2002). *Self-determination.* [Brochure]. Minneapolis, MN: Author.

Iwasaki, Y., & Mannell, R. C. (2000). Hierarchical dimensions of leisure stress coping. *Leisure Sciences, 22*, 163–181.

Lazarus, R. S., & Folkman, S. (1984). *Stress, appraisal, and coping.* New York, NY: McGraw-Hill.

Lyubomirsky, S. (2008). *The how of happiness: A scientific approach to getting the life you want.* New York, NY: Penguin.

Maddux, J. E. (2002). Self-efficacy: The power of believing you can. In C. R. Snyder & S. J. Lopez (Eds.), *Handbook of positive psychology* (pp. 277–287). New York, NY: Oxford University Press.

McKnight, J. (1987). Regenerating community. *Social Policy.* Winter Issue, 54–58.

McKnight, J. (1988). *Beyond community services.* Evanston, IL: Center for Urban Affairs and Policy Research.

Mead, M. (1935). *Sex and temperament in three primitive societies.* New York, NY: William Morrow & Co.

Mundy, J. (1998). *Leisure education: Theory and practice.* Champaign, IL: Sagamore.

National Council on Disability. (2007, October 1). *Issues in creating livable communities for people with disabilities: Proceedings of the panel.* Washington, DC: Author.

Nirje, B. (1992). *The Normalization principle papers.* Uppsala, Sweden: Centre for Handicap Research, Uppsala University.

Nirje, B. (1993). *The Normalization principle—25 years later.* Uppsala, Sweden: Centre for Handicap Research, Uppsala University.

Nirje, B. (1999a). How I came to formulate the Normalization principle. In R. J. Flynn & R. A. Lemay (Eds.), *A quarter-century of normalization and social role valorization: Evolution and impact* (pp. 17–47). Ottawa, ON, Canada: University of Ottawa Press.

Nirje, B. (1999b). Normalization. In R. J. Flynn & R. A. Lemay (Eds.), *A quarter-century of normalization and social role valorization: Evolution and impact* (pp. 112–113). Ottawa, ON, Canada: University of Ottawa Press.

O'Brien, J. (1986). *Discovering community.* Atlanta, GA: Responsive Systems Associates.

O'Brien, J., & Lyle O'Brien, C. (1996). *Members of each other: Building community in company with people with developmental disabilities.* Toronto, ON, Canada: Inclusion.

O'Connell, M. (1988). *The gift of hospitality: Opening the doors of community life to people with disabilities.* Evanston, IL: Center for Urban Affairs and Policy Research. Retrieved from http://www.northwestern.edu/ipr/publications/papers/goh.pdf

O'Hanlon, B. (2008). *The science of happiness: Four key findings from Positive Psychology research that can increase your life satisfaction.* Retrieved from http://www.billohanlon.com

Orsega–Smith, E., Payne, L., Mowen, A., Ho, C., & Godbey, G. (2007). The role of social support and self-efficacy in shaping the leisure time physical activity of older adults. *Journal of Leisure Research, 39*(4), 705–727.

Perrin, B., & Nirje, B. (1985). Setting the record straight: A critique of some frequent misconceptions of the Normalization principle. *Journal of Intellectual & Developmental Disability, 11*(2), 69–74.

Peterson, C. (2006). *A primer in positive psychology.* New York, NY: Oxford University Press.

Peterson, C., & Park, N. (2009). Positive psychology. In B. Sadock, V. Sadock, & P. Ruiz (Eds.), *Comprehensive textbook of psychiatry* (9th ed.). Baltimore, MD: Lippincott, Williams, & Wilkins.

Peterson, C., & Stumbo, N. (2000). *Therapeutic recreation program design: Principles and procedures* (3rd ed.). Boston, MA: Allyn and Bacon.

Pogrebin, L. C. (1987). *Among friends: Who we like, why we like them, and what we do with them.* New York, NY: McGraw-Hill.

Polk, L. V. (1997). Toward a middle-range theory of resilience. *Advances in Nursing Science, 19*(3), 1–13. Retrieved from http://www.pediatricnursing.org

Putnam, R. (2001). *Bowling alone: The collapse and revival of American community.* New York, NY: Simon & Schuster.

Putnam, R., & Feldstein, L. (2004). *Better together: Restoring the American community.* New York, NY: Simon & Schuster.

Reclaiming Youth International. (2012). *The Circle of Courage philosophy.* Retrieved from http://www.reclaiming.com/content/about-circle-of-courage

Ryan, R. M., & Deci, E. L. (2000). Self-determination theory and the facilitation of intrinsic motivation, social development, and well-being. *American Psychologist, 55*(1), 68–78.

Ryff, C. D., & Singer, B. (2003). Flourishing under fire: Resilience as a prototype of challenged thriving. In C. L. M. Keyes & J. Haidt (Eds.), *Flourishing: Positive psychology and the life well-lived* (p. xi). Washington, DC: American Psychological Association.

Search Institute. (2006). *40 developmental assets for adolescents (ages 12–18).* Minneapolis, MN: Author. Retrieved from http://www.search-institute.org/assets

Seligman, M. (1975). *Helplessness.* San Francisco, CA: W. H. Freeman.

Seligman, M. (1991). *Learned optimism.* New York, NY: Alfred A. Knopf.

Seligman, M. (2002). *Authentic happiness: Using the new positive psychology to realize your potential for lasting fulfillment.* New York, NY: Free Press.

Seligman, M. (2003). Foreword: The past and future of positive psychology. In C. Keyes & J. Haidt (Eds.), *Flourishing: Positive psychology and the life well-lived* (pp. xi–xx). Washington, DC: American Psychological Association.

Seligman, M. (2009). *Positive Psychology Center*, University of Pennsylvania. Retrieved from http://www.ppc.sas.upenn.edu/index.html

Shank, J., & Coyle, C. (2002). *Therapeutic recreation in health promotion and rehabilitation.* State College, PA: Venture Publishing, Inc.

Shank, J., Coyle, C., Boyd, R., & Kinney, W. B. (1996). A classification scheme for therapeutic recreation research grounded in the rehabilitative sciences. *Therapeutic Recreation Journal, 30*, 179–196.

Sheldon, K., Frederickson, B., Rathunde, K., Csíkszentmihályi, M., & Haidt, J. (2000). *Akumal Manifesto*, Positive Psychology Center: University of Pennsylvania. Retrieved from http://www.ppc.sas.upenn.edu/akumalmanifesto.htm

Space and Motion. (2010). *Leonardo da Vinci: On the philosophy, art & science of Leonardo da Vinci*. Retrieved from http://www.spaceandmotion.com/philosophy-leonardo-da-vinci-art-science-quotes.htm

Tugade, M. M., & Fredrickson, B. L. (2004). Resilient individuals use positive emotions to bounce back from negative emotional experiences. *Journal of Personality and Social Psychology, 86*(2), 320–333.

Wallis, C. (2004, January 17). The new science of happiness. *Time Magazine*. Retrieved August 10, 2009, from http://www.authentichappiness.sas.upenn.edu.

Wehmeyer, M. L., & Berkobien, R. (1991). Self-determination and self-advocacy: A case of mistaken identity. *The Association for Persons with Severe Handicaps Newsletter, 7*, 4.

Werner, E. E. (1995). Resilience in development. *Current Directions in Psychological Science, 4*, 81–85.

Wiersma, W. (1991). *Research methods in education*. Boston, MA: Allyn & Bacon.

Wikipedia. (2005, May 30). *1956 Hungarian Revolution*. Retrieved from http://en.wikipedia.org/wiki/Hungarian_Revolution,_1956

Wolfensberger, W. (1972). *The principle of Normalization in human services*. Toronto, ON, Canada: National Institute on Mental Retardation.

Wolfensberger, W. (1983). Social role valorization: A proposed new term for the principle of normalization. *Mental Retardation, 21*(6), 234–239.

Wolfensberger, W. (1999). A contribution to the history of Normalization, with primary emphasis on the establishment of Normalization in North America, circa 1967–1975. In R. J. Flynn & R. Lemay (Eds.), *A quarter-century of normalization and social role valorization*. Ottawa, ON, Canada: University of Ottawa Press.

World Health Organization. (2003). *ICF Checklist*. Retrieved from http://www.who.int/classifications

World Health Organization. (2012). *About WHO*. Retrieved from http://www.who.int/about/

Chapter 7
Principles that Guide Strengths-Based Therapeutic Recreation Practice

A lily represents simple elegance, signifying pure essence.

"The soul is dyed the color of its thoughts. Think only on those things that are in line with your principles and can bear the light of day ... Day by day, what you choose, what you think, and what you do is who you become."

—*Heraclitus, Sixth-century BC Greek philosopher*

Overview of Chapter 7

- Principles defined
- Principles to guide strengths-based therapeutic recreation practice
- Meaningfulness and application to therapeutic recreation practice

Focus Questions

- What principles guide a strengths-based approach in therapeutic recreation?
- How do strengths-based principles differ from those that guide a deficits, or medical model, approach?
- How does a strengths-based approach make our work in therapeutic recreation meaningful and relevant?

Principles Defined

A definition of "principle"
A basic or essential quality or element determining intrinsic nature or characteristic behavior; a basic generalization that is accepted as true and that can be used as a basis for reasoning or conduct

Principles provide direction and set standards for professional practice. They guide, in a proactive way, the professional behaviors of everyday practice as we endeavor to facilitate optimal well-being and quality of life for our participants. Principles not only lead practitioners—they inform participants and the general public about the values they can expect us, as therapeutic recreation professionals, to uphold.

Principles can also serve to unite a community of professionals under a common approach to practice. A unifying set of principles can inspire practitioners, provide a common language and orientation, and foster the continued development of the profession. To this unifying end, we offer these principles for strengths-based practice in therapeutic recreation based on the work of Dr. Dennis Saleebey (2006).

Principles to Guide Strengths-Based Therapeutic Recreation Practice

In the previous chapters in Part 1 of this book, we provided overviews of the strengths perspective and the sea change in health and human services and in therapeutic recreation. We defined strengths as the heart of therapeutic recreation practice, and we presented the prevailing theories that underlie and give credence to a strengths approach. In this final chapter of Part 1, we aim to distill the essence of the preceding chapters into eight guiding principles. As the calla lily on the top of the page represents simple elegance and essential being, these principles represent the essence of a strengths orientation to therapeutic recreation practice. Further, these principles guide the strengths-based therapeutic recreation process, which you will learn about in Part 2.

While it is challenging to offer principles that fit the entire range of settings in which therapeutic recreation specialists work, we believe these principles are grounded broadly enough in the rights of participants to apply meaningfully to all settings. As you examine these principles, think about the places where you work or volunteer and whether or not these principles are followed. If they are not followed, what changes could be made to align practice with strengths-based principles? Consider, too, how the principles presented here overlap and reinforce one another to create a unified orientation to therapeutic recreation practice.

PRINCIPLE 1:
Every individual, group, family, and community has strengths.

Fundamental to a strengths approach is the belief that every person and every group possesses strengths (Saleebey, 2006). On the surface, someone's strong points may not be apparent though they exist, and it is up to us as therapeutic recreation specialists to help participants discover their strengths and nurture them. We also need to reorient ourselves to see people's strengths, and we need to encourage our participants to recognize their own strengths in ways that empower them and give them hope.

In Chapter 5 *Strengths* you learned that strengths may be internal or external to the participant. That is, strengths may be present within the person in the form of talents, interests, character strengths and virtues, aspirations, and goals. Strengths may also take the form of external environmental resources, which can include friends, family members, pets, recreation materials, houses of worship, and wilderness areas, to name a few. Examining the many areas of potential strength inside and outside the participant can unearth a "treasure chest" of assets upon which to enhance a person's well-being and quality of life (see Figure 7.1, p. 148).

PRINCIPLE 2:
Difficulties are also sources of challenge and opportunity.

The word "crisis" derives from the Greek words *krisis*, or turning point, and *krinein*, which means to choose or decide. Thus, difficulty (e.g., illness, disability) presents us with a decision: How will I choose to respond to this hardship? Will I succumb to feelings of distress and negativity, or resolve to stay positive? Will I retreat, or draw upon my strengths and resources to open myself to the possibility of transformation?

When a participant struggles with loss, illness, or disability, professionals need to help them work through their feelings as well as see the positive aspects and opportunities a situation has to offer. This is no easy task, yet our optimism can inspire optimism in others. Our ability to tap into people's strengths and resources can ignite their hopefulness and set them on a new journey toward healing and thriving.

The concept of resilience is central to the idea that difficulties are also sources of challenge and opportunity. Resilience is defined as the "personal and community qualities that enable us to rebound from adversity, trauma, tragedy, threats, or other stresses—and to go on with life with a sense of mastery, competence, and hope" (President's New Freedom Commission on Mental Health, 2003, p. 5). Notice how this definition describes resilience as relevant not only for people but also for neighborhoods and communities, which can offer many supports and resources to boost citizens' well-being.

A prime example of someone who faced tremendous difficulty, yet chose to convert it to opportunity, is Winston Churchill, Prime Minister of the United Kingdom during the Second World War. His words of resolve, which inspired Allied forces to victory, capture the heart of this strengths principle: "The pessimist sees difficulty in every opportunity. The optimist sees the opportunity in every difficulty."

PRINCIPLE 3:
We do not know the upper limits of a participant's capacity to grow and change—only the participant knows.

"Risks must be taken because the greatest hazard in life is to risk nothing."

—*William Arthur Ward*

For centuries, the abilities of people with disabilities have been underestimated by those who thought they knew better, who thought they had the answers. Labels and diagnoses, based on a medical model, have reinforced this negative view. As we reorient ourselves to a strengths approach, we need to resist prejudging a participant's abilities and capacities. We need to refrain from sheltering participants from risks and challenges that are based, not on necessity or reality, but on fear of what may (or may not) happen. We need to listen to what participants think about their own capabilities. We need to listen to their dreams and encourage them along their own unique paths.

Risk is a natural part of growth, healing, and rehabilitation—as it is an inherent part of living. Rather than avoid risk, we need to embrace it and accept that a measure of uncertainty simply cannot be avoided if one is to live a full life. Ascertaining whether a risk is prudent or perilous is a skill of discernment that is important for participants to learn. Each of us has the right to determine for ourselves the kinds and levels of challenges we wish to undertake. We all have the right to what Perske and Perske (1981) call the "dignity of risk." In Table 7.1, you can read their eloquent perspective on this empowering concept, as well as their warnings about the hazards of overprotecting participants.

This third principle reminds us that it is not ours to decide the upper limits of what a person can do. If we do, we may restrict a person's opportunities and possibilities. The Life Story in Figure 7.2 tells of a practitioner who struggles against the involuntary reflex of prejudging a young man's potential. See which prevails: dignity of risk and self-determination, or the professional's need to have "the answers."

PRINCIPLE 4:
COLLABORATION (NOT EXPERT DOMINATION) IS THE BASIS FOR OUR INTERACTION WITH PARTICIPANTS.

The strengths approach calls for an unprecedented shift in the dynamic between the participant and the professional. In the deficits approach, the professional is seen as the expert, as the person in charge who has all the answers. By contrast, the strengths approach sees the participant as the expert and the one in control. It is the participant, after all, who is the expert on his or her own life, experiences, interests, wants, needs, and aspirations for the future.

In the deficits model, the professional molds, shapes, and imposes judgments upon the participant's life; by contrast, in the strengths model, the participant is the driving force behind the therapeutic process. Participants know how they want their lives to look. They set the direction, establish goals, and define the parameters for success. The role of the professional is to support participants through the process of achieving their goals and dreams. The professional facilitates therapeutic processes and interventions according to his or her training, expertise, professional judgment, and collaboration with other team members who also follow the lead of the participant. The professional does not do *for* or *to* the participant; rather, the professional does *with* the participant.

Table 7.2 presents a powerful statement of belief, "A Credo for Support," written by Canadian disability rights activist Norman Kunc. His candid perspective as a person with cerebral palsy lends insight into the necessity of collaboration with participants, not expert domination. Kunc and his wife Emma Van der Klift (1995) have developed this text into a DVD and poster, and information about their availability appears in the Resources section at the end of this chapter.

In summary, the relationship between the participant and the professional in a strengths-based approach is marked by collaboration, equality, mutual respect, and confidence in the participant's capabilities. The hierarchical, vertical relationship of the deficits approach gives way to a side-by-side, horizontal team approach. The participant is the most important member of the team—at the center—and, thus, the

Table 7.1 Robert Perske on Overprotection and the Dignity of Risk *(Perske & Perske, 1981)*

Overprotection may appear on the surface to be kind, but it can be really evil. An oversupply can smother people emotionally, and squeeze the life out of their hopes and expectations, and strip them away of their dignity.

Overprotection can keep people from becoming all they could become.

Many of our best achievements came the hard way: We took risks, fell flat, suffered, picked ourselves up, and tried again. Sometimes we made it and sometimes we did not. Even so, we were given the chance to try. Persons with special needs need these chances too.

Of course, we are talking about prudent risks. People should not be expected to blindly face challenges that, without a doubt, will explode in their faces. Knowing which chances are prudent and which are not—this is a new skill that needs to be acquired.

On the other hand, a risk is really only when it is not known beforehand whether a person can succeed. . . .

The real world is not always safe, secure, and predictable. It does not always say "please," "excuse me," or "I'm sorry." Every day we face the possibility of being thrown into situations where we will have to risk everything . . .

In the past, we found clever ways to build avoidance of risk into the lives of persons living with disabilities. Now we must work equally hard to help find the proper amount of risk . . . people have the right to take. We have learned that there can be healthy development in risk taking . . . and there can be crippling indignity in safety!

focus of all the other team members who work for her or his benefit.

PRINCIPLE 5:
Every environment is full of resources.

Just as every person has strengths, every environment contains resources. And just as we must train ourselves to see the strengths and assets of participants, we need to orient ourselves to notice supportive resources in the environments where participants regularly spend their time.

Most metropolitan areas have a range of organized services and resources for participants with disabilities, illnesses, and other challenging life circumstances. Yet, even if a community does not have all the resources of a large metro area, there are always people, places, and groups to draw on for support. This is also true of rural communities. In fact, many rural residents share particularly strong community bonds. They don't assume someone else will provide services, so they often create their own connections and supports.

What are some examples of people, places, and groups that may be tapped as supports for participants? *People* might include immediate family members and relatives, friends, neighbors, schoolmates, and co-workers, among others. *Places* might include schools, workplaces, community centers, coffee houses, places of worship, fitness centers, farmers markets, and homes of friends or neighbors, to name a few. And *groups* might include clubs and organizations that match the participant's interests—for example, Boy or Girl Scouts; 4-H; a softball team; cultural associations; or a ski, bridge, sports, dance, or birding club. The list of resources is limited only by our creativity to see the potential of environments and how to connect participants to them.

The fact that community resources and supports occur *naturally* in the context of a participant's life is a keen advantage. As the individual is involved

Primary Source Support:

Youth Protective Factors in South Africa

Bloemhoff, H. J. (2006). The effect of an adventure-based recreation programme (ropes course) on the development of resiliency in at-risk adolescent boys confined to a rehabilitation centre. *South African Journal for Research in Sport, Physical Education and Recreation, 28*(1), 1–11.

In 1997, Drs. Peter Witt and John Crompton developed a protective-factors framework to understand, explain, and evaluate the resiliency of at-risk youth. Thirteen protective factors were identified that, if present in an adolescent's life, could offset the negative influence of stressful conditions in home, school, or community environments. The protective factors they identified are as follows:

1. Interested and caring adults
2. Neighborhood resources
3. School and club involvement
4. High control against deviant behavior
5. Models for conventional behavior
6. Positive attitudes toward the future
7. Value on achievement
8. Ability to work with others
9. Ability to work out conflicts
10. Sense of acceptance
11. Church attendance
12. Quality schools
13. Cohesive family

Witt and Crompton then designed a questionnaire, *The Protective Factors Scale*, to measure resiliency outcomes of recreation programs for at-risk youth. The scale was also used to establish program goals and to design recreation programs that could support children's resiliency in the face of stressful life circumstances.

Dr. Bloemhoff (2006) used *The Shortened Protective Factor Scale* (addresses 10 instead of 13 protective factors) to measure the effect of an outdoor adventure-based ropes course program on the resiliency of 46 adolescent boys who lived at a rehabilitation center. Sixty adolescent boys were assigned to a control group and did not take part in the ropes course program. The questionnaire was administered as a pre- and post-test to both groups. The results showed that 8 of the 10 protective factors of the boys in the experimental group increased significantly ($p = < .05$) as a result of the program. These findings suggest that adventure-based recreation has the potential to improve the resiliency of adolescent boys, which can foster their successful transition into adulthood.

Figure 7.1 Primary Source Support: Youth Protective Factors in South Africa

Life Story:

Kevin's Story: Who's really in the "driver's seat"?

While working as an inclusion coordinator at a neighborhood community center, I enjoyed knowing a family with an athletic, easygoing son named Kevin. He had participated regularly in center programs for several years. Kevin had taken swimming lessons, performed in "Fiddler on the Roof," attended after-school day care, and gone to summer day camp—all with other children without disabilities his same age. Now Kevin is 12 and taking instructional basketball with other sixth-grade boys. They have spent every Sunday practicing basketball drills together for the past 2 years.

One Sunday afternoon in March, Kevin's mother Pat and I were sitting in the bleachers watching Kevin dribble, pass, shoot baskets, and give "high fives" with the other players. The inevitable question arose: "What will Kevin do next year?" You see, the following year all the boys would be in junior high, when it was customary for them to join competitive teams and play in leagues.

"What will Kevin do next year?" Pat wondered. "I'm not sure," I replied weakly. Neither one of us had the heart to say it aloud yet both of us were thinking, "Of course Kevin can't play competitive basketball. He has Down syndrome, his speech is sometimes hard to understand, and he often takes too many steps when he dribbles. He might not be much of an asset to his team, and the other players would probably resent him being there.

A few moments later I said resolutely, "We'll think of something" (after all, I was the expert and should have the answers). "Perhaps Kevin can keep score or work at the Pro Shop to check in the players," I suggested. "That's what another boy with a disability did last year."

"That would probably be best for everyone," Pat replied soberly. "Let me talk with Kevin."

A few days later Pat dropped by my office. "Well, I talked with Kevin." "Yes? What did he say?" "Well, he's assuming he'll be playing on a team next year. Everyone else will be on a team, so he assumed he would be too!"

Then it hit me. Of course, Kevin should play on the team. If that's what everyone else is doing, why shouldn't he? How could I forget to ask Kevin what he wanted to do?! Embarrassed by our oversight, all Pat and I could do was laugh—then agree we'd need to find a way for Kevin to play on a team next season.

I talked with the physical education director, who in turn talked with the volunteer coaches. One of the coaches, Scott, was particularly excited to have Kevin on his team. Scott emphasized sportsmanship, socialization, and teamwork during games and practices—not necessarily winning, although everyone always tried their hardest. With Kevin on the team, his teammates would have an opportunity to work together to support him. The coaches also agreed to grant Kevin one small rule adaptation: He could "travel" while dribbling the ball. Otherwise, all the other rules applied.

The following March, Pat and I sat in the bleachers once again, this time happily watching Kevin play with his team. Everyone in the stands, including us, seemed to hold their breath whenever Kevin had the ball, mentally willing it to go wherever Kevin aimed it. Even though he couldn't play quite as well as the others, Pat and I marveled at how much Kevin was a part of his team.

The game was coming to a close, and Kevin was sitting on the sideline. With only minutes to go and with a tied score, the coach signaled Kevin to play. Pat and I were surprised, and it looked like everyone else was too. Kevin wasn't surprised, however. He jaunted onto the court, alert and poised for action. A teammate who was positioned close to the basket decided not to take the shot, and instead passed the ball to Kevin. Everyone in the gym froze. No one said a word. Everyone was watching to see what Kevin would do next. Planting his feet firmly on the floor, from a distance of nearly 50 feet, Kevin leapt up and propelled the ball high into the air and through the hoop. The crowd went wild. We were all standing and cheering and waving, and Kevin's mother was wiping away tears. Kevin's teammates were slapping him on the back and whooping, and the coaches shook his hand proudly. The team went on to win, with Kevin's basket earning the game point.

That day was one of the highlights of my professional career. Kevin's thrilling basket and the crowd's affirming response is embedded in my memory forever. And just as poignant is the humbling lesson Kevin taught me about assumptions and who really is in charge in therapeutic recreation practice. What if I had gone with my initial instincts and kept Kevin from playing? What if I had never asked Kevin what he wanted to do? What if I had unwittingly limited his opportunities, protecting him from the risk of failure?

If I had kept Kevin from playing, he would never have known what it was like to be a star player and win a game for his team. And no one in that gymnasium would have ever seen Kevin play so adeptly and shoot that game-winning basket. Never again will I assume I know more than a participant about what is possible for him or her to achieve.

Now his mother tells me Kevin wants to learn to drive. If Kevin believes it's possible, then I do too!

Figure 7.2 Life Story: Kevin

Table 7.2 "A Credo for Support" by Norman Kunc *(Kunc & Van der Klift, 1995)*

Throughout history, people with physical and mental disabilities have been abandoned at birth, banished from society, used as court jesters, drowned and burned during the Inquisition, gassed in Nazi Germany, and still continue to be segregated, institutionalized, tortured in the name of behavior management, abused, raped, euthanized, and murdered. Now, for the first time, people with disabilities are taking their rightful place as fully contributing citizens. The danger is that we will respond with remediation and benevolence rather than equity and respect. And so, we offer you

A Credo for Support

Do not see my disability as a problem. Recognize that my disability is an attribute.

Do not see my disability as a deficit. It is you who see me as deviant and helpless.

Do not try to fix me because I am not broken. Support me.
I can make my contribution to the community in my way.

Do not see me as your client. I am your fellow citizen. See me as your neighbor.
Remember, none of us can be self-sufficient.

Do not try to modify my behavior. Be still and listen. What you define as inappropriate
may be my attempt to communicate with you in the only way I can.

Do not try to change me, you have no right. Help me learn what I want to know.

Do not hide your uncertainty behind "professional" distance. Be a person who listens
and does not take my struggle away from me by trying to make it all better.

Do not use theories and strategies on me. Be with me. And when we struggle
with each other, let that give use to self-reflection.

Do not try to control me. I have a right to my power as a person. What you call
non-compliance or manipulation may actually be the only way I can exert control over my life.

Do not teach me to be obedient, submissive, and polite.
I need to feel entitled to say no if I am to protect myself.

Do not be charitable to me. The last thing the world needs is another Jerry Lewis.
Be my ally against those who exploit me for their own gratification.

Do not try to be my friend. I deserve more than that. Get to know me. We may become friends.

Do not help me even if it does make you feel good.
Ask me if I need your help. Let me show you how to better assist me.

Do not admire me. A desire to live a full life does not warrant adoration.
Respect me, for respect presumes equity.

Do not tell, correct, and lead. Listen, support, and follow.

Do not work on me. Work with me.

---

consistently in community settings, seeing and interacting regularly with people and resources, his or her goals may be met to the point that professional services are reduced or even no longer needed. As a caring community surrounds the participant, she or he gains opportunities for greater independence, interdependence, and community belonging, as well as opportunities to contribute to society. As the participant is strengthened, the community is likewise made stronger by his or her contributions. In contrast to a deficits-based system that often results in a continued dependence on professional services, *natural supports* present a more sustainable solution for maintaining a participant's well-being.

PRINCIPLE 6:
Context matters.

One of the many gifts therapeutic recreation specialists bring to health and human services is a holistic perspective. We see the psychological, cognitive, social, emotional, physical, and spiritual dimensions of a person, as well as the potential that individuals have for involvement in a variety of recreation and other kinds of environments. These settings may include, for example, a playground, gym, park, beach, ski slope, workplace lunchroom, neighborhood recreation center, a friend's house, or one's own home, among many other places.

Just as looking at one dimension of a person in isolation is shortsighted, viewing participants apart from the relationships and environments in which they live, play, work, and learn is narrow and impractical. Knowing the social circles and places in which participants spend their time, either presently or in the future, helps us facilitate their involvement more realistically and fully. We can consider the demands that settings or social groups require, and draw on environmental resources as they are needed. We can assess how the participant will benefit from interaction within the setting, as well as how the participant might contribute. We can also address the practical realities of environmental barriers and find solutions that allow for participation. Planning with context in mind makes for more comprehensive, true-to-life solutions that improve and sustain a person's well-being over time (see Figure 7.3).

PRINCIPLE 7:
HOPEFULNESS MATTERS.

When participants sense they are viewed as a problem or a diagnosis—and not as a person—they will likely feel devalued and discouraged. Similarly, when

---

Primary Source Support:

Therapeutic Recreation and Youth Resiliency

Ellis, J., Braff, E., & Hutchinson, S. (2001). Youth recreation and resiliency: Putting theory into practice in Fairfax County. *Therapeutic Recreation Journal, 35*(4), 307–317.

This article describes a teen recreation program in Fairfax County, Virginia in which the Community and Recreation Services merged two of its departments, Therapeutic Recreation Services and Teen Centers, to support youth resiliency. Several reasons are given for involving therapeutic recreation services in youth development (Baldwin, 2000; Caldwell, 2000). Participants are involved in activities that are intrinsically motivating. The strengths, competencies, assets, and needs of participants are emphasized, not the negative behaviors or problematic nature of the person's situation. The specific contexts in which interventions will be most effective are considered. Therapeutic recreation assessment, planning, and implementation processes lead to targeted, documented outcomes. Further, therapeutic recreation outcomes are similar to outcomes sought in youth development, such as building resiliency, competence, appropriate social behaviors, and the constructive use of time.

The two departments merged to form a new entity, the Division of Therapeutic Recreation and Teen Centers (TRTC). A joint mission was developed:

> To provide individuals with physical, mental, and developmental disabilities an opportunity to acquire, restore, or apply leisure skills, knowledge, and abilities; to promote inclusion in community activities; and to foster community awareness and sensitivity for acceptance of individuals with disabilities. And to provide safe and drug-free centers where Fairfax County teens can participate in a variety of social, recreational, and community activities that facilitate the establishment of healthy and positive leisure participation patterns; develop a sense of ownership and responsibility for center activities; and develop the values and ethical behavior that enable productive and responsible community citizenship. (Fairfax County Department of Community and Recreation Services, 2000)

The key to TRTC's approach is youth-directed programming. Teens take on meaningful roles to develop and implement programs intended to support their own resilience and healthy psychological development. Programming centers around four key concepts tied to the literature on resiliency: (a) social competence, (b) problem solving, (c) autonomy, and (d) sense of purpose/belief in a bright future. Staff members surmise that, when youth participate in program development, they also mature in their social competence and problem-solving skills. When youth are given ownership of the program, they gain greater autonomy. And, as teens experience success through their decision-making and participation, their outlook for the future becomes brighter.

Programming consists of five service areas: (a) personal and social skill building, (b) exploring recreational interests, (c) substance-abuse prevention, (d) tutoring and other support for homework, and (e) service learning and career development. This meaningful and relevant self-directed curriculum resulted in a substantial increase in youth attendance. Participation in activities such as teen councils and service projects increased 30% between 1999 and 2000. Attendance in other service area programming increased 23%. Furthermore, referrals of teens to the centers increased by 13.3% as police, courts, and social service workers recognized the value of individualized therapeutic recreation services for positive youth development.

Figure 7.3 Primary Source Support: Therapeutic Recreation and Youth Resiliency

we professionals find ourselves looking exclusively at problems—at deficits, limitations, and what's wrong—we may grow disheartened and succumb to feelings of burnout. Participants and professionals may both feel dispirited when facing the enormity of perceived problems.

When we adopt a strengths approach that focuses on people's talents, assets, and aspirations, however, we tap into some powerful catalysts for hopefulness and positive change. Affirming a person's strengths empowers them. Reminding people of their positive traits, virtues, and beliefs can boost their optimism as they move through the therapeutic process. Likewise, if professionals listen well to participants, their stories, dreams, and goals can inspire us to feel hopeful about the possibilities for their futures. Their goals become our goals, their dreams our dreams. Dr. Patricia Deegan, co-founder of the Boston University Institute for the Study of Human Resilience and former patient at a psychiatric institution, gives us a moving story on the importance of hope in the healing process (see Figure 7.4).

Equally, families need hope. Too often family members hear what their loved ones can't do. We can encourage families to believe in real possibilities for their family member's future. We can help them by pointing out resources in the community that can support their family member in a consistent way.

Hopefulness plays an essential role in the healing and recovery process. Recovery, as defined by the President's New Freedom Commission on Mental Health (2003), incorporates hope as an integral part of leading people toward greater well-being:

> Recovery refers to the process in which people are able to live, work, learn, and participate fully in their communities. For some individuals, recovery is the ability to live a fulfilling and productive life despite a disability. For others, recovery implies the reduction or complete remission of symptoms. Science has shown that having hope plays an integral role in an individual's recovery. (p. 6)

Notice how this quotation emphasizes the context in which people participate, reinforcing the previous principle that, as hopefulness matters, so does context.

All in all, hope empowers us and makes the impossible possible. Disability activist and actor Christopher Reeve (2002) reminds us of the power of hopefulness in the following quote:

> When the unthinkable happens, the lighthouse is hope. Once we find it, we must cling to it with absolute determination.... Hope must be real, and built upon the same solid foundation, as a lighthouse; in that way it is different from ... wishful thinking. When we have hope, we discover powers within ourselves we may have never known—the power to make sacrifices, to endure, to heal, and to love. Once we choose hope, everything is possible. (p. 176)

How can we ignite a sense of hopefulness in our participants? As we explain in the next principle, we instill hopefulness by *intentionally* nurturing participants' strengths through the use of the therapeutic recreation process.

PRINCIPLE 8:
STRENGTHS CAN BE NURTURED—THUS, THEY MUST BE ASSESSED, PLANNED, FOCUSED ON, AND EVALUATED.

As noted previously in this book, what we focus on increases. If we focus on a problem, it is likely to become larger and more enmeshed. The problem may grow to the point of consuming our thoughts and causing us to lose perspective. Just as giving attention to problems encourages their growth, giving attention to strengths and positive outcomes helps them flourish. If we focus on a hopeful aspiration, we are likely to find ourselves filled with positive thoughts and energy that move us closer to its realization. By systematically centering on strengths through the therapeutic recreation process, we can help our participants reduce problem-oriented thinking while augmenting their strengths and capabilities.

What does it mean to nurture strengths in therapeutic recreation practice? You will find an in-depth answer to this question in Part 2 of this book, yet, in short, it means to keep strengths centrally in mind throughout the therapeutic recreation process. During the assessment phase, the participant's strengths and environmental resources are identified. Identifying strengths and resources leads to the development of specific goals and objectives around which the intervention is planned. As the intervention or program is implemented, strengths are accentuated and built upon to produce healthy outcomes. Documentation and evaluation show the extent to which a participant's own goals and dreams have been realized, as well as what steps need to be taken next. Focusing systematically on strengths in therapeutic recreation practice provides the participant with a hopeful framework to progress toward a flourishing life.

Life Story

Patricia's Story: "There is strength in vulnerability."

Patricia Deegan is only a teenager when she's admitted to a psychiatric institution for the second time and given the diagnosis of chronic undifferentiated schizophrenia. She senses that the staff members who worked with her in the past view her differently now. She sees hopelessness in their eyes. She sees they've branded her a recidivist—caught in the perpetual revolving door of readmissions to mental health institutions. Patricia fears if she succumbs to the hopelessness reflected in their eyes, she may be "lost forever."

Patricia has a dream to return to school. She vows to do whatever she can to be discharged from the hospital as soon as possible. She musters all her strength and, 3 weeks later, walks away from the institution in time to resume an English composition course at her community college. Sitting in the classroom Patricia knows she looks ragged. She knows her eyes have dark circles under them and her hands tremble. She knows the drugs she's taking cause her eyes to glaze over and make it difficult to concentrate. Yet she feels triumphant! Her spirit soars. She feels like she just climbed Mt. Everest to get there.

At the break, the professor approaches Patricia smiling. She thinks he's going to welcome her back to class and say he's glad to see her. Instead he says, "Pat, you look awful. Why don't you just go home tonight, and we'll see you next week." Her spirit sinks. She wonders why he can't see what she's just accomplished. Why is he focusing on what's wrong with her instead of seeing how strong she is? She goes home dejected and spends the next 9 months on the couch staring at the wall and smoking cigarettes.

Ultimately Patricia doesn't fault the professor for what he said because she believes he was trying to be helpful. Yet she points out that he wasn't helpful, for two reasons. First, his advice was offered without her input. He didn't realize that help is only helpful if it's created in partnership with the person asking for help. Second, the professor looked at what was wrong with her and didn't see the strength behind her vulnerabilities. He didn't see it was through her drive to not let her vulnerabilities limit her that she found the inspiration and strength to come to class.

Patricia recalls other mental health staff who have given similar advice—all with good intentions—not realizing they were focusing on people's deficits instead of their strengths:

"You should try a volunteer job because you're not ready for work."
"We recommend group home placement because you are not high-functioning enough to live in your own apartment."
"Avoid stress and stay on medications for the rest of your life."

Too many service providers see only deficits, Patricia writes, and as a result "too many people have put their dreams, hopes and aspirations on hold and are living marginal lives in handicaptivity." By using a strengths orientation, however, Patricia believes, "we learn that even when people present with obvious vulnerabilities, they also have strengths. Their strengths are in their passions, in their skills, in their interests, in their relationships, and in their environments."

Service providers, she says, need to recognize people's strengths and tap places in the environment where their strengths can be expressed and valued. Nurturing strengths activates a "radiating effect." As Patricia explains, "the strong part of the self begins to radiate outward, building a new life of meaning and purpose."

Today, Dr. Deegan is co-founder of the Boston University Institute for the Study of Human Resilience. She is known worldwide for her lectures, research, and publications that offer people hope and resources for mental wellness. See the Resources section at the end of this chapter to learn more about Dr. Deegan and her work.

Figure 7.4 Life Story: Patricia *(adapted from Deegan, 2006)*

To wrap up this section on strengths-based principles, we direct your attention to the Compare/Contrast feature in Figure 7.5, which summarizes the assumptions underlying the principles of strengths and deficits approaches. In this figure, you can see how the two approaches compare on multiple dimensions: focus, scope of practice, how the participant is viewed, overall framework and vocabulary, and the effectiveness of generating solutions. It is evident that the strengths approach capitalizes on the capacity and potential of the participant, which necessitates a new vocabulary and framework for practice. Notice also how, in the strengths paradigm, participants are viewed holistically, within the rich contexts of their lives. This holistic orientation leads more readily to practical and creative solutions to assist participants in reaching their goals and aspirations.

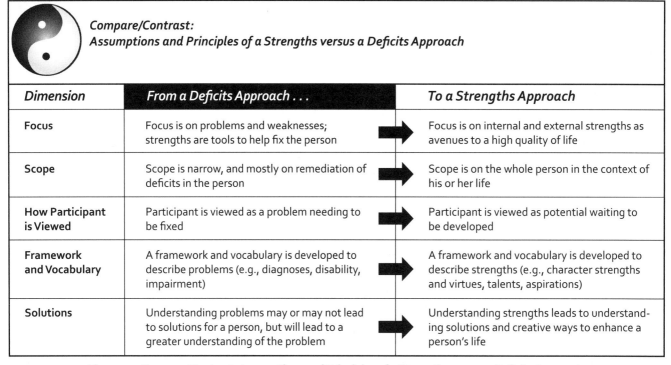

Figure 7.5 Compare/Contrast: Assumptions and Principles of a Strengths versus a Deficits Approach

Meaningfulness and Application to Therapeutic Recreation Practice

A strengths-based approach brings a new optimism and hopefulness to therapeutic recreation practice, making the process more meaningful for participants and practitioners alike. A strengths approach diverts attention away from problems, deficits, illness, and limitations to concentrate on the more refreshing possibilities, aspirations, and visions of how participants wish to live their lives (see Figure 7.6).

A strengths orientation doesn't imply that considering problems is never important. It doesn't mean we don't need to understand the nature of an illness, disability, injury, or other condition. Understanding a problem has its value for acknowledging the situation, understanding how the problem developed, and learning the likely prognosis. Yet how far can comprehending the problem or deficit take a participant along the continuum from illness to well-being? A problem-oriented approach may help correct an injury or alleviate an illness, but does it stretch beyond these ends to allow the participant to truly experience wellness? Further, in a problem-oriented approach, the participant is susceptible to being viewed as the problem or pathology—as someone who needs "fixing." This limited scope yields limited benefit. By contrast, the strengths approach allows us to keep the bigger picture of the person's life and lifestyle in mind in order to yield more abundant rewards for well-being and quality of life.

The focus of the strengths approach is forward-moving, and our perceptive powers and creativity are engaged to purposefully identify internal strengths, hopes, aspirations, and similar qualities. External resources are brought to bear to support the person along his or her journey toward well-being. Drawing upon the person's strengths adds a spiritual, even existential, dimension to practice. Richter and Kaschalk (1996) see the future of therapeutic recreation as encompassing existential outcomes, that is, as addressing the great questions that pertain to human existence. They say the "wise" therapeutic recreation specialist can help "answer the most important question of all, 'what makes a person tick?'" (p. 89). Richter and Kaschalk continue:

> Therapeutic recreation is the only discipline that actually stands as an *end*, not just a means. It is the only discipline seeking the person's "want to's" and not just the "have to's." It is a goal in itself, not just a stepping stone.... The therapeutic recreation specialist is the professional who can help people realize that what remains when they face disability and treatment is a life worth living. (pp. 86–87)

The strengths principles presented in this chapter can guide us toward these meaningful existential outcomes and assist our participants in finding that "life worth living."

Summary

Eight principles were presented to guide strengths-based practice in therapeutic recreation. These principles emphasize how every person, community, and environment has strengths and resources, and it is up to the therapeutic recreation professional to discover them, build upon them, and help participants to also see them. Difficulties that participants experience are viewed as sources of opportunity and growth, and hopefulness is essential for resilience and recovery to occur. Considering the home and community contexts in which people live, work, play, and learn is essential to arrive at practical solutions that enhance participants' well-being and quality of life.

Participants are at the center of our practice, and decisions are made through collaboration with them. Participants have the right to self-determination and the dignity of risk. In all respects, the participant leads; the professional follows. By focusing on a person's positive characteristics and resources, we can nurture strengths and encourage their growth, which lead to rich, existential outcomes for health, well-being, and a life worth living.

Resources

A Credo for Support
http://www.normemma.com

This philosophical statement by Norman Kunc, a Canadian disability rights activist with cerebral palsy, is presented in Table 7.2. He and his wife Emma Van der Klift have developed this credo into a provocative 5-minute DVD and poster, which are available through BroadReach Training & Resources.

Common Ground
http://www.patdeegan.com

Pat Deegan, Ph.D. & Associates developed this web-based software to encourage recovery-oriented practice and shared decision making among people with psychiatric disorders and their health and human services providers. The software allows people with psychiatric disorders to enter initial information and concerns, "Power Statement" goals, and "How I am doing" reports by touchscreen. Their input enables doctors and staff to collaborate with participants to make recovery decisions in an efficient, functional, and holistic way. A 9-minute video describing Common Ground is available at this website.

My Cultural Lens: Differences in Aspirations

Lily Dyson (2005) compared the personal aspirations of children from China who had recently immigrated to Canada with the aspirations of white native born children. Dyson asked both groups, "What do you want to do or to be when you grow up?" Because Chinese culture is collectivist-oriented compared to the individualistic orientation of Western societies, Dyson hypothesized that the aspirations of the two groups of children would be different.

Dyson discovered, however, that there were relatively small differences between the future career aspirations of the two groups. Most of the immigrant and native born children favored careers in three areas: (a) communication, arts, and culture; (b) health and sciences; and (c) social services and education. More of the immigrant children (4%) than the native born children (1%), however, preferred careers in business and economics. And more native born children (14%) than immigrant children (6%) saw themselves working in the fields of recreation, sports, or tourism. None of the immigrant children wanted to work in skilled occupations or industry compared to 4% of the native born children. Overall, the immigrant children aspired to professionally oriented careers more than the native born children. Dyson surmised that their immigrant status tends to drive them toward higher achievements than their native born peers.

How do you think your culture has influenced your aspirations? How has your family influenced them? Is there a clash between what your community and family expect of you and what you expect of yourself? Talk with people from cultures other than your own and ask them these same questions. How are their answers similar to or different from your own?

Figure 7.6 My Cultural Lens: Differences in Aspirations

President's New Freedom Commission on Mental Health
http://govinfo.library.unt.edu/mentalhealthcommission/index.htm

This Commission was established as part of an effort to promote equality for Americans with disabilities, particularly children and adults with mental illness and emotional disturbances. The Commission has established policies to promote community integration, coordinate services, and maximize the use of existing resources. You may access the Commission's final report to the President at this website.

Recovery and the Conspiracy of Hope
http://www.namiscc.org

In 1996, Dr. Patricia Deegan presented this paper at the Sixth Annual Mental Health Services Conference of

Self-Assessment of Learning

- In the introduction to the strengths-based principles, you were invited to think about a place where you work or volunteer as you read the principles. In what ways are the strengths principles followed in that setting? In what ways are they not followed? If some principles are not followed, what changes could be made at the agency to reflect a strengths orientation?

- Reread Table 7.1, which presents Robert Perske's views on Overprotection and Dignity of Risk. Make a list of the aspects of a "risky" activity that might realistically warrant caution or exemption from participation. Similarly, make a list of aspects of a "risky" activity that could contribute positively to a person's healthy development. How could you assist a participant in discerning the difference between a risk that is prudent and one that is too dangerous?

- The Life Story in Figure 7.2 tells of a professional who almost limited a person's choice and dignity of risk. Can you recall a time when you automatically prejudged a person's capabilities? What was your initial reaction? Where do you think your reaction came from? How could your orientation be adjusted to align more with a strengths approach?

Australia and New Zealand. It is her personal account of living with a diagnosis of chronic undifferentiated schizophrenia. She rejects asking what's wrong with people with psychiatric disorders in favor of changing environments and providing resources that offer people hope for gaining mental wellness.

References

Baldwin, C. K. (2000). Theory, programs, and outcomes: Assessing the challenges of evaluating at-risk youth recreation programs. *Journal of Park and Recreation Administration, 18*(1), 19–33.

Bloemhoff, H. J. (2006). The effect of an adventure-based recreation programme (ropes course) on the development of resiliency in at-risk adolescent boys confined to a rehabilitation centre. *South African Journal for Research in Sport, Physical Education and Recreation, 28*(1), 1–11.

Caldwell, L. L. (2000). Beyond fun and games? Challenges to adopting a prevention and youth development approach to youth recreation. *Journal of Park and Recreation Administration, 18*(1), 1–18.

Deegan, P. (1996). *Recovery and the conspiracy of hope*. National Alliance on Mental Illness—Santa Cruz. Retrieved from http://www.namiscc.org

Deegan, P. (2006). Foreword. In C. A. Rapp & R. J. Goscha (Eds.), *The strengths model: Case management with people with psychiatric disabilities* (2nd ed.). New York, NY: Oxford University Press.

Dyson, L. L. (2005). The lives of recent Chinese immigrant children in Canadian society: Values, aspirations, and social experiences. *Canadian Ethnic Studies Journal, 37*(2), 49–66.

Ellis, J., Braff, E., & Hutchinson, S. (2001). Youth recreation and resiliency: Putting theory into practice in Fairfax County. *Therapeutic Recreation Journal, 35*(4), 307–317.

Fairfax County Department of Community and Recreation Services. (2000). Teen centers 2000 annual report. Fairfax, VA: Author.

Kunc, N., & Van der Klift, E. (1995). *A credo for support* [DVD]. Available from BroadReach Training and Resources at http://www.normemma.com

Perske, R., & Perske, M. (1981). *Hope for the families: New directions for parents of persons with retardation and other disabilities*. Nashville, TN: Abingdon.

President's New Freedom Commission on Mental Health. (2003). *Achieving the promise: Transforming mental health care in America (final report)*. Rockville, MD: Department of Health and Human Services.

Reeve, C. (2002). *Nothing is impossible: Reflections on a new life*. New York, NY: Random House.

Richter, K., & Kaschalk, S. (1996). The future of therapeutic recreation: An existential outcome. In C. Sylvester (Ed.), *Philosophy of therapeutic recreation: Ideas and Issues* (Vol. II). Ashburn, VA: National Recreation and Park Association.

Saleebey, D. (2006). *The strengths perspective in social work practice* (4th ed.). Boston, MA: Allyn & Bacon.

Witt, P. A., & Crompton, J. L. (1997). The protective factors framework: A key for programming for benefits and evaluating for results. *Journal of Park and Recreation Administration, 15*(3), 1–18. Retrieved from https://www.sagamorepub.com

Part II

The Therapeutic Recreation Process in Strengths-Based Practice

---
Part II interprets the heart of our field
—the "therapeutic recreation process"—
in light of strengths-based practice.

"The real voyage of discovery consists not in seeking new landscapes but in having new eyes."

Marcel Proust

*The Green Gentian has four petals, like the four phases of the therapeutic recreation process.
It is an everyday flower, but beautiful and loved.*

Part II Overview

	Chapter 8	*Collaborative Practice in Therapeutic Recreation*	Therapeutic recreation practice is made stronger when we team with others – especially the participant. Learn how and with whom we team in this chapter.
	Chapter 9	*Assessment in Strengths-Based Therapeutic Recreation Practice*	It all starts with assessment. Here we describe assessment basics and principles, and what and how to assess. You'll discover some new strengths-based assessment instruments too.
	Chapter 10	*Planning in Strengths-Based Therapeutic Recreation Practice*	Strengths-oriented planning is person-centered. In this chapter we explain what that means, offer you guiding principles, and describe how to write goals and objectives, among other practical planning approaches.
	Chapter 11	*Implementation in Strengths-Based Therapeutic Recreation Practice*	How can we support participants' goals and aspirations by building on strengths and resources? Here you'll learn implementation strategies from a breadth of positive approaches with both the participant and the environment.
	Chapter 12	*Transition and Inclusion in Strengths-Based Therapeutic Recreation Practice*	When a participant leaves one setting or service for another, planning for transition and inclusion is key to successful flourishing. Learn how to help participants thrive in inclusive settings.
	Chapter 13	*Evaluation in Strengths-Based Therapeutic Recreation Practice*	Evaluation is the final stage in the therapeutic recreation process. You'll learn about evaluation basics, documentation, and strengths-based empowerment evaluation.

Chapter 8
COLLABORATIVE PRACTICE IN THERAPEUTIC RECREATION

A team is like a bouquet of flowers—together more effective than each flower alone.

"Hope is like a road in the country; there was never a road, but when many people walk on it, the road comes into existence."

—*Lin Yutang, Chinese writer and inventor*

OVERVIEW OF CHAPTER 8

- The importance of working on a team in therapeutic recreation practice
- The members of a team in a strengths-based approach
- Person-centered teams: the central role of participants and their circle of support
- Ways teams function: multidisciplinary, interdisciplinary, and transdisciplinary approaches
- An in-depth look at the transdisciplinary team approach
- Collaboration and networking as important competencies on teams
- Advocating for a strengths approach on the team, and using strengths-based language

FOCUS QUESTIONS

- Why are teams important for delivering high-quality therapeutic recreation services in recreation, health, and human services?
- Who are the typical team members with whom you will work in therapeutic recreation practice?
- Why is the participant the most important team member when planning, delivering, and evaluating services?
- What are the differences between multidisciplinary, interdisciplinary, and transdisciplinary teams, and what are the benefits of each approach?
- What skills will you need to be an effective team member in therapeutic recreation practice?

AN OVERVIEW OF TEAMS AND COLLABORATION

Definition of "team":
A distinguishable set of two or more individuals who interact dynamically, interdependently, and adaptively to achieve specified, shared, and valued objectives

Definition of "collaboration":
The act of working jointly; from the Latin word meaning to labor together

In therapeutic recreation, you will rarely work in isolation with a participant. In most settings where therapeutic recreation services are delivered, you will find other skilled and knowledgeable professionals to help ensure the best services for participants. Typically, the groups of professionals who help participants meet valued life outcomes have unique and specialized competencies. When that expertise is used in a collaborative process with the participant, the most effective outcomes are realized. Who are the team members? And what approaches do teams use? What skills do you need to be an effective part of the team? This chapter will explore these questions, and help you more fully appreciate the unique role you play as a therapeutic recreation specialist.

WHY IS A TEAM APPROACH USED IN HEALTH AND HUMAN SERVICES?

Working with a team takes extensive communication, time, energy, and effort on the part of all involved.

Teams may slow down progress, due to conflict or miscommunication, and teams can overwhelm participants and their families with expertise and information. So, with these drawbacks, why bother using a team approach? If you have ever been a part of any type of team, you may recall the frustrations, but also the great sense of purpose and accomplishment that resulted from your effort and participation. The benefits that result from providing services in a team approach far outweigh the drawbacks. Some of these benefits include:

- Teams offer diverse and numerous perspectives across multiple environments.
- Teams enrich the helping process through complementary areas of expertise.
- Teams provide a thorough information base from which to plan and design services and supports.
- Teams can generate more ideas and are more creative than one professional alone.
- Teams have increased resources, information, and expertise at their disposal to benefit the participant.
- When working in a team approach, goals and services are coordinated. Splintered, disjointed, or incomplete services can be avoided more effectively.
- Through the group process, teams can solve problems and resolve conflict more effectively than individual professionals.
- Teams provide needed therapeutic support.
- Teams can provide one point of contact for the participant and his or her circle of support, instead of having the participant work and communicate with several different professionals.
- A team of respected professionals, communicating high expectations, hope, and support, can be a powerful therapeutic change agent for the participant. *Hope is like a road in the country, created by a team that believes in its destination and its traveler.*

In health and human services, where we work with diverse people who have complex life situations, teams are an essential aspect of providing services. Each team member brings specialized knowledge and expertise to the services requested by participants, complementing and coordinating the knowledge and expertise of other team members. Like a beautifully designed quilt, in a collaborative team the whole is greater than the sum of its pieces. Together, collaborative team members can help participants create valued life outcomes. Who are the typical team members with whom you will work in therapeutic recreation, and what role does each member play on the team?

Team Members in Health and Human Services

The Participant and Circle of Support as Key Team Members

"Nothing about us without us" (United Nations, 2004). This tenet from the independent living movement sums up the importance of the role of the participant on a collaborative team. The most important member of any team is **the participant**. In an ecological approach, equally important on the team is the participant's circle of support. A **circle of support** is the network of people in the participant's life that helps him or her reach daily and life goals. The people in the network care about what happens to the participant, advocate for him or her when needed, and believe in what the participant wants for his or her life.

The **person-centered movement** in health and human services, where the participant's dreams and goals are the engine that drives the helping process, empowers participants and their circles of support to have control and responsibility for their own context-specific plans. The role of the rest of the team, whatever its composition, is to help participants make and achieve goals and outcomes that the participants themselves have chosen. Participants and their circles of support are the key decision-makers on an effective, collaborative team. The team, using its expertise, will help identify effective services and supports to help the participant meet valued life outcomes.

As the head of the collaborative team, the role of the participant (and his or her circle of support) is as follows:

- Express dreams and goals honestly and openly.
- Actively assist the team in identifying strengths and a plan that will help meet the goals.
- Clarify and understand all aspects of the plan as it is developed. The participant may need education and information to do this effectively, which the team is obligated to provide.
- Exercise basic rights to choose or decide against services and supports that do not

align with the participant's life situation—the participant (and/or circle of support) knows better than anyone what his or her particular needs and strengths are.

- Ensure that services and supports fit with the participant's culture, values, life situation, and strengths.
- Follow the plan as developed with the team, and communicate openly when any aspects of it do not feel right.
- Communicate openly, respectfully, and frequently with the team.

The team will assist the participant in fulfilling his or her role, providing whatever education, services, or supports are needed to do so.

Person-centered teams have emerged as vital to helping participants achieve their goals and have a high level of well-being. When we give the driver's seat to the participant, we fundamentally change how health and human services have traditionally been delivered. According to Tondora and colleagues (2005):

We must work together to move away from "medical necessity" toward "human need," away from managing illness to promoting recovery, away from deficit-oriented to strengths-based, and away from symptom relief to personally defined quality of life. Perhaps most critical is the fundamental shift in power involved in realigning systems to promote person and/or family-centered planning—the shift away from prioritizing "expert" knowledge over respect for individual autonomy and self-determination. (p. 3)

Therapeutic recreation specialists and other team members must not only learn and understand the strengths and dreams of the participant, they also must learn and understand the cultural context of the participant. Individual autonomy may or may not be something the participant values or strives to achieve, depending on culture. As team members develop cultural competence, they will be better able to empower participants and their supports to work toward the level of well-being they define for themselves (see Figure 8.1).

My Cultural Lens: The Impact of Cultural Incompetence

Dieser (2002) shared two personal narratives of his work as a White therapeutic recreation specialist with two participants from cultures different than his own, one American Indian and one African American. In both cases, the participants terminated services early, and through critical analysis, Dieser concludes that culture insensitivity was a primary cause for failure.

In the first narrative, Dieser describes his interactions with "Floyd," a participant who is American Indian and was at his treatment facility for assistance with addiction. The facility used a cognitive therapy approach, universally applied to all participants in treatment. Floyd struggled with the approach, the lack of acknowledgement of his culture on the part of the team, and the unwillingness of the team to be flexible and work with Floyd's desires to incorporate culturally relevant healing practices into his plan. Floyd eventually left treatment due to dissatisfaction with the program—the team concluded that Floyd was using his cultural differences to maintain denial of his substance abuse issues. Dieser, reflecting on the case, concluded that the team lacked awareness of cultural differences and that led to an inability to modify interventions to meet cultural needs. The team also made the mistake of believing that the facility's treatment program had universal, unilateral applications to all people, regardless of culture. They had difficulty comprehending Floyd's differences in interactional style and values orientation, as these differences did not fit with the worldview they held. Lastly, the team did not take the time to really get to know Floyd as an individual with a different cultural heritage. In sum, Dieser concluded that cultural insensitivity was the main reason Floyd terminated his care sooner than was helpful for him.

In the second narrative, Dieser shares his interaction with "Don," a participant who is African American. Dieser felt resentment from Don throughout the assessment and subsequent interventions. In leisure education groups, with a focus on self-awareness and independent leisure lifestyle, Don struggled to find meaning in the concepts. He shared with the team that his leisure was too intertwined with his family, friends, and church community for him to understand the relevance and meaning of the ideas. Throughout the treatment program, Don expressed the same discontent with the individualistic focus. He terminated services after two weeks without any notification. Dieser concluded that Don's cultural values of dependence in a cooperative group conflicted with the overarching goals of independence that cut across all aspects of treatment.

These two narratives highlight the negative consequences of cultural incompetence on the part of a team. Reflecting back to Chapter 1, where we talked about the five stages of cultural competence, in what stage would you place these two different teams in the narratives above? Cultural destructiveness? Cultural incapacity? Cultural blindness? Cultural pre-competence? Cultural competence? What could the teams in these two stories have done differently, to ensure more successful outcomes for Floyd and Don? What can you learn from these narratives as you work on teams with participants from different cultures?

Figure 8.1 My Cultural Lens: The Impact of Cultural Incompetence

Table 8.1a Typical Team Members in Therapeutic Recreation Practice

Team member	Role	Typical settings where TR works with this team member
Adapted physical educator	Provides physical education which may be adapted or modified to address the individualized needs of children and youth who have gross motor developmental delays (National Consortium for Physical Education and Recreation for Individuals with Disabilities, 2005) **Main focus:** *Physical activity skills*	Schools, adaptive sports programs
Architect	Provides the planning, design, construction, enlargement, conservation, restoration, or alteration of building or spaces (American Institute of Architects, 2006) **Main focus:** *Design of living spaces*	Community parks and recreation, community programs, military recreation, inclusion programs
Art therapist	Uses the creative process of art-making to improve and enhance the physical, mental, and emotional well-being of individuals of all ages (American Art Therapy Association, 2008) **Main focus:** *Expressive arts*	Mental health settings such as psychiatric hospitals or chemical-dependency treatment centers
Athletic trainer	Optimizes activity and participation of patients and clients through the prevention, diagnosis, and intervention of emergency, acute, and chronic medical conditions involving impairment, functional limitations, and disabilities (National Athletic Trainers Association, 2007) **Main focus:** *Physical injury in athletics*	Athletic events and venues, schools, community sports facilities, fitness facilities, colleges and universities
Case manager	Through a collaborative process of assessment, planning, facilitation, and advocacy, helps identify options and services to meet an individual's health needs through communication and available resources to promote quality, cost-effective care (Case Management Society of America, 2008) **Main focus:** *Coordination of services*	Most settings; therapeutic recreation specialists can and often do function as case managers in community-based services, and are able to focus on recreation as an important component of service options
Child Life Specialist	Provides play, preparation, education, and self-expression activities to assist children and families during hospitalization and other pediatric health care (Child Life Council, 2009). Therapeutic recreation specialists can pursue child life certification in addition to their certification in therapeutic recreation by meeting the Child Life Council requirements **Main focus:** *Medical play*	Pediatric hospitals
Dance/ movement therapist	Provides psychotherapeutic use of movement to further the emotional, cognitive, physical, and social integration of the individual; body movement as the core component of dance simultaneously provides the means of assessment and the mode of intervention for dance/movement therapy (American Dance Therapy Association, 2008) **Main focus:** *Movement and dance*	Mental health rehabilitation, medical, and educational settings, extended care facilities, day care, forensic, disease-prevention and health-promotion programs
Dietician	Provides expertise in food, nutrition and health; works on a broad range of issues to advance the nutritional status of people in seven priority areas: aging, child nutrition, food and food safety, health literacy and nutrition advancement, Medical Nutrition Therapy, nutrition research and monitoring, and weight management for health (American Dietetic Association, 2008) **Main focus:** *Nutrition*	Hospitals, extended care facilities, clinics, schools, prisons, public health programs, senior centers
Educator (special educator, teacher)	Provides specifically designed instruction and services to children with disabilities; adapts and develops materials to match the special needs of each student and use a variety of teaching strategies to ensure that students with disabilities reach their learning potential (Council for Exceptional Children, 2007) **Main focus:** *Academic learning of children with disabilities*	Schools, after-school programs, inclusion programs

Table 8.1b Typical Team Members in Therapeutic Recreation Practice (cont'd)

Team member	Role	Typical settings where TR works with this team member
Family and other circle of support members	Provides the substance of the helping relationship by articulating the dreams, goals, and aspirations of the participant; includes family members, close friends and invested professionals that make up the inner circle of support for a participant with a disability, are valued by the participant, and are a daily or very frequent part of the participant's life based on intrinsic motivation and caring **Main focus:** *Dreams and aspirations of participant; quality of life*	All settings
Music therapist	Uses music within a therapeutic relationship to address physical, psychological, cognitive, and social needs of individuals (American Music Therapy Association, 2008) **Main focus:** *Music*	Extended care facilities, psychiatric hospitals
Nurse	Focuses on the protection, promotion, and optimization of health and abilities, prevention of illness and injury, alleviation of suffering through the diagnosis and treatment of human response, and advocacy in the care of individuals, families, communities, and populations (American Nurses Association, 2004) **Main focus:** *Total health of the patient*	Medical settings, camps, schools
Occupational therapist	Helps individuals achieve independence in all facets of their lives; assists people in developing the "skills for the job of living" necessary for independent and satisfying lives (American Occupational Therapy Association, 2008) **Main focus:** *Functioning in occupational roles*	Physical rehabilitation hospitals, schools, psychiatric hospitals, general medical hospitals, extended care facilities
Orthotist and prosthetist (O&P)	Evaluates, fabricates, and custom fits artificial limbs and orthopedic braces (American Academy of Orthotists and Prosthetists, 2008) **Main focus:** *Prosthetic devices*	Physical rehabilitation hospitals and outpatient programs, adaptive sports and outdoor adventure programs, military recreation programs
Pastoral care	Ensures the provision of pastoral, spiritual, and religious care of patients and staff (Association of Professional Chaplains, 2005) **Main focus:** *Spiritual well-being*	Hospitals, extended-care facilities
Physical therapist	Diagnoses and treats individuals of all ages who have medical problems or other health-related conditions that limit their abilities to move and perform functional activities in their daily lives (American Physical Therapy Association, 2008) **Main focus:** *Physical functioning*	Physical rehabilitation hospitals, outpatient rehabilitation programs, adaptive sports and outdoor adventure programs, extended-care facilities
Physician	Diagnoses illnesses and prescribes and administers treatment for people suffering from injury or disease (Bureau of Labor Statistics, 2008a) **Main focus:** *Disease and disorders; medicine*	Medical settings, such as hospitals, clinics, extended-care facilities
Planner	Helps create a broad vision for the community; researches, designs, and develops programs; leads public processes; effects social change; performs technical analyses; manages and educates (American Planning Association, 2007) **Main focus:** *City and community planning*	Community parks and recreation, community programs, military recreation, inclusion programs, senior citizen housing and programs, advocacy associations; social service agencies
Psychiatrist	A medical physician who specializes in the diagnosis, treatment, and prevention of mental illnesses, including substance abuse and addiction (American Psychiatric Association, 2006) **Main focus:** *Mental illness, mental health*	Psychiatric hospitals, mental health centers, child and adolescent residential settings, prisons

Table 8.1c Typical Team Members in Therapeutic Recreation Practice (cont'd)

Team member	Role	Typical settings where TR works with this team member
Recreation professional	Develops and manages comprehensive recreation programs in parks, playgrounds, and other settings; serves as technical advisors to state and local recreation and park commissions; responsible for recreation and park budgets (Bureau of Labor Statistics, 2008b) **Main focus:** *Recreation facilities, programs, and services*	Parks and recreation departments, adaptive sports and outdoor adventure programs, community-based therapy programs, advocacy associations
Social worker	Assists individuals, groups, or communities to restore or enhance their capacity for social functioning, while creating societal conditions favorable to their goals (National Association of Social Workers, 2008) **Main focus:** *Social issues; social functioning; financial coordination (e.g., third party reimbursement)*	All settings
Speech language pathologist	Diagnoses and treats speech, language, cognitive-communication and swallowing disorders (American Speech-Language-Hearing Association, 2007) **Main focus:** *Communication*	Physical rehabilitation, extended-care facilities, schools
Vocational rehabilitation counselor	Assists persons with physical, mental, developmental, cognitive, and emotional disabilities to achieve their personal, career, and independent living goals in the most integrated settings possible through the application of the counseling process (American Rehabilitation Counseling Association, 2005) **Main focus:** *Work*	Developmental disabilities service settings, mental health treatment settings, day treatment programs

Other Team Members

The participant is the key member of a collaborative team. In addition to the participant, the team can be comprised of many different professionals. Table 8.1 provides a description of some of the typical team members with whom we work in therapeutic recreation. The exact composition of a team varies with the system (e.g., healthcare, human services, education, recreation), the agency, and the life circumstances of the participant. Table 8.1 also provides examples of typical settings where therapeutic recreation specialists may work with a particular discipline.

We present some real-life examples below to clarify even further the diversity of teams with whom we collaborate in therapeutic recreation:

Physical Rehabilitation Agency. Craig Hospital, in Denver, Colorado, specializes in spinal cord and brain injury rehabilitation. Craig Hospital uses the following team composition:

> Each patient and family has a consistent team of professionals that includes the *physician, nurses, physical therapist, occupational therapist, patient and family service counselor, therapeutic recreation specialist, psychologist, dietitian,* and when necessary, *speech and language pathologist, neuropsychologist, respiratory therapist,* and others. The team meets regularly with the patient and family to set goals, develop plans, review progress, and coordinate services needed at home following discharge. Craig provides a highly individualized and personal approach to services, focusing on the patient's physical, cognitive, and psychological well-being. Craig sets high expectations for patient participation and helps patients set high expectations for themselves. Therapeutic recreation specialists help patients develop lifelong leisure pursuits and activities. Rehabilitation is serious, but keeping fun in the process helps our patients stay motivated and active following injury. (Craig Hospital, 2010)

Mental Health Agency. Skyland Trail is a community-based residential and day treatment facility for adults with serious mental illness, located in Atlanta, Georgia. Skyland Trail uses the following team approach:

> Skyland Trail's unique philosophy emphasizes incremental progress through which the patient enjoys an improved quality of life, healthier relationships, and enhanced ability to reach his or her personal goals. Symptom containment is an integral part of our approach; however, key outcomes indicators relate mainly to the patient's ability to function effectively and experience quality of life. Multidisciplinary

teams integrate individual-specific interventions based on the client's overall recovery plan. This team includes *primary counselors and experts in nutrition, preventive medical care, psychiatry, pastoral counseling, adjunctive therapies (which include therapeutic recreation, art therapy, music therapy, and drama therapy), and employment/educational services.* (Skyland Trail, 2010)

Long-Term Care Agency. The Center for Nursing and Rehabilitation, a 320-bed skilled nursing facility in Brooklyn, New York uses a person-centered approach in its care. It uses the following team approach:

> The Center for Nursing and Rehabilitation is the first nursing home in New York City organized on the "neighborhood" model which focuses on residents' preferences rather than management's convenience. Living in a "neighborhood" with staff that includes *RNs, LPNs, CNAs, social workers, recreational therapists, dietitians and activity staff,* residents have greater independence in matters of daily living and participate in decisions about how their "neighborhood" will conduct itself. (Center for Rehabilitation and Nursing, 2010)

Educational Agency. Matheny Medical and Education Center, located in Peapack, New Jersey, is a special hospital and educational facility for children and adults with medically complex developmental disabilities. The team at Matheny involves the following personnel and approaches:

> A key to Matheny's educational philosophy is its interdisciplinary approach—integrating therapy treatment, social services, and psychology into the educational program. The expertise of *speech-language pathologists, physical, occupational, music and recreation therapists, social workers and psychologists* is always available and is provided in collaboration with the *classroom teachers*. Recreation Therapy at Matheny provides our patients with a variety of recreation opportunities and resources to improve their physical, emotional, cognitive, and social well being. The recreation therapy program encourages development of leisure, social and community skills through purposeful leisure activities and community trips. (Matheny Medical and Education Center, 2010)

Community Parks and Recreation Agency. The City of Eugene Parks and Recreation, in Eugene, Oregon, offers the Adaptive Recreation Services, which provides year-round, community-based recreational, social, educational, and inclusive programs for Eugene-area children, teens, and adults with disabilities. The department provides participants with the opportunity to develop new skills, enhance awareness of their community and natural environment, build self-confidence, and recognize personal potential. The team composition at Eugene Adaptive Recreation Services is composed of *recreation specialists, educators, outdoor educators, art specialists, fitness instructors, and other educational specialists, all supervised by therapeutic recreation specialists* (Eugene Parks and Recreation, 2010).

These examples highlight the variability in team composition across different service delivery systems. The role of the therapeutic recreation specialist may differ somewhat, depending on the setting, the needs of the participant, and the other members present on the team. However, the core of therapeutic recreation, leisure, well-being, and quality of life is constant and guides our practice as we work with a team of other professionals. We are obligated to learn about and understand what our fellow team members contribute, and how we can most effectively work together to meet the needs of participants, but we are also obligated to stay true to our professional core. As Shank and Coyle (2002) state, "we believe that the profession [therapeutic recreation] must remember its purpose within the community of health-related professionals: promoting and protecting the importance of play, recreation, and leisure in the lives of people with illnesses and disabling conditions" (p. 4).

Team Approaches or Models

In therapeutic recreation, you will experience variability in the team composition. You will also experience variability in the approaches teams use in working with participants and delivering services. There are three common approaches: multidisciplinary, interdisciplinary, and transdisciplinary. Multidisciplinary is the least person-centered and least sophisticated approach, and transdisciplinary is the most person-centered and most sophisticated approach (Rainforth & York-Barr, 1997). Figure 8.2 (p. 166) provides a graphic overview of the three approaches to teams.

In the **multidisciplinary approach**, multiple disciplines contribute to assessment, planning, and service provision, but each discipline works independently,

166 • Therapeutic Recreation Practice: A Strengths Approach

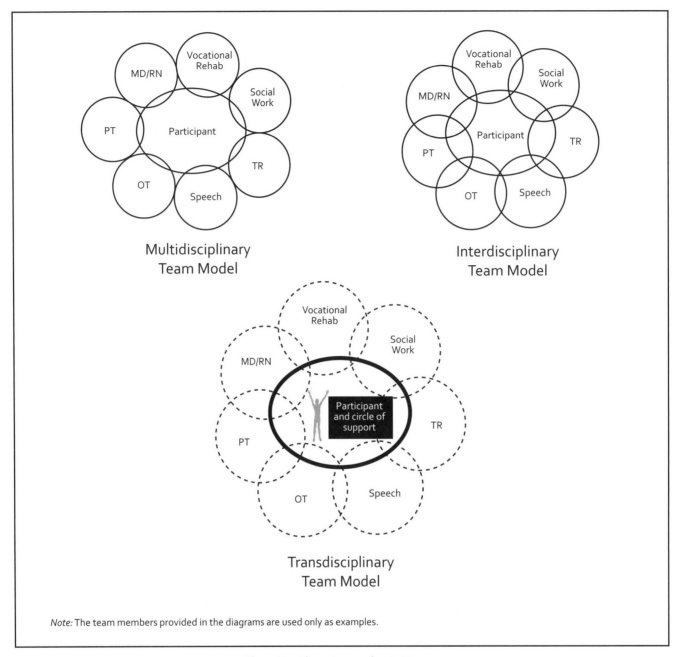

Figure 8.2 Three Approaches to Teams

with little communication across disciplines. In this approach, comprehensive services are provided, but the coordination and integration of services can be fragmented. There is a high risk for duplication of services or for gaps in services.

In the **interdisciplinary approach**, multiple disciplines contribute to assessment, planning, and service provision with formal communication between disciplines established. Services and efforts are coordinated and communicated in an ongoing manner. Though each discipline conducts its own assessment, there is a commitment to shared decision-making and the development of a unified plan. Each discipline then provides its disciplinary services independently of other team members. Because of the coordination and communication, there is less risk for duplication or gaps in services.

In the **transdisciplinary approach**, multiple disciplines work collaboratively to develop a joint plan for assessment, planning, and service implementation. Team members retain responsibility for the expertise of their home discipline, but information and competency from any single discipline is actively transmitted to members of other disciplines. Team members teach, learn, and work across disciplinary boundaries to plan and provide integrated services (see Figure 8.3).

In the transdisciplinary approach, **integrated services** stem from discipline-free goals set by participants

Life Story:

Culture Change at Perham Memorial Hospital and Home

With fishing trips, a private dining room for family gatherings, and a town center to meet up with friends, Perham Memorial Hospital and Home (PMHH), in Perham, Minnesota, looks more like a small community than a nursing home. Residents attend household council meetings and even participate in interviewing prospective employees.

This concept of a "household model" was developed in 2001. The model was implemented in 2004, as staff and residents were divided into six households of 16 residents, each with permanently assigned staff.

As a result of switching to the household model, residents have become more involved in how they live in their households. Residents tell the staff how they want to live: what time they want to get up; what they like to eat; what they want to do for the day; and when they would like to go to bed.

In addition to the households, a Town Center was created as a common meeting area for all residents. Included in the Town Center are a barber/beauty shop, a theatre, a gift store, a chapel, and a Courtyard Café. This gives residents the opportunity to leave their households and "go to town."

PMHH caregivers are cross-trained and certified as nursing assistants to respond quickly to resident needs, no matter what they are. Everyone works hard, doing whatever needs to be done to make PMHH the best possible home.

It's not just the residents and staff who are benefiting from the household model; family members of residents are being given peace of mind. Families don't have the same guilt that they used to have about putting their loved one in a nursing home. It gives them comfort knowing that there is a beautiful home for their family member who is in need of skilled care, and that home is situated in a caring community built by a well-trained team.

Figure 8.3 Life Story of a Culture Change at Perham Memorial Hospital and Home *(Perham Memorial Hospital, 2010)*

and their circles of support. Integrated services are provided in the context of natural environments, during typical daily routines, while doing typical activities. Services are provided by cross-trained team members, using "teachable or therapeutic moments" during a participant's daily life routine. For example, if a participant has a goal to strengthen recreation skills and is working with the occupational therapist on vocational skills, the therapeutic recreation specialist will have trained the occupational therapist on the leisure education program that is part of the participant's plan. The occupational therapist can then assist the participant in using recreation skills during the breaks or lunch hour in the workday, under the supervision of the therapeutic recreation specialist.

Table 8.2 (see p. 168), adapted from Garland and colleagues (1989), compares the three approaches to working with teams. The philosophy, roles, type of communication, and planning and delivery of services are much more integrated in the transdisciplinary approach. The next section will give you a deeper understanding of this approach, as it will likely become a more common model in the future in our field (see Figure 8.4, p. 169).

A Focus on the Transdisciplinary Team Approach

The use of transdisciplinary teams, which has emerged as a best practice, is more effective and more efficient than the other team approaches in helping participants reach their goals in a holistic and person-centered manner. Transdisciplinary teams can lead to the development of shared conceptual frameworks that not only integrate but transcend individual disciplinary perspectives (Mâsse et al., 2008). Transdisciplinary frameworks, which draw from several disciplines and integrate diverse concepts, have the greatest potential to generate novel and truly helpful ways of changing lives for the better. Transdisciplinary teams are characterized by joint decision-making, shared responsibility, frequent and joint evaluation of programs and services, and role release, discussed below. A transdisciplinary team is more complex and requires

Table 8.2 Three Approaches for Collaborative Teams *(Garland, McGonigel, Frank, & Buck, 1989)*

Component	Multidisciplinary	Interdisciplinary	Transdisciplinary
Philosophy of Team Interaction	Team members recognize the importance of contributions from several disciplines.	Team members are willing and able to share responsibility for services among disciplines.	Team members commit to teach, learn, and work across disciplinary boundaries to plan and provide integrated services.
Participant and Family Roles	Generally, participants and families meet with team members separately by discipline.	The participant and family may or may not be considered a team member. Families may work with the whole team or team representatives.	Participants and families are always members of the team and determine their own team roles.
Lines of Communication	Lines of communication are typically informal. Members may not think of themselves as part of a team.	The team meets regularly for case conferences, consultations, etc.	The team meets regularly to share information and to teach and learn across disciplines (for consultations, team building, etc.).
Staff Development	Staff development generally is independent and within individual disciplines.	Staff development is frequently shared and held across disciplines.	Staff development across disciplines is critical to team development and role transition.
Assessment Process	Team members conduct separate assessments by disciplines.	Team members conduct assessments by discipline and share results.	The team participates in an arena assessment, observing and recording across disciplines.
Plan Development	Team members develop separate plans for intervention within their own disciplines.	Goals are developed by discipline and shared with the rest of the team to form a single service plan.	Staff, participant, and family develop plan together based on participant and family goals, priorities, and resources.
Plan Implementation	Team members implement their plan separately by discipline.	Team members implement parts of the plan for which their disciplines are responsible.	Team members share responsibility and are accountable for how the plan is implemented by one person, with the participant and family.

more intentional collaboration, yet the benefits to the participant are powerful.

In the transdisciplinary approach, one team member is the **primary facilitator**, directly interacting with and providing services to a participant on a consistent basis. The primary facilitator can be from any discipline, but is usually chosen based on the needs of the participant and agency caseload. Other team members provide the primary facilitator with the skills and knowledge needed to implement that part of the plan that involves their discipline. The participant develops a consistent and stable relationship with the primary facilitator, rather than having a multitude of more superficial interactions with many different professionals. In essence, the primary facilitator implements the helping process, under the guidance and support of the team, to develop a high-quality and trusting, helping relationship with the participant. The transdisciplinary approach reduces confusion and anxiety for the participant, and reduces fragmented, overlapping, and inconsistent services.

There are six stages of development through which the transdisciplinary team works to achieve the most effective functioning. As a transdisciplinary team matures and reaches the upper levels of development, participants will receive the greatest benefit and quality of services centered on their life situation (Sable, Powell, & Aldrich, 1993/94). Table 8.3 (see p. 170) provides an overview of each level of development of a transdisciplinary team. The developmental process begins with **role extension**, having a deep understanding of one's own discipline. It then moves to **role enrichment**, where team members learn basic information and terminology about other disciplines. The next stage of development is **role expansion**, where team members begin to make observations, judgments, and recommendations within and outside their own disciplines. **Role exchange** is the next developmental level of a transdisciplinary team, where team members begin to implement each other's techniques with participants, under direct supervision of the disciplinary specialist.

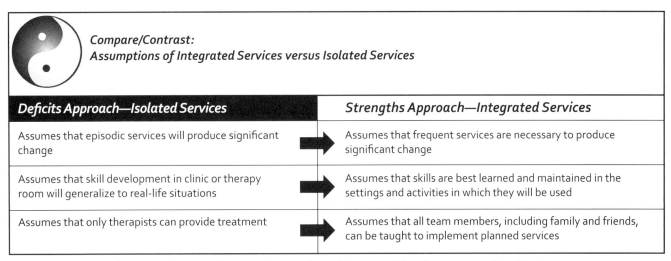

Figure 8.4 Compare/Contrast: Assumptions of Integrated Services versus Isolated Services

Role release is the level at which team members are able to implement the techniques of other disciplines, with consultation from the practitioners of those disciplines. In addition, each discipline is accountable for its services being implemented by other team members. Role release involves sharing general information, so other team members are knowledgeable about basic procedures and practices. A physical therapist might describe to other team members the role of muscle tone in positioning and other tasks. Role release involves sharing skills, so that others can make specific judgments and decisions. For example, a physical therapist teaches a therapeutic recreation specialist to look at a participant in a wheelchair and determine if the participant is positioned correctly. Lastly, role release involves helping other team members develop competencies, so that they can perform specific actions. A therapeutic recreation specialist might teach a parent how to do activity analysis, so the parent can choose activities for her or his child that will best meet the goals in a plan.

Role support is the level at which team members support other disciplines in providing transdisciplinary services. Throughout the transdiscplinary process, each team member provides his or her own discipline's services if they are too complex and not reasonable to transfer to other disciplines, or if they must legally be provided by a practitioner of the discipline.

For transdisciplinary teams to be effective, each team member must be able to clearly and concisely share information with others, and to ask for help without feeling diminished professionally (Kuhlmann, n.d.). Team members must put the goals and aspirations of the participant at the center of what they do, not their professional status or their professional boundaries. In the transdisciplinary approach, professionals retain responsibility for their expertise in a home discipline, but information and competency from any single discipline is actively transmitted to members of other disciplines with the higher goal being to provide the best, most effective service possible for the participant. Jones, Lombardo, and Putnam Boyle (2003) provide a nice example of the use of transdisciplinary teams in therapeutic recreation practice (see Figure 8.5, p. 171).

COLLABORATION AND NETWORKING AS IMPORTANT COMPETENCIES ON TEAMS

Regardless of the type of team or approach you use in your practice of therapeutic recreation, there are key competencies you will need to be an effective team member. Collaboration is one key competency, and networking is another. By developing these two key competencies, you will be a more productive and necessary member of any team.

Collaboration involves working together with others who are different in their expertise, perspectives, values, and communication styles. Collaboration is made up of a complex set of behaviors that you will need to learn and practice to be effective on a team (Anderson & Kress, 2003). Collaboration is more than cooperation with your team members. It can be thought of as a high level of assertive behavior and a high level of cooperativeness on the part of each team member. Figure 8.6 (p. 171) shows the relationship between assertiveness and cooperation.

"Assertiveness" is defined as the ability to express yourself confidently, openly, and honestly, meeting your own needs for contribution to the team while respecting the needs and communication of others. Assertiveness embodies confidence, flexibility, self-respect, and respect for others. "Cooperation" is defined as working toward the same goal with others. Cooperation is not

Table 8.3 Developmental Levels and Characteristics of Transdisciplinary Teams

Level	Characteristics	How Teams Develop and Nurture This Level
Level One: Role Extension	Increasing one's own knowledge and skills in one's own discipline	• Reading research journals and new books in the field • Attending conferences and research symposia • Joining professional organizations • Participating in clinical supervision within the profession
Level Two: Role Enrichment	Developing awareness and understanding of other disciplines; sharing terminology and basic information about each other's practices	• Team meetings and team conferences • Carefully listening to participants and team members • Participating in clinical supervision across disciplines • Attending workshops within agencies across disciplines
Level Three: Role Expansion	Learning how to observe and make judgments and recommendations outside one's own discipline; teaching other disciplines how to observe and make judgments in one's discipline	• Observing other disciplines working with a participant and discussing what was learned • Attending workshops in another field that include "hands-on" training • Rotating the role of primary team facilitator among all service providers
Level Four: Role Exchange	Team members have learned the knowledge and skills of other disciplines sufficiently to begin to implement techniques from these disciplines under direct supervision	• Working side-by-side with team members, providing co-facilitated services • Observing and providing feedback to each other to improve skills across disciplines • Checking for accuracy of judgments and techniques with the discipline being practiced
Level Five: Role Release	Team members put newly acquired skills and knowledge from other disciplines into practice with consultation from other disciplinary team members, who will be accountable for the techniques used	• Having one primary service provider carry out the entire plan with a participant, using approaches from many disciplines to help reach goals • Meeting frequently to discuss services, presenting the "whole" participant to the team and developing new or improved approaches together • Completing continual self-assessment of skills and techniques needed, and asking for help from other disciplines as needed to ensure high quality services • Understanding the limits of one's skills and knowledge, and using other team members to assist where needed
Level Six: Role Support	Team members support other disciplines in providing transdisciplinary services, or they provide services directly if the skills are too complex to reasonably transfer to another discipline or if the law requires it	• Asking for help when it is needed to give the highest quality services in a holistic manner • Offering help when a team member needs it within the discipline, when struggling with more complex interventions • Directly providing the interventions within the discipline which are required by law or are very complex, while sharing progress frequently and openly with the primary facilitator and participant/family

the same as collaboration—cooperation can involve working in a parallel or individual manner, as long as the team members are all pursuing a common goal with their activities. Collaboration involves actively and jointly working together toward a common goal.

When assertiveness and cooperation are both low, avoidance of issues and conflict can occur and less productive solutions are reached. When assertiveness is high and cooperation is low, competitiveness can occur, where individual team members pursue their own needs at others' expense. When assertiveness is low and cooperation is high, compliance and yielding to the dominant point of view can occur. When cooperation and assertiveness are both moderate, compromises can be reached, but it is often a "middle ground" or mediocre solution. These styles of communication and behavior on a team can lead to less productive and positive outcomes for service.

When both assertiveness and cooperation are high on a team, creative thinking occurs, joint decisions can be made, win-win solutions can be reached, and trust and respect are built. This leads to a positive

Primary Source Support: Transdisciplinary Teams in Rehabilitation

Jones, D., Lombardo, M., & Putnam Boyle, A. (2003). Recreational therapy operating within a transdisciplinary team—National Therapeutic Recreation Society-Maine Center for Integrated Rehabilitation. *Parks and Recreation, 38*, 3.

The Maine Center for Integrated Rehabilitation provides day-treatment programs for individuals who have acquired brain injury. Services are provided in participants' homes and communities, as well as at the rehabilitation center. The team at the center includes therapeutic recreation specialists, speech and language therapists, occupational therapists, physical therapists, social workers, neuropsychologists, physiatrists, case managers, nurses, and rehabilitation technicians. The team uses a transdisciplinary approach to services.

Goals are established by the participant and the team together, based on a holistic assessment. Therapeutic recreation specialists on the team oversee their home discipline's knowledge and practices in leisure awareness, interests and pursuits, as well as leisure skills development. They then work collaboratively with other team members to help participants meet short-term and long-term goals, using all aspects of the rehabilitation process. Collaborative practice occurs in many specialized groups and techniques as well, including aquatic therapy, therapeutic horseback riding, pet therapy, computer skills, communication skills, music therapy, art therapy, and other group modalities.

Through the transdisciplinary team, participants are able to improve the quality of their lives in all aspects, from their physical, emotional, and social functioning to self-care, leisure, and community living. The use of the transdisciplinary team approach helps the center and the participant address the complex and varied needs that can result from an acquired brain injury.

Figure 8.5 Primary Source Support: Transdisciplinary Teams in Rehabilitation

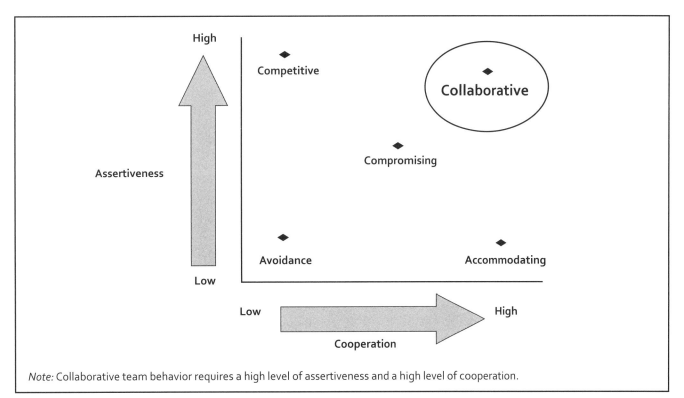

Note: Collaborative team behavior requires a high level of assertiveness and a high level of cooperation.

Figure 8.6 Collaborative Behavior on a Team

upward spiral of more collaborative work as a team. More collaborative teamwork leads to new, integrative frameworks for helping participants reach their desired outcomes (Choi & Pak, 2007).

You can learn and practice the communication and team skills that lead to cooperative and assertive behavior, and thus to high levels of collaboration. In Figure 8.7, we offer a short checklist of the interpersonal skills needed to collaborate on a team (Anderson & Kress, 2003). Complete the self-assessment and identify areas where you do well and where you would like to improve to become a more effective collaborator.

Networking involves connecting people and resources to better meet the needs of participants (Anderson & Kress, 2003). It is the ability to create and maintain a diverse system of resources and information for the purpose of achieving common goals (Lord, 2008). Networking is essential in therapeutic recreation practice due to the diversity of our interventions, our use of community resources in our practice, and our need to do our work across several service systems. Networks are built by learning all you can about your community and service area, having good working relationships, and maintaining the trust of those in your network. Networks provide many benefits, including enhanced services, improved communication, increased resources, increased diversity, and a greater ability to meet the wide variety of needs of the participants with whom we work. For example, you may work in a facility that does not have a swimming pool, yet many participants could benefit from aquatic therapy. The local YMCA, as a part of your network, allows you to use its swimming pool during a slow time in the schedule. In exchange, you help with disability awareness training for the YMCA staff on a monthly basis. This example of a mutually beneficial partnership is how networks are built and maintained.

Collaborative skills and networking are competencies you can continue to build in your practice of therapeutic recreation. The more you are able to master these competencies, building an effective team and a large network, the more effective you will be in your ability to help participants, as you will have amplified your impact with the help of many others.

Advocating for a Strengths Approach on the Team

In therapeutic recreation, you will work in many settings with a variety of differently trained team members. Many team members will have most of their experience and training in the deficits-based culture, using a medical model to plan and deliver services. The ideas, perceptions, and language used by other team members will reflect the past experiences they have had. In addition, you may work in a facility or service setting where services are driven by pathology. Funding and resources are procured through identifying a diagnosis or problem list. Of any member on the team, the therapeutic recreation specialist is best situated to advocate for a strengths approach, even when operating within a remedial model. Advocacy for a strengths approach on a team can take two forms: language and focus.

Language

Language is powerful. Our words can shape our perceptions and actions. Our actions in turn shape our habits and thus our culture. By changing language, we can begin to change the culture in which a team works. Figure 8.8 (p. 174) provides some examples of ways we can shift our language to a strengths approach in daily interactions with team members, regardless of our service setting or population. Reframing how we talk about the participants with whom we work can change the culture of our team and have a powerful impact on our perceptions of participants.

Because of your education and training in a strengths approach in therapeutic recreation, you may have more awareness and a higher sensitivity to the kind of language used on teams. It is important to advocate for the use of more positive and sensitive language in a consistent way. The first step you can take is to demonstrate how to use positive language in all interactions with team members.

Focus

Recall from Chapter 2 the concept from neuroscience that "what we focus on increases." It is imperative that, when helping others, we focus attention on dreams, strengths, and aspirations. In many settings, you will find yourself on teams where there is an overwhelming focus on dysfunction, pathology, and remediation. You may be the only team member who gives voice to the participants' strengths, dreams, and aspirations. The team may have narrowed its focus to what is weak and defective about participants, to the exclusion of what is strong and healthy, seeing abnormality over normality, or poor adjustment over healthy adjustment (Maddux, 2008). Drawing the focus of the team to the participant's strengths and dreams is a vital contribution therapeutic recreation can make. Doing so can help the team more effectively develop a productive relationship with the participant, one built on mutual respect.

Assess Your Interpersonal Skills for Collaboration

On a 5-point scale (1 = "I never do"; 2= "I seldom do"; 3= "I sometimes do"; 4= "I usually do"; 5 = "I always do"), rate yourself on the following skills:

FORMING SKILLS
(skills needed to build initial trust in a partnership)

____ I encourage everyone to participate.
____ I use members' names.
____ I use no "put-downs."
____ I get to meetings on time.
____ I ask for opinions and elaboration.

FUNCTIONING SKILLS
(skills needed to manage and organize team activities so that tasks are completed and relationships are maintained)

____ I offer ideas.
____ I state and restate the purpose of the meeting.
____ I offer procedures on how to most effectively do a task.
____ I volunteer for a task.
____ I express support and acceptance.
____ I ask for help, clarification, or technical assistance.
____ I offer to explain or clarify.
____ I show enthusiasm and optimism.
____ I am non-judgmental of others' contributions.

FORMULATING SKILLS
(skills needed to stimulate creative problem-solving and decision-making)

____ I summarize what has been discussed.
____ I encourage assigning of specific roles.
____ I seek accuracy of information by adding to summaries or questioning.
____ I ask for feedback in a non-confrontational way.

FERMENTING SKILLS
(skills needed to manage controversy and conflict and stimulate refinement of solutions)

____ I see ideas from other persons' perspectives.
____ I criticize ideas without criticizing people.
____ I integrate different ideas/opinions into a single position.
____ I ask for justification of others' conclusions or ideas.
____ I extend or build on others' ideas.
____ I help decide next steps.
____ I generate additional strategies.
____ I test reality of ideas by assessing the feasibility of their implementation.
____ I help compromise, harmonize.

Figure 8.7 Assess Your Interpersonal Skills for Collaboration *(reprinted with permission from Anderson & Kress, 2003)*

In therapeutic recreation, because our practice revolves around the leisure experience in naturalized, normal settings, we often have the opportunity to see the participant from a "strengths lens." Other team members, because of their roles, often only see pathology, deficits, and dysfunction. Our unique gift, as a transdisciplinary team member, is to constantly help the team focus on strengths.

SUMMARY

Therapeutic recreation specialists almost always work on a team of professionals from other disciplines when providing services to participants. A team approach provides many benefits, from increased coordination of services to improved outcomes. The composition of a team varies, depending on the service system and needs of the participant. However, the participant

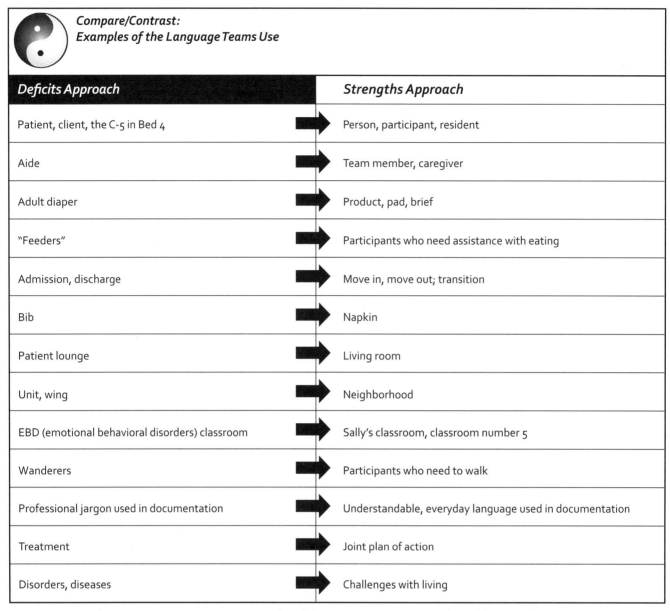

Figure 8.8 Compare/Contrast: Examples of the Language Teams Use *(adapted from Maddux, 2008)*

and his or her circle of support are the consistent key members of any team. Team members can range from nurses to occupational therapists to special education teachers. The approaches teams use can vary as well, from multidisciplinary, to interdisciplinary, to transdisciplinary. Transdisciplinary teams, where team members practice role release, provide the most integrated and person-centered services (see Figure 8.9). To be an effective team member, you must develop and use competencies in collaborative behavior and networking. You must also have a solid, confident grasp of your own disciplinary knowledge and skills (see Figure 8.10, p. 176). Lastly, as a therapeutic recreation specialist practicing from a strengths approach, you have a unique contribution to make to the team as a strengths advocate.

Working on a team is one of the great rewards of being a therapeutic recreation specialist. You grow and learn daily, extending your knowledge beyond your own discipline.

The next four chapters of the book will provide you with a clear understanding, from a strengths approach, of the heart of therapeutic recreation practice: assessment, planning, implementation, and evaluation.

Primary Source Support: Transdisciplinary Teams in Education

Sable, J., Powell, L., & Aldrich, L. (1993/94). Transdisciplinary principles in the provision of therapeutic recreation services in inclusionary school settings. *Annual in Therapeutic Recreation, 4,* 69–81.

Sable, Powell, and Aldrich describe a model of transdisciplinary teaming using a collaborative approach in an educational setting. In the model, the entire educational team, made up of teachers, parents, and related service providers (including therapeutic recreation), identifies one set of educational goals to be focused on in the IEP (Individualized Education Plan). The assessment is completed as a team, and a creative problem-solving approach is used to identify solutions for the student. The team uses the following collaborative skills:

- Creative problem-solving and brainstorming
- Obtaining and sharing information across disciplines
- Consensual decision-making
- Careful planning and coordination
- Creation of a sense of partnership by integrating assessments, plans, and techniques
- Constant communication within the team

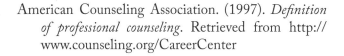

The team identifies environments seen as meaningful to the student across life domains such as work, school, leisure, community living, and home. Instruction occurs in those environments, in the most ordinary and typical settings possible. When needed, additional assessment may be completed by a particular discipline. For example, when the team observes that the student continues to be isolated on the playground and in the lunchroom, the therapeutic recreation specialist may complete a leisure assessment, such as the *Leisure Diagnostic Battery*, to help the student gain more leisure skills.

The transdisciplinary team, using collaborative skills, is able to best meet the needs of the student and parents, with the least amount of unnecessary duplication.

Figure 8.9 Primary Source Support: Transdisciplinary Teams in Education

Resources

The Center for Effective Collaboration and Practice
http://cecp.air.org/center.asp

The Center for Effective Collaboration and Practice has a wealth of information and resources, such as the best practices in collaborative practice, "mini-webs" on topics important to collaborative practice, interactive discussions, and information on topics ranging from strengths-based assessment to wraparound services. A network of "greenhouse" and "nursery" programs is provided. Greenhouse programs are those that have validated their best practices, and nursery programs are those that are demonstrating emerging best practices.

References

American Academy of Orthotists and Prosthetists. (2008). *AAOP position statement.* Retrieved from http://www.opcareers.org

American Art Therapy Association. (2008). *About art therapy.* Retrieved from http://www.arttherapy.org

American Counseling Association. (1997). *Definition of professional counseling.* Retrieved from http://www.counseling.org/CareerCenter

American Dance Therapy Association. (2008). *Who we are.* Retrieved from http://www.adta.org

American Dietetic Association. (2008). *What is a registered dietician?* Retrieved from http://www.eatright.org

American Institute of Architects. (2006). *UIA accord on recommended international standards of professionalism in architectural practice.* Retrieved from http://www.aia.org

American Music Therapy Association. (2008). *A career in music therapy.* Retrieved from http://www.musictherapy.org

American Nurses Association. (2004). *About nursing.* Retrieved from http://www.nursingworld.org

Life Story:

A Therapeutic Recreation Specialist's Experience on a Transdisciplinary Team

For many years, I worked closely with a team in a psychiatric setting. Our core team, led by a psychiatrist, was comprised of the participant and his or her family, therapeutic recreation specialist, nurse, occupational therapist, social worker, and dietitian. When needed, we brought other disciplines, such as psychologists, chaplains, art therapists, or physical therapists, onto the team to help us with unique needs of a participant. We used a therapeutic community model, where every aspect of the environment was an opportunity for helping, from meals to formal group therapy sessions.

Our core team was closely knit, and had evolved to a level of role release whenever possible. Many group sessions, from assertiveness skills to relaxation training to wellness, were facilitated across disciplines. We provided frequent in-services to each other on our own discipline's scope of practice and techniques. This approach furthered role enhancement and role exchange, and fostered a sense of invitation among team members to join in each others' practice. Obvious areas of care were always delivered by appropriate disciplines. For example, medications and vital signs were always completed by nursing staff, dietitians always completed complicated meal plans, and the like. On the team, the therapeutic recreation specialists almost exclusively delivered community integration and community-based modalities.

Often, when working with participants in the community, I would see a whole different person than the rest of the team. Because of the naturally occurring high expectations, natural supports, and consequences of being in a community setting, instead of in a hospital unit, participants would often rise to the occasion and show much more functional behavior. In team meetings, I would very purposefully share my observations of participants, focusing the team's attention to what the participant *could do* when in a setting that facilitated a higher level of behavior. This focus on capability was an invaluable contribution and was recognized as necessary by other team members as a corrective to the behavior they saw on the hospital wing.

When time permitted, which was rare, I would invite other team members to join me in a community integration activity. The effect was invariably the same, where team members shifted their expectations of the "patient" to a new, higher level—that of community member. This shift changed how they approached participants in their own work in a positive way.

Because of the level of trust, the constant sharing of information, and the use of role release, as a team, we were able to truly help people on their path to recovery. As a therapeutic recreation specialist, because of my focus on strengths, I was able to impact not only the quality of life of participants, but the quality of work of other team members.

Figure 8.10 Life Story: A Therapeutic Recreation Specialist's Experience on a Transdisciplinary Team

American Occupational Therapy Association. (2008). *What is occupational therapy?* Retrieved from http://www.aota.org

American Physical Therapy Association. (2008). *Who are PTs?* Retrieved from http://www.apta.org

American Planning Association. (2007). *About planning*. Retrieved from http://www.planning.org/aboutplanning/whatisplanning.htm#2

American Psychiatric Association. (2006). *Let's talk facts*. Retrieved from http://www.healthyminds.org

American Psychological Association. (2008). *What psychology is*. Retrieved from http://www.apa.org/topics/psychologycareer.html

American Rehabilitation Counseling Association. (2005). *Scope of practice for rehabilitation counseling*. Retrieved from http://www.arcaweb.org

American Speech-Language-Hearing Association (2007). *Speech-language pathology*. Retrieved from http://www.asha.org

Anderson, L., & Kress, C. (2003). *Inclusion: Including people with disabilities in parks and recreation opportunities*. State College, PA: Venture Publishing, Inc.

Association of Professional Chaplains. (2005). *Pastoral care providers are members of the healthcare team in accordance with the regulations of the Department of Health & Human Services*. Retrieved from http://www.professionalchaplains.org/index.aspx?id=228

Self-Assessment of Learning

Working on teams requires skills and knowledge in **collaboration** and **transdisciplinary approaches**. Take this assessment to see where you rate in terms of your comfort level, skills, and knowledge about collaboration. If you do not yet work on a health or human service team, rate yourself on teams you are currently a part of, such as class project groups. Scoring directions are given at the end of the scale.

Collaboration and Transdisciplinary Rating Scale

Please evaluate the collaboration within your team by indicating if the collaboration is
(1) inadequate, (2) poor, (3) satisfactory, (4) good, or (5) excellent by checking the appropriate box.

Collaboration within Your Team	1	2	3	4	5
1. Acceptance of new ideas					
2. Communication among collaborators					
3. Ability to capitalize on the strengths of different team members					
4. Organization or structure of collaborative teams					
5. Resolution of conflicts among collaborators					
6. Ability to accommodate different working styles of collaborators					
7. Involvement of collaborators from outside the center					
8. Involvement of collaborators from diverse disciplines					
9. Productivity of collaboration meetings					
10. Productivity in developing services and supports					
11. Overall productivity of collaboration					

Please rate your views about collaboration with respect to your team-related services by indicating if you
(1) strongly disagree, (2) somewhat agree, (3) are not sure, (4) somewhat agree, or (5) strongly agree with the statement.

Collaborative Team-Related Services	1	2	3	4	5
12. Collaboration has improved my productivity.					
13. Collaboration has improved the quality of my services.					
14. Collaboration has posed a significant time burden in my work.					
15. I am comfortable showing limits or gaps in my knowledge to those with whom I collaborate.					
16. I feel that I can trust the colleagues with whom I collaborate.					
17. I find that my collaborators are open to criticism.					
18. I respect my collaborators.					

Please rate the following attitudes about transdisciplinary teamwork by indicating if you
(1) strongly disagree, (2) somewhat agree, (3) are not sure, (4) somewhat agree, or (5) strongly agree with the statement.

Attitudes about Transdisciplinary Teamwork	1	2	3	4	5
19. I would describe myself as someone who strongly values transdisciplinary collaboration.					
20. Transdisciplinary teamwork interferes with my ability to maintain knowledge in my primary area.					
21. I tend to be more productive working on my own rather than working as a member of a transdisciplinary team.					
22. In a transdisciplinary team, it takes more time to produce results.					
23. Transdisciplinary teamwork stimulates me to change my thinking.					
24. I have changed the way I pursue an idea because of my involvement in transdisciplinary work.					
25. Transdisciplinary teamwork has improved how I work with participants.					
26. I am optimistic that transdisciplinary work among participants will lead to valuable outcomes that would not have occurred without that kind of collaboration.					
27. Participating in a transdisciplinary team improves the interventions that are developed.					
28. Because of my involvement in transdisciplinary teams, I have an increased understanding of what my own discipline brings to others.					
29. My transdisciplinary collaborations are sustainable over the long haul.					
30. I believe that the benefits of transdisciplinary work outweigh the inconveniences and costs of such work.					
31. I am comfortable working in a transdisciplinary environment.					
32. Overall, I am pleased with the effort I have made to engage in transdisciplinary teamwork.					
33. My team members as a group are open-minded about considering perspectives from fields other than their own.					

To score the Collaboration and Transdisciplinary Rating Scale, see p. 178

(adapted from Mâsse et al., 2008)

Self-Assessment of Learning

To score the Collaboration and Transdisciplinary Rating Scale:

_____ **Satisfaction with Collaboration** (Items 1–8)
Add the responses you have for items 1–8, divide the total by 8, and enter in the blank line. The higher the number, the more satisfied you are with the level and quality of collaboration on your team.

_____ **Impact of Collaboration** (Items 9–14)
Add the responses you have for items 9–14. For item 14, reverse the scoring (for example, if you answered 1, give yourself a 5). Divide the total by 6, and enter in the blank line. The higher the number, the more you feel collaboration has had a positive impact on your work.

_____ **Trust and Respect** (Items 15–18)
Add the responses you have for items 15–18, divide by 4, and enter in the blank line. The higher the number, the more you experience trust and respect on your team.

_____ **Transdisciplinary Integration** (Items 19–33)
Add the responses you have for items 19–33. For items 20, 21, and 22, reverse the scoring (for example, if you answered 1, give yourself a 5). Divide the total by 15 and enter in the blank line. The higher the number, the more your team has moved to using a transdisciplinary approach in an effective manner.

_____ **TOTAL SCORE**
Add all four scores above, and divide the total by 4.

Are there areas you would like to improve your experience and skills in being a member of a transdisciplinary team? What are your areas of strength?

Bureau of Labor Statistics. (2008a). *Occupational outlook handbook: Physicians and surgeons.* Retrieved from http://www.bls.gov/oco/ocos074.htm

Bureau of Labor Statistics. (2008b). *Occupational outlook handbook: Recreation workers.* Retrieved from http://www.bls.gov/oco/ocos058.htm

Case Management Society of America. (2008). *What is a case manager?* Retrieved from http://www.cmsa.org

Center for Rehabilitation and Nursing. (2010). *Culture change.* Retrieved from http://www.ipro.org

Child Life Council. (2009). *What is a child life specialist?* Retrieved from http://www.childlife.org/The%20Child%20Life%20Profession/

Choi, B., & Pak, A. (2007). Multidisciplinarity, interdisciplinarity, and transdisciplinarity in health research, services, education and policy: 2. Promoters, barriers, and strategies for enhancement. *Clinical and Investigative Medicine, 30*(6), E224–E232.

Council for Exceptional Children. (2007). *Your career in special education.* Retrieved from http://www.cec.sped.org/Content/NavigationMenu/ProfessionalDevelopment

Craig Hospital. (2010). *Teams.* Retrieved from http://www.craighospital.org/About/OverviewOfHospital.asp

Dieser, R. (2002). A personal narrative of a cross-cultural experience in therapeutic recreation: Unmasking the masked. *Therapeutic Recreation Journal, 36*(1), 84–96.

Eugene Parks and Recreation. (2010). *Adapted recreation.* Retrieved from http://www.eugene-or.gov/portal/server.pt?open=512&objID=234&PageID=0&cached=true&mode=2&userID=2

Garland, C., McGonigel, J., Frank, A., & Buck, D. (1989). *The transdisciplinary model of service delivery.* Lightfoot, VA: Child Development. Retrieved from http://www.cdl.unc.edu/

Jones, D., Lombardo, M., & Putnam Boyle, A. (2003). Recreational therapy operating within a transdisciplinary team—National Therapeutic Recreation Society-Maine Center for Integrated Rehabilitation. *Parks and Recreation, 38,* 3.

Kuhlmann, M. (n.d.). *Transdisciplinary teams: An evolving approach in rehabilitation.* Retrieved from http://pmch.utmb.edu

Lord, M. (2008). Professional opportunities in therapeutic recreation. In T. Robertson & T. Long (Eds.), *Foundations of therapeutic recreation: Perceptions, philosophies, and practices for the 21st century.* Champaign, IL: Human Kinetics.

Maddux, J. (2008). Positive psychology and the illness ideology: Toward a positive clinical psychology. *Applied Psychology: An International Review, 57,* 54–70.

Mâsse, L., Moser, R., Stokols, D., Taylor, B., Marcus, S., Morgan, G., Hall, K., Croyle, R., & Trochim, W. (2008). Measuring collaboration and transdisciplinary integration in team science. *American Journal of Preventative Medicine, 35*(2S), S151–S160.

Matheny Medical and Education Center. (2010) *About Matheny.* Retrieved from http://www.matheny.org

National Association of Social Workers. (2008). *Social work profession.* Retrieved from http://www.socialworkers.org/pressroom/features/general/profession.asp

National Athletic Trainers Association. (2007). *Definition of athletic training.* Retrieved from http://www.nata.org/about_AT/terminology.htm

National Consortium for Physical Education and Recreation for Individuals with Disabilities. (2005). *What is adapted physical education?* Retrieved from http://www.pecentral.org/adapted/adaptedwhatis.html

Perham Memorial Hospital. (2010). *Nursing home.* Retrieved from http://www.pmhh.com/content_106.php

Rainforth, B., & York-Barr, J. (1997). *Collaborative teams for students with severe disabilities: Integrating therapy and education* (2nd ed.). Baltimore, MD: Paul H. Brookes.

Sable, J., Powell, L., & Aldrich, L. (1993/94). Transdisciplinary principles in the provision of therapeutic recreation services in inclusionary school settings. *Annual in Therapeutic Recreation, 4,* 69–81.

Shank, J., & Coyle, C. (2002). *Therapeutic recreation in health promotion and rehabilitation.* State College, PA: Venture Publishing, Inc.

Skyland Trail. (2010). *Programs and services.* Retrieved from http://www.skylandtrail.org/programs-and-services

Tondora, J., Pocklington, S., Gorges, A., Osher, D., & Davidson, L. (2005). *Implementation of person-centered care and planning: From policy to practice to evaluation.* Washington, DC: Substance Abuse and Mental Health Services Administration. Retrieved from http://www.yale.edu/PRCH/pdf/ProgramReferences.pdf

United Nations. (2004). *Nothing about us without us.* Retrieved from http://www.un.org/esa/socdev/enable/iddp2004.htm

Chapter 9
ASSESSMENT IN STRENGTHS-BASED THERAPEUTIC RECREATION PRACTICE

*If one focuses on the thorn, the rose would be discarded.
If one focuses on the bloom, the rose is highly valued.*

"The greatest good you can do for another is not just to share your riches but reveal to him his own."

—Benjamin Disraeli, Nineteenth-century statesman and author

OVERVIEW OF CHAPTER 9

- The importance of assessment to therapeutic recreation practice
- Principles that guide assessment in strengths-based practice
- Assessment basics
- Process of assessment
- Focus of assessment in therapeutic recreation
- Assessment resources for therapeutic recreation practice

FOCUS QUESTIONS

- Why is assessment important to therapeutic recreation practice?
- What strengths-based principles guide assessment?
- What do you need to know about assessment to ensure quality?
- When and how do you complete the assessment process with participants?
- On what do you focus in assessment?
- What are some strengths-based tools available to help you with assessment in therapeutic recreation practice?

AN OVERVIEW AND RATIONALE FOR ASSESSMENT

A definition of "assessment":
The act of estimating the nature, quality, ability, extent, or significance of something

A definition of "discovery":
The process of making something known and visible

The therapeutic recreation process is a universal approach to working with participants, no matter where you work or which delivery system you use. The therapeutic process—assess, plan, implement, and evaluate (APIE)—is grounded by assessment. It is the first step in discovering who the participant is, what he or she aspires to, and how you may be able to help. Another way to conceptualize the therapeutic recreation process in a strengths-based approach is:

- Discover (assess)
- Dream, Design (plan)
- Deliver (implement)
- Deliberate (evaluate)

Remember that therapeutic recreation is the purposeful and careful facilitation of quality leisure experiences and the development of personal and environmental strengths that lead to greater well-being for people. In order to be purposeful, we need to learn all we can about participants and their environments in order to best help them achieve their goals and dreams. Because participants may have life circumstances, such as illness or disability, that necessitate individualized assistance, assessment helps us know what the most effective interventions will be. Assessment allows us to get to know the participant as a whole person in the environment, and find out what is meaningful for him or her. It helps us learn what makes a person "tick." The rest of the therapeutic recreation process is driven by what we discover about participants during assessment. The plan, how it is implemented, and what we evaluate, all rest on the foundation of a well-completed assessment process. There are several other reasons why assessment is important.

Builds a Positive Relationship

We begin the development of a positive relationship with the participant while completing the assessment. We can build rapport and trust in the initial assessment process that will contribute to the helping process over time. We can set the helping process in motion in a constructive way by underscoring strengths and dreams. We can communicate the need for a collaborative relationship, and involve the participant in a positive way as, together, we move toward planning.

Establishes a Baseline

Assessment allows us to establish a baseline before we begin services. We can document strengths and competencies and establish positive expectations. From this baseline, we are better able to determine the extent and impact of services, either to the person or to his or her environment. This in turn helps us evaluate outcomes from our services, and gauge the effectiveness of our approaches. Seeing change from baseline, or the start of services, helps participants gain insight and feel a sense of achievement as goals are reached.

Provides the Right Services

Assessment helps us provide the "right" services and supports to participants. When we know the person's strengths, interests, contexts, and goals, we can better plan with that person. We can orient services to fit the context and life view of a participant, to capitalize on strengths, and to help the participant move toward goals and dreams. We can provide targeted and well-thought-out interventions.

Is Solution-Focused

Assessment helps us focus on solutions and not on problems. By asking the right questions and learning about the whole person, we can discover what a person wants and how to best help. For some participants, this focus on strengths and solutions may be new, and may uncover things that help them reframe how they view themselves and their lives. Some of the participants with whom we work have been in the "system" long enough to start seeing themselves as their label, since this is often the focus of services and professionals. Focusing on labels, diagnoses, and problems in assessment only helps us get clearer on what is wrong and what the person does poorly, not what the person can do, or to help a person achieve their aspirations. A strengths-based, solution-focused view helps us shape hopeful and positive expectations.

Supports Team Collaboration

Assessment helps us along the path to strong collaboration with the team of professionals with whom we work. Assessment, when done with the participant and the team, provides a thorough and complete look into what the participant wants and who can best help. Other professionals gain a deeper understanding of therapeutic recreation services as they collaborate with us in the assessment process. We in turn learn more about other disciplines and their focus, and how we can best work together to help the participant.

Meets Professional Standards of Practice

Lastly, assessment is required by professional standards of practice in therapeutic recreation, and is often mandated by regulatory bodies that oversee services at health and human service agencies. In therapeutic recreation, professional standards of practice state that an individualized and systematic assessment must be completed in a timely manner and the results used to develop an individualized plan (ATRA, 2000; CTRA, 2006; NTRS, 2004).

WHAT IS ASSESSMENT?

Assessment is a treasure hunt! It is the systematic process of learning about a person and his or her strengths and aspirations for leisure and well-being. Here is a more formal definition of assessment:

> Assessment is a **systematic process** for gathering **specific information** about an **individual and his or her environment** for the purpose of identifying aspirations and strengths and **collaboratively making decisions** about the individual's **plans.**

Let's break this definition down and study it carefully. A ***systematic process*** means that the assessment process can be repeated in a consistent manner and is valid, reliable, and documented. A systematic process means that all therapeutic recreation staff approach assessment in the same manner and are able to train other transdisciplinary team members in that process. It means the results of assessments are reported in a consistent manner, to the participant and to the team. It means that the assessment process has been evaluated and continually improved.

Gathering specific information means that the assessment focuses on those areas of practice defined by a well-articulated service model. It means understanding the participant's dreams and goals, as well as his or her functional, leisure, and environmental strengths and resources available to help achieve aspirations.

About the individual and his or her environment means that the assessment is person-centered, focused on individual strengths, interests, expectations, and aspirations. The assessment also looks at the unique context of the individual, and takes into account his or her circle of support, community, and culture.

To collaboratively make decisions about the plan means that what we learn during the assessment process about aspirations and expectations will help us choose goals with the participant and other team members. What we learn about strengths and interests can help us choose approaches and interventions. What we learn about the environment can help us identify supports and resources. The gap, or difference, between the participant's aspirations and the current situation can help us identify needed services and help us prioritize efforts as a team.

A simple framework to think about assessment is shown in Figure 9.1. Assessment focuses on learning about the participant, learning about a person's goals and his or her environment, and identifying where necessary supports and services can be facilitated to bridge any gaps. Assessment is about amplifying the "well part" of the participant, to help mobilize him or her on the path to a flourishing life.

Assessment is like a treasure hunt in that you help to discover the strengths, interests, talents, and competencies of a participant. Assessment is like a treasure hunt in that you have a map, the systematic process, to guide you. Assessment is like a treasure hunt in that you start with the "whole island," the initial contact or screening, and when the exact location of the treasure is identified, you narrow down your search and become more specific, using more specialized tools and the help of your fellow treasure-hunters, your team. In this chapter, we give you many examples of specific and specialized strengths-based assessment tools you can use in therapeutic recreation. Assessment is like a treasure hunt in that, in the end, you find the richness of the treasure: a participant developing a flourishing life!

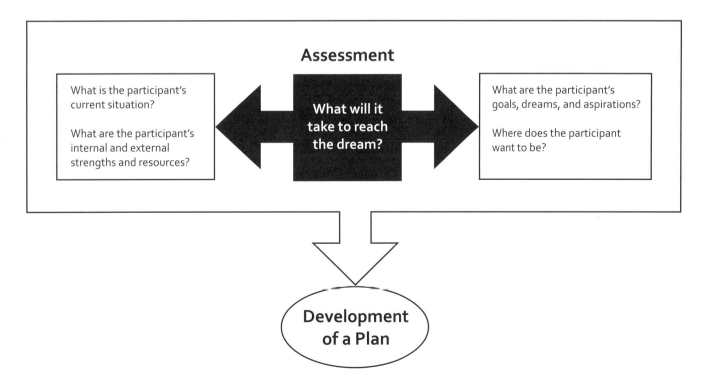

Figure 9.1 A Conceptual Diagram of the Components of Assessment

Principles to Guide Strengths-Based Assessment in Therapeutic Recreation Practice

Strengths-based assessment in therapeutic recreation is guided by assumptions and principles. Making these ideas explicit will help you as you work with all kinds of people in all kinds of environments. Because so much of assessment in health and human services has been oriented to deficits and problems, it is helpful to compare these two approaches (see Figure 9.2).

Cowger, Anderson, and Snively (2006), Rudolph and Epstein (2000), and Saleebey (2006) provide these important **guidelines** for strengths-based assessment:

- Give primacy to participants' perspectives. They are experts in their own lives.
- Believe participants. Support and validate their life story.
- Discover what participants want. What are their aspirations, goals, and dreams? Honor self-determination, which is so crucial to well-being.
- Direct assessment toward personal and environmental strengths. These are keys to creatively working toward goals and negotiating any obstacles.
- Make the assessment of strengths multidimensional, using the expertise of the whole team. When participants, their circles of support, and professionals with differing areas of expertise communicate among themselves, goals become more attainable through a comprehensive assessment of strengths and resources across one's life.
- Discover participants' uniqueness, and avoid labels and stereotypes as a shortcut to understanding a person. Understanding normative behavior is helpful only in that it enriches our understanding of a person's uniqueness.

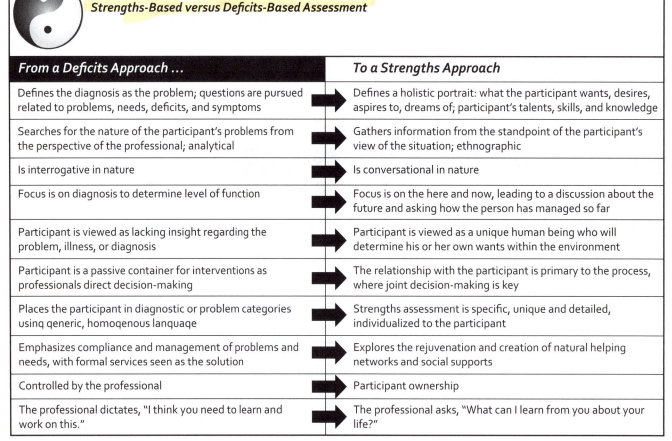

Compare/Contrast: Strengths-Based versus Deficits-Based Assessment

From a Deficits Approach …	To a Strengths Approach
Defines the diagnosis as the problem; questions are pursued related to problems, needs, deficits, and symptoms	Defines a holistic portrait: what the participant wants, desires, aspires to, dreams of; participant's talents, skills, and knowledge
Searches for the nature of the participant's problems from the perspective of the professional; analytical	Gathers information from the standpoint of the participant's view of the situation; ethnographic
Is interrogative in nature	Is conversational in nature
Focus is on diagnosis to determine level of function	Focus is on the here and now, leading to a discussion about the future and asking how the person has managed so far
Participant is viewed as lacking insight regarding the problem, illness, or diagnosis	Participant is viewed as a unique human being who will determine his or her own wants within the environment
Participant is a passive container for interventions as professionals direct decision-making	The relationship with the participant is primary to the process, where joint decision-making is key
Places the participant in diagnostic or problem categories using generic, homogenous language	Strengths assessment is specific, unique and detailed, individualized to the participant
Emphasizes compliance and management of problems and needs, with formal services seen as the solution	Explores the rejuvenation and creation of natural helping networks and social supports
Controlled by the professional	Participant ownership
The professional dictates, "I think you need to learn and work on this."	The professional asks, "What can I learn from you about your life?"

Figure 9.2 Compare/Contrast: Strengths-Based versus Deficits-Based Assessment *(adapted from Rapp & Goscha, 2006)*

- Use language participants can understand. This practice allows the assessment to be a shared process with the participants, giving them ownership over information that is about them and their lives (see Figure 9.3).
- Avoid blaming, cause-and-effect thinking, and labeling. Assessment is about learning about the whole person. Causal thinking, which focuses on the cause of problems, limits perspectives and can inhibit moving toward solutions and strategies to help participants reach their goals. Labeling focuses our attention on pathology, making it a central feature in the helping relationship, and limiting how a participant is perceived.

In Table 9.1, we summarize and offer these important principles to guide you in the assessment process in therapeutic recreation practice. Perhaps Dan Wilkins (n.d.) stated it best:

Table 9.1 Principles to Guide Strengths-Based Assessment

Principles to Guide Strengths-Based Assessment
Assessment . . . • is strengths-based and person-centered • is individualized, based on the participant's world view • focuses on well-being and quality of life through leisure • looks at the whole person in her or his environment (authentic and ecological) • is based on the aspirations and goals of the participant • uses multiple methods and seeks to understand multiple variables • always involves the participant and his or her circle of support

"I said to the child, 'Reach for the stars.'
And the child replied, 'I am the star, filled with wonder and possibility.'"

Primary Source Support: Authentic and Meaningful Assessment

Hornibook, T., Pedlar, A., & Haasen, B. (2001). Patient-focused care: Theory and practice. *Therapeutic Recreation Journal, 35*(1), 15–30.

Hornibook and colleagues were interested in what the assessment experience was like for both participants and therapeutic recreation specialists, and how person-centered theory was enacted, or not, in practice. Following the initial assessment period at a regional healthcare facility, they used action research by conducting in-depth interviews with the therapeutic recreation specialists and the participants.

The researchers uncovered several themes. First, they found that therapeutic recreation specialists were trained to use specific terminology or use specific assessment techniques that did not match up to the communication needs of the participants. For example, therapeutic recreation specialists would ask about "leisure" or "barriers," and the participants were confused by what was being asked. Another theme was that the therapeutic recreation specialists felt hurried to complete the initial interview, and they would often redirect or ignore participants' responses, in an attempt to finish quickly. As a result, participants felt a sense of invalidation. In addition, the use of rating scales and standardized assessments was confusing to the participants and frustrating for the therapeutic recreation staff. Lastly, an important theme was that the participants did not understand the role of therapeutic recreation in their lives, or why they interacted with the therapeutic recreation specialists. The researchers note,

"Many patients described feelings of anxiety about the assessments that they had undergone and the possible implications of these assessments, such as the determination of their ability to return home. Assessment implies a one-way flow of information from the patient to the therapist. A recreation therapist's role is to exchange information; the information they pass on to the individual is as important as the information they receive. Finally, assessment was seen as a very technical term implying measurement."

Based on the interview results, the therapeutic recreation staff decided to change the name of their assessment process to "Personal Leisure Profile." The therapeutic recreation specialists also put several assessment protocol recommendations into practice:

- Be truly present with individuals by listening, accepting, and empathizing with their reality.
- Use understandable language that is familiar to the participant.
- Ensure that the participant understands the purpose of therapeutic recreation questions and actions.
- Contribute personal experiences and ideas to the interaction.
- Eliminate assessment tools in the first exchange and focus on the participant's leisure interests.
- Provide real and meaningful opportunities for choice.

These recommendations led to more authentic and meaningful assessment on the part of the therapeutic recreation staff and more person-centered practice.

Figure 9.3 Primary Source Support: Authentic and Meaningful Assessment

Assessment Basics

The assessment, or discovery, phase of the therapeutic recreation process is the first step in the helping relationship with participants. It is a very important interaction, and the information exchanged forms the basis to move to the next phase of the process, planning. How will you know you have obtained the "right" information? How will you know you have truly heard and understood the participant? How will you know that you have learned about the context of the participant's life? These questions all relate to essential characteristics of assessment. Assessment must be authentic, ecological, valid or credible, reliable or trustworthy, fair, and usable in your setting. Before we look at each of these characteristics in more depth, it is important to differentiate whether you are seeking quantitative or qualitative information during assessment, and whether your information comes from a primary or secondary source.

Quantitative information means you have measured something and assigned a numeric value to it. When information is quantified, it allows for comparison from the beginning of services to another point in time, or from one person to another.

Qualitative information means you have obtained information in words. You have not measured something; instead you have described it, using the richness of words rather than the objectivity of numbers.

Neither quantitative nor qualitative information is superior to the other. Which approach you choose depends simply on what you need to know and why. If you want to truly understand the participant's point of view and describe that perspective to other team members, qualitative data may be richer. If you want to compare how the participant has changed, in relation to baseline or in comparison to peers, quantitative data may be richer. Often, both types of information are needed, and we combine our assessment methods to gather qualitative descriptions from the participant, as well as objective quantitative measures that help us evaluate change and our overall services.

Another characteristic of data that you collect in the assessment process is its source. Information can come directly from the participant or from some other source. When you get information directly from the participant, the data is from a **primary source**. When you gather information about the participant from others, such as family members, friends, other professionals, or from documented information such as a medical chart or social history, the data is from a **secondary source**. You should strive to gather information from participants themselves in relation to leisure and well-being. However, when working on a transdisciplinary team, one team member is often assigned to complete the assessment and collect the primary and secondary data for the rest of the team. Regardless of the type of information collected, assessment approaches need to have several characteristics to be useful to you and fair to participants. You will learn about these defining characteristics of assessment in the next section.

Assessment Characteristics

Authentic Assessment

Have you ever driven a friend's car, and could not find the light switch, turn signal, or other controls, because the car was so different from one that you usually drove? Now imagine that you had a driving examiner in the car with you, assessing your driving skills as you fumble to show your competence as a driver. This would not be a true, or authentic, assessment of your driving skills. Because you are being assessed in an unfamiliar setting, and being asked to demonstrate a real-world task in isolation from your usual environment, you are not able to show what you can really do as effectively as when you drive under your usual circumstances.

Authentic assessment means that real-world performance on valued activities is assessed in real-world environments, allowing participants to benefit from meaningful tasks with natural cues, feedback, and familiar contexts. In therapeutic recreation, for example, we could assess a participant's social skills on a paper-and-pencil test or we can observe the participant interact with peers in a recreation activity. Observation during a genuine social event would be a more authentic assessment of social skills than a multiple-choice test or even a contrived role-playing situation. Figure 9.4 illustrates further differences between more traditional assessment and authentic assessment.

Ecological Assessment

Ecological assessment considers the participant in his or her environment. The focus of the assessment is on the participant's goals, aspirations, and strengths, and the environmental resources and context in which the participant lives. When an assessment is ecological, it means that the therapeutic recreation specialist has spent time getting to know not only the participant, but also the participant's home, school, work, community, and other contexts of his or her life. It means understanding how the participant interacts with that context, and what changes might need to be made on the part of the participant or the environment, so that the specialist can help him or her reach goals and achieve

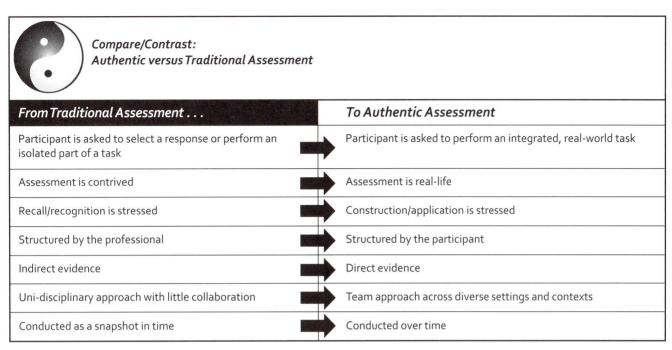

Figure 9.4 Compare/Contrast: Authentic versus Traditional Assessment *(adapted from Mueller, 2009)*

well-being. Later in this chapter, we will look closely at how to conduct an ecological assessment in therapeutic recreation.

Validity and Credibility

Are you assessing what you really think you are assessing when you use a particular assessment tool or method in your therapeutic recreation practice? Are you truly learning what you need to learn about the participant and his or her environment? **Validity** addresses these types of questions. For quantitative assessment, a valid assessment tool is one that measures what it is supposed to measure. In other words, you are able to infer from the assessment results to the real world in a meaningful way. For example, if you want to measure someone's height and you use a bathroom scale, is that a valid assessment of height? For a physical measurement, like height, we know that, of course, the bathroom scale is not a valid way to measure it. But what about more difficult concepts to measure, like self-determination? or self-esteem? or well-being? We need to use different approaches to determine the validity of measurements for concepts that we cannot physically measure. We use indicators of these types of concepts, and make an inference or logical judgment that we are measuring the actual notion. For example, what would be some indicators of high self-esteem? or of well-being? We have to list behaviors, thoughts, or feelings that indicate each of these concepts and then measure them. We have to take abstract ideas and make them measurable and more concrete. Once we have done that, there are varying ways to test the validity of measurement tools: face validity, content validity, criterion-related validity (including predictive and concurrent validity), and construct validity.

Face validity is the least rigorous method of determining if a measurement tool is valid. Face validity involves an expert review of the tool, and a judgment by experts that the tool measures what it says it measures. "At face value," the tool looks like it will measure what it is supposed to measure. It is an important first step in developing an assessment tool or method, but it may be subject to error or bias.

Content validity means that the assessment tool measures all aspects of whatever is being measured, in the same relative proportion or importance. For example, if an assessment measures physical fitness, it must measure all aspects of fitness proportionately: cardiovascular fitness, body composition, muscular strength, muscular endurance, and flexibility. If a fitness assessment measures only flexibility, for example, it lacks content validity as an overall measure of physical fitness.

Criterion-related validity means that the assessment tool compares favorably to a standard or "criterion" by which the tool can be judged. There are two ways to test for criterion-related validity: predictive and concurrent validity. **Predictive validity** means the score on the assessment tool will correlate highly with future performance. If an assessment has high predictive validity, it means the tool can predict success in the behavior being measured. For example, if we want to

Primary Source Support: Perceptions of Boredom in Leisure Scale

Iso-Ahola, S., & Weissenger, E. (1990). Perceptions of boredom in leisure: Conceptualization, reliability, and validity of the Leisure Boredom Scale. *Journal of Leisure Research, 22*(1), 1–17.

Drs. Iso-Ahola and Weissenger determined the need to develop an assessment tool to measure leisure boredom based on the large and growing evidence that leisure satisfaction, more than any other life area, supported a high quality of life. They reviewed many studies and found that boredom in leisure was a predictor of lower life quality and life satisfaction.

To be able to measure leisure boredom, the researchers first developed an operational definition: "Leisure boredom is the subjective perception that available leisure experiences are not sufficient to instrumentally satisfy needs for optimal arousal." Perceptions of leisure as boring are associated with negative affect, and stem from beliefs that leisure experiences are not frequent enough, involving, exciting, varied, or novel. Leisure boredom is a mismatch between desired arousal-producing characteristics of leisure and perceptual or actual availability of leisure experiences.

The researchers then hypothesized that leisure boredom would be negatively related to many other constructs: social competence, self-as-entertainment, intrinsic leisure motivation, leisure satisfaction, self-esteem, leisure participation, affinity for leisure, and physical and mental health. They developed the questions or items for the instrument and had experts determine face validity of the 28 statements to assess leisure boredom. Then, across three studies, they administered the *Leisure Boredom Scale*, and a mix of assessments that measured the various constructs listed above to over 750 participants. The researchers also tested for reliability of the Leisure Boredom Scale using a test for internal consistency.

Drs. Iso-Ahola and Weissenger found support for their hypothesis. The correlation coefficients across all the measures used were negative and significant. In other words, participants who scored high on the Leisure Boredom Scale (showing high leisure boredom) scored low on assessments of intrinsic leisure motivation, self-as-entertainment, social competence, leisure satisfaction, self-esteem, and the other variables tested. The researchers concluded that, "The fact that all constructs were significantly correlated in the predicted manner lends credence to the construct validity of the instrument" (p. 12). They also found internal consistency with reliability coefficients ranging from .85 to .88.

The researchers concluded that more testing is needed, but the Leisure Boredom Scale does appear to have validity and reliability, and does measure leisure boredom as defined in a consistent manner.

Figure 9.5 Primary Source Support: Perceptions of Boredom in Leisure Scale

determine the predictive validity of a tool that measures social skills, we would compare the score achieved on the social skills assessment tool to actual performance in a social setting. If the two measures (the assessment tool and the actual performance of social skills) correlate highly, we can infer predictive validity.

The other form of criterion-related validity, **concurrent validity,** means the score on the assessment tool correlates highly with other known or established measures of the same construct being measured. For example, if we develop an assessment tool to measure leisure well-being, we could compare the participants' results with results on previously validated tools that measure similar ideas, such as the *Leisure Diagnostic Battery* or the *Satisfaction With Life Scale*. These tools all measure some aspect of leisure well-being, and participants should score similarly on all measures.

Construct validity means that the developer of the assessment tool has formed and tested a hypothesis about what the tool will measure, in relation to a theoretical construct. Construct validity has two components: **convergent** (the items on the tool converge on the theoretical construct as expected) and **discriminant** (groups who are expected to score differently on the assessment tool, based on the construct being measured, do actually score differently). In other words, the assessment tool converges on items that should be similar and discriminates on items that should be different. To help you understand this type of validity, in Figure 9.5, we provide a study that investigated the construct validity of the *Leisure Boredom Scale*.

Validity is often reported as a correlation coefficient, a number that shows how strong the relationship is between the tool and other measures such as another similar tool. A perfect correlation is 1.0. In the social sciences, a correlation coefficient of .70 or higher is often considered rigorous enough to trust that the assessment tool is truly measuring what it says it measures.

When choosing an assessment tool to use in your own therapeutic recreation practice, look carefully at how validity was established, and how strong the reported correlation coefficient is.

Credibility is a similar concept to validity, if you are using a qualitative assessment such as an interview. A credible assessment means it describes what the participant wanted to describe in a believable way. From the perspective of the participant, the assessment results are credible if they truly describe what he or she wanted to convey to you. To judge if your assessment is credible, you must share the results with the participant for him or her to make that determination.

Lastly, **social validity** means that what we are assessing really matters to the participants we serve—it is something they care about, and want to know more about. Social validity means participants and their circles of support have given feedback that what you have measured and focused on is meaningful and important to them. It means that you, as a therapeutic recreation specialist, have asked for their input into the assessment process and, in response, you have continually modified the process.

Reliability and Dependability

If you want to measure your weight, you would use a scale, which is a valid tool to measure weight. Imagine you get on the scale and find you weigh 130 pounds. You immediately get on the scale again, and the scale shows 160 pounds. You step off and back on a third time, and find you weigh 100 pounds. The scale you are using is not reliable. It does not give you a consistent result that you can trust.

The assessment tools you use must have reliability to be usable. Reliability is defined as being consistent or dependable. It means that you will get approximately the same results each time you administer the assessment, given no other change. Reliability answers the question, "If the assessment is given two or more times, will the results be similar?" Reliability also answers the question, "If two different therapeutic recreation specialists administer the same assessment with a participant, will the results be similar?" Reliability is, in essence, how much error there is in relation to a true measurement, when using an assessment tool or method.

Reliability for quantitative assessment tools is often reported as a **reliability coefficient**. When choosing an assessment tool, a certain level of reliability is needed to be not only dependable, but valid as well. A correlation coefficient of 1.0 means the tool is perfectly reliable. This is very rare, as there is often some error anytime we measure things, especially social constructs or traits. Conversely, a reliability coefficient of 0.0 means the tool is perfectly unreliable. In the social sciences, a reliability coefficient of 0.70 is a minimally acceptable level of reliability for an assessment tool to be considered usable in a trustworthy manner.

Reliability of an assessment tool may be assessed in different ways. **Test-retest** reliability means the developers of the assessment tool have administered the same tool to the same group of participants at different points in time and, given that nothing else has changed, arrived at the correlation between the first and second testing situation. The higher the correlation between the first and second administration of the tool, the higher is the reliability coefficient.

The developers of an assessment tool may develop **alternate forms** of the same assessment tool (e.g., different order of questions, slightly different wording) and administer the two forms of the same tool to a group of participants. Again, the higher the correlation between the alternate forms, the higher is the reliability coefficient.

Another way to determine reliability is to assess the instrument's **internal consistency**, or how reliably the tool converges on or measures what it is intended to measure. One way to determine internal consistency is called **split-half**. In this method, half the questions on an assessment tool are correlated with the other half (e.g., even-numbered questions to odd-numbered questions). The higher the correlation between the two halves, the more reliable is the assessment tool. Another method to measure internal consistency is **Cronbach's alpha**. In this approach, every item on an assessment tool is correlated with every other item that measures the same construct. The higher the correlation, the more internal consistency the assessment tool has.

Lastly, reliability can be assessed using inter-rater or inter-observer methods. **Inter-rater reliability** is the degree to which two observers or raters give consistent estimates on the measure or assessment tool being used. For example, if two therapeutic recreation specialists are observing a child in the playroom in a group situation and rating the amount of cooperative behavior the child shows, both will rate the child's behavior similarly. There will be a high correlation between their ratings.

Reliability is necessary for an assessment tool to be considered valid. However, just because a tool has reliability, this does not ensure validity. Let's think back to our example with the bathroom scale. If you want to know how tall you are, and you use the bathroom scale to measure your height, it doesn't matter that the scale consistently gives you the same result when you step on it, because it isn't measuring the right construct. Even if it reliably gives you the same measurement, it isn't giving you a valid measurement. The same holds true for assessment tools we use in therapeutic recreation. The tools must have both validity and reliability.

Dependability is a similar concept to reliability, which applies when you use a qualitative assessment such as an open-ended interview. A dependable or trustworthy assessment means that the qualitative results of your assessment are consistent and accurate. Dependability is established through detailed notes about the participant, the context, and how you arrived at any conclusions drawn. These detailed notes are sometimes called an audit trail.

In sum, when you use an assessment in therapeutic recreation, you must pay attention to the validity or credibility of the assessment, as well as to its reliability or dependability. These are very important assessment characteristics and help to ensure that you are learning or discovering strengths in participants in a way that is meaningful and rigorous.

Fairness and Cultural Relevance

Imagine that someone asked you to complete an assessment that was going to determine something important about your future, and most of the assessment was in a language you did not comprehend, that used examples you could not understand, that made judgments about you that were different from your own values, or that asked you to complete tasks that were uncomfortable or exhausting. These kinds of issues all relate to the assessment characteristics of fairness, cultural relevance, and sensitivity. Fairness means you take into account the amount of time and effort the assessment will take, as well as how comfortable it will be for the participant. It means that every person should have an opportunity to complete an assessment successfully, regardless of background, gender, or culture. Cultural relevance means that you take into account how appropriate the tool or technique is for a participant in relation to culture, gender, generation, and other core differences. Figure 9.6 presents a situation where cultural differences were not taken into consideration during the assessment process.

Usability

Many excellent and well-tested assessment tools exist for use in our field. But if the tools or approaches are not usable in your setting or with the participants with whom you typically work, the other characteristics become less important. One consideration in practice is the practicality of using different tools and approaches, or their usability. For example, if the average amount of time you have to work with participants is 2 weeks, then you will need to choose an assessment approach that you can complete quickly. If you work in a setting where most participants receive services for a long period of time, you can choose an assessment method that is more in-depth and takes more time to complete.

You may also judge usability of an assessment method or tool based on what type of team approach you use. If you work on a high-functioning transdisciplinary team, for example, how you complete assessments will be different than if you work on a multidisciplinary team. On a transdisciplinary team, you will often share assessment tasks across disciplines and take a more holistic, integrated assessment approach.

Standardization

Standardization means that you are using an assessment tool the way the developers of the tool or method intend it to be used, following the guidelines, parameters, instructions, and other directions provided. For example, the *Leisure Diagnostic Battery* (*LDB*), discussed later in this chapter, is a standardized assessment tool. The manual that accompanies the *LDB* provides directions on how the assessment session should be conducted, from the amount of time given to the participant to complete the assessment to the verbal instructions that are provided. If you are using a standardized assessment tool, it is important to use it as intended so you do not threaten the validity or reliability of the tool. As a general rule, you cannot change an assessment tool any more than 10% without threatening its established validity and reliability.

Criterion-Referenced versus Norm-Referenced

Once results are obtained from an assessment tool, you can use those results in differing ways, depending on the purpose of completing the assessment and on the type of assessment. Two ways to use results are criterion-referencing and norm-referencing.

Do you remember standardized tests you took in school or to enter college? When you got the results of those tests, they often provided you with an indication of how you compared to all other people who took the test when you did or to some national norm. Tests or assessments that provide comparisons to a larger, similar group are called **norm-referenced**. The assessment results of the participant are compared to population results, and this comparison can help to make decisions about the plan. For example, you may ask a participant to complete the *Oxford Happiness Questionnaire* (discussed later in this chapter), and compare his or her score to national averages to compare levels of perceived well-being. Norm-referenced results are often reported

My Cultural Lens:

Self-Esteem and Differences in Cultural Orientation

I worked for a long period of time in a regional hospital that served a large geographical area. Several large American Indian reservations were a part of our service area. We often worked with youth from the reservations and found we needed to change the way we assessed common areas in therapeutic recreation. For example, we often focused on self-esteem as a targeted outcome. We asked youth to complete a self-esteem inventory when they first entered our program, and again when they were ready to leave. We also used observation as a common method of assessment and looked for behavioral indicators of improved self-esteem.

We noticed a trend in that many of the youth from the reservations did not show improvements in their self-esteem based on our assessment, even though they were happier and expressed feeling good about themselves and their attainment of goals. We looked more critically at how we were conceptualizing and measuring self-esteem, and talked with American Indian youth in our program. We quickly realized that it was not culturally appropriate for the youth who were from an American Indian culture to exhibit some of the behaviors we were using as indicators of positive self-esteem. For example, where we measured things like, "maintains eye contact," or "states positive things about self," we were not considering the cultural differences between youth from the more prevalent White American background and Native American background. According to the youth in our program, in the Sioux culture, it was considered disrespectful to make eye contact with an elder. It was considered boastful and vain to state positive things about oneself. On the other hand, we did not ask questions or look for behaviors related to generosity, something that the youth felt was an indicator of improved self-esteem for them. Thus, our assessment of self-esteem was not culturally relevant, neither was it valid for this group of youth. We modified our assessment approach to take into account Sioux cultural values, and more accurately assess how self-esteem may have changed by the end of services.

Can you think of other typical therapeutic recreation outcomes in which the indicators vary by culture? How can you ensure you are completing an assessment in a culturally relevant way? How will you know if you are not? Talk through these ideas with your colleagues or classmates.

Figure 9.6 My Cultural Lens: Self-Esteem and Differences in Cultural Orientation

as percentile scores and show the participant's relative standing in a group (e.g., in the 90th percentile). Norm-referenced assessments are sometimes used to help participants qualify for services they may need or for placement decisions.

When assessment results are **criterion-referenced**, it means you are comparing the results of the assessment to some standard or criterion. You are determining some level of skill mastery, behavior, knowledge, or emotion. For example, you may compare how well a participant performs a recreation skill in relation to the level of skill that is needed to successfully participate at the next level (e.g., a participant may need to show the ability to come to a complete stop 100% of the time in a mono-ski before progressing to the next level of difficulty on the mountain slopes).

Often, in therapeutic recreation, we use results in both ways. For example, it is useful to compare a participant's score on the *Oxford Happiness Questionnaire* to national norms and to compare how the participant changes over time, in relation to his or her own score as well as to the maximum score possible on the assessment. Both comparisons, norm-referenced and criterion-referenced, help us understand the participant better.

Availability

Availability refers to how easy it is to access an assessment tool for use in your practice in therapeutic recreation. Some tools are proprietary and must be purchased from the developer of the tool or from a vendor. Others are freely disseminated through research journals or websites. Still others are only available after you have undergone training on how to use the assessment or have a certain credential to purchase or have access to the tool. Later in this chapter, we will overview some assessment tools and methods that are useful for strengths-based therapeutic recreation practice and provide information on their availability.

Using Assessment Characteristics to Choose Assessment Tools or Approaches

The overview of assessment characteristics we have provided gives you a mental checklist of questions to ask yourself as you decide which tools or approaches you will use as you work with participants to discover their strengths, dreams, goals, interests, aspirations, and other factors that contribute to well-being in leisure. In Figure 9.7, we offer an actual checklist that you can use in your daily practice. Ascertaining the characteristics

Assessment Checklist

Name of assessment: _____
Focus (what it assesses): _____
Assessment developed with what group of people? _____
    (e.g., adults, children, adults with developmental disabilities)

Data collection method:
    ☐ Interview   ☐ Observation   ☐ Test/questionnaire   ☐ Multiple methods

Type of data collected:
    ☐ Qualitative   ☐ Quantitative   ☐ Both

If this is a quantitative assessment:
    Validity of assessment: _____ (coefficient)
    Type of validity:
      ☐ Face   ☐ Content   ☐ Predictive   ☐ Concurrent   ☐ Construct

    Reliability of assessment: _____ (coefficient)
    Type of reliability:
      ☐ Test-retest   ☐ Parallel forms   ☐ Split halves   ☐ Cronbach's alpha
      ☐ Inter-rater

    Assessment results can be referenced to:
    ☐ Norms   ☐ Criteria   ☐ Both
    If norm-referenced, what population? _____

If this is a qualitative assessment:
    ☐ Credible   ☐ Dependable and trustworthy
    How determined: _____

Assessment is: (check all that apply)
    ☐ Authentic   ☐ Ecological   ☐ Culturally relevant   ☐ Fair   ☐ Standardized

Usability:
    Amount of time needed to complete assessment: _____
    Place/space needed to complete assessment: _____
    Equipment/supplies needed to complete assessment: _____
    Cost of assessment: _____

Assessment is available from:
    Source: _____
    Criteria to obtain assessment (check all that apply):
      ☐ Available for free   ☐ Available for purchase
      ☐ Available after training is completed from: _____
      ☐ Available with these credentials: _____

Figure 9.7 An Assessment Checklist

of an assessment is one of the important steps you take in practice as you develop and use the assessment process. In the next section, we describe these steps in more depth, to ensure that the therapeutic recreation process rests on a solid foundation of a well-done assessment.

The Assessment Process

Assessment in therapeutic recreation practice follows a process that is typical in health and human services. Figure 9.8 shows the steps that are usually followed to complete a therapeutic recreation assessment. The process begins with a **referral**. Referrals can come from many sources and take many forms. In medical settings, the referral comes from a medical doctor. In residential settings, referrals are often standing orders, where all participants who move in to the home or facility will participate in assessment. In community settings, referrals can come from families, registration processes, case managers, and many other sources. In school settings, the referral can come from the team, the special education coordinator, or the family.

Once a referral has been received, you will make **initial contact** with the participant and typically conduct an **initial therapeutic recreation assessment**. In Table 9.2, we provide a sample initial therapeutic recreation assessment from an inpatient rehabilitation therapeutic recreation program and, in Table 9.3, a sample initial assessment from a community-based inclusion program.

The focus and scope of the initial assessment varies greatly depending on setting and team structure. The initial assessment may be completed, for example, by a case manager for all disciplines at your agency. Or, if the team uses a transdisciplinary approach, an arena assessment (discussed later in this chapter) may be completed, where only one assigned team member completes the initial assessment for all disciplines, including therapeutic recreation. Regardless of approach, the initial assessment is the starting point of the helping relationship and gathers enough information from the participant and family to move toward more in-depth assessment. The initial assessment is often an interview, to begin to develop rapport and put the participant at ease.

Table 9.2 A Sample Initial Therapeutic Recreation Assessment from a Rehabilitation Hospital *(Hornibook, Pedlar, & Haasen, 2001)*

The Personal Leisure Profile
1. What do you enjoy? (Past/present leisure interests)
2. What about that do you enjoy? (Characteristics of pursuits that are enjoyed)
3. Recently, what has brought enjoyment/happiness to your day? (Current leisure status)
4. What is stopping you from enjoying (or some of) those activities? (Barriers)
5. Is there something that you have always wanted to do? (Dreams)

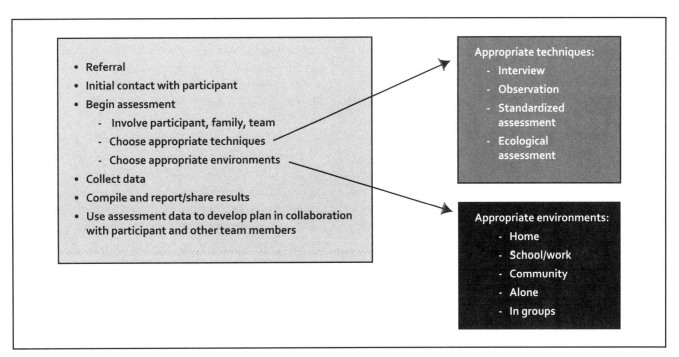

Figure 9.8 The Assessment Process

Table 9.3 A Sample Initial Therapeutic Recreation Assessment from a Community Inclusion Service
(Anderson, Penney McGee, Wilkins, & Roeder, 2008)

Recreation Referral Service of the Inclusive Recreation Resource Center

Getting to Know You Assessment

(completed with the participant *and* his/her support circle)

About your recreation!
1. What are your favorite activities or hobbies? What activities do you enjoy the most? (Supplement with activity checklists, if helpful to do so.)
2. What kinds of things are you really good at doing?
3. What are some goals or dreams you have for your recreation?
4. Who do you usually play or recreate with?
5. What recreation resources or programs do you use now or have you used in the past?
6. What new recreation programs or activities are you interested in doing?
7. Complete the Quality of Life Scale *(discussed in a later section of this chapter)*.

For your safety:
8. What type of communication do you use?
   __Verbal   __Limited verbal   __Facilitated/assisted communication   __Sign language   __Other
9. What types of supports, accommodations, or adaptive equipment do you use (wheelchair, assistive devices, hand-over-hand, etc.)?
10. Do you have any allergies, medications, or special precautions (bee stings, carries an epi-pen, peanut allergy, other food allergies, etc.)?
11. Is there any other information you would like to add (level of supervision, crowds, sensory needs, flight in the community, etc.)?
12. It may be helpful to schedule another time to meet with you while you are participating in an activity (work, school, program, etc.). If so, what are some times or places that I could come to see you and get to know you better?

Emergency Contact Information:

The next step in the assessment process is to choose the focus and method of the **in-depth assessment.** The initial screening or assessment helps you hone in on what you will assess further and how you will assess it. In-depth assessment asks you to choose appropriate tools, methods, and environments to gather needed information to truly learn about the participant. In the next sections, we will overview the common methods used to collect assessment information and focus areas for therapeutic recreation assessment. The in-depth assessment should include the collection of baseline data, which will help you and the participant evaluate progress toward goals as you work together.

The assessment methods and focus you choose will often dictate the **types of environments** you will need to use to collect information. For example, you may need to complete observation of social skills on the playground and lunchroom at school, if you are working with a child. You may need to interview family members, if you are working with a participant with Alzheimer's disease. You may need to accompany a participant on a community outing to understand competencies in using community resources. The assessment focus helps to determine the environment in which the assessment needs to be completed, to ensure it is authentic.

Once you have determined the focus, tools, methods, and environments to complete an in-depth assessment, your next task is to **implement the assessment and collect the data**. It is often necessary to have multiple interactions with a participant and his or her environment to get a true picture of strengths, goals, aspirations, skills, and other baseline information. Your setting and the amount of time you have to work with a participant will often dictate how much information you are able to collect to help you develop a plan. In an acute medical setting, for example, there are often major restrictions to completing quality assessments, because of the short amount of time available to work with participants. In residential or community settings, you will have time and flexibility to do a more thorough and authentic assessment. The art of assessment is in choosing methods and tools that give you the most information within the constrictions of your agency and setting. The science of assessment is in understanding the assessment characteristics and the rationale behind your choices.

Once your assessment is completed, you need to **compile the results** in a format that is understandable to the participant, his or her circle of support, and other team members. Agencies may have a specific format for reporting assessment results. Or you may need to

Table 9.4 Format of a Typical Assessment Report

Therapeutic Recreation Assessment Report Format
Participant Name:
Dates of the Assessment:
Reason for Referral:
Background Information:
Methods: *Methods used to complete the assessment across various environments (e.g., behavioral observation; interview; standardized assessment in home, work/school, community, or agency environments)*
Results of the Assessment:
Summary and Interpretation:
Recommendations:
Signature (of therapeutic recreation specialist completing the assessment):
Date of Signature:

write a brief assessment report. In Table 9.4, we offer a typical assessment report format. The report includes who completed the assessment, the methods used, and the results, or what was learned. The report should be written in plain language that the participant and his or her family members can easily understand.

Share results with the participant and other team members once your assessment results are compiled. If you have conducted a qualitative assessment, this is an especially crucial step in the process, since the participant must ascertain the credibility of the information you have compiled. Often, in an interdisciplinary team, each discipline will share assessment results at a team meeting. On a transdisciplinary team, the assigned primary team member will share results for all disciplines. Results can thus be shared in writing, in conversation with participants, and in team meetings. Assessment results become part of the record of the participant as well.

We would like to use the metaphor of a tree to sum up the assessment process. The "trunk" of the tree is the initial contact and assessment. What you learn about the participant in the initial assessment will determine how the rest of the assessment process unfolds. It will determine which "branches" will be explored in more depth. Not every participant will need every branch explored, some may need no other branches explored, and some may need them all explored. The initial assessment directs in-depth and more specialized assessment

to those areas most important to the participant, to help him or her reach goals and dreams for a flourishing life.

Assessment Techniques or Approaches

You collect assessment information using a variety of techniques or approaches. The most common methods of assessment include record review, interviews, observation, standardized assessments, such as questionnaires and tests, and ecological assessment. In addition, assessments can be completed by a single discipline or with a team. One approach, using a transdisciplinary team, is an arena assessment. Let's look at each of these approaches in more detail.

Record Review

Often, many other professionals will interact with and collect information from the participant. This information is contained in an official record, whether it is a medical chart, a case file, or an educational file. The information collected can range from medical tests to social histories. Reviewing the documented record of the participant is often a starting point for the assessment process. Record review will provide you with a context and history of the participant. However, it is important to remember that the information you collect in a record review is secondary source data and may have been collected from a deficit approach. Though record review will help you collect basic information, you must be cautious when forming any judgments or expectations about the participant from this information. As a therapeutic recreation specialist, the primary source information you collect from the participant will be more valuable to you.

Interviews

Interviews are one of the most powerful methods of assessment in therapeutic recreation. You are able to establish a relationship with a participant, gain in-depth information, modify your assessment based on the individual situation of the participant, and get a fuller picture of the person's life. However, interviews do take more time than some other methods of assessment, can be prone to bias, and may not allow for quantifiable results as easily.

Types of Interviews

You have a continuum of choices for interviewing, depending on the situation and the type of information you hope to gain from the assessment. Interview formats range from having less to more structure. The most unstructured type of interview is the **conversational interview**. In the conversational interview, though you have an overall purpose or focus, the topics and questions emerge during the natural course of a conversation with the participant. Neither the topics nor the wording of questions is predetermined. In therapeutic recreation, we often have many opportunities to conduct conversational interviews when participants are involved in casual or informal leisure activities, often with family members present.

The **interview guide approach** has more structure than the conversational interview, but is still conversational in nature. In this interviewing approach, the topics of the interview are decided in advance and used in an outline form to guide the interview. However, you decide the exact wording and sequencing of the interview as it unfolds—the interview is conversational and situational in nature and can be adapted to the communication style and perspective of the participant.

The **standardized open-ended interview approach** is more structured yet. The exact wording and sequence of the questions are developed in advance. The same questions are used in the same basic order each time you conduct the therapeutic recreation assessment interview. However, the questions are open-ended, meaning the participant can answer in his or her own words. This is a common interview approach used in therapeutic recreation. The interview assessments provided in Tables 9.2 and 9.3 are examples of standardized open-ended interviews. Both the interview guide and standardized open-ended interview approaches are considered semi-structured interviews.

The most structured approach to interviewing is the **standardized closed-ended interview**. In this interview approach, the questions and the response categories are predetermined. The responses are fixed, or closed-ended. In other words, the participant is given a question, and then closed-ended or fixed responses from which to choose. For example, you may ask, "During your recreation experiences, how often do you feel completely absorbed by the activity? All the time, some of the time, or never?" This approach is much like a standardized assessment tool that is orally administered.

Any of the four types of interview approaches can be used in therapeutic recreation practice. Both the advantages and disadvantages of the various methods are offered in Table 9.5. Despite having some disadvantages, interviewing is one of the most common methods of completing at least the initial assessment in therapeutic recreation. As a therapeutic recreation specialist, you will need to determine what interviewing approach will best help you discover the strengths, goals, dreams, and aspirations of the participant in the context of his or her life.

Phases of a typical interview

When conducting an interview, whether conversational or highly structured, you will follow a progression to be most effective. The phases of the interview are:

1. **Beginning phase**—introduction and opening. In this phase, you greet the participant, establish rapport, inform the participant of what will be asked, how the interview will progress, how the information will be used, confidentiality, and how you are recording (e.g., notes, audiotape) the interview.

2. **Working phase**—body of the interview. In this phase, you will use active listening skills to complete the assessment questions or purpose. Table 9.6 provides an overview of active listening skills you should be competent in using in therapeutic recreation. Table 9.7 provides some guidance in how interview questions should be sequenced to be most effective in gaining valid and reliable results.

3. **Termination phase**—closing the interview. In this phase, you thank the participant, encourage the participant to ask any

Table 9.5 Advantages and Disadvantages of Interviewing Approaches

Amount of Structure	Type of Interview	Advantages	Disadvantages
Least	Conversational Interview	• Builds rapport most effectively • Increases the salience and relevance of questions • Interview is built on and emerges from observations • Interview is matched to the participant and his or her situation	• Differing information is collected, depending on who is doing the interviewing • Less systematic • Data organization and analysis can be more difficult
	Interview Guide	• Having an outline of topics increases the comprehensiveness of the information collected • Flexible, yet more systematic than a conversational interview • Allows questions to be sequenced and worded in ways that best match the needs of the participant	• Ability to compare responses across interviews is difficult • Must have good interviewing skills • Consistency may vary, depending on the interviewers' skills
	Structured Open-Ended Interview	• All participants answer the same questions, so results can be compared across participants • Interviewer bias is reduced • Easier to organize and analyze the data	• Less flexibility in relating the interview questions to the participant's particular circumstances • Wording may constrain responses
Most	Structured Closed-Ended Interview	• Data analysis is simple • Responses can be directly compared and easily aggregated • Can ask many questions in a short amount of time	• Participants cannot answer in their own words about their own feelings and experiences • Categorical responses may not be valid • Limited response choices

questions, and let her or him know what will happen next.

In sum, interviewing is a useful and positive approach to therapeutic recreation assessment. It has many advantages over other assessment methods (see Table 9.10). It takes skill and knowledge to use this method, and it is an area of therapeutic recreation practice where you will constantly improve as you mature in the field.

Observation

"You can discover more about a person in an hour of play than a year of conversation."
Plato

Have you ever spent the afternoon at the park "people watching"? Or found yourself absorbed in observing a group of people interact as you waited for your order at a restaurant? Have you ever found yourself stepping back at a meeting or social gathering and observing the situation, its dynamics, and the behavior of others? Observation is a natural way for us to learn about the world around us and the people in that world. It is one of the first ways we learn to interact with our environment and is a natural skill we can develop to higher levels as therapeutic recreation specialists.

Observation, like interviewing, can range from unstructured and naturalistic, to highly structured and quantitative. In Figure 9.9, we provide the types of observation you can conduct as a part of assessment.

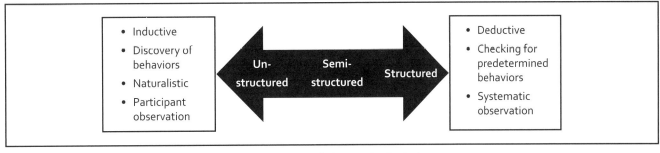

Figure 9.9 Range of Observation Techniques

Table 9.6 Basic Interviewing Skills *(adapted from Okun, Kantrowitz, & Kantrowitz, 2007)*

Purpose	Skills	Description and Example
Basic skills to facilitate authentic and empathetic listening	Attending	• Show the participant you are interested and paying attention • Use eye contact, posture, gestures, and verbal behavior.
	Paraphrasing	• Listen for the basic idea, restate the idea briefly, and note the participant's response. - For example: *Participant:* "I love being outside. I feel so much more attuned to myself when I do anything in nature. It is just so much more enjoyable than doing things indoors." *Therapeutic recreation specialist:* "You really love being in nature."
	Clarifying	• Ask for clarification. - For example: "I am not sure I understand. Would you say that again?" "Do you have an example of what you mean?"
	Perception checking	• Paraphrase what you heard, ask for confirmation, permit the participant to correct inaccurate information. - For example: *Participant:* "I think I am really good at being a leader in groups. I don't get to be a leader often, but when I do, I am great at it. I wish people would see that more so I could have a chance to be the softball team manager." *Therapeutic recreation specialist:* "You feel you are a good leader and want more opportunities to use that strength. Is that what I hear you saying?"
More advanced active listening skills to help the participant gain insight or learn new information	Reflecting	• Reflect the feeling or emotion, as well as the content that the participant is communicating to you.
	Summarizing	• Pull together the key points of what you have heard so far in the interview and invite the participant to correct or add to anything you have summarized.
	Informing	• Give information, advice, or suggestions. (This is useful if the participant has invited you to do so.)
	Leading	• If you feel there is information you still need to learn from the participant that has not been shared, ask questions, probe, and focus the interview.

Observation follows these basic steps, regardless of level of structure:

- First, choose the behavior(s) or situation you wish to assess, based on what you need to learn about the participant. You may use an observation checklist that has already been developed, such as the CERT Scale (described later in this chapter). Or you may need to define the behavior yourself so it is observable, and two or more observers would interpret it the same way.
- Next, you decide the type of observation needed—that is, qualitative or quantitative—and how you will record the information you collect. If you are going to collect quantitative data, you need to develop a recording form, if one is not already available.
- Choose when you will observe the participant, in what environments, and for how long.
- If more than one person will be observing the participant, you need to train the other observers and practice the observation method, to increase reliability and validity.
- While observing the participant, check for inter-rater reliability by comparing your observations to another observer's data to check for agreement.
- While observing, use the techniques presented in Table 9.8 to reduce the error and bias that can occur in observation.

There are several ways to conduct observation assessments, depending on what you need to learn about the participant. Table 9.9 provides an overview of these types, as well as some examples of when you would use each type.

Table 9.7 Content, Wording, and Sequencing of Interview Questions

Content or focus of interview questions	• *Fact and knowledge* questions: factual information the participant knows (e.g., "When you are back home, where can you go to do ceramics?") • *Experience or behavior* questions: what a participant is doing or has done; observable behaviors (e.g., "What recreation do you participate in on the weekends?") • *Sensory perception* questions: asks the participant to describe what he or she has seen, smelled, tasted, or touched (e.g., "Describe what you smell, see, taste, and hear when you go to the park.") • *Interests, preferences, and passion* questions: asks the participant to identify those things that he or she likes best (e.g., "What is your favorite recreation activity?") • *Attitudes, values, and opinion* questions: what the participant thinks about something (e.g., "What is your opinion of the inclusive softball team you play on?") • *Feelings/emotions* questions: emotional responses of the participant (e.g., "How did you feel after the dance Friday night?") • *Evaluative* questions: asks the participant to make a judgment about something (e.g., "How would you rate the quality of your community resources for recreation?") • *"Dream," "miracle," or "magic wand"* questions: what the participant wants to happen in her or his life (e.g., "If you woke up tomorrow and had the perfect recreation experience, what would it be like?") • *Demographic and descriptive* questions: information such as age, education, family structure, or residence
Wording of interview questions	• Be careful not to presuppose the participant's response (e.g., ask "how do you feel about . . ." instead of "how satisfied are you with . . .") • Avoid yes/no questions that force participants to reduce complex ideas into a dichotomous response and often yield little elaboration • Ask "how" or "what" questions that invite the participant to describe and explain • Avoid "why" questions which can create defensiveness; instead, ask "what are your reasons for..." or "what led you to decide to..." • Ask one question at a time, and keep each question clear and brief • Phrase questions in the participant's frame of reference • Use neutral versus leading questions (e.g., ask "How do you feel about recreation in your life?" instead of "I'm sure recreation is important in your life, isn't it?")

Sequencing of interview questions	• Start with "easy," non-controversial questions
	   - It is usually easier to talk about behaviors, activities, and experiences than about feelings, attitudes, or opinions
	   - It is usually easier to talk about the present than the past or the future
	   - Knowledge questions can be threatening (can feel like one is being tested or judged)
	• Move from the general to the specific in your questions
	• Ask demographic questions, if needed, unobtrusively throughout the interview or at the end
	• Have transitions to maintain flow of the interview
	• Be aware of nonverbal as well as verbal responses and note these

Table 9.8 Common Errors in Observation and How to Reduce Them

Observer Effects and Errors	Ways to Reduce Observer Effects and Errors
• Being observed changes the behavior of the participant or changes the situation	• Conceal the observer • Wait to collect observation data for a short period of time • Spend more time in the setting or with the participant
• The observer has personal bias about the participant or is overly swayed by first impressions (the "halo" effect)	• Define the behaviors to be observed clearly and objectively • Train the observer in the use of the tool • Use more than one observer
• Errors in collecting the observation data, such as being too lenient, always erring toward the middle of a rating scale, missing observations, or changing the way observations occur over time	• Practice the observation tool • Train and re-train observers • Check for inter-rater reliability on a routine basis • Use mechanical recording devices if possible

Table 9.9 Types of Structured Observation

Type of Observation	How the Observation Data is Collected	Example
Duration recording: Amount of time a behavior occurs	Stopwatch Recording form	Time how long a child stays on task in a play activity
Frequency count recording: Number of times a behavior occurs	Counter (or use tick marks) Recording form	Count how many times a participant initiates a social interaction with another adult
Interval recording: Noting whether a behavior occurs during a specified interval of time, such as every minute or every hour, and recording if the behavior occurs or not. This is a rough estimate of frequency and duration of a behavior.	On a recording form, have the specified intervals of time laid out in a grid. Check during each time interval whether the behavior occurs or not. [pre-set]	In 1-minute intervals, note whether a participant is fully engaged in a leisure experience over the course of a 2-hour activity ("engaged" is defined as focused fully on the activity)
Time sampling (spot checking): Use of any of the above techniques, but at randomly sampled times throughout the course of the observation period.	Recording form Dependent upon the type of observation chosen	Randomly sample the times you will observe the social interaction of a participant over the course of a week-long camping program
Continuous observation: Continuous, ongoing observation of the participant. Record a summary of your observations at the end of the session.	Checklists as a summary of the observation Narrative notes — write it out video taping	CERT Scale FIM Scale Narrative notes with emergent themes identified

Table 9.10 Advantages and Disadvantages of Assessment Methods

Method or Approach	Advantages	Disadvantages
Record review	• Can get the "big picture" of the participant's life • Can use the expertise of others • Quick method to get information • Avoid redundant collection of information	• Potential bias and inaccuracy • May have been collected from a deficits approach • Usually does not contain the information you need for therapeutic recreation assessment
Interviewing	• Person-centered • Allows in-depth discovery • Flexible • Establishes rapport and begins relationship	• Time-consuming • May have subjectivity and bias • Data difficult to reduce and report • Difficult to make comparisons between participants
Observation	• Authentic • Can see many behaviors • Naturalistic • Avoids self-report bias	• Time-consuming • May have subjectivity and bias on the part of the observer • Observer may affect behavior of participant
Standardized assessments (tests, scales, and questionnaires)	• Standardized • Allows for comparisons to norms and to baseline • Quick • Objective • Easy to reduce and report results	• No rapport established with participant; participant can feel anxious • Only get a "slice" of behavior • Not all participants can complete
Ecological assessment	• Person- and environment-centered • Allows greater understanding of the participant in her or his context • Provides direction for supports, services, and accommodations that will be needed • Strengths-based and authentic • Uses multiple methods (interview, observation, record review, and tests/questionnaires)	• Time-consuming • Difficulty accessing all environments needed for assessment

Observation is another powerful tool for assessment and is commonly used in therapeutic recreation. In Table 9.10, the advantages and disadvantages of observation are listed. Like interviewing, observation can produce a full and rich picture of the participant in the context of his or her life.

Standardized Assessment Tools and Measurement

Standardized assessment tools are those that have been developed to measure or focus on a particular aspect of an individual or the environment and gather data in a consistent and predictable manner. Standardized assessment tools can include observation checklists and interview protocols, which we have already discussed. Standardized assessment tools can also include a vast array of questionnaires, surveys, scales, and other written assessment forms. Often, a standardized assessment tool will focus on one idea or concept to measure, such as leisure satisfaction, passion, or orientation to reality. Other times, the standardized assessment will cover several areas and consist of several scales. These are sometimes called a **battery**, meaning the assessment contains multiple forms measuring different aspects of a person or a construct. Standardized assessment tools have been tested for validity and reliability, and often they must be administered according to set instructions and conditions with the population for whom they were developed.

Standardized assessments are particularly useful in therapeutic recreation practice to gather more in-depth assessment of targeted areas. For example, when working with a participant, after the initial assessment, you may find you need to gather more clear and specific information about leisure passions, social skills, or some other important life area. Standardized assessments allow you to precisely focus on and measure or assess the targeted area. Standardized assessments allow for clear documentation of baseline performance, which helps measure progress. They also allow for meaningful comparison to norms or to criteria.

There are as many standardized assessments as there are ideas to measure. Many questionnaires, surveys, scales, and tools have been developed to measure all sorts of human behaviors, emotions, attitudes, and knowledge. At the end of this chapter, we provide several resources you may possibly use to help participants along their paths to their aspirations. With the increased attention given to human flourishing in the social sciences and helping professions, we now have many more tools that have direct application to measuring strengths and other therapeutic recreation focus areas.

Ecological Assessment

Ecological assessment is an approach that looks at the person in the environment. Ecological assessment can be broad in scope or can focus specifically on a goal of the participant in relation to the environment. A variety of tools and approaches are used to complete an ecological assessment, from observation to interview to standardized assessment.

A **broad ecological assessment** is pictured in Figure 9.10. In this assessment approach, you gather information in two areas: "what we know about the person" and "what we know about the environment" (Arge Nathan, 2003, pp. 31–32). The information we gather about the person is focused on psychological/

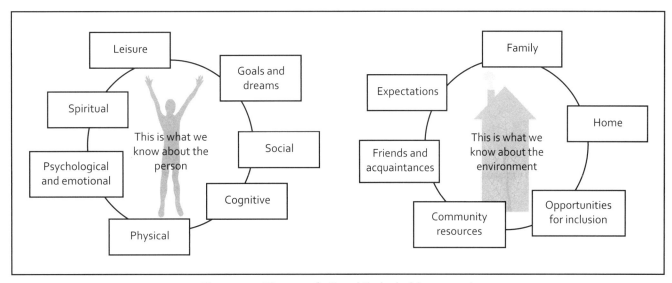

Figure 9.10 Diagram of a Broad Ecological Assessment

emotional, social, cognitive, physical, and spiritual strengths, as well as leisure experiences. The information we gather about the environment is focused on the external strengths surrounding the participant. Figure 9.10 provides a graphical way to summarize information collected, using a variety of other assessment tools and approaches, to provide an ecological perspective of the participant. Note that this approach uses the Flourishing through Leisure Model, a therapeutic recreation service model, to guide assessment practice.

A **focused ecological assessment** is used once you and the participant know the goals and activities she or he wants to pursue. Focused ecological assessment looks at the participant's abilities in relation to the demands of the environments in which he or she would be included for recreation. The gaps between what is needed to successfully participate in a particular recreation activity or environment and the participant's abilities are identified. From this assessment, you will determine the goals, modifications, supports, and strategies that will allow the participant to be successful.

The steps to complete a focused ecological assessment are as follows:

1. **Task-analyze the preferred recreation activity**. The task analysis includes each step required for participation. For example, if a participant wants to pursue a passion for swimming and join a water-exercise class at the local community center, you would identify every step or task in this activity, from registering to transportation to doing the actual activity to social interaction during the activity. The task analysis allows you to clearly understand the demands of the activity and the environment.

2. **Identify the abilities** (e.g., social, cognitive, psychological/emotional, physical, recreational) of the participant in relation to the task analysis.

3. **Identify the gaps**, where the participant will need instruction, coaching, supports, adaptations, or other changes for successful participation and inclusion.

4. **Identify the services, interventions, supports, or accommodations** that will bridge the gap.

5. Use this information to help **develop the participant's plan**.

Figure 9.11 provides a graphic of the focused ecological assessment. In essence, therapeutic recreation specialists are assessing the demands of the activity, the abilities of the participant, and identifying what is needed to bridge any differences.

Table 9.10 provides an overview of the advantages and disadvantages to the five approaches to assessment described in the preceding sections: record review, interviewing, observation, standardized assessments, and ecological assessment. There is no one "good way" or magic bullet to complete an assessment. You must choose an approach that best fits with your practice setting and the participants you serve and that best allows you to learn about the strengths, dreams, goals,

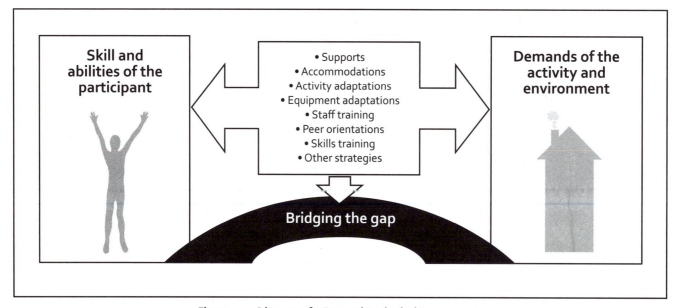

Figure 9.11 Diagram of a Focused Ecological Assessment

and aspirations of the participants. At the end of this chapter, we provide you with some exercises to help you think through this complex activity of choosing methods and tools for assessment.

Arena assessments

Recall that on a transdisciplinary team, you share roles and responsibilities across disciplines. Assessment is one task that can be shared by the team and accomplished through an arena assessment. In this type of assessment, one primary team member conducts the assessment, while the rest of the team observes and provides questions or input into the process guided by their own disciplinary knowledge. Usually the primary team member interacting with the participant is the one with whom the participant is most comfortable or familiar and could even be a family member. Arena assessments allow for more natural responses on the part of the participant, due to a higher comfort level and ability to establish rapport and trust with one professional versus several. However, gathering all team members together to complete the assessment can be an obstacle. Arena assessments tend to be used most often with young children, participants with significant intellectual disabilities, or frail older adults.

Other assessments that use a team approach will be discussed later in this chapter. They may or may not be completed in an arena approach, but they do promote coordinated interaction and focus between disciplines and lead to a unified and coordinated set of goals and priorities for participants. In practice, you may find yourself in an agency or setting that uses an arena approach to assessment, as it is a person-centered approach that is growing in attractiveness. As a therapeutic recreation specialist, you have the skills and knowledge to be a primary assessor on a transdisciplinary team. You must be prepared to learn from other disciplines and teach others about therapeutic recreation, to fully implement arena assessments.

ASSESSMENT FOCUS

You now have an understanding of what methods or approaches to use in completing an assessment, from observation to interviewing to standardized assessments. But what is the focus of the information you collect in therapeutic recreation practice? What is most important to discover about the participant? What guides you in your choice of assessment tools? Let's briefly explore how you make decisions about the assessment focus.

The Leisure and Well-Being Model and the Flourishing through Leisure Model: An Ecological Extension of the Leisure and Well-Being Model can provide guidance on where to focus your assessment. If the ultimate goal of therapeutic recreation is to help participants achieve a flourishing life based on well-being by enhancing the leisure experience and building strengths and resources, then those are areas that warrant assessment. The Flourishing through Leisure Model, pictured in Figure 9.12, is a road map to assessment. It provides a framework around which to organize therapeutic recreation assessment.

Enhanced Leisure Experiences; Internal and External Strengths and Resources

Assessment can focus on discovery of internal and external strengths and resources, the state or quality of a participant's leisure experience, passions, interests, preferences, and other indicators of enhanced leisure. Assessment can also clarify the environmental facilitators to an enhanced leisure experience and to environmental resources that help nurture well-being. Strengths and resources in psychological/emotional, cognitive, social, physical, and spiritual domains can be assessed. And assessment can focus on important indicators of well-being, such as self-determination, friends and social supports, community resources, recreation skills and interests, and personal goals. The "person in the environment" framework of the Flourishing through Leisure Model provides direction for assessment focus across several domains and in many life settings.

Outcomes of Well-Being and a Flourishing Life

The Flourishing through Leisure Model also provides a roadmap to the outcomes on which assessment could focus. If we are helping participants truly reach their goals, we can then assess changes in well-being and quality of life using a variety of tools and approaches. By assessing where a participant is at the start of our services, and where he or she is at the end of our services, we can document overall changes in happiness, well-being, and quality of life. We can also document changes in all the aspects of well-being, from leisure well-being to physical well-being. We can examine every petal of the flower, or only those that are most important to the participant and his or her perception of a high quality of life.

The next section in this chapter describes several specific assessment tools that you could use in

204 • Therapeutic Recreation Practice: A Strengths Approach

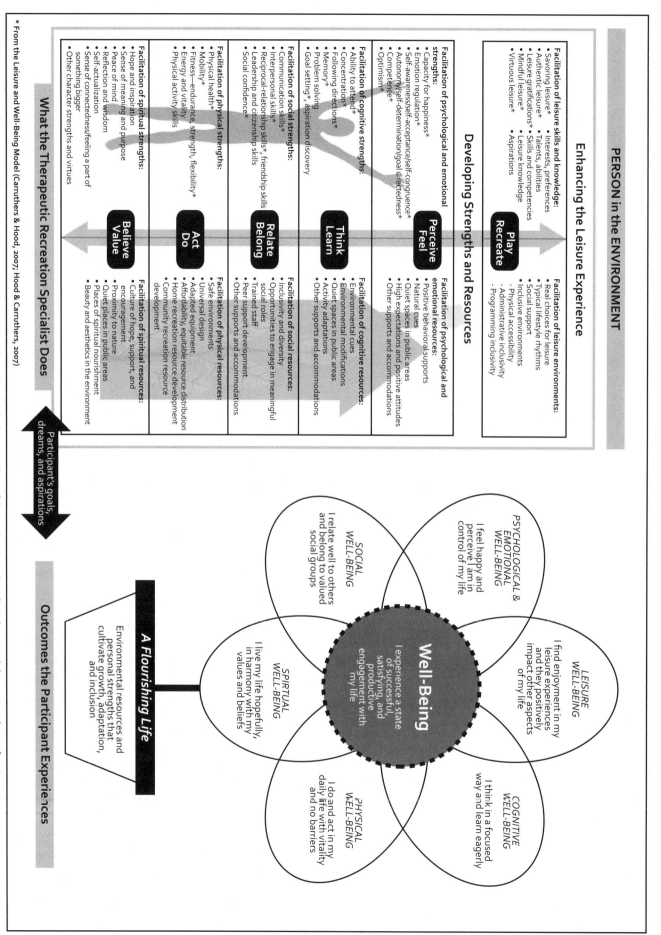

Figure 9.12 Flourishing through Leisure Model: An Ecological Extension of the Leisure and Well-Being Model as a Roadmap for Assessment

therapeutic recreation assessment. There are hundreds of assessment tools available to you—we will only introduce those that are commonly used by interdisciplinary or transdisciplinary teams, are strengths-based, and are important resources for you if you are guided in your practices by the Flourishing through Leisure Model or other strengths-based models of therapeutic recreation practice.

Common Team-Based Assessments

Often, in therapeutic recreation practice, you will participate in assessment as part of a team, working together to discover the strengths, context, and goals of participants. Depending on the setting, many agencies use a team-based approach to initial assessment. In addition, assessment tools and approaches may be mandated by regulators or other external groups in many of the agencies where you may work. These mandated or commonly used assessments are often global in nature and completed by all members of the team, under the leadership of a primary coordinator. Below, we give an overview of several common team-based assessments you will likely encounter in therapeutic recreation practice: the ICF, the FIM, the MDS, the GAF, the TPBA, as well as some examples of team-based interview protocols. As a therapeutic recreation specialist, you will likely complete a piece or section of this type of assessment, and you will often complete a more in-depth therapeutic recreation assessment in addition to the team-based assessment. Our intent is to *introduce* you to each of these team-based assessment tools. We hope that you will learn more about each tool as you use it in your work or through the resources we provide for further study.

International Classification of Functioning, Disability and Health Checklist (ICF)

The International Classification of Functioning, Disability and Health Checklist (the ICF Checklist) was developed by the World Health Organization (WHO). We introduced you to the ICF model in Chapter 5 *Strengths* and Chapter 6 *Theories*. The ICF Checklist is a practical tool to discover and record information on the functioning and disability of an individual. According to the WHO (2001), it is used for functional status assessment, goal setting, planning and monitoring, as well as outcome measurement. The ICF Checklist allows you to identify and qualify the individual's functioning profile in a simple and time efficient manner. According to the WHO (2001):

One of the major innovations in ICF is the presence of an environmental factor classification that makes it possible for the identification of environmental barriers and facilitators for both capacity and performance of actions and tasks in daily living. With this classification scheme, which can be used either on an individual basis or for population-wide data collection, it may be possible to create instruments that assess environments in terms of their level of facilitation or barrier-creation for different kinds and levels of disability. With this information in hand, it will then be more practical to develop and implement guidelines for universal design and other environmental regulations that extend the functioning levels of persons with disabilities across the range of life activities. (p. 8)

The ecological approach used by the ICF Checklist makes it an attractive and useful assessment tool for therapeutic recreation specialists, since we work to help participants achieve their aspirations in the context of their environment.

In Table 9.11, we present the broad areas the team assesses with the ICF Checklist. Within each of these broad areas are many specific sub-areas (only the Community, Social, and Civic Life section has the sub-areas listed due its relevance to therapeutic recreation). Part 1 of the ICF Checklist assesses the extent of impairment to body functions (the physiological functions of the body) and body structures (anatomical parts of the body). Part 2 (Activity and Participation) is a key area in which therapeutic recreation specialists can contribute to assessment. **Activity** is defined by the ICF as "the execution of a task or action by an individual," and **participation** is defined as "involvement in a life situation" (WHO, 2003, p. 4). **Performance** is defined as the level at which a person can do an activity in his or her real-life environment. **Capacity** is the level at which a person can do an activity in a standardized environment, like a clinic area or hospital room. As therapeutic recreation specialists, we can provide especially useful assessment information on the Community, Social, and Civic Life section of the ICF Checklist, especially given our use of the community environment as a routine part of the services we provide. The ICF Checklist is completed using observation and interview. You can learn more about the ICF Checklist on the World Health Organization website (http://www.who.int/classifications/icf/en/).

Table 9.11 The ICF Checklist

ICF PART 1: Body Function and Structure	
Function: • Mental functions • Sensory functions and pain • Voice and speech functions • Functions of the cardiovascular, hematological, • immunological, and respiratory systems • Functions of the digestive, metabolic, and endocrine systems • Genitourinary and reproductive functions • Neuro-musculoskeletal and movement-related functions • Functions of the skin and related structures	**Structure:** • Structure of the nervous system • The eye, ear, and related structures • Structures involved in voice and speech • Structure of the cardiovascular, immunological, and respiratory systems • Structures related to the digestive, metabolic, and endocrine systems • Structure related to genitourinary and reproductive systems • Structure related to movement • Skin and related structures
ICF PART 2: Activity and Participation	**ICF PART 2 Scale**

• Learning and applying knowledge
• General tasks and demands
• Communication
• Mobility
• Self-care
• Domestic life
• Interpersonal interactions and relationships
• Major life areas
• Community, social, and civic life
   - Community life
   - Recreation and leisure
   - Religion and spirituality
   - Human rights
   - Political life and citizenship
	First Qualifier: Performance
	Extent of participation restriction
	Second Qualifier: Capacity (without assistance)
	Extent of activity limitation
	  0 **No difficulty** means the person has no problem.
	
	  1 **Mild difficulty** means a problem that is present less than 25% of the time, with an intensity a person can tolerate and which happened rarely over the last 30 days.
	
	  2 **Moderate difficulty** means a problem is present less than 50% of the time, with an intensity that is interfering in the person's day-to-day life and which happened occasionally over the last 30 days.
	
	  3 **Severe difficulty** means a problem is present more than 50% of the time, with an intensity that is partially disrupting the person's day-to-day life and which happened frequently over the last 30 days.
	
	  4 **Complete difficulty** means a problem is present more than 95% of the time, with an intensity that is totally disrupting the person's day-to-day life and which happened every day over the last 30 days.
	
	  8 **Not specified** means there is insufficient information to specify the severity of the difficulty.
	
	  9 **Not applicable** means it is inappropriate to apply a particular code.

ICF PART 3: Environmental Factors	**ICF PART 3 Scale**

• Products and technology
• Natural environment and human-made changes to environment
• Support and relationships
• Attitudes
• Services, systems, and policies
	Qualifier in environment:
	  0 No barriers 0 No facilitator
	Barriers or facilitator:
	  1 Mild barriers +1 Mild facilitator
	  2 Moderate barriers +2 Moderate facilitator
	  3 Severe barriers +3 Substantial facilitator
	  4 Complete barriers +4 Complete facilitator

From World Health Organization (2003)

Functional Independence Measure (FIM)

The Functional Independence Measure (FIM) is most often used in physical rehabilitation facilities. The FIM refers to a scale that is used to measure a participant's ability to *function* with *independence*. A FIM score is typically collected within 72 hours after admission to a rehabilitation unit, within 72 hours before discharge, and between 80 to 180 days after discharge.

The FIM is used to assess several aspects of a participant's basic functioning. These are listed in Table 9.12. Therapeutic recreation specialists often assess areas such as social cognition or communication, but they provide feedback on all areas of the assessment. Each of these areas is assessed using the FIM Scale, provided in Table 9.13. Through interview and observation, the team assigns a value that best describes the participant's level of ability in each area.

You must be certified in the FIM system before assigning scores that rate people's functioning. Certification involves watching training videos, observing others in practice, and taking a test. Though as a therapeutic recreation specialist, you will likely focus on the social cognition area of the FIM assessment, you will also likely be involved in all aspects of the assessment (see Figure 9.13, p. 208).

The FIM uses interview and observation as the main approaches to collecting information. You can learn more about the FIM from the company that regulates its use, The Uniform Data Set for Medical Rehabilitation (http://www.udsmr.org).

Table 9.12 Team-Based Assessments Commonly Used in Practice

FIM — *Functional Independence Measure*	MDS 3.0 — *Minimum Data Set 3.0*
Commonly used in physical rehabilitation Areas assessed: • *Self-care:* eating, grooming, bathing, dressing (upper body), dressing (lower body), toileting • *Sphincter control:* bladder management, bowel management • *Transfers:* transferring (to go from one place to another) in a bed, chair, and/or wheelchair, transferring on and off a toilet, transferring into and out of a shower • *Locomotion:* locomotion (moving) for walking or in a wheelchair, and locomotion going up and down stairs • *Communication:* comprehension, expression • **Social cognition:** social interaction, problem solving, and memory	Commonly used in long-term care Areas assessed: • Section A: Identification information • Section B: Hearing, speech, and vision • Section C: Cognitive patterns • Section D: Mood • Section E: Behavior • **Section F: Preferences for customary routine and activities** • Section G: Functional status • Section H: Bladder and bowel • Section I: Active diagnoses • Section J: Health conditions • Section K: Swallowing and nutritional status • Section L: Oral/dental status • Section M: Skin conditions • Section N: Medications • **Section O: Special treatments and procedures (recreational and music therapy listed as a choice here)** • Section P: Restraints • Section Q: Participation in assessment and goal-setting • Section V: Care area assessment summary • Section X: Correction request • Section Z: Assessment administration
GAF — *Global Assessment of Functioning*	TPBA — *Transdisciplinary Play-Based Assessment*
Commonly used in mental health Areas assessed: • **Social functioning** • Occupational functioning • Symptoms of mental illness	Commonly used in pediatrics and school settings Areas assessed: • Sensorimotor development • Vision and hearing development • **Emotional and social development** • Communication development • Cognitive development

Note: Areas in bold type are likely to be assessed by a therapeutic recreation specialist.

Table 9.13 FIM Scale *(Wright, 2000)*

Levels	Independent 7 Complete independence (timely, safely) 6 Modified independence (using a device)	No Helper
	Modified Dependence 5 Supervision (participant does 100%) 4 Minimal assist (participant does 75%+) 3 Moderate assist (participant does 50%+) **Complete Dependence** 2 Maximal assist (participant does 25%+) 1 Total assist (participant does less than 25%)	Helper

Note: Leave no blanks. Enter "1" if participant is not testable due to risk.

Life Story:

Using the FIM in My Practice, by Janet Connolly, CTRS

I am a Certified Therapeutic Recreation Specialist (CTRS) currently working in a Long-Term Acute Care Hospital (LTACH) on an inpatient physical rehabilitation unit. As in short-term acute rehabilitation hospitals, we utilize the Functional Independence Measure (FIM) as a tool for measuring functional gains and outcomes. I completed my first training to become "FIM Certified" over 12 years ago while working in an acute rehabilitation hospital, and I continue to take the recommended refresher courses to maintain this certification.

The hospital I currently work at is unique in its approach to using the FIM. Only therapists/nurses with over one year of experience in rehabilitation are allowed to score the FIM independently. I agree with this practice, as it speaks to a base of knowledge that all who use the instrument should possess, especially when setting long-term goals or expected outcomes.

As a therapeutic recreation specialist, I am the designated professional at my hospital responsible for scoring *Social Interaction* on the FIM. I complete this section of the FIM by evaluating the patient for the first 3 days of their stay; gathering information in a variety of ways: observation of the patient, interview with the patient/family/caregivers, completing a skill assessment of the patient, documentation review, and behavior assessment. I assess the patient based on the timeliness of his or her responses, the appropriateness of the interaction, and how much assistance is needed to interact. I pay particular attention to social behaviors and level of assistance needed for interaction. It is also important for me to note if a patient is utilizing pharmacological interventions as part of treatment, as this too impacts a patient's FIM score. I feel it is a testimony to the expertise of our profession that we are charged with the responsibility of completing this section of the FIM, and I feel it should not be taken lightly.

In addition to our primary areas of focus, as a member of an interdisciplinary team, I can provide input on any area of the FIM. If I am working with a patient and he or she demonstrates particular skills with me that differ from the level demonstrated with the primary therapist who records progress in this area, it is important that I note these changes in function. If a patient demonstrates varying levels of ability, the lowest score prevails. Consistency is important; therefore, communication is critical among team members to ensure accuracy in scoring.

Having witnessed the FIM in action for over 10 years, I have learned that the FIM is widely accepted as "THE TOOL." It is used to compare hospitals' and clinicians' abilities to rehabilitate patients who have significant functional impairments. It is the responsibility of the professional to not only understand the FIM tool and how it is implemented, but to also question and affirm one's own understanding of assessment of function of each sub-category, particularly the one they are responsible for. In the case of therapeutic recreation, does it not speak to the need for therapeutic recreation professionals working in physical medicine and rehabilitation to adopt the standardized "tool of choice" for measuring Social Interaction in order to improve our skills, establish consistency of practice, and therefore accuracy in assessing and documenting function? I think it does and I look forward to it!

Figure 9.13 Life Story: Using the FIM in Practice

Minimum Data Set (MDS)

Used in long-term care, the Minimum Data Set (MDS) was developed by the Centers for Medicare and Medicaid Services (CMS). Nursing homes are required to use the MDS at the time of admission, at regular intervals throughout a participant's stay, and any time there is a change in status. The MDS is used to assist teams in developing a comprehensive care plan for each resident.

First developed in 1990, the MDS continues to be improved. In 2009, the MDS 2.0 was being used, and the MDS 3.0 was introduced in 2010. The MDS 3.0 provides increased opportunities for the transdisciplinary team to interview participants and their families, to increase the voice of participants in their own care.

The MDS measures several areas of a resident's life (see Table 9.12). One section of the MDS focuses specifically on activities and customary routines, based on the premise that nursing homes are not only healthcare facilities but also places where people live. Nursing homes thus serve multiple needs of residents, from rehabilitation to community living. Routines and activities make up an important aspect of quality of life in a nursing home, and therapeutic recreation plays an important role in assessing for this continuum of services for residents. Residents and their families have identified the following areas as important to them in their daily lives: choice and personal control over daily life activities, privacy, daily physical activity, access to adaptive or assistive devices, and participation in assessment and planning. Based on this feedback, the MDS includes an embedded assessment called the Preferences Assessment Tool (shown in Figure 9.14, p. 210), an interview-based assessment that gathers preferences for activities and routines. In addition, the MDS contains Section O, in which additional therapeutic recreation services that are more intensive and individualized can be documented.

You can learn more about the MDS from the Centers for Medicare and Medicaid Services website (http://www.cms.hhs.gov/NursingHomeQualityInits/).

Global Assessment of Functioning (GAF)

The Global Assessment of Functioning (GAF) is commonly used in the U.S. in mental health settings and by the Veterans Administration. It is a part of the Diagnostic and Statistical Manual of Mental Disorders (DSM). The DSM provides a framework for describing a participant's diagnosis and status in relation to mental illness and disability. It uses a deficits-based approach, and provides a label and description based on five axes: (a) clinical disorder(s), (b) underlying pervasive conditions, (c) acute medical conditions, (d) psychosocial or environmental factors contributing to disorder, and lastly, (e) a participant's score on the GAF.

The GAF is a *global* assessment of functioning. It is based on a numeric scale from 0 through 100 and is used to rate overall psychological, social, and occupational functioning of adults. The single measure is often determined by a psychiatrist or other mental health professional with input from the team, and is a subjective measure of how well a person is performing in several domains of his or her life. The scale provides a range of scores for each functional level (see Table 9.12 and Table 9.14). The GAF is a broad and non-specific indicator of mental health. As a therapeutic recreation specialist, you may provide input based on interview and observation to assist the team in arriving at a GAF score.

The DSM is a useful resource to learn more about the Global Assessment of Functioning, as is the website of the American Psychiatric Association (http://www.psych.org).

Transdisciplinary Play-Based Assessment (TPBA)

In pediatric and school settings, a common tool in use is the Transdisciplinary Play-Based Assessment (TPBA). Developed by Linder (2008) and colleagues, the TPBA looks at the overall functioning of children while they play. It is transdisciplinary and authentic, and it primarily uses observation. The TPBA looks at several areas of a child's functioning, as listed in Table 9.12. Information in all domains is collected by observing the child while playing and by talking with parents or caregivers. The data collected is both quantitative and qualitative. The assessment results provide guidance for building on a child's strengths and interests and identifying supports and accommodations. You can learn more about the TPBA by reading the published assessment tool manual, which is listed in the reference list at the end of this chapter.

Strengths-Based Interviews

Earlier, we discussed the use of interviews as a powerful assessment approach. In the strengths-based approach, protocols for team-based interviews have been developed that ask about the whole life of a participant and what he or she aspires to in each area. One common solution-focused interview approach is called

Resident _____ **Identifier** _____ **Date** _____

Section F — Preferences for Customary Routine and Activities

F0300. Should Interview for Daily and Activity Preferences be Conducted? - Attempt to interview all residents able to communicate. If resident is unable to complete, attempt to complete interview with family member or significant other

Enter Code ☐
0. **No** (resident is rarely/never understood *and* family/significant other not available) → Skip to and complete F0800, Staff Assessment of Daily and Activity Preferences
1. **Yes** → Continue to F0400, Interview for Daily Preferences

F0400. Interview for Daily Preferences

Show resident the response options and say: **"While you are in this facility..."**

↓ Enter Codes in Boxes

Coding:
1. **Very important**
2. **Somewhat important**
3. **Not very important**
4. **Not important at all**
5. **Important, but can't do or no choice**
9. **No response or non-responsive**

- ☐ A. how important is it to you to **choose what clothes to wear?**
- ☐ B. how important is it to you to **take care of your personal belongings or things?**
- ☐ C. how important is it to you to **choose between a tub bath, shower, bed bath, or sponge bath?**
- ☐ D. how important is it to you to **have snacks available between meals?**
- ☐ E. how important is it to you to **choose your own bedtime?**
- ☐ F. how important is it to you to **have your family or a close friend involved in discussions about your care?**
- ☐ G. how important is it to you to **be able to use the phone in private?**
- ☐ H. how important is it to you to **have a place to lock your things to keep them safe?**

F0500. Interview for Activity Preferences

Show resident the response options and say: **"While you are in this facility..."**

↓ Enter Codes in Boxes

Coding:
1. **Very important**
2. **Somewhat important**
3. **Not very important**
4. **Not important at all**
5. **Important, but can't do or no choice**
9. **No response or non-responsive**

- ☐ A. how important is it to you to **have books, newspapers, and magazines to read?**
- ☐ B. how important is it to you to **listen to music you like?**
- ☐ C. how important is it to you to **be around animals such as pets?**
- ☐ D. how important is it to you to **keep up with the news?**
- ☐ E. how important is it to you to **do things with groups of people?**
- ☐ F. how important is it to you to **do your favorite activities?**
- ☐ G. how important is it to you to **go outside to get fresh air when the weather is good?**
- ☐ H. how important is it to you to **participate in religious services or practices?**

F0600. Daily and Activity Preferences Primary Respondent

Enter Code ☐
Indicate primary respondent for Daily and Activity Preferences (F0400 and F0500)
1. **Resident**
2. **Family or significant other** (close friend or other representative)
9. **Interview could not be completed** by resident or family/significant other ("No response" to 3 or more items)

MDS 3.0 Nursing Home Comprehensive (NC) Version 1.10.4 Effective 04/01/2012

Figure 9.14 Section F of the Minimum Data Set

Table 9.14 The Global Assessment of Functioning Scale

GAF Score	Functional Level
91–100	Superior functioning in a wide range of activities; life's problems never seem to get out of hand; is sought out by others because of his or her many qualities. No symptoms.
81–90	Absent or minimal symptoms; good functioning in all areas; interested and involved in a wide range of activities; socially effective; generally satisfied with life; no more than everyday problems or concerns.
71–80	If symptoms are present they are transient and expectable reactions to psychosocial stresses; no more than slight impairment in social, occupational, or school functioning.
61–70	Some mild symptoms OR some difficulty in social, occupational, or school functioning, but generally functioning pretty well; has some meaningful interpersonal relationships.
51–60	Moderate symptoms OR any moderate difficulty in social, occupational, or school functioning.
41–50	Serious symptoms OR any serious impairment in social, occupational, or school functioning.
31–40	Some impairment in reality testing or communication OR major impairment in several areas, such as work or school, family relations, judgment, thinking, or mood.
21–30	Behavior is considerably influenced by delusions or hallucinations OR serious impairment in communications or judgment OR inability to function in all areas.
11–20	Some danger of hurting self or others OR occasionally fails to maintain minimal personal hygiene OR gross impairment in communication.
1–10	Persistent danger of severely hurting self or others OR persistent inability to maintain minimum personal hygiene OR serious suicidal act with clear expectation of death.
0	Not enough information available to provide global assessment of functioning.

the "Miracle Question" (see Figure 9.15, p. 212). The Miracle Question was first developed by O'Hanlon (1999) as an antidote to the usual problem-oriented approaches used to help people. The Miracle Question asks participants to identify what they most want to work toward in their lives, so it is a life they love. The Miracle Question approach has been used in a wide array of settings, from mental health to youth development. Since recreation and leisure are such important aspects of the "good life" that people dream about, asking the Miracle Question as a team often leads to information that will help you and the participant develop a plan for therapeutic recreation services.

Other strengths-based interviews that are conducted in a team approach, and which look at all aspects of a participant's life, have been developed. Tables 9.15 (p. 212) and 9.16 (p. 213) are two more examples of interview protocols that can be completed in a team approach, and provide valuable information to you in therapeutic recreation.

Many more team-based assessments are available or in use in agencies that work with participants in a helping relationship. We have touched on a few that are commonly used, and in which you will have an important role as a therapeutic recreation specialist. In the next section of this chapter, we want to provide you with some examples of assessment tools that are more specific to therapeutic recreation and that you will often complete on your own with participants. The tools we have selected to share with you are strengths-based, and can be used in multiple ways with participants to provide a baseline from which to evaluate change, discover strengths, set goals, and plan services, supports, and accommodations. We call this section of the chapter a "toolbox." Like a carpenter, you will need to understand each tool to know if it is appropriate for the job you have to do. You will need to develop the skills and practical wisdom to select the right tool for the task. We will end this chapter with a discussion of the process you can use to develop that level of practical wisdom.

A Toolbox of Assessment Resources for Strengths-Based Therapeutic Recreation Practice

In therapeutic recreation, we have many assessment tools we can choose from to help us understand and

The Miracle Question

I'd like to ask you a strange question.

Suppose that you go home tonight and go to bed and fall asleep as usual. And while you are sleeping, a miracle happens. The miracle is that the problems that brought you in here are gone and you don't know because you are sleeping.

What will you notice different tomorrow that will tell you that there has been a miracle?

What are the signs throughout the day (after the miracle occurred) that are evidence to you that the miracle occurred?

What are the signs throughout the day (after the miracle occurred) that will show your friends or family that the miracle happened?

What difference would it make in your life if the miracle did start happening?

Figure 9.15 The Miracle Question as a Transdisciplinary Strengths-Based Assessment Approach *(Positive Psychology, 2010)*

Table 9.15 Example of Transdisciplinary Team Interview Questions *(adapted from Saleebey, 2006)*

Sample Strengths-Based Initial Interview Questions for a Transdisciplinary Team

Strengths-discovery questions are endless. Here are some sample interview questions, to start your own thinking about what is important to learn from the participant.

Survival questions:
How have you managed to overcome the challenges that you have faced? What have you learned about yourself and your world during those struggles?

Support questions:
Who are the people that you can rely on? Who has made you feel understood, supported, or encouraged?

Exception questions:
When things were going well in life, what was different?

Possibility questions:
What do you want to accomplish in your life? What are your hopes for your future or the future of your family?

Esteem questions:
What makes you proud about yourself? What positive things do people say about you?

Perspective questions:
What are your ideas about your current situation?

Change questions:
What do you think is necessary for things to change? What could you do to make that happen?

A word of caution. Repeating these questions or filling out a strengths-based form does not mean that you are working from the strengths perspective. A profound belief in the participant's potential is intrinsic to any strengths-based assessment. Thinking about strengths begins with the understanding of what goals and dreams the person has and reflecting on the possibilities and hope in their lives. In this process, participants can discover or develop new possibilities for themselves and change toward a better quality of life.

Table 9.16 Transdisciplinary Strengths Assessment Worksheet

Domain	SEVEN LIFE DOMAINS The intrinsic purpose of this assessment is to "amplify the well aspects of the individual."		
	For each domain:		
	Resources Used in the Past	Current Status & Resources	Individual Desires & Aspirations
• Daily Living Situation • Financial/Insurance • Vocational/Educational • Social Supports • Health • Leisure/Recreation • Spirituality	What has worked well in the past for this domain/situation?	What is available now? What's going on today?	What do you want?

For a complete description of this tool as well as the process of conducting a strengths assessment, please see Rapp & Goscha (2006, p. 99).

discover a participant's strengths and resources. Many tools have been developed to discover a participant's problems or barriers, instead of focusing on strengths, facilitators, and assets. However, these same tools could be used in a strengths approach if you use them carefully, with the purposes of learning what the participant can do well and what the participant wants to do more of. One published work in therapeutic recreation that is an important assessment resource is the "Red Book," as it is often called. The "Red Book," *Assessment Tools for Recreational Therapy and Related Fields* by joan burlingame and Thomas Blaschko, is an encyclopedia of assessment tools available in the field. The volume contains a wealth of information about assessment in general, as well as about specific assessment tools. In Table 9.17 we provide a listing of some of the tools provided in the "Red Book," what the tools assess, and with whom. Some of these tools can be used in a strengths approach. We hope you will count the "Red Book" as one of the resources you have in your assessment toolbox.

In this section, we offer a wide variety of assessment tools that are strengths-based, newer, and not found in currently published assessment resources like the "Red Book." However, we do include some assessments that are published and widely available, due to their importance in the field and their potential strengths approach (i.e., the *Leisure Diagnostic Battery*, the *Leisure Competence Measure*, the *Leisurescope Plus*, and the *Home and Community Social Behavior Scales*). We organize this toolbox of assessments according to areas on which you will likely focus in therapeutic recreation practice: internal strengths (leisure and functional), external strengths and resources (leisure and functional), and outcomes (well-being and quality of life). For each tool, we provide a brief description of the tool and where you can access it. We hope you will use this information in addition to the existing published assessment resources in the field.

Internal Strengths

Leisure Assessments

Several excellent assessment tools are available to measure or assess the overall leisure functioning of participants. We will highlight only a few that are readily available, well-developed, and are, or can be, strengths-based.

Leisure Diagnostic Battery

The Leisure Diagnostic Battery (LDB) assesses several areas important to quality leisure experiences. Developed by Witt and Ellis (1989) and updated in 2008 to a computer-based version (Witt, Ellis, & Widmer, 2008), the LDB measures "leisure functioning," which is conceptualized as perceived freedom in leisure. Perceived freedom in leisure is defined as how the participant feels about his or her leisure experiences and the positive outcomes associated with them. Involvement in activity becomes leisure when certain conditions are met, which are measured by the LDB: perceived leisure competence, perceived leisure control, leisure needs, depth of involvement, and playfulness. The LDB is based on attribution theory, which helps explain motivation for and quality of leisure experiences. Table 9.18 provides a description of each scale of the LDB. A long and a short form are available for use—the short form combines scales A–E (the Perceived Freedom in Leisure scales) into one scale of only 25 items.

Leisure Competence Measure

The Leisure Competence Measure (LCM) was developed to document the outcomes of therapeutic

Table 9.17 Commonly Used Assessment Tools Featured in the "Red Book"*

Tool	What does the tool assess?	With whom?
LEISURE DOMAIN		
Leisure Attitude Measure (LAM)	Attitudes toward leisure	Adolescents and adults
Leisure Interest Measure (LIM)	Leisure interests in eight domains	Adolescents and adults
Leisure Motivation Scale (LMS)	Motivations for leisure involvement	Adolescents and adults
Leisure Satisfaction Scale/Measure (LSM)	Satisfaction of needs through leisure	Adolescents and adults
Leisure and Recreation Involvement (LRI)	Perception of quality of involvement in recreation activities	Adolescents and adults
Leisure Assessment Inventory (LAI)	Leisure activity involvement, leisure preferences and interests, barriers	Adults with developmental disabilities
Leisure Step Up	Quality and breadth of recreation participation	Adolescents and adults
STILAP	Leisure interests and leisure lifestyle balance	Adults with developmental disabilities
Recreation Participation Data Sheet (RPD)	Functional leisure abilities such as initiation, participation, and decision-making	Children, adolescents, and adults
Community Integration Program (CIP)	Knowledge and functional skills for using leisure resources in the community	Children, adolescents, and adults
FUNCTIONAL DOMAINS		
Comprehensive Evaluation in Recreational Therapy— Psych/Behavioral, Rev. (CERT-Psych/R)	Performance areas in general, individual, and group social skills	Adolescents and adults
Comprehensive Evaluation in Recreational Therapy—Physical Disabilities (CERT—Physical Disabilities)	Broad-based assessment in eight functional areas such as gross and fine motor function, locomotion and motor skills, sensory, cognitive, communication skills, and behavior	Adolescents and adults
FOX—Activity Therapy Skills Baseline	Social and affective skills	Individuals with developmental disabilities
Functional Assessment of Characteristics for Therapeutic Recreation, Revised (FACTR-R)	Functional skills in three areas: cognitive, physical, and social/emotional	Adolescents and adults
General Recreation Screening Tool (GRST)	Functional skills in all domains: cognitive, physical, social, and emotional	Children or individuals with developmental disabilities
Leisure and Social/Sexual Assessment (LS/SA)	Breadth and depth of understanding of social and sexual roles	Individuals with developmental disabilities
Recreation Early Development Screening Tool (REDS)	Functional skills in areas such as play, fine and gross motor skills, sensory, and social/cognition	Very young children or individuals with significant intellectual disabilities

*The "Red Book" is *Assessment Tools for Recreational Therapy and Related Fields* (burlingame & Blaschko, 2002)

Table 9.18 Areas Measured with the Leisure Diagnostic Battery *(Witt & Ellis, 1989)*

Leisure Diagnostic Battery	
Scale	Description
Scale A: Perceived Leisure Competence	Measures the level of perceived competence (the possession of required skills, knowledge, experience, or capacity for an activity) in leisure in social, cognitive, physical, and general terms
Scale B: Perceived Leisure Control	Measures the perception of stable, internal control over events or outcomes in leisure experiences
Scale C: Leisure Needs	Measures the ability to satisfy intrinsic needs through leisure experiences; needs include relaxation, surplus energy, compensation, catharsis, optimal arousal, status, gregariousness, creative expression, skill development, and self-image
Scale D: Depth of Involvement in Leisure	Measures how absorbed one can become in leisure, or experience flow (centering of attention, merging of action and awareness, loss of self-consciousness, perception of control over self and environment, clear demands from the activity)
Scale E: Playfulness	Measures how playful or spontaneous one is during leisure, including cognitive, social and physical spontaneity, and manifest joy
Total of Scale A–E	Perceived freedom in leisure
Scale F: Barriers to Leisure	Measures barriers: communication, social, decision-making, opportunity, motivation, ability, money, and time
Scale G: Leisure Preferences	Measures preferences for leisure in terms of activities (outdoor/nature, music/dance/drama, sports, arts/crafts/hobbies, mental linguistics; and style of participation (individual/group, risk/non-risk, active/passive)

recreation services in eight areas: leisure awareness, leisure attitude, leisure skills, cultural/social behaviors, interpersonal skills, community integration skills, social contact, and community participation (Kloseck & Crilly, 1997). Each of these subscales is described in Table 9.19. The LCM was designed to be used with other assessment tools and approaches. Assessment results are then recorded on the LCM using a rating scale very similar to the FIM discussed earlier in this chapter. The 7-point scale mirrors the FIM scale, using ratings that range from complete independence to total dependence and assistance. The Leisure Competence Measure has a leisure-based philosophy of therapeutic recreation, consistent with the Flourishing through Leisure Model.

Strengths-Based Group Interviews

In Chapter 10 *Planning* we will look closely at a planning process called MAPS, or Making Action Plans. A part of the MAPS process is collecting information about the participant through a group interview with the participant and her or his circle of support (Falvey, Forest, Pearpoint, & Rosenberg, 1997). You ask seven key questions that can be used specifically to focus on recreation and leisure in the participant's life:

1. What is this person's history or story?
2. What are this person's dreams for recreation and leisure?
3. What is your nightmare for this person? (can be omitted)
4. Who is this person?
5. What are this person's strengths, gifts, and talents?
6. What does this person need to achieve his or her dream (and avoid the nightmare)?
7. What is the plan of action?

Typically, you will capture the answers to these questions during the group interview on large paper with colorful images and pictures. The MAPS questions are a powerful tool to discover a person's dreams, talents, strengths, and supports for recreation. Because the last question asks how the dream will be achieved, the transition from assessment to planning with people who will be supportive of the participant is often successful. We will discuss the MAPS process in more detail in Chapter 10 *Planning*.

Table 9.19 Areas Measured with the Leisure Competence Measure *(Kloseck & Crilly, 1997)*

Leisure Competence Measure	
Scale	Description
Sub-scale 1: Leisure Awareness	Rating of knowledge and understanding of leisure
Sub-scale 2: Leisure Attitude	Rating of attitude toward leisure involvement
Sub-scale 3: Leisure Skills	Rating of skills that affect leisure involvement
Sub-scale 4: Cultural/Social Behaviors	Rating of cultural and social behaviors that affect ability to function well in leisure
Sub-scale 5: Interpersonal Skills	Rating of ability to participate in inter-individual and group situations
Sub-scale 6: Community Integration Skills	Rating of skills needed for successful involvement in community leisure activities
Sub-scale 7: Social Contact	Rating of types and duration of social contacts
Sub-scale 8: Community Participation	Rating of overall participation pattern in the community

Another variation of the MAPS questions is the friendship focus-group, based on the Framework for Accomplishment Profile (Amado, Conklin, & Wells, 1990). The questions are similar to MAPS, but with a stronger focus on friendships in leisure:

1. What have the person's life experiences been like?
2. Who are the people in this individual's life? What kinds of roles does the person play in those relationships?
3. Where does this person spend time? In what activities does the person participate?
4. What works and what doesn't work for this person?
5. What are the person's interests, gifts, and abilities?
6. What does this person contribute to others?
7. What assistance does the person need?

According to Amado and colleagues, these questions can help form a vision for a person's social life and help him or her form real and meaningful relationships in valued activities.

Strengths Discovery Assessment

The Strengths Discovery Assessment was developed by Clark (2007) as a way to help youth receiving services for emotional behavioral disorders focus on the strengths and assets in their lives, and clarify the life they want. The Strengths Discovery Assessment is an interview protocol, using a conversational style, which focuses on the following areas:

1. Interests and preferences
2. Values and traditions in one's life
3. Skills, abilities, and competencies
4. Personal attributes (e.g., sense of humor, resiliency)
5. Dreams/Aspirations
6. Strategies in the past that have worked best at home, school, or in the community
7. Settings which are most comfortable
8. Family members, relatives, friends, and other informal key players valued by and/or in this young person's life
9. Formal key players involved in his/her life
10. Priority needs and goals

Though the interview can focus on several different life domains, you can also focus specifically on recreation and leisure. The Strengths Discovery Assessment and self-guided training modules on its use are readily available (see the reference list at the end of this chapter for details).

Assessment of Leisure Interests, Preferences, and Passions

One of the most important areas you assess in therapeutic recreation practice is what participants love to do in leisure. This information is a key to helping participants enhance their leisure experiences, derive satisfaction, and enjoy life. Leisure interests, preferences, and passions were defined in Chapter 5 *Strengths*. Remember that you can use scale G of the Leisure Diagnostic Battery as one way to help participants clarify their preferences for leisure. Other tools we summarize for you in this section include the Passion Scale, the Passion Interview, the Leisurescope Plus, and the Person-Activity Fit Assessment.

Passion Scale

Developed by Vallerand and colleagues (2003), the Passion Scale measures how much passion a participant feels for a favorite activity. Passion can be harmonious, meaning an individual pursues an activity at a high level based on intrinsic motivation, positive emotion, and positive identity formation, and the activity is harmonious with other life activities. Passion can also be obsessive, meaning an individual pursues an activity at a high level based on some form of pressure (internal or external), disproportionate identity formation (where the activity becomes too significant), and a sense of uncontrollability with the activity in relation to other life activities. The Passion Scale helps participants identify favorite activities that truly add quality to their life, rather than those that may cause disruption. The Passion Scale is readily available on the website of the Research Laboratory of Social Behavior (see the reference list at the end of this chapter for more information).

Passion Interview

Some participants with whom you work will know their passions, and easily be able to identify them to complete the Passion Scale. Others will be unsure, and the "Discovering Your Passions" interview developed by McGill (1996) may be useful for the assessment process. The interview questions are provided in Figure 9.16. The questions can be asked directly in a conversational interview or can be answered through sustained observation over the course of time.

Discovering Your Passions!

The following questions can be asked in a conversational interview or through sustained observation over the course of time:

- What lights you up?
- What do you spend a lot of your time anticipating and getting excited about?
- When do you seem most focused and unaware of distractions?
- When do you seem and feel most alive?
- What helps you feel a sense of purpose?
- What gets you animated?
- What inspires you to talk and get excited?
- Do you remember a time when you really felt proud of yourself? What were you doing at the time?
- When was there a time that you felt at peace with yourself? What was happening?
- Have you ever been doing something and then realized that a lot of time had passed? What were you doing?
- Is there a time in your leisure when you can remember smiling a lot and feeling really happy? Describe that time.
- What do you do that really makes you smile, laugh, and feel happy inside?
- What do you remember doing in your leisure that made you stand up tall and feel really good about yourself?
- What have you tried in your leisure that you would give anything to try again?
- If you had lots of money, what would you want to do with it? Where would you go and what would you buy?
- What was your favorite thing to do as a child? Why was it your favorite thing? Who did you do it with?
- Is there anything that you used to do a lot of in your leisure that you would love to take up again?
- As a child, what did your family do together for leisure, on weekends and during vacations? With relatives?
- What does your family do together now?
- What is something you have always wanted to do in your leisure but were afraid to try?
- When are you most proud of yourself? How does it feel?
- What hidden talent do you have that no one but you seems to know about?
- If you could be someone special in your leisure who would you be?
- Did you ever see someone doing something on television that you wanted to learn to do yourself?
- Do you know of any neighbors/family members/friends/staff that have interesting hobbies or who do interesting things with their spare time? What makes it interesting to you?
- Who is your idol? Why is he or she your idol—what is it about him/her that you admire?
- If you were to go on a trip, where would you go and what would you do? Who would you take with you?
- Would you like to become a member of a club or organization? Which club or what kind of club? How do you know about that club? What do you think it would be like to be a member of that group? What would make that fun?

Figure 9.16 Discovering Your Passions Interview *(McGill, 1996)*

Leisurescope Plus

Leisurescope Plus and Teen Leisurescope Plus, developed by Nall Schenk (n.d.), is a pictorial assessment that measures the degree to which participants (teens or adults) have interest in 10 different broad areas of leisure: games, sports, nature, collection, crafts, art and music, entertainment, helping others/volunteerism, social affiliation, and adventure. The assessment uses visual comparisons to help participants clarify preferences for types of leisure activities, as well as emotional motivators for participation. Emotional motivators include accomplishment, excitement, companionship, relaxation, contentment/pleasure, tension reduction, health/fitness, rejuvenation, escape, and fun. Because the assessment is pictorial, it can be used with a wide range of individuals in a variety of ways, from group to individual administration and discussion.

Person-Activity Fit Diagnostic

How do you go about finding the activities that are an optimal fit for the participants with whom you work? How do you help the participant choose strategies for their leisure that will enhance their happiness and well-being? The Person-Activity Fit Diagnostic, developed by Lyubomirsky (2007), assists participants in determining which of the strategies for increasing happiness best fits for them—strategies that can be incorporated into their leisure. The Person-Activity Fit Diagnostic consists of 12 statements, each focused on a different strategy for improving happiness that can be infused in leisure experiences (we discuss these strategies in depth in Chapter 11 *Implementation*). For each statement, participants identify to what degree the strategy feels natural, brings enjoyment, is valued, is chosen because of guilt, and is done because of external situations. The Person-Activity Fit Diagnostic helps the participant and the therapeutic recreation specialist better match strategies that feel right for the participant to activities, in order to enhance the quality of leisure experiences. You can access the electronic, self-scoring version of the Person-Activity Fit Diagnostic on the How of Happiness website, listed at the end of this chapter, or in the book by Lyubomirsky.

Functional Assessments

Enhancing leisure experience is an important focus in therapeutic recreation. By enhancing leisure, participants will likely experience functional improvements as well. Assessing or measuring functional abilities or strengths provides a baseline as well as useful information for developing strategies for enhancing leisure. Functional areas were identified in the Flourishing through Leisure Model as psychological/emotional, cognitive, social, physical, and spiritual. There are innumerable assessments available to you in therapeutic recreation to assess any or all of these functional areas. We will highlight a few that are especially useful in a strengths-based approach to therapeutic recreation and that are also helpful in enhancing the leisure experience. Some of these assessments focus in one particular functional area, while others look at multiple areas.

Assessment of Psychological and Emotional Strengths

Positivity Self-Test

Fredrickson (2009), who developed the Broaden-and-Build Theory we discussed in previous chapters, has developed a tool to help people measure the level of positive to negative emotion they experience, called their "positivity ratio." When you help participants assess their positivity ratio, you can then help them monitor how much they increase that ratio as they incorporate strategies and goals to achieve well-being in their lives. When one's positivity ratio increases, one is able to benefit from the broaden-and-build effects of positive emotion. The Positivity Self-Test is meant to be a snapshot in time, which can be taken repeatedly to monitor change over time. It includes 10 items that measure positivity (amused, awe, grateful, hopeful, inspired, interested, joyful, love, proud, and serene), and 10 items that measure negativity (angry, ashamed, contemptuous, disgust, embarrassed, guilty, hate, sad, scared, and stressed). You can access the Positivity Self-Test online at the Positive Emotions and Psychophysiology Lab at the University of North Carolina, Chapel Hill, where the test is automatically scored, and assistance is given to interpret the results. See the Resources section at the end of the chapter for the website address.

Behavioral and Emotional Rating Scale (BERS)

The Behavioral and Emotional Rating Scale (BERS-2) is a helpful tool used to assess the emotional and behavioral strengths of children (Epstein, 2004). It is a 52-item scale that captures, through observation and interview, a child's strengths in five areas: interpersonal strength (ability to regulate emotions and behavior in social settings), family involvement (quality of relationship between the child and his or her family), intrapersonal strength (perception of competence, accomplishments, and interests), school functioning (competence in school), and affective strength (ability to express feelings and accept affection from others). The BERS-2 captures perceptions of strengths in these areas from the participant, the parent, and the professional. The assessment is available commercially from PRO-ED (see the reference list at the end of the chapter).

Culture-Free Self-Esteem Inventory

The Culture-Free Self-Esteem Inventory (CFSEI-3) measures self-esteem, or a person's overall appraisal of self-worth, in a culturally fair manner on a short self-report form (Battle, 2002). The CFSEI-3 assesses global self-esteem, as well as self-esteem in other areas as well: academic, general, parental/home, personal, and social. There is also an adult version of the Culture-Free Self-Esteem Inventory. The CFSEI-3 is useful to help measure change in self-esteem as participants work toward their goals. It is available commercially from several companies and is listed in the references at the end of the chapter.

Assessment of Cognitive Strengths

Learning Styles Inventory

Recall from Chapter 5 *Strengths* that all people learn in different ways and have cognitive strengths in differing areas. Learning styles are affected by multiple intelligences, as described in Chapter 5. These include linguistic, mathematical/logical, visual/spatial, body/kinesthetic, naturalistic, musical, interpersonal, and intrapersonal styles. Using a learning styles inventory can help you and the participant better plan strategies that will be most effective for him or her. Many variations of learning style inventories are available that provide a good indicator of how an individual best learns. One example of a short inventory, which is made available by the Learning Disabilities Resources Community (2009), is provided in Table 9.20. You can find several other learning style inventories on the Internet or in research journals.

Take a minute and complete the Learning Strengths Inventory. It is a useful exercise for both the helper and the participant. If you are aware of your own learning style, you also become more aware of how you tend to approach helping others learn, which is based on your own preferred style. You can stretch yourself to teach others in styles different from your own once you have increased your self-awareness.

Assessment of Social Strengths

Home and Community Social Behavior Scales

The Home and Community Social Behavior Scales (HCSBS) is a rating scale completed through observation of a participant in home and community settings (Merrell & Caldarella, 2008). Scale A of the tool focuses on social competence using a 5-point rating scale on frequency of each behavior, and can help identify areas of strength in peer relations and self-management in social situations. The tool can also clarify areas where a participant may want training, supports, or accommodations to achieve goals. There is a companion rating scale, the School Social Behavior Scale, which is designed to be used in school environments. The HCSBS is a useful observation tool for documenting social competence in typical recreation settings at home and in the community.

Assessment of Physical Strengths

Physical functioning is an area that is often assessed in collaboration with other team members, such as a physical therapist, a kinesiotherapist, or even a physician. However, physical functioning is important to full recreation involvement, and we often focus on helping people have a better quality of life through active leisure. It is important to help participants develop their own abilities to assess their level of physical exertion and fitness. According to Ratey (2008), the research clearly shows that being physically active every day to a point of exertion helps us think, learn, feel, and relate better. An easy and commonly used assessment we can use in therapeutic recreation to help participants assess their level of exertion is described next.

Borg Rating of Perceived Exertion Scale

Table 9.21 presents the Borg Rating of Perceived Exertion Scale (Borg, 1998). The scale is a useful and easy way for participants to determine how much effort they are putting into physical activity so that they can maximize the benefits of physical recreation. The self-assessed perception of exertion is based on sensations that one experiences during physical activity, such as increased heart rate, increased breathing rate, increased sweating, or muscle fatigue. According to the Centers for Disease Control (2009), perceived exertion ratings between 12 and 14 on the Borg Scale suggest that physical activity is being performed at a moderate level of intensity. Self-monitoring how hard your body is working can help you adjust the intensity of the activity by speeding up or slowing down your movements. This self-awareness or self-monitoring can help participants adjust their physical exertion to a level that will provide the most benefit to them. The Borg scale is an easy way to measure physical activity within therapeutic recreation services and activities, and has been shown to correlate highly with more sophisticated

Table 9.20 Learning Strengths Inventory *(http://www.ldrc.ca/projects/miinventory/mitest.html, by Greg Gay and adapted by J. Ivanco, 1998)*

What are my Learning Strengths?
Research shows that all human beings have at least eight different types of intelligence. Depending on your background and age, some intelligences are more developed than others. This activity will help you find out what your strengths are.

Verbal/Linguistic Intelligence	Logical/Mathematical Intelligence
___ I enjoy telling stories and jokes ___ I have a good memory for trivia ___ I enjoy word games (e.g., Scrabble and puzzles) ___ I read books just for fun ___ I am a good speller (most of the time) ___ In an argument I tend to use put-downs or sarcasm ___ I like talking and writing about my ideas ___ If I have to memorize something I create a rhyme or saying to help me remember ___ If something breaks and won't work, I read the instruction book first ___ For a group presentation I prefer to do the writing and research	___ I really enjoy math ___ I like logical math puzzles or brain teasers ___ I find solving math problems to be fun ___ If I have to memorize something I tend to place events in a logical order ___ I like to find out how things work ___ I enjoy computer and math games ___ I love playing chess, checkers, or Monopoly ___ In an argument, I try to find a fair and logical solution ___ If something breaks and won't work, I look at the pieces and try to figure out how it works ___ For a group presentation I prefer to create the charts and graphs

Visual/Spatial Intelligence	Bodily/Kinesthetic Intelligence
___ I prefer a map to written directions ___ I daydream a lot ___ I enjoy hobbies such as photography ___ I like to draw and create ___ If I have to memorize something I draw a diagram to help me remember ___ I like to doodle on paper whenever I can ___ In a magazine, I prefer looking at the pictures rather than reading the text ___ In an argument I try to keep my distance, keep silent, or visualize some solution ___ If something breaks and won't work I tend to study the diagram of how it works ___ For a group presentation I prefer to draw all the pictures	___ I like sports ___ I enjoy activities such as woodworking, sewing, and building models ___ When looking at things, I like touching them ___ I have trouble sitting still for any length of time ___ I use a lot of body movements when talking ___ If I have to memorize something I write it out a number of times until I know it ___ I tend to tap my fingers or play with my pencil during class ___ In an argument I tend to strike out and hit or run away ___ If something breaks and won't work I tend to play with the pieces to try to fit them together ___ For a group presentation I prefer to move the props around, hold things up, or build a model

Musical/Rhythmic Intelligence	Interpersonal Intelligence
___ I enjoy listening to music ___ I tend to hum to myself when working ___ I like to sing ___ I play a musical instrument quite well ___ I like to have music playing when doing homework or studying ___ If I have to memorize something I try to create a rhyme about the event ___ In an argument I tend to shout or punch or move in some sort of rhythm ___ I can remember the melodies of many songs ___ If something breaks and won't work I tend to tap my fingers to a beat while I figure it out ___ For a group presentation I prefer to put new words to a popular tune or use music	___ I get along well with others ___ I like to belong to clubs and organizations ___ I have several very close friends ___ I like helping teach other students ___ I like working with others in groups ___ Friends ask my advice because I seem to be a natural leader ___ If I have to memorize something I ask someone to quiz me to see if I know it ___ In an argument I tend to ask a friend or some person in authority for help ___ If something breaks and won't work I try to find someone who can help me ___ For a group presentation I like to help organize the group's efforts

Intrapersonal Intelligence	Naturalist Intelligence
___ I like to work alone without anyone bothering me ___ I like to keep a diary ___ I like myself (most of the time) ___ I don't like crowds ___ I know what I am good at and what I am weak at ___ I find that I am strong-willed, independent, and don't follow the crowd ___ If I have to memorize something I tend to close my eyes and feel the situation ___ In an argument I will usually walk away until I calm down ___ If something breaks and won't work, I wonder if it's worth fixing ___ For a group presentation I like to contribute something that is uniquely mine, often based on how I feel	___ I am keenly aware of my surroundings and of what goes on around me ___ I love to go walking in the woods and looking at the trees and flowers ___ I enjoy gardening ___ I like to collect things (e.g., rocks, sports cards, stamps) ___ I think I would like to get away from the city and enjoy nature ___ If I have to memorize something, I tend to organize it into categories ___ I enjoy learning the names of living things in our environment, such as flowers and trees ___ In an argument I tend to compare my opponent to someone or something I have read or heard about and react accordingly ___ If something breaks down, I look around me to try and see what I can find to fix the problem ___ For a group presentation I prefer to organize and classify the information into categories so it makes sense

TOTAL SCORE
Count the number of items you checked in each area and enter below. Higher numbers indicate areas of strength.

_____ Verbal/Linguistic	_____ Visual/Spatial	_____ Musical/Rhythmic	_____ Intrapersonal
_____ Logical/Mathematical	_____ Bodily/Kinesthetic	_____ Interpersonal	_____ Naturalist

Table 9.21 The Borg Rating of Perceived Exertion Scale

Instructions for Borg Rating of Perceived Exertion (RPE) Scale

While doing physical activity, we want you to rate your perception of exertion. This feeling should reflect how heavy and strenuous the exercise feels to you, combining all sensations and feelings of physical stress, effort, and fatigue. Do not concern yourself with any one factor such as leg pain or shortness of breath, but try to focus on your total feeling of exertion.

Look at the rating scale below while you are engaging in an activity; it ranges from 6 to 20, where 6 means "no exertion at all" and 20 means "maximal exertion." Choose the number from below that best describes your level of exertion. This will give you a good idea of the intensity level of your activity, and you can use this information to speed up or slow down your movements to reach your desired range.

Try to appraise your feeling of exertion as honestly as possible, without thinking about what the actual physical load is. Your own feeling of effort and exertion, not how it compares to other people's, is important. Look at the scales and the expressions and then give a number.

- 6   No exertion at all
- 7
-     Extremely light (7.5)
- 8
- 9   Very light
- 10
- 11   Light
- 12
- 13   Somewhat hard
- 14
- 15   Hard (heavy)
- 16
- 17   Very hard
- 18
- 19   Extremely hard
- 20   Maximal exertion

---

9   corresponds to "very light" exercise. For a healthy person, it is like walking slowly at his or her own pace for some minutes.

13   on the scale is "somewhat hard" exercise, but it still feels OK to continue.

17   "very hard" is very strenuous. A healthy person can still go on, but he or she really has to push him- or herself. It feels very heavy, and the person is very tired.

19   on the scale is an extremely strenuous exercise level. For most people this is the most strenuous exercise they have ever experienced.

©Gunnar Borg, 1998; from the Centers for Disease Control and Prevention (http://www.cdc.gov/physicalactivity/everyone/measuring/exertion.html)

and complicated measures of physical exertion (Borg, 1998).

Assessment of Spiritual and Psychological Strengths

Values in Action Strengths Assessment

The Values in Action (VIA) Strengths Assessment measures character strengths and virtues. Recall that we described the character strengths and virtues in depth in Chapter 5 *Strengths*. The VIA helps participants identify their strengths and virtues using a 5-point scale ranging from "very much like me" to "very much unlike me." The VIA allows the participant to identify her or his top five strengths, called signature strengths. Knowledge of a participant's character strengths is key to helping that person use those strengths every day, which in turn contributes to happiness and well-being. The VIA is available in a youth and adult version and in a short-form, long-form, and online version. The online version allows the participant to compare results to others in the region and the nation. The online version is available through the University of Pennsylvania's Authentic Happiness website or the VIA Institute on Character website. Details are at the end of this chapter.

Aspirations Index

Aspirations, the goals people hope to accomplish over the course of their lives, are important to strengths-based therapeutic recreation practice. Knowing a participant's aspirations will make planning and subsequent services meaningful and socially valid. To assess aspirations, we have already discussed qualitative approaches such as the Miracle Question or the

MAPS interview process. However, you may also want to ascertain and measure what type of aspirations a participant holds. The research clearly shows that extrinsic aspirations (wealth, fame, and image) do not contribute to happiness and well-being, while intrinsic aspirations (meaningful relationships, personal growth, and community contributions) do (Kasser & Ryan, 1993; 1996). Good health, a common aspiration for many people, is neither positively nor negatively correlated with well-being. The Aspirations Index is a tool you can use to help participants clarify their type of aspirations (extrinsic, intrinsic, and health) and how those may be related to their life quality. Participants rate the importance of each listed aspiration for them, their beliefs about the likelihood of attaining each aspiration, and the degree to which they have already attained each one. The Aspirations Index is available from the Self-Determination website at the University of Rochester, or from research journals, all referenced at the end of this chapter.

External Strengths

Assessment of Leisure Resources

Recall in Chapter 5 *Strengths* that we overviewed many resources available in a person's environment for the enhancement of recreation and leisure experiences. These resources are in the home and community. In this section, we present a sample of tools that assess these external resources for leisure.

Inclusivity Assessment Tool

The Inclusivity Assessment Tool assesses the physical and social inclusion of a recreation environment (Anderson, Penney McGee, & Wilkins, 2011). The Inclusivity Assessment Tool (IAT) assesses four major areas of a recreation resource: physical accessibility of the area or facility, administrative practices of the agency, program practices used by the staff, and adapted equipment. The IAT gives the participant and the therapeutic recreation specialist a clear picture of what the recreation amenity is like, and what changes, supports, or accommodations may be needed to facilitate full leisure involvement at the site. In order to use the IAT, the assessor must complete the training that accompanies the tool, which is called *Inclusion U*. Information about the tool and training is provided at the end of this chapter.

Ecological Assessment Tool

Numerous tools are available to complete an ecological assessment, which we described earlier in this chapter. One tool that is especially well developed is the Recreation Inventory for Inclusive Participation (RIIP) by Schleien, Ray, and Green (1997). The RIIP consists of the following sections: Part IA assesses the appropriateness of a recreation activity or setting. Part IB examines the general program and participant information. Part II is an activity analysis of the proposed activity in the setting and, lastly, Part III is a discrepancy analysis between the demands of the activity and the abilities of the participant. By completing the RIIP, the participant and the therapeutic recreation specialist will have a clear idea of what is required to participate in a recreation activity and setting, and what training, supports, or accommodations may be needed.

Leisure Resources Asset Mapping

Earlier in this chapter, in Figure 9.10, we presented a diagram of a broad ecological assessment approach. Through this approach, which is sometimes called community asset mapping, you can create a visual map of the recreation resources available to a participant. Information about the assets in the participant's community can be gathered through interviews with family and friends, field trips, the Internet, phone books, newspapers, tourism bureaus, the local chamber of commerce, and other community groups. The information is used to develop a community leisure profile that can be organized according to many different categories: physical resources; cultural assets; organizational assets; federal, state, and local recreation assets; neighborhood assets; human resources assets; and more (see Figure 9.17). The activity of creating a leisure resources asset map is like a treasure hunt and involves the participant in the process. This asset map can then be helpful in identifying supports, strategies, and actions to help put the participant's plan into place.

Assessment of Functional Resources

Circle of Support or Circle of Friends

Have you ever stepped back and thought about the kinds of people you have in your life and what role they play for you? About how many intimate friends versus acquaintances fill your life? The Circle of Support or Circle of Friends is a way to discover the current and potential network of friends in a participant's life (Falvey, Forest, Pearpoint, & Rosenberg, 1997). The Circle is basically a social scan that helps clarify who is in the participant's life and where he or she will want to add more relationships to improve well-being and quality of life.

Individual Assets Individuals and their • Skills • Talents • Experiences Consider assets in these areas: • Professional • Personal • Resources • Leadership • Networks	**Institutional Assets** Parks and recreation agencies Churches Colleges and universities Elderly care facilities Fire department Hospitals and clinics Mental health facilities Libraries Police department Schools Transportation	**Organizational Assets** Community centers Radio/TV stations Small businesses Large businesses Home-based enterprises Religious organizations Nonprofit organizations Clubs Citizen groups 
Governmental (State and Federal) Assets City government Land management agencies Park Service Forest Service Military facilities School service center State education agency	**Physical and Land Assets** Forests Lakes, ponds, streams Natural resources/landmarks Parks/recreation areas Vacant land Trails, roadways 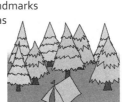	**Cultural Assets** Historic/arts groups Ethnic/racial diversity Heritage Crafts, skills Cultural traditions

Figure 9.17 Leisure Asset Mapping

To complete the Circle of Friends, four concentric circles are drawn and labeled, as shown in Figure 9.18. The participant puts him or herself in the middle, then fills in the people in each of the four circles, as indicated in Figure 9.18. This exercise is often completed with others who are a part of the participant's life.

- In *Circle 1: Circle of Intimacy*, the participant writes the names of all the people closest to her or his heart.
- In *Circle 2: Circle of Friendship*, the participant writes the names of people who are considered friends, but not as close as those listed in the first circle.
- In *Circle 3: Circle of Participation*, the participant writes the names of individuals or groups that they like, but who are not very close. This circle may include acquaintances, teammates, club members, and the like.
- In *Circle 4: Circle of Exchange*, the participant writes the names of people who are paid to be in their lives. This circle would include doctors, professors, housekeepers, mechanics, and the like. Often, for people with disabilities, this circle includes support staff and human service workers who are involved in their lives on a frequent basis.

Once the circles are completed, you can talk with the participant and his or her close supports about desired changes, especially if the participant wants to have more people in the inner circles of his or her life. In Chapter 11 *Implementation* we talk in depth about strategies to help participants build friendships in their lives. The Circle of Friends is a tool that you can use on an ongoing basis with participants to help them build strong social networks. Having done the Circle of Friends with numerous people, we have noticed that people with disabilities tend to have many more people marked on the outside circle, a visual that almost looks like a barbed-wire fence around the participant. One of our roles as therapeutic recreation specialists is to help participants nurture natural supports and friendships through leisure and recreation, strengthening the inner circles and de-emphasizing the outer circles.

Supports Intensity Scale

Developed and distributed by the American Association for Intellectual and Developmental Disabilities (AAIDD), the Supports Intensity Scale (SIS) is a way to assess the supports needed for a person to achieve their goals and dreams and be fully supported in

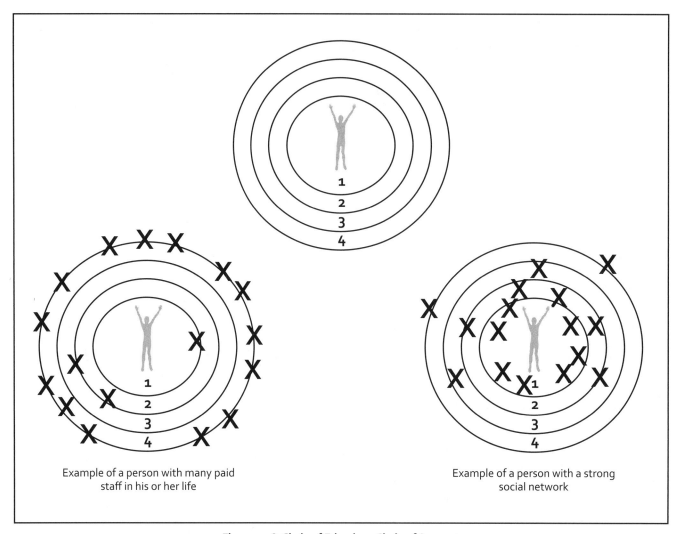

Figure 9.18 Circle of Friends or Circle of Support

community living (AAIDD, 2005). Section I of the SIS, the Supports Needs Scale, consists of 57 life activities grouped into 6 domains: home living, community living, lifelong learning, employment, health, and social activities. Through a semi-structured interview with the participant and his or her circle of support, the assessment determines what level of support is needed in the six life domains. The interviewer assesses what type (from monitoring to full physical assistance), frequency (how often), and intensity (amount of time needed to provide the support) of support would help the participant be fully included in the home and community environment. The SIS yields a Support Intensity Profile that will help the participant, his or her circle of support, and the therapeutic recreation specialist in planning and implementation of services. The SIS is available from the AAIDD in print or Web-based electronic formats. See the reference list at the end of the chapter for further information.

Assessment of Global Outcomes of Therapeutic Recreation Services

Well-being is a global outcome for participants in therapeutic recreation. Using a strengths approach, we want to know if our services are making a difference. One way to assess possible change is to measure global outcomes such as level of happiness, well-being, and quality of life at the beginning of services (baseline) and at the end of services (transition/discharge). Although we know that many other professionals provide many other services, and other changes are occurring in the participants' lives during our time with a participant, we can at least have a rough indicator of change that occurred. The next section focuses on tools that can help us measure a change in a participant's level of happiness, well-being, and quality of life. According to most models and definitions of therapeutic recreation, this is an ultimate goal of our profession as we work with all types of participants in all types of settings.

Happiness and Well-Being

Oxford Happiness Questionnaire and the Brief Happiness Questionnaire

The Oxford Happiness Questionnaire was developed by Hills and Argyle (2002) and updated by Lyubomirsky (2007). It measures a person's happiness level, or a person's perception of well-being. The 29 items on the scale focus on self-esteem, sense of purpose, social interest, and humor, and are rated on a 6-point scale, from "strongly disagree" to "strongly agree." The scale has been used widely to measure levels of happiness in research and in practice. You can obtain the Oxford Happiness Questionnaire in research journals or in the book by Lyubomirsky, listed at the end of this chapter.

Lyubomirsky (2007) developed and tested a shorter happiness questionnaire as well, the Brief Happiness Questionnaire. This tool also measures a person's level of happiness, but consists of only four items. It would be easier to use in practice, to assess happiness levels frequently throughout services. The Brief Happiness Questionnaire is available in Lyubomirsky's book and on the website, *The How of Happiness*, where it is in self-scoring electronic form.

Satisfaction with Life Scale

One of the oldest and most used measures of well-being is the Satisfaction with Life Scale (SWLS), developed by Diener (1984) and Pavot and Diener (1993). The SWLS is a short self-report measure that assesses the extent to which people think and feel that their life is going well for them. It has been used extensively in research and practice, and it can be administered repeatedly over time to assess changes in perceptions of well-being. We offer the SWLS in Table 9.22. You can learn the theory behind the scale in more depth, as well as how to score and interpret the scale, in the research article by Pavot and Diener (1993).

Perceived Wellness Survey

The Perceived Wellness Survey was developed by Adams, Bezner, and Steinhardt (1997) to measure a participant's perceived level of wellness, or well-being, across six domains: physical, spiritual, psychological, social, emotional, and intellectual. Each domain is represented by six items that are scored from 1, "Strongly disagree," to 6, "Strongly agree." Sub-scale scores in each of the six domains, as well as an overall wellness score, can be used in practice. The Perceived Wellness Survey is available in research journals and online at the Perceived Wellness website.

Quality of Life: A Flourishing Life

A global outcome that we hope participants will attain through the therapeutic recreation process is improved quality of life and a flourishing life. We have discussed these ideas in depth in previous chapters as being central and critical to the work we do in our field. How do we know a participant's level of quality of life has changed? How do we know if a participant feels that he or she has a good life, where thriving and positive emotion are a daily part of the texture and fabric of life? The following assessment tools help to measure this broad, more global area of a participant's life.

Table 9.22 The Satisfaction With Life Scale (SWLS) *(Pavot & Diener, 1993)*

The Satisfaction with Life Scale

Using the 1–7 scale below, indicate your agreement with each item by placing the appropriate number on the line preceding that item. Please be open and honest in your response.

7 - Strongly agree
6 - Agree
5 - Slightly agree
4 - Neither agree nor disagree
3 - Slightly disagree
2 - Disagree
1 - Strongly disagree

_____ In most ways my life is close to my ideal.
_____ The conditions of my life are excellent.
_____ I am satisfied with my life.
_____ So far I have gotten the important things I want in life
_____ If I could live my life over, I would change almost nothing.

The SWLS is free and can be used without permission from the authors.

WHO Quality of Life Scale

The World Health Organization developed a scale to measure quality of life across cultures. Called the WHOQOL-100, the WHO later developed a brief version of the scale, called the WHOQOL-BREF (WHO, 1998). Quality of life is defined by the WHO as "individuals' perceptions of their position in life in the context of the culture and value systems in which they live and in relation to their goals, expectations, standards and concerns" (p. 1570).

Using a 5-point scale, participants rate various aspects of their lives, including leisure. The four major domains assessed in the WHOQOL-BREF are physical, psychological, social, and environmental. The full scale, the WHOQOL-100, measures these four domains, as well as additional domains of level of independence and spirituality.

Toronto Quality of Life Profile

The Toronto Quality of Life Model was discussed in Chapter 3 *A Sea Change in Therapeutic Recreation* (see Table 3.3). The Toronto Quality of Life Model conceptualizes quality of life as having three dimensions: being, belonging, and becoming (Quality of Life Research Unit, 2009). The "being" dimension includes physical, psychological, and spiritual being. The "belonging" dimension of quality of life includes physical belonging, social belonging, and community belonging. The "becoming" dimension includes practical becoming, leisure becoming, and growth becoming.

The Research Unit has developed several tools to assess quality of life using this conceptualization with several populations: children, adolescents, adults, older adults, individuals with developmental disabilities, individuals with sensory or physical disabilities, and communities. All assessment tools are available on the Quality of Life Research Unit website at the University of Toronto. Also on the website is a free online version of the Adult Quality of Life Profile, which is interactive and self-scoring. We provide information to access the Quality of Life Profile at the end of the chapter.

Quality of Life Scale

Anderson (2007) developed a quality of life scale based on the work of Pavot and Diener (1993) and Schlalock (2004) to assess quality of life with individuals with developmental disabilities or with children. The Quality of Life Scale and scoring key are shown in Table 9.23. The Quality of Life Scale measures perceptions of life quality in the core domains of emotional well-being, interpersonal relationships, material well-being, personal development, self-determination, social inclusion, rights, physical well-being, and an overall assessment of satisfaction with life. The scale can be used in an interview format or self-administered, depending on the abilities of the participant. The Quality of Life Scale provides another way to measure changes over time in a global outcome of therapeutic recreation services.

Assessment Toolbox Summary

The toolbox of assessments we have introduced to you is just the tip of the iceberg of available resources. At the end of this chapter, we provide additional resources to search for assessment tools you may find useful in your practice. New assessment tools are being developed all the time, and it is important for you to read professional research journals in therapeutic recreation and related fields to stay current on new ways you can help participants discover their strengths and assets. The sea change in health and human services is reaching practice in many ways—a fundamental shift in what we assess and how we assess in therapeutic recreation is happening now.

PROCESS FOR ASSESSMENT SELECTION

With all the tools and approaches available to you for assessment in therapeutic recreation, how do you choose which to use? What will help you discover how you can best assist participants in making progress toward their goals and aspirations? In Table 9.24, we provide some guiding questions to assist you in the assessment selection process. As you gain experience in the field, you will develop what is called "practice wisdom," which is the "possession of practice experience and knowledge together with the ability to use them critically, intuitively and practically . . . these qualities, skills, and processes and their blending are built up through extensive introspection and critical reflection, and review of, practice" (Higgs & Titchen, 2001, p. 275). By learning about a variety of assessment tools, trying them out in practice, and reflecting critically on their utility, you will become a "wise treasure hunter"!

FINAL THOUGHTS ON ASSESSMENT

In closing, we would like to offer a succinct list of what we feel is essential advice in completing strengths-based assessment in therapeutic recreation practice—advice that has also been captured in part by other authors who have embraced a strengths approach (Forest, 2003; Arge Nathan, 2003):

Table 9.23 Quality of Life Scale

IRRC Quality of Life Scale

Could you read each statement and choose the answer that best describes you?

		Sounds Like Me	Doesn't Sound Like Me	Not Sure
1.	I feel happy and enjoy most things I do for recreation.	☺	☹	😐
2.	I like myself.	☺	☹	😐
3.	I feel in control of my recreation time.	☺	☹	😐
4.	I know people I can call or talk to in my free time.	☺	☹	😐
5.	I have family and friends I can do recreation activities with.	☺	☹	😐
6.	I have people in my life who help me with recreation when I need it.	☺	☹	😐
7.	I have enough money to do what I want for recreation.	☺	☹	😐
8.	I have a chance to learn new recreation activities.	☺	☹	😐
9.	I have recreation skills I use a lot.	☺	☹	😐
10.	I am good at recreation activities.	☺	☹	😐
11.	I exercise or do physical activity at least 20 minutes every day.	☺	☹	😐
12.	I know how to take care of myself.	☺	☹	😐
13.	I have hobbies and interests I like to do.	☺	☹	😐
14.	I do the recreation activities I like when I want.	☺	☹	😐
15.	I follow my dreams for recreation.	☺	☹	😐
16.	I choose my recreation activities.	☺	☹	😐
17.	I participate in recreation activities in my community.	☺	☹	😐
18.	I volunteer in my community.	☺	☹	😐
19.	I have people who help me participate in the community.	☺	☹	😐
20.	People around me treat me with respect.	☺	☹	😐
21.	I can access recreation activities and places in my community.	☺	☹	😐
22.	My recreation is everything I want it to be.	☺	☹	😐
23.	The things around me in my life are excellent.	☺	☹	😐
24.	I like my recreation.	☺	☹	😐
25.	I have the important things I want in my life.	☺	☹	😐
26.	If I could live my life over, I would keep it the same.	☺	☹	😐

___ Total score   ___ EW   ___ IR   ___ MW   ___ PD   ___ PW   ___ SD   ___ SI   ___ R   ___ SW

IRRC Quality of Life Scale - KEY

			Sounds Like Me	Doesn't Sound Like Me	Not Sure
1.	I feel happy and enjoy most things I do for recreation.	(EW)	3	1	2
2.	I like myself.	(EW)	3	1	2
3.	I feel in control of my recreation time.	(EW)	3	1	2
4.	I know people I can call or talk to in my free time.	(IR)	3	1	2
5.	I have family and friends I can do recreation activities with.	(IR)	3	1	2
6.	I have people in my life who help me with recreation when I need it.	(IR)	3	1	2
7.	I have enough money to do what I want for recreation.	(MW)	3	1	2
8.	I have a chance to learn new recreation activities.	(PD)	3	1	2
9.	I have recreation skills I use a lot.	(PD)	3	1	2
10.	I am good at recreation activities.	(PD)	3	1	2
11.	I exercise or do physical activity at least 20 minutes every day.	(PW)	3	1	2
12.	I know how to take care of myself.	(PW)	3	1	2
13.	I have hobbies and interests I like to do.	(SD)	3	1	2
14.	I do the recreation activities I like when I want.	(SD)	3	1	2
15.	I follow my dreams for recreation.	(SD)	3	1	2
16.	I choose my recreation activities.	(SD)	3	1	2
17.	I participate in recreation activities in my community.	(SI)	3	1	2
18.	I volunteer in my community.	(SI)	3	1	2
19.	I have people who help me participate in the community.	(SI)	3	1	2
20.	People around me treat me with respect.	(R)	3	1	2
21.	I can access recreation activities and places in my community.	(R)	3	1	2
22.	My recreation is everything I want it to be.	(SW)	3	1	2
23.	The things around me in my life are excellent.	(SW)	3	1	2
24.	I like my recreation.	(SW)	3	1	2
25.	I have the important things I want in my life.	(SW)	3	1	2
26.	If I could live my life over, I would keep it the same.	(SW)	3	1	2

Anderson (2007)

Core Concepts of Quality of Life (Schalock, 2004)

Emotional well-being (EW)
  Contentment (satisfaction, moods, enjoyment)
  Self-concept (identify, self-worth, self-esteem)
  Lack of stress (predictability, control)

Interpersonal relations (IR)
  Interactions (social networks, social contacts)
  Relationships (family, friends, peers)
  Supports (emotional, physical, financial, feedback)

Material well-being (MW)
  Financial status (income, benefits)
  Employment (work status, work environment)
  Housing (type of residence, ownership)

Personal development (PD)
  Education (achievements, status)
  Personal competence (cognitive, social, practical)
  Performance (success, achievement, productivity)

Physical well-being (PW)
  Health (functioning, symptoms, fitness, nutrition)
  Activities of daily living (self-care skills, mobility)
  Leisure (recreation, hobbies)

Self-determination (SD)
  Autonomy/personal control (independence)
  Goals and personal values (desires, expectations)
  Choices (opportunities, options, preferences)

Social inclusion (SI)
  Community integration and participation
  Community roles (contributor, volunteer)
  Social supports (support network, services)

Rights (R)
  Human (respect, dignity, equality)
  Legal (citizenship, access, due process)

Subjective well-being (SW) (Pavot & Diener)

- Meet and establish rapport with participants.
- Involve family, significant others, and the team.
- Be person-centered and capability-based in your approach.
- Be comprehensive—look at the whole person in relation to leisure functioning, in the context of the environment.
- Focus on participants' strengths, goals, aspirations, and general life situation.
- Recognize and respect cultural, educational, and experiential differences throughout the assessment process.
- Be sure your assessment is meaningful. Leisure is an integral part of life quality and a flourishing life; work with the participant and other team members to learn as much as you can about this important aspect of the participant's life.
- Always individualize your approach. There is no "one way" to do an assessment—it is based on the individual with whom you are working. Focus your assessment in more depth on those areas that make sense for each participant.
- Choose assessment methods and tools that are a good fit and are rigorous (i.e., valid, reliable, credible, and dependable); use multiple appropriate methods.
- Use an ecological approach; assess the participant's environment and larger community issues, such as attitudes, accessibility, and available resources.
- Understand that assessment is an ongoing process; participants will often share more with you as trust develops in the helping relationship.
- Always keep inclusion in meaningful lifelong leisure and overall well-being as ultimate goals for the participant.

Summary

In this chapter, we discussed several aspects of assessment in therapeutic recreation. Assessment is a key step in the therapeutic recreation process, and several guidelines were provided to ensure that it is strengths-based, valid, reliable, authentic, ecological, practical, and meaningful. The focus of assessment is framed by the practice model you use, and the system in which you work in therapeutic recreation. We discussed the

Table 9.24 Assessment Selection Questions

Questions to Guide You in the Assessment Selection Process
The Participant and Her or His Environment: • What do I know about the participant's cultural background, educational level, and life context? • How much time can I spend with the participant to complete an assessment? • Can I use an interview approach, or is observation more appropriate? • Can I use a standardized assessment? Will the participant understand and feel comfortable completing a standardized assessment? • Can I include the family or circle of support in the assessment? • Will the participant gain insight and discover strengths through the assessment? **My Agency:** • What is the overall mission of the agency where I provide therapeutic recreation services? • What is the service delivery system of my agency and how does that affect assessment? • What are the parameters of my agency (physical environment, time, cost, etc.)? • Does my agency use a transdisciplinary approach, with a team-based assessment? • Can I focus on strengths, goals, dreams, and aspirations of the participant as a valued aspect of assessment on the team? • What therapeutic recreation philosophy and model guide practice and does the assessment match these? **The Assessment Tool:** • What do I know about the assessment tool and its characteristics? (Use the Assessment Checklist provided earlier in this chapter.) • Does the assessment provide information that will help me develop a meaningful plan with the participant? • Does the assessment provide data to establish a baseline measurement from which to measure growth and change? • Do the assessment results add to what the team needs to know about the participant to give the most meaningful, holistic services?

assessment process, from referral to reporting the results, and provided a typical format for assessment reports. We surveyed the main assessment methods: record review, interviews, observation, standardized assessments, and ecological assessment. We asked you to think about the advantages and disadvantages of each of these approaches. We introduced you to assessment tools you will likely use in a team approach. We then gave you a sampling of several different strengths-based assessments in an "assessment toolbox." Last, we gave you a way to think about how to choose assessment methods and tools.

In Table 9.25, we offer a sample assessment completed by a therapeutic recreation specialist, to help you see how the steps in assessment come together to result in the final assessment report. Remember, assessment is a treasure hunt. You are helping the participant uncover his or her strengths, dreams, and aspirations. Once you and the participant have discovered the treasure, it is time to make a plan. The next chapter moves us to the second phase of the therapeutic recreation process, planning. All you learned during the assessment process will be put to use as you help the participant "dream and design" for a life that is good for him or her.

Resources

UPenn Authentic Happiness Questionnaire Center
http://www.authentichappiness.sas.upenn.edu/questionnaires.aspx

The Authentic Happiness Questionnaire Center offers a wealth of assessment tools for therapeutic recreation specialists working from a strengths approach, interested in measuring strengths and many different aspects of well-being. Available questionnaires include the Brief Strengths Test, the Meaning in Life Questionnaire, and the Life Satisfaction Questionnaire, among others. All questionnaires can be completed online, and many results can be compared to national and regional norms.

The Red Book
http://www.idyllarbor.com

This book, *Assessment Tools for Recreational Therapy and Related Fields*, commonly known as the "Red Book," is a must-have for therapeutic recreation specialists. Included in the "Red Book" is ample background and conceptual information about assessment, and several standardized assessment tools for use in therapeutic recreation practice. Assessment focus areas include attitudes, functional skills, participation patterns, community integration, leisure competence, and more.

Positive Psychological Assessment: A Handbook of Models and Measures
http://www.apa.org/pubs/books/index.aspx

This handbook, published by the American Psychological Association (APA), provides a scientific look at the measurement of several constructs related to positive psychology, happiness, and well-being. Several assessment tools are presented and discussed across variables such as quality of life, optimism, locus of control, hope, and creativity.

Venture Publishing
http://www.venturepublish.com

Venture Publishing offers many resources on therapeutic recreation assessment, including the Leisure Diagnostic Battery computer software and user's manual, several books written specifically on therapeutic recreation assessment, and more.

Test Link
http://www.ets.org

Managed by the Educational Testing Service, *Test Link* is the largest online database of existing tests and assessment tools in the world. Searchable in many ways, *Test Link* is a good resource to find standardized tools for assessment of areas such as well-being, self-esteem, among others.

Test Reviews Online
http://buros.unl.edu/buros/jsp/search.jsp

The Buros Institute of Mental Measurements, a long-time publisher of tests and other measures, manages an online test review service. Searchable by keyword, the online database provides summary information for over 3,500 commercially available tests and questionnaires. You can also purchase in-depth reviews of many of the assessment tools. The sources to purchase the assessments are also provided.

World Health Organization
http://www.who.int/classifications/icf/en

The World Health Organization has extensive resources on its website for learning and using the ICF Checklist (International Classification of Functioning, Disability

230 • THERAPEUTIC RECREATION PRACTICE: A STRENGTHS APPROACH

Table 9.25 An Example of a Completed Therapeutic Recreation Assessment Report

Example Assessment Write-Up—Meet Charlie

Participant Name: Charlie Jones   **Dates of the Assessment:** 1/30/10–2/2/10

Reason for Referral:
To establish a basis for the development of an inclusive recreation program plan for Charlie.

Background Information:
Charlie is a 25-year-old man who lives with his parents and three siblings in Hometown, NY. Charlie has a developmental disability, moderate speech difficulty, and mild vision impairment. Charlie graduated from Hometown High School in 2007 and currently works mornings at the sheltered workshop and participates in the Day Habilitation Program in the afternoons. As part of his Day Habilitation program, Charlie volunteers regularly at several community locations.

Methods:
An ecological assessment was completed by Sarah Sample, therapeutic recreation specialist. The purpose of the assessment was to identify Charlie's strengths and abilities, likes and dislikes, leisure interests, attitudes and motivations, and his goals for leisure and community inclusion. The assessment focused on home, workplace/day habilitation, and community environments. The following methods were used to complete this ecological assessment:

Home Environment: A brief behavioral observation of Charlie was done in his home environment (relaxing in living room with family members). An informal interview with Charlie's mother was completed to gain her input on Charlie's schedule, routines, interests, behaviors, and lifestyle. A baseline Quality of Life Scale interview was completed with Charlie and his family to gain insight into his recreation participation, quality of leisure, choice/self-determination, free-time usage, friends, community involvement, meaningfulness of life, health and fitness, self-esteem, and physical environment.

Day Habilitation/Workplace Environment: Behavioral observation of Charlie with his day-habilitation staff and peers was completed to learn about Charlie's social and interpersonal skills with peers and others in a variety of situations. Brief interviews were completed with Charlie, his workshop staff members, and his day-habilitation staff members to gain insight into Charlie's life, and specifically his strengths, leisure interests, and attitudes.

Community Environment: Behavioral observation of Charlie in the community (park, downtown) was completed to assess social skills and comfort level in the community. Informal interviews were completed with Charlie to identify leisure interests and disinterests, to assess his ability to express preferences and make choices and to identify a possible community inclusion activity for him.

Results of the Ecological Assessment:

Overall Quality of Life
Charlie scored in the high range on emotional well-being, material well-being, personal development, and rights. His scores on the interpersonal relations, self-determination, physical well-being, and social inclusion scales were lower. His overall subjective well-being score was 2 out of 3. These scores will provide a baseline measurement, and this scale will be repeated near the end of services.

Leisure/Recreation Interests, Attitudes, and Motivations
Charlie expressed that his recreation and leisure interests are listening to country music, shopping for CDs, watching TV, watching movies, arts and crafts, walking/hiking, and visiting individuals who reside in nursing homes. Charlie is able to indicate preferences for leisure activities. Charlie expressed he wished he had more time for recreation, leisure, and fun.

(cont'd)

Socialization/Friendship Skills
Charlie is cheerful, friendly, and polite. He is soft-spoken and often does not maintain eye contact. Charlie likes to joke and laugh, though his speech difficulty may be a challenge in social relationships. However, he is aware of this and uses methods to clarify himself, including sounding out words, spelling, and repeating. Observing his social skills with his peers at work and day habilitation, it seems Charlie is well-liked and enjoys socialization, yet he is not very talkative. Charlie's understanding of friends is unclear, as he referred to staff and case-workers only as friends.

Choice-Making/Decision-Making Skills
Charlie's decision-making skills need further development. Sometimes Charlie expresses preferences clearly and enthusiastically, while other times he is unsure of what he wants to do next.

Concept of Self and Environment
Charlie expresses that he is happy with himself. In terms of his living environment, he feels that he has lived at home too long and would like to possibly move to an ARC home. Charlie expressed that he did not want to change anything about himself. He expressed that he doesn't do a lot in the community now but wants to get out more.

Physical Health/Capabilities
Charlie noted that he wants to lose weight and get more exercise.

Summary and Interpretation
Based on this assessment of Charlie's strengths, goals, and interests in leisure as well as community participation, the following recommendations are provided for Charlie's successful inclusion in a community activity or setting:

Recommendations
1. Conduct a more in-depth assessment of Charlie's Circle of Friends, to learn how to expand his social network beyond his family.
2. Explore volunteer opportunities at a local long-term care facility, to capitalize on Charlie's desire to visit and socialize with residents of a nursing home in his community.
3. Explore long-term participation in an arts and crafts class, club, or group activity in the community.
4. Explore long-term participation in a walking or hiking club or program in the community.
5. Assist with developing more assertive social skills in order to capitalize on Charlie's warm and friendly personality and to help him meet others who participate in community activities who could become friends or acquaintances.

Recommendations also include continued communication with Charlie's family to facilitate his participation, as well as continued exploration of transportation and available finances for activity participation.

Signature: _____Sarah Sample, TR Student_____   Date: __2/2/10__

>
>
> *Self-Assessment of Learning*
>
> We provide four scenarios in Self-Assessment of Learning and ask you to apply what you have learned about assessment in this chapter. How would you approach Scenario #1 to complete a meaningful and careful assessment with the participant?
>
> *Scenario #1—Hometown Adult Day Program*
>
> You are the therapeutic recreation specialist at the Hometown Adult Day Program, a psychosocial program for older adults who have a variety of impairments or disabilities. There are three other professional staff members—another therapeutic recreation specialist, a social worker, and a nurse. A physician is on-call. Additionally, you have four paraprofessional activity assistants. The mission of the Hometown Adult Day Program is to maintain or improve the quality of life, including meaningful leisure, of retirees who have experienced functional limitations as a part of the aging process. Participants come to the agency daily for services and live at home with family members. Typically, you have about 20 participants at the program each week. Programs vary based on the interests and goals of the participants, but include a variety of exercise groups, leisure education, community inclusion, aquatic therapy, an ongoing bridge club, a children's group on a few days a week, and other activities.
>
> You have a new participant joining the program. Ernie is a 78-year-old who will be attending the program at least three times a week. His wife, Claire, is his primary caregiver, and she needs respite. In addition, Claire feels Ernie needs to get out of the house and increase his social interaction. Ernie had a stroke about 3 years ago, and now uses a wheelchair due to right side hemiparesis. At home, he has been mostly watching daytime television and napping. Claire tells you that he used to have many hobbies and interests and was always active and outdoors.
>
> Given the setting in which you work, and what you know from the referral for Ernie, how would you complete the assessment process? Remember, assessment is a treasure hunt, and you need to discover Ernie's strengths, dreams, and aspirations.
>
> What methods would you use? _____
>
> What would you focus on in the assessment? _____
>
> What specific assessment tools would you use? _____
>
> Who would you involve in the assessment? _____

and Health). Training materials, as well as the actual ICF checklist, are available on the website.

The Handbook of Multicultural Assessment
http://www.josseybass.com

This handbook provides a comprehensive look at the influence of culture on assessment. It includes reviews of assessment tools that can be used with culturally diverse populations.

Youthwork Links and Ideas
http://www.youthwork.com/activelistening.html

This website is loaded with resources and ideas for professionals in human services. One especially fun and useful feature on the website is an interactive series of games and exercises to learn and practice active listening skills. Use the site to practice your skills in reflective, attentive listening, which is needed to conduct good interviews in therapeutic recreation assessment.

Positive Emotion and Psychophysiology Lab
http://www.unc.edu/peplab/home.html

This website is full of resources on positive emotion and the theory, research, and practice behind building positive emotion to enrich people's lives. Based at the University of North Carolina at Chapel Hill, and headed by Dr. Barbara Fredrickson, the lab continues to make new discoveries on the important role positive emotion plays in well-being. Access the site for research, assessment tools, and more.

Self-Assessment of Learning

How would you approach Scenario #2 to complete a meaningful and careful assessment with the participant?

Scenario #2—Hometown Mental Health Services

You are a therapeutic recreation specialist at the Hometown Mental Health Services, an agency that provides services to adolescents and adults recovering from mental illness. The agency has a short-term hospital, a day treatment program, and follow-up services to individuals living in their homes or supported living. You are a therapeutic recreation specialist who works across the agency service settings—when a participant has recovered enough to move from the short-term hospital setting, you follow that person to the next level of services (e.g., day treatment and/or in-home follow-up services). You work with two other therapeutic recreation specialists, psychiatric nurses, social workers, psychiatrists, and an art therapist. The mission of Hometown Mental Health Services is to assist participants in improving their mental health and quality of life so as to resume functional and meaningful roles within their communities. The community milieu model is used in the hospital setting and the day treatment program. Typically you work with about 35 participants at one time, but only 10 of them are in the hospital setting or day treatment program. The typical hospital stay is about 4 days, and typical day treatment and follow-up services is about 6 months. Your agency offers a range of therapeutic recreation services: relaxation training, exercise and fitness groups, wellness groups, leisure education, community-based skills training, social skills and assertiveness training, and more.

Laura is a 15-year-old who was just admitted to the hospital. She was referred by the court system to Hometown Mental Health Services. Her record review shows that she has made several suicide attempts and cuts herself. Her family is scattered; she has lost contact with her father and her mother works full-time at two jobs and cares for her three younger siblings. Laura's mom, Janice, initiated the court order to have Laura receive treatment. She loves her daughter, but feels she has lost control. She misses the little girl she thought she knew, who loved to be helpful and spend time with her. Janice reports that Laura is rarely home, hangs out with a negative group of peers, is failing at many subjects in school, and does not help around the house or with her siblings. You will work with Laura from her hospitalization through to follow up in her home.

Given the setting in which you work, and what you know from the referral about Laura, how would you complete the assessment process? Remember, assessment is a treasure hunt, and you need to discover Laura's strengths, dreams, and aspirations.

What methods would you use? _____

What would you focus on in the assessment? _____

What specific assessment tools would you use? _____

Who would you involve in the assessment? _____

Self-Determination Theory Lab
http://www.psych.rochester.edu/SDT/index.php

This website is home to much original research by Deci and Ryan on self-determination, as well numerous resources for assessing self-determination and related constructs (competence, locus of control, aspirations, motivation, among others).

The How of Happiness
http://chass.ucr.edu/faculty_book/lyubomirsky/index.html

This website, based on the work of Dr. Sonja Lyubomirsky, offers electronic versions of the Brief Happiness Questionnaire and the Person-Activity Fit Diagnostic, as well as many other resources to help you incorporate scientifically tested happiness strategies into your therapeutic recreation practice.

Self-Assessment of Learning

How would you approach Scenario #3 to complete a meaningful and careful assessment with the participant?

Scenario #3—Hometown Rehabilitation Center

You are a therapeutic recreation specialist at the Hometown Rehabilitation Center, a free-standing non-profit 32-bed rehabilitation hospital that serves people needing rehabilitation from a variety of disabilities and impairments. Other than you, there is one part-time therapeutic recreation specialist and two recreation assistants. The transdisciplinary team includes nurses, orthotists, physical therapists, occupational therapists, speech language pathologists, social workers, and doctors. The mission of the Hometown Rehabilitation Center is to help those they serve to reach their highest level of functioning and quality of life following illness, accident, or injury. In the Therapeutic Recreation Services area, you offer a wide variety of interventions and activities, including community mobility skills, community inclusion activities, leisure education, cognitive retraining, and a transitional program with the local parks and recreation department focused on adapted sports and recreation (winter- and summer-based activities). The length of stay varies widely but averages around 14 days.

Jason is a 23-year-old who sustained a spinal cord injury as a result of a snowboarding accident in the terrain park. His injury was at the T-5 level and he has complete paraplegia. Jason recently graduated from college with a major in graphic arts and computer design. He was spending the winter snowboarding "before getting a real job." He has a girlfriend, who also is an avid snowboarder, and a supportive family who lives in the area.

Given the setting in which you work, and what you know from the referral about Jason, how would you complete the assessment process? Remember, assessment is a treasure hunt, and you need to discover Jason's strengths, dreams, and aspirations.

What methods would you use? _____

_____

What would you focus on in the assessment? _____

_____

What specific assessment tools would you use? _____

_____

Who would you involve in the assessment? _____

_____

Inclusive Recreation Resource Center
http://www.inclusiverec.org

The Inclusive Recreation Resource Center, headquartered at the State University of New York at Cortland, provides training on using the Inclusivity Assessment Tool, as well as training for the protocol for recreation inclusion services, called the Recreation Referral Service. The center has numerous online resources available.

References

Adams, T., Bezner, J., & Steinhardt, M. (1997). The conceptualization and measurement of perceived wellness: Integrating balance across and within dimensions. *American Journal of Health Promotion*, *11*(3), 208–218.

Amado, A., Conklin, F., & Wells, J. (1990). *Friends: A manual for connecting persons with disabilities and community members*. St. Paul, MN: Human Services Research and Development Center.

American Association for Intellectual and Developmental Disabilities. (2005, 2009). *The Supports Intensity Scale*. Washington, DC: AAIDD. Retrieved from http://www.siswebsite.org/page.ww?section=root&name=Home

American Therapeutic Recreation Association (ATRA). (2000). *Standards for the practice of therapeutic recreation and self-assessment guide*. Hattiesburg, MS: American Therapeutic Recreation Association.

Self-Assessment of Learning

How would you approach Scenario #4 to complete a meaningful and careful assessment with the participant?

Scenario #4—Hometown Parks and Recreation Department

You are the therapeutic recreation specialists at the Hometown Parks and Recreation Department, which provides parks, recreation facilities, and a broad array of programs to a community of 60,000 residents. You serve as the inclusion coordinator and ADA (Americans with Disabilities Act) point of contact for the Department. The mission of the Hometown Parks and Recreation Department is to enhance the quality of life to all residents, regardless of age, gender, ability, income, or ethnicity, through high-quality leisure programs and amenities. The Department offers programs for all ages, from playground programs to senior softball leagues. Programs include arts, sports, educational programs, a teen center, several large parks, a golf course, a community center with a full array of fitness programs, and special-interest groups (e.g., a cycling club, a hiking club, a bird-watching club). Several partnerships thrive between schools, hospitals, group-home systems, and other social service agencies in the community.

Christy is a 7-year-old who lives with her mom and brother in Hometown. She is interested in sports and playing outside. She loves to be around other children her age but has limited opportunities to play with them. Christy has an intellectual disability and uses a wheelchair and a communication device. She has limited social skills, but she notices others around her and smiles at them. Christy attends her neighborhood school and has an aide with her throughout the school day. She currently stays in the classroom during recess and eats with her aid at lunch. After school, Christy has an aide who picks her up, brings her home and watches TV with her until her mom gets home from work. Christy has a "Special Buddy" from the Easter Seals who comes once a month to take her out. Otherwise, she mostly stays home. Christy's mom called the Parks and Recreation Department to see if she can get Christy involved in sports, the playground program, and any other activities that will help her meet and be friends with other children her age, learn social skills, and get fresh air and exercise.

Given the setting in which you work, and what you know from the referral about Christy, how would you complete the assessment process? Remember, assessment is a treasure hunt, and you need to discover Christy's strengths, dreams, and aspirations.

What methods would you use? _____

What would you focus on in the assessment? _____

What specific assessment tools would you use? _____

Who would you involve in the assessment? _____

Anderson, L. (2007). *Quality of Life Scale.* Unpublished.

Anderson, L., Penney McGee, L., & Wilkins, V. (2011). *The Inclusivity Assessment Tool.* Cortland, NY: State University of New York at Cortland.

Anderson, L., Penney McGee, L., Wilkins, V., & Roeder, M. (2008). *The Recreation Referral Service manual.* Cortland, NY: State University of New York at Cortland.

Arge Nathan, A. (2003). *The art of recreation therapy: Using activities as assessment tools.* San Francisco, CA: Study Center.

Battle, J. (2002). *The Culture Free Self-Esteem Inventory* (3rd ed.). Lutz, FL: Psychological Assessment Resources.

Beard, J., & Ragheb, M. (1980). Measuring leisure satisfaction. *Journal of Leisure Research, 12*(1), 20–33.

Borg, G. (1998). *Borg's Perceived Exertion and Pain Scales.* Champaign, IL: Human Kinetics.

burlingame, j., & Blaschko, T. (2002). *Assessment tools for recreational therapy and related fields* (3rd ed.). Ravensdale, WA: Idyll Arbor.

Canadian Therapeutic Recreation Association (CTRA). (2006). *Standards of practice for recreation therapists and therapeutic recreation assistants.* Calgary, AB, Canada: Canadian Therapeutic Recreation Association.

Centers for Disease Control and Prevention. (2009). *Perceived exertion.* Retrieved from http://www.cdc.gov/physicalactivity/everyone/measuring/exertion.html

Clark, H. (2007). *Strengths Discovery Assessment Process for working with transition aged youth and young adults.* Tampa, FL: Florida Department of Education. Retrieved from http://www.fldoe.org

Cowger, C., Anderson, K., & Snively, C. (2006). Assessing strengths: The political context of individual, family, and community empowerment. In D. Saleebey (Ed.), *The strengths perspective in social work practice* (4th ed., pp. 93–115). Boston, MA: Pearson Education.

Diener, E. (1984). Subjective well-being. *Psychological Bulletin, 95,* 542–575.

Epstein, M. (2004). *BERS-2: The Behavioral and Emotional Rating Scale* (2nd ed.). Austin, TX: PRO-ED.

Falvey, M., Forest, M., Pearpoint, J., & Rosenberg, R. (1997). *All my life's a circle. Using the tools: Circles, MAPS and PATHS.* Toronto, ON, Canada: Inclusion.

Forest, C. (2003). *Empowerment skills for family workers.* Ithaca, NY: Cornell Family Development.

Fredrickson, B. (2009). *Positivity.* New York, NY: Random House.

Higgs, J., & Titchen, A. (2001). Towards professional artistry and creativity in practice. In J. Higgs & A. Titchen (Eds.), *Professional practice in health, education and the creative arts* (pp. 273–290). Oxford, UK: Blackwell Science.

Hills, P., & Argyle, M. (2002). The Oxford Happiness Questionnaire: A compact scale for the measurement of psychological well-being. *Personality and Individual Differences, 33,* 1073–1082.

Hornibook, T., Pedlar, A., & Haasen, B. (2001). Patient-focused care: Theory and practice. *Therapeutic Recreation Journal, 35*(1), 15–30.

Iso-Ahola, S., & Weissenger, E. (1990). Perceptions of boredom in leisure: Conceptualization, reliability, and validity of the Leisure Boredom Scale. *Journal of Leisure Research, 22*(1), 1–17.

Kasser, T., & Ryan, R. M. (1993). A dark side of the American dream: Correlates of financial success as a central life aspiration. *Journal of Personality and Social Psychology, 65,* 410–422.

Kasser, T., & Ryan, R. M. (1996). Further examining the American dream: Differential correlates of intrinsic and extrinsic goals. *Personality and Social Psychology Bulletin, 22,* 280–287.

Kloseck, M., & Crilly, R. (1997). *The Leisure Competence Measure.* London, ON, Canada: Marchand.

Learning Disabilities Resource Community. (2009). *The Learning Strengths Inventory.* Retrieved from http://www.ldrc.ca/projects/miinventory/miinventory.php

Linder, T. (2008). *Transdisciplinary Play-Based Assessment 2.* Baltimore, MD: Brookes.

Lopez, S., & Snyder, C. (2003). *Positive psychological assessment: A handbook of models and measures.* Washington, DC: American Psychological Association.

Lyubomirsky, S. (2007). *The how of happiness: A scientific approach to getting the life you want.* New York, NY: Penguin.

McGill, J. (1996). *Developing leisure identities.* Toronto, ON, Canada: Leisurability.

Merrell, K., & Caldarella, P. (2008). *Home and Community Social Behavior Scales (HCSBS).* Baltimore, MD: Paul Brookes.

Mueller, J. (2009). *Authentic assessment toolbox.* Retrieved from http://jonathan.mueller.faculty.noctrl.edu/toolbox/whatisit.htm

Nall Schenk, C. (n.d.). *Leisurescope Plus and Teen Leisurescope Plus.* Ravensdale, WA: Idyll Arbor.

National Therapeutic Recreation Society (NTRS). (2004). *Standards of practice for a continuum of care in therapeutic recreation.* Ashburn, VA: National Therapeutic Recreation Society.

O'Hanlon, B. (1999). *Do one thing differently: Ten simple ways to change your life.* New York, NY: HarperCollins.

Okun, B., Kantrowitz, R., & Kantrowitz, R. (2007). *Effective helping: Interviewing and counseling techniques.* Belmont, CA: Wadsworth.

Pavot, W., & Diener, E. (1993). Review of the Satisfaction With Life Scale. *Psychological Assessment, 5,* 164–172.

Positive Psychology. (2010). *The miracle question.* Retrieved from http://www.positive-psychology.info/miracle_questions.htm

Quality of Life Research Unit. (2009). *The Quality of Life Profile for Adults.* Retrieved from http://www.utoronto.ca/qol/

Rapp, C., & Goscha, R. (2006). *The strengths model: Case management with people with psychiatric disabilities.* New York, NY: Oxford University Press.

Ratey, J. (2008). *Spark: The revolutionary new science of exercise and the brain.* New York, NY: Little, Brown and Company.

Rudolph, S., & Epstein, M. (2000). Empowering children and families through strength-based assessment. *Reclaiming Children and Youth, 8*(4), 207–209, 232.

Saleebey, D. (2006). *The strengths perspective in social work practice* (4th ed.). Boston, MA: Pearson Education.

Saliba, D., & Buchanan, J. (2008). *Development and validation of a revised nursing home assessment tool: MDS 3.0.* Boston, MA: Harvard University/RAND Health.

Schlalock, R. (2004). The concept of quality of life: What we know and do not know. *Journal of Intellectual Disability Research, 48*(3), 203–216.

Schleien, S., Ray, M., & Green, F. (1997). *Community recreation and people with disabilities: Strategies for inclusion.* Baltimore, MD: Paul Brookes.

Suzuki, L., & Ponterotto, J. (2008). *Handbook of multicultural assessment: Clinical, psychological, and educational applications* (3rd ed.). San Francisco, CA: Jossey Bass.

Vallerand, R., Blanchard, C., Mageau, G. A., Koestner, R., Ratelle, C., Léonard, M., Gagné, M., & Marsolais, J. (2003). Les passions de l'âme: On obsessive and harmonious passion. *Journal of Personality and Social Psychology, 85,* 756–76. Retrieved from http://www.er.uqam.ca/nobel/r26710/LRCS/echelles_en.htm

Wilkins, D. (n.d.). *The nth degree.* Retrieved from http://www.thenthdegree.com/default.asp

Witt, P., & Ellis, G. (1989). *The Leisure Diagnostic Battery.* State College, PA: Venture Publishing, Inc.

Witt, P., Ellis, G., & Widmer, M. (2008). *The LDB computer software and user manual.* State College, PA: Venture Publishing, Inc.

World Health Organization. (2001). *International Classification of Functioning, Disability and Health, Short version.* Geneva, Switzerland: World Health Organization.

World Health Organization. (2003). *ICF Checklist.* Version 2.1a, Clinician Form. Geneva: World Health Organization.

World Health Organization. (1998). The World Health Organization Quality of Life Assessment (WHOQOL): Development and general psychometric properties. *Social Science Medicine, 46*(12), 1567–1585.

Wright, J. (2000). *The FIM(TM).* The Center for Outcome Measurement in Brain Injury. Retrieved from http://www.tbims.org/combi/FIM

Chapter 10
PLANNING IN STRENGTHS-BASED THERAPEUTIC RECREATION PRACTICE

The sunflower is bright, sunny, and hopeful. At its center are many seeds ready for germination.

"The future belongs to those who believe in the beauty of their dreams."

—*Eleanor Roosevelt*

OVERVIEW OF CHAPTER 10

- Overview of planning
- The link between assessment and planning
- Principles that guide strengths-based planning
- The planning process and the roles of the participant and team in that process
- Types of plans
- Goals and objectives
- Linking goals and objectives to effective actions and strategies
- Introduction to activity analysis as a part of planning
- Person-centered planning as an example of the planning process in action

FOCUS QUESTIONS

- Why is planning such an important part of the helping relationship?
- How do you use what you learned in the assessment phase to help participants plan? What "reasoning" or "practice wisdom" do you need to use as a therapeutic recreation specialist?
- What guiding principles can help you craft a strengths-based plan with a participant?
- "Not all goals are created equal." What do we mean by this? Besides goals, what elements are necessary to include in a plan?
- What are some examples of strengths-based planning processes you can use in therapeutic recreation practice?

AN INTRODUCTION TO PLANNING

A definition of "planning":
To formulate a scheme, program, or method beforehand for the accomplishment of an objective

A definition of "dreaming":
To conceptualize a condition or achievement that is longed for; to aspire

A definition of "designing":
To create or execute in an artistic or highly skilled manner

Recall that the therapeutic recreation process is a universal approach to working with participants, no matter the delivery system or service setting. In the last chapter, we offered an alternative way to think about the therapeutic recreation process—assess, plan, implement, and evaluate (APIE):

- Discover (assess)
- Dream and Design (plan)
- Deliver (implement)
- Deliberate (evaluate)

The first phase of the therapeutic recreation process, *assessment*, which we described in the last chapter, helps us discover the strengths, dreams, and aspirations of the participant. Assessment helps us and the participant see "where we are now." This chapter focuses on the *planning*, or the dreaming and designing, phase of therapeutic recreation services, the next step in the process. The planning phase helps us answer the question, "Where do you want to be and how will you get there?" Once you feel you truly understand the participant in relation to leisure well-being and life quality, you are ready to move from assessment to planning.

Rationale for Careful and Collaborative Planning

Remember that therapeutic recreation is the purposeful and careful facilitation of quality leisure experiences and the development of personal and environmental strengths that lead to greater well-being for participants. In order to be purposeful, we need to design a clear plan that can be followed by participants to reach their goals and dreams. There are many reasons for thorough and collaborative planning with participants in therapeutic recreation. Here we list some of those reasons, saving the most important two reasons for last.

Focuses Attention on the Participant as an Individual

Individualized planning with the participant keeps the participant at the center of our services. It helps us focus on the strengths, dreams, and aspirations of the individual that will drive how services are designed and delivered. Planning assures that we avoid making assumptions about what will best help a person based on a label or category. A well-crafted plan sees the person as a unique individual with his or her own constellation of strengths, resources, dreams, and goals. That unique constellation is what drives services, not our system, our "programs," or other cookie-cutter approaches. Planning helps us understand how each person can benefit—and benefit in different ways—from what we can provide in our agency, and when we need to look outside our agency for additional supports or services.

Provides a Systematic Approach to Helping

The process of planning ensures that each participant we serve will receive the full attention of the team in a consistent way. The planning process, like the assessment process, is documented and understood by all the staff members who work with a participant. It is implemented fairly and comprehensively with each participant in ways that allow for the most effective help to be given.

Assists All Staff in Understanding a Participant's Strengths and Goals

The planning process and the resulting written plan are important to developing channels of communication across the whole team. The plan provides ongoing and consistent information to diverse disciplines and helpers on the team, and allows the participant to have a voice in that communication process.

Develops the "Road Map"

The plan, developed with the participant and the team, helps us know how to get from *here* to *there*. Like a map, it tells us what will happen, when, with whom, and for how long. It helps us visualize our destination, the steps needed to get there, and how long our trip may be.

Assures the Appropriate Services Based on Assessment Results and Careful Reasoning

The process of planning is systematic and reflective. The planning process helps the participant, his or her circle of support, and team members think through in a clear and deliberate manner how best to meet the participant's goals. The process forces reflection that leads to more reasoned action, which in turn helps to improve the quality and appropriateness of services provided. The planning process assures that the right services are being used in relation to the participant's goals.

Increases the Likelihood of Success

If we have carefully identified goals and deliberately planned methods, we increase our likelihood that the participant will experience some level of success. In contrast, if we provide shotgun services or cookie-cutter programming based on agency and program goals, participant success will be hit and miss.

Assists in Documenting Outcomes

A plan helps us in our quest to document how our services impact the participant and his or her quality of life. The plan provides a blueprint for evaluating our efforts, and the participant's response to our efforts. As the saying goes, "If you don't know where you are going, how will you know if you ever got there?"

Meets Professional Standards of Practice

Planning is a required part of competent therapeutic recreation practice. Our professional standards require that we complete an individualized plan with each participant we involve in therapeutic recreation services (ATRA, 2000, CTRA, 2006; NTRS, 2004). Our agency's regulations and accreditation standards require the same.

Empowers the Participant

Imagine that you agree to go on a trip with a group of strangers, all who say they want you to have the best trip ever. Yet you are never quite sure where you are headed, what route you will take to get there, or even what method of travel you will be using. How would this make you feel? Even though you are excited to take the journey, you would likely feel a little anxious, confused, and disempowered. If, however, you were able to help the group plan the destination, the route to get there, and the method of travel, you would be much more excited and better able to put focused effort and energy into the journey. And you will enjoy the journey more fully. A plan does the same thing for a participant receiving help in a health or human services setting. It empowers the participant to have a voice in what the goals are and in what methods and strategies would best assist in reaching the goals. Receiving help in a health or human services setting is much like a journey and a plan is much like a trip itinerary that gives one control over the travel.

Inspires the Participant

If planning is approached with excitement and anticipation of desired positive change, and if the process is participatory, engaging, fun, and enjoyable, then planning can inspire people. It can help them envision a different future for themselves. It can help them mobilize their strengths, resources, and energy to realize what they want in their lives. Plans are essentially maps to dreams.

Plans, developed in a collaborative process, mobilize participants toward a vision they have for their lives. Using creativity, inspiration, and guided self-reflection, you can help participants begin to craft the life they want. In fact, in the life-coaching profession, plans are sometimes called "vision boards" or "treasure maps." In Figure 10.1 (p. 240), we share the life story of Pamela Moss, an artist who facilitates planning sessions called "Treasure Mapping." We offer this story to help you think about planning as something that can be full of hope, inspiration, and energy. Planning itself can be a leisure experience for those involved, and not just some mandated requirement of a bureaucracy. In strengths-based practice, when we focus on the positive aspects of all we do, planning becomes an exciting interaction between the team and the participant.

THE LINK BETWEEN ASSESSMENT AND PLANNING

Recall from Chapter 9 *Assessment* that identifying goals or clarifying dreams was often a part of the assessment process. For example, in the MAPS process, a key aspect is learning about a participant's dreams and goals. In most of the initial and specific assessment processes and tools we introduced, discovering what someone wants in life and in leisure is inherent in the assessment process. Assessment provides rich information about goals, dreams, aspirations, and valued life outcomes that move the therapeutic recreation process seamlessly into the planning phase. Taking what is learned from assessment about goals and dreams, and turning that information into a road map to get there, takes the skills and knowledge of the therapeutic recreation specialist in partnership with the participant, his or her circle of support, and the team.

The process of thinking through assessment results and coming up with a realistic achievable plan is called action-oriented critical thinking, or "clinical reasoning." The term **clinical reasoning** means that you are influenced by knowledge, experience, ethics, and critically reflective thinking as you holistically synthesize information to make decisions about practice (Benner, Hughes, & Sutphen, 2008). We will talk in more depth about clinical reasoning, or action-oriented critical thinking, in Chapter 15 *Building Your Strengths as a Therapeutic Recreation Specialist*. Here, we introduce this important thought process, since it is key to developing an effective plan.

In the assessment phase, you learn much about a participant, his or her strengths, resources, environments, and dreams. The dreams may at times seem unrealistic, and even outrageous, in the context of the person's life. But using action-oriented critical thinking, you can often find the kernel in every dream that can help guide planning. In Figure 10.2 (p. 241), we share Judith Snow's story of her dream. Judith's story highlights the critical importance of dreams and aspirations in the planning process. Later in this chapter, we provide further evidence about the importance of goals that are intrinsic and authentic for achieving well-being.

In summary, to move from assessment to planning, you need to consider all you have learned about the participant in the assessment phase, especially strengths, resources, dreams, and goals. As you work to develop a plan to achieve participant goals, you must incorporate practical considerations as well, such as the following elements:

- the setting and service delivery system in which you work
- the team members with whom you work
- the therapeutic recreation philosophy you use to guide your practice
- the environment in which the participant lives (e.g., urban versus rural)

Despite these variations, fundamental strengths-based principles will guide your work as you plan with

Life Story:

The Art of Visioning, by Pamela Moss

'Vision-Powered Life' Mentor Pamela Moss Ph.D. is a coach, transformational artist, and speaker. Her company, *Heart Vision*, helps people see what lights them up and grows their dreams into reality, so they can make the difference they are here to make.

Here is Pamela's story:

"I'm someone who discovered that what lights me up is helping others see what lights *them* up—I live to see and celebrate the light in each of us. Following that 'heart vision' has lead to my work being featured in international telesummits, private art collections across the U.S., and national TV.

"My idealistic dream is that this work will help people not only see their own light—their inner beauty and greatness and gifts—but also see the light *in others*, at home, our communities, and all over the world. If we all saw this consistently there would truly be peace on earth.

"Before I began following this 'heart vision,' I was an insecure homeschooling mom and the author of an ethics textbook.* I never imagined being a transformational artist or seminar leader or international speaker—much less one who helps people remember who they really are.

"So what happened? I had an inspired idea...and acted on it.

"During a powerful self-discovery course, I went to see an exhibit of Byzantine art. As I was marveling at an ancient icon, an idea struck me like a revelation: "Wouldn't it be incredible to paint *portraits of ordinary people in their divine aspects*, icons for the 21st century that show who we have the capacity to be?"

"But—I hadn't touched a paintbrush in over 20 years! (Like many people, I loved to draw and paint as a child, then later decided I couldn't be an artist.) I was so on fire with my idea, though, that I rushed home, bought paints and supplies, and turned our bedroom into an art studio. And as I interviewed my first subject and began painting the first "Possibility Portrait," I discovered a delight and purposefulness I'd last remembered as a young teen, counseling friends and drawing over my schoolwork. *So this is what I was meant to do!*

"Since then, continuing to take inspired action aligned with my 'heart vision' has led me to create vision board workshops, design a curriculum to help people grow their dreams, and attract mentors, partnerships, and a team that allow me to serve people all over the globe. I am so grateful to have found work that is profoundly fulfilling and fun for me, and also makes a big contribution to others. Who could ask for more?"

Possibility Portraits, Vision-Powered Goals, Treasure Mapping, Magic Mirror Kits, Grow Your Dreams Intensives, and other creative approaches developed by Pamela to help people realize their dreams are featured on her websites: www.innervisionportraits.com and www.growyourdreamsnow.com

* Here is Pamela's ethics textbook: Strike, K., & Moss, P. (2008). *Ethics and college student life: A case study approach (3rd ed).* Englewood Cliffs, NJ: Prentice Hall.

Figure 10.1 Life Story: The Art of Visioning

participants. It is imperative that you make these principles explicit and clear so you can facilitate a planning process that is consistent, authentic, and meaningful. In the next section, we provide a review of what we feel are essential guiding principles to help you make decisions with participants during the planning phase of therapeutic recreation practice.

Principles that Guide Strengths-Based Planning

In Chapter 7 *Principles* we overviewed several principles that guide therapeutic recreation practice. These same principles must be used as guideposts in the planning process. In Figure 10.3 (see p. 242), we provide a visual of the principles we have discussed in Part 1 of this

Life Story:

Judith Snow
Truck Driver?

Judith Snow is one of Canada's leading experts on inclusion and rights for people with disabilities and others who have been excluded. Judith uses a wheelchair and has no mobility except the use of her right thumb. Judith's dream was to be a truck driver!

Digging deeper into Judith's dream, the kernel or the North Star of her vision for her life wasn't necessarily to drive trucks. But all that went with truck driving was what she wanted: motion, movement, freedom, travel, adventure, and seeing the world from high up.

According to Judith, "My dream had important seeds in it. In my truck driver dream, my getting around and giving things to other people is an important part of my gift. I now travel internationally talking to people about how we can support all our diversities. My dream has come true and my life is satisfying to me. It is a life of contribution to other people. All the information we needed was in the dream about my being a truck driver" (Falvey, Forest, Pearpoint, & Rosenberg, 1997, pp. 64–65).

According to Judith, if we become good at listening carefully to what people's dreams are, we then become good at helping them find their way to that dream. We need to refrain from judging and limiting people. We need to look for the seed, the essence of what a person's real desire is and, from that, work on what is eventually feasible in the context of a participant's life.

Figure 10.2 Life Story: Judith Snow, Truck Driver? *(adapted from Falvey, Forest, Pearpoint, & Rosenberg, 1997)*

book. Remember that principles guide, in a proactive way, the professional behaviors of our everyday practice. They light our way as we work with participants to plan their future.

In a strengths-based approach to planning, the principles in Figure 10.3 will be used consistently throughout the process. Repeating the principles here helps us to keep them clearly in mind, to light our way (see also Figure 10.4, p. 242). In many settings in which you may provide therapeutic recreation services, you may well be the *only* team member practicing from a strengths approach. Planning has historically been a problem-oriented process. In Figure 10.5 (p. 243), we provide a comparison of a deficit-based approach to planning and a strengths-based approach. In the strengths approach, the focus is on goals, strengths, and using natural supports and resources to facilitate well-being. We also offer a life story in Figure 10.6 (p. 244) that illuminates the culture shift that occurs when an agency, the Sarah Neuman Center, moves from a deficit-based approach to a strengths approach in planning and the subsequent benefits of the shift to participants.

One important principle and practice in strengths-based planning is the use of strengths-based language. In strengths-based planning, the language of the plan must align with the principles that guide the creation of that plan. Instead of using the third-person (e.g., he, she, him, her), a formal tone, and medical jargon, the plan can use "I" statements, from the participant's point of view. The plan can be written in plain language understandable by the participant, the circle of support, and all staff (including assistants). In Figure 10.7 (p. 245), we offer a comparison of a sample plan written in a traditional approach with a sample plan written in a strengths approach. Using "I" statements instead of third-person statements humanizes and personalizes the plan, helps the team see life more fully through the eyes of the participant, and improves communication and motivation on the team (Krugh & Bowman, 2006).

Planning Process

The planning process is a systematic and logical means of moving from assessment to developing an effective plan with participants, their circles of support, and the team. The planning process is a roadmap to plan for change. In Figure 10.8 (p. 246), we offer a visual of the planning process and each step that is involved in the journey.

Determine Direction

The planning process involves determining direction, actions, and evaluation. When you work with a participant to illuminate direction, you are often working not only with the participant, but the participant's circle of support and other team members. You are getting clear together on what is most important to address in

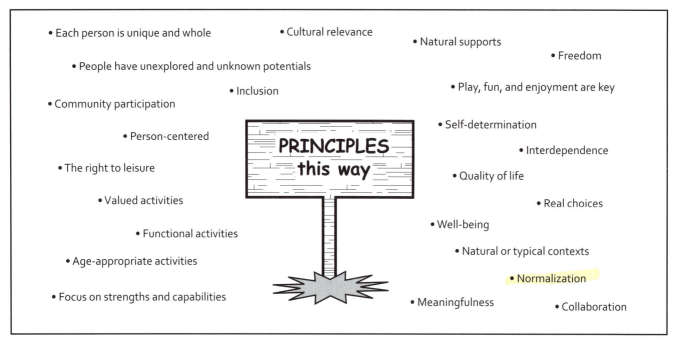

Figure 10.3 Principles that Guide Strengths-Based Planning

My Cultural Lens: Assumptions of Helpers

When we help participants plan, Leakes, Black, and Roberts (2004) ask us to examine the assumptions we hold due to our cultural perspective. The authors bring to light several assumptions held by professionals who come from a Western perspective:

- An individualistic versus a collectivistic perspective, where independence and self-reliance are valued more highly than dependence and group reliance
- A strong focus on self-determination and individual choice, embedded in an individualistic approach versus group or hierarchical decision-making
- Individual competitiveness and personal achievement versus group competitiveness and group achievement
- Independent living and self-reliance versus living with kin, interdependence, and possibly being cared for
- Creating a plan on paper versus a verbal plan that is established in the context of close personal relationships between family and professionals

Leakes and colleagues offer four steps to increase cultural sensitivity in planning:

- *Step 1:* Identify your cultural values underlying interpretations of the participant's situation. For example, you may realize that values like independence and self-reliance lead to recommending that a participant with developmental disabilities move from the family home to supported living and, eventually, independent living.
- *Step 2:* Find out the extent to which your values and assumptions are recognized and accepted by the participant and family. If they do not view independence as important, then this may not be an appropriate goal.
- *Step 3:* Acknowledge any cultural differences identified and explain to the participant and family how and why mainstream American society promotes different values. How the value of independence has benefited other participants and families might be described, helping the participant and family to understand the cultural basis for your recommendations.
- *Step 4:* Through discussion and collaboration, you, the participant, and the circle of support collaboratively determine the most effective way of adapting your interpretations and recommendations to the family value system.

Discuss these assumptions with a colleague or fellow student. What cultural values do you hold? How would they affect your ability to help a participant plan for enhanced leisure and well-being? How could you use the steps offered above to increase your own cultural sensitivity?

Figure 10.4 My Cultural Lens: Assumptions of Helpers

Compare/Contrast:
Strengths-Based Approach to Planning versus a Deficits-Based Approach

Focus	From a Deficits Approach . . .	To a Strengths Approach
Purpose of plan	A list of problems the participant must fix; inflexible	A living document that provides a framework for the helping process
View of participant	Participant known by his or her diagnosis or label	Participant known through a personal relationship and a circle of support
Role of participant in developing plan	Little to no involvement and input Expertise of the professional prevails and is most respected	Direct involvement; the plan is based on participant input and what it is he or she wants to achieve Expertise of the participant and circle of support is honored and respected
Outside or community resources	Underutilized or not utilized at all; may even be seen as a hindrance	Integrated into the plan; a key component of wrap-around services and cultivation of natural supports
Problems	Form the foundation of the plan; often a plan is focused solely on remediation of the problem	Problems are not the focus of the plan; problems are seen as unsuccessful attempts at negotiating a life situation
Strengths	Minimized or relegated to a back part of the plan Assessments do not measure strengths Viewed as the opposite of weaknesses	Placed at the forefront of the plan; the plan is built around strengths Assessment measures strengths Viewed as contextual
Goals	Focuses mainly on the problems Often worded negatively, e.g., "the participant will stop doing [something negative]" Language follows a clinical or medical model	Integrates participant's strengths Worded positively, e.g., "the participant will do more of [something positive]" Language is understood by all participants in the process
Planned interventions	Based on diagnoses and standards of practice, as well as program structure and routine of the facility	Unique interventions that focus on the goals and strengths of the participant, as well as standards of practice

Figure 10.5 Compare/Contrast: Strengths-Based Approach to Planning versus a Deficits-Based Approach *(adapted from Brasler, 2001)*

therapeutic recreation and other services. To help you clarify priorities, pose the following kinds of questions:

- What goals or dreams are most important to the participant? Are there some goals that should be addressed first, that would allow for a more logical route to reach other goals?
- What could the participant accomplish on his or her own, without assistance from the team?
- What goals would benefit from the help of the team?
- What strengths and resources (both internal and external) does the participant have to help him or her reach goals? What interests and passions does the participant have that can be put into play to help reach a goal as well as ensure the right to leisure participation?
- What expectations do the participant and circle of support have in the planning process?

Recall the story of Judith Snow's dream to be a truck driver and how it took careful and thoughtful probing and exploring to get at the kernel of a goal in

Life Story:

*A Culture Change
at Sarah Neuman Center for Healthcare & Rehabilitation
Mamaroneck, New York*

As part of an ongoing culture change at the Sarah Neuman Center for Healthcare & Rehabilitation, the care planning process underwent significant change. In coordination with families, the interdisciplinary team adopted a "Strengths-Based Care Planning Model." The model emphasizes each resident's strengths instead of using a problem, or weakness-oriented approach. Essential in the model is its reliance on what a resident can still do rather than what he or she cannot.

For example, with residents who have a diagnosis of dementia, there was so much attention paid to deficits that the strengths of the individual were forgotten or overlooked. When the focus was shifted to the residents' strengths, the team saw an improvement in residents' self-esteem and confidence, and a decline in what were considered problem behaviors, such as wandering, yelling, or repetitive verbalizations. Working from a strengths perspective, the focus shifted to the positive aspects of the residents' lives. The interventions and goals are now based on skills that the residents are still able to maintain. Residents' strengths can include a specific leisure activity, or physical or cognitive skills.

Families are an integral part of the Strengths-Based Care Planning Model at Sarah Neuman, from the day of admission. They help the staff identify ongoing strengths and help reinforce identified strengths. That reinforcement of strengths is a powerful tool to maintain abilities, de-emphasize losses, and enhance residents' lives, according to the team. It also helps incorporate family members in the care-planning team.

Strengths-Based Care Planning helps the Sarah Neuman Center implement its mission of improving the quality of life for all residents.

Figure 10.6 Life Story: A Culture Change *(adapted from Gallagher, 2005)*

that dream. Use this "detective-like" approach to help participants get clear on what direction they want to take with their goals. Once you are clear, you will help the participant form more concrete goals and measurable objectives. We discuss how to effectively develop goals and objectives later in this chapter. In Figure 10.9 (p. 247), we present a "Primary Source Support" of ongoing research by Claire Forest (2009) on how families set goals with assistance from family coaches.

Determine Actions

The next step in the planning process is to determine what methods, approaches, environments, and resources will be needed to help a participant reach his or her clearly formulated goals. In this step, you, the participant, and the team determine strategies, services, interventions, and activities that will be most effective in helping the participant and the environment grow and change toward goals. Together, you will decide who will provide services, where they will be provided, and for how long.

Determine Evaluation

A part of planning is deciding how the participant, you, and the team will decide when the goals are achieved at a level that feels successful. You will plan the way you collect information and feedback, and how you will analyze it, to come to a decision with the participant about success. We will discuss evaluation in more depth in Chapter 13 *Evaluation*.

The planning process is influenced by your own practice wisdom and that of your team. As a collective group, you will have many perspectives, experiences, and levels of expertise to help you develop a plan that truly helps participants accomplish their dreams. Other factors may also influence the planning process:

- The amount of time you have to spend with the participant
- The mission of your agency
- The resources you have available
- The other disciplines available on the team to assist you and the participant

The most important influence on the planning process is the participant and his or her circle of support. In the next section, we explore the important role of the participant in planning, as well as the roles of the family, other social support, and other team members.

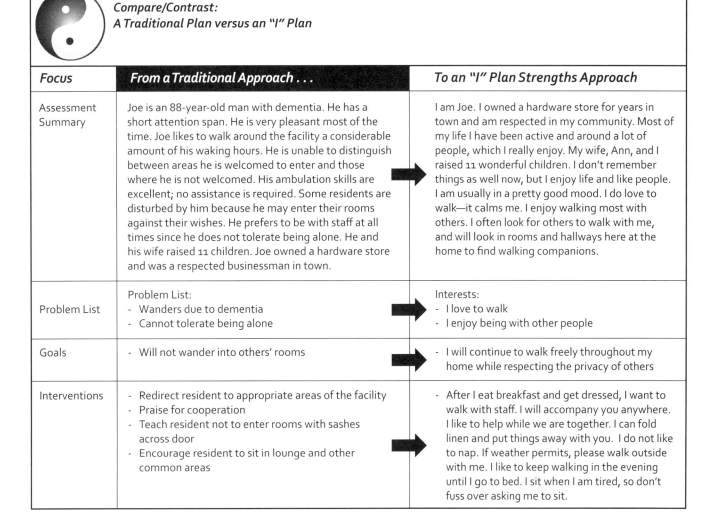

Figure 10.7 Compare/Contrast: A Traditional Plan versus an "I" Plan *(adapted from Krugh & Bowman, 2006)*

ROLE OF THE PARTICIPANT, CIRCLE OF SUPPORT, AND TEAM IN PLANNING

"Nothing about us without us." Recall those words from self-advocates that we presented in Chapter 8 *Collaborative Teams*. In strengths-based planning, the participant is the key member of the planning team. The role of the participant is to identify dreams and goals; to help form the smaller steps, the objectives, which show progress toward the goals; and to help identify passions and interests that can be promoted to build strengths and, more importantly, to enhance leisure. The participant can help make decisions about services and interventions. After all, the participant is the only team member that can say, "This plan is credible and meaningful for me." If the participant is unable to make that judgment, then the family or circle of support can do so. When the participant is fully involved in joint decision-making in planning, better outcomes and greater satisfaction result (Briggs, 2004).

The role of the collaborative team, especially in a transdisciplinary approach, is to work with each other to help the participant achieve the goals he or she identifies. The role of the team is to empower participants—using our skills, knowledge, and resources—to set and reach their goals. Forest (2009) stated, "The cornerstone of the empowerment approach is that empowerment is not something anyone can do for someone else, nor can it be forced. Empowerment happens when people set their own goals. The role of helping systems, whether family, friends, or agencies, is to support that goal, not to set it for the person" (para. 5).

Goals are set not only with the participant, but with the team's help. Recall from Chapter 8 *Collaborative Teams* that there are many ways to function as a team, from multidisciplinary to interdisciplinary to transdisciplinary. Whatever model of teamwork is used in planning, clear communication and sharing is needed. In some settings, you will develop a single, comprehensive, unified plan, with one set of goals and interventions.

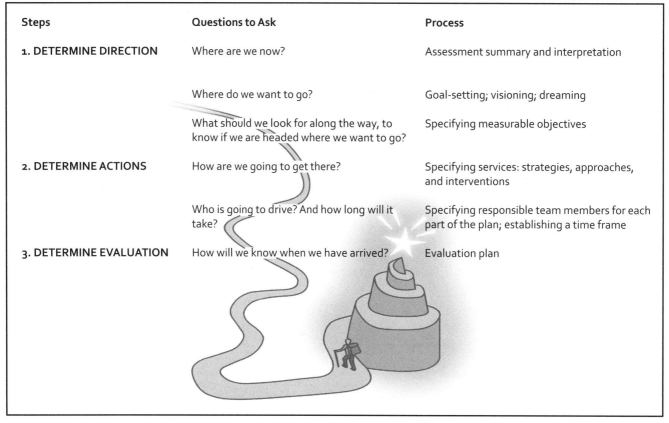

Figure 10.8 The Planning Process—A Journey Toward Change

In other settings, each discipline will develop its own interventions, in relation to a unified set of goals. And in yet other settings, each discipline will develop its own plan, with its own set of goals. We introduced you to Janet Connolly, CTRS, and her work using the FIM assessment on a rehabilitation interdisciplinary team in Chapter 9 *Assessment*. In Figure 10.10 (p. 248), we share Janet's experience developing goals as part of a team.

Types of Plans

Plans can be developed in two ways: as a unified team plan, called *comprehensive plans*, or individually within each discipline, called *discipline-specific plans*. You may encounter many variations in these two approaches, depending on the setting and service delivery system in which you work.

Comprehensive Team-Based Plan

A comprehensive plan is developed by the whole team, with each discipline contributing to the plan. The comprehensive plan typically includes a **summary of the participant's basic information** (e.g., family contact information, emergency information, medications), a social history, what was learned in the assessment process from each team member (either by discipline or combined into one summary), and the team members involved in the plan (including consultants).

The comprehensive plan largely consists of the **working plan**. It is a comprehensive, integrated plan of action developed by the participant, his or her circle of support, and the team. A comprehensive plan typically includes the following components:

- A prioritized list of main goals and objectives
- The activities/interventions for that goal
- The person(s) responsible for that action or intervention
- The due date for the action or intervention

In some settings, each discipline may develop a separate set of objectives and interventions, directed by that particular discipline, to contribute to the goal. In other settings, all the interventions are combined in one master plan, with responsible disciplines delineated in the master plan.

Depending on where you provide therapeutic recreation services, the comprehensive plan will be called many different things. In Table 10.1 (p. 248), we provide an overview of some of the common comprehensive plans in use today.

Primary Source Support:
How Do Families Set and Reach Goals?

Forest, C. (2009). Preliminary research findings on "How do Families Coached by Family Development Credentialed Workers Set and Reach Goals?" Current Family Development Credential Research, http://www.human.cornell.edu

Forest conducted a study to determine how families coached by Family Development Credential workers set and reach goals. Families from urban and rural areas were invited to participate in the study if they had met with a family worker three times, set a major goal and smaller goals, and completed goal-setting plans with the worker. The final family sample included 25 families (11 rural, 14 urban) that ranged in age from 18 to 74, and represented diverse races, ethnicities, and family compositions. Seventy-five percent of families who participated had a yearly income under $20,000. Forest then conducted in-depth interviews with each of them. The results of the study showed the following:
- Families reported that learning to set goals was a key skill in building their sense of greater self-reliance.
- Families perceived that receiving information and encouragement from workers was critical to reaching their goals.
- Workers reported that using family development skills had changed how they perceived and worked with families.
- The majority of families who participated in the study had experienced "socially toxic environments" (experienced at least one of the following: physical, verbal, or sexual abuse; foster care placement; psychiatric illness; unemployment; illiteracy; alcoholism; incarceration; substance abuse; or homelessness).
- Family members reported there were significant differences in their relationships with strengths-based family development workers as compared with other family workers who worked from a deficit approach. They stated that strengths-based family development workers confirmed what the family was doing right, were the first ones to ask what their goal was, explained things and taught skills for self-reliance, demonstrated genuine concern and empathy, were nonjudgmental, provided consistent encouragement, followed up, conveyed respect, and were genuinely open and patient.

Family member also reported that they felt that deficit-based workers
- Perceived they were lazy
- Were judgmental about what the family needed
- Gave intensive short-term support but didn't follow up
- Gave the sense they were "better than the families"

The strengths-based approach to helping families set and achieve goals was a powerful agent in creating positive change.

Figure 10.9 Primary Source Support: How Do Families Set and Reach Goals?

Discipline-Specific Plan

In some settings, discipline-specific plans are developed. Typically this kind of plan is used in settings where only one discipline is providing services, or where services are provided on more of a consulting basis. Some agencies still function using a multidisciplinary approach, where each discipline works in isolation from the other disciplines, developing plans and delivering services with little coordination between professionals. This is much less common today due to standards of practice, accreditation, and regulations. In service settings where therapeutic recreation is the only discipline providing primary services, a discipline-specific plan is developed that contains all the same elements of a comprehensive plan. In Figure 10.11 (p. 249), we share a model therapeutic recreation service, PATH, which uses a discipline-specific planning process, but engages many community services in the process.

Regardless of the type of plan being developed, the heart and soul of any plan are the goals. In the next section, we look at goals in detail, because not all goals are created equal!

Not All Goals Are Created Equal

Have you ever had someone say to you, "You should [do this]" or "You should [do that]?" Have you ever had someone say to you, "You shouldn't do so much of [this]"? When another person tells you what your goals ought to be, it can have a negative and disempowering effect (in fact, the word "should" indicates that an action is considered by the speaker to be obligatory on the part of the receiver of the communication, implying a form of external control). Goals that are not intrinsic, authentic, appropriate, or positive are not effective for most people.

In this section, we explore the powerful activity of goal-setting. If done correctly, setting goals and committing to them is one of the proven strategies for building well-being and happiness (Lyubomirsky, 2007). But what makes goal-setting effective? What do we need to do to help participants set goals that lead to higher well-being? Understanding that the process of setting and working toward a goal is as important to

Table 10.1 Types of Comprehensive Plans

Type of Plan	Typical Setting
Individualized Family Service Plan (IFSP)	Early intervention services for children with disabilities from birth to 3 years old; mandated by federal law (Individuals with Disabilities Education Act or IDEA)
Individualized Education Plan (IEP)	School setting for children from 4–21 years old; mandated by federal law (IDEA)
Individualized Transition Plan (ITP)	Part of the IEP in the school setting; initiated when the participant is 14 years old or in 9th grade
Individualized Service Plan (ISP)	Used in many settings, but particularly in community-based services for people with developmental or other disabilities who receive Medicaid funding (formerly called an individualized program plan before the paradigm shift to services rather than programs); also called an Individualized Support Plan
Individual Habilitation Plan (IHP)	Developmental disabilities services, such as group homes, day habilitation programs, and human services
Comprehensive Treatment Plan	Medical settings, such as general hospitals, rehabilitation hospitals, psychiatric treatment centers, and chemical dependency treatment centers
Critical Pathway (or Clinical Pathway)	Medical settings, particularly cardiology, diabetes management, and other physical conditions; also used occasionally in physical rehabilitation and psychiatry, but there is controversy over the utility of critical pathways in these settings
Comprehensive Care Plan	Long-term care settings, adult day services; usually organized around the Minimum Data Set (MDS) as the comprehensive assessment in nursing homes
"I" Care Plan	Long-term care settings; used as a person-centered alternative to a traditional comprehensive care plan
Inclusion Plan	Community-based settings, such as schools, parks and recreation departments, youth-serving organizations, and the like; inclusion plans can be developed for the agency as well as the individual

Life Story:

Team Planning Using the FIM
By Janet Connolly, CTRS

I am a Certified Therapeutic Recreation Specialist (CTRS) currently working in a long-term acute care hospital (LTACH) on an inpatient physical rehabilitation unit. As in short-term acute rehabilitation hospitals, we utilize the Functional Independence Measure (FIM) as a tool for measuring functional gains and outcomes (see Chapter 9, Figure 9.13).

After the FIM is administered and scored by the team, we create goals for the patient. There are several factors that I must consider when designing goals. A CTRS must consider the practice standards of the facility where he or she works, which somewhat guide the "acceptable" length of stay for patients based on the acuity of their condition.

The success of a program is often judged by internal and external reviewers in relation to the number of patients who have achieved the FIM goals set upon admission. This is a challenge in long-term acute care hospital settings, where patients have three or more medical areas of significance.

Discharge goals, as measured with the FIM, are often based on one's hope for recovery/rehabilitation (and hope that insurance will allow for the appropriate length of stay to allow for this recovery/rehabilitation to take place). As a general practice, the CTRS relies heavily on previous years of experience to guide the setting of these goals. The general length of stay for patients in LTACH facilities is generally longer than acute rehabilitation due to the complicating factors of the care of the patients. However, the outcomes (FIM scores) continue to be very good, with most patients being discharged to the community having met or surpassed their goals, as measured with the FIM.

Figure 10.10 Life Story: Team Planning Using the FIM

Primary Source Support: Project PATH

Sable, J., & Gravink, J. (2005). The PATH to community health care for people with disabilities: A community-based therapeutic recreation service. *Therapeutic Recreation Journal, 39*(1), 78–87.

Janet Sable and Jill Gravink present a therapeutic recreation service modeled using an ecological approach. The PATH, or Promoting Access, Transition, and Health, protocol was developed to assist individuals with physical disabilities achieve healthy lifestyles centered on recreation in the community.

The protocol for PATH begins with a referral from a health maintenance organization, or HMO. Once the referral is received, a therapeutic recreation specialist completes an ecological assessment with the participant in his or her home and community. The interests, goals, strengths, and resources of the participant are identified through the assessment.

The goals of the participant often revolve around these areas: individual fitness, wellness, improved functional skills in the community, community inclusion, network and resource development, and recreation skill development. The therapeutic recreation specialist assists the participant in developing a plan that focuses on the environment as well, including accessibility improvement and community inclusion.

PATH is an evidence-based approach to working with the whole individual, in his or her environment, building strengths and resources. It is a discipline-specific plan, developed with the participant and a therapeutic recreation specialist. However, to put the plan into action, the participant and therapeutic recreation specialist rely on community-based team members, such as parks and recreation professionals, fitness professionals, and other recreation providers.

Figure 10.11 Primary Source Support: Project PATH

well-being as the attainment of that goal is an important first step.

Goal pursuit has been shown to have many positive benefits, supported by a strong body of research (Ryan & Deci, 2001). Goal pursuit . . .

- Provides a sense of purpose and a feeling of control over our lives; gives us something to look forward to or to work for
- Bolsters our self-esteem; the accomplishment of sub-goals or objectives on our way to accomplishing the goals provides further boosts
- Adds structure and meaning to our daily lives
- Helps us master our use of time; learning to develop higher-order goals and subdividing them into smaller steps with a schedule to accomplish them is a life-enhancing skill
- Helps us cope better with problems
- Helps us engage with other people in positive ways, especially if we share a common goal

What types of goals are the most powerful in promoting well-being? Recall in Chapter 9 *Assessment* that we presented the Aspirations Index. Those aspirations that focus on wealth, image, and fame are not related to well-being, while those that focus on meaningful relationships, personal growth, and community contributions are related (Kasser & Ryan, 1993; 1996). Here are six important findings that the research tells us about goals that promote well-being (Lyubomirsky, 2007):

Intrinsic Goals

Goals must be freely chosen, personally involving, and rewarding. Intrinsic goals are those that are inherently satisfying and meaningful to the participant. Sometimes we will pursue extrinsic goals, but only insofar as they help meet intrinsic goals. The research is clear that intrinsic goals make us happier and more motivated to action.

Authentic Goals

Authentic goals are those that are rooted in a person's lifelong, deeply-held interests and core values. They are goals that come from the heart, and not from parents, professionals, spouses, or others. Authentic goals come from a clear sense of your desires, interests, preferences, and guiding values. They are goals that "fit" with who you are.

Approach Goals

Approach goals are those that are framed to help us reach a desired outcome. Compare this to avoidance goals, which are those that are framed in terms of avoiding an undesirable outcome. For example, we can frame a goal about our leisure in two ways: to be fully engaged in meaningful and stimulating activities with others *or* to pursue activities to avoid boredom and loneliness. The research is clear that people who frame their goals in approach terms are much happier and healthier than people who frame their goals in avoidance terms.

Harmonious Goals

Goals that complement one another versus goals that conflict with one another are important to well-being. For example, to have competing goals, such as "spend more time at my job to work my way up the ladder" and "spend more time outdoors kayaking" will cause stress and anxiety. The research is clear that competing goals usually lead to failure in both areas, and that it is better to sacrifice one goal than try to pursue goals that are not harmonious.

Flexible and Appropriate Goals

Goals that fit the place, time, culture, and life-stage are more likely to lead to well-being than those that do not match the right task with the right time. When we adapt our goals to the opportunities that open up before us, due to changes in our environment or ourselves, we will be happier. This is an especially important concept for some participants with whom we work, who may be newly injured and whose view of the future is altered due to changes in functional ability.

Activity Goals

The research clearly shows that taking up activities that allow us to continuously experience new challenges, take on new opportunities, or meet new people, lead to well-being more than goals that focus on changing our circumstances (e.g., moving to a new house, buying new things, or changing roommates). The process of pursuing activity goals directly contributes to well-being. According to Lyubomirsky (2007), "find a happy person, and you will find a project" (p. 205). Part of this is explained by what is called "hedonic adaptation." We get used to our new circumstances, and return to our happiness set point. With activity, we are engaged, stimulated, and experiencing a steady inflow of positive feelings and experiences.

Therapeutic recreation, with its focus on preferences, interests, passions, strengths, and activity, is perhaps the discipline that can best help participants achieve well-being, regardless of functional ability. Table 10.2 summarizes the important aspects of goals that you need to keep at the forefront as you work with participants to form the goals for their plan. You can use this checklist with participants to help them evaluate their own goals. If participants find that the goals they have formed mostly fit the descriptors on the right-hand side of the table, they may want to reformulate their goals to be more enriching for their well-being.

Remember that you are taking the dreams that the participant and his or her circle of support have articulated, and helping them "mine" or distill goals from those dreams. Besides asking if the goals meet the above attributes, you can also ask these questions to help you clarify goals:

- Are the goals clear statements of desired outcomes?
- Do the goals capitalize on the strengths of the participant and his or her environment?
- Are the goals valued outcomes for the participant? Are they important changes that will enhance leisure and quality of life?
- Are the goals written in terms of outcomes for the participant, and not the processes or activities of the staff working with the participant?
- Are the goals achievable with the resources available and the services you provide? If not, what other resources will you need to garner? Or what referrals might you need to make?

Goals are statements of desired outcomes. They are higher-level statements and often broadly written to capture the essence of the participant's valued outcomes. In order to work toward the goal, you and the participant must break it down into smaller sub-goals, or steps, to reach the higher-level goal. These sub-goals are called objectives, and they provide a way for the participant and the team to monitor whether the goals are being achieved. The next section looks at the process of writing effective objectives.

Table 10.2 Important Goal Attributes to Consider in Forming a Plan with a Participant and the Team *(Lyubomirsky, 2007)*

Descriptors of Goals that Support Well-Being	Descriptors of Goals that Do NOT Support Well-Being
☐ Intrinsic	☐ Extrinsic
☐ Authentic	☐ Inauthentic
☐ Approach-oriented	☐ Avoidance-oriented
☐ Harmonious	☐ Conflicting
☐ Flexible/appropriate	☐ Rigid/inappropriate
☐ Activity-based	☐ Circumstance-based

OBJECTIVES

"Goals are dreams with deadlines."

—*Diana Scharf-Hunt*

Goals are dreams with deadlines, and it is behavioral objectives that provide the deadlines. Where a **goal** is a broad statement of intent, objectives are narrower and measurable. Objectives are sub-goals that break the larger goal into small, achievable steps. An **objective** is a statement in specific and measurable terms that describes what the participant will know, feel, think, or be able to do. For objectives to be effective, they need to be SMART (Centers for Disease Control and Prevention, 2009). SMART is an acronym that describes the attributes of strong and useful objectives. Let's look at each element of SMART objectives:

S—Specific

Specific objectives use only one specific and observable action verb. In a specific objective, it is clearly stated who should do what and under what conditions.

M—Measurable

The objective states how much of a behavior is needed, or how much change is expected, to determine whether the objective is met or not. Objectives provide a concrete way to measure a change in behavior or performance.

A—Achievable

Well-written objectives are attainable within the time frame and with the resources available. The objectives specify appropriate levels of outcome, given the participant's context and abilities.

R—Relevant

Objectives are meaningful and truly show progress toward the participant's goals and dreams. They ask the participant to engage in activities or interventions that fit the context of their lives.

T—Time-Framed

The objectives provide a timeline or deadline by which it is realistically expected that the objectives will be met. The time frame fits the participant, the setting, and the services being provided.

SMART objectives must be carefully written. To ensure that objectives are well-formed, they must include three key components: a specific behavior, a criterion (also called a standard), and a condition. In essence, the three components answer these questions (Mager, 1997):

- What should the participant be able to do or know? (behavior or action)
- How well must it be done? (criterion or standard)
- Under what conditions do you want the participant to do it? (condition)

Here is an example of a goal, contrasted with a corresponding objective that contains all three elements:

Goal: Kari wants to increase her recreation involvement in the community.

Objective: Kari will successfully complete one full 4-week session of Aquacize at her neighborhood YMCA with support from the therapeutic recreation specialist.

The goal, increased community-based recreation involvement, is not measurable. It is a broad statement of intent. The objective provides specific, measurable, achievable, relevant, and time-framed activity. The objective states that Kari will complete a specific community-based recreation activity, Aquacize, that she will complete a full 4-week session, and that the therapeutic recreation specialist will provide supports to help her do so. Let's look in depth at the anatomy of an objective and its three key elements. For each of these key components, you must consider several factors to craft objectives that will truly help you and the participant measure progress toward the goal.

Measurable Objective Key Element #1 - Behavior or Action

A measurable objective clearly states the behavior or action that needs to be demonstrated to show progress. Behaviors need to be observable and measurable in some way. Behaviors can be physical, affective, cognitive, or be an integrated performance of any or all of these domains (see Figure 10.12). For each domain, differing types of behaviors at differing levels of complexity can be specified.

The **physical or psychomotor domain** is the most simple to define, observe, and measure. In Table 10.3, note how psychomotor behavior can range from simple to more complex. It is important to understand at what level of complexity you are asking the participant to do a behavior or task in relation to his or her current level to keep objectives achievable. Here are two objectives with a psychomotor focus, with the **behavior** bolded and underlined:

- *Sara will **walk** one mile each day with her neighbor or her husband.*
- *John will **make** 3 out of 5 **free throws** during drills at the wheelchair basketball practice session.*

The **cognitive domain** is more difficult to observe and tasks or activities must be specified to show what someone has learned or is thinking in order to measure it. Like the psychomotor domain, the cognitive domain can be conceptualized from simple to complex ways of thinking and learning. In Table 10.4 (p. 254), note how cognitive levels range from remembering, the most simple level, to creating, the most complex level. Again, when developing an objective, be sure the level of complexity of the task matches the abilities of the participant. Here are two examples of cognitive objectives, with the **behavior** bolded and underlined:

- *Sara will **describe how to take her pulse** correctly after walking, when asked by staff.*
- *John will **design** three **new plays** for his wheelchair basketball team when asked by the coach.*

The **affective domain** focuses on how one feels, what one values, and the beliefs one holds. In Table 10.5 (p. 255), we provide the taxonomy of the affective domain to assist in developing objectives. The affective domain ranges from receiving to internalizing feelings,

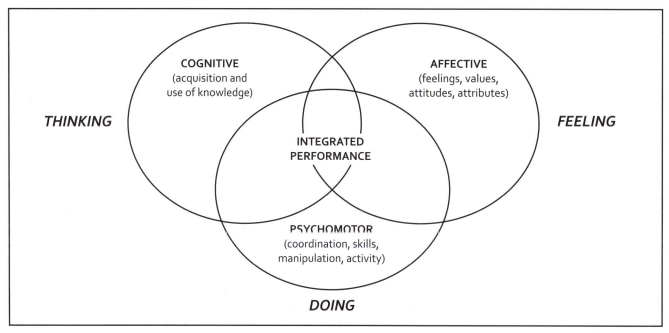

Figure 10.12 The Three Domains of Behavioral Learning and Performance

Table 10.3 The Taxonomy of the Psychomotor (Behavioral or Physical) Domain *(adapted from Dave, 1970)*

	Level or Category	Behavior Description	Example of Activity	Key Words (verbs to describe)
Simple ↓ Complex	Imitation	Copy action of another; observe and replicate	Watch and repeat an action, process, or activity	Copy, follow, replicate, repeat, adhere, attempt, reproduce, organize, sketch, duplicate
	Manipulation	Reproduce activity from instruction or memory	Carry out a task from written or verbal instruction	Re-create, build, perform, execute, implement, acquire, conduct, operate
	Precision	Execute skill reliably, independent of help; activity is quick, smooth, and accurate	Perform a task or activity with expertise and to a high quality without assistance or instruction; able to demonstrate an activity to others	Demonstrate, complete, show, perfect, calibrate, control, achieve, accomplish, master
	Articulation	Adapt and integrate expertise to satisfy a new context or task	Relate and combine associated activities to develop methods to meet varying, novel requirements	Solve, adapt, combine, coordinate, revise, integrate, develop, formulate, modify, master
	Naturalization	Instinctive, effortless, unconscious mastery of activity and related skills at strategic level	Use activity to meet strategic need	Construct, compose, design, specify, manage, invent, originate

beliefs, and attitudes. Here are two objectives that focus on the affective domain, with the **behavior** bolded and underlined:

- Sara will **express feelings of enjoyment** at least once during her walk, when asked by staff.

- John will **choose** wheelchair basketball over passive activities in his free time at least twice a week. *For how many weeks?*

In sum, for each objective, you must identify a behavior that is observable and measurable, that shows the participant is making progress toward the goal, and that is at the appropriate level of specificity and complexity. In Figure 10.13 (p. 256), we offer you a "recipe," or some simple steps, to assist in taking a goal and breaking it down into manageable slices of behavior. Think of the goal as the "whole pie," and the objectives as the slices—each slice has the same flavor, texture, and ingredients as the entire pie, but is more manageable than eating the whole pie!

Measurable Objective Key Element #2: Criterion or Standard

A measurable objective clearly states the amount or expected level of performance of the behavior or action that needs to be demonstrated to show progress. A criterion provides the exact amount or nature of the behavior that can be taken as evidence that the objective has been met. The criterion answers the question, "How well must the behavior be done in order to say the participant has been successful?" Some of the forms that criteria can take appear below:

Criteria
- Number of trials (e.g., 3 out of 4 times)
- Level of accuracy (e.g., within 1 yard of the green)
- Speed (e.g., within 5 minutes)
- Amount of time (e.g., within 5 sessions)
- Percentage or fraction (e.g., ½ the game; 25% of the group session)
- Form, according to a standard (e.g., performs the sidestroke according to the Red Cross standard)
- Characteristics that describe the behavior (e.g., shows enjoyment as characterized by laughing and smiling in an authentic manner)

The bottom line is that two people should have no problem making the same decision about whether or not a desired behavior has occurred at a level that shows success.

Table 10.4 The Taxonomy of the Cognitive Domain *(adapted from Anderson et al., 2001)*

	Level or Category	Behavior Description	Example of Activity	Key Words (verbs to describe)
Simple ↓	Remember	Recall or recognize information	Multiple choice test, recount facts or statistics, recall a process, rules, definitions, quote procedures	Arrange, define, describe, label, list, memorize, recognize, relate, reproduce, select, state, repeat
	Understand	Understand meaning, restate data in one's own words, interpret, extrapolate, translate	Explain or interpret meaning, suggest reaction or solution to given problem, create examples or metaphors	Explain, reiterate, reword, critique, classify, summarize, illustrate, translate, review, report, discuss, rewrite, estimate, interpret, theorize, paraphrase, reference, example
	Apply	Use or apply knowledge, put theory into practice, use knowledge in response to real circumstances	Put a theory into practical effect, demonstrate, solve a problem, manage an activity	Use, apply, discover, manage, execute, solve, produce, implement, construct, change, prepare, conduct, perform, react, respond, role-play
	Analyze	Interpret elements, organizational principles, structure, construction, internal relationships; quality, reliability of individual components	Identify constituent parts and functions of a process or concept, or deconstruct a methodology or process, making qualitative assessment of elements, relationships, values and effects; measure requirements or needs	Analyze, break down, catalogue, compare, quantify, measure, test, examine, experiment, relate, graph, diagram, plot, extrapolate, value, divide
	Evaluate	Assess effectiveness of whole concepts, in relation to values, outputs, efficacy, viability; critical thinking, strategic comparison and review; judgment relating to criteria	Review options or plans in terms of efficacy or practicability; assess sustainability; calculate the effects of a plan or strategy; perform a detailed analysis with recommendations and justifications	Review, justify, assess, present a case for, defend, report on, investigate, direct, appraise, argue, manage, rate, rank, value
Complex	Create	Develop new unique structures, systems, models, approaches, ideas; creative thinking; operations	Develop plans, design solutions, integrate methods, resources, ideas, parts; create new approaches; write new material	Develop, plan, build, create, design, organize, revise, formulate, propose, establish, assemble, integrate, rearrange, modify

In each of the following objectives, we have bolded and underlined the **criterion**. See if you can identify what type of criterion is used in each objective:

- Sara will walk **1 mile each day** with her neighbor or her husband.
- John will make **3 out of 5** free throws during drills at the wheelchair basketball practice session.
- Sara will describe how to take her pulse **correctly** after walking when asked by staff.
- John will design **three** new plays for his wheelchair basketball team when asked by the coach.
- Sara will express feelings of enjoyment **at least once** during her walk, when asked by staff.
- John will choose wheelchair basketball over passive activities in his free time **at least twice a week**.

Measurable Objective Key Element #3: Condition

A measurable objective clearly states the condition or circumstances under which the behavior will occur, if it is not implied in the behavior or criterion. The objective specifies the situation or circumstances in which you expect to see the behavior displayed. In each objective below, we have bolded and underlined the **conditions**:

- Sara will walk one mile each day **with her neighbor or her husband**.

Table 10.5 The Taxonomy of the Affective Domain *(adapted Anderson et al., 2001)*

	Level or Category	Behavior Description	Example of Activity	Key Words (verbs to describe)
Simple ↓ Complex	Receive	Awareness, willingness to hear	Listen to others, take interest in session, take notes, participate passively, attend, make time for session	Ask, listen, focus, attend, take part, discuss, acknowledge, hear, be open to, retain, follow, concentrate, read
	Respond	React and participate actively	Participate actively in group discussion, active participation in activity, interest in outcomes, enthusiasm for action, question and probe ideas, suggest ideas	React, respond, seek clarification, interpret, clarify, contribute, question, present, cite, become animated or excited, help others, perform
	Value	Accept a value as a belief and express it to others	Decide the worth and relevance of ideas, accept or commit to a particular idea or action	Argue, challenge, debate, refute, persuade, criticize, justify
	Organize	Reconcile internal conflicts, develop value system	State personal positions, state beliefs, clarify personal views	Favor, prioritize, contrast, compare, defend, build, develop, discriminate, relate
	Internalize	Adopt a belief system and philosophy	Act consistently with personal value set, self-reliance	Integrity, act consistently, influence, practice

- *John will make 3 out of 5 free throws **during drills** at the wheelchair basketball practice session.*
- *Sara will describe how to take her pulse correctly **after walking, when asked by staff**.*
- *John will design three new plays for his wheelchair basketball team **when asked by the coach**.*
- *Sara will express feelings of enjoyment at least once **during her walk**, **when asked by staff**.*
- *John will choose wheelchair basketball over passive activities **in his free time** at least twice a week.*

In sum, an objective is a smaller part of the goal, breaking the goal down into manageable steps. By including a behavior, a criterion, and a condition, you will help the participant and his or her circle of support easily spot and celebrate progress and change.

Taking a goal, and breaking it down into measurable sub-goals, or objectives, takes practice and patience. It takes thoughtful inclusion of the participant in the process. You will have the expertise to make a goal measurable, and will need to use guiding questions to help the participant form authentic objectives. Once objectives are developed, carefully evaluate them. Are the objectives measurable? Do they contain verbs or actions at the appropriate level of complexity? Do the objectives inspire the participant, but not overwhelm her or him? Are they achievable? Are the objectives set primarily by the participant and his or her circle of support, or are they prescribed by you? Do the objectives embrace theories of social role valorization, person-centeredness, and a strengths approach?

The next step in the planning process is choosing actions and strategies, such as activities, approaches, interventions, supports, accommodations, and other services, that make the objectives achievable and the dream a step closer. The next step is necessary to move goal-setting from a feel-good exercise to real and important change for the participant and his or her environment.

LINKING GOALS TO EFFECTIVE ACTIONS AND STRATEGIES

"What you do speaks so loudly I cannot hear what you say."
—*Ralph Waldo Emerson*

Earlier, we shared research that shows that the act of identifying goals and setting objectives can be therapeutic in and of itself. The next step in the planning process, however, truly helps mobilize the participant and the team toward making positive change. The planning process is where the participant, with your help, decides what to do to put the plan into motion, to work toward attainment of the goal. It is where you decide on

An objective is like a slice of pie, wherein the whole pie represents the overall goal. Follow this simple recipe for reducing a goal to behavioral objectives:
1. Write down the goal.
2. Ask, "How will I know success when I see it? What will the participant be doing or saying?"
3. List the behaviors or performance which would tell you the goal has been achieved.
4. Eliminate behaviors from the list that are not important, socially valued, or age-appropriate.
5. Remove any broad goal statements from the list that are difficult to measure.
6. Ask, "Would I be willing to say the participant is progressing toward the goal based on the remaining behaviors on my list?"
7. If yes, use these behaviors to create objectives. If no, start over on this recipe. Repeat the process until you feel the slice represents the pie!

Figure 10.13 Reducing a Goal to Behavioral Terms

specific actions and strategies that you and the participant will use to make the goal a reality and to achieve the objective. Actions and strategies include deciding which activities, approaches, strengths, and resources to put into play. Your planning will also consider interventions, equipment, supports, services, and whatever tools are available to support goal attainment.

Moving from goals to objectives to actions and strategies is an iterative process. The word, "iterative," means that an action is characterized by or involves repetition, recurrence, or reiteration. An **iterative process** means that, as your understanding of the participant and his or her environment evolves, you continually revisit and revise the objectives and maybe even the goals. An iterative process means that as you identify interventions, activities, approaches, services, supports, and other approaches you think will help the participant, you will likely go back and modify the objective to more tightly align it with the activity. In an iterative process, you continually look at the participant and his or her immediate circle of support (the micro- or "small" level); the relationships and the community in which the participant lives (the meso- or "middle" level); the systematic policies, practices, and external networks (the exo- or "outward" level); the larger culture and norms of the participant's context (the macro- or "long" level); and lastly the natural environment in which all is situated (the natural environment level) (Bronfenbrenner, 1979; Bronfenbrenner & Evans, 2000; Forest, 2009). Figure 10.14 provides a way to visualize the iterative process between goals, objectives, and actions/strategies at the four levels of a person's life.

Here are some questions to ask as you choose actions and strategies in relation to goals in this iterative process:

- What are the participant's passions, preferences, and interests that can be used as priority actions? For example, if a participant loves being outdoors, hiking in the woods, and observing plants and animals, and has a goal to increase a sense of peace and relaxation, this passion for the outdoors becomes a very important tool in the plan. If a participant loves to be around people, loves sports, and wants to increase fitness and vitality, then wheelchair sports may become an important tool.

- What strengths and resources are available in the environment, the circle of support, and the participant on which to capitalize in the actions and strategies phase?

- What specifically needs to be done to meet the objective? What tasks or actions?

- What approaches or strategies will work best to address the objectives? In what settings or environments? Who is most appropriate to help?

- When will the actions happen, and what are the target dates to achieve the goals and objectives? How much of the action is needed to meet that target? for how long? how often?

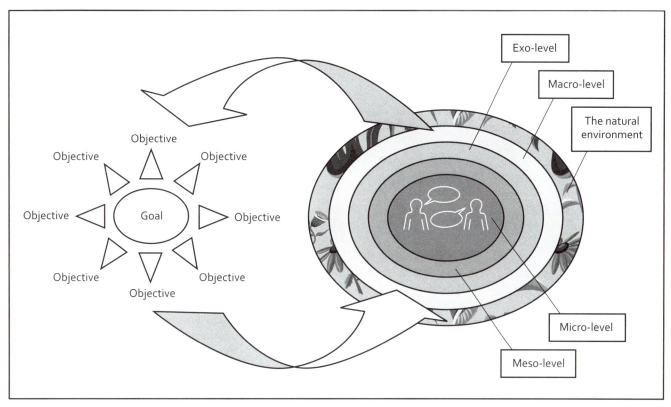

Figure 10.14 The Iterative Process of Determining Objectives and Actions for the Plan

- What objectives can be addressed by recreation activities (situated learning, contextualized learning, or "in vivo therapy") and which need specialized, targeted education, training, or other interventions?
- What are the choices for methods, interventions, or approaches? Who besides you on the team or in the circle of support can help with the various choices for action?
- Will the strategies and actions be focused on the participant, on the environment, or both?
- What theoretical perspective will guide your choices? ecological? strengths-based? person-centered?

These types of questions will help you and the participant get clear on what action to take to mobilize toward the goals. In Figure 10.15 (p. 258), we offer a mental checklist to use as you consider the actions, strategies, and activities you will choose in a plan.

Analyzing the goals, the objectives, and the strengths and resources of the participant will lead you to the final step in the plan: specifying specific actions, responsibilities, and timelines. In this step, you identify the content of the activities (what you will do) and the process of the activities (how you will do it). Regardless of setting, you will need to document the following for each objective:

- The action, strategy, method, experience, or activity
- The person responsible to take a leadership role in implementing the activity
- The timeline or target date for achievement

Once you have documented the actions and strategies, ask yourself and the participant (or circle of support) this question to be sure you have developed the right plan of action:

"Is this the right service, at the right time, in the right place, at the right level of intensity, and for the right amount of time for this participant?"

If you can answer yes to these questions, you are ready to move on to implementing the plan!

> ### A Mental Checklist for Selecting Actions and Strategies for a Plan
>
> ☐ Are you considering the micro-, meso-, exo-, and macro-levels of the participant's context as you choose actions and strategies?
>
> ☐ Are you considering the resources? the strengths? the rest of the team? the circle of support?
>
> ☐ Are you considering the participant's culture, and using the strengths of that culture to help meet goals?
>
> ☐ Are you using activity analysis to help you choose activities with the participant? to help you modify equipment or the environment? to help you choose supports and accommodations that may be needed?
>
> ☐ Are you using recreation activities *and* specific educational or therapeutic approaches if needed? do you have other team members who can assist? or natural supports in the participant's environment?
>
> ☐ Are you using a variety of leadership strategies and helping behaviors?
>
> ☐ Are you using varying approaches with the participant and the environment, from brief, frequent contact for establishing trust to advocacy in the environment/community?
>
> ☐ Are you considering safety? medications and their possible side effects? risks in the environment (social, emotional, and physical)?

Figure 10.15 A Mental Checklist for Selecting Actions and Strategies

Introduction to Activity Analysis as a Part of Planning

One very important step in choosing actions and strategies based on recreation is to understand recreation activity as it is typically experienced. This skill is called **activity analysis** and is an important part of clinical reasoning in therapeutic recreation practice. Activity analysis is the process of determining the inherent skills and knowledge needed to participate successfully in a recreation activity. Activity analysis includes all aspects of participation: physical, cognitive, social, emotional, spiritual, and environmental. Activity analysis is often used in conjunction with **task analysis**, which identifies the sequence of skills or tasks needed to complete a recreation activity.

If a participant has identified a passion or strong recreation interest, activity analysis can be used to capitalize on the intrinsic motivational aspects of the activity. By using activity analysis, you can identify inherent aspects of the activity that can help build strengths. For example, if a participant loves to paint on canvas, and she also wants to increase her range of motion, you can alter the painting activity set-up so she reaches further than usual for brushes or the palette. The repetitive, functional activity of reaching slightly beyond the participant's usual range of motion will help her with that goal.

Activity analysis helps you identify where an activity, equipment, or environment may need to be adapted, or where differing teaching or leadership techniques may be needed, to help facilitate successful participation. By using activity analysis, you become clear on what the demands of the activity are, and that analysis helps you make adaptations or accommodations that will help the participant experience the activity at the highest level of independence and enjoyment. This in turn contributes to well-being.

In Chapter 11 *Implementation* we will talk in more depth about activity analysis, as it is a competency you use repeatedly as you implement varying activities, strategies, and approaches. Activity analysis is an important part of practice wisdom, and becomes "second nature" thinking as you gain competence and experience in the field.

DOCUMENTING THE PLAN

The last step in the planning process is to pull everything together with the participant, the participant's circle of support, and others on the team. The plan you develop becomes a roadmap and communication tool more readily when it is clearly documented. Typically, the team will hold a planning meeting to finalize the plan with the participant and then document it according to agency mandates.

Recall in Table 10.1 that we provided examples of types of plans you may help design, depending on your setting and service-delivery system. Each of these types of plans has a different method of compiling the results of your planning efforts. All documented plans contain goals, objectives, actions or strategies, responsible parties, and specifics about service delivery (such as when, how much, how often, and where services are provided). How this information is documented varies greatly by setting. In many settings, plans are electronic, and completed through software applications. In other settings, plans are hand-written documents on agency-specific forms. And in still other settings, plans take a narrative form. Some service-delivery systems have mandated planning and documentation processes, such as the comprehensive care planning system used in long-term care, required by the Centers for Medicare and Medicaid (CMS).

We want to end this discussion on documentation of the plan with a note on standardized plans based on *labels* or *diagnoses*. Called **clinical pathways** (or critical pathways or care maps), this form of planning is used in some medical and rehabilitation settings. In essence, a standardized plan is written for all participants who share a diagnosis or label. When a participant is admitted to the facility, and has a diagnosis made, the standardized plan is used with *exceptions* or *variations*. In other words, instead of starting out with learning about who the participant is as a person, the team starts out with who the participant is as a label. Then exceptions are applied, based on any uniqueness the participant has in relation to the diagnosis. There is controversy about this approach to planning. First, the obvious controversy is that the process is deficits-oriented and not person-centered. The rationale for using this approach is its efficiency, low cost, and ability to make planning more consistent. With simple, acute, or urgent medical conditions, such as response to an asthma crisis in the emergency room, this is logical. However, when the critical pathway model is applied to complex and more encompassing human conditions, the clinical pathway may not be as useful. In fact, the research shows that clinical pathways in complex situations have typically not saved time or money, have reduced patient satisfaction and quality of life, and are not person-centered (Kwan & Sandercook, 2005; Taylor, Wong, Siegert, & McNaughton, 2006). If you work in a setting that uses critical pathways, you will likely need to advocate more vigorously for a strengths-based focus and a person-centered approach. You will need to carefully analyze clinical pathways used at your agency to find places where a strengths approach can be inserted and used effectively. Fortunately, therapeutic recreation is the discipline most suited to do so, with our focus on well-being and quality of life through enhanced leisure experiences.

In sum, the planning process is comprehensive, thoughtful, and provides a clear roadmap for the participant and team to follow to reach goals and dreams. Documenting the plan allows all involved to have a shared vision. In Figure 10.16 (pp. 260–261), we provide a sample assessment summary and plan written for a participant receiving therapeutic recreation services as part of an Individualized Education Plan (IEP) in a school system. We hope this example will help to bring the planning process to life for you. In the next section, we share one specific planning process, Personal Futures Planning, to give you a sense of the whole process using best practices in the strengths-based approach.

PERSONAL FUTURES PLANNING AS AN EXAMPLE OF THE PLANNING PROCESS IN ACTION

Personal Futures Planning encompasses many best practices in strengths-based planning. It is an interactive style of planning that is capability-based, person-centered, and ecological. Personal Futures Planning is a more generic approach to planning than other similar models. We introduced you to one of those models in Chapter 9 *Assessment*, the MAPS approach (Making Action Plans). Another similar approach is called PATH, or Planning Alternative Tomorrows with Hope (Falvey, Forest, Pearpoint, & Rosenberg, 1997). Where Personal Futures Planning and MAPS are broader in scope, PATH is a more focused planning process that puts emphasis on the development of a working plan of action to achieve the participant's North Star Dream.

Carly Jones
Therapeutic Recreation Portion of the Individualized Education Plan (IEP)

Referral

Carly is a 12-year-old who lives with her parents in Hometown, USA. Carly completed 5th grade in an inclusive classroom at North Elementary School this past spring and will be attending South Middle School this fall. Transitioning to middle school and early adolescence is creating major life changes for both Carly and her family, especially in the area of recreation, socialization, and friendships, so Carly's family felt it necessary to focus on this area of her life very specifically in her IEP, as a related service provided by therapeutic recreation.

Assessment Summary

Jane Doe, CTRS, completed a therapeutic recreation assessment to identify Carly's strengths and goals in relation to leisure. Jane also identified opportunities in Carly's environment that would allow her to achieve her full potential for recreation and socialization as she transitions from the primary grades to middle school and adolescence. Carly, her family, and others in her circle of support were interviewed in home, school, and community environments to learn Carly's recreation skills and interests, socialization skills, and environmental resources for recreation.

Recreation Skills and Interests: Based on observation, interview, and a standardized assessment, the Teen Leisurescope, Carly has broad interests in a wide variety of recreational areas, especially nature activities, sports, and art/music. She enjoys being around others her age. Her family would like her to belong to a school group once she starts school. In general, Carly shows strengths in physical skills and, during structured activities, she is able to participant fully. She is able to make adaptations for her physical limitations on her own. During physical activities, Carly's differences in verbal communication skills become less important.

Friendship/Socialization, Choice-Making, Decision-Making, and Planning Skills: In unstructured activities, Carly chooses to play with young children and activities that are not necessarily age-appropriate. These choices do not allow her to develop friendships as fully with her own peers. This is an area where she could use some support in learning more effective choice-making and social skills so she can reach her goal of having more friends. If the group activity setting is prepared and properly structured and supervised, group activities could bring much enjoyment and friendships for Carly.

Environmental Opportunities: Carly has many opportunities available to her. At school, Club REC, an after-school program, provides recreation activities with peers in the middle school. Students must sign up independently on the day of the activities, and go from their last class to the scheduled activity. This may be difficult for Carly, at least initially. The program coordinator for Club REC is very open to working with Carly in the program. The Middle School Intramural Program offers many sports activities as well. These activities would match Carly's interests and allow her numerous opportunities for social interaction with peers. At intramurals, attendance is not taken and students come only if they want to come. Supports (e.g., additional staff, a trained peer inclusion advocate) would need to be in place for intramurals to be successful for her. One last activity, PAWS (Positive Activities With Students), is a scheduled time during each school day where a group of students meets with their advisor to work on activities together. This would be another opportunity for Carly to get to know her peers in a more structured setting.

Figure 10.16a Carly's Assessment Summary

In Figure 10.17, we briefly describe the steps used in a PATH planning process. This process is completed with the circle of support identified by the participant.

Personal Futures Planning is a broader planning approach than PATH but equally effective. It consists of three phases (Mount & Zwernik, 1988). The first phase is the development of a personal profile that comprehensively describes the participant, his or her circle of support, and context. The second phase is the development of a plan with the participant, based on the information from the personal profile. The third phase is a commitment from the circle of support to form a social network of support for the participant to carry out the plan.

In the first phase, **developing a personal profile**, the circle of support and the participant gather these types of information:

- The participant's background (e.g., positive and negative experiences, major moves, critical events, current dynamics that are affecting the future, family situation, general health, and ethnic and community ties)

- The participant's capacities and accomplishments (e.g., community participation, community presence, choices, rights, respect, competence, skills, and talents)

Carly Jones
Therapeutic Recreation Portion of the Individualized Education Plan (IEP)

Plan

Goal 1: *Carly will communicate and engage effectively across her environments in order to interact successfully with her peers in all activities.*

(This comprehensive goal was set by the IEP Team, including the family; it is an overall comprehensive goal in the plan and is one of four goals; the other goals focus on academic areas.)

Objectives	Actions/Strategies
1a. Carly will learn and use leisure/recreation choice-making, planning, and decision-making skills, incorporating after-school recreation activities in her plan, as evidenced by: (a) completion of a weekly leisure plan (during PAWS), completed each Thursday for the following week (b) follow-through with the leisure plan 90% of the time, using necessary supports to get to the activity (c) development of at least three new recreation/leisure skills during the planned activities	Leisure education in the most inclusive environments (PAWS in classroom, after-school program) with a focus on leisure and recreation skills, choice-making/decision-making skills, and socialization/friendship skills Teacher training on leisure education Peer advocate training, staff training, and an ecological inventory to determine and implement necessary supports to ascertain success for Carly in inclusive settings (lunchroom, Club Rec, intramurals) Increased staff ratios to teach recreation skills as needed; use adapted equipment as needed; implement other supports or accommodations as needed
1b. Carly will use age-appropriate social and friendship skills in recreation/leisure settings (Club REC, Intramurals, lunch period), as evidenced by: (a) using cooperative skills in group activities (turn-taking, and compromising) 100% of the time (b) initiating and reciprocating social interaction during less structured leisure/recreation activities that facilitate development of friendships at least 3 times during each after-school program session (c) strong affiliation or friendship with at least two peers during after-school programs as judged by Carly when asked after 4 weeks in the program	Social skills training and supports in classroom, lunchroom, Club Rec, and intramurals Sensitivity training/disability awareness activities with peers, classroom teacher, and staff Support with developing natural friendships in recreation activities, fading out as relationships are nurtured, formed, and sustained; use a sociometric inventory if needed Monitor and evaluate social inclusion; modify supports as needed; fade out support as friendships are formed and natural supports develop

Therapeutic Recreation Service Intensity: 180 minutes per week or as needed
Starting Date: 9/1/12; Target Completion Date: 12/1/13

Figure 10.16b Carly's Plan

- The participant's preferences and desires (passions, activities, goals, dreams, hopes, etc.)

The questions presented in Chapter 9 about MAPS are very useful at this point. This profile is completed in a meeting with the entire circle of support, and a "group graphic" is produced that shows a picture and tells the story of who the participant is and what he or she dreams about.

The second phase, **planning a personal future**, follows these steps, again in a group meeting with the entire circle of support present:

1. Review the personal profile.
2. Review the trends in the environment (at the meso-, exo-, and macro-levels).
3. Find desirable images of the future, where all members present contribute their vision.
4. Identify obstacles and opportunities, and brainstorm ways to convert the obstacles into opportunities.
5. Identify strategies or action steps for implementing the visions from Step 3.
6. Get started, with every group member identifying and committing to at least five actions they can start today.

A Brief Overview of the PATH Process *Planning Alternative Tomorrow's with Hope*	
Step 1: Dream	Situate yourself positively in the future; touch the dream, the "North Star."
Step 2: Goal	For the next year, what do you want to accomplish?
Step 3: Now	Where are you now? Where are we now?
Step 4: People to enroll	Identify people who need and want to be on the journey.
Step 5: Ways to build strengths	Identify ways to build on strengths.
Step 6: Chart actions	Chart actions that need to be taken in the next few months.
Step 7: Next month's work	Be specific and plan work that needs to happen in the next month.
Step 8: Commit to the first step	Be determined to take the first steps; assign responsibilities.

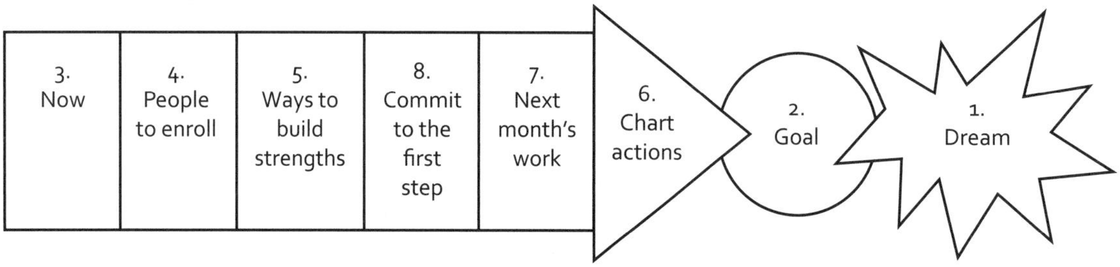

Figure 10.17 The PATH Planning Process *(adapted from Falvey, Forest, Pearpoint, & Rosenberg, 1997)*

7. Identify the need for systems or environmental change, listing changes that must be made in the participant's context for the plan to take shape.

These steps again produce a "group graphic" that lays out the plan in an inspiring, colorful picture. This facilitates action toward the vision.

The third phase, **forming the social network**, entails strengthening the circle of support, and ensuring commitment from members of that circle, as well as broadening and building the circle. These principles are used in forming effective social networks:

- Form the network around a participant who truly desires change in his or her life.
- Form the network around a few people who have a very strong relationship with the participant and can advocate for the participant.
- Build an honest and committed network—the participant will grow in direct relationship to the strength of the network.
- Define the purpose and direction of the network according to the participant's dreams and goals.
- Base the size of the network on the amount and speed of change the participant desires—too big and people get bored and drop out, too small and people get overwhelmed.
- Crisis can help form a committed network, as the participant and the environment are often more ready for change.
- Facilitate action when the network and the participant seem stuck.

Personal Futures Planning, MAPS, and PATH are strengths-based, ecological, and action-oriented planning processes that can inspire a team of people to help make real and positive change in a participant's life. To close this section on strengths-based planning processes, we offer a life story written by Toni Boelter, CTRS, who had the honor of being part of Jeffrey's circle of support. Read the story of Jeffrey's PATH in Figure 10.18.

Lastly, to illustrate the cross-cultural use of strengths-based planning, in Figure 10.19 we describe a

Life Story:

The Fabulous Life of Jeffrey James

By Toni Boelter, CTRS
Dakota Communities, Minneapolis, Minnesota

When I first met Jeffrey, he had just moved into a home that was built for him and five other young people, coming from a facility that was home to 48 people. I was just beginning my career working in human services, and therapeutic interventions based on strengths were a few years away. The human services system dealt with deficits. There was something wrong with people and it was our job to figure out what those things were and how to "fix them." We dealt with people in terms of their vulnerabilities, their negative target behaviors, and their failures in their cognitive and physical abilities. A few years later that would all change for me, as my life would again intersect with my friend Jeffrey.

As fate would have it, I would begin to pursue my career in therapeutic recreation, and I needed a job that would allow me the flexibility to finish my degree. That job would lead me to being the Program Coordinator of the home in which Jeffrey lived. By this time, Jeff had lived at a group home of one kind or another for approximately 10 years. Jeff was diagnosed with significant physical and cognitive disabilities, but I saw someone very different; I saw a sports fan, a wrestling fan, lover of music, and a practical joker. As was the norm, all of Jeff's assessments and subsequent programming dealt with his deficits and disabilities. He had a behavior program that collected data on all of the "bad" things he did. He had a program to correct his management of his wheelchair. He had therapy programs to correct range of motion deficits and effects from his spina bifida, and his community programs consisted of shopping at the local discount store. He was 18 years old.

Jeffrey was blessed in more ways than one, and I was subsequently blessed to be working with him. He had an incredibly supportive and loving family. Much of what was lacking in his programming and structure in his group home was made up for by his family. He was surrounded by "professionals" for so many years of his life, yet it was his family who was the most educated about how to offer him quality of life. It was from their lead that a group of new and dedicated staff and I began the course to assist Jeffrey with reaching his dreams. We worked to offer him the opportunities in his life that were most important to him, not the service system in which he had fallen for half of his life.

In October one year, a new phase in Jeffrey's life began. His team meeting occurred that day, but it was a process in which none of us had ever been involved. Instead of reviewing and filling out forms that evaluated progress in deficit areas, we began on a PATH that talked about dreams, adventures, and the things that Jeffrey felt were important in his life. This PATH (Planning Alternative Tomorrows with Hope) process was a new tool in our organization that focused on the person and what they saw as important. It focused on positive planning, positive outcomes, and positive supports to reach the dreams that Jeffrey had never been asked to dream of before. It was October 9th, 1996, and Jeffrey's life was about to take on a whole new meaning, not just to him, but to those involved in his life as well.

Jeffrey's PATH

Of course, as with any type of gathering, you must have rules. But these rules were quite different than we had experienced in the past. They were simple, yet effective.

- Rule #1: The right people are here.
- Rule #2: It begins when it begins, and ends when it ends.
- Rule #3: Whatever happens is the only thing that could have.
- Rule #4: The Golden Rule: Be nice or get out!

Once the ground rules were established, the process began. Jeffrey was joined by those in his life who he felt meant the most to him. He was in charge of the invitations, and if he did not want you there, you were not there. Not surprisingly, there were no doctors present, no therapists present, no psychologists present, and no behavioral analysts present. He wanted those people there who he knew would help him dream: his mother, his teacher, and the direct support professionals who had recently joined him to make positive changes in his life. He had set the stage, and we were now ready to make his dreams come true.

We began with his North Star. What would he do in a perfect world with no limitations, no disabilities, and no barriers of any kind? We asked Jeffrey to dream. We asked his mother and his friends to dream. His dreams were positive. His dreams were about getting away from his disability, about soaring above it. His dreams were about family, recreation, travel, and friends. Not one of his dreams involved a behavior support plan, adaptive equipment, learning to unload the dishwasher, or put away his laundry. He wanted to go to college, travel to Florida for Spring Training, go to as many sporting events as possible, own his own house, be a father, build a greenhouse, own his own car, own his own dog or cat, remain close to his family, and last, but one of his biggest dreams of all, m~ Celine Dion!

Figure 10.18a Life Story: The Fabulous Life of Jeffrey James

The Fabulous Life of Jeffrey James (cont'd)

Jeffrey had several other dreams as well. Once he was asked about his own life, the floodgates opened. Soon he was not just talking about his dreams, but demanding them! All the years of being told what to do, being programmed according to his deficits and disabilities, all those walls that had been placed in front of him were starting to come crashing down. From his dreams, he began to take First Steps. He talked about what he could have accomplished from his dreams in one year's time. We all focused on what was positive and possible for Jeffrey, and how we, as those he had chosen to join him in this process, would help him to reach his North Star. Everyone used words to describe the process that were rarely heard in annual planning meetings for people. We used words such as "thrilling," "positive," "doable," "meaningful," "complete," "fun," "ambitious," "groundbreaking," "pioneering" and "all about Jeffrey"! We could not remember the last time we had heard the word "groundbreaking" describe a planning meeting for someone with a disability. But that is what this was for Jeffrey. It was groundbreaking. It was about him, about his dreams and focusing on the positive outcomes that would take Jeffrey all the way to his North Star and beyond.

Positive and Possible

The key to the success of this process was to have commitment from the team that had come to support Jeffrey. Working on a PATH takes a great deal of commitment; commitment beyond paper, beyond assessments, and beyond collecting data. Jeffrey had chosen people that he knew would follow through on his dreams. What we did not expect was that other people, those who had not been involved in the process, wanted in on Jeffrey's dreams. When we began to work with people focusing on positive outcomes and not negative deficits, everyone wanted to be involved. Jeffrey was excited about his plan for the first time in his life. And along with that excitement and the progress towards his North Star, we saw something that none of us expected. We saw the negative aspects of Jeffrey's disability begin to disappear. It seemed that when the focus was on the positive and not the negative, the negative began to fade. And his dreams were coming true!

The beauty of the PATH process, and other processes that focus on people and their strengths, and the benefits that it brought to Jeffrey's life, could never have been imagined with the old system's negative focus. The PATH simply took the therapeutic recreation process and based it on positive outcomes. The PATH itself was the initial assessment; the First Steps the programming; the 3-month, 6-month, and 1-year follow-up required documentation; and his 1-year celebration the evaluation of the process. While several more steps were involved on a daily and monthly basis, it was not surprising that when people were asked to dream, their dreams focused on recreation and relationships—the very core of what therapeutic recreation could bring to their lives.

Jeffrey's life was cut short in January of 2000. But the last 4 years of his life were filled with his dreams. He created his own garden in his backyard; he attended more sporting events than we ever thought possible; he redecorated his room, purchased his own car, and most importantly saw Celine Dion not once, but twice! The last day of his life he spent surrounded by family at a favorite restaurant. He reached for his North Star, he dreamed and helped all of us around him realize that dreaming was a necessary part of helping people to become everything they wanted to be.

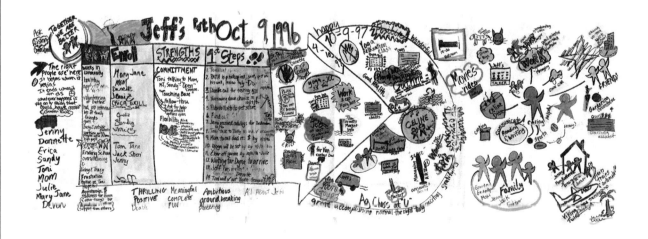

Figure 10.18b Life Story: The Fabulous Life of Jeffrey James (cont'd)

My Cultural Lens:

Anticipation Dialogues: A Finnish Approach to Person-Centered Planning
Co-authored with Heikki Autere

Finnish social services give us a uniquely comprehensive method of person-centered planning called *Anticipation Dialogues* (YARi PROJECT, 2006). This method brings together the "network bond" of a participant to support his or her vision for the future in a solutions-oriented way. Because diverse perspectives and authorities are included in the discussion, multiple resources can be mobilized to realize the participant's vision. Representatives from four kinds of support contribute to the Anticipation Dialogue:

1. Family members (such as children, parents, and grandparents) and friends
2. Social service providers who work closely with the participant
3. Supervisors of service providers who have the authority to allocate resources
4. Municipal authorities who have the power to contribute funding to help actualize the participant's vision for the future

Participation in Anticipation Dialogues by representatives from the last two groups is a recent development in Finland. Their involvement is made possible through public welfare funding financed through taxes and guided by Finnish laws and professional ethics. The ability of supervisors and municipal authorities to grant funding, makes *real* change possible for participants and challenges service providers and professionals to change too.

The dialogue, which is led by a facilitator, centers on the participant's imagined future. Instead of discussing present concerns and problems, the facilitator encourages group members to fully invest themselves to support the participant's future life vision. The dialogue starts as the participant describes his or her view of "utopia"—what he or she *anticipates* for the future. The participant imagines every barrier or worry removed, and describes the future as if anything is possible. This step is referred to as "recalling the future."

Next, representatives from the four groups each elaborate his or her subjective point of view, indicating how they might contribute to realizing the participant's utopia. "Reflecting aloud" in this way helps others understand the speaker's perspective and discipline, as well as the interrelated nature of the participant's support network. Times for speaking and listening are kept separate. No one responds after a person speaks, and individuals address only the aspects for which they are responsible. As helpful measures are suggested, they are recorded. After everyone has spoken, the group discusses whether or not everyone can commit to the plan that has emerged. Agreements are reached on the next steps to be taken, and responsible persons are identified. If needed, follow-up sessions are scheduled.

This method cultivates respect and tolerance for others' viewpoints. It also creates a climate that transcends disciplinary boundaries to support a common vision for the participant's future. Thus, the dialogue helps *everyone* to change, not just the participant!

To learn more about Anticipation Dialogues, see the Resources at the end of this chapter.

Heikki Autere is Senior Lecturer at HAMK University of Applied Sciences, Hämeenlinna, Finland.

Figure 10.19 My Cultural Lens: A Finnish Approach to Person-Centered Planning

process used in Finland called Anticipation Dialogues. More information on this interesting planning approach is available in the *Resources* section at the end of this chapter.

Final Thoughts on Planning

Now the cards I've drawn's a rough hand, darlin'
I straighten my back and I'm working on a dream
I'm working on a dream. Come on!
—*"The Boss," Bruce Springsteen*

Planning, or dreaming and designing, is an exciting step in the therapeutic recreation process, and recreation is an area of life that elicits more dreams and goals toward well-being than almost any other area. As one of the three great realms of life—work, love, and play—it is in play where we can most choose our outcomes, our "North Stars." If those around us are inspired by our dreams, then the possibilities become even greater for dreams to come true in some shape or form. Planning should be approached with this hopeful frame of mind. Recall the story of Hilary Lister from Chapter 2. Hilary's dream, despite having no physical movement in her whole body, was to sail solo around the British Isles. With a group of committed people who did not doubt her dream, she began to make it happen. We offer one final life story of a group of people who are "working on a dream": the band Flame. Read their story in Figure 10.20.

Summary

Planning, or dreaming and designing, is the phase in the therapeutic recreation process where you work with participants to identify and develop their goals and dreams. In this chapter, we provided you with a rationale for the importance of planning, a process for planning, the important link between assessment and planning, and several principles to guide you in that process. We reiterated the important role the participant, the participant's circle of support, and the team play in planning, as well as the different types of plans you may craft. We looked in depth at goals, and how critical it is to form meaningful, quality goals, and then break them down into SMART objectives that are measurable, achievable, and socially valid. Moving from goal-setting to concrete planning is an iterative process, and we discussed the interactivity of choosing actions and strategies in relation to goals and objectives in the context of the participant's life. Documenting the plan clearly allows all team members and the circle of support to share the vision and help implement the steps to reach the vision. Last, we provided a more in-depth look at one planning approach, Personal Futures Planning, and its kindred approaches, MAPS and PATH. Now, we challenge you to become a "treasure mapper," a professional who believes that dreams are possible, and that it is our ethical responsibility to help make it so.

Resources

Person-Centered Planning Online Educational Modules
http://www.ilr.cornell.edu/edi/PCP/courses.html

Cornell University has several self-paced online courses that will teach you about several aspects of person-centered planning, from PATH, to transition planning, to self-determination. Each course module consists of an introduction, activity, quiz, in-depth reading, links,

---

FLAME—Working on a Dream

FLAME, a band from upstate New York made up of 11 people with developmental/physical disabilities, including autism, Down syndrome, mental retardation, and blindness, is capturing the world's attention, but success has not changed the band's aim. The band wants to change the world through music. They are a phenomenon that inspires people and changes the way the general public views people with disabilities. People of all ages and backgrounds connect with this rock band, especially those who have a disability. Parents are often overcome with emotion watching FLAME, seeing that it's possible to have their child achieve great things and, even more importantly, have a fun, fulfilling life.

FLAME began in 2003 from a recreation program at Lexington Center ARC in Gloversville, NY. The plan was to have the band play at the agency and around town. However, the profound effect they have on their audiences made it impossible to keep FLAME within the confines of Fulton County. Word spread and requests for hire began pouring in. FLAME now averages over 90 paid performances per year, including concerts in 16 different states, Canada, and Europe. They perform for national and statewide conventions, corporate conferences, civic events, school functions, dances, and private parties. Their song list contains over 100 classic hit rock, country, and blues songs from the past five decades.

FLAME is now an international touring band in high demand. They have released four CDs, travel on a custom tour bus, and are entertaining many offers from documentary filmmakers, who want to tell FLAME's story to the world. Major events have catapulted FLAME into the national spotlight. Performances at Manhattan's Gracie Mansion for NYC Mayor Bloomberg, the Eunice Kennedy Shriver wake, a feature on ABC TV's "Good Morning America," and a feature article in *People* magazine have positioned FLAME to greatly expand their scope of influence.

As FLAME continues their quest to change the world, their following of adoring fans and grateful parents continues to grow. If you would like more information or would like to book FLAME, contact Tim Fiori at Lexington Center at 518-762-0024 or visit the band's web site at www.flametheband.com.

Figure 10.20 Flame: Working on a Dream

and a resource page. Though the focus is on work more than recreation, you can learn several core concepts that are easily applied to therapeutic recreation practice.

Person-Centered Planning Workbook
http://ici.umn.edu

The University of Minnesota's Institute on Community Integration has developed many tools to assist person-centered planning and transition planning.

Creating Your Self-Directed Life Plan Workbook
http://www.psych.uic.edu/uicnrtc/self-determination.htm#tools

The National Research and Training Center, housed at the University of Illinois at Chicago, has a rich collection of tools available online to help you and participants plan their own life, including recreation. One very nice workbook available on the site is the *Self-Directed Life Plan*, which walks the participant through the planning process. The workbook and several other tools are available at this website.

All My Life's a Circle
http://www.inclusion.com

This manual by Mary Falvey, Marsha Forest, Jack Pearpoint, and Richard Rosenberg is a treasure of detailed information on how to conduct a circle of support assessment, a MAPS planning process, and a PATH planning process. Simply but effectively illustrated, you can use this manual to implement these best practices immediately.

Anticipation Dialogues
http://opko.laurea.fi/youth_at_risk/English_final.pdf

This collaborative planning process, developed through Finnish social services, is designed to help realize a participant's "utopia" of the future. A crucial feature of the Anticipation Dialogues method is the authority that municipal personnel and supervisors of social service providers have to allocate resources to support the participant's future vision. The URL below takes you to a manual entitled *YARi Working Model for Working with Young People*. (Information about Anticipation Dialogues appears in Chapter 3 of this manual.)

REFERENCES

American Therapeutic Recreation Association. (2000). *Standards for the practice of therapeutic recreation.* Hattiesburg, MS: American Therapeutic Recreation Association.

Anderson, L., Krathwohl, D., Airasian, P., Cruikshank, K., Mayer, R., Pintrich, P., Raths, J., & Wittrock, M. (2001). *A taxonomy for learning, teaching, and assessing: A revision of Bloom's Taxonomy of Educational Objectives.* New York, NY: Longman.

Benner, P., Hughes, R., & Sutphen, M. (2008). Clinical reasoning, decisionmaking, and action: Thinking clinically and critically. In R. Hughes (Ed.), *Patient safety and quality: An evidence-based handbook for nurses.* Rockville, MD: Agency for Healthcare Research and Quality. Retrieved from http://www.ahrq.gov/QUAL/nurseshdbk/

Brasler, P. (2001). *Developing strengths-based treatment plans.* Richmond, VA: United Methodist Family Services. Retrieved from http://www.unified-solutions.org

Briggs, L. (2004). Patient-centered advance care planning in special patient populations: A pilot study *Journal of Professional Nursing, 20*(1), 47–58. Retrieved from http://linkinghub.elsevier.com/retrieve/pii/S8755722303001789

Bronfenbrenner, U. (1979). *The ecology of human development: Experiments by nature and design.* Cambridge, MA: Harvard University Press.

Bronfenbrenner, U., & Evans, G. (2000). Developmental science in the 21st century: Emerging questions, theoretical models, research designs, and empirical findings. *Social Development, 9*(1), 115–125.

Canadian Therapeutic Recreation Association. (2006). *Standards of practice for recreation therapists and therapeutic recreation assistants.* Calgary, AB, Canada: Canadian Therapeutic Recreation Association.

Centers for Disease Control and Prevention. (2009). *Writing SMART objectives.* Washington, DC: Department of Health and Human Services. Retrieved from http://www.cdc.gov/healthyyouth/evaluation/pdf/brief3b.pdf

Dave, R. (1970). Psychomotor levels. In R. J. Armstrong (Ed.), *Developing and writing educational objectives*. Tucson, AZ: Educational Innovators.

Falvey, M., Forest, M., Pearpoint, J., & Rosenberg, R. (1997). *All my life's a circle: Using the tools Circles, MAPS & PATH*. Toronto, ON, Canada: Inclusion.

Flame the Band. (2010). *About Flame*. Retrieved from http://www.flametheband.com/bio.cfm

Forest, C. (2009). *Cornell Family Development Credential Program empirical foundations*. Retrieved from http://www.human.cornell.edu

Gallagher, C. (2005). Strengths-based care planning: Coordinating quality care. *Communities of Caring, 4*(4), 5.

Kasser, T., & Ryan, R. M. (1993). A dark side of the American dream: Correlates of financial success as a central life aspiration. *Journal of Personality and Social Psychology, 65*, 410–422.

Kasser, T., & Ryan, R. M. (1996). Further examining the American dream: Differential correlates of intrinsic and extrinsic goals. *Personality and Social Psychology Bulletin, 22*, 280–287.

Krugh, C., & Bowman, C. (2006). *Changing the culture of care planning: A person-directed approach*. Milwaukee, WI: Action Pact.

Kwan, J., & Sandercook, P. (2005). In-hospital care pathways for stroke: An updated systematic review. *Stroke, 36*, 1348–1349. Retrieved from http://stroke.ahajournals.org/cgi/content/full/36/6/1348

Leakes, D., Black, R., & Roberts, K. (2004). Assumptions in transition planning: Are they culturally sensitive? *Impact, 16*(3), 1, 24.

Lyubomirsky, S. (2007). *The how of happiness: A scientific approach to getting the life you want*. New York, NY: Penguin.

Mager, R. (1997). *Preparing instructional objectives: A critical tool in the development of effective instruction*. Atlanta, GA: The Center for Effective Performance.

Mount, B., & Zwernik, K. (1988). *It's never too early, it's never too late: A booklet about Personal Futures Planning*. St. Paul, MN: Minnesota Developmental Disabilities Planning Council.

National Therapeutic Recreation Society. (2004). *Standards of practice for therapeutic recreation*. Ashburn, VA: National Recreation and Parks Association.

Ryan, R., & Deci, E. (2001). On happiness and human potential: A review of research on hedonic and eudaimonic well-being. *Annual Review of Psychology, 52*, 141–166.

Sable, J., & Gravink, J. (2005). The PATH to community health care for people with disabilities: A community-based therapeutic recreation service. *Therapeutic Recreation Journal, 39*(1), 78–87.

Schwarz, J. (2008). *The vision board: The secret to an extraordinary life*. New York, NY: Harper Collins.

Taylor, W., Wong, A., Siegert, R., & McNaughton, H. (2006). Effectiveness of a clinical pathway for acute stroke care in a district general hospital: An audit. *BMC Health Services Research, 6*, 16. Retrieved from http://www.biomedcentral.com/1472-6963/6/16

YARi PROJECT. (2006). *YARi working model for working with young people*. Naples, Italy: Cooperativa Social earl Litografi Vesuviani. Retrieved from http://opko.laurea.fi/youth_at_risk/English_final.pdf

Self-Assessment of Learning

Activity #1: What are Your Goals and Do They Contribute to Your Well-Being?

In this chapter, we looked at goals as being a powerful influence on well-being. Here is an exercise to see how your own personal or professional goals meet the criteria we discussed in this chapter. List your goals below. For each goal, decide which of the descriptors best fit. The more your goals are intrinsic, authentic, approach-oriented, harmonious, activity-based, flexible, and appropriate, the more they will contribute to your overall happiness.

Goal: _____

    Is this goal: ☐ intrinsic ☐ authentic ☐ approach-oriented ☐ harmonious ☐ activity-based ☐ flexible/appropriate

Goal: _____

    Is this goal: ☐ intrinsic ☐ authentic ☐ approach-oriented ☐ harmonious ☐ activity-based ☐ flexible/appropriate

Goal: _____

    Is this goal: ☐ intrinsic ☐ authentic ☐ approach-oriented ☐ harmonious ☐ activity-based ☐ flexible/appropriate

Goal: _____

    Is this goal: ☐ intrinsic ☐ authentic ☐ approach-oriented ☐ harmonious ☐ activity-based ☐ flexible/appropriate

Goal: _____

    Is this goal: ☐ intrinsic ☐ authentic ☐ approach-oriented ☐ harmonious ☐ activity-based ☐ flexible/appropriate

Activity #2: Practice Writing Goals Using the Scenarios from Chapter 9: Assessment

Using what you have learned about planning in this chapter, describe how you would approach each scenario we introduced at the end of Chapter 9, and extended here, to complete a meaningful and careful plan with the participant.

Scenario #1—Hometown Adult Day Program

Recall Ernie, a 78-year-old who will be attending the adult day program at least three times a week. His wife, Claire, is his primary caregiver, and she needs respite. In addition, Claire feels Ernie needs to get out of the house and increase his social interaction. Ernie had a stroke about three years ago, and now uses a wheelchair due to right side hemiparesis. At home, he has been mostly watching daytime television and napping. Claire tells you that he used to have many hobbies and interests, and was always active and outdoors. Your assessment results found that Ernie was passionate about hunting and fishing. He also loves music, games, and bird watching. Prior to his stroke, he played saxophone for many years in the Community Band. He wants to get out more, to do more outdoor activities, and to reconnect with his music. He is articulate and loves children. His church, which he no longer attends, has a musical program, and is two blocks from his home. His neighborhood community center has an active bird-watching group. Other community resources are available as well. On the Satisfaction with Life Scale, Ernie scored 2 out of 7.

Write one goal with Ernie, for his plan:

_____

For this goal, write two objectives (be sure each has a behavior, a criterion, and a condition):

1. _____
2. _____

Determine at least one action or strategy for each objective:

1. _____
2. _____

What team members or members of Ernie's circle of support will you rely on?

_____

# Self-Assessment of Learning

Scenario #2—Hometown Mental Health Services

Recall Laura, a 15-year-old who was just admitted to the hospital. She was referred by the court system to Hometown Mental Health Services. Her record review shows that she has made several suicide attempts and cuts herself. Her family is scattered; she has lost contact with her father and her mother works full-time at two jobs and cares for her three younger siblings. Laura's mom, Janice, initiated the court order to have Laura receive treatment. She reports that Laura is rarely home, hangs out with a negative group of peers, is failing at many subjects in school, and does not help around the house or with her siblings. You will work with Laura from her hospitalization through to follow-up in her home. In the assessment, you learned that Laura used to love sports, and was a rising star on the school track team. She loves being with friends but expresses feeling much peer pressure to drink and skip school with her current peer group. Her dream is to someday be a social worker and help kids who don't have much support from their parents find things they love to do. She wants to make new friends that are more helpful to her and to get reconnected with positive school activities. She is tired of making bad choices, and wants more positivity in her life. Laura scored in the "very low self-esteem" on the Culture-Free Self-Esteem Inventory, and scored well below the mean on the Leisure Diagnostic Battery. Her score on the Positivity Self-Test was 1 out of 10, giving Laura a positivity ratio of .1 (out of 1.0).

Write one goal with Laura, for her plan:
_____

For this goal, write two objectives (be sure each has a behavior, a criterion, and a condition):
1. _____
2. _____

Determine at least one action or strategy for each objective:
1. _____
2. _____

What team members or members of Laura's circle of support will you rely on?
_____

Scenario #3—Hometown Rehabilitation Center

Jason is a 23-year-old who sustained a spinal cord injury as a result of a snowboarding accident in the terrain park. His injury was at the T-5 level and he has complete paraplegia. Jason recently graduated from college with a major in graphic arts and computer design. He was spending the winter snowboarding "before getting a real job." He has a girlfriend who also is an avid snowboarder, and has a supportive family who lives in the area. From the assessment, you learned that Jason loves outdoor adventure activities of all sorts, listening to alternative rock music, interacting with his pet dog, Bugs, and playing online computer games. He scored below average on the Leisure Diagnostic Battery, and his Oxford Happiness Scale score was 2 out of 6. He wants more than anything to get back out on the snow, to have a little adventure back in his life, and to pursue his career in graphic arts.

Write one goal with Jason, for his plan:
_____

For this goal, write two objectives (be sure each has a behavior, a criterion, and a condition):
1. _____
2. _____

Determine at least one action or strategy for each objective:
1. _____
2. _____

What team members or members of Jason's circle of support will you rely on?
_____

Self-Assessment of Learning

Scenario #4—Hometown Parks and Recreation Department
Recall Christy, a 7-year-old who lives with her mom and brother in Hometown. She is interested in sports and playing outside. She loves to be around other children her age, but has limited opportunities to play with them. Christy has an intellectual disability and uses a wheelchair and a communication device. She has limited social skills, but notices others around her and smiles at others. Christy attends her neighborhood school, and has an aide with her throughout the school day. She currently stays in the classroom during recess and eats with her aide at lunch. After school, Christy has a different aide who picks her up, brings her home and watches TV with her until her mom gets home from work. Christy has a "Special Buddy" from Easter Seals who comes once a month to take her out. Otherwise, she mostly stays home. Christy has strengths in many areas, but needs support in communication, initiating social interactions, giving and receiving feedback, obtaining environmental cues to choose her own behavior, offering and receiving assistance, and turn-taking. Christy scored 50 out of 78 on the Quality of Life Scale completed with Christy and her mom. Christy's mother called the Parks and Recreation Department to see if she can get Christy involved in sports, the playground program, and any other activities that will help her meet and be friends with other children her age, learn social skills, and get fresh air and exercise.

Write one goal with Christy and her mom, for Christy's plan:
_____

For this goal, write two objectives (be sure each has a behavior, a criterion, and a condition):
1. _____
2. _____

Determine at least one action or strategy for each objective:
1. _____
2. _____

What team members or members of Christy's circle of support will you rely on?
_____

Chapter 11
IMPLEMENTATION IN STRENGTHS-BASED THERAPEUTIC RECREATION PRACTICE

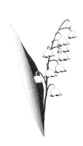

The Lily of the Valley, on a single stem, has many blooms – much like the therapeutic recreation specialist has many approaches and strategies clustered around the single stem of "leisure, well-being, and quality of life."

Whatever you can do, or dream you can, begin it. Boldness has genius, power and magic in it.

—Goethe

OVERVIEW OF CHAPTER 11

- General implementation principles using a strengths approach
- Using the Flourishing through Leisure Model to organize and choose implementation strategies for building internal strengths and external strengths and resources
- Strategies to build leisure strengths and resources
- Strategies to build strengths and resources across domains for well-being: psychological/emotional, cognitive, social, physical, and spiritual
- An in-depth look at supporting positive behavior, friendship development, and building community
- Other implementation strategies commonly used in therapeutic recreation

FOCUS QUESTIONS

- What is a strengths orientation to implementation within the therapeutic recreation process?
- How can the Flourishing through Leisure Model help us sort out and select implementation strategies to meet the goals and aspirations of participants?
- How can we build the internal and external strengths and resources of our participants in the domains of leisure, psychological/emotional, cognitive, social, physical, and spiritual well-being? What strategies and interventions are available to us?
- What other implementation strategies are commonly used in therapeutic recreation?

AN INTRODUCTION TO IMPLEMENTATION

A definition of implementation:
To carry out or fulfill something; to put something into effect or action

A definition of deliver:
To provide or produce something; to do what has been promised

The therapeutic recreation process is a universal approach to working with participants, no matter the delivery system or service setting. We have offered an alternative way to think about the therapeutic recreation process of assessment, planning, implementation, and evaluation (APIE):

- Discover (assess)
- Dream and Design (plan)
- Deliver (implement)
- Deliberate (evaluate)

This chapter focuses on the *implementation* or the delivery phase of therapeutic recreation services, the next step in the process. Implementation is where the plan is put into action using carefully selected strategies, interventions, and approaches. It is the step in the therapeutic recreation process where you must use practice wisdom and draw on all you know about helping others. One of the many reasons therapeutic recreation is such an exciting profession in which to practice is the myriad of choices available to enable participants to reach their goals and aspirations. However, this same breadth of choices can be overwhelming for the professional and the participant, and can make it difficult to select interventions, methods, and approaches that are most effective and appropriate in creating desired change.

In this chapter, we provide a framework to help you and participants choose activities and interventions to reach desired goals and outcomes. We then provide a brief introduction to a selected set of strategies available to therapeutic recreation specialists that are newer and strengths-based in their focus. Lastly, we provide a listing of other common strategies and interventions used in therapeutic recreation. Because whole textbooks are written about interventions alone, the purpose of this chapter is not to provide a comprehensive look at implementation, but to provide a way to think about choosing interventions as well as to introduce you to newer interventions in therapeutic recreation.

As with every phase in the therapeutic recreation process, we can orient our interventions from a strengths or a deficits perspective. In Figure 11.1, we compare these two different orientations. In a strengths approach, we focus on goals and aspirations versus problems as the basis to choose strategies. The therapeutic recreation specialist, in collaboration with the participant, chooses approaches and resources to make desired changes that are seen as important, drawing on internal and external strengths. Strategies and interventions for change focus on the participant's environment as much as on the self. Small change is celebrated and is seen as the initiation of the "spiral effect." In the **spiral effect**, the participant takes a step in the right direction, others in the context respond differently, the participant feels empowered and is encouraged to make further changes, which leads to another step in the right direction and an energizing of the spiral of change (Corcoran, 2005).

As a therapeutic recreation specialist, in order to effectively implement plans with participants using a strengths approach, you need to understand:

- the nature and diversity of recreation and leisure activities

Compare/Contrast:
Implementation Using a Strengths versus Deficits Perspective

From a Deficits Approach ...	To a Strengths Approach
We pay attention to deficits and use deficits to guide our interactions and interventions	We pay attention to what works and continually identify and build strengths to guide our interactions and interventions
The ability and resources for change reside in the professional and the service delivery system (health, human, and social services)	The ability and resources for change reside in the participant, his or her circle of support, and community resources which include not only the service delivery system, but naturally occurring supports and networks in work, recreation, and school settings; in neighborhoods; and in other social institutions
The focus is on what is urgent	The focus is on what is important
The professional practices from a deficits-based philosophy (fixing the participant) at all levels of implementation of interventions	The whole community practices from a strengths-based philosophy at all levels of implementation of interventions
Helping depends most on techniques and professionals	Helping depends most on relationships and natural supports nurtured with the help of professionals
Professionals identify participant problems and choose interventions to address the problems	Professionals partner with participants to help them identify and use their own strengths and resources to find opportunity in challenges and to live empowered lives, choosing interventions in a collaborative process
Change must be significant and under the control of the professional to be justifiable under a medical model	Change occurs systematically, but small change is all that is necessary for a positive spiral effect to begin to take place; much change happens outside the control of the professional as the spiral effect continues

Figure 11.1 Implementation Using a Strengths versus Deficits Perspective
(adapted from Dunst & Trivette, 2009; Corcoran, 2005)

- how to select activities to help participants reach their goals
- how to analyze and modify activities
- how to select and effectively use facilitation techniques, approaches, modalities, and interventions (NCTRC, 2012)

Shank and Coyle (2002) identify interventions as a combination of activity and education-based strategies, a supportive and accommodating environment, and a therapeutic relationship.

We use the Flourishing through Leisure Model: An Ecological Extension of the Leisure and Well-Being Model as a framework for thinking about, organizing, and selecting activities and interventions. Table 11.1 provides a listing of the interventions and approaches we have chosen to introduce in this chapter, structured around the domains of the Flourishing through Leisure Model. We chose to discuss these select few interventions because they are evidence-based, reflect the most recent thinking in the literature (especially from positive science), and are newer to therapeutic recreation. The interventions are also strengths-based and important to have in one's repertoire of helping skills. In Table 11.1, we have categorized strategies by the most potent outcomes that can be met by using the strategy: enhanced leisure (which in turn enhances functional outcomes) or increased psychological/emotional, cognitive, social, physical, or spiritual functioning (which in turn enhances leisure functioning). However, many of the strategies listed improve functioning across many domains. We merely list the particular strategy under a domain to assist you in selecting implementation strategies.

Before introducing many of the interventions listed in Table 11.1, we offer general implementation principles that guide interactions with participants, regardless of the strategy or approach used. The general implementation principles are universal ways to work

Table 11.1 Using the LWM and the Flourishing through Leisure Model to Categorize Selected Strategies and Interventions

Well-Being Domain	Strategies to Build Internal Strengths	Strategies to Build External Strengths and Resources

Leisure	• Leisure education
	  - Savoring leisure
	  - Pursuing authentic leisure
	  - Increasing flow and leisure gratifications
	  - Increasing mindful leisure
	  - Pursuing virtuous leisure
	  - Building interests
	  - Building skills
	  - Building knowledge
		• Building recreation strengths and resources
		  - Enhancing real choices for recreation
		  - Facilitating typical rhythms
		  - Creating inclusive environments and services
		• Adapting activities, equipment, and environments

Psychological/ Emotional	• Learning and cultivating optimism • Acting happy • Being self-determined • Being a self-advocate • Developing coping strategies • Identifying character strengths and virtues	• Identifying/supporting diverse individuals and groups that enhance emotional and psychological well-being • Identifying/creating quiet spaces in public places • Building positive accepting attitudes • Enhancing natural cues • Identifying/developing positive behavioral supports
Cognitive	• Avoiding overthinking • Committing to goals and aspirations	• Identifying/creating environmental cues
Social	• Practicing acts of kindness • Nurturing social relationships • Learning positive behavior	• Identifying/building positive behavioral supports • Building and nurturing social supports and friendships • Building community • Identifying/supporting family resources
Physical	• Taking care of the body and physical activity	• Using adapted equipment • Using universal design • Creating and sustaining livable communities
Spiritual	• Learning to forgive • Expressing gratitude • Practicing spirituality • Practicing meditation • Clarifying values • Clarifying goals and aspirations • Using character strengths and virtues	• Building and sustaining a culture of hope and high expectations • Identifying supporting nature-based activities • Identifying/creating quiet spaces • Enhancing beauty and aesthetics in the environment

Primary Source Support:

"Your Life Isn't Over...You Can Actually Do Fun Stuff"

Sable, J., & Bocarro, J. (2004). Transitioning back to health: Participants' perspectives of Project PATH. *Therapeutic Recreation Journal, 38*(2), 206–224.

This qualitative research study looked at the experiences of men and women who recently transitioned back to their home communities after rehabilitation for spinal cord injuries. The researchers conducted in-depth interviews to understand the meaning that therapeutic recreation services, delivered in a program called Project PATH (Promoting Access, Transition and Health) had in their lives and their recovery. Results of the interviews showed that the participants perceived environmental constraints to pursuing a healthy lifestyle, but that the social and emotional support from therapeutic recreation specialists empowered them to do things in their communities. The individualized and holistic approach used by therapeutic recreation also assisted in regaining a healthy lifestyle based on recreation. Lastly, participants described how important it was to have access to adapted equipment and activities to pursue their recreational passions, like bi-skiing, hand cycling, and kayaking. The researchers conclude that therapeutic recreation programs like Project PATH are important to individuals with disabilities because they empower people to take control of their lives through physically and socially active recreation pursuits, which are so important in their quality of life. As one study participant stated, "Your life isn't over... you can actually do fun stuff."

Figure 11.2 Primary Source Support: "Your Life Isn't Over...You Can Actually Do Fun Stuff"

with participants across settings, ages, abilities, and service delivery systems.

General Implementation Principles

Implementation Principle #1: Recreation is at the core of therapeutic recreation services.

Throughout this book, we have emphasized that recreation is at the heart of therapeutic recreation practice. Recreation is our greatest resource to help participants reach their goals and enjoy a high quality of life. Many other researchers and writers in therapeutic recreation have made the strong case for the central and valuable role recreation plays in well-being and life quality (Carruthers & Hood, 2007; Hood & Carruthers, 2007; Pedlar et al., 1999; Sable & Bocarro, 2004; Sylvester, Voelkl, & Ellis, 2001; Wilhite, Keller, Hodges, & Caldwell, 2004). In Table 11.2, we again revisit why recreation and leisure are the most important tools we have in our repertoire. The ability to have full and satisfying leisure involvement is a keystone to well-being. Remember that recreation is a strength and a context in which to build strengths (see Figure 11.2).

Implementation Principle #2: The helping relationship is more important than technique.

Recall from Chapter 5 *Strengths* that the helping relationship is the most powerful factor in aiding people to make positive change. Dunst and Trivette (2009) reviewed 40 years of research and found the best predictor of successful change was engagement in meaningful relationships and engagement in meaningful activities. They found, in a meta-analysis, that 83% of positive change involved these two factors. In therapeutic recreation, we help people find meaningful recreation activities, and we develop a trusting, supportive relationship. This is the most important work we do. Techniques we may use add some, but not much, to helping people make changes they want. Though we present many techniques, strategies, and interventions in this chapter, remember that it is meaningful activity and meaningful relationships that are the most potent and effective in helping people reach their goals and dreams.

Nurturing a meaningful and helpful relationship can be accomplished by seeing the participant with unconditional positive regard. We define **helping** as the means by which you assist a participant in mobilizing his or her resources to reach a goal or to satisfy a need. An authentic belief in the strengths and resources of participants is essential in the helping relationship. In Table 11.3, we provide other characteristics of effective helpers.

The helping relationship is not only cultivated with individuals, but with groups as well. In therapeutic recreation, many activities and interventions involve the use of groups. Not only does interaction with groups help build on the social nature of recreation, developing helping relationships in the context of groups has many other benefits for well-being. In Figure 11.3, we present a rationale for using groups to nurture meaningful relationships, as well as a list of how groups help people.

Table 11.2 Recreation—Core to Therapeutic Recreation Interventions

Recreation...

- Has the power to help people feel good about their lives, increasing positive emotion
- Provides a context for the experience of positive emotions, which are directly linked to health and well-being
- Helps people make the positive changes they want to see in their lives
- Provides opportunities to fully engage in activity and acts as a stimulus to health
- Helps people feel alive, vibrant, strong, and complex as a human being when they exercise their interests, preferences, talents, and passions
- Directly meets the creative-expressive needs of people
- Helps make people's lives textured and interesting, infused with meaning and purpose
- Contributes to the development of resources and strengths in one's life, from physical to social to cognitive to environmental resources
- Provides a natural vehicle to promote inclusion in community and develop friendship circles, essential to well-being
- Directly impacts self-development and self-determination, again essential to well-being
- Leads to growth and adaptation
- Can be pursued by everyone, everyday, everywhere, infusing well-being in anyone's life – regardless of "functional ability"
- Changes communities, making communities healthier and more welcoming of differences, including disability and illness
- People, all people, have a fundamental right to leisure!

Table 11.3 Characteristics of Effective Helpers

Effective helpers are:

- Self-Aware
- Altruistic
- Compassionate
- Open
- Flexible
- Genuine
- Empathetic
- Courageous
- Supportive

Effective helpers have:

- Stamina
- Positive regard and respect for others
- A basic belief in the competence of others
- A belief in the value of recreation and leisure in quality of life and well-being

Effective helpers are skilled in:

- Analyzing one's own feelings
- Creating collaborative, empowering partnerships with participants
- Using self-disclosure and therapeutic use of self
- Advocacy
- Cultural competence
- Communication competence (active listening, communication across cultural differences, alternative forms of communication, touch)

Groups facilitated by therapeutic recreation specialists can be of many types:

- Recreational groups (e.g., shared leisure interests, clubs, hobby groups)
- Educational groups (e.g., leisure education, relaxation training)
- Functional skills groups (e.g., daily living skills, transportation skills, self-advocacy skills)
- Psycho-educational groups (e.g., pet therapy, remotivation, therapeutic adventure, medical play)
- Support groups (e.g., social clubhouse groups, autism support groups)

Each type of group calls for differing types of leadership on the part of the therapeutic recreation specialist (e.g., instructor, therapist, facilitator, coach), all of which are within the scope of therapeutic recreation practice. Whether nurtured individually or in

Why use groups?	How do groups help people?
• Therapeutic support • Develop a feeling of belonging • Increase awareness of others and ways to relate • Increase socialization skills • Experience self-confidence • Offer opportunities for exchange of ideas • Increase opportunities for immediate and multiple feedback • Experience everyday life situations in a controlled setting (e.g., peer pressure, social influence, need to conform)	• Share information • Gain hope • Share problems • Help one another • Experience group as family or friends • Develop social skills • Imitate behavior modeled by others • Learn interpersonal behaviors • Feel a sense of belonging and group cohesion • Express feelings and experience catharsis

Figure 11.3 The Rationale for and Benefits of Using Groups in Therapeutic Recreation

groups, meaningful relationships with participants are fundamental to helping them achieve dreams and goals through positive change.

Implementation Principle #3: Contextualized and authentic learning is rich and effective.

One of the strengths of therapeutic recreation is its use of recreation to help people learn and grow. Recreation takes place in many environments, and can range from solitary to highly social. Recreation is authentic activity that takes place in authentic settings with authentic co-participants and authentic feedback from fellow recreators, the activity, and the environment. What do we mean by authentic? Table 11.4 provides the characteristics of authentic learning situations and activities.

Research has shown that learning is most effective in the settings in which a skill, behavior, or attitude will be needed. Learning that takes place in isolated settings, like a clinic or hospital, can be difficult to apply in a new or different setting from which it was learned (Slavkin, 2004). As therapeutic recreation specialists, we need to provide opportunities for participants to apply learned information and practice complex behaviors in their naturally occurring settings. When using the lens of situational or authentic learning, the importance of inclusion and community integration/reintegration is clarified. Though some foundational knowledge may need to be provided to participants in isolated clinical settings, the most effective learning and change will likely occur in natural and authentic settings.

Contextual or situational learning often uses community environments. Exceptions are facilities and programs such as "Easy Street" (see Figure 11.4, p. 280). Given the importance of community-based activities, therapeutic recreation specialists must have a deep knowledge of community, and its resources, niches, providers, and networks. Therapeutic recreation specialists, perhaps more than any other professional, must be community treasure hunters and community experts.

Implementation Principle #4: Wraparound services are desirable as they are person-centered and sustainable.

Historically, systems of services were developed with the system at the center. Participants were expected to conform to the demands, settings, and schedules of the system-driven services. One of the sea changes occurring in health and human services is the shift to wraparound services, driven not by the needs of the system, but by the aspirations and needs of the participant. **Wraparound services** "surround" a participant with services that are holistic, strengths-based, and individualized instead of surrounding him or her with institutional walls (Behar, 1986). Wraparound is a comprehensive method of engaging with participants so that they can live in their homes and communities and realize their hopes and dreams (Walker & Bruns, 2006). For example, instead of moving participants from setting to setting as their status or needs change, they continue to live in their home with appropriate services and supports provided there. Wraparound services and supports fit the lives of participants and tap into their personal and environmental strengths, thus assuring sustainability. Figure 11.5 (see p. 281) provides

Table 11.4 Characteristics of Authentic Learning Situations
(adapted from Herrington and Oliver, 2000; Reeves, Herrington, and Oliver, 2002)

Characteristic:	Description:
Real-world relevance	Activities are contextualized and use real world tasks in real-world environments; activities are meaningful to participants.
Real-world feedback	Activities take place in real-life settings with rich situational feedback during participation.
Participant-defined	Activities require participants to define tasks and subtasks to successfully complete the activity. Activities are "whole" and not simplified or fragmented.
Complex and sustained	Activities are completed over time rather than in minutes or hours. They require significant investment of time and other personal resources.
Opportunities for vicarious learning and modeling	Activities provide opportunities to observe others in various stages of learning and expertise in the activity as it occurs.
Collaborative	Activities provide opportunities for participants to work in concert with others as well as opportunity to share narratives and stories about the activity.
Value-laden	Activities provide opportunities to reflect and involve participants' beliefs and values.
Authentic and multiple possible outcomes	Activities have outcomes that are valued in their own right rather than as preparation for something else. Activities allow a range and diversity of outcomes rather than one correct response.

an example of wraparound services and supports called "Aging in Place."

Wraparound services and supports are important initiatives of many service providers, including several federal agencies that direct policy and funding (e.g., Centers for Medicare and Medicaid Services, Administration on Aging, Administration for Children and Families, Office of Disability). In 2010, the U.S. Department of Health and Human Services reaffirmed its focus on community living and wraparound services in its broad-reaching *Community Living Initiative* (U.S. Department of Health and Human Services, 2010). As therapeutic recreation specialists, we are uniquely poised to be leaders in collaborative teams as wraparound services and community living becomes the norm and institutional and hospital-based care diminishes.

Implementation Principle #5: Activity analysis and activity adaptation are effective tools to support other techniques and to enhance leisure.

A core competency in therapeutic recreation is the ability to analyze activities and use that information to facilitate participants' successful recreation involvement, as well as to enhance those aspects of an activity that can build participants' strengths. Activity analysis is a fundamental skill and way of thinking that permeates all areas of therapeutic recreation practice, regardless of setting, and is an invaluable tool to help you link a participant's goals and aspirations to specific activities. Activity adaptation, in turn, helps you facilitate recreation for all people and makes it more feasible for participants to reach their goals, bridging the gap between what they want and what they can do.

Activity analysis is the process of breaking down and identifying the capabilities, skills, and knowledge inherent in an activity and necessary for successful participation (Gunn & Peterson, 1984; Stumbo & Peterson, 2004). It is studying an activity and all its properties (Wilkins, n.d.). Activity analysis is a generic process, and activities are examined as they are typically done. Activity analysis has several benefits that help you:

- Understand the simplicity or complexity of an activity
- Understand more clearly how to adapt or modify an activity if needed
- Decide what type of instruction, intervention, or leadership would be most effective
- Clarify the therapeutic benefits that may be inherent in an activity (e.g., movement of a certain body part repeatedly in an activity will strengthen that body part)
- Clarify elements of an activity that may cause harm for a particular participant
- Improve safety

Primary Source Support:

"Easy Street" – A Controlled Authentic Environment

McClusky, J. (2008). Creating engaging experiences for rehabilitation. *Top Stroke Rehabilitation, 15*(2), 80–86.

For many years, rehabilitation centers were designed for usability and function, resembling medical or institutional gyms. The sterile and medical environments were neither motivating nor like any real-world settings participants would later use in their lives. To learn to reach or lift or transfer, participants would use medicalized contraptions or isolated movements with props that had no relation to real life.

Slowly, rehabilitation centers are moving toward designs that use more authentic and contextualized activity to learn or relearn skills and build strengths. McClusky shares designs for rehabilitation centers by Patricia Moore and David Guynes that are inspired by real community settings. Moore and Guynes' designs include "Easy Street," a simulated built community inside a rehabilitation hospital. "Easy Street" can contain such amenities as a real automobile to practice transfers, a produce section of a grocery store to practice shopping, or a section of a swimming pool at a community center, complete with locker room, to practice accessing and using a recreation environment. The designs simulate real-life situations to help participants connect the early phase of their rehabilitation to the life they aspire to have—a full life in their own community doing activities they love. McClusky shares an example of an "Easy Street" element, a fishing boat tied to a dock, used to practice balance. Participants must adjust to the rocking of the boat (a spring versus real water) as they load up to go on a simulated fishing trip. According to McClusky, "[This] helps patients and therapist incrementally develop the patients' balance capabilities within the motivational context of a recreational activity. Success in this sort of situation is controlled and directly connected to an independent living situation, thus boosting patients' desires to participate and succeed in their rehabilitation exercises" (p. 83).

Designs like "Easy Street" help to bridge the gap between the isolated clinical setting void of context to the real and rich world of the community. Other designs developed by Moore and Guynes include "Independence Square," "Rehab 1-2-3," "Our Towne," and more. These contextualized designs have proven to be highly effective in motivating participants in their rehabilitation. According to McClusky, "They have accomplished this by developing a clear understanding of patients' values and designing centers in which they can directly relate their rehabilitation activities with the activities that they aspire to continue upon completing their rehabilitation. This accomplishment requires a design emphasis that extends beyond mere functional needs and physical fit. It also requires an emphasis that seeks to serve deeper human values" (p. 85).

Figure 11.4 Primary Source Support: "Easy Street" – A Controlled Authentic Environment

When analyzing an activity, examine the activity as it is normally engaged in by others (Stumbo & Peterson, 2004). Rate the activity compared to all other recreation activities. For example, rate the physical effort of reading in comparison to all other recreation activities, including those that take high physical effort. Do not consider disability when analyzing an activity, as the analysis focuses on the activity, not the participant. Complete your analysis using traditional patterns of participation. When determining skills or capabilities for successful participation, identify the minimal skills needed in order to be successful at the activity.

Therapeutic recreation specialists typically examine four components or behavioral domains as a way to deconstruct an activity to learn its requirements. We have added a fifth domain, spiritual, in line with the Flourishing through Leisure Model: An Ecological Extension of the Leisure and Well-Being Model. In Table 11.5 (p. 282), we provide a listing of the aspects within each of the five domains that can be a part of the activity analysis. As well, activity analysis includes understanding the administrative and leadership aspects of an activity. In Figure 11.6 (p. 283), we provide a more detailed description of the social interaction patterns (Avedon, 1974) that are a part of activity analysis.

Primary Source Support:

Aging in Place

Kunstler, R. (2002). Therapeutic recreation in Naturally Occurring Retirement Community (NORC): Benefitting aging in place. *Therapeutic Recreation Journal, 34*(2), 186–202.

In this interesting research case study, Kunstler followed 12 participants who lived in neighborhoods in which a majority of the residents were over 60 years of age. To counteract the tendency of older adults to become isolated, physically inactive, and unable to care for themselves, in-home therapeutic recreation services were delivered in conjunction with other services such as nursing and social services. Results showed that therapeutic recreation services helped to stimulate participants' social interaction, cognitive functioning, and interest in the larger community. According to Kunstler, in-home therapeutic recreation services gave a level of power and control in the participants' lives not possible in a long-term care facility. Being in their own homes and communities created comfort and control over their recreation experience, and participants felt safe and free to follow their own choices. This in turn contributed to many other positive functional outcomes. Refer to this case study to read about Kunstler's many recommendations for the practice of therapeutic recreation using a wraparound approach in home and community settings.

Figure 11.5 Primary Source Support: Aging in Place

Task analysis, related to but different from activity analysis, is another competency often used by therapeutic recreation specialists. Task analysis is commonly completed after activity analysis and includes a description of the sequence in which skills and responses must occur during an activity for a participant to experience success. For each identified step in the task analysis, the therapeutic recreation specialist will determine a teaching method or an instructional cue to use. Task analysis, then, is a teaching or coaching tool, delineating what the participant must do, and in what order, to be successful at an activity. Like activity analysis, task analysis can help you clarify if and how activities may need to be adapted for individual participants. We discuss task analysis again later in this chapter when we address positive behavioral supports.

Activity adaptation is altering some aspect of a recreation activity or environment to allow for more successful participation by all. Recall from Chapter 9 *Assessment* that, when you do an assessment, you focus on the person and his or her environment (see Figure 9.11). Activity adaptation is one of the ways that you can help participants bridge the gap between what they can currently do and what they want to do. Activity adaptation helps participants meet the demands of the activity more successfully. Activity analysis helps you get clear on what those demands are. Assessment of the participant helps you get clear on what changes may need to occur for full and successful participation. With the information from activity analysis and participant assessment, you can adapt the activity to increase success and inherent therapeutic benefits. In Table 11.6 (p. 284), we provide principles and areas of activity adaptation.

Implementation Principle #6: Advocacy and self-advocacy are important to initiate and sustain change.

Advocacy is an important concept and skill for therapeutic recreation specialists. Advocacy is speaking, writing, and/or acting on behalf of the sincerely perceived interests of others. It requires a passionate desire to see positive change, a sound understanding of the issue or idea for which you are advocating, and a willingness to "go public" to effect change. We often find ourselves in a position where we must champion change at many levels, whether it is for the participants we serve, the communities in which they reside, or even to ensure the use of a strengths approach or the provision of therapeutic recreation services. As the paradigm shifts from a medical model to an ecological strengths approach, you will find yourself using advocacy more than in the past. Chapter 14 *Advocacy* provides an in-depth look at advocacy and self-advocacy. Here, we want to reinforce that advocacy is a fundamental principle when implementing therapeutic recreation services with participants.

Implementation Principle #7: All interventions require thoughtful planning and delivery to increase effectiveness.

In therapeutic recreation practice, you will find yourself repeating the therapeutic recreation process—assess, plan, implement, and evaluate (or discover, dream and design, deliver, and deliberate)—as you implement services with participants. Every strategy, intervention,

Table 11.5 Activity Analysis Domains
(adapted from Avedon, 1974; Gunn and Peterson, 1984; Stumbo and Peterson, 2004; Sylvester, Voelkl, and Ellis, 2001; Wilkins, n.d.)

Physical Aspects – Act, Do, Move

- ☐ Primary body position (prone, kneeling, sitting, standing)
- ☐ Body parts involved
- ☐ Movements (fine motor, gross motor)
- ☐ Primary senses (sight, hearing, touch, smell, taste)
- ☐ Coordination
- ☐ Hand-eye coordination
- ☐ Strength
- ☐ Speed
- ☐ Endurance (muscular, cardiovascular)
- ☐ Energy
- ☐ Cardiovascular
- ☐ Flexibility

Social Aspects – Relate, Belong

- ☐ Number of participants
- ☐ Physical proximity/spacing
- ☐ Physical contact level
- ☐ Primary social interaction pattern (see Table 11.6)
- ☐ Amount of structure
- ☐ Communication style (verbal, non-verbal, formal, casual)
- ☐ Opportunity for casual conversation
- ☐ Opportunity for sharing
- ☐ Turn-taking
- ☐ Noise level
- ☐ Clothing and other cultural norms
- ☐ Types of rewards (immediate, delayed, extrinsic)

Cognitive Aspects – Think, Learn

- ☐ Number and complexity of rules
- ☐ Complexity of thought processes (strategy, sequencing, matching, decision-making, problem-solving, planning)
- ☐ Verbalization of thought processes
- ☐ Memory (long-term, immediate recall)
- ☐ Concentration (consistent, intermittent)
- ☐ Discrimination skills (colors, objects, spatial, gestures)
- ☐ Directionality (up/down, left/right, over/under, etc.)
- ☐ Judgment
- ☐ Ability to listen and follow directions
- ☐ Academic skills (reading, writing, math)
- ☐ Specific knowledge areas needed for activity
- ☐ Orientation to person, place and time

Affective Aspects – Perceive, Feel

- ☐ Emotions the activity may most likely elicit
    - Joy, gratitude, serenity, interest, hope, pride, amusement, inspiration, awe, love, guilt, pain, anger, fear, frustration
- ☐ Opportunities for expressing emotions
- ☐ Need to control emotions
- ☐ Self-esteem enhancement
- ☐ Group esteem enhancement
- ☐ Level of perceived risk
- ☐ Consequences (success/failure, pride/embarrassment)
- ☐ Level of stress/relaxation
- ☐ Opportunities to make choices

Spiritual Aspects – Believe, Value

- ☐ Opportunities for reflection
- ☐ Opportunities to use character strengths and virtues
- ☐ Opportunities to build quiet spaces into activity
- ☐ Opportunities for aesthetic appreciation
- ☐ Proximity to nature
- ☐ Level of meaningfulness of activity to participant
- ☐ Opportunity to share beliefs and values with others

Leadership/Administrative Aspects

- ☐ Leadership style and skills
- ☐ Equipment needed
- ☐ Facility or environment needed
- ☐ Cost of the activity
- ☐ Duration of activity
- ☐ Number of participants required
- ☐ Age or gender restrictions

Intraindividual Actions take place in the mind of the individual, or involve the mind and a part of the body, requiring no contact outside oneself (e.g., daydreaming, meditation, jumping jacks)	
Extraindividual Actions directed by a person to an object in the environment requiring no contact with another person (e.g., watching TV, playing Solitaire, crafts, computer games)	
Aggregate Action directed by a person to an object in the environment while in the company of others doing the same thing but requiring no interaction (e.g., watching a movie, Bingo)	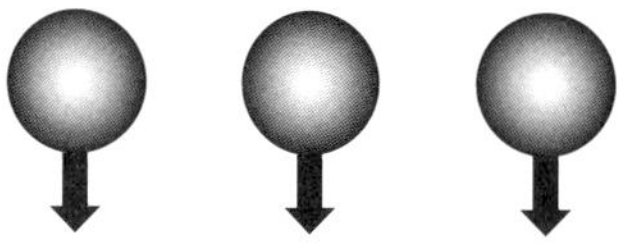
Interindividual Action of a competitive nature by one person directed toward another (e.g., tennis, chess)	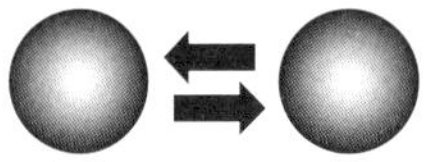
Unilateral Action of a competitive nature with three or more people; the focus is on one antagonist (e.g., tag, hide-and-seek)	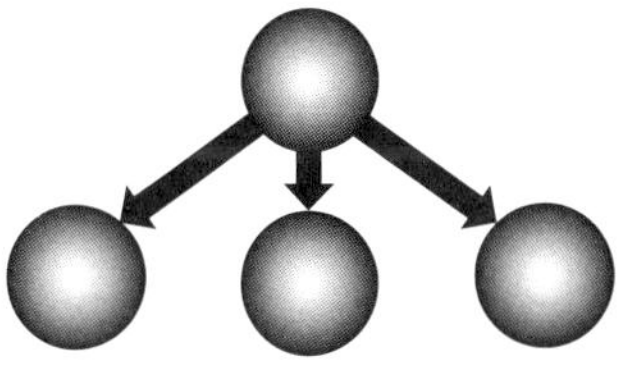
Multilateral Action of a competitive nature, with three or more people and no one antagonist; everyone is "in it for themselves" (e.g., Scrabble or other board games, marathons)	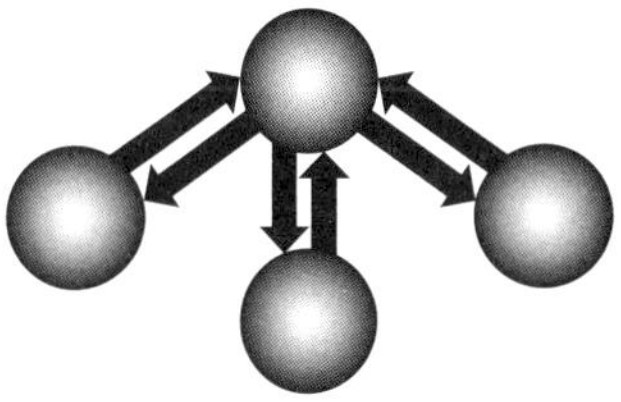
Intragroup Action of a cooperative nature by two or more people who want to obtain a mutual goal; requires interaction (e.g., choir, performing a play)	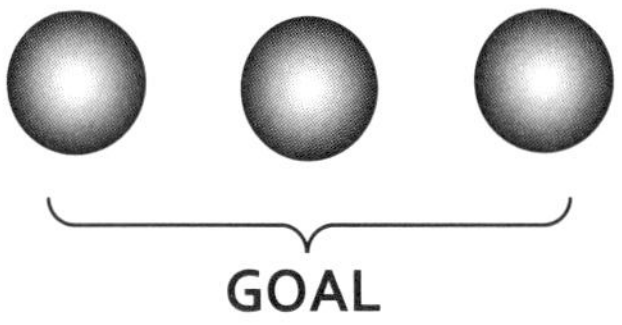
Intergroup Two or more intragroups working competitively against each other (e.g., team sports)	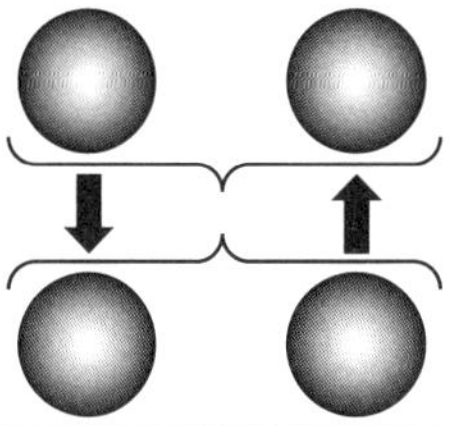

Figure 11.6 Elliot Avedon's Social Interaction Patterns *(Avedon, 1974)*

Table 11.6 Considerations for Adapting Activities
(adapted from Anderson & Kress, 2003; Schleien, Green, & Ray, 1997)

What is Activity Adaptation?

Altering some aspect of a recreation activity or environment to allow for more successful participation by all.

Why Adapt Activities?

- To enable maximum participation
- To increase the therapeutic outcomes of an activity

Principles for Adapting Activities

- As much as possible, have participants make their own adaptations (participants will feel more empowered and in control, will know best what adaptations are needed, and will learn the process of adapting activities)
- Make only necessary changes to the activity to increase participation, success, and enjoyment; do not "over adapt"
- View adaptations as transitional and temporary, if possible, as participants gain skills and strengths (unless the adaptation is inherently needed based on functional differences)
- Make adaptations on an individual basis to meet specific participant needs for a specific activity
- Maintain the integrity of the activity so that the original activity is not lost and the modifications are respectful
- Make sure activity modifications are age-appropriate
- Make sure adaptations do not segregate participants from others
- Make sure you have support from the community or environment in which adapted activities will take place
- Make sure others participating in the activity are not uncomfortable with or resentful of the adaptations

Areas of Activities that Can be Adapted

• Skill Level	Change how the activity is executed, such as using different body parts, slower movements, or different movements (e.g., sit-skiing versus stand-up skiing, wheel versus run, cones further apart on a bicycle obstacle course)
• Skill Sequence	Rearrange the components or steps of an activity to enhance participation (e.g., place pizza in oven then, for safety, turn oven on)
• Lead-up Activity	Develop a simplified version of the original activity as a lead-up (e.g., cooperative volleyball as lead-up to team volleyball)
• Rules	Change rules or procedures to simplify an activity (e.g., time, substitutions, points, equipment allowed)
• Equipment or Materials	Change the characteristics of equipment or materials by making them lighter or heavier, larger or smaller, lower or higher, emit sounds, or other modifications (e.g., use t-stand, raise or lower nets, enlarge handles, use beeper balls, provide assistance with gripping, use card holders)
• Environment	Change space requirements (e.g., boundaries, more or fewer players, restrict players to a certain spot)
• Method of Instruction	Change the way the activity is taught (e.g., break down activity into smaller steps taught more sequentially, use alternative forms of communication)
• Type of Leadership	Change the amount of supervision or style of leadership provided
• Facility Alteration	Reconstruct or remodel a facility for accessibility (e.g., ramps, harder surfaces, wider doors, better lighting, lower tables)

action, service, or program you deliver requires careful and thoughtful planning. A typical interaction with participants, whether it is a recreation activity, a psycho-educational group, or any other intervention, requires careful steps for preparation and implementation. In Table 11.7 (p. 286), we provide some fundamental steps that are a part of every activity, interaction, or session that takes place with participants during therapeutic recreation services. By completing these simple tasks, and assuring goal-oriented planning and reflection, you will increase the effectiveness of therapeutic recreation services during the implementation phase of the therapeutic recreation process.

Introduction to Implementation Strategies

You will choose and use strategies and approaches that are meaningful to the participant and effective in creating positive change by using the principles described in the previous section. In addition, the factors listed in Table 11.8 (p. 286), delineated by Shank and Coyle (2002), should be considered as you determine what interventions to use in helping participants reach their goals. Choosing strengths-based interventions is a creative process, where you design strategies that tap into a participant's assets while also balancing needs created by illness or disability. When choosing interventions or approaches, you should ask yourself these two questions:

- Is this activity, approach, or intervention based on an assessment of participants' strengths, interests, and goals?
- Is this the right service at the right time in the right setting at the right level of intensity for the right length of time for this participant?

In the end, effective interventions will help participants reach goals and aspirations and prepare them for successful participation in life.

In the remainder of this chapter, we briefly introduce several strategies, tools, and techniques available to therapeutic recreation specialists. We have organized the strategies according to the Leisure and Well-Being Model and the Flourishing through Leisure Model: An Ecological Extension of the Leisure and Well-Being Model. While we have categorized strategies into usually only one of the six Flourishing through Leisure Model domains, you will see that the approaches often produce benefits across multiple domains, reflecting the integrated nature of well-being. As you learn about each strategy, reflect back to Table 11.1 (p. 275) and decide which other domain(s) a particular approach would be effective in enabling desired change.

Building Leisure Strengths and Resources

In Table 11.1, under the Leisure Domain, we provide a listing of strategies most salient in assisting participants in building internal and external strengths and resources. Here, we provide a brief overview of some of these strategies.

Supporting Internal Leisure Strengths through Leisure Education

Savoring Leisure

Savoring leisure is defined as consciously paying attention to the positive aspects of leisure involvement, including positive emotions, and purposefully seeking leisure activities that create positive emotions (Hood & Carruthers, 2007). Lyubomirsky (2008) defines savoring as any thoughts or behaviors capable of generating, intensifying, or prolonging enjoyment. You can help participants increase savoring by teaching them to use specific strategies, which we offer in Figure 11.7 (p. 287). Savoring will help participants become absorbed in the present, and gain maximum enjoyment in the moment. Used in balance with other strategies, savoring will enhance leisure experiences and well-being.

Pursuing Authentic Leisure

Pursuing and facilitating authentic leisure is defined as the purposive selection of leisure involvement that reflects essential aspects of the self (Carruthers & Hood, 2007). Authentic leisure involves increasing self-awareness of interests, preferences, values, beliefs, feelings, and thoughts, and carefully choosing leisure involvement that allows for the full expression of those essential aspects. Authentic leisure results in part from helping participants identify their character strengths and virtues, their passions, and their talents, and then helping them pursue leisure experiences where they can express those strengths on a consistent basis in their daily lives. Table 11.9 (p. 288) provides strategies that can be used to facilitate authentic leisure.

Increasing Flow and Leisure Gratifications

Flow and leisure gratifications are defined as leisure experiences that are optimally engaging and challenging,

Table 11.7 Deliberative Planning for Implementation Strategies

Preparation	☐ Analyze the activities that will be used in the session ☐ Analyze the environments where the activity or session will occur; thoroughly understand any inherent risks in the environment and use strategies to manage those risks (e.g., bring extra sunscreen and water on a hot day, provide a quiet space for participants who may need it) ☐ Analyze social supports and other socio-political factors in the activity environment; work to enhance supports prior to the activity if possible (e.g., disability-awareness training, peer orientations) ☐ Gather all needed supplies, equipment, and other resources ☐ Orient and train any additional staff or volunteers

Implementation	☐ Opening and introduction of the session or interaction
	   • Clearly communicate the goals of the session or activity in relation to each participant
	   • Clearly communicate any ground rules or social norms for the activity, as well as any precautions, in a respectful manner
	
	☐ During the session or interaction
	   • Use well-researched content (the substance of your interaction, such as leisure resources, social skills, stress management techniques, or activity rules and skills)
	   • Use active listening skills
	   • Use observation skills
	   • Pay attention to and manage group dynamics and use group leadership skills
	   • Use advocacy skills as needed in a community environment
	   • Be a role model
	      - For participants (demonstrate skills, behaviors, attitudes according to the social norms of the setting and activity)
	      - For other community members (demonstrate acceptance, positive attitudes, and egalitarian norms in relationship to participants with disabilities)
	
	☐ Closure and debriefing
	   • End every session in a positive way (e.g., give compliments, reinforce goal attainment); the research is clear that the last part of an experience tends to color and strongly influence our overall memory or sense of that experience, so ending positively increases motivation for further interactions (Redelmeier & Kahneman, 1996)
	
	   • End every session or interaction with reflection and debriefing. Some example strategies for debriefing include the following:
	      - "What? So What? Now What?" where participants share what they learned, what it means to them, and how they will use or apply it to their own lives
	      - "Muddy/Clear" where participants share what is still unclear to them as well as what they understand clearly from the session
	      - Journal writing and sharing, using a structured entry that includes actions (what the participant did) and reactions (what the participant thought and felt)

Table 11.8 Factors to Consider in Selecting Interventions *(adapted from Shank and Coyle, 2002)*

Additional factors to consider when choosing strategies, approaches, and interventions:

☐ Participant interests, needs, strengths, and priorities

☐ Participant values (cultural, religious, other)

☐ Participant choice

☐ Participant and family understanding of the intervention

☐ Carry-over value after services with professionals have ended

☐ Contact time needed to effectively implement the approach or intervention

☐ Competence of the therapeutic recreation specialist

☐ Specialized training needed to use the approach, technique, or intervention

☐ Supervision needed during the intervention

> *Teach participants these skills to experience savoring in leisure:*
>
> - Share with others: Share leisure experiences with others; share the positive feelings and thoughts openly with fellow participants to increase the positive impact of the experience.
>
> - Fleetingness of experience: Focus on the fleetingness of an experience to enhance savoring and increase its positive impact. Remind yourself that it won't last, so enjoy it while you can.
>
> - Humor: Find the funny or enjoyable aspect of the leisure experience; look for the incongruent.
>
> - Focus: Do not multi-task. Focus on just one activity with full concentration in the current moment, looking for and being aware of all the positive and joyous aspects of that one experience.
>
> - Take pleasure in the senses: Luxuriate in seeing, smelling, touching, tasting, and hearing all the experience offers. Pay close attention to all five senses as you participate in the leisure experience.
>
> - Name positive emotions: Consciously put descriptors or words on the positive feelings you are experiencing during an enjoyable moment. Find words to describe the positive. Do you feel awesome, joyous, energized, uplifted, mellow, serene, thrilled, pleased, inspired, proud, amazed, happy, empowered, content, elated? Name the positive feelings to savor the experience more deeply.
>
> - Congratulate yourself: Savor not only the moment and the emotion, but your accomplishment or full immersion in an experience.
>
> - Take time off: Give yourself the space and time to savor experiences; slow your life down; take a mini-vacation.
>
> - Be proactive: Look for joy in every moment; instead of waiting to react, create experiences throughout the day that provide for positive emotion.
>
> - Be open to beauty and excellence: Stop and not only smell the roses, but see the rich deep color and the perfect form. Marvel at excellence; be awestruck by beauty, talent, performance, or virtue.
>
> - Recount leisure experiences: Tell stories, write in a diary, sketch, or daydream about positive leisure experiences, capturing the positive emotions involved to deepen savoring of the positive aspects. Do this to savor reminiscence about leisure experiences that have brought you joy in the past.

Figure 11.7 **How to Facilitate Savoring in Leisure** *(adapted from Bryant and Veroff, 2007; Lyubomirsky, 2008)*

require sustained effort and commitment, and lead to the development of strengths and personal attributes that are meaningful and rewarding for the individual. Flow provides a conceptual framework for leisure gratifications. In Chapter 6 *Theories* you learned about the theory of flow and the conditions under which it occurs. Recall that flow is a state in which you feel entirely absorbed in an activity and where your skills are keenly matched with the level of challenge required by the activity (Csíkszentmihályi, 1997). You are so present to the task, in fact, that your perspective of time takes on an eternal quality: You are "in the zone."

Csíkszentmihályi (1990) maintains that we have the power to cultivate the flow experience within ourselves at will using a three-step process which we can share with participants to transform stress and adversity into flow, strength, and enjoyment (see Table 11.10). Following these three steps can help participants grow and learn from any challenging situation they encounter. Csíkszentmihályi (1990) also encourages us to cultivate what he calls the *autotelic self*, from the Latin words *auto* meaning "self or directed from within," and *teleo* meaning "completion, fulfillment, or being an end unto itself." The autotelic self is "one that easily translates potential threats into enjoyable challenges [i.e., flow], and therefore maintains its inner harmony" (p. 209). Csíkszentmihályi gives us a simple yet practical framework we can use to help participants develop their autotelic self: set goals, become immersed in the activity, pay attention to what is happening, and learn to enjoy the immediate experience. If we help participants practice this straightforward method regularly, they will engage more meaningfully with life and experience flow more frequently. Moreover, they will emerge stronger from adversity.

Table 11.9 How to Facilitate Authentic Leisure

Participants can enjoy authentic leisure through these actions:
☐ Identify character strengths and virtues
☐ Identify passions, preferences, and leisure interests
☐ Identify leisure activities where strengths can be exercised and passions can be pursued
☐ Identify resources and opportunities for those leisure activities
☐ Create a leisure plan incorporating authentic leisure
☐ Support follow through on the plan, where a positive spiral effect is put into action and self-reinforcing authentic leisure behavior is initiated and sustained

Lyubomirsky (2008) similarly maintains that we can train ourselves to experience flow and that doing so will actually make our lives happier. "Finding flow," she says, "involves the ability to expand your mind and body to its limits, to strive to accomplish something difficult, novel, or worthwhile, and to discover rewards in the process of each moment, indeed in life itself" (p. 183). She offers recommendations, presented in Table 11.10, which we can facilitate with participants. Lyubomirsky warns us, however, that it will require effort, creativity, and persistence to be effective.

Lastly, Ellis, Witt, and Aguilar (1983) provide practical strategies for helping participants experience flow during therapeutic recreation services, also listed in Table 11.10. By assisting participants in achieving flow experiences, they will experience leisure gratifications; that is, participants will develop strengths and personal attributes that are meaningful and rewarding.

Increasing Mindful Leisure

Mindful leisure is defined as being fully immersed in the moments of the current leisure experience, and using one's full attention and awareness to enhance the present moment during the experience. Mindful leisure implies full attention to the current experience—all its sights, sounds, smells, feelings, and the like—without judgment and with a total disengagement from thoughts, feelings, or concerns about other things in one's life. Mindfulness differs from savoring. In savoring, we purposefully seek out positive emotions and sensations. In mindfulness, *all* aspects of the immediate experience are the focus of our attention, not just those that provide positive emotions or sensations (Carruthers & Hood, 2007). When a person is mindful during leisure, the experience is enhanced, or amplified, and beneficial to the individual in multiple ways.

Formal mindfulness training is often 8 weeks long, and intensive. However, recent research has shown that even simple steps taken toward mindfulness are as effective as in-depth meditation (Langer, 2009). Therapeutic recreation specialists can facilitate mindfulness during leisure using the strategies listed in Table 11.11 (p. 290).

Pursuing Virtuous Leisure

> "Happiness is the aim of life, but virtue is the foundation of happiness."
>
> —*Thomas Jefferson*

Virtuous leisure is defined as using one's strengths and leisure interests in the service of something larger than one's self (Hood & Carruthers, 2007). Sylvester (2010) tells us that virtue pertains to the moral habits, qualities, or characteristics of an individual, such as honesty, fairness, and compassion, the sum of which constitutes the individual's moral character. Helping participants pursue virtuous leisure, then, can be thought of as helping them develop moral habits that are routinely expressed in their leisure. Virtuous leisure can include volunteering, participating in community or environmental organizations and activities, among other enterprises. It can also include informal leisure, like reading to an elderly neighbor or doing random acts of kindness. Facilitating these types of opportunities for participants may involve matching participant strengths with service opportunities in their environments and supporting them in enduring engagement in those opportunities. Phoenix, Miller, and Schleien (2002) offer an example of virtuous leisure in Figure 11.8 (p. 290).

Table 11.10 How to Facilitate Flow in Leisure

According to Csíkszentmihályi (1990), you can teach participants these steps to facilitate flow in leisure:

- **Cultivate unselfconscious self-assurance.** To explain "unselfconscious self-assurance," Csíkszentmihályi recalls survivors of extreme ordeals such as imprisonment in a concentration camp or being lost in the Arctic. He observes that survivors tend to share a common attitude during highly stressful situations: "My destiny is in my own hands." Rather than rely on something external to save them, or willfully forcing their personal goals onto the situation, they adapt and work with their environment to find a way out of the crisis. Csíkszentmihályi maintains that, similarly, we must trust ourselves, our environment, and our place in the environment, and marshal the confidence that we can handle whatever situation we encounter.

- **Focus your attention to the world.** When faced with a stressful situation, Csíkszentmihályi advises us to resist the natural response to draw inward and become preoccupied with ourselves and our predicament. Turning inward exacerbates our inner turmoil, compromises our ability to cope, and isolates us from others. Instead, he directs us to shift our attention to our surroundings. If we look outward and stay in tune with the environment, our minds have the opportunity to open to new possibilities, which keeps us engaged with the situation, and with life. We will then be able to notice potential solutions in the environment that, otherwise, we may have overlooked.

- **Discover new solutions.** Csíkszentmihályi holds that there are basically two ways to cope with a difficult situation. The first is to use a problem-oriented strategy: We focus on the obstacles that stand in the way of achieving our goals, then explore how to remove those obstacles. Or, second, we can follow a strengths approach: We focus on the entire situation, including ourselves within the context of the situation. We are then in a position to ask ourselves if other goals might actually be more appropriate and, ultimately, more satisfying to us. Through this process we are able to seek alternative solutions that may, in fact, add more enjoyment to our lives.

According to Lyubomirsky (2008), you can teach participants these actions to facilitate flow in leisure:

- **Control your attention.** What you pay attention to is your experience – indeed, it is your life. Cultivate flow, then, by directing your attention fully to the task before you, to the exclusion of extraneous thoughts such as "I wonder what time it is" or "What's for dinner?" Concentrating intensely means gaining control over your attention and thoughts – essentially, your consciousness. By controlling consciousness, we control the quality of our experience.

- **Adopt new values of openness and learning.** Flow comes naturally to children, who tend to be present to each new moment; adults, however, need to work at it. We can adopt two new values to increase our happiness and sense of flow: (a) be open to new and different experiences, and (b) keep learning every day. Adopting these values will allow us, like children, to be more in tune with our surroundings and to take in wonderful new experiences and knowledge each day.

- **Learn what flows.** If we recognize when we are in states of flow, we can duplicate those conditions and activities to experience flow more frequently. In one of her studies, Lyubomirsky gave participants a pager that beeped at regular intervals at which time they were asked to record their level of concentration; if they wanted to continue the activity; and how strong, confident, and happy they were feeling. If we ask ourselves these same questions throughout our day, we can identify those activities that naturally produce flow in us, then increase our involvement in them.

- **Transform routine tasks.** We can transform seemingly boring activities, such as sitting in traffic, waiting for a bus, or standing in line at the grocery store, into experiences that are meaningful and stimulating. To do this, we can create in our heads "microflow activities" with specific goals and rules. We could solve a puzzle, create a painting, design a dream home, practice meditation, or engage in a similar activity that absorbs our attention.

- **Flow in conversation.** Recreation offers many opportunities for socialization and conversation. To experience flow during conversations, focus intently on what the other person is saying to you, giving him or her space to elaborate, and following up by asking questions.

- **Smart leisure.** Lyubomirsky challenges our choices during our leisure time. Do the activities we choose really require us to use our minds, exercise our skills, and absorb our concentration? Or do we opt to decompress by watching television or reading a mindless magazine? Choosing the former activities are more apt to lead to flow experiences.

- **Strive for superflow.** We can strive to experience superflow, that is, those moments when we are so engrossed in what we are doing that we lose track of time and place, and which leave us feeling invigorated, creative, and happy. Seeking out a flow experience in a conscious way helps to increase its occurrence.

According to Ellis, Witt, and Aguilar (1983), you can facilitate flow with these strategies:

- Enhance novelty, complexity, and dissonance in activities
- Attract participants' full attention through meaningful activities that are preferred and desired
- Match activity challenges to participants' skills and abilities
- Limit the amount of extraneous stimulus during activities to help focus attention
- Minimize external rewards, and assist participants in reflecting on intrinsic rewards
- Minimize the focus on the outcomes of activities (winning, getting something) to assist in focusing attention on the activity as it occurs

Table 11.11 How to Facilitate Mindful Leisure

Help participants to experience mindful leisure through these steps:

- ☐ Have participants focus attention on the target observation (e.g., moving, breathing, walking, nature)
- ☐ Be aware of the target observation in each moment
- ☐ When emotions, sensations, or thoughts intrude, observe them non-judgmentally, then return attention to the present moment
- ☐ If the mind wanders, notice thoughts and feelings, but do not become absorbed in their content (note the content or nature of the thoughts, then turn attention back to the present moment)
- ☐ Sustain these actions for the duration of the recreation experience, if possible

Primary Source Support:

Volunteering: An Example of Virtuous Leisure

Phoenix, T., Miller, K., & Schleien, S. (2002). Better to give than receive. *Parks & Recreation, 37*(10), 26–33.

In this study, the researchers wanted to understand what benefits people with disabilities would accrue as the providers of volunteer services, versus the recipients, as is traditional. According to the researchers, "Inclusive volunteering necessitates a paradigm shift from viewing people with disabilities as recipients of services to contributors of service. This type of paradigm shift will ultimately result in benefits to persons with and without disabilities, agencies and communities as a whole. The key is to focus and build on the strengths and interests that volunteers with disabilities bring to the agency using a systemic and holistic approach to inclusion." In the study, the research team found that participants with disabilities gained a sense of hopefulness, learned new skills, enjoyed social support networks, and were able to "show people what we can do."

Figure 11.8 Primary Source Support: Volunteering: An Example of Virtuous Leisure

Building Leisure Interests

We have discussed leisure interests and passions in great depth throughout this book. Helping participants build leisure interests involves several strategies. Recall that **interests** are a feeling of having your attention and curiosity particularly engaged by something. **Preferences** are liking something better, or setting or holding it above other things. Preferences drive your choices or selections. **Passion** is what compels us to pursue and devote ourselves to certain goals and activities, and is a strong inclination toward an activity that individuals like or love, that they find important, and in which they invest time and energy. The passion becomes a part of a person's identity, and can even become a central feature of self identity.

At times, participants need assistance identifying and choosing leisure interests. They may have lost touch with their interests due to illness, disability, or other life circumstances. They may need to develop new interests due to an altered level of functioning, such as paraplegia, aphasia, vision loss, or even sobriety. Or, they may have never developed healthy leisure interests due to such things as a life of institutionalization or a chronic disability. For example, some youth who experience substance abuse from a very young age have never been exposed to leisure activities that weren't chosen for chemical use. For these and many other reasons, participants may need assistance choosing and then building leisure interests.

Figure 11.9 provides some guidelines to help participants choose leisure activities when they need support and guidance in doing so.

Building Leisure Knowledge

Knowledge is defined as an acquaintance with facts, truths, or principles. Knowledge means having a clear and certain understanding of a topic or subject area. People can have knowledge in many different topics or subjects. Knowledge of leisure can be categorized as leisure knowledge, self-awareness in leisure, leisure and play attitudes, and related participatory and decision-making skills. Several resources are available for leisure education, to assist in you in helping participants build leisure knowledge. Some of these resources are listed

> Help participants choose leisure interests and activities using these guidelines; think of this process like a treasure hunt for richness in their lives:
>
> - **Explore activities that reflect preferences, abilities, and strengths** – Use leisure interest assessments, strengths assessments, interviews, observation, and other tools to help participants discover what they love; try a wide variety of activities as a "sampler" to explore what fits and brings pleasure and meaning.
>
> - **Explore activities that contribute to dreams and goals of participants** – Look at all aspects of an activity and its many forms; a participant may not be able to sing on Broadway, as she dreams, but she may find happiness in singing with her community choir.
>
> - **Explore activities that reflect personal and environmental characteristics** – Look for activities that fit participants' personal lives as well as their environment. For example, if a participant lives in an inner city environment, some outdoor recreation activities may be difficult for that person to pursue, at least on a regular basis, especially if the participant's family and friends are not interested in those types of activities.
>
> - **Explore valued activities** – Identify activities that are valued by and respected by the peer groups of participants, by the family, or by the neighborhood or community; shared values will facilitate social inclusion and friendship development.
>
> - **Explore activities that are functional, transferable, and age-appropriate** – Functional skills are those required frequently in natural environments that enhance independence or interdependence. Transferable activities are those that can be enjoyed across many different environments, or skills that can be applied to different life domains. Age appropriate activities are those that fit with one's age group, are socially relevant, do not stigmatize, and complement and reinforce a positive social image.
>
> - **Explore activities that provide a balance** – Activities that can be done easily every day should offset special or grand activities to provide balance in a participant's life.
>
> - **Explore activities that are realistic** – Cost, access to materials, transportation, and other resources that will be needed to pursue a leisure interest should be explored and, if they are limiting, alternatives explored as well. For example, a participant may want to pursue boating, but does not have a boat or the income level to support owning a boat. Instead, you can explore volunteering at a local marina or volunteering to crew with a local sailing club. A word of caution: Don't assume to know the limits or creativity of a participant when pursuing a passion.
>
> - **Presume competence** – Explore new leisure interests with the assumption that the participant is capable of whatever he or she dreams of doing, then look for ways to make involvement possible, even if it means starting with just a small part of the dream.

Figure 11.9 How to Facilitate Choosing Leisure Interests

in Table 11.12 (p. 292), and more are being tested on a routine basis. Whatever resources you choose to use for leisure education and building leisure knowledge, it is important that you spend adequate time with participants to truly learn, especially for those who may take longer to absorb and retain information due to a functional difference (e.g., traumatic brain injury, intellectual disability, chronic mental illness, dementia-related disorder, learning disability).

Building Leisure Skills

Building leisure skills is the next step after leisure interests are identified. Given that a skill is the ability to do something well, arising from talent, training, or practice, therapeutic recreation specialists are charged with providing instruction and opportunity for participants. Building leisure skills involves systematic instruction in natural environments with naturally occurring social supports. Opportunities for practice involve access and time to truly develop proficiency in typical environments. One-shot or sporadic opportunities to pursue a leisure skill, or isolated instruction in artificial settings, will not be enough to truly help participants develop competency. Later in this chapter, we provide more specific information on teaching skills using a behavioral approach.

One effective strategy to help participants build skills for a recreation pursuit is leisure coaching. **Leisure coaching** is contextualized instruction and support to a participant as he or she learns a recreation activity that is faded out as the participant becomes independent at the activity or natural supports are developed. A leisure coach system has the following steps:

- A leisure coach directly supports a participant with disability.

Table 11.12 Resources for Teaching Leisure Knowledge in Leisure Education

An Introduction to Recreation Services for People with Disabilities: A Person-Centered Approach By Charles Bullock, Michael Mahon, and Charles Killingsworth Sagamore Publishing, 2010	*Leisure Education Program Planning: A Systematic Approach* By John Dattilo Venture Publishing, Inc., 2008	The following resources by Norma Stumbo (published by Venture Publishing, Inc.): *Leisure Education I: A Manual of Activities* (2002) *Leisure Education II: More Activities and Resources* (2002)
TimeWise: Taking Charge of Leisure Time By Linda Caldwell ETR Publishing, 2004	*Leisure Education* By Jean Mundy and Linda Odum Sagamore Publishing, 1998	*Leisure Education III: More Goal-Oriented Activities* (1997) *Leisure Education IV: Activities for Individuals with Substance Addictions* (1998)

Life Story:

"Inclusion U" - Strengthening Leisure Resources in the Community

Offered by the Inclusive Recreation Resource Center at SUNY Cortland, *Inclusion U* is a model for strengthening leisure resources in the community for participants of all abilities. *Inclusion U* is a one-day workshop that teaches participants how to be an *Inclusivity Assessor*. Inclusion U is based on these principles:

- Recreation is critical to quality of life and well-being
- Choice matters – self-determination is key to quality recreation
- Strengths approach – all people have capabilities waiting to be developed
- Honor interests – people want to recreate based on their interests, not their disability
- Celebration of differences – disability is a variation in the human condition that enriches us
- Natural supports – natural supports are most effective at sustaining inclusion and recreation
- Inclusion is a right – not a privilege
- Person-centered – services are supports, individualized, and based on strengths and goals

Inclusion U is provided to parks and recreation professionals, self-advocates, tourism professionals, human services professionals, families, and anyone interested in increasing opportunities for inclusive recreation. Once participants have completed *Inclusion U*, they are able to complete accessibility surveys and submit the results to the Center to be included in an online recreation access database available at this link: www.inclusiverec.org

With the user-friendly tool, the *Inclusivity Assessment Tool*, the center helps programs and facilities assess both physical accessibility and programmatic inclusion. All programs or facilities that are assessed using the *Inclusivity Assessment Tool* are entered into an extensive online database. The database is a comprehensive bank of information, sorted by region, on how inclusive and accessible recreation resources are around the state, to help people with disabilities better plan their recreation.

The center also provides assistance in improving program or facility accessibility. It also helps individual agencies as they work to increase inclusion of people with disabilities and other differences into their parks, programs, or facilities. The Center has numerous partnerships to promote full inclusion in recreation.

The mission of the Inclusive Recreation Resource Center is to promote and sustain participation by people with disabilities in inclusive recreation activities and resources. Leisure resources in the environment are strengthened and ALL people are helped to play wherever they choose!

Figure 11.10 Life Story: Inclusion U

- The coach helps the participant develop skills and make friends.
- Support from the coach fades out as the participant develops skills and makes friends.

Supporting External Leisure Resources

As participants build quality recreation and leisure experiences in their lives, using strategies like savoring, mindfulness, flow, increased leisure interests, skills and knowledge, and the like, they may also need assistance with building external strengths and resources for leisure. This assistance can range from changing environments to be more physically accessible to helping staff at a community center understand how to provide positive behavioral supports. In Table 11.13 (p. 294), we provide a listing of common strategies you will use as a therapeutic recreation specialist to build external leisure resources with participants. When you complete an ecological assessment with a participant, you often identify areas in the environment of the participant that could be strengthened—you then focus your attention there to bridge the gap between the participant's dreams and goals and the ability of the environment to support them. You may need to work with an agency to learn and implement these strategies, providing education, training, and technical assistance. In Chapter 12 *Transition and Inclusion* we describe some of these strategies in more depth. These strategies will lead to positive, thriving community resources.

BUILDING PSYCHOLOGICAL AND EMOTIONAL STRENGTHS AND RESOURCES

Enhancing positive leisure involvement often leads to enhanced psychological and emotional strengths and resources. Positivity gained through leisure broadens and builds us (Fredrickson, 2009). Dr. Barbara Fredrickson, architect of "broaden-and-build" theory, has identified these reasons why a positive emotional and psychological state is so beneficial:

- Positivity feels good and is pleasant to experience, versus negativity
- Positivity changes how your mind works; it broadens your outlook and you see, feel, hear, and learn more
- Positivity accrues other resources (e.g., physical, social)
- Positivity, which Dr. Fredrickson calls our "reset button" or the "undo effect," counteracts the deleterious effects of negativity and is a key to resiliency.
- Positivity has a tipping point, from which the benefits to participants spiral to accrue in a dramatic fashion
- You can increase your positivity with simple and daily activities

In this section, we share more strategies you can use to help people build psychological and emotional strengths to a more positive life.

Supporting Internal Psychological and Emotional Strengths

Cultivating Optimism

In Chapter 6 *Theories* we discussed the concept of "learned optimism" developed by positive psychologist Dr. Martin Seligman. Seligman (1999) believes an optimistic attitude is essential for coping with adversity and assuming control over our reactions in ways that support our well-being. If our outlook is negative, we are likely to feel discouraged and develop unproductive, self-defeating behaviors. If our outlook is positive, however, we tend to view situations in proportion to reality, refrain from minimizing or belittling our abilities, and are prompted to act in ways that are constructive and benefit our well-being.

So how exactly can we help participants overcome patterns of pessimistic thinking and learned helplessness that have become engrained? Seligman (1991, 2002) suggests we use a process he refers to as ABCDE: *adversity, belief, consequences, disputation, and energization*. This process is outlined for you in Figure 11.11 (p. 295).

Lyubomirsky (2008) also recommends strategies for cultivating optimism, described in Table 11.14 (p. 296). The first exercise, the Best Possible Selves diary, has been proven to increase positive moods, boost feelings of happiness, and reduce physical ailments among those who wrote in their diaries every day for several days. The second strategy, the Goals and Subgoals diary, is similar to the first exercise except that it pinpoints specific actions a participant can take to attain his or her dreams. The final exercise, identifying barrier thoughts, can help us reappraise automatic pessimistic thinking.

With practice and persistence, we can help participants learn to replace pessimistic thinking with optimistic thoughts. This does not imply that participants

Table 11.13 Common Strategies to Build Strengths and Resources in Leisure Environments from A to Z

Strategy	Description
Accessible agency website	Website that provides information about programs, services, and facilities for recreation complies with Section 508 of the Rehabilitation Act and is usable by all
Adapted equipment availability	Adapted equipment is available; how to access it and any restrictions in its use are clearly communicated
Advisory boards	Advisory boards include people with disabilities and other minority groups to help plan, promote, and evaluate recreation services
Advocacy	Agencies that provide recreation services and facilities have skills to advocate for funding and resources to serve all people in their community
Alternative forms of communication	Agency uses all forms of communication (e.g., large print, sign language, Braille, oral, pictorial, languages other than English)
Dietary accommodations	Agency is prepared to make accommodations for those who cannot have certain foods or need certain foods (e.g., peanut allergies, gluten-free, sugar-free)
Disability awareness training	Staff and other participants are trained in understanding functional differences and common ways to adapt to include people with functional differences
Documentation and evaluation of best practices	Inclusive and effective practices are documented and shared in staff training and with participants and their families
Inclusion point of contact	A staff member is designated to serve as a single point of contact to facilitate inclusion at the agency
Inclusive agency mission statement	Agency mission statement reflects a belief about serving all people in a community, regardless of ability level
Inclusive marketing	Agency marketing portrays people with disabilities, indicates the availability of adapted equipment and supports, and is available in alternative forms of communication
Modified staff ratios	Additional staff or volunteers are available to assist in including participants with disabilities who need extra support to be involved
Partial participation	Staff are trained in analyzing activities and identifying parts of activities in which participants can be successful if they are unable to participate in the whole activity
Partnership development	Agency develops partnerships with disability groups and other community groups to enlarge its expertise and resources, and to reach out to the disability community
Peer orientation	Sometimes called similarity training, an orientation to others in an activity in which a participant will be included to educate, address issues, and facilitate social inclusion
Physical accessibility	People with disabilities can approach, enter, and use a facility (e.g., ramps, wide doors, firm and stable surfaces, good lighting, elevators)
Policy and procedure modification	Policies/procedures take into account people of varying ability (e.g., policies about service animals, personal care attendants, evacuation) and staff are trained in and know the policies
Positive behavior supports	Supports are in place to help participants with more challenging behaviors be successful in the activity and environment (see section later in this chapter for details)
Program goal modification	Agency shift program goals from highly competitive to more cooperative structures to facilitate inclusion of participants with differences if possible
Quiet spaces	Quiet spaces are created/provided to allow for individuals who need a place to relax, calm down, or reintegrate senses
Staff hiring and training	Staff are chosen based on a positive attitude toward including all people and are trained in disability awareness, inclusion principles, and other relevant areas
Structured social interaction	Staff purposefully ensure there is time and opportunity for structured social interaction regardless of the activity
Team or group formation	The way teams or groups are formed in activities is structured to be inclusive versus based on ability level, and the activity is then modified to allow full participation by all participants (e.g., age grouping versus ability grouping)
Zero tolerance	Agency policy that does not allow behavior that hurts or disadvantages another person (e.g., bullying, sexual harrassment)

We Can Learn to Be Optimistic

Martin Seligman's research (1991, 2002) has proven we can cultivate optimism by using his ABCDE method, described below. Through regular, conscious practice of this method we can help participants notice habitual self-defeating reactions, correct them, and create a more optimistic outlook that activates behaviors which enhance their well-being. Use the following method with participants:

A = Adversity
The adverse event is described in neutral, factual terms.
   Example: *My anatomy and physiology professor returned our exams and I received a D.*

B = Belief
When an adverse event occurs, we react spontaneously by thinking about it. Our thoughts rapidly turn to beliefs which directly cause what we feel, and what we will do next. Our beliefs can make the difference between becoming dejected and giving up, or taking constructive action that strengthens our well-being.
   Example: *I'm just not very smart. Colleen got a B on the exam, and so did David. I studied hard for that exam. No matter what I do I can't seem to grasp the material. I'm worried this course is going to affect all my grades this semester. And, if I don't pass this course, I won't be able to sit for the certification exam next year. Then what will I do?!*

C = Consequences
Consequences result from our beliefs. If we are prone to pessimism, our reactions may be to give up, take on too much blame, belittle ourselves, withdraw, magnify adversity out of proportion, get angry, or act out in some way. Seligman says, to move toward optimism, we need to make the connection between adversity, beliefs, and consequences, as well as notice how the ABC's operate in our everyday lives.
   Example: *I feel really discouraged. Studying seems futile and overwhelming. I am going to take the next couple nights off and watch DVDs with friends. I feel like dropping the course.*

D = Disputation
In this phase we dispute the inaccurate, routine, catastrophizing beliefs we have about ourselves and the adverse event. We recognize our pessimistic thoughts and refute them as if some external person who is intent on making us miserable spoke them. Dispute them as if your best friend were by your side defending you.
   Example: *I get As and Bs in my other classes, so I know I'm a good student. The truth is the exam was really hard and a number of students said they failed it. At least I didn't get an F. It's still early in the semester. I have lots of time to pull up my grade, and it's an entire year before I need to sit for the certification exam. This is just a temporary setback. Now I know I need to study harder.*

E = Energization
When you dispute pessimistic beliefs effectively, energization occurs. Your reaction shifts from dejection to hope and constructive action.
   Example: *I still feel disappointed about my grade, but I know I can do better. Tonight I'll join the study group Dr. Taylor told us about and tomorrow I'll sign up for tutoring. I want to do well in this course and I know, with some extra effort, I can!*

Figure 11.11 We Can Learn to Be Optimistic

will deny all negative information or permanently wear blinders to the point of self-deception. You will need to help participants practice optimism judiciously and in a way that mirrors the reality of the situation. However, in everyday living, optimism is a choice we make to see the world in a different light, and to adjust our thoughts to benefit our well-being rather than erode it.

Building Portfolios of Positive Emotions

Dr. Barbara Fredrickson, Distinguished Professor at the University of North Carolina-Chapel Hill, has researched a method to increase positive emotion in one's life (2009). In her "toolkit" she recommends many of the strategies we present in this chapter. In addition, she recommends and has researched the use of positive emotions portfolios. Participants can hunt for photos, words, objects, songs, video clips, or any other artifact that can be put into a portfolio with care and creativity. Dr. Fredrickson recommends and provides guiding questions for participants to make a portfolio for each of these emotions: joy portfolio, gratitude portfolio, serenity portfolio, interest portfolio, hope portfolio, pride portfolio, amusement portfolio, inspiration portfolio, awe portfolio, and love portfolio. Construction of these positivity portfolios, which could be part of a leisure education program, is the first step. Using the portfolios involves keeping them close at hand to pull out and be reminded often about the good things in one's life,

Table 11.14 How to Facilitate Optimism and Positive Thinking

Help participants with these strategies to cultivate optimism and positive thinking:

Best Possible Selves diary. Lyubomirsky provides these instructions for keeping a Best Possible Selves diary:

> ...sit in a quiet place, and take twenty to thirty minutes to think about what you expect your life to be one, five, or ten years from now. Visualize a future for yourself in which everything has turned out the way you've wanted. You've tried your best, worked hard, and achieved all your goals. Now write down what you imagine. (p. 108)

Repeating this method over several days and returning to it regularly does more than help a person imagine his or her model future, says Lyubomirsky. It activates the desire to be the best possible self today that will make that vision come true tomorrow.

Goals and Subgoals diary. Similar to the Best Possible Selves diary, this method asks you to identify your long-range goals and the subgoals that will help you accomplish them. To do this, Lyubomirsky suggests you recognize the personal strengths and resources that have helped you be successful in the past. Drawing from your strengths and resources can motivate and inspire you to actualize your current aspirations.

Identify barrier thoughts. We can also increase optimism by identifying our automatic pessimistic thoughts and challenging ourselves to reinterpret situations and the conclusions we reach. Say, for instance, you think, "My friend didn't e-mail me today; she must not like me anymore" or "Since my relationship ended, I feel unattractive and unlovable." Lyubomirsky proposes that we counter this type of negative thinking by asking ourselves the following questions:

- What else could this situation or experience mean?
- Can anything good come from it?
- Does it present any opportunities for me?
- What lessons can I learn and apply to the future?
- Did I develop any strengths as a result? (p. 109)

Lyubomirsky advises us to wait until we are in a neutral or positive mood to ask ourselves these questions, and to write down our answers.

---

and the positive emotions that are a part of those good things.

Acting Happy

Can just acting happy make you happier? The empirical research says yes! Repeated studies have shown that merely pretending to be happy can actually change your level of happiness (Fredrickson, 2009; Lyubomirsky, 2008). All the benefits of positivity begin to accrue as one does such simple things as smiling more, laughing more, acting more engaged, and showing more energy and enthusiasm. Participants can do these simple things, with support from the therapeutic recreation specialist, on a routine basis and on a small scale. Although it may not seem natural to smile or laugh when under adversity or stress, pretending to be happy is a simple action that can begin an upward spiral for people and become a habit resulting in many benefits. As you appear more positive, others will respond more positively toward you. They will smile back and engage with you, bringing you even greater joy and happiness.

Enhancing Self-Determination

Self-determination, as you learned in Chapter 6 *Theories*, implies being in charge of life and able to make one's own decisions. You also learned that self-determination is both an individual issue and a function of one's environment, including recreation environments. Bullock et al. (2010) identify several ways therapeutic recreation specialists can enhance a participant's self-determination in recreation and leisure settings (see Table 11.15).

As you can see from Table 11.15, self-determination is an empowering concept for strengths-based practice. This theory encourages us, as therapeutic recreation specialists, to develop programs and arrange environments that maximize participants' self-awareness, capabilities, decision-making skills, intrinsic motivation, and sense of autonomy—all faculties tied to the development of self-determination.

Building Self-Advocacy

Self-advocacy, which is a natural extension of self-determination, asserts that people with disabilities can be responsible for making decisions about the human and social services that affect them. In recent years curricula have been developed to teach individuals with disabilities self-advocacy skills related to self-awareness, knowledge of individual rights, communication, leadership, and the like. You will read more about techniques to teach self-advocacy competencies in Chapter 14, which is devoted to the topic of *Advocacy*.

Table 11.15 Enhancing Self-Determination through Recreation

> Bullock et al. (2010) suggest several ways to enhance self-determination through recreation and other kinds of settings:
>
> 1. Teach decision-making skills that include setting goals, weighing options, identifying resources and supports, identifying consequences, and solving problems.
> 2. Provide opportunities for choice-making across environments – schools, homes, and communities.
> 3. Identify and establish with the individual the necessary and appropriate supports.
> 4. Provide opportunities for challenge and success.
> 5. Project belief in a person's ability to succeed as well as in the person's ability to survive failure.
> 6. Provide individuals the opportunity to take risks.
> 7. Provide individuals the opportunity to make mistakes and/or fail, and to learn from those mistakes.
> 8. Provide specific, positive feedback to facilitate self-awareness, confidence, and self-efficacy.
> 9. Encourage the individual to accept and take responsibility for his [or her] decisions and actions.
> 10. Provide environments that are accessible and promote individual's utilization of strengths and abilities.
> 11. Offer reinforcement and acknowledgment of efforts and process of achieving goals.

Strengthening Coping Strategies

Coping strategies are varied and diverse. All humans experience stress and, at times, at levels that are not helpful for growth and development. Hood and Carruthers (2010) identify four main ways that we can teach participants to cope with unhealthy stressors in their lives, which we list in Table 11.16. Learning to cope with stress is another path to building a good life, and because recreation inherently provides many coping strategies, it is a positive and life-enhancing way to help participants handle stress while building strengths.

Identifying Character Strengths and Virtues

Character strengths and virtues are the positive traits that define who we are as human beings. Peterson and Seligman (2004) assert that strength-congruent activity represents an important route to the psychological good life. When participants are able to exercise their character strengths, they will experience higher levels of well-being. Recreation and leisure is an ideal arena for people to employ their strengths, due to the level of choice people have to express themselves, leading to authentic leisure. In Chapter 5 *Strengths* we introduced

Table 11.16 Methods of Coping *(Hood and Carruthers, 2010)*

Emotion-Focused Coping	
• Challenge irrational thoughts	Targeting and challenging irrational thoughts and feelings and changing them to positive perceptions can lead to reduced stress levels.
• Divert attention	Diverting attention away from one issue and focusing attention on another, so a person is not thinking about a potential threat, will reduce the physiological stress response and possibly increase the relaxation response.
• Accept the situation	When a solution is beyond a person's control, accepting a situation for what it really is, without defense or distortion, and just letting it be.
Problem-Focused Coping	
• Target problems with direct action	Identifying the targeted actions needed to reduce a stressor, and having a willingness to act to implement those actions (e.g., joining a study group to do better on an exam), can support effective coping.
• Build resources	Building internal and external strengths and resources can help people to better cope with life's demands.
Relaxation	Learning and using various relaxation techniques and activities can induce the relaxation response. Techniques can range from guided imagery, deep breathing, and progressive muscle relaxation techniques to physical activity and walks in nature.
Leisure-Based Coping	Leisure can be used to induce relaxation and decrease stressors. Leisure-based coping can include leisure palliative coping (e.g. going for a run), leisure mood enhancement (e.g., watching a funny movie), and leisure companionship (e.g., spending an evening with friends).

you to character strengths and virtues. In Chapter 9 *Assessment* we shared the Values in Action (VIA) assessment tool to help participants become more aware of their own strengths. An important strategy in therapeutic recreation is to guide participants into understanding and then using their own strengths, not just in recreation but in all aspects of their lives.

Supporting External Psychological and Emotional Resources

In the ecological perspective, therapeutic recreation specialists help build not only internal psychological and emotional strengths of participants, but external resources as well. When participants can live and play in environments that nurture psychological and emotional well-being, they have improved quality of life. Each of the strategies that follow, only briefly introduced here, can be used to strengthen external psychological and emotional resources.

Identifying Supportive Individuals and Groups

Through leisure education and advocacy, you can assist participants in discovering and accessing family, neighborhood, and community groups that provide positive experiences, relationships, and places for participation and support. As well, some Internet-based resources, such as social networking, if used carefully, can provide a resource for psychological and emotional support and enhancement of well-being. One such resource is *Disaboom*, an online community for people whose lives are touched by disability, listed in the Resources section at the end of the chapter.

Identifying or Creating Quiet Spaces in Public Places

Some participants, due to the nature of their disability, can participate in community activities, but may need a quiet space available to do so. A quiet space allows participants to relax or calm themselves when an activity becomes too stressful. For a participant with sensory integration differences (e.g., someone with autism), a quiet space may provide a place to regroup, reintegrate, and reduce incoming stimuli for a brief period before rejoining the group. Quiet spaces need not be "special" or segregating. Perhaps it is an unused staff office or the lounge/reading area in a community center. As a therapeutic recreation specialist, you can assist recreation providers in understanding the need for quiet spaces, how to create them, and how to use them appropriately with participants.

Building Positive Accepting Attitudes

One of the roles you may play as a therapeutic recreation specialist is coach or mentor to those providing recreation services in the community, especially in helping to change attitudes about disability and inclusion, and how to structure activities to promote positive attitudes. One way to do that is disability awareness training, discussed earlier. Another powerful approach is to structure the social environment using contact theory as a guide (Anderson, 1994; Anderson & Kress, 2003). In Table 11.17, we provide the main principles you can use, based on contact theory, to build more positive and accepting attitudes toward participants with differences you support and assist them in being included in positive environments, programs, and services in the community. Table 11.18 (p. 300) provides the numerous ways you or another leader can structure interdependence, an important principle for promoting positive attitudes toward differences.

Enhancing Natural Cues to Support Learning

We discussed contextualized or authentic learning earlier in this chapter. We also presented design concepts like "Easy Street" to enhance natural cues to support learning early in the rehabilitation process. Another powerful strategy to enhance natural cues in the environment is the use of the therapeutic community or therapeutic milieu. In this model, every aspect of the rehabilitation environment is part of the learning, from the custodial staff to the other participants to operation, policies, and procedures of the community. The amount of responsibility assumed by each community member directly relates to the amount of privilege each member experiences. The more responsible one becomes, the more privileges one enjoys. In the therapeutic community, the entire milieu is part of the intervention to help a person grow and learn.

These are a sampling of strategies that can be used to help participants build internal and external strengths and resources for psychological and emotional well-being.

BUILDING COGNITIVE STRENGTHS AND RESOURCES

Cognitive strengths and resources are those we use to think and learn. Supporting and building internal cognitive strengths can include strategies such as avoiding overthinking, strengthening goal commitment, and reminiscing about positive life events. Developing external resources to support cognitive strengths can

Table 11.17 Principles to Structure the Social Environment to Promote Positive Attitudes toward People with Differences *(Anderson, 1994)*

Principle	Description	Examples
Frequent and consistent opportunities to get acquainted	Structure the recreation activity so that participants can get to know each other.	• Ice breakers • Name tags • Using pairs or partners in activities
Equal status	Structure the recreation activity and situation so that each participant has equal status in the group, including the participant with a disability.	• Make everyone a part of the decision-making • Mix up groups and responsibilities • Change format in which information is given • Assign roles in activities—everyone gets to try a role
Mutual goals	Structure the recreation activity so participants perceive they all share a common goal.	• Accent teamwork to reinforce equal status • Leader sets mutual goals and sets the tone • Ask the group to set mutual goals • Give feedback on progress toward goals • Everyone participates; rotate positions or roles
Cooperation and interdependence	Structure the recreation activity to include active cooperation and a feeling that each individual's success depends on the successes of the other group members.	• Assign duties or tasks, all of which are needed to successfully complete the activity • Use groups to promote team spirit and group identity • Use team nicknames, T-shirts, other group identifiers • Keep verbal communication clear • Use cooperative structure, where each person completes a part of the whole
Receiving accurate (not stereotyped) information about the person with a disability	Structure the recreation activity so that all participants receive information about the participant with a disability that is accurate and doesn't perpetuate stereotyped beliefs about the disability.	• Explain disability at initial session • Do ice breaker (similarities vs. differences) • Assume a "can do" attitude • Create an environment of open communication • Individual determines what should be shared with group • Draw attention to the participant with a disability when she or he is doing something very well
Fair and tolerant norms	Structure the recreation activity so that the situation favors group equality and fairness. Create and reinforce norms that promote fair and caring behavior and tolerance of diversity on the part of the leaders, participants, and spectators.	• Don't patronize and don't "over help" • As the leader, role model positive accepting behavior • Rotate positions and roles • Accent positive attributes and skills • Emphasize teamwork • Get diverse input from all group members • Reinforce rules and fairness • Equal out or balance skill levels

Table 11.18 Ways to Structure Interdependence *(Anderson, 1994; Johnson, Johnson, and Holubec, 1991)*

There are many different ways to structure interdependence:

- ☐ *Positive Goal Interdependence*
  Participants perceive they can achieve their goals if and only if all members of their group also obtain their goals. They have a mutual set of goals.

- ☐ *Positive Reward Interdependence*
  Each participant receives the same reward for completing the task. A joint reward is given for successful group work. Everyone is rewarded or no one is rewarded.

- ☐ *Positive Resource Interdependence*
  Each participant has only a portion of the information, resources, or material necessary for the task. The participants resources have to be combined in order for the group to reach its goal.

- ☐ *Positive Task Interdependence*
  The actions of one participant must be completed if the next participant is to complete her or his part.

- ☐ *Positive Role Interdependence*
  Each participant is assigned complementary and interconnected roles that specify responsibilities that the group needs in order to complete a joint task.

- ☐ *Positive Identity Interdependence*
  The group establishes a mutual identity through a name, flag, motto, and the like.

- ☐ *Positive Outside Enemy Interdependence*
  Groups are placed in competition with each other. Group members then feel interdependent as they strive to beat the other groups.

- ☐ *Positive Fantasy Interdependence*
  A task is given that requires members to imagine that they are in a life or death situation and must collaborate to survive. Many initiatives or challenge activities use this approach.

- ☐ *Environmental Interdependence*
  Group members are bound together by the physical environment in some way.

include use of environmental cues to support learning and orientation, among many others. We focus on these four strategies in this section.

Supporting Internal Cognitive Strengths

Avoiding Overthinking

In Chapter 2 *Paradigm Shifts* we presented the fundamental concept, "What we focus on increases." So too with overthinking. Dwelling on problems, pondering meanings, obsessively thinking too much—what psychologists call self-focused rumination—rarely helps us find solutions; in fact, overthinking worsens and sustains sadness, pessimism, and a distorted sense of reality (Lyubomirsky, 2008).

Nolen Hocksema (2003) proposes a three-step process to keep rumination in check, which we can teach participants through therapeutic recreation: (a) break free of overthinking, (b) take action to solve problems, and (c) avoid future traps. In the first phase, participants can tell themselves plainly to stop ruminating, distract themselves with an engrossing activity, unburden their worries through writing, talking with a trusted person, or allowing themselves a few minutes to ruminate—and no longer. Participants can begin action toward a solution by taking even a small step to change their situation. By brainstorming all the possible solutions, they can imagine or consider what action someone they respect might take. Following-up through action can break the cycle of passivity and boost their self-confidence. To ward off future temptations to overthink, participants can avoid the people and situations that trigger rumination, adopt a new leisure activity, and work on boosting their self-worth.

Additionally, Lyubomirsky recommends that one looks at the big picture, by asking, "Will this matter a year from now?" "Will it matter when I'm on my deathbed?" Helping participants gain perspective and glean the lessons they can learn from the situation can help move them forward toward a happier life.

Strengthening Goal Commitment

Happy people are those who are engaged in life and who have strong personal goals and aspirations. Goals give us a sense of purpose, add structure and meaning to our lives, bolster our self-esteem, and involve us with other people. Deliberative cognitive focus on goals that are intrinsic, personally meaningful, authentic, activity-based, harmonious with our other goals, and flexible is particularly conducive to enhancing happiness (Lyubomirsky, 2008). Therapeutic recreation specialists can support participants in choosing goals with these qualities, commit to them with passion, break them down into achievable steps, and track their own progress.

Remembering or Reminiscing Positive Life Events

Another proven strategy to increase well-being is to reminisce about or replay positive past experiences and events—a form of savoring. Therapeutic recreation specialist can facilitate positive reminiscence by encouraging participants to remember a shared memory with a friend or family member, to use guided imagery to sharpen one's recall of details of the memory, or to conjure up a mental image of a previous peak experience. Bryant, Smart, and King (2005) have shown that when people write down their positive memories and gather personal mementos (e.g., photographs, souvenirs, gifts) to reminisce about their happy memories on a regular basis, their levels of happiness increase substantially. The more vivid the memories, the greater the happy feelings.

Other techniques therapeutic recreation specialists can use to enhance internal cognitive well-being is to help participants celebrate good news, appreciate beauty and excellence, cultivate mindfulness and awareness in the present moment, and tune into experiencing the world through one's senses.

Supporting External Cognitive Strengths and Resources

Use of Environmental Cues to Enhance Learning and Orientation

The environment surrounding us can play a major role in nurturing cognitive strengths. Have you ever been on vacation, or in a place where you lost track of what day or date it was? The environment cues us and helps us reorient. Some participants live in environments that are institutionalized; others have a functional difference that may impair orientation to person, place, or time. As therapeutic recreation specialists, we play a major role in tapping into environmental cues to enhance orientation and learning.

Some typical strategies for enhancing environmental cues include decorating for the holidays, bulletin boards with upcoming and current events, daily group activities that integrate current events and news, and adding personalized signage to residents' doors (photos, memorabilia).

BUILDING SOCIAL STRENGTHS AND RESOURCES

Social strengths and resources help us to relate and belong. Supporting and building internal social strengths can include strategies such as practicing acts of kindness and learning effective social skills. Positive behavior is a key strength for participants and, because it is so critical to relating and belonging, we devote significant attention to it in this section. As well, developing external resources to support social strengths is vitally important to the well-being of the participants with whom we work, and we focus in-depth on how to enhance social support, childhood and adult friendships, and inclusive and livable communities.

Supporting Internal Social Strengths

Two proven strategies for increasing the ability to relate and belong are practicing acts of kindness and developing effective social skills.

Practicing Acts of Kindness

Several researchers have documented how kindness, when expressed on a routine basis, increases one's social well-being (Fredrickson, 2009; Lyubomirsky, 2008). Acts of kindness may be small (e.g., holding the door for someone, doing a roommate's dishes, helping someone carry a heavy package) or relatively large (e.g., tutoring a student, visiting a sick neighbor, volunteering at a hospital). One need not look beyond one's own family, workplace, or community for occasions to practice kindness. Opportunities are all around us. Lyubomirsky has found that certain circumstances surrounding acts of kindness yield especially high levels of happiness to those who practice them. For example, choosing one particular day of the week to engage in an act of kindness and varying the kinds of acts one performs are most apt to heighten one's well-being. Ultimately, however, you need to help participants choose the acts of kindness that suit them best, as well as how often and how much they are able to do. Research shows that these random acts bolster self-regard, positive social interactions, and charitable feelings toward others. Further, when participants see that others appreciate their kindness, they begin to see themselves as compassionate and altruistic, increasing their sense of confidence, optimism, and self-worth.

Social Skills Training to Nurture Social Relationships

Social skills training is an important part of nurturing social relationships. At times, participants may not have had the opportunity to develop social skills or, due to the nature of their disability, may need more support with social skills. Several social skills training programs are available to therapeutic recreation specialists. Most share the common goal of helping participants learn the basics of interacting with others in an appropriate way using typical skills found in social situations. These skills include basic communication skills, relationship-building skills, and self-presentation skills (Stumbo, 2002) (see Figure 11.12). Teaching social skills in natural contexts with natural cues and consequences is most effective, but classroom-based instruction is useful as well for basic skills or early in a participant's rehabilitation.

Related to social skills training is the important area of positive behavior. We now provide an in-depth look at positive behavioral supports, so crucial for some of the participants with whom we work to be included and accepted, and to begin to experience the well-being that social connections provide.

Supporting Positive Behavior— An In-Depth Look

One of the biggest challenges to participation in recreation and leisure by participants with disabilities is behavior that disrupts the environment and prevents the participant and everyone else from having a positive experience. In recent years, researchers have developed a strengths-based ecological orientation toward challenging behavior called *positive behavior support*, much of it coming from the educational research community. The most important aspect of positive behavior support is its emphasis on altering environmental factors to promote appropriate social behavior. In fact, according to Siegel (2008), at least 80% of behavioral interventions should stem from modifying systems so all participants, staff, and settings work together to support positive behavior. Threaded throughout this section you will find many strategies that engineer environmental factors (e.g., responses from others, teaching procedures, physical aspects of the setting) to address behavior change within an individual. As you read this section, call your attention to these environmental strategies and how they are used to cultivate positive behavior.

Here are some questions for you to consider as you read about positive behavior supports: What are the principles of positive behavior support? When does behavior need to be changed and when does it not? What does it mean to understand behavior within its context? How can an environmental systems-wide approach be used to address behavior? What are the terms and definitions used in positive behavior support? Let us begin by examining the assumptions that underlie positive behavior support.

Assumptions of Positive Behavioral Support

The positive behavioral support movement shares some underlying assumptions, which we describe in Table 11.19, along with an example of a common scenario.

What Do We Mean by "Challenging Behavior"?

Traditionally, challenging behavior has been described as behavior that is aberrant, maladaptive, excessive, disordered, disturbed, or problem behavior—language that

---

Communication Skills
- Conversational skills
- Active listening and responsive behavior
- Expressing feelings and thoughts
- Information seeking and information giving skills
- Skills involving negotiation, disagreement, conflict, and compromise
- Assertiveness skills
- Social proximity and distance; body language; gestures; eye contact; touching
- Empathy and perspective taking skills

Self-Presentation Skills
- Skills involving politeness, etiquette, and manners (e.g., sharing, taking turns)
- Body image and body awareness
- Hygiene, health, and grooming skills
- Appropriate attire and dressing for height, weight, weather, and activity
- Responsibility for self-care

Relationship-Building Skills
- Greeting and initiation skills, such as locating leisure partners
- Forming appropriate attachments to and connections with people
- Friendship development skills
- Self-disclosure and privacy issues
- Cooperation and competitive skills
- Developing and maintaining social networks
- Helping others in time of need
- Reciprocal social support (e.g., expressing care and concern for others and vice versa)

Figure 11.12 Social Skills to Enhance Social Well-Being *(Stumbo, 2002b)*

Table 11.19 Assumptions Underlying Positive Behavioral Supports *(adapted by Crimmins et al., 2007)*

- **Challenging behavior serves a function**
  While challenging behavior can be frustrating for those nearby, it makes sense to the person who is doing it. She or he benefits in some way from engaging in the behavior—that is, it serves a purpose, or function. Positive behavioral support acknowledges four primary functions of behavior:
  - *Tangible:* The behavior results in acquiring a desired object or activity.
  - *Sensory:* The behavior is driven by a desire to meet a sensory need, either for more or less sensory input.
  - *Attention:* The behavior results in desired attention from others.
  - *Escape:* The behavior allows the participant to escape from undesirable activities or settings.

  Sometimes the behavior serves more than one function, such as gaining attention and avoiding a task that is perceived as difficult. If the environment continues to support the behavior, over time the behavior may become so ingrained that it develops into a habit.

  Imagine an afterschool recreation program, where Evan gradually stops working on his art project and begins talking in a loud voice. Whether he intends it or not, he interrupts the recreation leader and distracts the other participants, who begin to laugh. The leader reprimands Evan. Consider these questions: Do the consequences in this scenario influence the likelihood that Evan will talk in a loud voice in the future? Has he learned a lesson, or will he repeat the behavior the next day? In Evan's case, he probably experienced something in the environment previously that reinforced talking in a loud voice. Perhaps he enjoyed the reader's attention or making the other participants laugh. Further study of the behavior in the context of the afterschool program may be needed to truly understand the reasons behind Evan's behavior.

- **Reducing challenging behavior requires offering more alternatives**
  Once you understand the function of the challenging behavior and how it meets a person's need, the next step is to change the participant's environment by offering a better way to meet that need. If the alternative is to succeed, it needs to work as well or better than the target behavior. Ideally, the alternative should tap into and use the participant's strengths. Participation in recreation is a powerful positive alternative. When people engage in recreation that is interesting and meaningful to them, their inappropriate behaviors commonly subside or disappear.

  Evan's short attention span and low tolerance for frustration may be contributing to his outburst, which has been useful for getting himself out of tasks that he finds difficult. An effective behavioral support plan would teach Evan the necessary communication skills to request attention, as well as enhance his ability to complete work independently. His art project could be broken down into smaller sets of tasks with short, structured breaks.

- **Challenging behavior emerges in context**
  A traditional view sees challenging behavior as arising from factors that are intrinsic to the individual such as genetics, early environmental factors, and social and cultural influences. A positive behavioral support approach, by contrast, sees the emergence of challenging behavior as emanating from the interaction between underlying influences and any number of factors occurring in the environment. Combined factors might include the participant's learning history and style, personal aspects, environmental triggers, and ensuing consequences.

  Because of the interplay between intrinsic and environmental factors, during an assessment with Evan, we would assess where his challenging behavior occurs and where it does not occur, and the situational factors present in each instance. We would look carefully at Evan's behavior, the setting, and the relationship between Evan and the environment to better understand how environmental factors contribute to prosocial or undesirable behavior.

- **A team approach is needed to address challenging behavior**
  Because behavior often varies from setting to setting, include various people's perceptions of the behavior across multiple environments. Using a team approach to address challenging behavior allows for shared perspectives as well as shared responsibilities. One of those responsibilities might include a review of previous evaluations, assessments, and interventions to discover what behavioral methods have failed in the past and which have succeeded. A team can also generate more creative solutions than one person working alone.

  In Evan's situation, the team would include the group leader, the parent(s), the inclusion facilitator, the director of the afterschool program, and if possible, Evan. Together, they would focus on understanding the behavior, ascertain how to prevent the behavior from occurring, and determine how to replace the behavior with more positive means to meet Evan's needs and desires.

is clearly rooted in a deficits and problems paradigm. Aggression (e.g., hitting, pinching, pushing), property destruction, self-injury, and tantrums all fall within this category.

As we have shifted toward more humanizing language, challenging behavior has become the preferred terminology in the literature. Sigafoos, Arthur, and O'Reilly (2003) offer this definition of challenging behaviors:

Challenging behaviors are ... destructive, harmful, disruptive or otherwise unacceptable behaviors that occur with sufficient frequency and/or severity to be of major concern. ... Challenging behaviors are pervasive and persistent, not sporadic ... [They] tend to stand out against the background of other less noxious behaviors. (p. 7)

Lowe and Felce (1995) note that challenging behavior is more than an aspect of the person who engages in the behavior. That is, the concern over challenging behavior is equally shared by the participant and those individuals in the environment who need to understand and address the behavior. The ability of people in various settings to change, tolerate, or minimize the behavior is part of the context in which challenging behavior occurs and, thus, must also be understood.

How do we know if the behavior is challenging enough to require behavioral support? At one time or another, most children and youth will misbehave (Crimmins, Farrell, Smith, & Bailey, 2007). "Typical" misbehavior might include, for example, refusing to share, running indoors, talking out of turn, splashing water, and similar behaviors. In most cases these behaviors are harmless and usually do not require serious behavioral support. Sometimes a participant with a disability engages in these typical behaviors and it appears that, because she or he has a disability, people are more upset than if a person without a disability acts similarly. When discerning whether behavior needs support or not, here is a good question to ask yourself: "Is this behavior typical for a participant *without a disability* in the same age group and in a similar setting?" If yes, then you can address the behavior as you typically would in that setting. If no, then a team will need to be gathered to assess the participant's behavior and environmental factors that contribute to it, and generate a plan for support. Other questions to determine whether behavioral support is necessary appear in the next section.

Identifying and Describing Behavior

To identify and describe a target challenging behavior, as well as decide if it is important to change, ask yourself the questions that appear in Table 11.20.

Once you have identified the challenging behavior, you will need to define it by describing it in a way that two or more independent observers would recognize it. This means you will need to *operationally define* the behavior based on *observable* behavior—that is, what you can see versus what is not visible, such as intentions or feelings. For example, let's take "running indoors" as the target behavior. As you develop your operational definition you will need to consider observable factors such as how far and how fast the participant needs to run and how much time the participant needs to be engaged in the behavior to qualify as "running indoors." Describing the behavior precisely will enable multiple observers to look at the participant and agree whether the behavior has occurred or not. Accurate descriptions are also critical for documenting behavior change precisely and evaluating the effectiveness of the behavioral plan.

Understanding Behavior within Its Context—The ABC Model

The positive behavior support approach, similar to other strengths-based approaches in this book, views behavior within the contexts in which participants spend their time. To understand why a challenging behavior occurs, it is important to determine how environmental conditions might be supporting the behavior. What conditions exist before the behavior occurs? What conditions exist afterwards? A simple yet effective model for understanding behavior within its context is widely known as the ABC model (see Figure 11.13).

In the ABC model, an *antecedent*, (A) is defined as "a specific environmental condition that precedes behavior" (Crimmins et al., 2007, p. 26). The assumption here is that most behavior occurs as a response to some prior stimulus, or cue. Identifying the prior stimulus is critical to understanding the behavior and how to respond to it. Thus, we ask ourselves, "What environmental events or interactions precede the behavior to influence its appearance?" Challenging *behavior* (B) defined earlier, refers to any targeted action (or non-action, such as refusing to participate or follow directions) determined to be detrimental to the participant, others, or the program. A *consequence* (C) refers to what occurs in the environment immediately following the behavior that serves to reinforce, or increase, the behavior. The Life Story in Figure 11.14 (p. 306) tells a story of how the ABC Model was used at a day camp to decipher and remedy behavior that posed a safety concern and hindered a camper's involvement.

Behavioral principles have a unique vocabulary, with meanings particular to the field of behavioral psychology. While a strengths approach tends to minimize the use of professional jargon when communicating with participants and their circles of support, knowing language associated with a positive behavioral approach is useful and important. You will frequently find yourself working on teams and will need to be familiar with behavioral terms and meanings so you can communicate effectively with other team members. Table 11.21 presents some of the key terminology used to convey behavioral principles, as well as examples to illustrate their meanings within the context of recreation.

Teaching and Strengthening Positive Behaviors

To decrease challenging behavior, one must increase appealing alternatives for meaningful engagement. It would be unrealistic to expect a person to stop a target

Table 11.20 Identifying and Describing Challenging Behavior *(adapted from Kaplan and Carter, 1995; McConnell, 2001)*

When identifying and describing challenging behavior, it is helpful to ask yourself the following kinds of questions, which addresses factors both within the individual *and* the environment:

1. How frequently does the behavior occur?
2. How long does the behavior last?
3. How intense is the behavior?
4. When and where does the behavior occur? When and where is the behavior least, and most, likely to occur?
5. With whom does the behavior occur?
6. Which staff is most effective at managing the behavior?
7. Does the behavior vary significantly from the behavior of other participants?
8. Does the behavior endanger the safety of the participant or others?
9. Does the behavior interfere with important learning?
10. Are medical problems (e.g., toothache, cold, ear infection, constipation, side effects of medication) masquerading as challenging behavior?
11. Does the participant have the necessary communication skills to gain attention, meet his or her needs, ask for assistance, or reject undesired activities or interactions? Is the behavior the participant's attempt to make his or her wishes known because no other mode of communication is available?

behavior without replacing it with something more interesting to do. Freely chosen, preferred recreational activities are ideal alternatives to challenging behaviors. In fact, researchers have documented that, as participants acquire preferred leisure skills, their challenging behaviors decrease (Schleien, Kiernan, & Wehman, 1981). Not only are such behaviors reduced, building leisure skills expands one's leisure repertoire and taps into a wealth of benefits across the realms of human well-being.

In this section we focus on two aspects of teaching positive behavior related to recreation participation: providing instructional prompts, or cues, to encourage independent participation in recreation, and the value of positive reinforcement techniques to strengthen prosocial behavior and learning.

Instructional cue hierarchy. When you teach a new leisure skill, it is important to be aware of how you provide both verbal and non-verbal instructional cues. A **cue** is a signal, or stimulus, that the instructor provides to prompt the participant to perform a particular behavior. Because instructional cues vary in their level of intrusiveness, you need to recognize the intrusiveness of the prompt you are using so you can guide the participant to eventually perform the task independently, if possible. Figure 11.15 (p. 308) shows this range of instructional cues, which is often referred to as a "cue hierarchy."

When providing instruction, always start with the least intrusive cue first. Looking at the first cue in Figure 11.15, you will provide the participant with the opportunity to engage in the activity independently, that is, solely in response to the natural cues that exist in the environment. It is critical that the participant be given the opportunity to first perform the task without any kind of prompt. If the participant does not respond, then you will move to the second level of intrusiveness and provide a gestural prompt. If the gesture does not elicit a response, then you will try the third level of the hierarchy, a verbal prompt. You will continue through the cue hierarchy, ending with physically guiding the participant through the activity if necessary, until he or she is able to successfully complete the task.

At each stage of the hierarchy, wait to give the participant adequate time to respond (some participants may need time to comprehend the instruction or filter sensory input). As you get to know individual

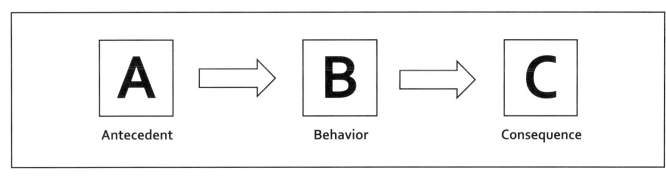

Figure 11.13 ABC Model for Understanding Behavior

Life Story:

Positive Behavioral Support at Day Camp: Getting Everyone Involved!

I am coordinating inclusion at a summer day camp and am faced with a challenging, potentially dangerous, situation. Sam, age 12, loves camp but is continually wandering away from his group. His infectious personality has made him popular with staff all over camp. The camp director and I are concerned, not only because Sam isn't staying with his group, but because the camp is situated on a lake surrounded by many acres of woods, with no enclosure. If Sam wanders off, he could easily get lost or injured and it would be very difficult to find him.

Some counselors are suggesting that Sam's family withdraw him from camp. I'm determined to find a way to keep him at camp, but I'm not sure how to approach the situation. Fortunately, our budget allows us to hire a licensed consulting psychologist who can give us onsite behavioral assessments and recommendations. I call the psychologist and the next day he joins me at camp and we observe Sam continually leaving his group to go talk to someone else. Sam is rarely where he's supposed to be and his counselors are getting pretty frustrated.

The psychologist comes up with a plan, one that involves the entire camp staff. Whenever Sam is not with his group, his counselors should refrain from calling or chasing after him. Whenever the other staff members see Sam away from his group, they should resist greeting him as they usually do. In fact, they should completely ignore him. If Sam returns to his group, the counselors and other campers should welcome him warmly, and immediately encourage his involvement in whatever activity they happen to be doing.

So that afternoon, at the staff meeting, I enlist the help of the entire camp staff. I explain the psychologist's plan, and everyone agrees to try. We're all eager to see how the approach will work.

The next day, as predicted, Sam starts the day with his group but soon wanders off. When his counselors do not call to him to return, Sam pauses and looks back over his shoulder with a quizzical look, then proceeds toward another group. When Sam greets them, the counselors all ignore him and keep on doing what they are doing. Their acting ability is impressive!

Sam just stands there for a few moments, not knowing what to do. He sees another group, and approaches them. They also ignore him. Suddenly Sam turns on his heels and, with a scowl on his face, stomps back to his group. Everyone welcomes him back, and his expression quickly brightens into a big smile. Soon he sees how much fun it is to be with his own group, and he never wanders away from them again. This experience showed us all what well-planned and cooperatively executed behavioral support can do to teach appropriate social behavior and completely change a frustrating situation into a positive one for everyone.

Figure 11.14 Life Story: Positive Behavioral Support at Day Camp: Getting Everyone Involved!

participants, you will learn to gauge the amount of time you will need to wait.

Whenever you provide an instructional cue, consider how you will fade, or withdraw, the cue. Fading should occur gradually and systematically. Timing is of the essence. If you fade the cue too soon, the participant may lose the response and you will need to start the cue sequence over. If you delay fading too long, the participant may become dependent on you to provide the prompt. The more dependent the participant becomes, the more difficult it will be in the long run for him or her to perform the task independently. Fading an instructional cue is an art—an art you will acquire with experience and paying close attention to the participant's responses.

Positive reinforcement provides feedback that the behavior has been performed correctly, and increases the likelihood the behavior will occur again. Once the participant responds correctly to the cue, no matter where it falls on the cue hierarchy, it is important to provide positive reinforcement. When provided to participants who perform tasks correctly, positive reinforcement is a powerful tool to increase and strengthen desirable behaviors. Naturally occurring positive reinforcement, that comes from the activity or the environment, is always preferred to that given by you or another instructor. If the participant is experiencing naturally occurring positive reinforcement, external reinforcers may not even be desirable (Deci, Koestner, & Ryan, 1999).

Table 11.21 **Key Behavioral Principles and Terminology** *(adapted from Crimmins et al., 2007, pp. 22–23)*

Category	Behavioral Principle	What is it?	Example
Conditioning	Operant conditioning	Form of learning in which voluntary behavior is developed or inhibited in response to environmental cues and consequences	A person tells a joke; the listener's response determines whether the joke teller is likely to repeat it
	Classical conditioning	Form of learning in which involuntary or automatic responses become associated with specific environmental cues	A veteran hears the bang of firecrackers at a 4th of July celebration, startles, and crouches defensively
ABC Model	Antecedent	An event or cue that precedes behavior and relates to its occurrence	The tae kwan do instructor assists someone in the class other than the participant
	Behavior	Targeted skill or behavior that is observable and measurable	The tae kwan do participant begins to wander around the room
	Consequence	An event that follows a behavior and relates functionally to its future occurrence	When the tae kwan do participant wanders, the instructor approaches the participant
	Contingency	A specific temporal relationship between a response and a consequence	The tae kwan do participant begins to wander aimlessly whenever the instructor assists someone else
Reinforcement	Reinforcement	A response from the environment increases the future likelihood of behavior	A program leader smiles at a participant who is focused on painting a portrait
	Positive Reinforcement	A positive experience follows a behavior, thereby increasing its future likelihood	A guitar teacher praises the clear tone the participant makes by plucking the strings of a guitar
	Negative Reinforcement	A negative experience ceases after a behavior, thereby increasing its future likelihood	The annoying buzzer of an alarm clock stops when a sleepy camper presses the snooze button
	Chaining	The reinforcement of successive elements of a behavior chain	Teaching and reinforcing a participant for going immediately to the front desk upon entering a fitness center, greeting the attendant, showing a membership card, proceeding to the locker room, and so forth.
	Shaping	Reinforcing successive approximations of target behavior	In an art class, reinforcing a participant for picking up a pencil to mark on the paper; when the participant marks the paper, prompting and reinforcing the participant for making a line; when the participant draws the line successfully, prompting and reinforcing the participant for drawing a tree, and so forth.
	Punishment	A response from the environment decreases the future likelihood of behavior	A participant interrupts the program leader to ask a question and the program leader becomes annoyed and unhelpful
Other Behavioral Terminology	Baseline	The level at which the target behavior occurs naturally, before intervention	The team determines that the participant's target behavior occurs an average of 6 times an hour during the recreation activity.
	Fading	The gradual removal of an instructional prompt in order to develop independent performance of a behavior	When teaching a participant to choose a toy, gradually fade a verbal prompt to a gestural prompt until the participant is able to perform the task independently
	Task analysis	Breaking down a complex skill or task into its component behaviors, subskills, or subtasks. Each component is stated in order of occurrence and sets the occasion for the occurrence of the subsequent behavior.	To teach a recreation activity such as tossing a Frisbee, the task is broken into steps: pick up Frisbee, step forward with one foot, lean forward extending dominant hand forward while holding Frisbee, and so forth.

Least Intrusive ↑↓ Most Intrusive	Instructional Cue	Description	Example: Board Game
	1. Independent performance	Provide access to the recreation activity and materials; participant engages in the activity based on the natural cues in the environment	A board game is spread out on a table, where Kerry and two other people are sitting. Kerry takes her turn rolling the dice.
	2. Gestural prompt	Gesture (e.g., point) toward the recreational materials to indicate it is time to play	Instructor stands near Kerry and gestures as though shaking a pair of dice.
	3. Verbal prompt	Provide a verbal instructional cue to indicate what the participant needs to do	Instructor says, "Kerry, roll the dice."
	4. Model	Demonstrate how to do the task and repeat the verbal cue	Instructor says, "Here, let me show you," and rolls the dice. "Now you try."
	5. Physical prompt	Touch the participant lightly to indicate what the participant needs to do	Instructor touches Kerry's hand lightly while saying, "Kerry, it's your turn to roll the dice."
	6. Physical guidance	Physically guide the participant through the task	Instructor places her hand over Kerry's hand and guides it to pick up the dice, shake them, and roll them, while saying, "This is how you roll the dice. Now you try."

Figure 11.15 Instructional Cue Hierarchy *(adapted from Schleien, Wehman, and Kiernan, 1981; and Horner and Keilitz, 1975)*

Reinforcers fall into two categories: primary reinforcers and secondary reinforcers. A *primary reinforcer* is reinforcement that meets an innate need, such as food when one is hungry, beverage when one is thirsty, and sleep when one is tired. Food and beverages need to be used judiciously, however, since they have the potential to lead to unwanted weight gain and an unhealthy relationship with food. If food or beverage is used, seek out low-fat, healthful choices such as fruit, whole grain crackers, and juice. A *secondary reinforcer* is reinforcement whose value is acquired, or learned, rather than innate. Examples include a sense of accomplishment from successful participation, money, points, or tokens that are exchanged for goods or privileges that are inherently rewarding to the individual. Social interactions such as authentic compliments from other participants, giving a "high five," a pat on the back, or a thumbs up are also forms of secondary reinforcers whose value is learned.

As a general rule, when giving positive reinforcement, only provide it *contingently*, that is, upon the participant's correct response. Providing reinforcement when the participant has not met the criteria leads to confusion about what is expected and perpetuates low expectations. Further, when providing positive reinforcement, be very clear and specific about why you are reinforcing the participant's behavior by providing *behavior specific positive feedback*. For example, instead of making a generic statement such as "good job" or "nice work," indicate specifically what it is you appreciate about the behavior. You might say, "Sandy, I noticed how you chose your own recreation activity when you came home from work today—that's terrific!" Being precise in your feedback and emphasizing natural reinforcers increases the likelihood that the participant will repeat the aspect of the behavior you are praising. Additionally, *how* you provide feedback is as important as *what* you say to the participant. Here are some tips to ensure that your verbal and your non-verbal communication support each other:

- Deliver feedback immediately following the behavior so the participant sees the direct relationship between your words and his or her behavior.
- Always emphasize and draw attention to natural reinforcers in the activity or environment.
- Use a relaxed tone of voice, with enough magnitude and energy to draw attention to your words.
- Stand close to the participant, while respecting his or her personal space, and make eye contact.
- Use facial expressions, hand gestures, and body posture that match the content of your words.

In the following section on external social resources we continue this discussion by offering some ways we, as therapeutic recreation specialists, can set the stage for supporting positive behavior in the context of recreation activities.

Supporting External Social Resources

Enhancing Positive Behavior in the Environment

This section looks at other approaches that we, as therapeutic recreation specialists, can use to establish an environment that optimizes positive and cooperative behaviors among participants, whether or not they have a disability. Table 11.22 describes some tips to maximize the likelihood that positive social behaviors will occur. While these methods cannot guarantee positive behaviors by participants all the time, they help create a safe and secure environment that encourages positive social interactions.

Enhancing Social Support

In the Flourishing through Leisure Model, and throughout this book, we have emphasized the importance of social relationships for human thriving. Recreation is an ideal environment for encouraging social relationships (Abery, 2003; Schleien, Green, & Ray, 1997). In fact, one of the principal reasons people participate in recreation is for social purposes – to meet people and to share activities with others who also enjoy them (Green & Heyne, 1997; Schleien, Green, & Ray, 1997).

However, people with disabilities tend to have limited social networks that seldom include people without disabilities, unless they are family members or service providers. Further, the lack of a partner has been cited as the number one barrier preventing youth and young adults with disabilities from engaging in community recreation (Ittenbach et al., 1994). Because of its importance for personal well-being, helping participants foster relationships needs to be one of our key focal areas in therapeutic recreation.

Abery (2003) says that people who report feeling socially included experience three phenomena: a sense of belonging, a sense of presence and active participation in the community, and an ability to take part in activities based on their preferences. Several qualities of recreation and leisure programs make them conducive to supporting social relationships. First, recreation and leisure programs bring people together who have similar interests or preferences, which is often a first step to finding and selecting friends. Common recreation interests and preferences among friends is often more important than other factors such as work roles, socio-economic status, political views, or religion. Recreation activities are also entered into voluntarily, as are our social relationships. Another quality of recreation that encourages social relationships is that programs tend to be ongoing, allowing people to move beyond myths and stereotypes to connect as people who are passionate about the same activities.

How can we support social relationships for people with disabilities through therapeutic recreation? In Chapter 9 *Assessment* we told you about one approach for social inclusion called Circle of Friends, or Circle of Support. This process allows a participant to discover who exists within his or her social network on four levels: intimacy, friendship, participation (in groups and clubs), and exchange (of goods or services). This social scan may also be used to identify in which circles one would like to add more social relationships.

In Chapter 10 *Planning* you learned about another process to strengthen social support, PATH, or

Table 11.22 Ways to Maximize Positive Social Behavior

- ☐ *Provide structure and schedules.* Give visual and verbal reminders of schedules to increase on-task behavior, create a sense of predictability, and reduce anxiety.

- ☐ *Ease transitions from one environment to the next.* Sometimes a participant will experience anxiety about moving from one setting to another. Again, provide verbal reminders of upcoming activity or venue changes, particularly as they draw nearer. Reassure the participant during the transition, and provide reinforcement as he or she successfully reorients to the new environment.

- ☐ *Communicate expectations clearly.* Expectations that are stated clearly reduce anxiety and minimize confusion, which can potentially trigger undesirable behaviors.

- ☐ *Clearly define rewards and consequences.* Explaining rewards for positive behavior and consequences for inappropriate behavior, with timely reminders, can curtail oppositional behavior.

- ☐ *Catch them being good!* Sometimes the sole reason a participant acts out is because he or she needs assistance from the instructor and has no better means to communicate it, or the participant simply wants attention. Providing positive reinforcement frequently (and contingently) keeps participants on track and reduces the likelihood they will act out. It also keeps you nearby and available to provide help when needed.

Planning Alternative Tomorrows with Hope. Recall that in this process the participant identifies his or her North Star dream and gathers a circle of support to help reach that dream. Starting with the present point in time, strengths are identified along with ways to build upon them. Members of the circle of support are then engaged in a series of specific actions and timelines designed to help the participant realize his or her dream.

In the following section, we continue this discussion of social support by addressing how to encourage friendships for participants with disabilities.

Building Friendships

Friendship is an area that is often neglected for people with disabilities. As with any other important life skill, we need to give careful attention and structured support to building friendships. Friendship is a magical thing that happens between people. It doesn't occur automatically simply because people with and without disabilities happen to be in the same space together. The mysterious nature of friendship also means there is no guarantee that friendship will result from our efforts. However, there is much we can do to create environments in which friendships have an opportunity to take root and blossom.

Children's Friendships

In Chapter 6 *Theories* we introduced you to a study in which the relationships of children with and without disabilities were followed for 2 years while they participated in a variety of recreational activities (Heyne, Schleien, & McAvoy, 1993; Heyne, Wilkins, & Anderson, 2012). An activity that was especially conducive to promoting social closeness was the "lunch bunch," where a small group of four to six children, including one with a disability, met once a week to share lunch and play together. The children themselves, rather than the group leader, decided what they wanted to do after lunch—play a game in the gym, make a craft project, paint, bake cookies, among many other creative pursuits. The group leader's role was to facilitate the children's interactions, gather whatever supplies the activities required, and more or less let the children form their own relationships, intervening only when necessary. After two years of leading and observing lunch bunches, research staff developed guidelines for leading small group activities to promote socialization and friendship. These guidelines are presented in Figure 11.16 (pp. 311–312).

Again, these guidelines cannot guarantee friendships will occur. However, they are useful for creating supportive environments where friendships can develop—where children see each other regularly, play together, form their own relationships, and have adults encouraging and reinforcing their friendship behaviors. As a result of attending the lunch bunches, many of the children visited each other in their homes—an indication that friendships were becoming established.

Supporting children's friendships takes a coordinated effort by parents (which includes anyone who functions in the parent role) of children with and without disabilities, school personnel, and recreation staff (Heyne, McAvoy, & Schleien, 1994; Heyne, Schleien, & McAvoy, 1993). Table 11.23 (p. 313) presents recommendations from children, parents, and school/recreation personnel on how to support friendships.

Adult Friendships

Amado (1993) suggests an approach to help adults with disabilities socialize and make friends by building on their internal strengths within the context of external community resources. Her approach takes an adult's unique capacities, interests, and talents and shapes external resources around them. When assisting adults with disabilities to make social connections with other community members, Amado emphasizes three principles:

- *Act as if almost anything can happen.* Most successful matches between adults with and without disabilities begin with a strong, confident belief in the benefits of the relationship for both parties involved.

- *Start small—one-to-one.* Assisting participants in developing friendships may take substantial time, effort, ingenuity, and perseverance. Further, it is often more effective if community members relate to one person at a time rather than to several people at once.

- *Believe in the capacities of the participant.* Making friends requires appreciating the positive attributes and gifts of each other and recognizing the contributions each person has to offer the relationship.

When supporting community connections and friendships for adults with disabilities, each person's individual situation and unique strengths must be carefully considered. No one method will work for everyone. Amado (1993) offers a four-part process, described in Table 11.24 (p. 314), which considers context as well as each person's uniqueness.

The following guidelines are designed to facilitate friendship between children with and without disabilities in small group recreational activities:

☐ **Prepare an activity plan**

As basic as this guideline seems, one of the most common reasons an activity falls apart is due to insufficient planning. When an activity loses structure, often the first person to be excluded is a participant with a disability. Be certain the activity is appropriate for the chronological age level of the children, and have all the required materials available. Plan so the activity fills the entire time available and, if the activity happens to end early or if the children lose interest, be prepared with a "bag of tricks" to offer alternative activities. Involving children in planning activities helps keep children engaged and interested.

☐ **Select an appropriate setting and room arrangement**

Unless the activity requires a large space such as a gym or multi-purpose room for gross motor movements, select a small area where the children can sit close together and easily see and hear each other. This kind of intimate setting encourages conversation and interaction.

☐ **Let interactions evolve naturally and, if needed, involve the children in establishing guidelines for conduct**

If rules are established by adults too early, children's playfulness and creativity may be hampered, as well as their sense of group ownership. When organizing the group, tell the children they're there to "have fun" and "make friends" (not to "win" or "be first"). Encourage the children to listen to each other, respect each other's space, and notice when someone else has done something well. Then let the children's interactions develop naturally, intervening only when necessary. If the group dynamics get out of hand, invite the children to establish their own rules. It's surprising how mature children can be when coming up with rules for their own behavior and, because they develop the rules themselves, they are more likely to follow them.

☐ **Arrange seating to promote social interaction**

Invite the children to sit in a circle, on the floor, or around a table. Adults should avoid sitting next to a child with a disability, if practical, so the child has an opportunity to interact with peers on either side. If some of the children start to form a clique, seat them apart from each other to encourage more inclusive interactions.

☐ **Select activities that promote cooperation**

Choose cooperative, rather than competitive or individualistic activities, where all the children can work together toward a common goal. Examples of cooperative activities include painting a mural, baking cookies, going on a scavenger hunt, making a pizza, parachute games, cake decorating, acting in plays, playing in a band, going snowshoeing, among many others.

☐ **Equalize interactions among the children**

Set the tone for equal and natural interactions among the children by emphasizing similarities and treating all the children the same. If a child tries to dominate the group, make sure everyone has an equal opportunity to be heard. If a child is shy, attempt to draw him or her out by encouraging participation in the activity. Otherwise, let the children direct their own interactions as much as possible. Have high expectations for participation by all the children, and select activities where everyone can take an active, contributing role.

☐ **Change "object-oriented" activities to "people-oriented" activities**

Often recreational activities require children to look at a board game, ball, computer screen, or some other play material instead of at each other. Think of ways to shift the focus away from an object and toward people by building in opportunities for social interaction. For example, you can remind the children to greet each other, take turns, share materials, provide feedback, offer encouragement, or engage in conversation about the activity.

☐ **Adapt activities to meet individual needs**

One of the best ways to maximize participation by a child with a disability is to invite group members to brainstorm ideas for adapting activities. This approach allows group members to take the perspective of the person with a disability, contribute creatively to solutions, and develop an inclusionary attitude. To minimize singling out the group member with a disability as the only person who requires accommodation, take advantage of the times when children without a disability require special assistance and have the group brainstorm adaptations for them as well.

Figure 11.16a Facilitating Children's Friendships in Small Group Recreational Activities

☐ **Keep the activity child-oriented**

Too many adults in the environment can sometimes restrict children's imagination and creativity, and keep them from directing their own conversations and interactions. Sometimes adults can be overprotective and do "for" a child rather than let a child do for him or herself. Participants may also be tempted to talk "through" an adult, rather than talk directly to a group member with a disability. Adults should assume facilitator roles, giving guidance while allowing children to come up with their own ideas, to work out their own solutions to problems that arise, and to establish their own connections with each other.

☐ **Establish continuity between sessions**

Friendships take time to develop. To create a sense of continuity and strengthen relationships over time, involve the children in activities that take more than one session to complete. Activities might include gardening, sewing, carpentry, or craft projects, as well as community volunteering.

☐ **Remain flexible**

Even the best plans sometimes go awry for any number of reasons. Maintain an attitude of flexibility, fluidity, and fun. Be in tune with the children's energy and dynamics, and be ready to shift gears to keep interactions positive.

Figure 11.16b Facilitating Children's Friendships in Small Group Recreational Activities (cont'd)
(adapted from Heyne, Schleien, and McAvoy, 1993; Heyne, Wilkins, and Anderson, 2012)

Empowering Families in Leisure

Families can play a fundamental role in supporting individuals with disabilities and influencing their involvement in recreation and the life of the community. Family members may include parents (or anyone who functions in the parent role), siblings, aunts and uncles, grandparents, among other individuals who are close to the participant. In this section we highlight some resources that support families and their family members with disabilities.

Parent-Professional Partnerships

A strong alliance between parents and professionals in therapeutic recreation is critical for supporting the involvement of family members in recreation (Schleien, Rynders, Heyne, & Tabourne, 1995). Forming a trusting relationship allows professionals to tap into the hopes, needs, and visions of parents and family members with disabilities, and to utilize them to ensure the maximum participation and benefit for a participant.

In any alliance, or collaboration, it is important to acknowledge each partner's gifts and contributions. What do parents have to offer a partnership with therapeutic recreation professionals? Parents provide a wealth of knowledge about their children with disabilities. They know intimately their children's strengths, abilities, needs, learning styles, idiosyncrasies, and likes and dislikes. Parents are acquainted with how to interact and communicate most effectively with their children, and can pass that information on to professionals who can further convey it to program instructors and other participants. Parents provide a cultural context for the child, and view the child in a holistic and relational light. Their child is not only a son or daughter, he or she is a sibling, a grandchild, a citizen of the community. Perhaps most important, a parent brings hopes and dreams for a child's overall growth and well-being. Knowing these hopes and dreams can instill tremendous motivation in professionals to help them come true.

And what do therapeutic recreation professionals bring to the partnership? They bring their desire to help others, their expertise, their knowledge of recreation and community resources, high expectations, and an ability to negotiate the system to get things done. Professionals validate the dreams and desires of parents and participants, and offer support and encouragement to fulfill them. Table 11.25 (p. 315) provides several suggestions on how therapeutic recreation specialists can strengthen partnerships with families. Ongoing collaboration and dialogue with parents make us, as therapeutic recreation specialists, better helpers and keeps our practice relevant and responsive.

The Family Development Credential Program, directed by Dr. Claire Forest, is an example of a family support program founded on strengths-based principles. This program supports families living in poverty whose children are susceptible to insufficient environmental supports. In Figure 11.17 (p. 316), Forest describes the Family Development Credential Program, and in Figure 11.18 (p. 317), she provides a life story drawn from her research. To learn more about this credential program, which would be valuable supplemental training for a certified therapeutic recreation specialist, refer to the Resources section at the end of this chapter.

Enhancing and Building Community

As you learned in Chapter 5 *Strengths* and Chapter 6 *Theories*, community building offers many opportunities to enrich the lives of people with and without disabilities. Because therapeutic recreation specialists must focus on the environment as much as the participant to facilitate positive change, community building becomes a critical knowledge and skill area. In this section, you will learn various approaches for building communities that are inclusive, that honor the rights of people with disabilities to advocate for themselves, and that are created from contributions by all community members.

Asset-Based Community Development

According to Kretzmann and McKnight (1993), there are two ways to build stronger communities. The first, and most frequently traveled way, is to seek solutions by focusing on a community's needs, deficiencies, and problems. A community needs survey is administered and analyzed, followed by an array of services upon which the community grows to rely. Residents come to believe their well-being depends upon being a "client" and a consumer of services. Their recovery depends on outsiders—experts with credentials who "know better." While not intentional, plans based on community needs and deficiencies ultimately teach residents they

Table 11.23 How Families, Schools, and Community Recreation Personnel Can Support Children's Friendships *(adapted from Heyne, Schleien, and McAvoy, 1993)*

Home-school-community connections are important for building friendships between children with and without disabilities: Families, school personnel, and community recreation staff can all play a role in encouraging friendship.

How Families Can Support Children's Friendships
- Make friendship development a family priority
- Become acquainted with other families in the neighborhood
- Schedule regular times for your child and his or her friends to get together
- Learn about individual needs of children with disabilities so you feel comfortable having them in your home
- Invite children into your home and on outings in the community
- Talk about your child's friendships at home
- Encourage positive social interactions through supporting communication and arranging cooperative activities when children play at home
- Learn about recreation opportunities in the community for your child and his or her friends

How School Staff Can Support Children's Friendships
- Include social and recreation skills in the curriculum
- Assign children who like each other to the same classroom; otherwise their relationships may fall away due to lack of regular contact
- Offer disability awareness training to parents, staff, and peers without disabilities to promote accepting attitudes
- Provide opportunities such as open houses, potluck meals, and open swim or gym times so families can get to know each other
- Train teachers and staff on friendship skills and how to support socialization and relationship building in the classroom and other school environments
- Let parents know when their children develop friendships at school so parents can encourage them at home

How Community Recreation Staff Can Support Children's Friendships
- Welcome all children in recreation programs and advertise programs directly to families whose children attend local schools
- Coordinate the times when afterschool programs are offered with school dismissal times
- Ensure architectural and programmatic accessibility
- Educate recreation staff to meet individual needs of participants
- Provide cooperative activities that promote positive peer interactions

Table 11.24 A Process to Support Community Connections and Friendships for Adults *(Amado, 1993)*

Step One: Identify the person's interests, gifts, and contributions.
Because friendships are often formed around common interests, it is important to learn what gives meaning to a person's life. For some people, interests may be obvious. They may be able to tell or show you their leisure preferences or their favorite kinds of music, food, or movies. For others, you may need to spend time with the person to detect the more subtle ways interests are expressed. You may also need to talk to people who know the person well, on a day-to-day basis, such as family members or residential staff, to discover the person's interests. Gifts are those attributes that attract people to you. A gift may be a positive attitude, a good sense of humor, accepting others just as they are, or being industrious, among many others. Recognizing gifts calls attention to what the person has to offer, and helps to identify places in which gifts can be expressed and appreciated by others. Additionally, calling attention to a person's positive attributes in the planning stages of friendship development allows those inherent qualities to grow and flourish throughout the relationship.

Step Two: Explore and identify possible connections with people and places in the community.
Amado suggests a variety of highly personal approaches to exploring potential connections:
1. Generate a list of all the places in the community in which the person expresses an interest, as well as those places in which his or her interests and gifts can be expressed. Ask yourself: Who do I know in these places? Who can I ask to be involved?
2. Identify places and opportunities where the person will see and interact with the same people on a regular basis. Ongoing opportunities to meet people might include joining a club, volunteering, attending a place of worship, taking a community education class, or participating on a sports team.
3. Look for settings that would welcome the person, and assess their receptivity to people with disabilities. To start, all you need is one person, and one environment. Potential settings could include a community recreation center, neighborhood groups and clubs, a food co-op, places of business, and public agencies and institutions (e.g., parks, libraries, universities, hospitals, associations, faith communities, meditation centers).
4. Identify people who may be interested in becoming friends with the person with a disability. Consider people in your own social networks, even if they haven't had prior interaction with a person with a disability. Ask people directly if they would be interested in being a friend to the person, with the understanding that friendship is different from volunteering. That is, volunteers are usually involved on a time-limited basis and do for someone else; friends genuinely like each other and benefit mutually from the relationship.

Step Three: Introduce the person to new people in the community setting.
The most effective introduction is personal and one-to-one. The manner in which introductions are made, as well as what is said, will naturally affect how community members view the person, so you must think carefully about what and how much to say. Emphasize the person's interests, gifts, and qualities that others appreciate, and give just enough information so both the participant and community member feel comfortable and can build upon what you tell them. If the participant is being introduced to a group of people, such as a club or association, identify a group member who is well-connected and can serve as the participant's "host." A host can help the participant gain entry into the group by introducing him or her to other group members.

Step Four: Continue to support the relationship.
Amado suggests three principles to support relationships. First, you must genuinely care about the well-being of the participant. Second, you need to trust in the openness and willingness of community members to extend themselves to people with disabilities. And third, you must believe in the value of building community for people with disabilities, as well as for society as a whole. Relationships will vary in the kind and amount of support they will require. Some relationships will require considerable encouragement, while others develop best if left to grow on their own. Sometimes the relationship will never grow into a friendship, and that must be respected too.

themselves are fundamentally deficient—powerless to take charge of their lives and the future of their communities.

The second way to rebuild and revitalize community is called *asset-based community development* (Kretzmann & McKnight, 1993). This path leads to community activities and policies, built from the inside out, that are rooted in the capacities, abilities, and assets of all its residents. As a first step, Kretzmann and McKnight recommend identifying all the available assets in the community, paying particular attention to the assets and gifts of people who are typically marginalized:

Each community boasts a unique combination of assets upon which to build its future. A thorough map of those assets would begin with an inventory of the gifts, skills and capacities of the community's residents. Household by household ... the capacity mapmakers will discover a vast and often surprising array of individual talents and productive skills, few of which are being mobilized for community-building purposes... It is essential to recognize the capacities, for example, of those who have been labeled mentally handicapped or disabled, or of those who are marginalized

Table 11.25 Developing and Strengthening Partnerships with Families *(Heyne and Schleien, 1997)*

Welcome families of children with disabilities. Barrier-free environments, printed materials that include photographs of people with disabilities, and inclusive philosophies all communicate that families with children with disabilities are welcome.

Offer a single point of contact. Avoid requiring parents to repeatedly explain their children's and families' needs to multiple professionals at your agency. Instead, provide a single parent contact that can gather all pertinent information and transmit it to others who work directly with the child.

Conduct assessments with parents and participants. Because parents possess the most complete information about their children with disabilities, it is important to involve them and their children in the assessment process. As you read in Chapter 9 *Assessment*, questions should be culturally relevant and in a language the family understands. Jargon and technical language should be avoided.

Invite parents to collaborate. Look for key ways that willing parents can be involved at your agency. For example, you can invite them to sit on a board of directors or an advisory council, or ask them to give feedback about a particular policy or procedure.

Maintain open communication. Relationships are built through frequent contact and interaction. Similarly, the best way for professionals to form trusting relationships with parents is through regular communication, whether it be in person at the agency, by telephone, or by e-mail.

because they are too old, or too young, or too poor. In a community whose assets are being fully recognized and mobilized, these people too will be part of the action, not as clients or recipients of aid, but as full contributors to the community-building process. (p. 6)

Just as individual community members are tremendous assets for building community, so are associations and institutions. Associations usually operate in an informal manner and provide a vehicle for people to connect around common religious, cultural, athletic, recreational, political, historical, or other interests. People in associations are accustomed to working together to tackle issues, and often their original purposes can be extended to encompass processes for building community. Institutions such as schools, recreation agencies, libraries, parks, police and fire stations, hospitals, and social service agencies are also important assets to enlist in community building. All three forms of assets—individuals, associations, and institutions—need to accept a sense of responsibility for the well-being of the community. Other local assets can also be drawn upon, such as the features of the land, buildings, and infrastructure (see Figure 11.19, p. 318).

Kretzmann and McKnight (1993) advise, "The key to neighborhood regeneration... is to locate all of the available local assets [and] to begin connecting them with one another in ways that multiply their power and effectiveness" (p. 5). The way in which assets are connected is through relationship building—relationships that are grounded in people's strengths and capacities, never in their needs or weaknesses. Community members need to know they can count on their neighbors and neighborhood resources for support, and that interdependence is the basis of effective community building.

To learn more of the particulars of how asset-based community development works, we refer you to the guidebook by John Kretzmann and John McKnight entitled *Building Communities From the Inside Out*, which is listed in the references at the end of this chapter.

Cultural Shifting

In Chapter 6 *Theories* we introduced you to Al Condeluci's thoughts on the ingredients that comprise community: a common theme, an avenue to membership, rituals, cultural and behavioral patterns, jargon, a collective memory, and gatekeepers. You also read about the *community approach to disability* in which "commonalities and connections" are the bridge that guides a person with a disability and his or her aspirations, skills, and capacities across the river of deficits into a community. Condeluci (2002) says that, whenever attempting to incorporate a person or new idea into an existing culture, a kind of *cultural shifting* needs to occur that allows the group to accept the person (or idea).

The key catalyst for the kind of cultural shifting necessary to include a person with a disability into the community or to champion a new strengths-based concept is the *gatekeeper*. You will recall that a gatekeeper is someone who is a member of a culture and who has some power of influence (either positive or negative) on the culture. Condeluci (2002) says that a positive gatekeeper "is the single most critical element to building community" (p. 95). Whether you are looking for a positive gatekeeper to strengthen a sense of community

A Strengths Approach in Family Practice

by Claire Forest, Ph.D.

The fields of family development and social work have been leaders in developing the strengths approach. Prior to the paradigm shift toward the strengths model, which began in the 1990s, social work was based on a deficit model in which an expert diagnosed a client's problem then recommended (or in the case of people receiving public services, required) expert-driven solutions. One pioneer in moving the field toward a strengths-based empowerment approach was the Cornell Family Development Credential (FDC) program. Developed in 1996 in anticipation of the federal Welfare Reform, the FDC program has trained and credentialed thousands of family workers from a wide range of public agencies to coach families to set and pursue goals for self-reliance.

Agencies apply to send trainers to learn to teach the 90-hour course *Empowerment Skills for Family Workers* (Forest, 2003) offered at University of Connecticut and in 19 states with affiliated FDC programs. After completing a week-long train-the-trainers course, FDC trainers return to their communities to establish interagency FDC programs. They teach the FDC course, offer field advisement, including portfolio development, and administer a written exam developed by Cornell. Workers who successfully complete the course, portfolio, and exam earn the Family Development Credential awarded by Cornell Continuing Education or a respected university in an affiliated state. Continuing education credit and college credit through local community colleges or the PONSI (National Program on Noncollegiate Sponsored Instruction) system is available.

FDC credentialed workers, who remain employed by their agencies as case workers or home visitors, help families develop their own long- and short-term goals then find the resources needed to pursue them. At weekly sessions, credentialed workers help clients review and update their Family Development Plans, then celebrate when goals are met. The term "coach" denotes a life coach, not a sports coach or physical education teacher. While life coaching is more common among business executives, the Cornell Family Development Credential program encourages welfare agencies, homeless shelters, child protective agencies, and similar organizations to train free "life coaches" to help women living on low incomes to set and pursue goals within their communities. The Family Development Credential program is built on the following core principles:

Core Principles of Family Development

1. All people and all families have strengths.
2. All families need and deserve support. How much and what kind of support varies throughout life.
3. Most successful families are not dependent on long-term public support. They maintain a healthy interdependence with extended family, friends, other people, spiritual organizations, cultural and community groups, schools and agencies, and the natural environment.
4. Diversity (race, ethnicity, gender, class, family form, religion, physical and mental ability, age, sexual orientation) is an important reality in our society, and is valuable. Family workers need to understand oppression in order to learn to work skillfully with families from all cultures.
5. The deficit approach, which requires families to show what is wrong in order to receive services, is counterproductive to helping families move toward self-reliance.
6. Changing from the deficit model to the family development approach requires a whole new way of thinking, not simply more new programs. Individual workers cannot make this shift without corresponding policy changes at agency, state, and federal levels.
7. Families need coordinated services in which all the agencies they work with use a similar approach. Collaboration at the local, state, and federal levels is crucial to effective family development.
8. Families and family development workers are equally important partners in this process, with each contributing important knowledge. Workers learn as much as the families from the process.
9. Families must choose their own goals and methods of achieving them. Family development workers' roles include helping families set reachable goals for their own self-reliance, providing access to services needed to reach these goals, and offering encouragement.
10. Services are provided so families can reach their goals, and are not themselves a measure of success. New methods of evaluating agency effectiveness are needed to measure family and community outcomes, not just the number of services provided.
11. For families to move out of dependency, helping systems must shift from a "power over" to a "shared power" paradigm. Human service workers have power (which they may not recognize) because they decide who gets valued resources. Workers can use that power to work with families rather than use power over them.

Claire Forest, Ph.D., is Director of the Family Development Credential Program, University of Connecticut Center for Culture, Health & Human Development, Storrs, CT (www.familydevelopmentcredential.org).

Core Principles of Family Development used with permission from Forest, C. (2003). *Empowerment Skills for Family Workers*. Ithaca, NY: Cornell Family Development Press.

Figure 11.17 A Strengths Approach in Family Practice

Life Story:

Family Empowerment Skills:
A Mother Overcoming Barriers of Poverty

by Claire Forest, Ph.D.

The following Life Story illustrates how credentialed Family Development coach Sue Trank uses a strengths approach to help an isolated woman attempting to overcome poverty-induced stress. This narrative is adapted with permission from the study, *Mothers Overcoming Barriers of Poverty: The Significance of a Relationship with a Credentialed Coach* (Forest, 2009). This study employs a new research method called "Profile Pairs," which combines the narratives of mothers overcoming poverty with narratives of the credentialed life coaches who help them. The following example shows how outdoor physical exercise suggested by the credentialed coach helps an isolated rural mother avoid repeating negative patterns that had resulted in founded cases of child abuse.

Jessica Cooper (mother) and Sue Trank (coach): *"Always chaos!"*

"Jessica" came to the attention of Child Protective Services (CPS) when, after many frustrated days isolated in her rural house trailer with her hyperactive preschooler, an object she threw broke glass in a china cabinet while her children slept. Jessica recalls that night, then speaks about her work with Sue:

> My husband and I were arguing with each other so we just said, "Okay, we need some help here." Amy at the Department of Social Services suggested Sue. We have four boys, so it was always busy, always chaos, and the three-year-old was just very busy! We were having some behavior issues with him.

> When Bobby totally falls apart with his temper tantrums, I'm glad Sue's here. She has come when I've had, like, four loads of laundry stacked up on the couch and we just kind of kick them off… She doesn't judge us. Bobby was really kind of running the whole household until she started coming.

Credentialed coach Sue recalls:

> I got a referral from CPS. An incident was reported, and the CPS report was founded because the children were in the home, not in the room but in the home, sleeping. The mom got angry and hit a glass window in a china cabinet. So I'm working with this family who has four boys [who are] 8, 7, 4, and 18 months [old].

> Jessica is a very busy woman. When I went for my first visit, I noticed that her four-year-old was very active, jumping off the furniture. Jessica is stressed out a lot. We talked about taking time for herself when Dad came home from work. Maybe to take a walk or something along that line.

Although Jessica is unlikely to find the transportation, time, child care, or money necessary to join a gym or a formal therapeutic recreation program, her relationship with credentialed coach got Jessica out walking. This informal outdoor exercise became part of the plan that enabled this mother to remain safely at home instead of being remanded to foster care.

Figure 11.18 Life Story: Family Empowerment Skills

that includes people with disabilities, or you wish to become a gatekeeper yourself, Figure 11.20 (p. 319) offers strategies you can use to promote cultural shifting.

Change is never easy and, even if we engage in all the actions listed in Figure 11.20, we may not meet with success. However, change essentially begins by *one person* doing something differently. It only takes one individual to step outside the norm and try something new to initiate cultural shifting. As others observe that one person, they may think, "I can do that too." Soon their actions affirm the viability of the gatekeeper's message and, as others also adopt the change, the culture gradually shifts toward the new orientation.

Five Commitments that Build Community

O'Brien and Lyle O'Brien (1996) believe that community happens for people with disabilities when "people step outside the roles prescribed by the formal and informal administrative assumptions that typically organize life" (pp. 80–81). As people involve themselves in shared goals and actions, the distinctions between staff, participants, family members, and ordinary citizens begin to dissolve: "Community building is an intentional move into a new space" (p. 81).

Stepping outside prescribed roles means that individuals make a person-to-person commitment

Primary Source Support:

"Tapping the Power of Community" to Prevent Substance Abuse

Benson, P., Roehlkepartain, & Sesma, Jr., A. (2004, March). Tapping the power of community: Building assets to strengthen substance abuse prevention. *Search Institute Insights & Evidence, 2*(1), 1–14.

Substance abuse prevention programs are widespread across the U.S., with 90% of high schools providing information about alcohol, tobacco, and other drug (ATOD) use. However, little evidence exists about whether these programs are (a) implemented properly and (b) effective in making a meaningful difference in young people's lives. The authors suggest it is difficult for program-based prevention programs alone to address the multiple factors that influence young people to use ATODs. The authors recommend building the capacity of communities as an integral part of supporting young people in their healthy development.

The Search Institute, as you learned in Chapter 2 *Paradigm Shifts* and Chapter 6 *Theories*, has developed a framework of 40 scientifically based developmental assets that strengthen resiliency in adolescents. Their research has shown that the presence of developmental assets is strongly linked to substance abuse in the following ways:

- The more developmental assets youth have, the less likely they are to engage in ATOD use.
- The protective nature of developmental assets to resist ATOD use holds true for all youth regardless of differences in gender, race/ethnicity, socioeconomic status, grade in school, and type of community (i.e., rural, suburban, urban).
- Developmental assets play a role in reducing all ATOD use, including alcohol, tobacco, illicit drug use, and driving while intoxicated.
- Ample developmental assets in childhood and adolescence delays initial ATOD use.
- Developmental assets have a greater impact on ATOD use than demographic factors.

Rather than rely on centrally-run programs and models, the Search Institute sees community building as a grassroots movement that responds to the challenges and dynamics of local communities. The focus is on encouraging the interaction of human capital, social capital, and organizational resources to support the broad-based accumulation of developmental assets by young people. Four asset-building targets are recommended to communities:

☐ *Vertical accumulation of assets:* The young person experiences an increase in the total amount of developmental assets in her or his life.

☐ *Horizontal accumulation of assets:* The young person experiences developmental assets in multiple contexts – families, schools, parks, playgrounds, faith communities, retail centers, and other places young people typically spend their time.

☐ *Chronological accumulation of assets:* The young person's assets are renewed and reinforced across time.

☐ *Developmental breadth of assets:* Asset-building efforts are extended to all young people, not just those identified as needing support.

The Search Institute recommends the following framework for increasing a community's capacity for asset-building:

1. *Cultivate community readiness, energy, and commitment:* The creation of a normative culture in which a network of individuals and groups supports youth's healthy development is encouraged by cultivating a shared vision, common purpose, social trust, and a belief in personal and collective efficacy to contribute meaningfully to asset-building.

2. *Create an operational infrastructure:* An asset-building infrastructure links, promotes, and supports asset-building efforts in the community. These activities typically include planning and governance, access to resources, networking, broad communication, training and technical assistance, and the documentation and evaluation of outcomes.

3. *Build community capacity:* Five actions are recommended for building asset-rich communities: (a) engage adults from all walks of life in forming supportive relationships with youth; (b) mobilize young people to positively influence peers to adopt healthy behaviors; (c) create an asset-building culture by activating all sectors of the community in asset-building; (d) encourage prevention programs to become more asset rich and accessible to all children and youth; and (e) influence community leaders to give financial, media, and policy resources to asset-building.

This synopsis shows how communities can be the "source of life-giving nutrients" (p. 12) for children and adolescents. Tapping the "power of community" creates a culture that supports developmental assets, prevents ATOD use, and builds young people's resilience and engagement in community life.

Figure 11.19 Primary Source Support: "Tapping the Power of Community" to Prevent Substance Abuse

to provide support to another person. O'Brien and Lyle O'Brien (1996) identify five commitments that individuals can make to build community, which are outlined in Figure 11.21 (p. 320). They note that people with disabilities are often on the "receiving end" of the five commitments, however they may also be on the "giving end," contributing to someone else's life.

Building Physical Strengths and Resources

Physical strengths and resources focus on being able to move, act, and do. Surprising new research is showing us just how critical it is for people to move, as often and as much as possible. Internal physical strengths, like fitness and health, allow us to do that. External physical resources, like the design, livability, and accessibility of environments, allow us to move freely as well. As therapeutic recreation specialists, having strategies to help participants move more will help them not only be physically stronger, but socially, emotionally, and cognitively stronger as well.

Supporting Internal Physical Strengths

Taking Care of the Body through Physical Activity

The surprising new research on the benefits of physical activity has been made possible through new technologies in studying the brain. This research has found that physical activity does much more than strengthen heart, lungs, and muscles. It has profound effects on brain function, which in turn affects thinking, feeling, learning, and a host of other functional abilities (Ratey, 2008). According to research by Dr. Ratey, clinical professor of psychiatry at Harvard University, physical activity improves the ability of the brain to learn, improves mood, decreases anxiety and depression, improves the ability to concentrate (especially for those with attention deficit disorder), guards against stress, and reverses the aging process. Through neuroscience, Dr. Ratey and many colleagues have documented the huge benefits of exercise to the brain, and thus to other functional areas.

Given the magnitude of benefits to participants that cut across all aspects of their lives, strategies that provide opportunities for physical activity for participants are crucial. Getting participants to move *more* is a step in the right direction, as many may have been

---

- **Be positive.** Look for the good around you and keep in mind the positive attributes of your community, and you will set the tone for capacity-oriented activity. If you keep your cultural shifting agenda foremost in mind and visualize your outcomes, you will be more likely to attain them.

- **Reach out.** Positive gatekeepers reach out to others. They are open, hospitable, and genuinely care about others. They welcome people, smile and greet them, and introduce themselves. These are the kinds of behaviors that foster relationship building, inclusion, and community building.

- **Take risks.** Little can be gained without taking risks. A positive gatekeeper is someone who believes enough in the goodness of what she or he is doing to withstand the risk of failure.

- **Be enthusiastic.** Your enthusiasm will incite others to join you in moving toward a cultural shift. Even if you don't have the personality of a cheerleader, your enthusiasm can show in your excitement about what you are doing and in your consistent, committed actions.

- **Stay flexible.** A positive gatekeeper is open to other possible routes to the ultimate goal and is willing to compromise to get there.

- **Be action-oriented.** Change agents are active in body, mind, and spirit. You will need to move beyond words, and even passion, to act on behalf of another person or in pursuit of your vision.

  - **Be brief.** To inspire others, be able to articulate your goal in just a few sentences. Your message needs to be communicated clearly and easily understood.

  - **Be creative.** Use your creativity, which comes in many forms and styles, to engage others in the process of culture shifting. Creativity itself will capture people's attention and rouse them to action.

Figure 11.20 Strategies to Promote Cultural Shifting *(Condeluci, 2002)*

leading sedentary lifestyles. Iwasaki, Coyle, and Shank (2010) suggest that we conceptualize active living more broadly than just physical activity and exercise, and help those who have been sedentary find leisure experiences that provide meaning and more movement in their lives as a way to promote healthier living. Dr. Ratey and colleagues agree (Sattelmair & Ratey, 2009) and recommend that a program of physical activity emphasize cognitively, socially, and aerobically demanding activity on a daily basis. Physical activity progrms should focus on personal progress and lifelong fitness activities, and include modes of physically strenuous play that are engaging, challenging, and enjoyable to participants.

Dr. Ratey, in his revolutionary book, *Spark*, provides a recipe, or "regimen" to follow to help people get started on the path to receiving the benefits of physical activity. We provide Dr. Ratey's suggestions in Figure 11.22, as a template from which to weave in many other strategies that include meaningful leisure. In many settings where therapeutic recreation services are provided, physical activity opportunities can be offered in many ways, such as walking or jogging clubs, yoga sessions, Dance Dance Revolution, Wii, or bicycling groups. Using leisure interests as a starting point and evolving physical activity opportunities to reflect interests will ensure success.

Supporting External Physical Resources

Universal Design

"The intent of universal design is to simplify life for everyone by making products, communications, and the built environment more usable by as many people as possible at little or no extra cost."

—*Ron Mace*, Founder, The Center for Universal Design

Have you ever carried a big load of boxes and wondered how you would manage to open the door? Have you ever seen a person with a stroller struggle to get off a bus? Have you ever encountered an elderly person

---

Five Commitments That Build Community

O'Brien and Lyle O'Brien (1996) recommend these five roles individuals can assume to reach out to others, person-to-person, and build community connections:

1. **Anchor**

An *anchor* is someone who commits to loving the person and is concerned about his or her well-being over time. An anchor is there during the ups and downs of life, and is committed to protect the person from wrongdoing. An anchor seeks to know more about the person – especially about their strengths and talents – and preserves the person's most treasured memories. Family members often act as anchors, though any other individual who sincerely loves the person may assume this role.

2. **Allies**

An *ally* commits to share time and resources to support the person in a change he or she would like to make. Allies offer practical help, assist with problem-solving, network with others, and provide useful information. They help build a future that the person will look forward to.

3. **Assistance**

An individual who provides *assistance* helps another person cope with the effects of a disability, so he or she can focus energy and gifts on the change he or she would like to make. An assistant may help the person with daily activities such as eating, dressing, housework, and participating in community events, or find funding to hire a personal assistant. An assistant may also support the person's communication, movement, learning, problem-solving, or coping with problematic behaviors and feelings.

4. **Associations**

Associations are defined as those formal and informal "social structures groups of people create to further their interests" (p. 84). Associations may focus on social change, a political objective, or any of the person's interests. Including people with disabilities in association membership brinqs considerable untapped energy to that association.

5. **Agendas**

People with disabilities, their families, and allies can develop *agendas* to organize political action that ensures just and effective public policy. Community in the form of political coalitions address concerns such as inclusive education, family support services, safe and affordable housing, employment, accessible transportation, adaptive technology, and the like.

Figure 11.21 Five Commitments That Build Community *(adapted from O'Brien and Lyle O'Brien, 1996)*

slowly climb a lengthy flight of stairs because there is no elevator? These are the kinds of scenarios addressed through *universal design*, a broad-spectrum approach to architecture, products, and environments.

As people live longer and as modern medicine increases survival rates after significant injury or illness, more and more people are becoming interested in universal design. The term "universal design" was coined by the late Ronald Mace when he observed that the design features that make environments more accessible for people with disabilities also make life easier for everybody. According to The Center for an Accessible Society (2010), universal design is based on the following premises:

- Disability is not a special condition of a few;
- It is ordinary and effects most of us for some part of our lives;
- If a design works well for people with disabilities, it works better for everyone;
- Usability and aesthetics are mutually compatible. (p. 1)

According to the Universal Design Alliance (2010), Universal Design has two meanings:

- The design of products and environments to be usable by all people, to the greatest extent possible, without adaptation or specialized design
- A user-friendly approach to design in the living environment where people of any culture, age, size, weight, race, gender and ability can experience an environment that promotes their health, safety and welfare today and in the future (p. 1)

The Center for Universal Design at North Carolina State University in Raleigh has developed seven principles of universal design (see Table 11.26, p. 322) to guide architects and designers to extend usability to as many different kinds of people as possible. Examples of universal design are all around us. Table 11.27 (p. 323) presents just a few.

One distinct advantage of universal design is that it allows for lifestyle changes as people move through the lifespan. It considers the needs of the complete population—small children, elders, people with disabilities, those with no physical limitations, among other variations. And universal design allows people to live in their homes as long as possible, an initiative

---

Spark! Getting Participants Moving for Overall Well-Being

John J. Ratey, M.D., author of *Spark: The Revolutionary New Science of Exercise and the Brain*, confirms the value of aerobic exercise to optimize brain function. Aerobic exercise indisputably encourages neurogenesis, or the growth of new brain cells. The higher your fitness level, the sharper your cognition will be, the more positive your mood, and the lower your feelings of anxiety and stress. Exercise sparks a plethora of reactions in the body for cardiovascular health including the release of mood-stabilizing serotonin, increased metabolism, and the coursing of oxygen throughout the body and brain.

How much exercise is ideal for yielding these kinds of health benefits? Ratey agrees with neuroscientists who have studied the positive effects of exercise that "A little is good, more is better" (p. 250). For optimal mind-body well-being, however, Ratey recommends:

- 45 to 60 minutes of aerobic exercise 6 days a week
- Four of the days should include an hour of moderate intensity exercise such as jogging (at 65% to 75% of your maximum heart rate)
- Two of the days should include 45 minutes of high-intensity activity such as running (at 75% to 90% of your maximum heart rate)

If you're not ready for such a vigorous regimen, you will be glad to hear that many studies champion the value of walking. Research concludes that you can begin to build up your aerobic base and get in shape by walking an hour a day using between 55% and 65% of your maximum heart rate. This means exerting yourself enough that it's difficult to carry on a conversation. You may also walk over your lunch hour, take stairs instead of an elevator, or fasten a pedometer to your waistband and challenge yourself to take 10,000 steps a day (about 5 miles).

Working out with others redoubles the benefits of aerobic exercise. Social interaction, particularly in groups, is complex and challenging, and also supports neurogenesis. Combining social interaction and exercise in therapeutic recreation programs is a powerful way to help participants get and stay healthy in mind and body.

Figure 11.22 Spark! Getting Participants Moving for Overall Well-Being

often referred to as "Aging in Place." This idea is closely linked with the concept of livable communities, which you will read about in the next section.

Creating and Sustaining Livable Communities

In the social well-being section above, you will remember our discussion of community building strategies as external sources of support. In this section we offer a similar approach to building community called livable communities, which was introduced in Chapter 6 *Theories*.

To summarize briefly, the initiative Livable Communities is a partnership between elders and people with disabilities, represented by the American Association of Retired Persons (AARP) and the National Council on Disability (NCD). Both groups share the common goals of affordable and appropriate housing, adequate mobility and transportation options, and access to community health and support services. They also seek inclusive and accessible physical environments; work, volunteer, and education opportunities; and participation in civic, cultural, recreational, and social activities.

Accomplishing these mutual goals requires the coordination of many facets of community planning and decision-making, across numerous issues such as land development, zoning, housing policy, road design, or transportation planning (Oberlink, 2008). The NCD (2007) proposes four general strategies, or "policy levers," that planners at any level of government can use to facilitate livable communities:

1. Consolidate administration and pool funds of multiple programs to improve ease of access to and information about benefits and programs.

2. Use tax credits and other incentives to stimulate change in individual and corporate behavior and encourage investment in livable community objectives.

3. Provide a waiver or other authority to help communities blend resources from multiple public funding streams to provide and coordinate different services.

4. Require or encourage a private sector match to leverage public funding and stimulate public-private sector partnerships.

As challenging as it may be to address the needs of elders and people with disabilities in a comprehensive and coordinated manner, doing so offers a unique opportunity to change the way in which government operates so more residents can experience improved quality of life. Change would embrace an interdependent network for how resources are organized and managed, how government interacts with the business community, and how government responds to the evolving interests, needs, and preferences of community members. This coordinated system would enable people to live in the community with greater independence, choice, and control.

Table 11.26 Principles of Universal Design *(Copyright © 1997 NC State University, The Center for Universal Design)*

PRINCIPLE ONE: Equitable use
The design is useful for people with a wide range of abilities.

PRINCIPLE TWO: Flexibility in use
The design accommodates a wide range of individual preferences and abilities.

PRINCIPLE THREE: Simple and intuitive use
Use of the design is easy to understand, regardless of the user's experience, knowledge, language skills, or current concentration level.

PRINCIPLE FOUR: Perceptible information
The design communicates necessary information effectively to the user, regardless of ambient conditions or the user's sensory abilities.

PRINCIPLE FIVE: Tolerance for error
The design minimizes hazards and the adverse consequences of accidental or unintended actions.

PRINCIPLE SIX: Low physical effort
The design can be used efficiently and comfortably and with a minimum of fatigue.

PRINCIPLE SEVEN: Size and space for approach and use
Appropriate size and space is provided for approach, reach, manipulation, and use regardless of user's body size, posture, or mobility.

Oberlink (2008) offers several examples of communities that have developed innovative solutions to increase livability for their residents through coordinated efforts. For example, affordable housing options have been expanded by constructing attached or separate living units to existing homes. Additional living units can provide rental income for older adults, which may make it feasible for them to stay in their homes. These units can also provide affordable housing for older parents who wish to down-size and live near their children and grandchildren. These kinds of housing options, which draw from existing infrastructure, also support a community's effort to maintain a small ecological footprint.

Another example that encourages livability in the home is the concept of "visitability." For example, certain physical design elements, such as steps leading to the entrance of a home, may prevent people with disabilities from visiting and socializing with family, neighbors, and friends. A solution to a this commonplace physical barrier is to require new housing developers to have at least one step-free entrance, 32 inches of clear passage through all interior doors, and a full or half bathroom on the main level of the home. Universal design approaches of this sort build the social fabric of society as they promote social and psychological well-being of individuals so they can continue to live at home.

Additionally, as an alternative to traditional van services that are often used to take seniors to doctors' offices and senior centers, communities have successfully experimented with giving older people transportation vouchers—a set amount of funding that may be used any way a person pleases to purchase rides. Seniors may hire a friend or family member to drive them, take a taxi, or ride a bus or train. This program is less expensive than traditional van service and gives people more freedom to decide when and where they want to go.

Several other strategies for realizing livable communities may be found in the References section at the end of this chapter.

Building Spiritual Strengths and Resources

Spiritual strengths and resources are those that help us see our connection to something larger than ourselves, help us gain a better perspective on life, and help us feel hopefulness and love. Internal strengths can be developed through several actions well-documented by scientific study and centuries of anecdotal evidence. External strengths and resources can be developed to support participants in their continual spiritual growth.

Supporting Internal Spiritual Strengths

Here we provide several strategies that lead to spiritual growth that have been well researched. These strategies can be infused in many therapeutic recreation programs and services. Often, we provide these types of activities

Table 11.27 **Examples of Universal Design**

Example of Universal Design	Usability
Automatic door opener	Allows access for people who use wheelchairs and those who carry items that make it difficult to open a door
Door levers	Allows people to open doors with minimum effort and gripping strength, as a more practical and functional substitute for door knobs
High contrast signs	Allows readability by people with visual impairments and provides clearly visible signage for the entire population
Ramp	Provides access to buildings by people who use wheelchairs, push strollers, walk bicycles, pull luggage, or use dollies
Smooth surfaces of entranceways	Provides safe access to buildings while eliminating the need to climb stairs
"Undo" command in computer software programs	Allows people to fix inadvertent errors easily
Utensils with large, easy-to-grip handles	Allows safe and easy handling of utensils, regardless of a person's dexterity and gripping strength
Wide interior doorways and hallways	Allows easy and safe interior access for people with varying abilities
"Universal design benefits people of ALL ages and abilities." The Center for Universal Design (2010, p. 1)	

in collaboration with other team members, such as chaplains, counselors, or social workers.

Learning to Forgive

> Holding on to anger is like grasping a hot coal with the intent of throwing it at someone else; you are the one getting burned.
>
> —*The Buddha*

Perhaps one of the most difficult of human endeavors, learning to forgive, has tremendous benefits to well-being (Lyubomirsky, 2008). As the Buddha implies in the quote above, holding onto bitterness or hatred harms you more than the object of your resentment. For this reason, forgiveness is something one does for oneself more than for the perpetrator. This wisdom is borne out in research. Studies with people who have experienced interpersonal hurts have shown that lessons in forgiveness led to lower anxiety, negative emotion, and blood pressure as well as higher self-esteem, hope, and a sense of control over one's emotions.

How can we help participants practice forgiveness? Lyubomirsky (2008) offers several proven strategies which may be undertaken through a journal, letter, conversation, or by simply using one's imagination. Here are two strategies participants can use:

- Write a letter seeking forgiveness for a wrong you did to another person, whether or not you actually send it. You can remember a situation when someone else has forgiven you, and reflect on what they said or did and, as a consequence, how you felt. You can ruminate less on the offense thus weakening its power over you.

- Write a detailed letter of forgiveness to someone who wronged you, ending the letter with an explicit statement of forgiveness such as "I realize now you did the best you could at the time, and I forgive you." Without excusing the person's behavior, you can adopt a perspective of empathy, charity, and compassion toward him or her.

Expressing Gratitude

Feeling grateful, or counting your blessings, enables you to let go of worry and irritation, and to appreciate your life as it is today. One of the most effective ways to facilitate the expression of gratitude is through keeping a gratitude journal (Lyubomirsky, 2008; Seligman et al., 2005). We can ask participants to use these strategies:

- Journal daily, weekly, or whenever best fits your lifestyle and disposition. Choose a time of day when you have a few minutes to reflect on your life and, in your journal, write down three to five things for which you feel grateful. You may write about anything, large or small, including individuals who matter to you, your surroundings, goals you have accomplished, the beauty of the night sky—anything that is meaningful to you. Instead of writing, you may choose a regular time to sit and contemplate your reasons for being grateful.

- Catch yourself when you have an ungrateful thought about a person, and replacing the thought with an appreciative one.

- Express your gratitude directly to someone—by phone, letter, or in person—to boost your level of well-being. Convey your gratitude in concrete terms, indicating what the person did for you and how it affected your life. Even if you don't send the letter, the benefits to your well-being will still be felt.

Practicing Religion and Spirituality

Lyubomirsky (2008) and others have documented the benefits of belonging to a faith community, regularly practicing a form of spirituality, disciplined meditation, prayer, or regular and reverent contact with nature. Practicing religion and spirituality has many returns for one's happiness. People tend to live healthy lifestyles, have a sense of purpose, enjoy a consistent social network, derive meaning from both ordinary and traumatic events, and are able to cope effectively with life's issues. Through therapeutic recreation, we can assist participants in connecting with a form of religion or spirituality that they can sustain in their daily lives. For example, depending on their inclinations, we can help them locate a faith community, dedicate a period of time each day to prayer, or find the sacred in the ordinary aspects of everyday life.

Practicing Meditation

Meditation is a mind-body spiritual practice that helps people to understand that their lives are constantly changing, to accept the futility of striving for control, to cultivate attention and a sense of awareness in the present moment, and to practice detachment. Keeping the mind anchored in the present helps people refrain from replaying painful memories of the past and from preoccupation with the future. Meditation takes various forms including concentrative, mindfulness, scientifically contemplative, and loving-kindness meditation. Lyubomirsky (2008) recounts the scientifically proven benefits of meditation, ranging from the physiological effects of reduced symptoms of illness to the improved mental health benefits of a heightened sense of peace and reduced depression and anxiety. As therapeutic recreation specialists, we can encourage participants to take a class on meditation, visit a meditation website, or purchase a book or compact disc that provides meditation instruction.

Clarifying Values, Goals, and Aspirations (Values Clarification)

A common strategy embedded in many leisure education programs, clarification of values helps participants make life and leisure choices that align with what is most important to them. Values clarification often leads to a clearer vision of goals and aspirations that are more true to the self, and thus more attainable and meaningful. Many of the leisure education programs listed in Table 11.12 (p. 292) provide values clarification exercises in them and can be used to facilitate this strength with participants.

Using Character Strengths

According to Seligman (2002), once we have identified our unique character strengths and virtues, and put them into use serving something bigger than ourselves, we will find authentic happiness and a sense of purpose and meaning. Helping participants find avenues to exercise their signature strengths is an important strategy for therapeutic recreation specialists to help nurture spiritual well-being. It is often during leisure that participants will be able to apply their strengths, as it is the area of life with the most choice and self-determination.

Supporting External Spiritual Strengths and Resources

Spiritual growth can be nurtured by resources in the environment. Here we offer a few ways that we can support this growth through building external strengths for spirituality.

Building and Sustaining a Culture of Hope and High Expectations

High expectations are those attitudes and messages that surround people in their environments, and influence aspirations for them and their quality of life, as well as the expectations of others in their social network. As therapeutic recreation specialists, we must send a strong message that we expect people to do well and prevail through whatever difficulty brought them to us for services. This message of high expectations translates into hope and a focus on possibilities.

Research repeatedly shows that hope and high expectations are powerful in helping people thrive. In Chapter 5 *Strengths* we talked about the importance of a culture of hope. Here, we remind you of its critical role in helping people make positive changes in their lives. As a professional, you have enormous influence in participants' outlooks on their own lives. This influence and unavoidable power comes with a serious responsibility to nurture hope and convey high expectations for positive outcomes.

Identifying and Supporting Nature-Based Activities

Richard Louv (2008), in his bellwether book, *Last Child in the Woods*, makes the case for the fundamental importance of the human-nature connection. Research has documented not only significant problems from a lack of contact with nature, but significant benefits as well. In Figure 11.23 (p. 326), we offer not only some of the researched benefits of connecting with nature, but some simple strategies that therapeutic recreation specialists can infuse in their programs, services, and settings.

Enhancing Beauty and Aesthetics in the Environment

Have you ever spent any length of time in an environment that was devoid of beauty? Think of what it would be like to live in an institutional setting where everything is designed for function, and not for aesthetics or beauty. This kind of living situation can wear down the spirit and create a sense of dreariness and apathy. In fact, recent neuroscience research has shown that the brain is more active when in a pleasing or aesthetic environment.

One of the important tasks of therapeutic recreation in institutional and other settings is to ensure that beauty and grace are a part of that setting. Color, art, furnishings, windows, plants, animals, and light all combine to create a livable and nurturing environment versus a deadening and sapping environment. In institutional settings, assisting participants in creating a milieu that is aesthetically pleasing and inviting is particularly important in sending a message of respect and hope. Leisure activities that are creative and expressive can often enrich environments, whether through participants' artwork, music, plants, or animals. Therapeutic recreation is in a unique position to facilitate a beautiful and aesthetically pleasing environment that helps build a stronger sense of peace and spirituality.

Cleanliness and maintenance of an environment is just as crucial. In the "broken window syndrome" theory, the effects of unmaintained environments can lead to apathy and further degradation of the environment, starting a downward spiral of negativity for all who live in that environment (Gladwell, 2002). Taking a leadership role in your setting, and helping other staff members and participants contribute to a well-maintained and aesthetically pleasing environment can contribute to the well-being of all who use that space.

In sum, as therapeutic recreation specialists, we have an exciting array of new strategies and interventions available to us to facilitate enhanced leisure and well-being with participants. We can add these strategies to the wealth of those already commonly used in therapeutic recreation.

Other Implementation Strategies Commonly Used in Therapeutic Recreation

We would like to end this chapter with a listing of other common strategies and interventions used in therapeutic recreation. Because whole textbooks are written about these interventions, our purpose is to simply raise your awareness of what is available. In Table 11.28, we provide a listing of common interventions.

Lastly, we share a beautiful life story about Aune, from Finland (see Figure 11.24, p. 328). Aune's story highlights how leisure and well-being, across all domains, are inextricably linked and how an upward spiral can begin with the smallest of activities if they have meaning and purpose for the participant.

Benefits of Connecting with Nature:

Physical
- Increased physical activity
- Increased motor abilities and coordination
- Lower body weight
- Decreased blood pressure
- Increased exposure to sunshine and less vitamin deficiencies
- Decreased asthma
- Decrease in the prevalence of many diseases
- Decrease in perception of pain

Cognitive
- Increased creativity
- Increased capacity for problem-solving
- Increased focus and attention span

Psychological/Emotional
- Relaxation and stress reduction
- Increased happiness
- Appropriate risk-taking
- Enhanced self-esteem
- Increased self-confidence
- Increased initiative

Social
- Increased cooperative behavior
- Decreased aggression
- Self-control

Spiritual
- Sense of connection to the larger world
- Awe, a sense of vastness
- Perception of beauty and serenity
- A sense of caring for the natural world; an increased environmental ethic
- Sense of the enduring cycle of life

Strategies for Connecting with Nature:

- Take a daily walk
- Explore neighborhood trails
- Plant a garden and take care of it daily
- Open up views out windows
- Feed, watch, and count birds
- Have numerous plants throughout your living area
- Have animals (aquarium, aviary, pets)
- Camp
- Fish and hunt
- Explore and learn a variety of outdoor recreation activities: backpacking, kayaking, canoeing, skiing and snowboarding, cross-country skiing, swimming, snorkeling, rafting
- Bicycle instead of driving a car
- Have a porch, patio, or outdoor area to relax in on a daily basis
- Teach outdoor skills (map reading, using a compass, how to dress) to increase comfort level in outdoor environments
- Advocate for parks and trails in your community
- Play in water – swim at a lake, wade in a creek, splash in puddles
- Start and build a collection: rocks, seashells, pressed flowers, leaves, insects
- Become a nature photographer
- Keep a nature journal, with observations, sketches, pressed flowers, and the like
- Spend a little quiet time each day in nature

Figure 11.23 Benefits of and Strategies for Connecting with Nature *(The Children and Nature Network, 2010)*

Summary

In this chapter we discussed the implementation phase of the therapeutic recreation process in terms of building internal and external strengths and resources across the Flourishing through Leisure Model domains of well-being: leisure, psychological/emotional, cognitive, social, physical, and spiritual. We emphasized how recreation and the helping relationship are at the center of therapeutic recreation services, and we provided implementation approaches that are universal, such as the helping relationship, advocacy, wraparound services, the use of activity analysis, and contextualized learning that depends on natural cues.

We chose the strategies discussed in this chapter because they are strengths-based, they are proven techniques based on research, they represent the best thinking arising from recent literature in psychology, human services, and leisure studies, and they are newer—and also important—to the field of therapeutic recreation. While we have usually categorized strategies into only one of the six Flourishing through Leisure Model domains, you found that the approaches often produce benefits across multiple domains, reflecting the integrated nature of well-being. To review the strategies that were presented across the six well-being realms of the Flourishing through Leisure Model, revisit Table 11.1 at the beginning of this chapter.

There are many more strategies, approaches, and interventions available to you as a therapeutic recreation specialist. One of the many reasons therapeutic recreation is an exciting profession in which to practice is the diversity of tools available to us. In therapeutic recreation, you can be a lifelong student, as new approaches and techniques are constantly emerging from research and practice, and there is always more to learn and master in those we already know how to use.

Resources

Disaboom: Live Forward
http://www.disaboomlive.com

This website is an online community for people whose lives are touched by disability. Whether you have a disability, are a caregiver, a family member or friend, you will find a community of people sharing stories, photos, advice, and words of encouragement, as well as facts and research about advances in improving the lives of those with disability.

Family Development Credential Program
http://www.familydevelopmentcredential.org

This strengths-based credential program is designed to train "frontline workers" from public, private, and non-profit agencies to coach low-income families in developing healthy self-reliance. Trainees attend 90 hours of training based on the curriculum, *Empowerment Skills for Family Workers* (Forest, 2003), complete a portfolio documenting their ability to apply Family Development Credential concepts and skills, and pass a standardized exam. For more information about this program, and to find out how you can earn this credential, visit the website.

National Wraparound Initiative
http://www.nwi.pdx.edu

The National Wraparound Initiative, a Web-based collaborative community of practice, emerged from a research team focused on evidence-based practice and has grown into a national center for promoting high quality wraparound service provision. The website includes resources, tools, research and other information to help implement quality community-based care.

Table 11.28 Common Interventions and Approaches used in Therapeutic Recreation

☐ Adventure Therapy	☐ Relaxation Training	☐ Therapeutic Use of Expressive Arts
☐ Aquatic Therapy	☐ Remotivation	☐ Therapeutic Use of Play
☐ Assertiveness Training	☐ Reminiscence/Life Review	☐ Therapeutic Use of Sport
☐ Bibliotherapy	☐ Sensory Stimulation	☐ Validation Therapy
☐ Humor	☐ Social Skills Training	☐ Wilderness Therapy
☐ Horticulture Therapy	☐ Tai Chi	☐ Yoga
☐ Medical Play	☐ Therapeutic Use of Animals	
☐ Reality Orientation	☐ Therapeutic Use of Electronic Games (e.g., Wii)	

My Cultural Lens:

Well-Being through Finnish Handicrafts
Co-authored with Petra Karttunen and Jari Aho

Aune, age 87, is a widow who lives in Helsinki, Finland. Because she can no longer take care of herself at home, she lives in a nursing home. The staff is concerned because Aune appears depressed and shows no interest in anything. She spends most of her time either sitting or sleeping. She has no real physical problems but she is overweight and it's difficult for her to move.

The staff at the nursing home meets to discuss how they might help Aune. There is one therapeutic recreation staff member at the nursing home named Petra, and Auna is scheduled to meet with her for an assessment in the Craft and Recreation Unit in early January. During the assessment Aune expresses an interest in handicrafts, indicating that she has had a loom on display at her home.

In Finland, handicrafts are a common hobby for people Aune's age, as well as for younger people. Because of the popularity of handicrafts, many therapeutic recreation personnel* specialize in arts and crafts and teach them to participants who are interested in them.

Aune tells Petra she would like to make Christmas presents for each member of her family. She has 25 family members in all—including children and grandchildren, their spouses, and grandchildren. With Petra's support, Aune decides she would like to make individually printed pillow cases for each family member.

Petra and Aune set up weekly sessions to make the pillow cases. Each week Aune walks to her session at the Crafts and Recreation Unit, which is excellent physical rehabilitation because she needs to walk down three long corridors to get there. Printing the pillowcases strengthens her hand-eye coordination and taps into her creativity. Aune strengthens her cognitive ability when she talks with Petra and when she checks the results of her handwork and plans the next pillow case. Emotional well-being also improves as Aune reminisces about her past life, thinking and talking about each family member, their lives, and the joys and sorrows they have brought her.

At the beginning of the program, Petra works one-to-one with Aune. As the sessions continue, however, Aune gets involved in group activities at the residence, increasing her opportunities for socialization. Gradually Aune's cognition grows sharper, and the depression and hopelessness she experienced lift. She plans her next session several days ahead of time, and talks about her experience for days afterward. The nurses let her know how important her work is, and report that Aune no longer needs so much help or medication. Aune has found new meaning and motivation for her life. She feels she is still important.

By December of the same year Aune has twenty presents ready and packed as Christmas gifts. The following spring Aune continues printing pillow cases, but suddenly she dies peacefully at the nursing home. Her remaining pillow cases remind the staff about her passion and motivation during the last year and a half of her life.

---

* Therapeutic recreation does not exist as a profession in Finland per se, however many recreation-oriented staff work at facilities and use recreation to promote well-being and quality of life.

Petra Karttunen is a Therapeutic Recreation Coordinator, Medivire Hoiva Ltd Senior Services, Helsinki, Finland. Jari Aho is a Psychology Lecturer at JAMK University of Applied Sciences, Teacher Education College, Jyväskylä, Finland)

Figure 11.24 My Cultural Lens: Well-Being through Finnish Handicrafts

Opportunities for Creating Livable Communities
http://assets.aarp.org/rgcenter/il/2008_02_communities.pdf

Mia Oberlink authored this report for the AARP Public Policy Institute, which presents a number of strategies for facilitating livable communities. Novel approaches are provided to support affordable housing, universal design, mobility and transportation, civic engagement, as well as other activities that increase people's independence, choice, and control. The entire document is available online.

Technical Assistance Center on Positive Behavioral Interventions & Supports
http://www.pbis.org

This website provides many resources for understanding and implementing positive behavioral interventions and supports with a focus on effective school-wide interventions. In addition to Positive Behavior Support, topics include self-assessment, evaluation processes, and bullying prevention (in Spanish and English). Educational videos, newsletters, PowerPoint presentations, conference and training information, and a resource catalog are among their many forward-thinking resources.

Self-Assessment of Learning

LEARNED OPTIMISM

In Chapter 6 *Theories* you learned that optimistic people "make *permanent* and *universal* explanations for good events, as well as *temporary* and *specific* explanations for bad events" (Seligman, 2002, p. 93). Pessimistic people do just the opposite; they give temporary and specific explanations for good events, and permanent and universal explanations for bad events. During the next week, use Seligman's ABCDE model (see Figure 11.11) to address the adverse events that naturally arise in your life. Don't necessarily look for them; simply notice them as they occur. Tune in carefully to your internal dialogue. When negative thoughts and beliefs crop up, notice them and complete the ABCDE exercise.

1. Adversity: _____
2. Belief: _____
3. Consequences: _____
4. Disputation: _____
5. Energization: _____

How might you use this exercise with a participant in your strengths-based therapeutic recreation practice?

SELF-DETERMINATION

Review Table 11.15 in which Bullock et al. (2010) suggest several ways to enhance self-determination through recreation. Drawing from their ideas, give specific examples of how you could encourage self-determination with a participant you know. Describe the conditions under which the opportunity for self-determination and instruction would be given.

Self-Assessment of Learning

12 PROVEN STRATEGIES FOR WELL-BEING
Lyubomirsky (2008) has used rigorous research to document strategies that lead to enhanced well-being and happiness for those who implement those practices in their daily lives. For each strategy listed below, describe how you could integrate this practice into your own life. Describe how you could help participants implement the strategy in their lives through the therapeutic recreation services you provide.

Strategy for Well-Being	How can you implement this strategy in your own life?	How could you implement this strategy with participants into therapeutic recreation services?
Expressing Gratitude		
Cultivating Optimism		
Avoiding Overthinking		
Practicing Acts of Kindness		
Nurturing Social Relationships		
Developing Strategies for Coping		
Learning to Forgive		
Increasing Flow Experiences		
Savoring		
Committing to your Goals		
Practicing Religion and Spirituality		
Meditation		
Physical Activity		
Acting Like a Happy Person		

Self-Assessment of Learning

ASSESS YOUR STRENGTHS-BASED PRACTICES

Green, McAllister, and Tarte (2004) developed the Strengths-Based Practice Inventory to help us assess our ability to implement the strengths approach in our services and programs with participants. Here are items adapted from the inventory that you can use to measure how well you are doing in putting the strengths-based approach into practice. Rate yourself from Strongly Agree (4) to Strongly Disagree (1). The higher your score, the more you are implementing the strengths approach (total possible points equals 64 points).

Empowerment Approach	Strongly Agree (4)	Agree (3)	Disagree (2)	Strongly Disagree (1)
1. I help participants see strengths in themselves they didn't know they had.				
2. I help participants use their own skills and resources to reach goals.				
3. I work together with participants to help them meet their needs.				
4. I help participants see they are good at things.				
5. I encourage participants to think about their own goals or dreams.				
Cultural Competence				
6. I encourage participants to learn about their own culture and history.				
7. I respect participants' cultural and/or religious beliefs.				
8. I have materials for participants that positively reflect their cultural background.				
Sensitivity and Knowledge				
9. I know about other programs participants can use if they need them.				
10. I give participants good information about where to go for services they need.				
11. I understand when something is difficult for participants.				
12. I support participants in the decisions they make about themselves.				
Relationships and Support				
13. I encourage participants to share their knowledge with others.				
14. I provide opportunities for participants to get to know others in the community.				
15. I encourage participants to go to friends and family for help and support.				
16. I encourage participants to get involved in their community.				

The Center for Universal Design
http://www.design.ncsu.edu/cud

According to their website, "The Center for Universal Design (CUD) is a national information, technical assistance, and research center that evaluates, develops, and promotes accessible and universal design in housing, commercial and public facilities, outdoor environments, and products." Their mission is "to improve environments and products through design innovation, research, education and design assistance." The website is based at North Carolina State University.

Therapeutic Recreation Directory
http://www.recreationtherapy.com

The Therapeutic Recreation Directory serves as an online resource for therapeutic recreation specialists who want to share activities, strategies, ideas, and resources. One section of the website is specifically focused on resources, including activity intervention ideas.

References

Abery, B. (2003). Social inclusion through recreation: What's the connection? *Impact, 16*(2), 2–3, 32–33.

Amado, A. N. (1993). *Friendships and community connections between people with and without developmental disabilities.* Baltimore, MD: Paul H. Brookes.

Anderson, L. (1994). *Outdoor adventure recreation and social integration: A social-psychological perspective.* Unpublished dissertation, University of Minnesota. (is available on microfilm, Pub. # 9428906, Ann Arbor, MI: UMI, Inc.).

Anderson, L., & Kress, C. (2003). *Inclusion: Including people with disabilities in parks and recreation opportunities.* State College, PA: Venture Publishing, Inc.

Avedon, E. (1974). *Therapeutic recreation service: An applied behavioral science approach.* Englewood Cliffs, NJ: Prentice-Hall.

Behar, L. (1986). A state model for child mental health services: The North Carolina experience. *Children Today, 15*(3), 16–21.

Benson, P., Roehlkepartain, E. C., & Sesma, Jr., A. (2004, March). Tapping the power of community: Building assets to strengthen substance abuse prevention. *Search Institute Insights & Evidence, 2*(1), 1–14.

Bryant, F., & Veroff, J. (2007). *Savoring: A new model of positive experience.* Mahwah, NJ: Erlbaum and Associates.

Bryant, F. B., Smart, C. M., & King, S. P. (2005). Using the past to enhance the present: Boosting happiness through positive reminiscence. *Journal of Happiness Studies, 6*, 227–260.

Bullock, C., Mahon, M., & Killingsworth, C. (2010). *Introduction to recreation services for people with disabilities: A person-centered approach.* Champaign, IL: Sagamore Press.

Caldwell, J., & Heller, T. (2003). Management of respite and personal assistance services in a consumer-directed family support programme. *Journal of Intellectual Disability Research, 47*(4/5), 352–366.

Caldwell, L. (2004). *Timewise: Taking charge of leisure time.* Scotts Valley, CA: ETR Publishing.

Carruthers, C., & Hood, C. (2007). Building a life of meaning through therapeutic recreation: The Leisure and Well-Being Model, part I. *Therapeutic Recreation Journal, 41*(4), 276–297.

Center for an Accessible Society. (2010). *Universal Design.* Retrieved from http://www.accessiblesociety.org/topics/universaldesign

Center for Universal Design. (1997). *The principles of universal design, version 2.0.* Raleigh, NC: North Carolina State University.

Center for Universal Design. (2010). *About UD.* Retrieved from http://www.design.ncsu.edu/cud/about_ud/about_ud.htm

Children and Nature Network. (2010). *Health benefits to children from contact with nature and the outdoors.* Santa Fe, NM. Children and Nature Network.

Condeluci, A. (1995). *Interdependence: The route to community.* Winter Park, FL: G. R. Press.

Condeluci, A. (2002). Cultural shifting: Community leadership and change. St. Augustine, FL: Training Resources Network.

Corcoran, J. (2005). *Building strengths and skills: A collaborative approach to working with clients.* New York, NY: Oxford University Press.

Cox, K. (2008). Tools for building on youth strengths. *Reclaiming Children and Youth, 16*(4), 19–24.

Crimmins, D., Farrell, A., Smith, P., & Bailey, A. (2007). *Positive strategies for students with behavior problems.* Baltimore, MD: Paul H. Brookes Publishing Co.

Csíkszentmihályi, M. (1990). Flow: *The psychology of optimal experience.* New York, NY: Harper and Row Publishers.

Csíkszentmihályi, M. (1997). *Finding flow: The psychology of engagement with everyday life.* New York, NY: HarperCollins Publishers.

Dattilo, J. (2000). *Facilitation techniques in therapeutic recreation.* State College, PA: Venture Publishing, Inc.

Dattilo, J. (2008). *Leisure education program planning: A systematic approach* (3rd ed.). State College, PA: Venture Publishing, Inc.

Deci, E. L., Koestner, R., & Ryan, R. M. (1999). A meta-analytic review of experiments examining the effects of extrinsic rewards on intrinsic motivation. *Psychological Bulletin, 125*, 627–668.

Dattilo, J., & Murphy, W. (1987). *Behavior modification in therapeutic recreation.* State College, PA: Venture Publishing, Inc.

Dunst, C., & Trivette, C. (2009). Capacity-building family-systems intervention practices. *Journal of Family Social Work, 12*, 119–143.

Ellis, G., Witt, P., & Aguilar, T. (1983). Facilitating "flow" through therapeutic recreation services. *Therapeutic Recreation Journal, 27*(2), 6–15.

Forest, C. (2009). *Mothers overcoming barriers of poverty: The significance of a relationship with a credentialed coach.* Ithaca, NY: Family Development Credential Program.

Fredrickson, B. (2009). *Positivity.* New York, NY: Random House.

Gladwell, M. (2002). *Tipping point: How little things can make a big difference.* New York, NY: Little, Brown, and Company.

Green, F., & Heyne, L. (1997). Friendship. In S. J. Schleien, F. P. Green, & M. T. Ray, *Community recreation and people with disabilities: Strategies for inclusion* (pp. 129–150). Baltimore, MD: Paul H. Brookes Co.

Green, B., McAllister, C., & Tarte, J. (2004). The Strengths-Based Practices Inventory: A tool for measuring strengths-based service delivery in early childhood and family support programs. *Families in Society: The Journal of Contemporary Social Services, 85*(3), 326–334.

Gunn, S., & Peterson, C. (1984). *Therapeutic recreation program design: Principles and procedures* (2nd ed.). San Francisco, CA: Pearson Education, Inc.

Herrington, J., & Oliver, R. (2000). An instructional design framework for authentic learning environments. *Educational Technology Research and Development, 48*(3), 23–48.

Heyne, L., McAvoy, L., & Schleien, S. J. (1994). Focus groups: Bringing people together in therapeutic recreation. *Palaestra, 10*(2), 19–24.

Heyne, L., & Schleien, S. J. (1997). Teaming up with parents to support inclusive recreation. *Parks and Recreation, 32*(5), 76–81.

Heyne, L., Schleien, S. J., & McAvoy, L. (1993). *Making friends: Using recreation activities to promote friendship between children with and without disabilities.* Minneapolis, MN: Institute on Community Integration, University of Minnesota.

Heyne, L., Wilkins, V., & Anderson, L. (2012). Social inclusion in the lunchroom and on the playground at school. *Social Advocacy and Systems Change Journal, 3*(1), 54–68.

Hood, C., & Carruthers, C. (2010). Managing stress to enhance well-being. In Human Kinetics (Ed.). *Dimensions of leisure for life: Individuals and society.* Champaign, IL: Human Kinetics.

Hood, C., & Carruthers, C. (2007). Enhancing leisure experience and developing resources: The

Leisure and Well-Being Model, part II. *Therapeutic Recreation Journal, 41*(4), 298–325.

Horner, R. D., & Keilitz, I. (1975). Training mentally retarded adolescents to brush their teeth. *Journal of Applied Behavior Analysis, 8*, 301–310.

Ittenbach, R., Abery, B., Larson, S., Spiegel, A., & Prouty, R. (1994). Community adjustment of young adults with mental retardation: Overcoming barriers to inclusion. *Palaestra, 10*(2), 32–42.

Iwasaki, Y., Coyle, C., & Shank, J. (2010). Leisure as a context for active living, recovery, health and life quality for persons with mental illness in a global context. *Health Promotion International, 25*(4): 483–494.

Johnson, D., Johnson, R., & Holubec, E. (1991). *Cooperation in the classroom.* Edina, MN: Interaction Book.

Kaplan, J. S., & Carter, J. (1995). *Beyond behavior modification: A cognitive-behavioral approach to behavior management in the school.* Austin, TX: Pro-Ed.

Kretzmann, J. P., & McKnight, J. L. (1993). *Building communities from the inside out: A path toward finding and mobilizing a community's assets.* Evanston, IL: Institute for Policy Research.

Kunstler, R. (2002). Therapeutic recreation in Naturally Occurring Retirement Community (NORC): Benefitting aging in place. *Therapeutic Recreation Journal, 34*(2), 186–202.

Langer, E. (2009). *Counterclockwise: Mindful health and the power of possibility.* New York, NY: Random House, Inc.

Louv, Richard. (2008). *Last child in the woods: Saving our children from nature deficit disorder.* Chapel Hill, NC: Algonquin Books.

Lowe, K., & Felce, D. (1995). How do carers assess the severity of challenging behavior? A total population study. *Journal of Intellectual Disability Research, 39*, 117–29.

Lyubomirsky, S. (2008). *The how of happiness: A scientific approach to getting the life you want.* New York, NY: The Penguin Press.

McClusky, J. (2008). Creating engaging experiences for rehabilitation. *Top Stroke Rehabilitation, 15*(2), 80–86.

McConnell, M. (2001). *Functional behavioral assessment.* Denver, CO: Love Publishing Co.

Mundy, J., & Odum, L. (1998). *Leisure education: Theory and Practice.* Champaign, IL: Sagamore Publishing.

National Council for Therapeutic Recreation. (2012). *Information for the certified therapeutic recreation specialist and new applicants.* New City, NY: NCTRC.

National Council on Disability. (2007, October 1). *Issues in creating livable communities for people with disabilities: Proceedings of the panel.* Washington, DC: Author.

Nolen-Hoeksema, S. (2003). *Women who think too much: How to break free of overthinking and reclaim your life.* New York, NY: Holt.

Oberlink, M. R. (2008). *Opportunities for creating livable communities.* AARP Public Policy Institute: Washington, DC. Retrieved from http://assets.aarp.org/rgcenter/il/2008_02_communities.pdf

O'Brien, J., & Lyle O'Brien, C. (1996). *Members of each other: Building community in company with people with developmental disabilities.* Toronto, ON, Canada: Inclusion Press.

Pedlar, A., Hayworth, L., Hutchinson, P., Taylor, A., & Dunn, P. (1999). *A textured life: Empowerment and adults with developmental disabilities.* Waterloo, ON, Canada: Wilfrid Laurier University Press.

Peterson, C., & Seligman, M. (2004). *Character strengths and virtues: A handbook and classification.* New York, NY: Oxford University Press.

Peterson, C., & Stumbo, N. (2000). *Therapeutic recreation program design: Principles and procedures* (3rd ed.). Boston, MA: Allyn and Bacon.

Phoenix, T., Miller, K., & Schleien, S. (2002). Better to give than receive. *Parks & Recreation, 37*(10), 26–33.

Ratey, J. (2008). *Spark! The revolutionary new science of exercise and the brain.* New York, NY: Little, Brown and Co.

Redelmeier, D., & Kahneman, D. (1996). Patients' memories of painful medical treatments: Real-time and retrospective evaluations of two minimally invasive procedures. *Pain, 116*, 3–8.

Reeves, T., Herrington, J., & Oliver, R. (2002). Authentic activity as a model for Web-based learning. *Annual Meeting of the American Educational Research Association*, New Orleans, LA. Retrieved from http://pbl-online.org/About/characteristics.htm

Rizzolo, M., Hemp, R., Baddock, D., & Schindler, A. (2009, May). Family support services in the United States: 2008. *Policy Research Brief, 20*(2), 1–11.

Sable, J., & Bocarro, J. (2004). Transitioning back to health: Participants' perspective of Project PATH. *Therapeutic Recreation Journal, 38*(2), 206–224.

Sattelmair, J., & Ratey, J. (2009). Physically active play and cognition: An academic matter? *American Journal of Play, Winter*, 365–374.

Schleien, S. J., Green, F., & Ray, T. (1997). *Community recreation and people with disabilities: Strategies for inclusion.* Baltimore, MD: Paul H. Brookes Co.

Schleien, S. J., Kiernan, J., & Wehman, P. (1981). Evaluation of an age-appropriate leisure skills program for moderately retarded adults. *Education & Training in Mental Retardation & Developmental Disabilities, 16*(1), 13–19.

Schleien, S. J., Rynders, J., Heyne, L., & Tabourne, C. (1995). Powerful partnerships: Families and professionals building inclusive recreation programs together. Minneapolis, MN: Institute on Community Integration, University of Minnesota.

Schleien, S. J., Wehman, P., & Kiernan, J. (1981). Teaching leisure skills to severely handicapped adults: An age-appropriate darts game. *Journal of Applied Behavior Analysis, 14*(4), 513–519.

Seigel, R. (2008). *Positive behavior supports.* Retrieved from http://www.pbis.org

Seligman, M. (1991). *Learned optimism.* New York, NY: Alfred A. Knopf.

Seligman, M. (2002). *Authentic happiness: Using the new positive psychology to realize your full potential for lasting fulfillment.* New York, NY: Free Press.

Seligman, M., Steen, T., Park, N., & Peterson, C. (2005). Positive psychology progress: Empirical validation of interventions. *American Psychologist, 60*, 410–421.

Shank, J., & Coyle, C. (2002). *Therapeutic recreation in health promotion and rehabilitation.* State College, PA: Venture Publishing, Inc.

Sigafoos, J., Arthur, M., & O'Reilly, M. (2003). *Challenging behavior & developmental disability.* Philadelphia, PA: Whurr Publishers.

Slavkin, M. (2004). *Authentic learning.* Lanham, MD: Rowman and Littlefield Publishing.

Stumbo, N. (1997). *Leisure education III: More goal-oriented activities.* State College, PA: Venture Publishing, Inc.

Stumbo, N. (1998). *Leisure education IV: Activities for individuals with substance addictions.* State College, PA: Venture Publishing, Inc.

Stumbo, N. (2002a). *Leisure education I: A manual of activities.* State College, PA: Venture Publishing, Inc.

Stumbo, N. (2002b). *Leisure education II: More activities and resources.* State College, PA: Venture Publishing, Inc.

Stumbo, N., & Peterson, C. (2004). *Therapeutic recreation program design: Principles and procedures* (4th ed.). San Francisco, CA: Pearson Education, Inc.

Sylvester, C. (2009). A virtue-based approach to therapeutic recreation practice. *Therapeutic Recreation Journal, 43*(3), 9–25.

Sylvester, C., Voekl, J., & Ellis, G. (2001). *Therapeutic recreation programming: Theory and practice.* State College, PA: Venture Publishing.

Test, D., Fowler, C., Wood, W., Brewer, D., & Eddy, S. (2005). A conceptual framework for self-advocacy for students with disabilities. *Remedial and Special Education, 26*(1), 43–54.

U.S. Department of Health and Human Services. (2010). *Community Living Initiative.* Retrieved from http://www.hhs.gov/od/topics/community/keyadvances.html

Universal Design Alliance. (2010). *What is Universal Design?* Retrieved from http://www.universaldesign.org/universaldesign1.htm

Walker, J., & Bruns, E. (2006). Building on practice-based evidence: Using expert perspectives to define the wraparound process. *Psychiatric Services, 57*, 1579–1585.

Wilhite, B., Keller, J., Hodges, J., & Caldwell, L. (2004). Enhancing human development and optimizing health and well-being in persons with multiple sclerosis. *Therapeutic Recreation Journal, 38*(2), 167–187.

Wilkins, V. (n.d.). *Activity analysis: Fine-tuning an essential skill.* Unpublished manuscript.

Chapter 12
TRANSITION AND INCLUSION IN STRENGTHS-BASED THERAPEUTIC RECREATION PRACTICE

The iris is a transition plant, growing in the rich zones between land and water, and is a sign that summer is here at last.

"When everyone is included, everyone wins."
—*Jesse Jackson*

OVERVIEW OF CHAPTER 12

- Transition and inclusion: A common purpose
- Transition services
  - Transition defined
  - Transition planning
- Inclusion
  - What is inclusion?
  - What does inclusion mean?
  - Rationale for inclusion
  - Inclusion as a therapeutic intervention
  - Inclusion and the therapeutic recreation process

FOCUS QUESTIONS

- What do planning for transition services and planning for inclusion have in common?
- What does transition mean, and what benchmarks can we use to gauge successful transition?
- What is inclusion, and why is it important?
- What are the proven beneficial outcomes of inclusive recreation?
- How can inclusive recreation be used as a means of therapeutic intervention using the therapeutic recreation process?
- How is inclusive recreation facilitated and how do we judge its effectiveness?

TRANSITION AND INCLUSION: A COMMON PURPOSE

A participant who is preparing to be discharged from a facility (i.e., transition) and a participant who wishes to participate in a public recreation program in the community (i.e., inclusion) face many of the same issues and questions: How and where can I participate in my favorite recreational activities? What recreation resources are available to me in my community? What accommodations and supports will I need to participate as fully as possible? What barriers to participation might I experience, and how can they be negotiated or removed? Whether a participant is connecting with community recreation services for the first time, or reconnecting after a serious illness or injury, both share a common purpose: participation in community recreation. Because of this mutual objective, we address the topics of transition and inclusion together in this chapter. As you will see, inclusion is an aspect of transition, and transition is an aspect of inclusion as it is, in itself, a kind of transition.

Similar to any other therapeutic recreation service, planning for transition and inclusion requires close attention to the internal strengths of participants and to the external strengths and resources of the community. We begin this chapter by presenting an overview of transition services, and then look at inclusion as a core principle and value that is relevant to transition. Strategies for connecting participant's goals and aspirations with community resources—central to both transition and inclusion—are then presented. Since there is no one cookie-cutter approach to transition or inclusion services, we provide more Life Stories in this chapter than in previous chapters to illustrate the many creative ways therapeutic recreation specialists can help shape individualized transition services.

Transition Services Defined

A definition of transition:
A process of change; a process or period in which something undergoes a change and passes from one state, stage, form, or activity to another

"Transition is not a discrete time in life affecting only the individual and one aspect of his or her functioning. Rather, transition is part of a lifelong process that begins at birth, relates to all life roles and affects the individual, family and community."

—Edna Mora Szymanski (1994)

What do we mean by transition? In broad terms, transition is a lifelong process of passing through the developmental stages of the life cycle—from childhood, through adolescence, and into adulthood and the elder years. For the purposes of this book, transition is a participant's movement from different types of services or from one setting to another. Participants typically transition to services or a setting in which they can enjoy greater independence such as to their own home, to an independent living arrangement, or from inpatient to outpatient services. Unfortunately, if a participant's condition worsens, she or he may need to move to a facility that offers more intensive services, such as to assisted living, a nursing home, or hospice care, if those intensive services cannot be provided in the current living situation. The broad transitions of the human life cycle and a participant's transition to new services or settings can carry a similar mix of emotions and implications: uncertainty, challenge, opportunity, and hope, to name a few. For these reasons, careful planning is essential during times of transition, so a participant's vision of how she or he wants to experience life is reflected in the new situation.

Educational services for students with disabilities give us a well-developed model and definition of transition, which translates well to other settings where therapeutic recreation is practiced. Transition in educational settings refers to the movement of students from school life to adult community life. The Individuals with Disabilities Education Act (IDEA) of 2004, originally Public Law 94 142 the Education for All Handicapped Children Act of 1975, requires schools to include transition goals in the Individualized Education Plans of students by the age 16. IDEA 2004 offers a definition of transition that is both person-centered and strengths-based. The portion of the definition that is the most relevant for therapeutic recreation services follows:

The term "transition services" means a coordinated set of activities for a child with a disability that… is designed to be within a results-oriented process that is focused on improving the academic and functional achievement of the child with a disability to facilitate the child's movement from school to post-school activities, including postsecondary education, vocational education, integrated employment (including supported employment), continuing and adult education, adult services, independent living, or community participation. (U.S. Department of Education, 2010)

As you can see, this definition emphasizes the importance of *coordinated* activities for successful transition as well as a focus on *results* and *community inclusion*. Community connections are particularly relevant to recreation services. Connecting activities refers to a "flexible set of services, accommodations, and supports that help youth gain access to and achieve success within chosen post-school options" (NASET, 2010, p. 12; see Figure 12.1). Among these options is "participation in leisure or recreational activities." Examples of partnering agencies in the area or leisure and recreation include parks and recreation, community events, community education, YM/WCA and other fitness and educational facilities, special education, transition services, among others. The coordinated and comprehensive approach to educational transition services offers therapeutic recreation a model for transition planning across the multiple settings in which we work.

Transition Planning

Transition planning, also called discharge planning (particularly in inpatient, outpatient, and residential facilities), is a vital part of the therapeutic recreation process. While transition occurs toward the end of the therapeutic recreation process, planning for discharge and transition should begin during the first few days of service (Bullock & Mahon, 1997; Shank & Coyle, 2002).

According to Bullock and Mahon (1997), transition planning provides an important sense of continuity for the participant. The therapeutic recreation specialist and the participant review the progress that has been made toward accomplishing goals and objectives, and anticipate future challenges and supports that may be needed in the new situation. Ideally, early planning allows the participant to visit the settings or experience the services she or he will experience upon discharge. Bullock and Mahon elaborate,

"Comprehensive transition planning involves exploration of the places, people, opportunities, and resources that will be part of the individual's life; exploration of the supports available to him; and identification of 'next steps' for his development" (p. 337).

From Barriers to Solutions

When planning for transition, one inevitably encounters barriers (Bogenschutz & Breitenstein, 2010; Bullock & Mahon, 1997). Obstacles may be internal or external. Obstacles that are internal to the participant might include a perceived lack of ability, fear of failure, lack of motivation or energy, limited finances, or doubts about the importance of leisure, among others. Common external barriers could include a lack of transportation, poor psychosocial support, or limited leisure resources. Bogenschutz and Breitenstein (2010) emphasize the importance of focusing on solutions, not problems, when one comes across transition barriers. Figure 12.2 presents suggestions for how therapeutic recreation specialists can respond to hurdles creatively

A leader in setting the tone for results-oriented collaborative partnerships is the National Alliance for Secondary Education and Transition (NASET), a national coalition of over 40 organizations and advocacy groups related to education, career development, youth development, and multiculturalism. NASET calls for an interagency team process in which decision-making is shared with youth and families to link youth to the services, accommodations, and supports needed to participate successfully in community activities as an adult.

Based on recent research, NASET has developed national standards and quality indicators for successful post-school transition for students with disabilities in five main content areas: schooling, career preparatory experiences, youth development and leadership, family involvement, and community connections.

You can download the national standards at http://www.nasetalliance.org/index.htm.

Figure 12.1 NASET – A Leader in Transition Planning

Compare/Contrast: From Transition Barriers to Solutions

TRANSITION BARRIERS	TRANSITION SOLUTIONS
Internal Barriers and Solutions	
"I can't do what I want to"	Identify adaptations to support participation
"I only want to focus on PT/OT"	Incorporate PT/OT goals into TR
"I am afraid to go out"	Start small with a local outing
"How will recreation help me?"	Talk about changes in time usage
"I'm not motivated to do anything"	Work on activities that the participant enjoys
"I don't have any money"	Look into programs or activities that offer scholarships, are low-cost, or free
External Barriers and Solutions	
"I live in a small town"	Encourage participation at the local active YMCA or other community center
"I don't have any transportation"	Teach participant to use public transportation; help family members find incentive to drive; explore car pools and other natural supports
"I don't have enough social support"	Provide peer support from other participants or other natural supports in the community

Figure 12.2 Compare/Contrast: From Transition Barriers to Solutions *(adapted from Bogenschutz and Breitenstein, 2010)*

and collaboratively based on their professional expertise. As you will discover later in this chapter, the same creativity and coordinated services that are necessary for realizing effective transitions are also indispensable when planning for successful inclusion.

Transition Planning Process

Transition planning will vary from agency to agency and from individual to individual. Benzanson (2005) suggests a systematic approach to transition planning that may be used across multiple settings based on her experience assisting nursing home residents who are moving back to the community. She emphasizes that transitions are most effective when a participant is highly invested in the transition process and motivated to do well. Beyond that, transition requires planning, planning, and more planning. This preparation means methodically thinking through everything the participant will need to succeed in the new setting or with new services. It also means involving, as much as is possible, all the diverse stakeholders in every stage of the process. Benzanson recommends the following approaches for effective transition planning:

- Explore with the participant all the options that are available to her or him.
- Listen to the participant's story and make certain she or he has a strong voice in expressing preferences and making decisions.
- Emphasize that community living arrangements can provide healthier outcomes than institutional placements and lead to greater life satisfaction.
- Actively share resources and collaborate with families, professionals, and providers.
- Explore the degree to which the community infrastructure can support individuals through transition.

Wherever the formal infrastructure does not support the participant, the gaps in services may be filled in by tapping into the informal supports that arise naturally through relationships with family and friends and through volunteers from community groups such as social clubs and faith communities. It is important to acknowledge that the more complex the participant's needs, the longer the transition process is likely to take. Benzanson recommends that a comprehensive transition plan include the following components:

1. Participant interview focused on transition goals, dreams, and hopes
2. Person-centered planning based on transition goals
3. Development of the transition team (e.g., participant, family, friends, other supportive people)
4. Assessment of medical needs
5. Assessment of support needs
6. Assessment of gaps in community infrastructure
7. Solutions to fill community gaps
8. Concrete plan
9. Contract with participant
10. Timelines and checklists
11. Quality assurance and improvement
12. Planning for the transition day(s)

Even with the most careful transition planning, therapeutic recreation specialists need to expect the unexpected. Follow-up services are important to assure the participant has the supports and confidence they need to work through unexpected challenges. In most instances participants will need time to adjust to their new lives and gradually gain independence. Therefore, transition needs to be seen as a dynamic process that may require long-term follow-up. The best transition services provide follow-up procedures in an ongoing way as support is needed.

Documenting the Transition or Discharge Plan

A discharge summary is typically the final form of documentation and evaluation that a participant receives at an inpatient or outpatient facility. While most agencies provide their own guidelines for the format and content of a discharge plan (Peterson & Stumbo, 2000), discharge plans typically include some common elements. In Chapter 13 *Evaluation* we identify the necessary aspects of a written discharge plan. Because of its relevance to this discussion on transition, we preview this information here by providing a summary of the key components of a therapeutic recreation discharge plan:

- Therapeutic recreation assessment summary
- Summary of therapeutic recreation services provided

- Comparison of pre-assessment scores with post-assessment results
- Progress toward goals, objectives, and other outcomes, and dates when achieved
- Status at discharge or end of service
- Any remaining areas the participant would like to focus on
- Recommendations, including any follow up, referrals, community resources, and post-discharge instructions

Transition Life Stories

As noted earlier, because the procedures for discharge and transition planning vary across settings, we offer several Life Story features in this chapter to give you a sense of how transition planning differs for various individuals and circumstances. Life Stories that emphasize transition planning from "day one" in adult and adolescent behavioral services appear in Figures 12.3 (pp. 343–344) and 12.4 (p. 345), respectively. Figure 12.5 (p. 346) provides a cultural perspective on transition planning. Figure 12.6 (p. 347) depicts transition in physical rehabilitation services, and Figure 12.7 (p. 348) describes an example of transition and inclusion through the Inclusive Recreation Resource Center. Figure 12.8 (p. 349) tells the story of DeMario Chandler who fulfills a dream to attend college through the postsecondary educational program, Beyond Academics, in collaboration with the University of North Carolina at Greensboro. We hope these stories inspire you to give therapeutic recreation transition and inclusion planning the careful attention they deserve to help participants live full and active lives in their home communities.

INCLUSION

As stated earlier, inclusion is an important aspect of transition and represents, in itself, a kind a transition in a participant's life. Recent trends in human services, and on a larger scale, societal attitudes, have led us to a place where inclusion of all people in the life of the community is valued (see Table 12.1, p. 342). In the remainder of this chapter, we explore the concept of inclusion and its significance to therapeutic recreation practice.

What is Inclusion?

A definition of inclusion:
Being a member of a whole; encompass or embrace as part of a whole

Inclusion is a word that has evolved from two previous terms that had a similar meaning, *mainstreaming* and *integration*. The term mainstreaming first came into usage in the 1970s with the enactment of Public Law 94-142, the Education for All Handicapped Children Act in 1975. This landmark legislation mandated a free and appropriate public education for children and youth with disabilities in the least restrictive environment. Now codified as the Individuals with Disabilities Education Act, or IDEA, this law has revolutionized the way in which educational services have been delivered for nearly four decades. When educators and other professionals first attempted to "mainstream" youth with disabilities into regular education classrooms and recreation settings, teachers, students, families, classrooms, schools, and communities were largely unprepared for this social experiment. Before long, stories emerged of students with disabilities showing up in classrooms and programs without the supports they needed and with professionals ill-equipped to include them. While administrators had good intentions, professionals and families perceived that people with disabilities were being "dumped" into settings without adequate preparation.

To dispel the negative implications of the word mainstreaming, a new term was coined, *integration*, borrowed from the Civil Rights Movement from 1955 to 1968. The emphasis on people's rights made integration a term that inspired many professionals in the 1980s to work tirelessly to develop practical strategies and approaches to support the education and recreation of children with disabilities in typical settings. Professionals were trained, curricula adapted, related services (including therapeutic recreation) provided, alternative communication devices put in place, and information shared about people with disabilities. It was a fruitful and creative time, which enabled many people with disabilities to participate with their peers without disabilities. However, people again began to notice shortcomings in this approach: Although students with disabilities were *physically* in the setting, they really were not an integral *part* of the group. They rarely interacted with others without disabilities and, in a sense, remained segregated from the majority.

While the integration innovations of the 1980s were indeed impressive, professionals and parents began to realize that the proponents of IDEA had more in mind than the physical placement of students with disabilities in typical settings. They recognized it was not enough for youth with disabilities to be in the same material space as peers without disabilities;

Table 12.1 Position Statement on Inclusion

National Recreation and Parks Association (NRPA)
(produced by the National Therapeutic Recreation Society,
a former branch of NRPA)

Position Statement on Inclusion

The following is an excerpt from the Position Statement on Inclusion, approved by the Board of Directors of the National Therapeutic Recreation Society on October 30, 1997:

Purpose

The purpose of the National Therapeutic Recreation Society's (NTRS) Position Statement on Inclusion is to encourage all providers of park, recreation, and leisure services to provide opportunities in settings where people of all abilities can recreate and interact together.

This document articulates a commitment to the leisure process and the desired outcomes. Accordingly, the NTRS Position Statement on Inclusion encompasses these broad concepts and beliefs:

Right to Leisure

- The pursuit of leisure is a condition necessary for human dignity and well-being.
- Leisure is a part of a healthy lifestyle and a productive life.
- Every individual is entitled to the opportunity of express unique interests and pursue, develop and improve talents and abilities
- People are entitled to opportunities and services in the most inclusive setting.
- The right to choose from the full array of recreation opportunities offered in diverse settings and environments and requiring different levels of competency should be provided.

Quality of Life

- People grow and develop throughout the lifespan.
- Through leisure an individual gains an enhanced sense of competence and self-direction.
- A healthy leisure lifestyle can prevent illness and promote wellness.
- The social connection with one's peers plays a major role in his/her life satisfaction.
- The opportunity to choose is an important component in one's quality of life; individual choices will be respected.

Support, Assistance and Accommodations

- Inclusion is most effective when support, assistance and accommodations are provided.
- Support, assistance and accommodations can and should be responsive to people's needs and preferences.
- Support, assistance and accommodations should create a safe and fun environment, remove real and artificial barriers to participation, and maximize not only the independence but also the interdependence of the individual. People want to be self-sufficient.
- Support, assistance and accommodations may often vary and are typically individualized. Types of support, assistance and accommodations include, but are not limited to: qualified staff, adaptive equipment, alternative formats for printed or audio materials, trained volunteers, or flexibility in policies and program rules.

Barrier Removal

- Environments should be designed to encourage social interaction, "risk-taking," fun, choices and acceptance that allow for personal accomplishment in a cooperative context.
- Physical barriers should be eliminated to facilitate full participation by individuals with disabilities.
- Attitudinal barriers in all existing and future recreation services should be removed or minimized through education and training of personnel (staff, volunteers, students, and/or community at-large).

Life Story:

A Strengths Approach to Discharge or Transition Planning in Adult Mental Health

Co-authored with Maureen Fessenden, CTRS and Stacey Caskey

On the adult behavioral services unit at Cayuga Medical Center (CMC), where we provide acute care, discharge planning starts from the moment we know a client will be coming on the unit. Transition planning continues during the assessment process, throughout planning and implementing interventions, up until the person is ready to leave the unit, and even after the person has been discharged. By considering discharge in every phase of treatment, we can help ensure a client's needs and hopes for the future are supported.

A diverse team of specialists is involved in discharge planning: a psychiatrist, psychologist, nurse, social worker, therapeutic recreation specialist, dietitian, chaplain, program director, and program manager. However, the most important member of the discharge planning team is the client. Input from clients is crucial to the success of their treatment, and they are involved in every step of the therapeutic process.

Our assessment consists of three parts: (a) a historical and physical assessment conducted by the physician, (b) a psychosocial assessment conducted by the social work assistant, and (c) the recreation assessment conducted by the therapeutic recreation specialist. As the team gets to know the client through the assessment, team members are already planning for discharge. Every discipline has a role in discharge planning, whether it is by providing informational handouts, referrals, or direct services. Therapeutic recreation services, for instance, build self-awareness, self-confidence, leisure awareness, and coping skills through leisure education. We also provide information about community recreation resources and inform agencies if a client could benefit from their services. Following are some of the other unique features of discharge planning at CMC.

Individualized Treatment Plan

As part of the planning process, each client develops a personal Individualized Treatment Plan. In the plan clients identify their primary issues, goals, strengths, and hopes for the future. They sketch their top three stressors in the form of a pie chart, indicating the magnitude of the stressor by the size of the slice of pie. Stressors commonly revolve around relationships, living situations, support services, mental or physical illness, finances, work, and/or college life. Alleviating these top stressors, along with building upon the person's strengths and hopes for the future, become integral components of the individual's treatment plan.

Community Resources Group

We are fortunate to collaborate with several community organizations that offer our clients a variety of support services. Rather than simply giving clients a list of community resources, we have found it much more effective to invite agency representatives to the unit once a week to meet clients and talk directly with them. Here are some of the agencies that participate regularly in the Community Resources group:

- *Advocacy Center*, an agency that supports individuals who have experienced domestic violence or child sexual abuse
- *Alcoholics Anonymous* (AA), which offers a fellowship of men and women who help each other achieve sobriety and stay sober
- *Compos Mentis*, an organization that offers adults with mental illness opportunities to engage in community farming as a means of developing patience, orderly discipline, self-confidence, hope, and a connection with nature.
- *Emotions Anonymous*, a 12-step organization similar to AA that helps individuals recover from emotional difficulties
- *Finger Lakes Independence Center*, which seeks to empower people with disabilities while creating an inclusive society
- *Mental Health Association*, an agency that provides mental health services to recipients, families, and providers
- *The Learning Web*, an organization that offers young people opportunities for exploration, building skills, and meaningful participation in the community based on the Developmental Assets model of the Search Institute

Clients who have already used some of the community services that are represented at the meeting often discuss their experiences and offer "peer counsel" to other group members. We've found that peer recommendations are particularly effective in motivating clients to seek services upon discharge. Our clients often teach *us* about new community resources!

Figure 12.3a Life Story: A Strengths Approach to Discharge or Transition Planning in Adult Mental Health

Life Story (cont'd):

A Strengths Approach to Discharge or Transition Planning in Adult Mental Health

Co-authored with Maureen Fessenden, CTRS and Stacey Caskey

Wellness Recovery Action Plan

Just prior to discharge, each client receives a packet of materials called the Wellness Recovery Action Plan (WRAP), which the client individualizes towards their life situation and treatment. The packet includes information clients have contributed about their "triggers," their reflections on the reasons that brought them to the unit, how they want their futures to look, and strategies to improve their emotional well-being and mental health when they return to the community. Clients are encouraged to share the WRAP with people in their support network, who can then notice if the client isn't doing well, talk with them, and remind them of the supports they identified while on the unit that will help get them back on track.

Assertive Community Treatment

Everything about our treatment and discharge services is designed to help people live independently, build connections with people and resources in the community, and cope successfully with the stressors they encounter. Sometimes, however, clients return home and have difficulty making the transition. On the unit there was structure, someone to cook meals, social support, and medication that was administered regularly. Some people find it difficult to suddenly be responsible for providing all these things for themselves. This is where Assertive Community Treatment (ACT) comes in. ACT is a mobile hospital, independent from CMC, whose services we rely upon heavily when our clients need them. ACT is staffed by a psychiatrist, psychologist, nurse, social worker, and vocational counselor that travels to wherever the client lives. Those who use the program usually live in rural areas, have no transportation, and have had repeat hospitalizations. Twice a week ACT meets clients at their homes, or takes them out for coffee or lunch, and provides the support they need until they gain self-sufficiency.

As a final transition service, all clients are called within 5 days of returning home to see how they are doing and whether they need anything. If a person requires extra support, additional information on resources and referrals are provided.

Recently, clients who had been on our unit completed a survey about their stay and treatment. Of all the professionals on the unit, the recreation therapy department was given the highest rating! Therapeutic recreation was considered the most effective service the unit had to offer. We think this feedback was due not only to the care clients received on the unit, but also to the ways clients are involved in discharge planning so they have the support they need for the transition back home.

Maureen Fessenden is a Recreation Therapist and Stacey Caskey is a Social Work Assistant with Behavioral Services at Cayuga Medical Center in Ithaca, NY.

Figure 12.3b Life Story: A Strengths Approach to Discharge or Transition Planning in Adult Mental Health (cont'd)

social interaction and relationships also needed to occur. Consequently, a new term was proposed, *inclusion*, implying that people with disabilities need to be physically *and* socially included in programs. Creating learning environments in which all people are welcome, valued, and accepted, and who interact together on a regular basis, took on a new emphasis. As such, inclusion signifies a deeper connection to others than the terms mainstreaming or integration; it implies community belonging.

The development of inclusion philosophy and practice in recreation services has paralleled the trajectory of services in inclusive education. While you may still hear people use the terms mainstreaming and integration in educational and recreational settings, the preferred term today is inclusion. Using this term conveys to others that you are knowledgeable about the distinctions among the three terms and that you are aware of the intent and philosophy associated with the inclusion movement. It also conveys to others that you are familiar with the theories associated with inclusion that you learned in Chapter 6 *Theories*—theories such as Normalization, social role valorization, self-determination, and self-advocacy—and how they support inclusivity. In the following section we explore more deeply the implications of inclusion.

What does Inclusion Mean Today?

"Inclusion means recognizing we are all one, even though we are not the same."

—*Shafik Abu Tahir*

Life Story:

Involving Families in Discharge or Transition Planning in Adolescent Mental Health

by Debbie Seligman Kratil, CTRS

At the adolescent behavioral services unit at Cayuga Medical Center (CMC), like the adult unit (see Figure 12.2), discharge planning starts upon admission. A good discharge takes time to plan as all options need to be reviewed and all individuals need to agree on the plan. We have the same transdisciplinary team members as the adult unit, and we use the same assessment process. An element that adds to the difficulty in effective discharge planning is that there are fewer services and programs for adolescents than adults, and at least 50% of the clients we serve are not from our community or county. In 2009, only 35% of our clients were from Tompkins County, where our hospital is located, and the other 65% represented 19 other counties.

Our goal is to support teens on the unit by helping them build various internal skills and attitudes they can use upon discharge. Through leisure education, we focus on improving communication and social skills, stress management, self-esteem, developing healthy boundaries, and reducing negative thinking. We also have an hour and half recreation group every day, where the teens can learn new skills and games, and practice how to share, negotiate, and be a good sport. To further support the client, the CTRS may research the availability of recreation and leisure programs such as Big Brothers/Big Sisters, summer camp, 4-H, YMCA programs, and intramural sports.

For us, discharge planning would amount to nothing without including the families – what they are willing and able to do, what resources are available, and what other support services they will need when the teen is discharged. Because most of our clients will return to their family and home, a focus of their treatment is on improving family relationships. Sometimes teens come to the unit wanting staff to find them a new family or convince their family members to change. As part of the discharge planning process, the doctor and social worker hold family meetings to address everyone's concerns and problem solve solutions. Sometimes there may be two or three of these meetings before everyone feels comfortable with the treatment and discharge plan.

When families need extra support upon discharge, we may recommend family therapy, dialectical behavior therapy groups, anger management groups, working with the Committee on Special Education (CSE), and/or an application for other services through Single Point of Access (SPOA). Every school district has a CSE that can review, address, and plan for a teen's school needs, with services ranging from in-home tutoring or instruction to alternative school programs. SPOAs are county-based committees that work with youth who need extra outpatient services from multiple service systems to help them succeed in their home communities. SPOAs review referrals for case management, waiver services, and mental health, special education, legal, probation, child welfare, health, or family services. Teens are also offered supports through respite, family advocates, and evaluations for out-of-home placements.

The hope of the adolescent transdisciplinary team is to provide comprehensive treatment for teens while they are on the unit and a discharge plan that supports them and their families in maintaining overall health and wellness.

Debbie Seligman Kratil is a Recreation Therapist with Behavioral Services at Cayuga Medical Center in Ithaca, NY.

Figure 12.4 Life Story: Involving Families in Discharge or Transition Planning in Adolescent Mental Health

Inclusion is a far-reaching concept with subtle implications for how people with and without disabilities relate to each other. According to researchers in inclusive recreation (Anderson & Kress, 2003; Anderson, Penny McGee, & Wilkins, 2010; Dattilo, 2002.; Heyne, Schleien, & McAvoy, 1993; Schleien, Ray, Green, 1997), inclusion has the following connotations:

- Everyone has the same choices and opportunities for recreation participation.
- People with disabilities participate with others that share their interests, not their disability.
- People are welcomed, appreciated, and accepted for who they are, regardless of their ability level.
- Participants have the supports and accommodations they need to participate in recreation as fully as possible.
- Opportunities exist to interact socially and make friends.
- Recreation areas and facilities are architecturally accessible.
- Inclusive recreation creates a sense of belonging.

My Cultural Lens:

Planning Transition Services that are Culturally Sensitive

Leake, Black, and Roberts (2004) note that educational transition services often assume that youth with disabilities and their families value the individualistic outcomes typically associated with mainstream U.S. culture. For example, these outcomes usually include self-determination, self-reliance, and independent living. Many youth and families, however, do not value these outcomes and, instead, attach special significance to a collectivist orientation. The authors draw the following distinctions between individualistic and collectivist oriented cultures:

Individualism: people are viewed as distinct entities; as people mature into adulthood, they are expected to move from dependence to independence and self-reliance; emphasis is placed on individual rights, pursuing personal interests and goals, and adhering to one's values and beliefs; individuals create relationships according to their preferences and interests

Collectivism: people are seen as part of the fabric of a group, such as a family, neighborhood, or tribe; maturation into adulthood requires that people move from dependence to interdependence; emphasis is placed on the obligations of the person's role in the group, working in an interdependent fashion to achieve group success, and adhering to the group's traditional values; people have a sense of shared biographies and are defined by their relationships with others

The authors also compare individualistic values with ones that are collectivist in nature:

Individualistic Values
- Individual competitiveness
- Personal achievement
- Self-determination and individual choice
- Postsecondary education
- Independent living and self-reliance
- Creating a transition plan on paper

Collectivist Values
- Group competitiveness
- Group achievement
- Group or hierarchical decision-making
- Contributing to family through wages
- Interdependence and residing with family
- Establishing close personal relationships among youth, family, and professionals

Because there is so much variation among the cultural values of different racial and ethnic groups and subgroups, the authors stress that each person's situation needs to be considered individually. They encourage professionals to examine their own cultural values and assumptions, to explain the implications of individualistic and collectivist goals, and to work collaboratively with youth and families to develop the most appropriate transition plan.

When planning for transition we need to be especially careful to accommodate collectivist values and behaviors, to offset the individualistic cultural assumptions we often bring to our work. Which orientation – individualism or collectivism – is most closely aligned with your own values? Which orientation do the people with whom you work or study value? How can you make sure your own orientation doesn't override a participant's values? What are the implications of each orientation for transition planning?

Figure 12.5 My Cultural Lens: Planning Transition Services that are Culturally Sensitive

Another way to understand what inclusion means is to ask what it does not mean (Anderson & Kress, 2003; Anderson, Penney McGee, & Wilkins, 2011). Inclusion does not mean having large groups of people with disabilities in one program. Inclusion does not mean disrupting the natural proportion of individuals with and without disabilities as reflected in the community. For every five people in America, roughly one of them will have a disability (Disabled in Action, 2010), and this 1 to 5 proportion needs to be mirrored when forming recreational groups (see Figure 12.9, p. 350, for a Life Story about applying the concept of natural proportions). Additionally, inclusion does not mean taking a vanload of people with disabilities on a community outing. Planning for inclusion should always occur on an individualized, not a group, basis. In sum, the spirit of inclusion calls for both individualization of services and social interaction with people with varying abilities.

Rationale for Inclusion

Sometimes a student will ask us, "What's the big deal about inclusion? Of course, people with disabilities should be able to go to whatever recreation program they choose." For those who have grown up in the last 20 years, it may not be apparent that any other model has existed for delivering recreation programs and services but inclusion. Sadly, however, this has not always

Life Story:

Helping with Transition from Rehabilitation to Community Living

by Whitney Mayer, CTRS

I am a therapeutic recreation specialist and I love my job! I am excited to go to work every day and, although it takes a lot of patience and the right kind of person to do it, it does not really seem like work at all. I work at Sheltering Arms Physical Rehabilitation Hospital in Richmond, Virginia in a day therapeutic recreation program called *Club Rec*. Through a holistic approach, Club Rec focuses on enhancing the quality of life for individuals who can benefit from a supervised social, recreational, or wellness program. We offer structured programs, organized and implemented by therapeutic recreation specialists, to help individuals transition from the rehabilitation hospital, adapt to life after injury or illness, and lead a healthy life.

Club Rec members have access to
- Organized recreation programs
- Health and leisure education
- Coping skills group
- Use of recreation/adaptive equipment
- Access to the computer lab
- Use of the onsite fitness center *(equipment designed for people with limited movement)*
- Use of the therapeutic pool
- Group outings
- Accessible travel program
- Community service projects
- Communication group

Most of the members of the group have had a stroke or a brain injury, while some have other disabilities. Most of our participants are referred after receiving services at the hospital. When they are getting discharged from the hospital, they come over and check out our program to decide if they would like to try it out. Members come for 1 to 5 days per week. There is a charge, but we have a sliding scale to accommodate people with financial needs. We do all sorts of programs – basically whatever the members request is fair game. We have offered everything from skiing to an accessible travel program which goes on a cruise every other year! The participants are so appreciative and really love coming to the program. It is very well supported by the hospital. Every day about 20 people tell me "thank you" for working here and I really should be thanking them.

One weekend we went camping on the Potomac River. While it was a nice time, it was not anything out of the ordinary. On the way home, one of the members started crying. She is a 40-year-old woman who had a stroke. I asked why she was crying and she said that she was just so happy because it was the best weekend of her life. Things like that happen every day and it makes me so appreciative that this is my job! If you are considering therapeutic recreation as a profession I would strongly recommend it. It is one of the few jobs where you can go home every day and feel that you really made a difference in someone's life!

Figure 12.6 Life Story: Helping with Transition from Rehabilitation to Community

been the case in our society. Historically speaking, inclusion is a very recent concept and phenomenon and, for this reason, it is crucial that therapeutic recreation specialists develop the competencies to practice in this area of service from which so many people—both with and without disabilities—can benefit. Therapeutic recreation professionals need to be educated in inclusion methods to affect social justice and provide equal opportunities for recreation participation for everyone, with all the ensuing beneficial outcomes.

When people with disabilities predominantly lived in institutions (and many still do), participation in any kind of activity was entirely hidden and separate from conventional society. When the unspeakable conditions of institutions were exposed in the 1960s, and people with disabilities began to move to community residences, no community recreation programs and services were available to them. This transitional period, which marked the beginning of the movement from institutional to community living for people with disabilities, would have been an ideal time to initiate inclusion as the preferred model for delivering services. Public outrage against the appalling circumstances in institutions was high, and a full humanitarian response could have called for embracing people with varying abilities in all walks of life, including recreation. Due to the myths, stereotypes, and misconceptions prevalent at the time, however, society opted for a variation of the

Life Story:

Successful Transitions Through Therapeutic Recreation

by Laurie Penney McGee, CTRS

As a Certified Therapeutic Recreation Specialist, I feel that it is an honor and a privilege to get to know people through their recreation and play. I have been lucky to work in this field with people of all ages in many settings, including both after school programs and community recreation centers. Once I was surprised and delighted to learn that a child who had not been permitted to attend his after school program without the assistance of an inclusion staff had just won a basketball trophy at the center's weekend program, a program he was attending on his own. In another instance, one of the teens in the inclusion program took one of his art projects and submitted it to the school's art contest. His piece was featured in the local newspaper!

At the Inclusive Recreation Resource Center, the Recreation Referral Service utilizes the therapeutic recreation process to assist people to discover their recreation goals and dreams and then identify resources in the community to facilitate their involvement in inclusive recreation activities. This program has had significant impact on the life of one particular individual. After spending 4 years in a long-term care setting as a result of sustaining a traumatic brain injury, this gentleman is now living in an apartment. Before meeting his inclusion advocate, his only community outings involved doctor's appointments and social service meetings. After conducting a recreation assessment, the advocate worked with this individual to identify a scholarship at a local community center, a pool that had a lift for assisting with transfers, and additional recreation activities. This person is now volunteering at a local animal shelter and swimming at his community center. His quality of life has drastically improved as a result of therapeutic recreation!

I can think of no better venue for people to learn and grow than through their recreation and play. While there is plenty of research to document the value and outcomes of our field, it is a pleasure to watch firsthand the friendships that are made, the skills people develop, and the improvement in people's overall quality of life as they transition beyond our services to recreating on their own.

Figure 12.7 Life Story: Successful Transitions through Therapeutic Recreation

familiar model of segregation. Similar to other human service providers and educators, recreation personnel focused on developing segregated recreation programs and services.

The first recreation programs for people with disabilities in the U.S. were initiated largely by parents who wanted their children to have opportunities for a normalized lifestyle that included recreation participation. Parents worked with recreation staff and advocacy organizations as pioneers to design and deliver recreation programs for people with disabilities. These programs were typically delivered to participants who all had the same kind of disability (e.g., cerebral palsy, intellectual disability, autism, hearing loss, visual impairment), sometimes regardless of the differing ages of participants. Remnants of this model still exist today. While arguably a realistic option at the time, as society has come to value inclusivity and multicultural diversity, inclusion has become the preferred mode of delivering community-based recreation services. The therapeutic value and benefits of inclusive recreation are manifold, which you will read about in the following section. See Figure 12.10 (p. 351) for a comparison of the defining characteristics of segregated versus inclusive recreation.

The relevance of the concept of inclusion reaches far beyond exclusion based on ability. People from many groups have experienced marginalization and prejudice, had their rights called into question, and have faced the pain of social exclusion. Marginalized groups include those who have experienced discrimination on the basis of their race, creed, color, gender, culture, national origin, sexual orientation, or other defining characteristic. Discrimination may also be founded on stereotypes and assumptions about a particular segment of society. Level of ability, of course, cuts across all these groups, potentially culminating in a multiple layer of exclusion. The principles of inclusion can teach us much about bringing all peoples into the fabric of community belonging. As you read further in this chapter about inclusion as a way of living and relating, consider how this concept might be applied to break down prejudices, perhaps toward yourself or those at your workplace or at your college or university. What might you do to create social environments that are welcoming of all peoples?

Inclusion as a Therapeutic Intervention

Therapeutic recreation intervention delivered through inclusionary services can be a powerful catalyst for change for people with disabilities, people without disabilities, and for society at large. In this section, we present some of the positive outcomes of inclusion, as

Off the Bench and Into the Game

DeMario's Story

by DeMario Chandler

A younger brother watches as his older sister goes through the transition process of visiting and applying for colleges, the anticipation of beginning a new life phase, moving onto a beautiful campus, and experiencing myriad opportunities that college life offers. Excitement abounds as the entire family is involved and it is not long until the young man informs his parents that he can't wait "to go to college just like his older sister." They never envisioned their son with an intellectual disability having college aspirations. He grew up receiving special education services and the school professionals had all but squelched any hopes or dreams of a similar college experience. Once over the initial shock, they began to question this unfair disparity. While their peers are heading off to exciting college experiences, why are high school students with developmental disabilities often hitting a dead-end when services from the school system end and part-time underemployment begins? The concept for Beyond Academics (BA) was born.

BA is a post-secondary educational program for young adults with intellectual and developmental disabilities offered in partnership with The University of North Carolina at Greensboro (UNCG). BA offers a socially inclusive, college-based experience that aims to enhance the development of individual potential and encourages students to become contributing members of the university community and society. Students in the 4-year program reside in university apartments with roommates enrolled at UNCG, take independent living classes on campus, participate in an inclusive leisure education class alongside their UNCG peers, serve with their peers in community service projects, participate in campus activities (e.g., homecoming activities, clubs, cheering on UNCG athletic teams), and develop relationships with peers they otherwise would not have access to. Here is the story of one BA student who was part of the initial cohort of students and is currently a junior.

At the age of 20, DeMario entered his first year of college at UNCG. Like most college students he was excited about all of the new opportunities that lay before him. However, he had not been anticipating his college career for very long. Following graduation from high school, DeMario remained in his hometown of Winston-Salem, North Carolina doing volunteer work and "just hanging out." He says that due to his intellectual disability he did not know that college was an option for him. He believed that he would remain on the sidelines during this important aspect of a young adult's life. It was not until a peer mentor from the BA program spoke with him that DeMario realized he could get into the game and attend college. A peer mentor and employee of BA, who also has a developmental disability, explained how this alternative college program would give him the opportunity to live with UNCG students, take classes on campus, explore his interests in college sports, and make new friends.

"The most important thing for me about being in Beyond Academics is that when I'm on campus I'm just a college student; people can't tell that I have a disability." Through this alternative college program, DeMario has learned a great deal about being a self-advocate and capitalizing on his strengths. People who know DeMario describe him as mature, independent, and dependable. His experiences in BA and at UNCG have helped him grow into this capable and well-adjusted adult.

At UNCG, DeMario keeps busy. His love for sports, especially college basketball, led him to the UNCG Spartans basketball team for which he now serves as team manager. DeMario developed a genuine and close relationship with the head coach and hangs out with the team on weekends. They meet to watch sports, have team dinners, and attend award ceremonies. These activities have been a great source of enjoyment and have given DeMario many opportunities to work on his friendship skills.

In the classroom, DeMario has excelled. He has not only taken the required BA classes, but elected to take typical university courses taught by UNCG professors. DeMario plans to graduate early from the BA program at the end of this academic year, rather than the scheduled 4 years. In the fall semester he plans to attend a local community college to pursue a degree in Entertainment Technology. He hopes to one day become the "tech guy" at concerts and sporting events. When DeMario graduated from high school he never believed that he could attend college due to his disability. The opportunity to become a part of the university has helped him realize that people do not see him as an individual with a disability visiting campus, but as a UNCG college student with much to offer. DeMario is a successful, respected, and hardworking individual, and that is the way that people throughout his future schooling and career will view him. He is in the game.

With collaboration from Laura Bocko, Kimberly D. Miller, M.S., CPRP, and Stuart J. Schleien, Ph.D., LRT/CTRS, CPRP

Figure 12.8 Life Story: Off the Bench and Into the Game—DeMario's Story

Life Story:

A Lesson about Natural Proportions

I was freshly graduated from my Master's program at the University of Minnesota and working my very first job as a therapeutic recreation specialist at a community recreation center in St. Paul. I was enjoying the challenge of starting up an inclusion program, working with families and staff, and applying the inclusive recreation concepts and strategies I had learned at the university to a real life setting.

One of the inclusion principles I had learned was the concept of natural proportions. At that time, we adhered to a ratio of 1 to 10; that is, for every 10 people in a recreation program, only one of them should have a disability. This principle purports that, if the same ratio of people with disabilities to people without disabilities as occurs in society is mirrored in programs, the group will be more accepting of people with disabilities and not stressed by too many individual needs.

We had already successfully included a dozen children in recreation programs over the previous year using the principle of natural proportions, and I was beginning to plan for the upcoming fall season. One boy with a disability was already enrolled in a swimming class, which had a cap of 8 participants, when I received a call from a parent requesting that her daughter be enrolled in the same class. Fortunately, I caught myself before I blurted out what I was thinking, "I'm sorry but we can't accept your child in the program because we would be *violating the concept of natural proportions.*" How could I say that to a parent?! Even if the principle was an important and legitimate one, how could I deny a child the opportunity to learn to swim in an inclusive program?

I told the parent I would look into the situation and call her the next day, then immediately scheduled a meeting to talk with my supervisor. I believed strongly in the principle of natural proportions – I had seen it work effectively – but I wondered if there was a way to accommodate a second participant. My supervisor and I weighed all the variables and potential dynamics of the situation. We noted that the boy who was already enrolled in the course had taken the class before. Both his assistant and the instructor knew him very well and how best to teach him, and inclusion had gone smoothly. We also noted that the girl who wanted to take the class would be able to participate in the class without assistance. She could learn directly from the instructor, with support from the boy's inclusion facilitator. The tipping point in the decision was when we learned the instructor was certified as an adapted aquatics instructor and had taught swimming to youngsters with varying abilities for several years. We asked for her input and, without hesitation, she said she felt comfortable including both children in the class. The decision was cinched.

I called the parent and gave her the good news, the only news I knew I could give. The moral of this story? Not to ignore the principle of natural proportions, but to use it as a guideline and, at times, to look beyond it to the other important factors at play. Every situation and group has its own dynamic, and every situation, like every person, needs to be assessed on an individualized basis.

Figure 12.9 Life Story: A Lesson About Natural Proportions

established through research. First, however, let's take a look at the detrimental effects of exclusion.

Negative Outcomes of Exclusion

Many have written of the ill effects of social exclusion, ranging from sadness to sociopathy (Eisenberger & Lieberman, 2004; Goffman, 1963; Harris, 2009; House, Umberson, & Landis, 1988; Lynch, 1977; Stillman et al., 2009). Social anxiety, depression, and low self-esteem have all been found to result from social isolation (Leary, 1990). Marginalization has been linked to feelings of loneliness among people with disabilities and retirees (Beresford, 2005), and also among older adults (Social Exclusion Unit, Office of the Deputy Prime Minister, Great Britain, 2005). Twenge, Baumeister, DeWall, Ciarocco, and Bartels (2007) found that social exclusion led to decreased prosocial behaviors such as empathy, cooperation, and charity toward others. Similarly, Harris (2009) noted reduced empathy and self-control, and increased instances of aggression, as a result of social segregation. Stillman et al. (2009) determined that social exclusion produced a global perception that life was less meaningful.

In his seminal work, *The Broken Heart: The Medical Consequences of Loneliness*, physician James Lynch (1977) helped establish the link between social exclusion and health. He concluded that, if one lacks human relationship and feels isolated from others, one's health and ability to resist disease will also suffer. Similarly, in 1988, House, Umberson, and Landis reviewed a series of studies, controlling for such factors as physical health, socioeconomic status, smoking, alcohol, exercise, obesity, race, life satisfaction, and healthcare. They made the startling discovery that individuals with few or weak social ties were found to be twice as likely to die as those with strong social connections. Clearly,

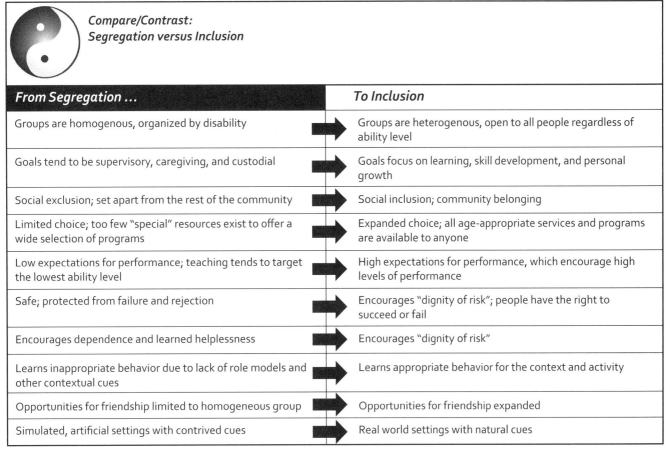

Figure 12.10 Compare/Contrast: Segregation versus Inclusion *(adapted from Schleien, Ray, and Green, 1997)*

one's overall health and well-being are related to the degree of one's social connectedness.

Recent research in neuroimaging sheds further light on the tie between physical well-being and social well-being. Eisenberger and Lieberman (2004) conducted a study in which they compared the brain scans of those who experienced social exclusion with those who experienced physical pain. In their experiment, research participants played a virtual ball-tossing game in which they were ultimately excluded, and neuroscientists scanned their brains at the point of exclusion. The scientists discovered that the anterior cingulated cortex (ACC) was more active during the period of exclusion than during inclusion, a phenomenon that paralleled results from physical pain studies. Both situations activated a kind of neural alarm system that sent a distress signal to the brain. Thus, social pain, as interpreted by the brain, is as "real" a hurt as physical pain.

Positive Outcomes of Inclusion

Inclusive recreation has been shown to produce numerous positive benefits for participants with disabilities across the domains of well-being. By choosing and participating in preferred recreational activities, participants with disabilities can enhance their self-determination and self-advocacy skills (Dattilo, 2002). Through inclusive recreation supports, they can learn a variety of new socially valid leisure skills, thus expanding their leisure repertoires (Peniston, 1998; Schleien, Ray, & Green, 1997). Inclusive recreation helps participants develop social interaction skills, build social networks, and form friendships (Heyne, Schleien, & McAvoy, 1993; Komro & Stigler, 2000; Meyer, 2001). Youth with disabilities are able to cultivate leadership skills during structured recreational and social development activities such as clubs, service organizations, sports, and fine arts (Larson, 2000; Wehman, 1996). Through involvement in inclusive sports and other physical activities, people with disabilities gain physical health and fitness (Anderson & Heyne, 2010). Inclusive recreation can be used as a venue for individuals with disabilities to contribute to society through volunteerism (Miller, Schleien, Rider, Hall, Roche, & Worsley, 2002). And inclusive recreation programs help create a sense of belonging for participants with disabilities, the ultimate goal of inclusion (Abery, 2003; Komro & Stigler, 2000). Because of these documented benefits, therapeutic recreation specialists can collaborate with participants to set goals aimed at achieving these kinds of therapeutic outcomes through inclusive recreation.

Another exciting facet of inclusive recreation is that people with disabilities are not the only ones who benefit from the experience. People without disabilities also profit in important ways that expand their awareness and openness toward others. Many studies have shown heightened or maintained acceptance of individuals with disabilities after interacting with them in inclusive recreation programs (Anderson, Schleien, McAvoy, Lais, & Seligmann, 1997 [see Figure 12.11]; Schleien, Ray, & Green, 1997). School-based inclusive recreation programs have helped peers without disabilities take the perspective of participants with disabilities as well as gain self-esteem through assisting them (Heyne, Schleien, & McAvoy, 1993; Heyne, Wilkins, & Anderson, 2012). As participants with and without disabilities benefit, so do communities. Inclusion, when it is well done, sends a "ripple effect" throughout the community, creating a more accepting and welcoming society (Heyne, 2006). Table 12.2 summarizes the evidence-based outcomes from inclusion.

Inclusion and the Therapeutic Recreation Process

As with any other therapeutic recreation service, inclusion services are delivered using the therapeutic recreation process, or APIE: assessment, planning, implementation, and evaluation (or discover, dream/design, deliver, and deliberate). As you can see from Figure 12.12 (p. 354), the inclusion process involves (a) program promotion or referral; (b) *assessment* of the participant's needs and abilities, as well as *assessment* of the program environment; (c) *planning* for individualized supports such as accommodations, staff training,

Primary Source Support:

Efficacy of Inclusive Outdoor Adventure

Anderson, L., Schleien, S. J., McAvoy, L., Lais, G., & Seligmann, D. (1997). Creating positive change through an integrated outdoor adventure program. *Therapeutic Recreation Journal, 31*(4), 214–229.

This 2½-year study investigated the efficacy of an integrated outdoor adventure program for creating positive change for participants with and without disabilities. The research participants included 12 people with disabilities and 14 people without disabilities who took part in a variety of outdoor adventure experiences through Wilderness Inquiry (WI) of Minneapolis, MN. Outings included 2-hour canoe skills lessons and 3- and 6-day wilderness-based canoe trips.

Data were collected on four variables: (a) the attitudes of the participants without disabilities toward individuals with disabilities, (b) relationship development during the wilderness experiences, (c), canoe skill acquisition, and (d) perceptions of the trip experiences on quality of life areas. The results were recorded as follows:

- *Attitudes:* The attitudes of the participants without disabilities toward their peers with disabilities were high in acceptance at the beginning of the study and remained high until the end of the study.

- *Relationship Development:* Nearly all the participants with and without disabilities were chosen as a friend more often at the end of the wilderness experiences than during baseline. Group expansiveness increased, meaning that groups grew more willing to include others as friends. Groups also gained in cohesiveness, which includes elements of closeness and cooperation, through the experience.

- *Canoe Skills:* Participants with disabilities acquired substantial canoe skills. By the end of the study, they were able to execute from 82% to 95% of the canoe skills correctly and independently, as outlined on a task analysis.

- *Quality of Life:* When participants with and without disabilities were interviewed 4 to 6 months after their wilderness experiences, they reported a positive impact related to quality of life. Personal growth was reported by both participants with and without disabilities in the following areas: self-confidence, tolerance of others, increased comfort meeting new people, increased involvement with groups, more relaxed and less perfectionistic, increased self-esteem and self-acceptance, better able to clarify values and set priorities, improved social and interpersonal skills, and an increased sense of well-being. Participants with disabilities especially gained in terms of increased social activity and the development of interpersonal relationships. Participants without disabilities grew most in the areas of employment, recreation, and tolerance for stress.

This study provides evidence that inclusive outdoor adventure experiences can enrich the lives of both participants with and without disabilities across multiple measures related to personal well-being.

Figure 12.11 Primary Source Support: Efficacy of Inclusive Outdoor Adventure

and peer orientations; (d) program *implementation*, which includes monitoring and consultation with individuals such as the participant, parent/guardian, family members, and staff; and (e) documentation and *evaluation*. You will notice that *transition services* are not specifically identified as a component of this process, since the entire process supports a kind of transition from no or minimal involvement to increased involvement in community recreation.

While it is beyond the scope of this book to identify all the approaches and strategies that are available to successfully include a participant with a disability in community recreation programs, we offer in the following section a detailed framework, based on APIE, to portray the careful planning and collaboration that is needed to accomplish inclusion and its resulting benefits. Additional sources of information about inclusion practices may be found in the resources and references sections at the end of this chapter.

Assessment

Before assessment is undertaken, the participant is referred to the inclusive recreation program. Referrals for inclusive recreation tend to be informal and personal, based on the preferences and desires of the particular individual or family seeking services. Referrals may be made by any individual involved in the participant's life, as well as the participant him or herself. A referral may come through a parent or other family member, school teacher, therapeutic recreation specialist or other allied health care professional, recreation provider, social worker, or another parent whose child has been involved in inclusive recreation, among others. Often

Table 12.2 Examples of Therapeutic Outcomes of Inclusive Recreation

WELL-BEING DOMAIN	EXAMPLES OF THERAPEUTIC OUTCOMES
Leisure	• Examine and understand leisure attitudes, preferences, participation, and/or barriers • Build leisure participation skills • Expand one's leisure repertoire • Tap into leisure resources
Psychological and Emotional	• Learn to set goals related to leisure and well-being and to meet them • Gain competence through participation in leisure activities • Learn optimism • Develop self-determination through prioritizing and choosing one's recreation activities
Social	• Build communication and social interaction skills during recreation activities such as initiating and holding conversations, making eye contact, learning to cooperate, describing feelings, developing conflict resolution skills, supporting others, etc. • Develop friendship skills • Invite friends to participate in recreation activities
Cognitive	• Learn to count money and change when making recreation purchases, buying tickets, or eating at a restaurant • Learn to keep score during a team game • Calculate points earned or spaces moved during a board or dice game • Learn to read a map of a park • Reminisce about cherished childhood leisure pursuits • Plan one's weekend leisure activities or summer vacation
Physical	• Learn self-help skills such as grooming and dressing in a locker room before and after participation in a recreation program or workout • Develop transportation skills by learning bus routes and riding the bus • Develop mobility skills by navigating the neighborhood or a local park • Enhance physical fitness by developing cardiovascular endurance, strength, and flexibility at a fitness center • Plan healthy snacks to maintain overall health and vitality
Spiritual	• Nourish spirituality during free time through religion, meditation, reading, reflection, or other spiritual practices • Engage in meaningful leisure pursuits • Gain a greater appreciation for nature by spending time in wilderness recreation areas • Volunteer in one's community

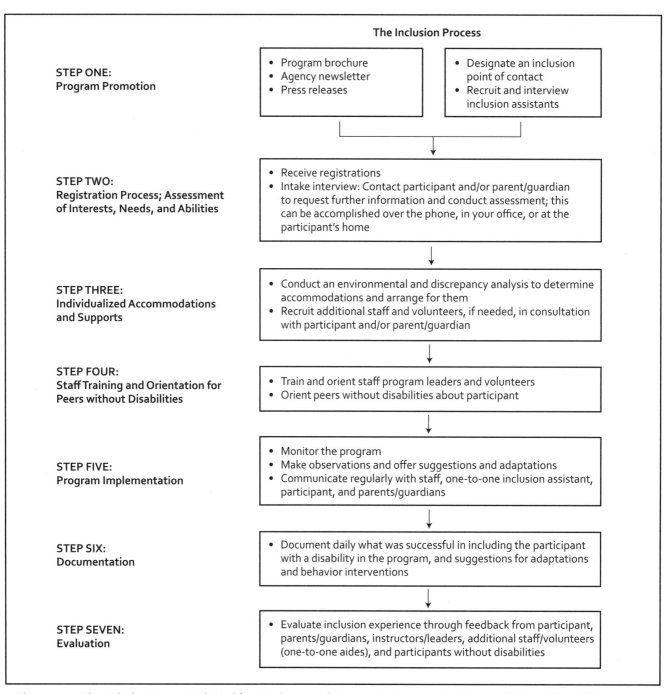

Figure 12.12 The Inclusion Process *(adapted from Anderson and Kress, 2003; Heyne, 1987; Wagner, Wetherald, and Wilson, 1994)*

community recreation agencies advertise inclusion opportunities in their brochures, neighborhood newspapers, or advocacy organization newsletters which initiate the referral process.

Similar to other therapeutic recreation assessments, there are two aspects to assessment in inclusive recreation services: assessment related to the *participant* and assessment related to the *environment*. Participant assessment entails meeting with the participant, along with a parent or guardian if the participant is a minor. Interviews, observation, and questionnaires are common methods of assessing a participant's interests, needs, abilities, goals, and preferred recreational activities. Depending on the individual, gathering information about the following areas may also be important: communication with peers and staff, promoting positive social behaviors, maximizing independent and interdependent participation, physical positioning, administration of medications, among other individual considerations.

Assessment of the environment is accomplished through an ecological assessment or inventory, also known as an environmental analysis. You will recall this approach from Chapter 9 *Assessment* (refer especially to

Figure 9.10, Diagram of a Broad Ecological Assessment and Figure 9.11, Diagram of a Focused Ecological Assessment). In an ecological assessment, participation in every aspect of the program is identified. The program is broken down into a task analysis which records all the necessary steps for participation in the activity, including transportation to and from the facility. Aside from its value for assessment purposes, ecological assessments are useful for planning and for documenting and evaluating participant progress.

Planning

The participant assessment and the ecological assessment come together during the planning phase of the therapeutic recreation process when you develop a discrepancy analysis based on the ecological inventory. In a discrepancy analysis, the abilities of the participant are compared with the requirements of the individual steps on the ecological inventory task analysis. Wherever the participant is unable to complete a step on the task analysis independently, the planning process requires that arrangements be made for individualized instruction, additional support, or an accommodation to bridge the gap. Individualized instruction may take the form of repeating instructions, providing a verbal or physical prompt, or modeling the behavior that is required. Individualized accommodation may take the form of adapted equipment (e.g., built-up paint brush handle, color-coded keyboard, ramp to enter swimming pool); a rule or procedure modification (e.g., two-handed dribble instead of one-handed, shorter distance to throw a Frisbee or toss a ball); or assistance from a peer, staff member, or aide.

Planning decisions are made in consultation with the participant, anyone else involved in the assessment process, as well as the program director and instructor who have special expertise in the activity skills and procedures. In addition to the arrangements that are made based on the assessment, planning involves training staff and assistants in inclusion practices as well as how to best teach and include the participant in the context of the program.

Another aspect of planning can involve providing a peer orientation, which is an opportunity to share information about the participant and his or her disability to the other program participants. Peer orientations provide accurate information about the person and the disability in a way that emphasizes similarities with peers and typical aspects of the participant's life. Orientations also give peers an opportunity to ask questions, which is beneficial for promoting understanding, acceptance, and perspective-taking. There are several aspects to consider when planning a peer orientation: Is an orientation necessary? What information will be shared? Who will share the information? How will information be shared? When will it be shared? When making decisions about peer orientations, it is essential to seek input from the participant and/or the parent/guardian. They have the best sense of what information needs to be shared to maintain privacy and promote acceptance and interaction among group members. Typically, peer orientations are most effective when they are given at the beginning of the first program session, with subsequent questions answered as they arise during the program.

Implementation

Once the program is underway, inclusion needs to be carefully monitored to ensure that everyone involved has a good experience. The key to successful inclusion is communication and close observation. Listening to feedback from the participant, family members, and staff is imperative, as well as following up on their suggestions. Successful inclusion implementation essentially requires building rapport and a trusting relationship among the therapeutic recreation specialist, the participant, any family members, and staff.

Some questions to consider during the implementation phase of the therapeutic recreation process are as follows: Is the participant involved in the activity as fully as possible? Is social interaction taking place? Is the participant learning effectively? Are the goals of the participant being met? What outcomes are taking place? Are peers accepting of the participant? Does staff feel comfortable meeting the needs of the participant in the program? Is there any resistance to inclusion? Are inappropriate or challenging behaviors adequately addressed? Can anything more be done to support the participant in the program? Communicating openly and regularly about these kinds of programmatic aspects, and following up in a proactive way, will help ensure a positive experience for everyone.

Evaluation

As you will learn in Chapter 13 *Evaluation*, the therapeutic recreation process involves both ongoing and summative approaches to evaluation. Ongoing evaluation occurs in part while monitoring the program during the implementation phase as the therapeutic recreation specialist carefully observes and communicates with others, as described in the previous section. Ongoing evaluation also occurs through recording any

Table 12.3 Quality Indicators of Inclusive Recreation Programs

Quality Indicators of Inclusive Recreation Programs

How can you be certain an agency has a commitment to inclusive recreation, and the knowledge and strategies necessary to accomplish it? Characteristics that reflect the effectiveness of services, or quality indicators, can help us evaluate the strengths and weaknesses of an agency's inclusion practices. The following quality indicators for inclusive recreation programs are adapted from Schleien and Rynders (1996).

Quality Indicator #1: Administrative Policy and Practice

- ☐ Agency's mission statement, as presented in brochures and advertising, reflects a commitment to inclusive recreation
- ☐ Policies and procedures comply with laws that pertain to serving individuals with disabilities in settings that are inclusive and in the least restrictive environment
- ☐ Collaboration occurs between staff and inclusion-oriented individuals such as participants, parents, and representatives from advocacy and advisory groups
- ☐ Staff are trained in inclusion philosophy and strategies
- ☐ Funding is adequate to provide adaptations, one-to-one aides, interpreters, equipment, and other supports necessary for inclusion

Quality Indicator #2: Logistical and Environmental Considerations

- ☐ Facilities are architecturally accessible
- ☐ Participants take part in programs that are chronologically age-appropriate and include participants with varying abilities
- ☐ Costs related to programmatic adaptations are reasonable
- ☐ Continued communication occurs among the key players

Quality Indicator #3: Techniques and Methods

- ☐ Participants and family members feel welcome at the agency
- ☐ Participants' interests, preferences, needs, abilities, and goals are assessed
- ☐ Activities and materials are modified to accommodate the needs of participants, and modifications are withdrawn as they are no longer needed
- ☐ Participants without disabilities are given information about the participant and his or her disability, presented with a "Person First" orientation
- ☐ Program instructors structure activities to encourage cooperation among group members
- ☐ Staff are adequately trained in how to involve the participant socially in programs
- ☐ Participant progress is documented
- ☐ Program evaluation is ongoing

Quality Indicator #4: Individualized Programming

- ☐ Activities represent the full range of recreation options offered to the public
- ☐ Activities are selected based on participant's interests, preferences, strengths, and needs
- ☐ Adaptations are individualized, designed to increase independence and allow for maximum participation, and slowly withdrawn as they are no longer needed
- ☐ Misunderstandings, disruptive behaviors, and similar challenging situations are addressed promptly and positively
- ☐ Participant is able to transfer skills and knowledge to other settings

programmatic adjustments (e.g., adaptations, instructional techniques, behavior interventions) as they occur and through documenting participant progress toward achieving goals and objectives. The task analysis of the ecological inventory is an especially useful tool for documenting successful skill acquisition. Adding dated columns for each program session next to the task analysis facilitates documenting when the participant learns a new skill and is able to perform it independently. Relevant comments related to performance, interactions, and other therapeutic outcomes may also be documented.

Summative program evaluation information is typically gathered from participants, family members, and staff through the use of questionnaires and surveys. Questions may relate to satisfaction with the agency's inclusion process, the occurrence of therapeutic outcomes, and suggestions for programmatic changes. The therapeutic recreation inclusion process is often cyclic in nature in that a participant may enroll in a number of programs consecutively at the same neighborhood facility. When this is the case, feedback gathered through summative evaluation may be immediately incorporated into the assessment process for the next program.

Self-Assessment of Learning

- You are a therapeutic recreation specialist responsible for discharge or transition planning for individuals with spinal cord injuries at a physical rehabilitation center. How would you go about planning for discharge? Who would be the members of your planning team? What aspects would you consider during the assessment? What community resources would you involve?

- Jennifer York (1993) states that inclusion is a value which, to be relevant to each of us on a personal level and to be the basis for thought and action, we must try to define in our own words. Drawing from your personal beliefs, values, and experiences, as well as the information presented in this chapter, answer the following questions: "How do I define inclusion?" "Why is inclusion important to me?"

- Table 12.2 presents how participation in recreation activities can contribute to the development of important life skills. What are some other examples of how inclusive recreation can build life skills? Consider the domains of the Flourishing through Leisure Model: leisure, psychological/emotional, cognitive, social, physical, and spiritual.

- Collaboration, creativity, flexibility, and resourcefulness are important competencies to cultivate to help us figure out how to remove barriers and structure environments to successfully include people with disabilities in recreation programs. With one or two other people, brainstorm how you might address the following scenarios adapted from Anderson and Kress (2003, p. 98). Remember that structuring environments involves not only architectural modifications; it also considers modifying programmatic features related to staffing, room selection, participants, curriculum, equipment, and information shared, to name a few.

Scenario #1: A staff member from a psychosocial rehabilitation center for people with mental illness calls you to see if one of his clients can join the painting class your agency sponsors. How should you proceed with the situation?

Scenario #2: A child who uses a wheelchair and has a developmental disability wants to participate in your playground program. He does not speak very clearly and also drools. On the first day of the program, the other kids in the group begin to ask you questions about this child: "Why does he use a wheelchair?" "Why does he drool?" "Why can't he talk right?" How would you handle this situation?

Scenario #3: There is an adult in your aerobics class who consistently wants to touch (e.g., hug, pat heads) the other participants and staff. This draws attention to the participant and bothers the others. How would you handle this situation?

Quality Indicators of Inclusive Recreation

To conclude this section on the role of the therapeutic recreation process in supporting inclusion, we present Table 12.3 Quality Indicators of Inclusive Recreation Programs developed by Schleien and Rynders (1996). Quality indicators are yardsticks by which the merit of inclusion services may be measured. They fall into four categories: administrative policy and practice, logistical and environmental considerations, techniques and methods, and individualized programming. Using this checklist of quality indicators, how prepared are the recreation agencies in your community to open their doors to participants with disabilities?

Summary

This chapter emphasized the common purposes of transition and inclusion, both of which revolve around planning for participants' successful engagement in recreation in their home communities. Definitions of transition and inclusion were presented, along with their applications in diverse therapeutic recreation settings. You learned that collaborative and coordinated services that focus on purposeful participant outcomes are central to successful transition and inclusion. The need for therapeutic recreation specialists who are trained to use the therapeutic recreation process in inclusive recreation settings was underscored as a means to effect social change and to promote therapeutic outcomes for individuals with disabilities.

Resources

Disabled Peoples International (DPI)
http://v1.dpi.org

DPI is a network of national organizations of people with disabilities established to promote human rights through participation and equal opportunity. Based at Mount Pearl, Newfoundland, the DPI website posts international reports on a wide range of current topics including self-empowerment, social inclusion, employment, women's rights, aging, and HIV/AIDS, among others.

Healthy Transition: Moving from Pediatric to Adult Health Care
http://healthytransitionsny.com

Sponsored by the New York State Institute for Health Transition Training for Youth with Developmental Disabilities Ages 14–25, Families, Service Coordinators, and Health Care Providers, this invaluable website provides interactive online training, checklists, and videos for learning skills related to health care and community living. Training modules include scheduling a medical appointment and transportation, speaking up at the doctor's office, acquiring health insurance, deciding about guardianship, understanding your disability, and finding community resources. Community resources include information about summer camp, job placement, independent living centers, building a circle of support, and more.

Inclusion Press International
http://www.inclusion.com

Inclusion Press International offers a variety of excellent materials (e.g., articles, books, videos, DVDs) for promoting inclusion, especially social inclusion, in recreational and educational settings. They sell workbooks for the processes of Circle of Friends, MAPS, and Planning Alternative Tomorrows with Hope (PATH), discussed in Chapter 10 *Planning*.

Inclusive Recreation Resource Center
http://www.inclusiverec.org

Based at the State University of New York at Cortland, under the direction of Dr. Lynn Anderson, the Center offers comprehensive training in inclusive recreation through the Inclusion U curriculum. To earn Inclusion U certification, trainees assess the programmatic and architectural accessibility of a community recreation resource (e.g., art gallery, community recreation center, health club, museum, nature center, ski resort, state park, theater). Accessibility findings are uploaded to the Center's website, so the public can see the extent to which facilities are accessible before venturing there. The Center also provides technical assistance, inclusivity assessments, and recreation referrals.

Institute on Community Integration (ICI)
http://ici.umn.edu

This institute is a University Center for Excellence in Developmental Disabilities at the University of Minnesota. Through collaborative research, training, and information sharing, ICI seeks to improve policies and practices that enable individuals with developmental disabilities to be involved in and contribute to their communities. ICI's website provides information about their research projects, services, and products (e.g., curricula, resource guides, newsletters, multimedia). Particularly informative and timely is the quarterly newsletter, *Impact*, which may be downloaded at no cost at http://ici.umn.edu/products/newsletters.html#impact.

National Alliance for Secondary Education and Transition (NASET)
http://www.nasetalliance.org

This national alliance is comprised of more than 40 organizations and advocacy groups from the areas of special education, general education, career and technical education, youth development, multicultural perspectives, and parents. Based on results from current research, the Alliance identifies and prioritizes quality indicators for successful postsecondary transition. *A Transition Toolkit*, designed to improve transition systems, is available for free download.

References

Abery, B. (2003). Social inclusion through recreation: What's the connection? *Impact, 16*(2), 2–3, 32–33.

Anderson, L., & Heyne, L. (2010). Physical activity for children and adults with disabilities: An issue of "amplified" importance. *Disability and Health Journal, 3*(2), 71–73.

Anderson, L., & Kress, C. (2003). *Inclusion: Including people with disabilities in parks and recreation opportunities.* State College, PA: Venture Publishing, Inc.

Anderson, L., Penney McGee, L., & Wilkins, V. (2011). *The inclusivity assessment tool and guide.* Cortland, NY: SUNY Cortland and the Inclusive Recreation Resource Center.

Anderson, L., Schleien, S. J., McAvoy, L., Lais, G., & Seligmann, D. (1997). Creating positive change through an integrated outdoor adventure program. *Therapeutic Recreation Journal, 31*(4), 214–229.

Benzanson, L. (2005). Strategies for meeting the needs of persons moving out of nursing homes. *Impact, 18*(1). Retrieved from http://ici.umn.edu/products/impact/181/default.html

Beresford, P. (2005). Solitary confinement. *Community Care, 1577,* 22.

Bogenschutz, D., & Breitenstein, J. (2010, March). *Transcending barriers to community access after discharge.* Paper presented at the American Therapeutic Recreation Association Mid-Year conference, Biloxi, MS.

Bullock, C., & Mahon, M. (1997). *Introduction to recreation services for people with disabilities: A person-centered approach.* Champaign, IL: Sagamore Publishing.

Bullock, C., Mahon, M., & Killingsworth, C. (2010). *Introduction to recreation services for people with disabilities: A person-centered approach.* Champaign, IL: Sagamore Publishing.

Dattilo, J. (2002). *Inclusive leisure services: Responding to the rights of people with disabilities.* State College, PA: Venture Publishing, Inc.

Disabled in Action. (2010). *Facts about disability in the U.S. population.* Retrieved from http://www.disabledinaction.org/census_stats.html

Eisenberger, N. I., & Lieberman, M. D. (2004). Why rejection hurts: A common neural alarm system for physical and social pain. *Trends in Cognitive Sciences, 8*(7), 294–300.

Goffman, E. (1963). *Stigma: Notes on the management of spoiled identity.* Englewood Cliffs, NJ: Prentice-Hall, Inc.

Harris, M. J. (2009). Bullying, rejection, and peer victimization: A social cognitive neuroscience perspective. In A. W. Crescioni & R. F. Baumeister (Eds.), *Alone and aggressive: Social exclusion impairs self-control and empathy and increases hostile cognition and aggression* (pp. 251–277). New York, NY: Springer Publishing Co.

Heyne, L. (1987). *Integrating children and youth with disabilities into community recreation agencies: One agency's experience and recommendations.* St. Paul, MN: The Jewish Community Center of the Greater St. Paul Area.

Heyne, L. (2006). Inclusion retrospective: Participant, peer, parent, and staff perspectives on long-term inclusive recreation. *Leisure Research Symposium Abstracts,* National Recreation and Park Association.

Heyne, L., Schleien, S. J., McAvoy, L. (1993). *Making friends: Using recreation activities to promote friendship between children with and without disabilities.* Minneapolis, MN: Institute on Community Integration, University of Minnesota.

Heyne, L., Wilkins, V., & Anderson, L. (2012). Social inclusion in the lunchroom and on the playground at school. *Social Advocacy and Systems Change Journal, 3*(1), 54–68.

House, J., Umberson, D., & Landis, K. (1988). Structures and processes of social support. *Annual Review of Sociology, 14,* 293–318.

Komro, K. A., & Stigler, M. H. (2000). *Growing absolutely fantastic youth: A review of the research on "best practices."* Minneapolis, MN: Konopka Institute for Best Practices in Adolescent Health, University of Minnesota.

Larson, R. W. (2000). Toward a psychology of positive youth development. *American Psychologist, 55*(1), 170–183.

Lawson, L. M., Coyle, C. P., & Ashton-Shaeffer, C. (2001). *Therapeutic recreation in special education: An IDEA for the future.* Alexandria, VA: American Therapeutic Recreation Association.

Leake, D. W., Black, R. S., & Roberts, K. (2004). Assumptions in transition planning: Are they culturally sensitive? *Impact, 16*(3). Retrieved from http://ici.umn.edu/products/impact/163

Leary, M. R. (1990). Responses to social exclusion: Social anxiety, jealousy, loneliness, depression, and low self-esteem. *Journal of Social and Clinical Psychology, 9*, 221–229.

Lynch, J. (1977). *The broken heart: The medical consequences of loneliness.* New York, NY: Basic Books.

Meyer, L. H. (2001). The impact of inclusion on children's lives: Multiple outcomes, and friendship in particular. *International Journal of Disability, Development and Education, 48*(1), 9–31.

Miller, K., Schleien, S. J., Rider, C., Hall, C., Roche, M., & Worsley, J. (2002). Inclusive volunteering: Benefits to participants and community. *Therapeutic Recreation Journal, 36*(3), 247–59.

National Alliance of Secondary Education and Transition. (2010). *National standards & quality indicators: Transition toolkit for systems improvement.* Retrieved from http://www.nasetalliance.org/docs/TransitionToolkit.pdf

Peniston, L. (1998). *Developing recreation skills in persons with learning disabilities.* Urbana, IL: Sagamore Publishing.

Peterson, C., & Stumbo, N. (2000). *Therapeutic recreation program design: Principles and procedures.* Boston, MA: Allyn and Bacon.

Rizzolo, M., Hemp, R., Baddock, D., & Schindler, A. (2009, May). Family support services in the United States: 2008. *Policy Research Brief, 20*(2), 1–11.

Schleien, S. J., Ray, M. T., & Green, F. P. (1997). *Community recreation and people with disabilities: Strategies for inclusion* (2nd ed.). Baltimore, MD: Paul H. Brookes Publishing Co.

Schleien, S. J., & Rynders, J. (1996). *Inclusive recreation: A parents' guide to quality.* In Heyne, L., Schleien, S. J., & Rynders, J. (Eds.). *IMPACT: Feature issue on inclusive recreation and families.* Minneapolis, MN: Institute on Community Integration, University of Minnesota.

Shank, J., & Coyle, C. (2002). *Therapeutic recreation in health promotion and rehabilitation.* State College, PA: Venture Publishing, Inc.

Social Exclusion Unit, Office of the Deputy Prime Minister, Great Britain (2005). Supporting excluded older people. *Working with Older People: Community Care Policy & Practice, 9*(2), 2–3,5.

Stillman, T. F., Baumeister, R. F., Lambert, N. M., Crescioni, A. W., DeWall, C. N., & Fincham, F. D. (2009). Alone and without purpose: Life loses meaning following social exclusion. *Journal of Experimental Social Psychology, 45*(4), 686–694.

Szymanski, E. M. (1994). Transition: Life-span and life-space considerations for empowerment. *Exceptional Children, 60*(5), 402–410.

Twenge, J. M., Baumeister, R. F., DeWall, C. N., Ciarocco, N. J., & Bartels, J. M. (2007). Social exclusion decreases prosocial behavior. *Journal of Personality and Social Psychology, 92*(1), 56–66. doi: 10.1037/0022-3514.92.1.56

U.S. Department of Education. (2010). *Building the legacy: IDEA 2004.* Retrieved from http://idea.ed.gov

Wagner, G., Wetherald, L., & Wilson, B. (1994). A model for making county and municipal recreation department programs inclusive. In S. Moon (Ed.), *Making school and community recreation fun for everyone* (pp. 181–192). Baltimore, MD: Paul H. Brookes Publishing Co.

Wehman, P. (1996). *Life beyond the classroom: Transition strategies for young people with disabilities.* Menlo Park, CA: SRI International.

York, J. (Spring/Summer 1993). What is inclusion really? Define it for yourself. *What's working in inclusive education?* Minneapolis, MN: University of Minnesota, Institute on Community Integration, p. 2.

Chapter 13
EVALUATION IN STRENGTHS-BASED THERAPEUTIC RECREATION PRACTICE

The gardenia is multi-faceted yet elegant.

"Everything that can be counted does not necessarily count; everything that counts cannot necessarily be counted."
—Albert Einstein

OVERVIEW OF CHAPTER 13

- An overview of evaluation
- Introduction to empowerment evaluation
- Evaluating individual participant progress
- Documentation basics (the what, why, when, and how of documentation)
- Overall therapeutic recreation service evaluation in the context of quality management

FOCUS QUESTIONS

- What is the difference between formative and summative evaluation? Why are both approaches important in therapeutic recreation practice?
- What is empowerment evaluation and what makes it strengths-based?
- Why is documentation such an important part of services?
- How is documentation of individual participant progress related to overall or comprehensive service evaluation?

AN INTRODUCTION TO EVALUATION

A definition of "evaluate":
To ascertain or fix the value or worth of; to examine and judge carefully; appraise

A definition of "deliberate":
To think carefully and often slowly, as about a choice to be made; to consult with others in a process of reaching a decision; to consider (something) deeply; ponder; think over

A definition of "empowerment":
The giving or delegation of power or authority; the giving of an ability; enablement or permission

Recall that the therapeutic recreation process is a universal approach to working with participants, no matter the delivery system or service setting. We have presented the therapeutic process—assess, plan, implement, and evaluate (APIE)—and offered an alternative way to think about the therapeutic recreation process:

- Discover (assess)
- Dream, Design (plan)
- Deliver (implement)
- Deliberate (evaluate)

This chapter focuses on the evaluation phase of therapeutic recreation services, the final step in the process. The first step, *assessment*, helps us discover the strengths, dreams, and aspirations of the participant. Assessment helps us and the participant see "where are you now?" The next phase, *planning*, helps us answer the question, "Where do you want to be and how will you get there?" The third phase, *implementation*, helps us answer the question, "How are you going to get there?" The fourth phase, *evaluation*, answers these questions, "Have you gotten there yet? What is left to do? How well did it go? What difference did this process make in your life?"

Remember that therapeutic recreation is the purposeful and careful facilitation of quality leisure experiences and the development of personal and environmental strengths that lead to greater well-being for participants. In order to be purposeful, we need to complete a careful and thoughtful assessment, design a clear plan that can be followed by participants, and implement actions that will help participants reach their goals and dreams. But how will you and the participant know when a goal has been reached? a milestone achieved? a dream brought a little closer? How will you know if you are using the right kinds of actions? in the right places, at the right time, and in the right amount? How do you know if changes in the plan are needed? if participants are satisfied with the plan and services? These are many of the questions that careful documentation and valid evaluation can help you and the participant answer.

In this chapter, we will explore forms of evaluation, at the individual level and the service or program level. We will describe documentation, its importance in providing quality services and in empowering participants. Additionally, we will challenge you to think about new ways to involve participants in strengths-based evaluation.

EVALUATION IN THERAPEUTIC RECREATION

"Evaluation" is defined, in its simplest terms, as judging the importance, value, worth, or status of something. In therapeutic recreation, as in many human services fields, we make continual judgments about how well our services are helping a participant and how well he or she is progressing toward goals. We also make decisions about how well participants achieve outcomes at the end of our services. And we must step back, look at the bigger picture, and continually judge how effective we are as we work with many participants across time. Evaluation, then, must encompass these aspects:

- Be formative *and* summative; in other words, provide feedback during and at the end of services
- Focus on the individual participant *and* our overall ability to provide quality services to all participants
- Focus on the process (what we do) *and* the outcomes achieved by the participant

How do we make these judgments? A more sophisticated definition of evaluation gives us greater insight to answer this question. **Evaluation** is the systematic collection and analysis of data to address some criteria to make judgments about the worth or improvement of something (Henderson & Bialeschki, 2002). In other words, evaluation is making decisions based on identified criteria and supporting evidence. Figure 13.1 shows the components of evaluation delineated in this definition. You can see that evaluation is driven by explicit criteria and systematically collected data that allow you to make sound judgments. Evaluation helps to correct inherent biases in our thinking. It also serves these functions:

- Compare to a baseline
- Document attainment of goals
- Determine keys to success or failure
- Improve quality of services
- Set future direction
- Comply with external standards, from our profession and from regulatory agencies

Thus, evaluation is an important part of therapeutic recreation practice. Whether conducted for formative or summative feedback, at the individual or service/program level, or focused on process or outcomes, evaluation helps us make data-driven decisions to guide our actions. Evaluation helps us be accountable for our services and actions. In Table 13.1, we provide an overview of the levels and foci of evaluation, and the type of documentation we use in practice. In the next section, we look more closely at formative and summative evaluation, both critical to quality services and an important part of the helping process.

Formative versus Summative Evaluation

"When the cook tastes the soup, that's formative; when the guests taste the soup, that's summative."

—*Robert Stakes*

Have you ever been a student in a class and not received any feedback on how you were doing until you got the final course grade? Contrast that experience with a time you may have taken a class and received continuous feedback throughout the class on your performance. How was the learning experience different for you? What effect did the differing approaches have on your investment and motivation in the subject and the class itself? How did the quality of the relationship with the teacher differ in each case? How did feedback change your ability to learn and grow? Formative evaluation is an ongoing evaluation process that occurs as we work with a participant. It is a feedback loop that provides information to the participant on how well he or she

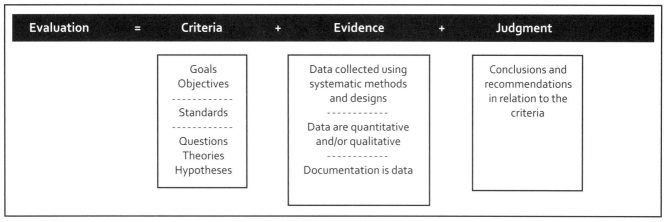

Figure 13.1 What is Evaluation?

is progressing toward goals, and also to the therapeutic recreation specialist on how well services are contributing to that progress. Formative evaluation is used to identify gaps and improve services or readjust goals and objectives. It allows us to make adjustments to what and how we implement services and allows participants to adjust their goals, objectives, and strategies as well. Formative evaluation is a collaborative process with the participant and team. It is a process-oriented form of evaluation, with the goal of maximizing the time spent with the participant. It becomes a part of the interaction with the participant, an important part of our strategies for helping.

Summative evaluation, on the other hand, is used at the end of services. It helps us be accountable for our services, and what was accomplished with the participant. Summative evaluation is primarily focused on outcomes and impact. It can also focus on process, in that we may scrutinize process when outcomes are not achieved. Summative evaluation helps us make judgments about the effectiveness of our services and the success the participant has experienced in reaching goals. Both forms of evaluation are important as we work with participants. In Figure 13.2 (p. 364), we provide a graphic representation of how formative and summative evaluation are used as we work with individual participants in therapeutic recreation services.

A key part of the formative evaluation process is constant feedback and communication between the participant, the therapeutic recreation specialist, and the team. Feedback is, in fact, an important catalyst in the therapeutic process. Formative evaluation feedback increases intrinsic motivation, clarifies goals and outcomes, enhances growth and learning, corrects misunderstandings, and increases self-determination. Feedback is important at all levels, but especially at the level between the therapeutic recreation specialist and the participant. Do you recall that in Chapter 10 *Planning* we presented research that showed that not all goals are created equal? The same holds true for feedback: For it to be truly effective in making positive change, it must meet certain criteria. These criteria,

Table 13.1 Levels and Focus of Evaluation

	Formative Evaluation	Summative Evaluation
Participant Level (Individual)	☐ Referral (P) ☐ Assessment (P & O) ☐ Individualized plan (P & O) ☐ Progress notes (P & O) ☐ Plan updates (P & O)	☐ Post-assessments (O) ☐ Discharge summary (O) ☐ Transition summary (O) ☐ Participant satisfaction survey (P & O)
Service Level (Comprehensive)	☐ Service or program plans and protocols (P) ☐ Logic models (P & O) ☐ Continuous quality improvement reports (P & O) ☐ M & E (monitoring and evaluation) reports (P & O)	☐ Final evaluation reports (O) ☐ Accreditation survey results (O) ☐ Annual reports (O) ☐ Audit reports (O)
P = process O = outcome		

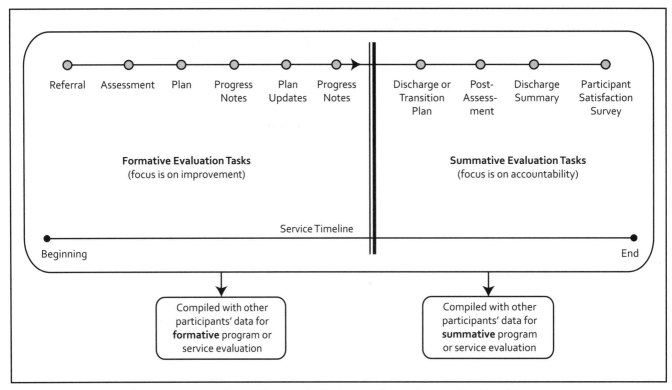

Figure 13.2 Formative and Summative Evaluation Tasks with Individual Participants

Effective feedback given to participants is…	
Solicited	Ask permission to give feedback, or create opportunities for feedback to be solicited; unsolicited feedback is generally resented and not listened to.
Goal-oriented	Provide feedback that is related to or helps clarify goals and helps identify gaps where more change is needed or to see progress, growth, and change.
Descriptive	Use clear, unambiguous language; be factual.
Specific	Give specific, targeted feedback, using examples and observations.
Focused on behavior	Focus feedback on behaviors or actions, not on the participant or the participant's personality.
Directed toward changeable behavior	Focus feedback on behaviors or situations that realistically can change, that are actionable.
Well-timed	Provide feedback as close as possible to the action that elicits it; the shorter the delay the less chance the feedback will get distorted and the more relevant the feedback will be.
Given in limited amounts	Give enough feedback to be meaningful, but not so much that you overwhelm the participant.
Mostly positive	Since the purpose of feedback is to support and improve the efforts of the participant, think about the range of activities the person has performed and not just the problems or issues. Highlight strengths and positive actions.
Given in a friendly, supportive environment	Create a trusting relationship that is authentic and accepting.
Followed up on	Comment on the performance that follows your feedback; make feedback a cyclical process.

Figure 13.3 Effective Feedback as Part of Formative Evaluation and the Helping Relationship

which appear in Figure 13.3, help ensure that feedback used during formative evaluation does indeed contribute to fulfilling participants' goals.

Both formative and summative evaluation processes are important to quality assurance in therapeutic recreation practice. Also important to quality is a focus on both the outcomes of services and the process used to achieve the outcomes.

Process versus Outcome Evaluation

Evaluation can focus on process (methods and activities) and outcomes (what effect methods and activities have on participants). In Figure 13.4, we offer a visual to conceptualize our interactions with participants using a systems approach. In this approach, we identify the inputs, process, and outcomes of our services, within a larger context. **Inputs** are those resources that are identified as necessary to implement the activities or methods. Inputs include such things as staff, facilities, participants, monetary resources, equipment, supplies, and the like. **Process** and **outputs** are what we actually do as we interact with the participant. Process includes specific actions, interventions, programs, and services. Outputs include amount of time spent in activities, number of participants served, number of programs offered, and the like. **Outcomes** are what participants achieve with our support, and include objectives, goals, and dreams.

When we focus evaluation on process, we are systematically collecting data about how well we are implementing services. Data can include such things as post-session report forms, debriefing with participants and other staff on what went well and what didn't, observation, interviews, and the like. When we focus evaluation on outcomes, we listen to the voice of the participant in judging the value, worth, importance, or status of services provided and outcomes experienced.

Fundamental to evaluation is a strengths approach. Empowerment evaluation is one type of evaluation approach that embraces a strengths and person-centered perspective. In the next section, we provide you with an introduction to empowerment evaluation, which is being used with increasing frequency in health and human services (Fetterman & Wandersman, 2007).

EMPOWERMENT EVALUATION IN THERAPEUTIC RECREATION

We started this chapter with a definition of empowerment: to give or delegate power or authority, or to enable. The World Bank, which is an international financial institution that seeks to reduce poverty by giving loans to developing countries, defines empowerment this way: "Empowerment is the process of increasing

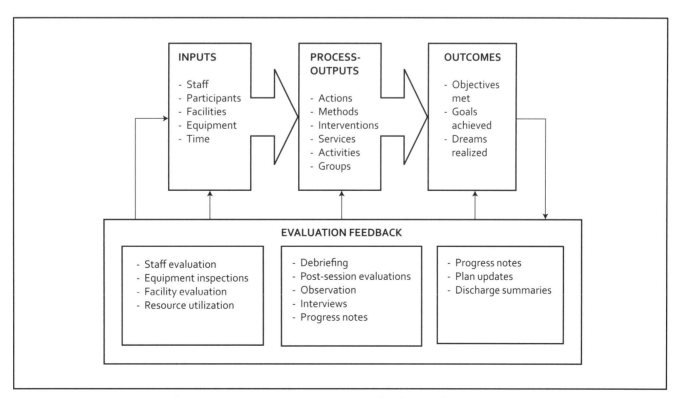

Figure 13.4 Input-Process-Outcomes-Feedback Model for Evaluation

the capacity of individuals or groups to make choices and to transform those choices into desired actions and outcomes" (2009, para. 1). When empowerment is applied to evaluation, it integrates the preceding two definitions: **Empowerment evaluation** is an approach that aims to increase the success of achieving outcomes by providing participants with the tools for ~~assessing~~ *evaluating* the planning, implementation, and self-evaluation of progress and services (Fetterman & Wandersman, 2007). Whereas traditional evaluation is professional-centered and driven, empowerment evaluation is driven by the participant, and is participatory in nature. In Figure 13.5, we compare and contrast traditional evaluation to empowerment evaluation.

Empowerment evaluation is conducted by the participant and the therapeutic recreation specialist, and is driven by 10 principles (Fetterman & Wandersman, 2005):

1. *Improvement*—The evaluators (the participant and therapeutic recreation specialist) want to see positive change and success. This differs from traditional evaluation, where the evaluator remains neutral and objective.

2. *Ownership*—The participant has a right to have the most control in actions and decisions that affect his or her life; the participant controls the evaluation process and puts the evaluation findings to use. The therapeutic recreation specialist helps the participant develop skills and knowledge to conduct evaluation and make good, data-driven decisions.

3. *Inclusion*—The participant, his or her circle of support, the team, and any other stakeholders are a part of evaluation planning and decision-making. Inclusiveness leads to better ideas, better communication, and better follow-through.

4. *Democratic participation*—Decisions about evaluation and the use of evaluation results are clear, understandable, and transparent to the participant and other stakeholders. Decisions are made as a group. In therapeutic recreation, decisions will often happen in planning meetings, such as care conferences, IEP meetings, or other team meetings.

5. *Social justice*—Results of evaluation are used to challenge inequities, inaccessible or unwelcoming environments or groups, and systemic unfairness. Empowerment evaluation is used to make positive change for the participant and the environments in which he or she lives, works, and plays. This principle firmly roots evaluation in an ecological approach, where change often needs to happen in environments and not just in participants. In Chapter 14 *Advocacy* we will explore in more depth the roles therapeutic recreation specialists can take in advocating for change in communities and agencies with the participant.

6. *Knowledge*—Participants and therapeutic recreation specialists recognize different forms of knowledge, from scientific to intuitive, held by the participant and by the professional, and use all forms of knowledge as decisions are made in evaluation.

7. *Evidence-based strategies*—While all forms of knowledge are respected, evidence-based strategies, or empirically tested "best practices" are especially valuable when used sensitively with participants. Therapeutic recreation specialists have a responsibility to know the research literature, and to share important evidence-based strategies with participants, helping them integrate evidence-based practices within their own context and culture.

8. *Capacity building*—Evaluation results are used to make changes at the participant and environment level, and at the therapeutic-recreation-service level, to reach goals and to improve well-being and quality of life. Changes are focused on building strengths and capacities that become more clear as services and progress are evaluated as a team. Participants are better able to identify capacities as they learn evaluation skills, methods, and techniques that are user-friendly from professionals.

9. *Organizational learning*—This kind of learning includes developing a culture of reflection on and improvement in the participant and his or her circle of support, as well as the agency in which therapeutic recreation services are delivered. Organization learning is an attitude of all

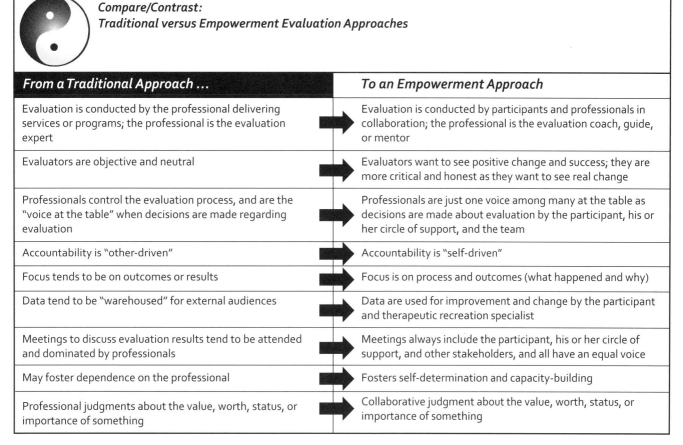

Figure 13.5 Compare/Contrast: Traditional versus Empowerment Evaluation Approaches

involved to want to reflect, learn, and grow using insights gained from evaluation.

10. *Accountability*—Everyone involved in a therapeutic recreation service—the professional, the participant, his or her circle of support, and the team—is responsible for the outcomes of that service. Everyone has a stake in improving the process and the outcome. Empowerment evaluation has more accountability than traditional evaluation methods because power is shared and decisions are made collaboratively based on data. Participants who are empowered to evaluate services and outcomes hold professionals highly accountable.

A fundamental premise of empowerment evaluation, underlying these 10 principles, is that people who engage in the act of conducting their own evaluations are more likely to find the results credible and to act on the recommendations.

When you use an empowerment evaluation approach in therapeutic recreation practice, you are guided by these principles. You plan how you will evaluate participant progress *with* the participant, teaching him or her methods and techniques of evaluation that may be needed. You implement the evaluation plan *with* the participant, who helps you collect data or information to make decisions. You analyze the evaluation data *with* the participant, and use it collaboratively to evaluate progress and make changes. You continually use feedback to *share* what each of you is learning, and you continually adjust actions and goals *with* the participant. You decide *together* when a goal has been met or an outcome achieved. You facilitate the full participation of the participant in any team meetings that focus on evaluation and planning updates. This may mean you advocate for the participant at these meetings. You involve the participant in documenting progress, and openly share documentation *with* the participant. Putting empowerment evaluation principles into practice means you become *a partner with* the participant as you decide how well things are going and how much outcomes are being met. With this important idea of partnership in mind, let's discuss how you evaluate individual participant progress.

Evaluating Individual Participant Progress

Recall the therapeutic recreation process—assess, plan, implement, and evaluate (or discover, dream and design, deliver, and deliberate). Formative evaluation starts at the first step of the process, and continues until you terminate services with the participant. In formative evaluation, we focus on these main areas: evaluating the referral, the assessment, the plan, the implementation, progress toward goals, and plan updates (including transition or discharge plans). In summative evaluation, once services end, we determine the outcomes of services with the participant, and document those outcomes in a discharge or other end-of-service summary.

The first step in formative evaluation is the **referral.** How we initiate services with a participant must be clearly documented. This will vary in form by service delivery system, but its function remains consistent—to clearly state who initiated the referral and why. Formative evaluation asks these questions: Is this referral appropriate? Is it asking for the right services in the right place at the right time for the participant? The referral must be carefully documented to provide data to answer these questions.

The next step is **assessment.** If we do not have a benchmark of where our services started, we have no basis for comparison as we implement services. Assessment provides the starting point, in addition to helping us develop the plan with the participant. Thus, assessment forms part of the basis for formative and summative evaluation. As we presented in Chapter 9 *Assessment*, the assessment results must be clearly and thoroughly documented.

The **plan** is the next important step in formative evaluation. Recall in Chapter 10 *Planning* the criteria we provided to judge the effectiveness of the plan, including the goals, objectives, and actions. In formative evaluation, we continually ask if the goals, methods, and timelines are appropriate. In order to evaluate how well our services worked, and what outcomes were achieved, we need a clear and well-written plan with clear goals and objectives. The plan provides the roadmap for evaluation and must be carefully documented.

Once the plan is implemented, **progress reports** capture in writing how the participant is doing in relation to the goals and objectives in the plan, as well as any other unintended outcomes. Progress reports can take many forms, including progress notes, attendance records, goal attainment scaling forms, and more. We will present detailed information on how to document progress in the next section, *Documentation Basics*. Here, it is important to note that progress reports are a critical part of formative evaluation. Progress reports provide the feedback needed to clarify if the participant is progressing toward goals and if the services are effective.

In a formative evaluation plan, we also collect information on how well we implemented the plan. We document any incidences that may have occurred or any deviations from the planned actions. This part of formative evaluation focuses on the work of the therapeutic recreation specialist, rather than on changes in the participant.

In most settings, the way we record data as we work with participants is through documentation, sometimes called clinical writing. Next, we provide an in-depth look at the skills you need to thoroughly and accurately create a record of your services and their impact on the participant.

Documentation Basics

Evaluation relies on data—without data, we cannot judge the value, worth, status, or importance of something. In therapeutic recreation practice, we often collect data through documentation. In this section, we overview what we mean by documentation, why it is so important, when it must be done, and how you document. Regardless of service delivery system, whether you are in a healthcare setting or a community-based program, documentation is critical to communication, collaboration, rigorous evaluation, and service improvement. Documentation may vary in its form across these differing delivery systems, but its function remains the same—to put into record the services provided and their impact on the participant.

What Is Documentation?

"If it's not in writing, it didn't happen."

Documentation is putting in writing the elements of the therapeutic recreation process described above. In every setting that therapeutic recreation services are delivered, this maxim holds true: "If it's not in writing, it didn't happen." In Figure 13.6, we show the forms of documentation you complete at each step of the process.

The following components are included in documentation:

- Referral
- Assessment summary
- Plan
- Progress reports or progress notes

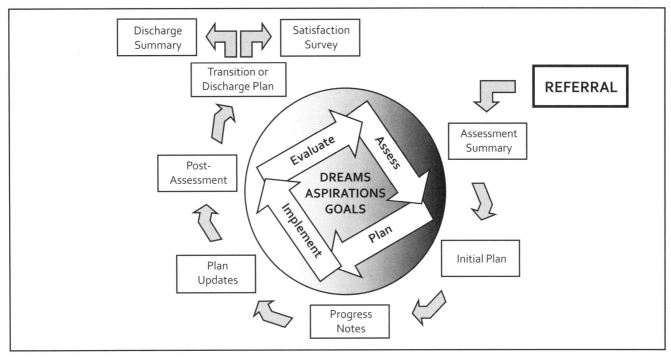

Figure 13.6 The Therapeutic Recreation Process and Documentation

- Plan updates
- Discharge summary

In Chapter 9 *Assessment* and Chapter 10 *Planning* we provided detailed information on how to document the assessment and plan. Referrals, progress reports, and discharge summaries are described here.

Referral

A referral varies by the service system in which you are providing therapeutic recreation services. However, regardless of setting, how we initiate services with a participant must be clearly documented. The referral must clearly state who made the referral and why. In a medical setting, a referral must come from a physician. In other settings, the referral can be made by many different professionals, by family members, and even by the participant. The typical elements of a referral appear below:

- Referral date
- Identifying information for the participant
- Reason for the referral
- Referral request (general services, specific services, assessment, etc.)
- Precautions, special needs, medications, and other important information
- Signature and contact information of the person making the referral

In Figure 13.7, we provide three different examples of referrals. One is a typical referral form that you may see in a medical setting. The second is a referral form from a community-based inclusion service. And the third is a typical "self-referral" on a registration form for a recreation program, where the participant or his or her circle of support asks for therapeutic recreation or inclusion services.

A referral initiates an assessment and the development of a plan, which have been described in previous chapters. Once the plan is implemented, regular progress reports are the next form of documentation.

Progress Reports or Notes

Progress reports, often called progress notes, are a form of clinical writing that documents in the permanent record current information about a participant and his or her response to services. Progress reports vary widely by setting. Often, progress notes are written in narrative form, but may also be in the form of checklists, graphs, numeric ratings, and other methods of documenting participation in and response to services provided. Progress notes can be written with the help of the participant.

Narrative Progress Notes

Narrative progress notes are written in free form. According to Shank and Coyle (2002), narrative progress notes are written in any logical order, so long as they address the goals and objectives of the participant. Narrative progress notes are less commonly used than other forms of notes.

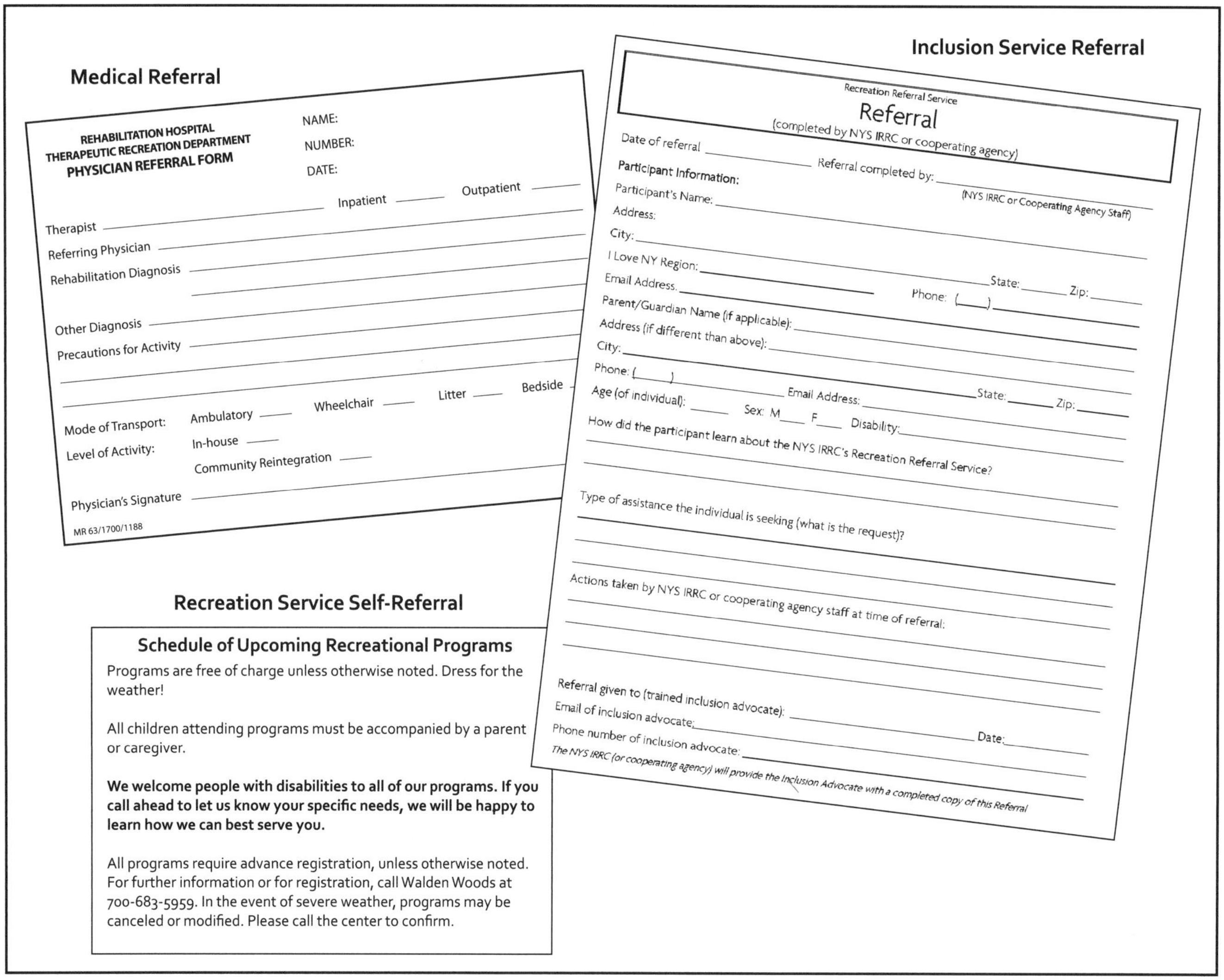

Medical Referral

REHABILITATION HOSPITAL
THERAPEUTIC RECREATION DEPARTMENT
PHYSICIAN REFERRAL FORM

NAME:
NUMBER:
DATE:

Inpatient ___ Outpatient ___
Therapist ___
Referring Physician ___
Rehabilitation Diagnosis ___
Other Diagnosis ___
Precautions for Activity ___
Mode of Transport: Ambulatory ___ Wheelchair ___ Litter ___ Bedside ___
Level of Activity: In-house ___
Community Reintegration ___
Physician's Signature ___
MR 63/1700/1188

Inclusion Service Referral

Recreation Referral Service
Referral
(completed by NYS IRRC or cooperating agency)

Date of referral ___ Referral completed by: ___
(NYS IRRC or Cooperating Agency Staff)
Participant Information:
Participant's Name: ___
Address: ___
City: ___ State: ___ Zip: ___
I Love NY Region: ___
Email Address: ___ Phone: ( ) ___
Parent/Guardian Name (if applicable): ___
Address (if different than above): ___
City: ___ State: ___ Zip: ___
Phone: ( ) ___ Email Address: ___
Age (of individual): ___ Sex: M___ F___ Disability: ___
How did the participant learn about the NYS IRRC's Recreation Referral Service?
Type of assistance the individual is seeking (what is the request)?
Actions taken by NYS IRRC or cooperating agency staff at time of referral:
Referral given to (trained inclusion advocate): ___
Email of inclusion advocate: ___ Date: ___
Phone number of inclusion advocate: ___
The NYS IRRC (or cooperating agency) will provide the Inclusion Advocate with a completed copy of this Referral

Recreation Service Self-Referral

Schedule of Upcoming Recreational Programs

Programs are free of charge unless otherwise noted. Dress for the weather!

All children attending programs must be accompanied by a parent or caregiver.

We welcome people with disabilities to all of our programs. If you call ahead to let us know your specific needs, we will be happy to learn how we can best serve you.

All programs require advance registration, unless otherwise noted. For further information or for registration, call Walden Woods at 700-683-5959. In the event of severe weather, programs may be canceled or modified. Please call the center to confirm.

Figure 13.7 Examples of Referrals

SOAP Notes

A more typical format for progress notes is a SOAP note. SOAP notes include these components: subjective data, objective data, an assessment or analysis of that data, and a plan update. In Table 13.2, we provide an explanation for each element of SOAP, as well as an example progress note. Other variations of SOAP notes include SOAPIE or SOAPIER (subjective, objective, analysis/assessment, plan, intervention/implementation, evaluation, revision to plan). The addition of intervention/implementation, evaluation, and revision provide additional documentation of the specific services you provide and how those services are impacting a participant.

Focus Charting and DARP Notes

Another typical format for progress notes is focus charting using DARP notes. Focus charting is a form of documentation that "focuses" the clinical record on important elements of services, often goals or objectives. The focus is written next to the progress note entry, to provide a form of indexing to the note, showing the content of that particular entry. DARP notes include these components: data, action, response, and a plan update. In Table 13.3, we offer an example of a DARP note, using the same scenario with Joanna that was used in Table 13.2. Focus charting allows for more efficient, accountable documentation that helps to avoid repetitious entries, facilitates communication among team members, and focuses on both the services provided and the participant's goals and responses.

PIE Charting and Charting By Exception

Other formats that you may use for documenting participant progress include PIE charting and charting by exception. PIE charting is problem- or deficit-oriented and associated with the medical model. PIE stands for problem, intervention, and evaluation. Progress notes are written based on identified problems. Charting by exception is a method of documenting participant

Table 13.2 SOAP Progress Notes

Elements of SOAP Notes	Example of a SOAP Note
S = Subjective What the participant said	S: "I want to stay in my room. Leave me alone."
O = Objective What behaviors you observe or other factual data	O: Joanna refused to attend the planned group activity today; she remained in bed with her face turned to the wall; she avoided eye contact and her voice was monotone.
A = Assessment or Analysis The conclusions or interpretation you make	A: Joanna is withdrawn and sad today; she seems very fatigued after her chemotherapy session.
P = Plan Based on the interaction, what immediate steps you plan to take	P: Approach Joanna later today after she has rested; bring her favorite music to listen to as she regains energy, as well as photos of the flowers blooming in the terrace garden that she helped plant. Assess her ability to participate in the horticulture group tomorrow.

Table 13.3 Focus Charting and DARP Progress Notes

Elements of Focus Charting and DARP Notes	Example of a DARP Note	
D = Data What the participant said; what behaviors or factual data you observe; your conclusions or interpretation	Focus: Goal to increase satisfying leisure everyday	Data: Joanna was in her room after lunch and didn't come to her favorite group, horticulture therapy. She usually attends early and stays late.
A = Action What you did		Action: I approached Joanna in her room to assist her to the group session, if needed.
R = Response How the participant responded to what you did		Response: "I want to stay in my room. Leave me alone." Joanna refused to attend the horticulture group activity today; she remained in bed with her face turned to the wall; she avoided eye contact and her voice was monotone. Joanna is withdrawn and sad today; she seems very fatigued after her chemotherapy session.
P = Plan Based on the interaction, what immediate steps you plan to take		Plan: Approach Joanna later today after she has rested; bring her favorite music to listen to as she regains energy, as well as photos of the flowers blooming in the terrace garden that she helped plant. Assess her ability to participate in the horticulture group tomorrow.

progress in relation to a particular standard. If the participant's progress deviates from what is considered normal or routine, then that is charted. Both these approaches are used in medical settings more so than other health or human service agencies.

Progress Note Content

Whether using narrative, SOAP, focus notes with DARP, or other methods, progress note content typically focuses on the progress a participant is making toward goals and objectives in relation to the services you provide. Other focus areas can include setbacks from meeting goals, new patterns of behavior, consistency of behavior, successful or unsuccessful attempts at tasks or activities, follow through on plans, attendance, participation, environmental changes, supports put in place, and the like. Progress notes are the record of the "implementation" phase of the therapeutic recreation process with a participant. In an empowerment approach, you will invite the participant to assist you in completing progress reports. The participant may have a different perspective on what is important to document. The inclusion of the participant's voice in documentation will provide a fuller, richer, and more credible record of the therapeutic recreation process in action.

Progress notes provide ongoing evidence or data that we can use to evaluate that the plan is being implemented as agreed upon and written, the strategies and services are having a positive impact for the participant or, if not, the plan is being revised to better help him or her reach goals and dreams.

Discharge Summary or End-of-Service Summary

The final component of documentation is the discharge or end-of-service summary. In essence, you begin discharge planning the first day you begin to work with a participant. You are constantly "working to work yourself out of a job," to help the participant develop natural supports, enhanced leisure, and ongoing well-being. We discussed this in depth in Chapter 12 *Transition and Inclusion*. When you reach the point where the participant's goals are achieved, or when the participant leaves your agency for other reasons (discharged to another setting, moving, or unfortunately, lack of payment or other negative reasons), you will complete a discharge summary. The components of a discharge summary include:

- Reason for referral (from the initial referral form)
- Summary of the therapeutic recreation assessment and pre-assessment scores
- Summary of the therapeutic recreation services provided
- Post-assessment results in comparison to pre-assessment scores
- Progress toward goals, objectives, and other outcomes, and dates when achieved
- Status at discharge or end of service
- Any remaining areas the participant would still like to work on
- Recommendations, including any follow-up, referrals, community resources, and post-discharge instructions
- Signature of therapeutic recreation specialist and, ideally, the participant

The format of the discharge summary will vary by agency, but typically includes the areas listed above. The discharge summary provides a summative evaluation of the outcomes gained by the participant while receiving services at your agency. It provides a picture of how the participant changed from pre- to post-assessment. In Figure 13.8, we offer some examples of typical discharge summary forms.

How Do You Document?

Documentation Organization

Documentation is typically completed and compiled as a team, and the participant's record is organized around the goals in the plan. In medical settings, the record is still commonly organized around the problems of the participant. This is called "problem-oriented" documentation. Both goal-oriented and problem-oriented documentation are interdisciplinary or transdisciplinary in nature, and the sections of the official participant record contain entries from many different disciplines organized by problem or goal.

Another way the participant record may be organized is by discipline or source. This is called "source-oriented" documentation. In this format, therapeutic recreation would have a section in the official record, and all documentation completed by therapeutic recreation specialists would be contained in that section. The difficulty with source-oriented documentation is a lack of unity or integration of the documented progress of the participant. This is a less common approach to documentation, but it may still be used in settings where only a few disciplines are working. Regardless of how the information is organized, you must follow very specific guidelines for clinical writing.

Writing Guidelines for Documentation

Documentation is a particular and precise form of writing. It includes all information recorded by a team member in a professional capacity in relation to the provision of services to the participant. Figure 13.9 provides a graphic of what are called the "C's" of documentation. Let's look at each of these characteristics of clinical writing:

- **Comprehensive, concise, and complete.** The entries you make in the participant's record include what services you provided and how the participant responded to the services. Entries act as evidence of your contributions to the overall service provision to the participant and the clinical judgments you made in collaboration with the participant. The entries document how the participant responded to services and the impact they had. Documentation must be complete but not duplicative of information already contained in the overall participant record. Entries must be dated and clearly signed by you as the professional completing the documentation, with both your name and your professional title.

Chapter 13–Evaluation in Strengths-Based Therapeutic Recreation Practice • 373

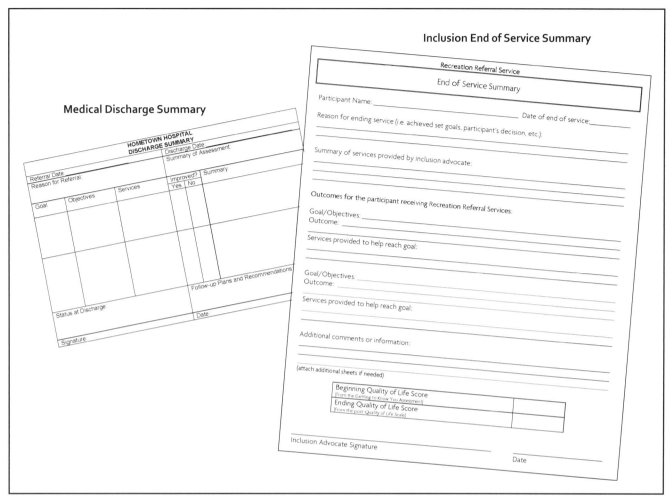

Figure 13.8 Examples of Discharge Summaries

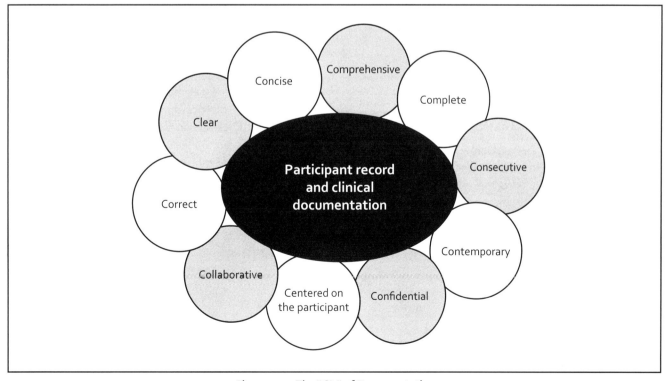

Figure 13.9 The "C's" of Documentation

- **Correct and clear.** The entries you make in the participant's record must be factual, accurate, true, and honest. Your entries must be easily understood over time and after services have ended. If documentation is hand-written versus electronic, you must write legibly in black ink. You must use correct grammar, spelling, and punctuation, and avoid slang. You must correct errors appropriately (strikethrough the error and initial it), and not use erasure or white-out. You must use only those abbreviations approved by your agency. All these actions will ensure a correct and clear entry in the participant's record.

- **Contemporary and consecutive.** Documentation that you complete as soon after the interaction with the participant as possible will be more accurate and complete, as you will remember it most clearly. "Contemporary documentation" means current and timely documentation. Documentation should also be completed in the consecutive or chronological order that services are provided to the participant. If a late entry is entered in the participant's record, it should be clearly identified as such, and should provide both the date the interaction occurred and the date the documentation was completed. If the entries are hand-written, no blank spaces should be left in the record and, if there is a blank space, a line should be written through it. Back entries or entries squeezed in between other entries should never be made. All these actions ensure that documentation is contemporary and consecutive.

- **Centered on the participant and collaborative.** The entries you make in the participant's record are based on valid, honest, and accurate observations and interpretations. Avoid biased, unfounded, and judgmental interpretations of the participant and his or her progress. Entries should be written in everyday language that is respectful of the participant, and they should be shared with the participant (and circle of support if permission is given) openly. If it is feasible in your setting or agency, the participant can assist in completing documentation, or reviewing documentation for accuracy. Not only can you collaborate with the participant, you can also collaborate with other team members in completing documentation. These actions ensure documentation that is collaborative, respectful, and person-centered.

- **Confidential.** All entries in the participant's record are confidential. As a therapeutic recreation specialist, you have ethical, professional, and legal obligations to maintain confidentiality of information about the participant. Confidentiality means that you safeguard the information you collect about individual participants and that you do not share that information with those not authorized to have access to it. Table 13.4 provides you with an overview of the ethical and legal mandates that apply to confidentiality. Our profession provides guidance on confidentiality in our codes of ethics. Federal law, the Health Insurance Portability and Accountability Act, or HIPAA (CDCP, 2003), mandates confidentiality of health information that applies to all entities that collect and store information about participants and their health. All these resources help guide us as we document our interactions with participants. However, it is important to be aware of our own values about privacy and how they may affect how we treat the privacy of the information of the participants we serve (see Figure 13.10, p. 376).

In summary, clinical documentation must meet many criteria to be considered of high quality. In Figure 13.11 (p. 376), we offer a checklist to help you evaluate the quality of your documentation. Use this checklist to develop or refine your level of competency to meet the standards of not only our own discipline, but those of the agency and service system in which you work.

Streamlining and Improving Documentation

Documentation is meant to not only permanently record, but also to improve the quality of services to participants. Yet, because of the amount of time it can take to complete, as well as its complexity, documentation is often perceived as a hindrance to quality interaction with participants. To decrease the burden of

Table 13.4 Ethical and Legal Obligations for Confidentiality of Documentation

Ethical Obligation: Professional Code of Ethics	**American Therapeutic Recreation Association Code of Ethics (2009)** *Principle 8: Confidentiality and Privacy* Recreational Therapy personnel have a duty to disclose all relevant information to persons seeking services; they also have a corresponding duty not to disclose private information to third parties. If a situation arises that requires disclosure of confidential information about an individual (i.e., to protect the individual's welfare or the interest of others) the professional has the responsibility to inform the individual served of the circumstances. **Canadian Therapeutic Recreation Association Code of Ethics (2005)** *Principle 2: Obligation to the Individual and Society* In advocating the importance of leisure, recreation and play, professionals are committed to equal opportunity and promote balance between the needs of the individual and the needs of others. Professionals are loyal to and committed to the well-being of the individuals they serve. They maintain privacy and confidentiality of the individual being served by practicing informed consent and seeking permission prior to the release of information. **National Therapeutic Recreation Society Code of Ethics (2001)** *Principle 2: The Obligation of the Professional to the Individual* **Privacy**: Professionals respect the privacy of individuals. Communications are kept confidential except with the explicit consent of the individual or where the welfare of the individual or others is clearly imperiled. Individuals are informed of the nature and the scope of confidentiality.
Legal Obligation: Health Insurance Portability and Accountability Act (HIPAA) *Privacy Rules*	*The Privacy Rule (2003) requires covered entities to:* • notify individuals regarding their privacy rights and how their protected health information is used or disclosed • adopt and implement internal privacy policies and procedures • train employees to understand these privacy policies and procedures as appropriate for their functions within the covered entity • designate individuals who are responsible for implementing privacy policies and procedures, and who will receive privacy-related complaints • establish privacy requirements in contracts with business associates that perform covered functions • have in place appropriate administrative, technical, and physical safeguards to protect the privacy of health information • meet obligations with respect to health consumers exercising their rights under the Privacy Rule. (para. 19) Individual rights include: • the right to receive access to protected health information • the right to request amendments to protected health information • the right to receive adequate notice; with limited exceptions, individuals have the right to receive a notice of the uses and disclosures the covered entity will make of their protected health information, their rights under the Privacy Rule, and the covered entity's obligations with respect to that information • the right to receive an accounting of disclosures, including the name of the person or entity who received the information, date of the disclosure, a brief description of the information disclosed, and a brief explanation of the reasons for disclosure or copy of the request • the right to request restrictions on certain uses or disclosures of their protected health information

Note: In 2010, the National Therapeutic Recreation Society became the Inclusion and Accessibility Network, still affiliated with the National Recreation and Park Association.

documentation and to decrease the amount of error or miscommunication in it, many agencies use streamlined documentation systems, such as electronic records, checklists, and other methods.

Electronic Records

A major thrust of many health and human service agencies is to convert all paper documentation to an electronic format, and to use computers and other electronic devices as the main method of documentation (Mehta & Partin, 2007). Reasons for the conversion to electronic records include:

- Improved communication and ability to share information among professionals and the participant more clearly and quickly
- Improved legibility and access for multiple users from multiple locations

My Cultural Lens:
The Ethics of Privacy

According to the National Therapeutic Recreation Society's Code of Ethics (2001), "The value placed on privacy varies greatly among people of different personality type, family background, and ethnic group. This does not usually present serious ethical problems in dealings among peers; but in the therapeutic setting, professionals hold power over clients and are in a position to impose their values. They thus have the obligation to be cognizant of the many different ways of viewing privacy and to carefully guard the spatial and informational privacy of those they serve. Since much information of a very private nature is needed in order to offer effective treatment, great pains must be taken to share that information only with other professionals, and then on a need-to-know basis. Although the law protects confidentiality of patient information, ethical practice requires that such information be held in a spirit of reverence" (p. 8)

What cultural differences may affect values of privacy? What are your own values about the privacy of others? How do your values represent your cultural background? How are your values different from others you know? Discuss these questions with colleagues or classmates.

Figure 13.10 My Cultural Lens: The Ethics of Privacy

Documentation Checklist

Comprehensive, Concise, Complete
- ☐ Does the entry include all the important facts about your interaction with the participant? Does it include the services you provided and the participant's reaction to the services?
- ☐ Did you avoid redundant entries? Do you stay focused on the important aspects of the interaction with the participant?
- ☐ Are all elements of documentation present in the official record? Referral? Assessment? Plan? Progress notes? Any incidents, variances, or accidents? Discharge or transition summary?
- ☐ Is the entry signed by you, with your professional title after your name? Is the entry dated? Is the participant's name on every page of the record?

Correct, Clear
- ☐ Is the entry accurate, honest, and factual?
- ☐ Is the entry easily understood using clear language? Will that be true over time?
- ☐ Did you write legibly with black ink (if hand-written)?
- ☐ Did you use correct grammar, spelling, and punctuation? Did you avoid slang?
- ☐ Did you use only those abbreviations approved by your agency?
- ☐ Did you correct any errors by drawing a line through the error, and initialing the error (if hand-written)?

Contemporary, Consecutive
- ☐ Did you complete the entry as soon as possible after your interaction with the participant?
- ☐ Are all your entries in chronological order? If not, are those entries that appear out of order clearly labeled as "late?"
- ☐ If you entered a late entry, did you provide the date of the documentation and the date of service accurately? Did you label it "late entry"?
- ☐ Did you draw a single line through any blank spaces in the participant's record, if hand-written, and initial it? Did you evenly space all entries, with none squeezed in between others?

Centered on the Participant, Collaborative
- ☐ Is the entry written in plain language, and in a respectful manner, so it can be shared with the participant?
- ☐ Are there opportunities for the participant to collaborate with documentation?

Confidential
- ☐ Have all steps been taken to assure the confidentiality of the information in the participant's record? If electronic, password protected? If hand-written, in a secure area?
- ☐ Have appropriate releases been obtained? Appropriate disclosures?

Figure 13.11 A Checklist to Evaluate the Quality of Your Documentation

- Automated reminders and alerts can be part of the documentation process
- Decreased risk of error and duplication of services, and increased safety for the participant
- Improved storage and retrieval of information, as well as the ability to integrate records from many sources into one record more easily (this integrated record that follows the participant is called the Electronic Health Record, or EHR)

Electronic records are a powerful method to streamline documentation and make information more usable and accessible for the team and participant. In order to ensure confidentiality of documentation in electronic formats, team members must take extra precautions than with a paper record. These precautions include keeping information password-protected, changing passwords often, using privacy screens on computer monitors, fully logging off when documentation is completed, never deleting information, and the like. Every agency will have policies and procedures in place to safeguard confidentiality when electronic documentation is used.

Checklists, Rating Scales, Flow Sheets, and Other Forms of Documentation

Many agencies develop checklists, rating scales, flow sheets, and other abbreviated methods of documenting information instead of using narrative data. These forms of documentation are used for recurring or routine activities or standardized activities. Documentation forms such as checklists or rating scales can be completed in collaboration with the participant more easily than narrative notes. Checklists and other forms of documentation can foster more complete records, as the checklists act as cognitive prompts when recording data (Hales, Terblanche, Fowler, & Sibbald, 2008). However, checklists can also limit individualization and richer data, if no space is provided for narrative. Often, checklists and narrative documentation are combined. In Figure 13.12 (p. 378), we offer some sample documentation forms that incorporate checklists, flow charts, or rating scales. In Figure 13.13 (p. 379), we present an interesting study that documented the common elements of therapeutic recreation practice across several spinal cord injury units. Once the common elements were identified, a streamlined method of documentation could be developed, based on the FIM (discussed in Chapter 9 *Assessment*).

When Is Documentation Completed?

When documentation is completed varies depending on your agency. In short-term acute settings, such as inpatient hospitals, you may document every time you interact with a participant. In long-term settings, you may document once a week. Each agency will have guidelines for the timeliness of documentation, often mandated by agency accreditation standards.

Referrals are completed immediately, to begin services. Assessment results and plans are documented within the time allotted at the agency, but often within a short time frame from the referral. Progress notes are written as you interact with the participant, on a daily, weekly, or even monthly basis, depending on the setting. Discharge or end-of-service summaries are written within the designated amount of time set by the agency, when you end services with the participant.

Any incidents that involve accidents or injuries, or variances from policies or procedures of the agency, are documented immediately and with a high level of factual detail. Often, you will need to ask others present as witnesses to also document what happened, or at least collect their names and contact information.

Remember the "C's" of documentation—contemporary and current entries are the most valid and reliable. The closer you document your interaction with a participant to the time it occurs, the more accurate your writing will likely be.

Why Is Documentation Important?

Documentation is vitally important to develop a permanent record of services and provide data for evaluation. It is important for several other reasons as well.

Documentation...
- Helps assure quality services by providing data for feedback and improvement.
- Facilitates communication with the team and the participant; this is especially important in settings or agencies where many different staff are working with the participant during varying times and may not have opportunities to meet in person on a regular basis.
- Provides a legal record of your services and their impact on the participant; this protects the participant, you as the professional, and the agency.

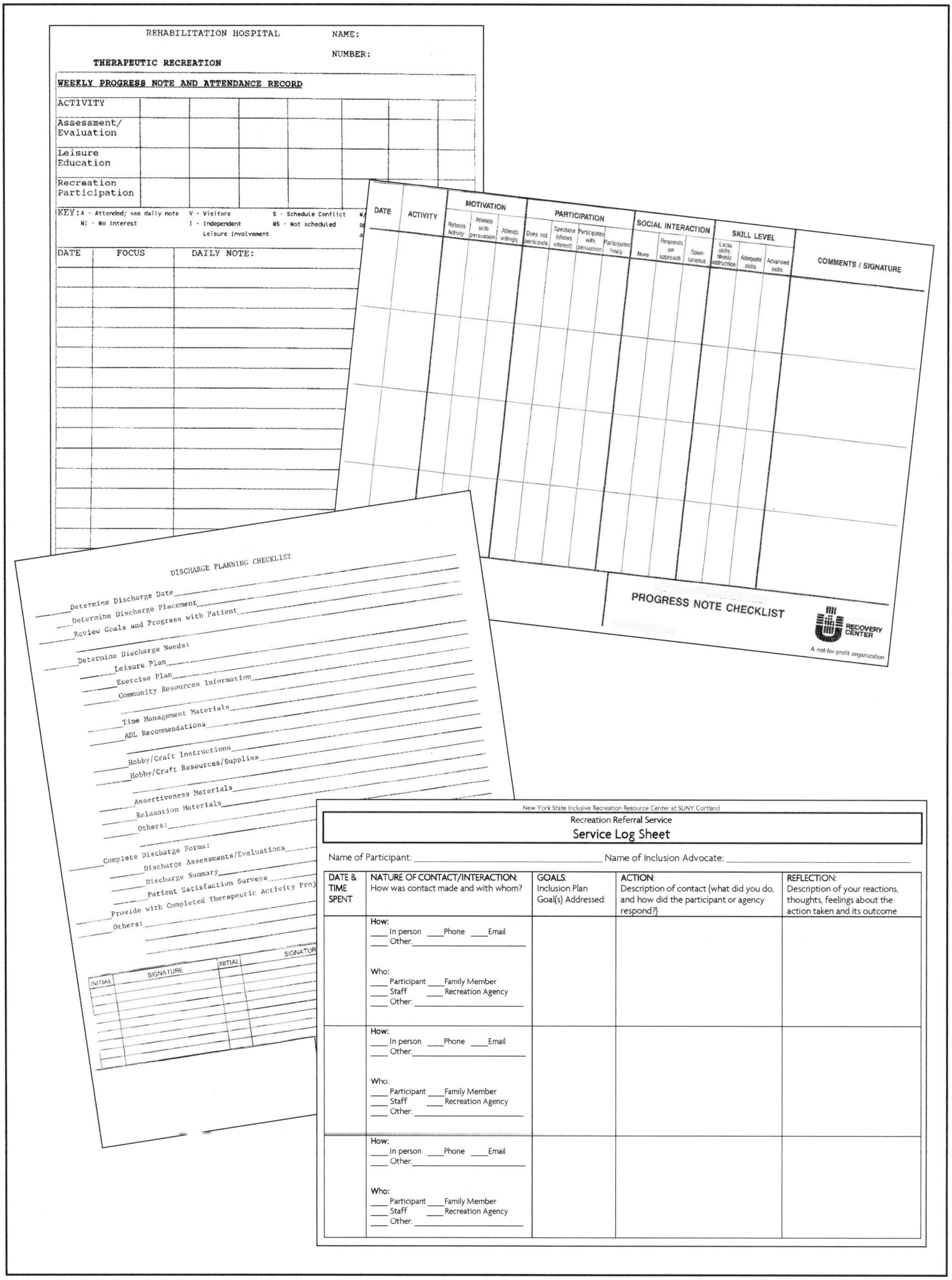

378 • Therapeutic Recreation Practice: A Strengths Approach

Figure 13.12 Examples of Checklists and Rating Scales

Primary Source Support: A Uniform Taxonomy for Therapeutic Recreation

Cahow, C., Skolnick, S., Joyce, J., Jug, J., Dragon, C., & Gassaway, J. (2009). SCIRehab Project Series: The therapeutic recreation taxonomy. *The Journal of Spinal Cord Medicine, 32*(3), 298–306.

The researchers who conducted this study were practicing therapeutic recreation specialists at six different spinal cord injury (SCI) rehabilitation hospitals around the United States. This study was a part of a larger effort to tie rehabilitation activities and interventions to outcomes for people with spinal cord injury, across the many disciplines involved. In this study, the therapeutic recreation specialists developed a therapeutic recreation documentation system that described all aspects of therapeutic recreation services across six different large rehabilitation hospitals. The methods involved describing and classifying all activities and services offered to 1,500 different participants with spinal cord injury.

The results of the research led to the development of a taxonomy of therapeutic recreation services and activities. Five broad categories were identified that captured general session information and activity-specific detail:

- Leisure education and counseling
- Leisure skill development in the rehabilitation center
- Leisure skill development in the community (outings)
- Community outings
- Social activities

In addition, time spent on activities and other session and administrative variables were categorized. Variables included type of session, missed session information, patient/family participation, individual factors impacting sessions, and administrative information (e.g., name, date).

The therapeutic recreation taxonomy is accompanied by a scale of how much assistance is needed for participation, which aligns with the FIM Scale. The scale ranges from total assistance from more than one person to independent performance.

By using the taxonomy and the Level of Assistance scale, therapeutic recreation specialists in most SCI rehabilitation centers should be able to document the type of services provided and then study in a consistent way the outcomes of services. The most interesting finding of the study was that, despite differing contexts in the six rehabilitation hospitals (e.g., large therapeutic recreation staff versus small, differing lengths of stay), the researchers were able to create a uniform taxonomy that documented all therapeutic recreation services.

Figure 13.13 Primary Source Support: A Uniform Taxonomy for Therapeutic Recreation

- Ensures compliance with standards set by the agency, by the profession, and by state and federal law. Our profession has standards of practice for documentation in therapeutic recreation that specifically outline our obligation to complete accurate, routine documentation (ATRA, 2000; CTRA, 2006; NTRS, 2004).

- Is necessary to meet accreditation standards (such as the Joint Commission, the Commission on Accreditation of Rehabilitation Facilities, and other accrediting bodies).

- Provides "PR for TR"; documentation helps you educate others about what you do in therapeutic recreation and the positive impact it has on the participant's well-being. When other team members read your entries in the participant's record, they gain a deeper, richer understanding of the value of your services.

Documentation may be your only method of remembering what happened in your interactions with a participant over time. If there is ever any question about the services you provided, and how effective they were, the documentation you completed may be all you have to rely on to answer questions. In Figure 13.14, we summarize the important information we have provided about documentation of the individual participant's status and progress. The who, what, when, where, how, and why of documentation provide the framework in which to develop and refine documentation skills. From a legal, professional, and ethical standpoint, documentation matters. Further, documentation matters because it provides us with a source of data that, when compiled across individuals, allows us to evaluate our services from an agency perspective.

WHO?	• First-hand, direct knowledge, observation, actions, decisions, and outcomes recorded by: 　- Therapeutic recreation specialist 　- Other team members (e.g., doctor, nurse, OT, PT, SW, teacher, case manager) 　- Participant and circle of support
WHAT?	• Complete information on all aspects of service • Subjective and objective information • Observations, assessment, plans, actions, and outcomes • Variances from expected outcomes • Rationale for decisions and actions • Collaboration and shared responsibilities between team members • Critical incidences
WHEN?	• As a chronological record of actions • At the time of or as soon as possible after: 　- the action or event 　- collaborations 　- variances to unexpected outcomes 　- critical incidents 　- an identified late entry
WHY?	• Basis of communication between team members and circle of support • Is a record of services provided • Used to evaluate practice as a part of quality improvement • Demonstrates accountability • Valuable source of data for research • Helps with funding and resource allocation • Educates others about therapeutic recreation professional practice
HOW?	• Concise, accurate, and true record • Participant-centered and respectful • Clear, legible, permanent, and identifiable • Chronological, current, and confidential • Based on observations, evidence, and assessment • Consistent with guidelines, organizational policy, and legislation • Avoids abbreviation, white space, and ambiguity

Figure 13.14 A Snapshot of the Elements of Documentation *(adapted from WHO-SEARO, 2007)*

Evaluating Therapeutic Recreation Services or Programs at the Agency Level

"We need to focus more on how services and supports lead to actual improvement in people's lives, as they define them. We need to count smiles, not just service units delivered."

—*Diana Jones Ritter (2008)*

In all systems where you provide therapeutic recreation services, you will be asked to show the outcomes and impact of your services, not to just one participant, but to all who are served by the agency. Whether it is a healthcare system, a human service or education system, or a community recreation system, services that do not make a positive documented difference are not supported in the long term. Thus, evaluation becomes critically important for therapeutic recreation services to flourish, regardless of setting or system. Program or service evaluation provides the empirical and documented outcomes you need to show how well your services work, as well as how to improve them. Recall from Figure 13.1, we defined evaluation as judging the value, worth, or effectiveness of something based on evidence you collect and compare to criteria. In Table 13.1, we provided the levels and focus of evaluation. At the service or program level, we can again conduct formative and summative evaluation, just as we did at the individual participant level.

In this section, we provide an introduction to evaluation, quality assurance, and performance improvement processes to help you document outcomes from therapeutic recreation services. We address this topic area only to help you understand how evaluation of the individual participant's progress ties into overall program or service evaluation. It is important for you to be familiar with therapeutic recreation standards of practice on evaluation, which we offer in Table 13.5. While it is beyond the scope of this book to provide detailed information about these topics, in the Resources and References section at the end of this chapter, you will find websites and books that will provide you with the knowledge and tools needed to conduct program or agency evaluation.

Program or Service Evaluation and the Use of Logic Models

To understand how individual participant data relates to program or service evaluation, in this section we introduce an approach in evaluation using logic models. This approach is being used by many non-profit and human service agencies. A **logic model** is a roadmap or graphic presentation that captures the key elements of a program or service, from inputs to outputs to outcomes, and helps you choose evaluation criteria and methods. The logic model shows the relationships between program or service elements and outcomes. In Figure 13.15, we offer a simple representation of a logic model as a roadmap.

In the logic model, we first delineate inputs to a program. Recall earlier in the chapter, we identified inputs as resources that go into a program or service, including things like staff, facilities, equipment, participants, and the like. Processes and outputs include activities or interventions we use, and participation, that is, who we reach with those activities. Outcomes are short-term (immediate results for the participant), medium-term (intermediate results for the participant), and long-term, often called impacts. Short-term outcomes are what the participant learns, or becomes aware of, or values. Medium-term outcomes are what the participant does, what actions he or she takes. Long-term outcomes are the ultimate impact or benefit.

Table 13.5 Professional Standards of Practice Related to Evaluation of Outcomes

American Therapeutic Recreation Association (2000)
  Standard 4: Re-Assessment and Evaluation
    The therapeutic recreation specialist systematically evaluates and compares the client's response to the individualized treatment plan. The treatment plan is revised based upon changes in the interventions, diagnosis and patient/client responses.

  Standard 10: Quality Management
    Within the therapeutic recreation department, there exists an objective and systematic quality improvement program for the purposes of monitoring and evaluating the quality and appropriateness of care, and to identify and resolve problems in order to improve therapeutic recreation services.

  Standard 12: Program Evaluation and Research
    The therapeutic recreation department engages in routine, systematic program evaluation and research for the purpose of determining appropriateness and efficacy.

Canadian Therapeutic Recreation Association (2006)
  Standard Five: Evaluation
    The process of determining whether the goals and objectives from the intervention plan were met by analyzing the effectiveness of the service or intervention and by receiving feedback from all involved.

  Standard Eight: Research
    Applying current applicable literature, studies and/or findings to enhance the recreation therapy profession. Where feasible the creation of a new study relating to a significant aspect in the recreation therapy profession.

National Therapeutic Recreation Society (2004)
  Standard Five: Outcomes
    The therapeutic recreation specialist records data on the participant's response to the therapeutic recreation process in the behavioral areas, cognitive, physical, social, emotional, spiritual; leisure functioning; personal development; and, quality of life variables and uses these results to enhance the therapeutic recreation process.

  Standard Eight: Quality Management
    The therapeutic recreation specialist implements management policies and procedures in order to maintain the quality of therapeutic recreation programs and services. These protocols comply with governmental, accreditation, professional, and agency standards and regulations. Evaluation and research are conducted to enhance the therapeutic recreation process; and, management practices and research initiatives are compatible with agency protocols and professional standards.

Note: Professional standards of practice are in constant revision as the profession evolves and grows. The standards provided throughout this book were the most current at the time of publication. In 2010, the National Therapeutic Recreation Society became the Inclusion and Accessibility Network, still affiliated with the National Recreation and Park Association.

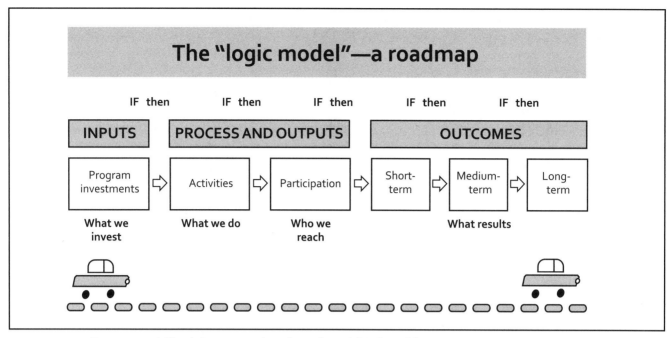

Figure 13.15 A Simple Representation of a Logic Model *(adapted from Taylor-Powell & Henert, 2008)*

The model is driven by process, answering the repeated question, "If this, then this?" In other words, if we have these resources, then we can provide this service; if we provide this service, then we will have this level of participation; if we have this level of participation, then we will have these short-term outcomes; if we have these short-term outcomes, then we expect these intermediate outcomes and long-term impacts. In Figure 13.16, we offer a sample logic model for a leisure education program for adults with chronic mental illness who desire more enriched leisure experiences for increased well-being.

The model provides a road map for inputs, process/outputs, and outcomes. It also provides a road map to evaluate each of these areas, which helps to empower not only you, but also participants, to clearly understand evaluation. Inputs are measured by the development of valid assessments and plans, as well as pre-assessment data. Recall the checklists we provided in Chapter 9 *Assessment* and Chapter 10 *Planning* to evaluate the quality of assessments and plans. These checklists could be used as tools to collect data on the quality of assessments and plans.

Data or evidence to judge the quality of process and outputs include those that are gathered about the activities and interventions used, and how well they were delivered. Data could be collected by peer observations and supervision, by evaluating if protocols or curricula were delivered as designed, and the like. Output evaluation also focuses on participation. Attendance records, flow sheets, progress notes, completion of homework assignments, and satisfaction surveys are examples of data that can be collected to evaluate participation.

Outcomes are evaluated by progress notes, goal attainment, discharge or end-of-service summaries, and evaluations by the participant. An important part of data collected for outcomes are post-assessments, which can be compared to pre-assessment results. For example, for the leisure education program in the example in Figure 13.16, we could administer the Oxford Happiness Questionnaire before the program starts and after it ends.

The logic model provides a simple, clear method of depicting program or service evaluation. It helps elucidate how individual participant data can be compiled with other data to evaluate overall services. Logic models help us see where we may need to make improvements in our services as they are implemented, as well as provide solid evidence of outcomes of services. We encourage you to use the resources provided at the end of this chapter to learn more about how to use logic models in your own therapeutic recreation practice. In the next section, we will look briefly at another common approach to evaluation in clinical practice: quality assurance, quality improvement, and performance improvement.

Quality Assurance and Performance Improvement Processes

"Do something. If it works, do more of it. If it doesn't, do something else."
—*Franklin D. Roosevelt*

INPUTS →	PROCESS & OUTPUTS →		OUTCOMES		
	Activities →	Participation →	Short-Term (what participants learn)	Medium-Term (what participants do)	Long-Term (the ultimate benefit or impact)
Staff

Leisure Education Protocol

Participants desiring enhanced leisure and well-being

Money

Facility

Equipment and supplies | Leisure Education Module on Mindfulness in Leisure

Leisure Education Module on Learning/Using Strengths in Leisure

Leisure Education Module on Friendship Skills

Leisure Education Module on Home and Community Resources | 80% of participants attend all four modules

80% of participants complete all homework assignments

100% of participants who attend rate the modules positively on a satisfaction survey | Participants understand mindfulness practices

Participants identify individual strengths and leisure activities that can put their strengths into practice

Participants learn strategies to make and keep friends and expand social support network

Participants identify leisure resources in their neighborhood and community | Daily practice of mindfulness techniques during leisure experiences

Leisure involvement that uses strengths each day

Use friendship skills at each leisure activity

Access and participate in a community leisure resource on a routine basis | Enhanced leisure experiences and overall well-being

Self-confidence and happiness in leisure

Friends and a social support network for leisure

Welcoming and accessible community leisure resources |
| EVALUATION – What do we want to know? (Criteria, goals, focus) | | | | | |
| What amount of money, time, and staff resources were invested? | What is the quality of modules?

How many sessions were held?

What is the quality of delivery? | Who/how many attended/did not attend?

Did they attend all sessions?

Did they complete homework?

Were they satisfied?

Why or why not? | To what extent did knowledge, awareness, and skills increase? For whom? Why? What else happened? | To what extent did behaviors and daily practices change? For whom? Why? What goals were met? What else happened? | To what extent are leisure experiences improved?

Well-being?

Friendships?

Community inclusion?

What else happened?

What dreams and aspirations were reached? |
| EVALUATION – How will you know it? (Data, evidence) | | | | | |
| Assessment results and plans

Pre-tests or pre-assessments | Protocol used as intended

Evaluation of facilitation skills

Peer supervision or clinical supervision | Flow sheets

Attendance records

Treatment units

Homework assignments

Progress notes

Satisfaction surveys | Progress notes | Progress notes | Discharge summaries

Post-tests or post-assessments |

Figure 13.16 An Example of a Logic Model for a Leisure Education Program

Figure 13.17 The Quality Assurance Triangle

Quality assurance and performance improvement are related but slightly different processes used to evaluate services and ensure quality in many health and human service settings. These approaches are most commonly associated with medical settings, though they had their roots in industry and business. Here, we provide a brief overview of quality assurance and again provide resources for further study at the end of the chapter.

Quality assurance (or QA) can be conceptualized as three interrelated activities: defining quality, measuring quality, and improving quality. In Figure 13.17, we offer a visual representation of the quality assurance triangle (Bornstein, 2001). **Defining quality** is much like developing inputs, process/outputs, and outcomes in a logic model. Defining quality means setting the goals and standards that must be met in order for

Life Story:

Using Research to Justify a New Service in a Health-Care Setting

A large body of research has developed in our field that provides evidence that nature-based adventure activities provide therapeutic benefits to people with a variety of differences, from children to older adults, to those with and without disabilities (Anderson & Hayes, 2001).

Working in an inpatient psychiatric setting, I very much wanted to introduce nature and adventure activities into the services we provided in therapeutic recreation. I was convinced that getting people into a natural setting, away from the clinical medical environment, would help them grow and heal more quickly. However, I knew that I needed to convince my team that it was safe, effective, and would bring about targeted growth and change in participants.

To justify the service I was proposing, I used the documented research to make my case. I developed a proposal for a one-day extended off-ward adventure-based activity program using empirical and peer-reviewed studies as the basis of the proposal. I incorporated pre- and post-assessments of key variables that the research showed could be impacted by adventure-based activity, such as self-esteem and self-efficacy. I used similar activities as those presented in the research, adapted to the setting (a local state park) and the participants (people with mental illness). I used a transdisciplinary team model that included an art therapist and a psychiatric nurse as other disciplines helping to deliver the program. The nurse was able to provide medical assistance as well as help facilitate activities, and the art therapist assisted with innovative methods of debriefing and other activities.

I presented my proposal to the medical director of our facility, who was the key decision-maker for our hospital, as well as the professional who would make referrals to the program. The medical director asked for a meeting where he asked many questions about the program; he was particularly concerned that, if participants could be away from the hospital setting for a full day, then perhaps they were well enough to just be discharged. He was concerned that insurance companies would question the program. In the end, he was swayed by the empirical support for the program, the documented changes that could occur for participants, as well as the rigorous evaluation plan that would be implemented with it. He approved the new program!

Using research results and a rigorous evaluation plan were essential to my efforts to bring a valuable new service to participants. Participants were able to experience nature and adventure as an important and powerful addition to the services they were receiving during their hospitalization.

Figure 13.18 Life Story: Using Research to Justify a New Service in a Health-Care Setting

ultimate outcomes to be realized. **Measuring quality** is like determining the evaluation focus and data in a logic model. Measuring quality involves choosing the methods and data to determine if goals and outcomes have been achieved or compliance with standards has occurred. **Improving quality** means that you engage in ongoing activities to close the gap between what you want to occur and what actually does occur, or between expected quality and current quality. Measuring and improving quality are often called monitoring and evaluation in quality assurance.

Quality improvement (or QI) uses a fairly standard four-step process in many settings (Bornstein, 2001). First, areas where the agency wants to improve are identified. Then, a careful analysis of the areas is conducted, using a variety of analytic tools. The third step is to identify what changes will improve the areas (this step is often called developing hypotheses). Last, the change is implemented, using a process that tests its effectiveness (Plan, Do, Study, Act). This process allows the agency to test the hypothesized change and, if it doesn't bring about the desired results, then the change can be modified or discarded, and the process starts again.

Performance improvement is very similar to quality improvement, with some differences (Bornstein, 2001). **Performance improvement** is a method used to improve the quality of agency and individual performance. Quality improvement is more broad and comprehensive, where performance improvement tends to focus more narrowly on determining whether services were delivered as planned and staff did their jobs as expected. This puts stronger focus on human resources, job expectations, and performance. Quality improvement tends to look more comprehensively at performance, taking many factors into account in determining quality, not just staff performance. You will likely hear these terms used interchangeably as you work in the field, depending on the agency and service system in which you work. Both use a systematic approach and are data-driven, so are valuable approaches to evaluation. Either will help you improve services and document outcomes. Both use individual participant documentation as part of the data collected, and both are centered on improving services and quality for participants.

In closing, whatever process or approach is used in evaluation, it is vitally important to carefully document participant progress and the services you provide. And it is vitally important to document outcomes for individual participants and for your program and services as a whole. Through research and evaluation, we are able to improve the quality of services we provide, and increase our ability to help participants thrive. Evaluation helps us justify and promote the services we provide, which in turn increase participants' access to the services. Whether used to develop new programs and services, or to secure resources to continue programs, evaluation provides the ammunition necessary to make your case! In Figures 13.18 and 13.19, we provide two different examples of the importance of documenting outcomes from services. In the first life story, documented outcomes published in research journals help to justify a new service. In the second life story, documented outcomes within an existing program helped to secure funding and ongoing support for that program.

SUMMARY

Evaluation and documentation are essential aspects of therapeutic recreation practice. Evaluation has several dimensions and foci. Evaluation is conducted at the individual participant level and at the program, service, and agency level. Evaluation is formative, in that it is conducted on an ongoing basis, providing data-driven feedback to improve services. And, evaluation is summative, in that it is conducted at the end of services to determine outcomes and impacts. Evaluation can focus on inputs, process, outputs, and outcomes.

At the individual level, the information you provide in the official legal record of the participant is called documentation. Documentation is essential in evaluating individual progress and, when compiled across participants, helps us evaluate services and programs. Documentation consists of the referral, the assessment, the plan, progress notes, and the discharge or end-of-service summary. Documentation must be completed in a very specific way, using rigorous writing guidelines. At the program or service level, evaluation can use varying approaches. Two common approaches in health and human services are the use of logic models and quality assurance/quality improvement.

Evaluation helps us improve services, document outcomes, and add to the body of knowledge in the field of therapeutic recreation. When conducted with the participant, using an empowerment approach, evaluation helps to bring about positive and desired changes in people and places.

Life Story:

Using Evaluation to Continue Program Funding

Part of my responsibilities as an inclusion coordinator at a community recreation center was to secure continuation funding for the program. Start-up funding for the first year had come from a state Developmental Disabilities Planning Council, and the following 2 years we had a U.S. Office of Special Education and Rehabilitative Services grant. Funding for the next few years, however, was uncertain.

Our ongoing evaluation methods proved key to keeping the program intact. I found it interesting how different funding sources valued different forms of evaluation in their grant applications. Foundations were swayed by the quantitative data we collected on leisure and social skill acquisition, using a task analytic approach. They were also impressed by the number of individuals we served in the program and the systematic way in which inclusion was implemented and evaluated. They intuitively understood the merits of inclusion, but it was the quantitative "hard" data that convinced them to fund the program.

The United Way, on the other hand, valued the "soft" qualitative stories that came out of inclusion. They were interested to learn how the program made a *difference* in people's lives. So we told the story of how Jorge, who had cerebral palsy, and Ben, a boy without a disability, became best friends through taking swimming and day camp together. We recounted how Ben often introduced Jorge to other children, letting them know it was okay to "goof around with him . . . he won't break." We told of Kristin and how her mother had noticed she had begun to isolate herself, which prompted her to bring her to the community center. Through participating in youth programs with her peers without disabilities, over time Kristin became outgoing enough to perform a prominent role in the production of *Fiddler on the Roof*. We told about Sandy, who was blind yet daringly jumped solo off the diving board into the arms of a swim instructor treading water below. These were the kind of stories that moved the United Way representatives to recommend the center for an allocation.

Eventually, the community center incorporated the program into its operating budget, which was substantially supported through United Way. In the meantime, however, our documentation and evaluation methods, which proved real and tangible outcomes, were vital to the program's vibrancy.

Figure 13.19 Life Story: Using Evaluation to Continue Program Funding

Resources

The American Health Information Management Association
http://www.ahima.org

This professional organization's website is loaded with resources on documentation, coding, HIPAA, confidentiality, and other useful information to learn more about health records.

The Kellogg Foundation
http://www.wkkf.org

The Kellogg Foundation has developed numerous tools and resources for evaluation. One excellent resource is an evaluation handbook written for youth, to assist young people in being a part of participatory evaluation. The evaluation resources are all downloadable books and pamphlets in pdf versions.

The University of Wisconsin Program Development and Evaluation Unit
http://www.uwex.edu/ces/pdande

The Program Development and Evaluation Unit at the University of Wisconsin system provides training and technical assistance that enables agencies and groups to plan, implement, and evaluate high-quality programs and services. Many useful tools on logic models and evaluation designs are provided that can be downloaded and customized to your agency needs.

The Health Care Improvement Project
http://www.hciproject.org

The Health Care Improvement Project, administered by the U.S. Agency for International Development (USAID), has developed a rich resource on its website to train healthcare providers around the world on quality assurance and quality improvement. Several online tutorials are provided on the website to learn how to

Self-Assessment of Learning

Documentation Practice

Progress Note: Using this scenario, write a progress note using the SOAP format.

Today, Mary came to the Leisure Skills Group on her own for the first time since her hospitalization. She was on time and said hello to the staff as she entered the clinic area. She even maintained eye contact and smiled at me, which is also a first.

The focus of the group today was on planning skills for leisure. I had participants analyze their favorite leisure activity and identify all the necessary skills, resources, time, energy, talents, and social networking required to do that particular activity. Mary identified her favorite activity as sewing. She was unable to identify all the necessary aspects of participation. When other group members gave her ideas on where to get the resources and skills to pursue sewing on a regular basis, she acknowledged their ideas by nodding and writing some information down on her worksheet. One group member told her about a quilting guild in town that meets regularly to design and sew quilts. Mary listened intently and asked for more information about it. She stated, "I need to find something like that. Since I've been so depressed, I don't even leave my house for days and weeks. I get so lonely, but I feel scared and embarrassed to go out. If I had a group I could go to that was small and liked to do the things I do, maybe that would help me not be such a hermit." Mary smiled at me. "Do you know where I could find out more about this quilting club?" This is the first time Mary had asked me a question directly or shown any interest in the planned group discussion since she had started attending the group 2 weeks ago. I told her I would help her get more information about the guild and that we could work on it together tomorrow, if she wanted.

I asked Mary what had changed for her recently as she seemed brighter and more interested in things. She stated that she was just starting to feel comfortable in this group and was really enjoying the companionship. "Maybe I can get that same feeling from a group when I get home. That would help me stay more healthy and help keep me from getting so down and lonely." I told her it was great to see her smile and express interest in things. A few other people in the group gave her some compliments also. Mary and I arranged a time to meet tomorrow to find out more information on the quilting guild and ways she could access one of their meetings while she was still hospitalized.

S: _____

O: _____

A: _____

P: _____

---

apply QA and QI methods to a variety of health and human service settings.

Evaluation Books in Therapeutic Recreation and Leisure Services

- Henderson, K. (2006). *Dimensions of choice: Qualitative approaches to parks, recreation, tourism, sport, and leisure research* (2nd ed.). State College, PA: Venture Publishing, Inc.

- Henderson, K., & Bialeschki, D. (2002). *Evaluating leisure services: Making enlightened decisions* (2nd ed.). State College, PA: Venture Publishing, Inc.

- Malkin, M., & Howe, C. (Eds.) (1993). *Research in therapeutic recreation: Concepts and methods*. State College, PA: Venture Publishing, Inc.

- Riley, B. (1991). *Quality management: Applications for therapeutic recreation*. State College, PA: Venture Publishing, Inc.

- Stumbo, N. (Ed). (2003). *Client outcomes in therapeutic recreation services*. State College, PA: Venture Publishing, Inc.

- Stumbo, N., & Peterson, C. (2009). *Therapeutic recreation program design: Principles and procedures* (5th ed.). Needham Heights, MA: Allyn and Bacon.

References

American Therapeutic Recreation Association. (2000). *Standards for the practice of therapeutic recreation and self-assessment guide.* Hattiesburg, MS: American Therapeutic Recreation Association.

American Therapeutic Recreation Association. (2009). *Code of ethics.* Hattiesburg, MS: American Therapeutic Recreation Association.

Anderson, L., & Hayes, G. (Eds.). (2001). *Best of adventure programming in therapeutic recreation.* Ashburn, VA: National Recreation and Park Association.

Bornstein, T. (2001). Quality improvement and performance improvement: Different means to the same end? *Quality Assurance Brief, 9*(1), 6–12.

Cahow, C., Skolnick, S., Joyce, J., Jug, J., Dragon, C., & Gassaway, J. (2009). SCIRehab Project Series: The therapeutic recreation taxonomy. *The Journal of Spinal Cord Medicine, 32*(3), 298–306.

Canadian Therapeutic Recreation Association. (2005). *Code of ethics.* Calgary, AB, Canada: CTRA. Retrieved from http://www.canadian-tr.org/pdf/CTRA%20Code%20of%%20Ethics.pdf

Canadian Therapeutic Recreation Association (2006). *Standards of practice for recreation therapists and therapeutic recreation assistants.* Calgary, AB, Canada: Canadian Therapeutic Recreation Association.

Centers for Disease Control and Prevention. (2003). *HIPAA Privacy Rule and public health: Guidance from CDC and the U.S. Department of Health and Human Services.* Retrieved from http://www.cdc.gov/mmwr/preview/mmwrhtml/m2e411a1.htm

Fetterman, D., & Wandersman, A. (2005). *Empowerment evaluation principles in practice.* New York, NY: Guilford.

Fetterman, D., & Wandersman, A. (2007). Empowerment evaluation: Yesterday, today, and tomorrow. *American Journal of Evaluation, 28*(2), 179–198.

Hales, B., Terblanche, M., Fowler, R., & Sibbald, W. (2008). Development of medical checklists for improved quality of patient care. *International Journal of Quality in Health Care, 20*(1), 22–30.

Henderson, K., & Bialeschki, D. (2002). *Evaluating leisure services: Making enlightened decisions* (2nd ed.). State College, PA: Venture Publishing, Inc.

Mehta, N., & Partin, M. (2007). Electronic records: A primer for practicing physicians. *Cleveland Clinic Journal of Medicine, 74*(11), 826–830.

National Therapeutic Recreation Society. (2001). *Code of ethics and interpretive guidelines.* Ashburn, VA: National Recreation and Park Association.

National Therapeutic Recreation Society. (2004). *Standards of practice.* Ashburn, VA: National Recreation and Park Association.

Ritter, D. (2008). *Putting people first.* Albany, NY: Office of Mental Retardation and Developmental Disabilities.

Shank, J., & Coyle, C. (2002). *Therapeutic recreation in health promotion and rehabilitation.* State College, PA: Venture Publishing, Inc.

Taylor-Powell, E., & Henert, E. (2008). *Developing a logic model: Teaching and training guide.* Madison, WI: University of Wisconsin Board of Regents. Retrieved from http://www.uwex.edu/ces/pdande

World Bank. (2009). *Empowerment.* Retrieved from http://www.worldbank.org

World Health Organization-SEARO. (2007). *Guidelines for medical record and clinical documentation.* Geneva, Switzerland: WHO. Retrieved from http://www.searo.who.int/index.htm

Part III

PROFESSIONALISM AS A STRENGTHS-BASED THERAPEUTIC RECREATION SPECIALIST

In Part III we explore concepts related to professionalism particular to strengths-based practice in therapeutic recreation.

"No person ever reached to excellence in any one art or profession without having passed through the slow and painful process of study and preparation."

Horace
Roman poet

The Rocky Mountain Columbine is a vigorous flower that has a wide range of habitats and thrives in many zones.

Part III Overview

Chapter 14   *Advocacy in Strengths-Based Therapeutic Recreation Practice*

Practicing therapeutic recreation with a strengths orientation can be challenging and require you to be an advocate—for your participants, for your profession, and for yourself. Learn how to strengthen your advocacy skills in this chapter.

Chapter 15   *Building Your Strengths as a Therapeutic Recreation Specialist*

Many professional resources are at your disposal for building your strengths as a therapeutic recreation specialist. Here you will learn about some of them, including credentialing, mentoring and clinical supervision, networking, ethical practice, and continuing education.

Chapter 16   *Looking Ahead*

You will help us write this chapter by articulating your vision for strengths-based therapeutic recreation practice. Take some time to clarify your own values and principles as you review what you have learned in this book.

Chapter 14
ADVOCACY IN STRENGTHS-BASED THERAPEUTIC RECREATION PRACTICE

*The Bird of Paradise is bold, exotic, and aspiring.
Its strong form draws positive attention.*

"Action is the catalyst that creates accomplishments. It is the path that takes us from uncrafted hopes to realized dreams."

—*Thomas Huxley, Biologist*

OVERVIEW OF CHAPTER 14

- An overview of advocacy and the skills needed to be an advocate
- Facilitating and supporting self-advocacy
- Advocating for and with the participant using individual and systems advocacy
- Advocating for positive changes in the participant's environment
- Advocating for the strengths approach on your team and in your agency
- Advocating for the profession of therapeutic recreation
- Balancing your roles as a helper, a team member, and an advocate
- Resources for advocacy

FOCUS QUESTIONS

- Why is advocacy an important concept and skill for therapeutic recreation specialists?
- How do you decide what level of advocacy is needed to help participants reach their goals? Should advocacy be at the individual level, the team level, the community level, or at all levels?
- What approaches might you use to advocate for a strengths approach in health and human services, where you may find a deficits-oriented approach in practice? Why is it important for you to advocate for a strengths approach in therapeutic recreation?
- Therapeutic recreation provides important services to participants. How will you champion our profession, when needed, to ensure services?
- Is advocacy always the right approach? How do you decide?

AN INTRODUCTION TO ADVOCACY

A definition of "advocacy":
The practice of supporting someone to make his or her voice heard;
active support; campaigning for, upholding one's rights

A definition of "lobbying":
To try to influence the thinking of legislators or other public officials for or against a specific cause

A definition of "charity":
Aid given to those in need; public provision for the relief of the needy

Advocacy is an important concept and skill for therapeutic recreation specialists. We often find ourselves in a position where we must champion change at many levels, whether it is for the participants we serve, the communities in which they reside, or even to ensure the use of a strengths approach or the provision of therapeutic recreation services. As the paradigm shifts from a medical model to an ecological strengths approach, you will find yourself using advocacy more than in the past. In the medical model, participants are seen as having the problem, in isolation from the context of their environment. The model assumes that change is needed in the participant. In the ecological model, participants are viewed in the context of their social system. It assumes change is needed in the environment as much or more than in the participant. Advocacy is one tool to help make that change. In this chapter, we give you some clear, concise methods you can use as you fulfill the role of advocate throughout your professional career.

To begin, we provide an overview of what advocacy is and clarify how it is different from other change approaches such as lobbying or charity. Advocacy can happen at many levels. In this chapter, we explore advocacy at these levels:

- Self-advocacy
- Individual advocacy
- Community or systems advocacy, including lobbying
- Advocacy for the strengths approach in services
- Advocacy for the provision of therapeutic recreation services

What is Advocacy?

Advocacy is speaking, writing, and/or acting on behalf of sincerely perceived interests of a disadvantaged person or group, without conflict of interest. Advocacy requires three things: a passionate desire to see positive change, a sound understanding of the issue or idea for which you are advocating, and a willingness to "go public" to effect change.

A desire to see change is fueled by the gap between what a participant aspires to in his or her life and the conditions in the environment that must be changed to lessen that gap. Thus, the passion to see desired change must be rooted in what participants want to achieve, not the ideology or personal beliefs of the helping professional. In addition, the professional must not have a conflict of interest that puts pressure on the ability to act effectively for the participant. For example, if you work for a particular therapeutic recreation program that provides services, you must be clear that you are not trying to get a participant engaged in your particular program instead of one that would align better in the participant's life.

Advocacy is based on having sound and well-researched information on which to make decisions and choices. As an advocate, it is your responsibility to ensure the quality and completeness of information the participant needs to make decisions regarding actions and changes. Involving the participant in the information-gathering phase further builds self-advocacy skills and helps the participant truly understand a particular issue or needed change.

Lastly, a willingness to take a stand or "go public" is an important part of advocacy. Openly communicating with participants, collaborating partners, policymakers, community members, and others in position of power or control is an integral part of advocacy. At times, going public involves taking a position against commonly held beliefs or cultural biases and requires a certain amount of courage. Advocates are assisted in going public by having clear and accurate information about the issue and a passion for the desired change that is person-centered.

The purpose of advocacy, then, is to effect positive change that improves the well-being of participants. This change must often happen in the social structures that surround participants as much as any changes participants themselves need to make. Advocacy differs from providing charity-based helping in that you are not only addressing a need, you are also addressing the larger social injustices that created that need. In Figure 14.1, we provide further comparisons between more traditional charity-based helping and advocacy-based helping. The shift from charity or benevolence to advocacy is an important one, as the outcomes of advocacy can be sustained as participants gain skills and confidence and as systems shift to support more equitable services and policies. Advocacy empowers participants to do more for themselves, lessens dependency on others, and reduces marginalizing or oppressive social structures.

Historically, many attempts at helping people with disabilities have been situated in the charity model. Assistance has been couched in pity and has cast people with disabilities as helpless victims. In the charity model, people with disabilities are seen as broken, sick, and in need of being fixed (Kluth, 2006 [see Figure 14.2, p. 394]). Even in the field of therapeutic recreation, roots of the charity model run deep in programs and services, and stigmas associated with the model have been hard to change (Storey, 2004). Advocacy, and in particular self-advocacy, is changing the helping relationship by couching it in a human-rights model that promotes equal rights, dignity, respect, and social justice. In the next section, we explore self-advocacy in depth.

Self-Advocacy

Self-advocacy, a concept closely associated with self-determination, is founded on the idea that people with disabilities want to and can be responsible for making decisions about their lives, including the human and social services that affect them. According to the Harvard

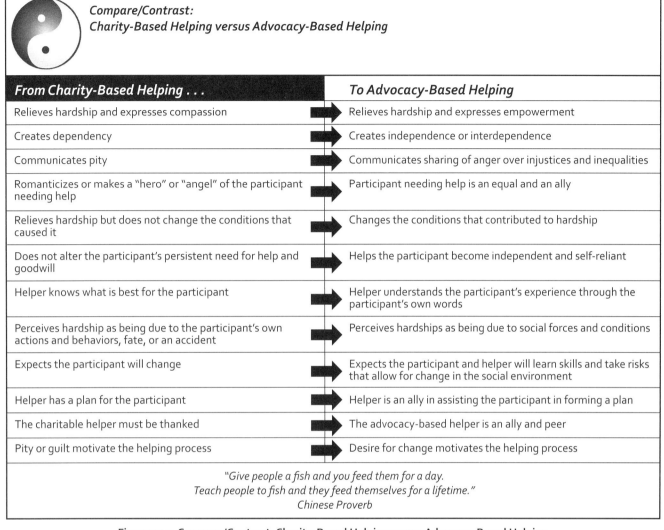

Figure 14.1 Compare/Contrast: Charity-Based Helping versus Advocacy-Based Helping

Project on Disability (2008), self-advocacy is when you speak up for yourself and work together with others to make change happen. Self-advocacy has been defined as a civil rights movement of individuals and organizations to empower people with disabilities to speak for themselves, make their own decisions, and stand up for their rights (Advocating Change Together, 2009).

When advocacy is needed, self-advocacy is the first area on which to focus in the helping relationship. As a therapeutic recreation specialist, you can teach, facilitate, and support self-advocacy skills with participants. If a participant needs additional support beyond self-advocacy, then you can provide additional advocacy efforts for and with the participant.

Building Self-Advocacy

The first training model to develop self-advocacy was developed when Nirje (1992) introduced the term *self-determination* in his writings on normalization. Since then, researchers, policymakers, and people with disabilities have developed a framework for teaching self-advocacy skills based on best practices in the field (Test, Fowler, Wood, Brewer, & Eddy, 2005; Harvard Project on Disability, 2008). The basic framework for self-advocacy includes four content areas that identify competencies that can be built into the design of therapeutic recreation programs and services. Below, we provide the four curricular areas for self-advocacy training with sample subcomponents. Notice how many of the subcomponents identified in Figure 14.3 reflect the internal strengths you learned about in Chapter 5 *Strengths*.

1. *Knowledge of Self*. This area of self-awareness, along with *knowledge of rights*, is the backbone of self-advocacy. Participants need to know and understand themselves and what they want before letting others know what they want. Common areas

My Cultural Lens: Self-Advocacy and the Jerry Lewis Telethon

Every year for several decades, people in the U.S. have experienced a Labor Day weekend tradition—the Jerry Lewis Telethon, a fundraiser for research for a cure for muscular dystrophy. In 2009, Jerry Lewis was given the Humanitarian Award at the Academy Awards ceremony in Hollywood for his years of work with the telethon. Yet, many in the disability community have crusaded against the telethon and its master of ceremonies for years. Why?

According to Mike Ervin, a disability rights advocate, a former head of the U.S. Equal Employment Opportunity Commission, and a person with a disability, the Jerry Lewis Telethon perpetuates the charity model of disability and portrays people with disabilities as objects of pity. Ervin stated, "The damage Lewis has done to the disability community goes far beyond name-calling. He and his telethon symbolize an antiquated and destructive 1950s charity mentality. This says that people with disabilities have no hope and nothing to offer unless we are cured, so the whole focus should be raising money for behemoth charities that can find that cure."

Self-advocates in the disability community have fought for years to have the telethon shift its focus from portraying people with disabilities as pitiful "poster children" to a more realistic story of people with disabilities as "having aspirations beyond mere cure, of the beauty of adaptation, of political activism, of demands for equality and inclusion." Every year, grassroots protests from self-advocates like "Jerry's Orphans" accompany the Telethon across the U.S. One self-advocate, Bill Bolte (1993), stated, "The phrase 'Jerry's kids' insults us just as deeply as 'boy' offends African American men or 'Jew boy' cuts Jewish men. Most of us committed the unforgivable sin of growing up, despite all predictions. Not only are we adults, not kids, but we are happily not descendants of Jerry Lewis. We are, therefore, in no sense Jerry's kids."

Despite widespread criticism of the charity model on which the annual Telethon is based, it continued to be held for many years and raised large sums of money. Why? What cultural values supported the continuation of this event? Why were disability self-advocates ignored in this conflict? Discuss these questions with your peers with and without disabilities.

Figure 14.2 My Cultural Lens: Self-Advocacy and the Jerry Lewis Telethon *(Ervin, 2009)*

of instruction focus on goal-setting, interests, preferences, strengths, needs, and learning style. Self-advocates also learn about the attributes of their disability; learning about one's disability supplies the necessary information to advocate for accommodations and to identify approaches to support involvement and contribution.

2. ***Knowledge of Rights***. Becoming a self-advocate involves knowing one's rights as a citizen, as an individual with a disability, and perhaps as a student who receives services under federal law. Instruction in this area of self-advocacy can include learning about the United Nations Convention on the Rights of Persons with Disabilities (see Table 14.1, p. 396), the American with Disabilities Act of 1990, as well as the Individuals with Disabilities Education Act and its amendments. It can include learning basic rights in health care, such as those developed by the Joint Commission (see Table 14.2, p. 396). Recognizing a violation of one's rights and seeking restitution are also a part of developing self-advocacy skills in this area.

3. ***Communication***. Once the foundation—knowledge of self and rights—is in place, participants can focus on effective communication. Figure 14.3 presents subcomponents of communication skills related to self-advocacy. Learning to communicate in groups and in meetings is also important.

4. ***Leadership***. The final component of self-advocacy is the development of leadership skills. Leadership involves understanding the roles of team members, group dynamics, learning how to function in a group, and performing one's duties as a team member. Political lobbying skills may also be addressed. It should be noted that one can be an effective self-advocate without necessarily assuming a leadership role.

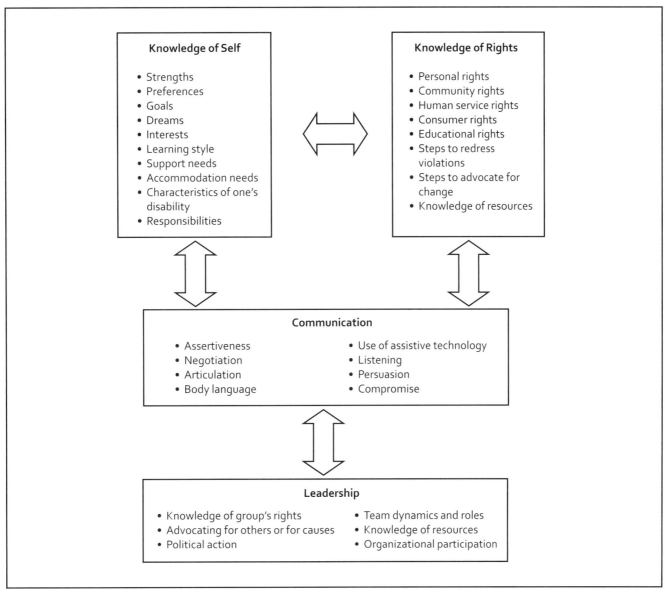

Figure 14.3 Conceptual Framework of Self-Advocacy *(adapted from Test et al., 2005)*

Self-advocacy often follows a common set of action steps to put skills and competencies into practice. In Table 14.3, we provide the steps you can teach participants to make the social changes they want to see in their lives. By supporting participants in following these 10 steps, therapeutic recreation specialists can facilitate the self-advocacy process and indirectly assist in making positive social change, as well as give lasting confidence and skills to participants.

Based on this framework and these common action steps, how can we, as therapeutic recreation specialists, build self-advocacy skills within the context of our services? Here are some suggestions:

- Invite people with disabilities to serve on your Board of Directors, advisory council, or resident activity board so they have an opportunity to give regular input into services and programs.

- During assessments, pay close attention to assessing areas identified as promoting self-advocacy, such as interests, preferences, goals, and dreams.

- When working on community recreation inclusion, help participants identify areas where they can use self-advocacy to make changes at the recreation agency or program so inclusion can happen for them.

- For participants with significant disabilities, provide training and opportunities for frequent choice-making about when things happen and what happens in their lives.

Table 14.1 The Convention on the Rights of Persons with Disabilities from the United Nations *(The Harvard Project on Disability, 2008)*

The United Nations Convention on the Rights of Persons with Disabilities (CRPD) says people with disabilities have human rights, including the right to:

- Be treated as equals (Article 5)
- Equal treatment for women with disabilities (Article 6)
- Equal treatment for children with disabilities (Article 7)
- Change attitudes about people with disabilities (Article 8)
- Access (Article 9)
- Life (Article 10)
- Assistance in emergencies (Article 11)
- Be treated equally by the law (Article 12)
- Access to justice (Article 13)
- Be free and safe (Article 14)
- Not be tortured or treated cruelly (Article 15)
- Not be used or abused (Article 16)
- Be free from medical exploitation (Article 17)
- Move around freely (Article 18)
- Independent living and be part of the community (Article 19)
- Get around (Article 20)
- Be free to express needs and wants and to get information (Article 21)
- Respect for their privacy (Article 22)
- Marry and have children (Article 23)
- Education (Article 24)
- Health (Article 25)
- Services to be independent (Article 26)
- Work (Article 27)
- A decent standard of living (Article 28)
- Be involved in politics (Article 29)
- Be involved in sport and leisure (Article 30)

Read the full Convention on the Rights of Persons with Disabilities (CRPD): http://www.un.org/disabilities

---

Table 14.2 Participant Rights in Health Care *(Joint Commission, 2009)*

Advocacy for Participants – Rights in Health Care

Participants have rights and a role regarding their treatment and care. Knowing basic rights can help participants make better decisions about their care.

Here is a list of basic rights you can help participants understand and use:

What are your rights?

- ☐ You have the right to be informed about the care you will receive.
- ☐ You have the right to get information about your care in your language.
- ☐ You have the right to make decisions about your care, including refusing care.
- ☐ You have the right to know the names of the caregivers who treat you.
- ☐ You have the right to safe care.
- ☐ You have the right to have your pain treated.
- ☐ You have the right to know when something goes wrong with your care.
- ☐ You have the right to get an up-to-date list of all of your current medicines.
- ☐ You have the right to be listened to.
- ☐ You have the right to be treated with courtesy and respect.

Ask for *written information* about all of your rights as a patient.

Table 14.3 Ten Concrete Steps for Self-Advocates *(based in part on the United Nations Change your Life with Human Rights Self-Advocacy Curriculum from Harvard Project on Disability, 2008)*

STEP 1: YOUR GOAL
- Spell out your goal, what you want to happen, in clear terms.
- What does victory look like?

STEP 2: YOUR RIGHTS
- Know your rights and be ready to stand up for them.
- Enlist assistance from your circle of support and from self-advocacy groups.

STEP 3: YOUR PARTNERS
- Identify your collaborators and friends.
- Who can help you make the changes you want? Who else can benefit from the same change? Who are your allies? Who has a position of influence or power that supports the change?
- Are there professionals on your team who can help (such as the therapeutic recreation specialist)?
- Are there self-advocacy groups you can call upon to assist you?

STEP 4: THE FACTS
- Get your information together; become knowledgeable about the issue, need, or goal.
- Draw on the expertise of professionals, community groups, published research, websites, and advocacy groups.
- Compile your information; keep it in an organized notebook for easy access during phone conversations, meetings, e-mail, or Skype interactions.

STEP 5: THE CHOICES
- Who makes what decisions? Who decides what will happen?
- Which government agency, business, or group has a say or influence in the situation?
- Figure out what your choices are and make them.

STEP 6: THE PLAN OF ACTION
- Write down the specific actions you will take.
- Who will do them? Where and when will these actions happen?

STEP 7: PREPARE AND PRACTICE
- Make sure that everyone involved understands the action plan and what roles and responsibilities they will have. Role-playing can be one way of doing this.
- Write out and practice telling your story and your goal to a friend or advocate. Be sure to include all the main points you want to make. Be positive and respectful.

STEP 8: TAKE ACTION
- Carry out your plan.
- Bring a friend or advocate for support to any meetings; have them take notes.
- Be persistent and patient.

STEP 9: EVALUATE AND FOLLOW-UP
- Check your notes. What happened? What were the results? How do you feel about what happened?
- Do you need to follow-up with anyone to be sure the change you advocated for is implemented?
- Share the outcomes with all your partners.

STEP 10: CELEBRATE
- Even small victories should be celebrated.
- Congratulate yourself for a job well done, regardless of the outcome, and be ready for the next advocacy effort!
- Remember, change can happen slowly. Don't give up even if things didn't work out how you planned.

- Provide leadership opportunities for participants with disabilities within your programs and services, which may include a leadership role in a club or sports team.
- Involve participants in hiring and evaluating staff. Involve them in administrative tasks such as documentation and charting, planning and conducting meetings, and the like.
- Invite local self-advocacy organizations to provide trainings for participants, including those with and without disabilities. People First is a national self-advocacy organization with many chapters in states across the country that can offer participants training in self-advocacy.
- Include modules on self-advocacy in your leisure education sessions, including choice-making and assertiveness skills.
- Sponsor a family education session on how families can support self-advocacy.

In the *Resources* section at the end of this chapter, you will find additional information and Web links for several organizations that support self-advocacy and have developed training materials that can be used within services you provide.

Advocating for and with Participants

The purpose of advocacy is to assist the participant and his or her circle of support in achieving their goals and dreams for a high quality of life and well-being. When participants need additional assistance beyond self-advocacy, you may be called upon to do advocacy work with and on their behalf. This type of advocacy can be at the individual level or the systems level.

Individual Level Advocacy

At the individual level, advocacy involves one person or group working on behalf of another person (Hutchinson & McGill, 1992). Individual advocacy requires a strong belief in the goals of the participant and no conflict of interest with the services or settings where advocacy must happen (see Figure 14.4). Individual advocacy also involves the following:

- A strong, consistent, and caring relationship with the participant
- An ability to listen to, understand, and support the participant's dreams and goals for recreation
- An ability to communicate not only with the participant, which may require the use of alternative forms of communication, but with the community and system
- A commitment to work with the participant to ensure the issue or need is addressed and resolved
- A high degree of independence from the agencies or services that the participant is needing or questioning (Hutchinson & McGill, 1992)
- A plan of action based on the goals of the participant and well-researched information

The steps in individual advocacy are much the same as those followed in self-advocacy (see Table 14.3). First, however, you may be required to address any acute needs of the participant before planned action that utilizes advocacy can occur. For example, before assisting a participant in making social connections and building friendships at a community recreation center where she has been excluded due to past behavior, you may need to coach her on some basic social skills and use of positive behavioral supports.

A key step for therapeutic recreation specialists in advocacy is to build strong partnerships and networks in the community that endure over time. Advocacy can then be more persuasive and less confrontational, and allow for more sustainable change. In Table 14.4, Teipel (2001) provides useful tips for persuasive self-advocacy that have been effective in her role as an advocate.

Table 14.4 Tips for Persuasive Advocacy *(adapted from Teipel, 2001)*

- With the participant, get clear on the goals and the needs for which advocacy is necessary.
- Identify the target audience where advocacy and change is needed; be sure to seek out those who are best able to make decisions or changes in the agency or system for the individual participant.
    - Once you are clear on the audience, learn about them, their beliefs, what matters to them, and how they feel about the issue you are advocating for.
    - Frame your message and request around what you learn about the audience and what is important to them and interests them to "hook" them into listening.
    - Identify allies and champions within the target audience and be sure your message reaches them.
    - Identify opponents within the target audience and try to understand the basis of their opposition; identify ways to diffuse their resistance if possible; know your opposition as well as you know your issue.
- Frame your request for change or support in ways that connect to the values of the target audience.
- Develop a clear concise message based on the facts you have researched and the personal story and needs of the participant.
- Prepare responses to opposition or challenges to your request to be prepared to handle them as they arise.
- Plan the delivery of your message, and determine the best spokesperson—depending on the target audience, the request may be better delivered by the participant or the therapeutic recreation specialist.
- Be persistent.
- Be flexible and willing to compromise (often, something is better than nothing).
- Always be respectful of others in interactions, even the opposition you may face; build a lasting working relationship if possible.
- Whenever possible, assist the participant in taking a leadership role in your advocacy efforts, and support him or her throughout the process.

Life Story:

Advocating for a Recreation Goal: Freedom to Swim . . . Slowly

Jen, a therapeutic recreation specialist, worked with Millie, who had a goal to get back on track with regular exercise that she enjoyed. She had been sedentary for several years and was certain it contributed to her depression and anxiety. Millie had always loved swimming, not only for the physical exercise, but the relaxing feel of the water and the mesmerizing sounds of swimming laps.

Together Jen and Millie identified a local community center near Millie's apartment that she could walk to and that had a pool. The community center offered lap swimming from 6 a.m. to 9 a.m., which worked well for Millie's schedule. They made a visit to the center to learn about registration, cost, the lap-swimming schedule, and to tour the locker room, all of which alleviated Millie's anxiety and boosted her confidence. Jen and Millie watched the lap swimming for a while, with its quiet and orderly activity. Upon talking to the aquatics director, they learned that the morning lap swimming time was primarily used by competitive swimmers, and all the lanes were used by fast swimmers. The aquatics director discouraged Millie from coming at that time because she would be too slow for any of the designated lanes and it would upset the "regulars" who swam at that time and had been doing so for years. The director instead recommended that Millie come to open swim in the evenings, where she could swim at her own pace, even if it wasn't designated as a lap swimming time.

Jen and Millie visited the pool in the evening to observe the open swim session and decide if it would work for Millie. The pool was very loud, with several youth jumping off the diving board, balls bouncing, and the like. There was only a small area of the pool where swimming laps would be possible, and even that had sporadic activity in it. Millie was upset that her plans to swim were looking less feasible.

Jen encouraged Millie to advocate for herself to be able to swim in the morning session, which met her needs perfectly except for the lack of a slow lane. Together, they developed a plan of action that included a proposal to the aquatics director to designate only one lane for slow swimmers, and for only the last hour of the lap swimming time. They talked with some of Millie's friends who were interested in joining her if they too could swim more slowly and rest in the lane often. Jen also talked with a few of the competitive lap swimmers, who agreed that it was a reasonable request and they would support it, even if it meant their lanes were slightly more crowded for part of the time. As a group, Jen, Millie and a few of her friends approached the aquatics director with their proposal and support statements from other swimmers.

The aquatics director was hesitant but agreed to talk with more of the core swimmers about the idea. She called Millie a few days later to tell her she would try the arrangement for a month to see how it went. Millie was thrilled, and her friends were eager to support her as well.

After a month, Jen spoke with the aquatics director about the changes in the morning lap swim. Not only was it working out great for Millie and her friends, but several other community center members had also started coming to the morning lap swim. Upon seeing that there was room for more ability levels at that time, more people felt "invited" to participate. The aquatics director had decided to extend the "slow lane" to two lanes and to the whole lap swim time.

Figure 14.4 Life Story: Advocating for a Recreation Goal: Freedom to Swim . . . Slowly

Systems or Community Level Advocacy

When you engage in systems advocacy, you are concerned with changing policies, rules, laws, or cultural beliefs and attitudes that disadvantage or discriminate against those you serve. Systems advocacy means taking action, usually as a part of an organized group or community, to create positive change and increase social justice (Kansas University, 2010).

Systems advocacy can occur at the grassroots level, where you join with other community members in advocating for a particular change, through many different avenues, such as organized communication, media events, protests, rallies, attending and testifying at public meetings, providing public input on proposals, letters to the editor, and more. Or systems advocacy can be more formal, where you work with organizations to change laws, rules, and policies (see Figure 14.5, p. 400).

Changing laws requires knowledge of the political arena and the legislative process. In Figure 14.6 (p. 401), we provide a checklist of how to approach systems advocacy focused on legislation. Though the process is similar to those used in self-advocacy and individual advocacy, systems advocacy requires stronger coalitions and partnerships, a more sophisticated plan, and, often, more time and persistence.

Lobbying is a form of advocacy that is focused on influencing decision-makers, usually elected and other officials, in supporting the specific law or rule you want

Primary Source Support: Social Change and Institutions

Hutchinson, P., & Potschaske, C. (1998). Social change and institutions: Implications for recreationists. *Therapeutic Recreation Journal, 32*(2), 130–156.

Peggy Hutchinson and Christiane Potschaske were interested in learning how young recreation professionals working in institutions, who start their careers hoping to "change the world," experience social change in their work. They were asked several questions:

- What social change issues were being addressed by professionals working in institutions?
- What was the source of impetus for social change?
- Were front-line professionals able to initiate and implement social change?
- What were any constraints to social change?

They interviewed nine recreation professionals in three different large institutions that provided therapeutic recreation. They found that social change was happening, especially the shift from institutional-based services to community-based services, but that the recreationists played a relatively minor role in initiating the changes. Most impetus for change came from participants and their families, as well as a societal and legislative shift to serve people in the community rather than in an institution. Though the recreationists did not feel they played a large role in initiating change, they did play an important role in implementing change.

Constraints to social change included resistance of the service system to change, negative attitudes toward participants (especially on the part of those staff who had worked at the institution a long time), skepticism of their ability to live independently in the community, and lastly, that change happened too slowly.

The researchers and study participants identified personal qualities needed to be effective advocates and change agents: good communication, empathy, active listening, continuous monitoring of change, enthusiasm for change, flexibility, and openness to new ideas. They also identified concrete strategies needed to effectively initiate and manage needed social change. These included being strategic (forming a plan of action and knowing how to present it in a convincing way), involving all stakeholders in planning and decision-making, educating others on social change issues, and clear and effective leadership.

The researchers made several recommendations to help therapeutic recreation specialists be more effective as advocates and change agents:

- Shift the philosophy and roles of recreationists from the medical model to a human-rights model and learn about the social change process
- Recognize that change is complex, but recreation plays an important role in supporting bottom-up social change due to the importance of recreation to quality of life
- Strengthen relationships and build partnerships in order to build a common societal change agenda that improves the quality of life and well-being of participants
- Conduct action research that provides answers to important questions about the social change process; involve participants as active research partners

Figure 14.5 Primary Source Support: Social Change and Institutions

to see changed in a particular way. Direct lobbying is regulated by government, and funding that comes from government entities to your agency or organization cannot be used for lobbying activities. Whereas lobbying has a narrow, specific focus to change or pass a particular law according to your views, advocacy is a broader range of less specific actions that are sustained over time (NRPA, 2009).

Systems advocacy is an effective way to address social injustice and make lasting change. It requires much more sustained and focused effort than any one individual can give to it. If you are involved in systems advocacy, it will usually be in collaboration with professional or advocacy organizations, such as those listed in the *Resources* section at the end of this chapter.

Advocating for Changes in the Participant's Environment

Recall from Chapter 11 *Implementation* and Chapter 12 *Transition and Inclusion* that helping participants have the leisure lifestyle they want may necessitate changes in the environments in which recreation happens. You can draw upon the skills and knowledge you have in the

When working with your community, your professional association, or other organizations to bring about legislative change, here are some steps to use in accomplishing your goals:

- [ ] Clarify need (legislative, policy)
    - Do you need help with a program or service?
    - Do you want to make a policy or legislative change?
- [ ] Organize
    - Identify allies and develop partnerships.
    - Clarify motives and goals among partners.
- [ ] Background research
    - Who are your representatives and elected officials? What are their passions, their records, their political affiliations?
    - Who is in control and power?
    - Gather complete and thorough information about your proposed policy or legislative change.
- [ ] Message development
    - Tell a compelling story.
    - Know your facts.
    - Be positive.
- [ ] General message delivery
    - Decide on communication methods: letters, phone calls, faxes, rallies, in-person meetings, Skype, e-mails, Twitter, and more.
    - Decide who is the best spokesperson for the message.
    - Develop a clear, well-written and well-thought-out message that is truthful, factual, and forceful without being rude.
    - Be prepared to answer questions about opposing arguments.
- [ ] Effective meetings
    - Set up meetings with elected officials through aids and professional staff.
    - Bring a small but carefully selected number of people to the meeting.
    - Be prepared to deliver your message in 5 minutes and in any location chosen by the official.
    - Have a short, concise, written summary to leave with the official at the end of the meeting.
    - Be sure to give complete contact information.
- [ ] Effective written communication
    - Make communication thought-provoking, personal, and accurate.
    - Limit your written communication to the key points or most important elements of the request.
    - Ask for a response and provide accurate contact information.
- [ ] Effective phone calls
    - Practice your message.
    - Have key information at hand when you place the call.
- [ ] Following up
    - Send a thank-you note to the staff and official soon after the meeting.
    - Wait at least 3 weeks for a response before calling.
    - Be persistent but respectful.

Figure 14.6 Legislative Advocacy Checklist *(adapted from Vance, n.d.)*

area of community building, as described in Chapter 11. Additionally, you can focus on the individual participant and make changes at that level to facilitate his or her aspirations for recreation. Advocating for the person to be more readily included in the environment can focus on any of these areas:

- *Physical accessibility*: To be included and participate fully, participants must be able to approach, enter, and use a recreation amenity. You may need to advocate to help a recreation or community agency become more physically accessible.

- *Administrative accessibility*: Policies, procedures, and practices must accommodate people who have differences to allow full inclusion and participation. This can range from communication and marketing, policies about personal care attendants and service animals, inclusive mission statements, vision and strategic plans, staff training for inclusion, and more. Your role as an advocate may range from giving the agency technical assistance on needed changes, to actually working with a board of directors to mandate change with staff and administrators based on rights and laws.

- *Programmatic and service accessibility*: Program structure, staffing, activity modifications, equipment modifications, and the like may need to change to be more inclusive and available. Again, your role as an advocate may range from providing staff training, to assisting the agency in locating adapted equipment, to helping create a quiet space at the agency. You may need to support a participant in the initial phase of being included, as you train agency staff and other attendees how to support the participant on their own.

Advocating for changes in the participant's environment can involve individual advocacy or systems advocacy, depending on the gap or need. For example, you may work with a recreation agency to allow an exemption to a policy for an individual participant, or you may work with a board of directors to have the policy changed now and in the future for all people with a similar need.

When you advocate for the person in the environment, you draw on your skills and knowledge as a recreation professional and a therapeutic recreation specialist. Your unique educational background, with courses and training in the recreation delivery system and the health and human service system, make you particularly qualified to be an advocate for environmental change. One of the strengths of our field is to have our feet in both worlds so we are able to make positive change not only for the individual participant, but for the agency and community as well.

Advocating for a Strengths Approach

In many settings in which you may work in therapeutic recreation, the medical or deficits model continues to dominate service provision. You will likely be part of an interdisciplinary or transdisciplinary team, and because this collaboration requires working closely with one another, you may experience a divergence in philosophical orientation with other team members. Often, in medical settings, the dominant discipline on the team is the medical profession, whose members are trained in the disease orientation. Given this context, it is important for you to be prepared to advocate for the strengths perspective on the team.

How can you advocate for the strengths approach? There are several strategies you can use to assist the team in understanding the strengths approach. First and foremost, recall from Chapter 3 *A Sea Change in Therapeutic Recreation* that our field is the ideal, most logical discipline from which to practice a strengths approach. Reaffirm with yourself how well this approach aligns with the values and strengths of therapeutic recreation.

Next, be prepared to educate other team members on the strengths approach. Ideally, provide an in-service or workshop on the strengths approach, including the philosophy and orientation in assessment, planning, implementing approaches, and evaluation. Also present the research and self-advocacy literature that supports positive outcomes with the strengths approach.

During the course of providing services, and especially at team meetings, continually offer evidence of participants' strengths. Share assessment results focused on strengths; plans developed in collaboration with participants that highlight dreams, goals, and aspirations; and progress participants demonstrate that highlights strengths. It may be artwork the participant has created or a physical skill she has demonstrated. It may be generosity shown with other participants or a courageous show of assertiveness in a community integration activity. Invite team members to groups, activities, and services you provide, to help them see participants in action, pursuing their interests or displaying their passions. Use artifacts, with permission, from groups or activities to decorate the agency, whether it is artwork, or poetry, or photos of recreation involvement. All these actions will help other team members see participants in a different light, through a strengths-based lens instead of a problem-oriented one. This in turn may help them see how important it is to focus on strengths in their practice as well.

You may also help participants develop skills and strategies to more assertively share their strengths with other team members and help them feel a sense of control over their own plan. As discussed earlier in this chapter, supporting participants in their own efforts at advocacy is the most powerful way to change systems. You can also help participants reaffirm their own strengths, dreams, and goals, when they experience disempowerment in the medical model.

These strategies are important to use, as the dominance of the deficits-based approach is entrenched in the helping professions. Russo (1999) described some of the obstacles encountered in implementing a strengths approach. For one, it is often a diagnosis or deficit that makes a person eligible for services to begin with. Funding for services is often tied to documentation of problem areas. Participants may be socialized into the deficits approach, and have difficulty verbalizing their own strengths. Given these obstacles, it is more important than ever to fully commit to a strengths approach, to advocate for it, and to advocate for changes in systems that trap people into stigmatized labels and disempowering roles. It is important to provide therapeutic recreation services that bolster strengths, enhance interests, skills, and passions, and improve well-being. In the next section, we offer a rationale for the importance of advocating for strengths-based therapeutic recreation.

Advocating for the Profession of Therapeutic Recreation

Therapeutic recreation is an amazing profession that does much good! Those of us who practice in therapeutic recreation know how much we help people and communities and how positive our approaches are. Yet, at times, others with whom we interact do not know much about our field or have not heard of it at all. Still others may have an inaccurate perception of therapeutic recreation based on past experiences or just plain misunderstanding of the nature of the field. We at times find ourselves in a position of needing to advocate for our own profession.

In this section, we share some practical tips on advocating for therapeutic recreation. We feel it is important to preface these tips with a caution. Advocacy for the field is solely for the good of the participant and the assurance that our services are accessible and available to those who benefit from our work. Advocacy for the field is *not* to improve our status or image for self-serving purposes. If your own image, importance, and status are at the heart of your efforts for professional advocacy, then your efforts are misaligned. If your desire is to be sure that our services are provided to the widest possible audience in the widest possible settings and systems at the highest level of quality so that many can benefit, then your advocacy efforts are sincere and good. With these reasons in mind, we offer the following tips to advocate for therapeutic recreation (see Figure 14.7, p. 404).

It Starts with You

Your appearance, your communication, your actions, and your interactions with participants, families, and other team members convey each day a strong message about the profession of therapeutic recreation (Szydlo & Fisher, 2009). Each time you meet a new participant and family, always introduce yourself *and* your profession. For example, "Hello, I am Jane, and I am a therapeutic recreation specialist. I look forward to helping you enhance your recreation, build your strengths, and increase your well-being while you are with us." Compare this to, "Hello, I am Jane, and I will be working with you every day while you are here with us." By specifically sharing your profession with participants, you also share your expertise and focus. You inform participants and family that you have a unique set of skills and knowledge that you are eager to put at their disposal.

If you consistently and persistently do the best work you can with each participant, and if your work is strongly person-centered and based on the participant's aspirations for enhanced leisure and quality of life, you will provide a highly valued service. The strongest advocacy for the field of therapeutic recreation often comes from participants and families themselves. It is common for a groundswell of support to rise up from families when therapeutic recreation services are being targeted for reduction or elimination. Recreation is very important to many and, if you are doing good work centered squarely on the participant and his or her circle of support, advocacy often comes from your constituents themselves.

You also convey much information about the profession of therapeutic recreation in your everyday interactions with your own family, friends, and old and new acquaintances. When someone asks you what you do for a living, be ready to share what you do in therapeutic recreation, how it benefits participants, and stories of important differences you have made in people's lives. Be ready to clarify the importance of play, and how you work every day to ensure that all people can benefit from positive leisure experiences. Avoid comparing yourself to other professions; instead, speak clearly and proudly about the unique and important services a therapeutic recreation specialist provides. Recall in Chapter 3 *A Sea Change in Therapeutic Recreation* that we asked you to write a letter to a close relative about your field, and to have an "elevator speech" ready to share. This is an important part of advocacy for the profession. Be ready to clearly and easily share the strengths and benefits of therapeutic recreation to any audience, including your own circle of support.

Self-Education

Learn as much as you can about therapeutic recreation. Engage in training, go to conferences, read the journals and newsletters in the field, and visit professional websites. Keeping up with best practices strengthens the field and your own practice and makes advocacy for the

Life Story:

Advocating for Adventures in Sobriety: You Can't Have REcovery without REC
By Lori Pilosi, MS, CTRS

Back in 1991, I accepted a position as a therapeutic recreation specialist at Marworth Treatment Center in Waverly, Pennsylvania. Marworth is a 91-bed inpatient alcohol and chemical dependence treatment center. During my interview, I remember asking what the facility's therapeutic recreation program consisted of, and my interviewers explained that I would be starting this modality as an addition to the overall treatment program offered. The first part of Marworth's mission statement spoke to improving the physical, spiritual, and emotional health of persons with chemical dependency. As a therapeutic recreation specialist I may be biased, however I wondered if this could ever be accomplished without therapeutic recreation. Perhaps it was possible, but in my heart I believe that the program has been greatly enhanced with the addition of therapeutic recreation over the past 18 years. Based on patient focus groups and satisfaction surveys from a participant standpoint, it is one of the most popular parts of the treatment day! Therapeutic recreation first helps participants identify how their leisure was impacted by their addiction. From there, they help each other in a group setting develop healthy leisure skills and experience healthy leisure participation. Marworth now offers a complete therapeutic recreation program, which includes the following interventions: a low elements challenge course, trust activities, team sports activities, nature activities, exercise programming, leisure education, relaxation, new games, art activities, off-ground activities (community reintegration), and special events on holidays.

Although the program is popular with participants, it was a challenge to introduce it to the rest of the treatment team. I had to sell a skeptical staff on the belief that therapeutic recreation in treatment would not be a diversion. My first way to convince them was by reminding them to put the word "therapeutic" before recreation. Then the next step in convincing them was to have them participate! Learning by doing seems to give people the best insight—the same was true for my colleagues. One of the highlights of the therapeutic recreation program is our low elements challenge course. With this being said, the treatment team staff was the first to test it out! Involving my colleagues in therapeutic recreation has helped them see the many benefits and positive outcomes of what I do.

The challenge course continues to be one of the highlights of the program. The low elements challenge course is a series of goal-oriented physical tasks designed to be accomplished by groups. It is an exciting and challenging opportunity for team building, goal setting, healthy risk-taking, and personal growth. Participants learn to ask for help in solving problems. They find out that they cannot do the activities or recovery alone, and that they need support and help from one another. They experience the power of the group. After the challenge-course activity, the tasks are processed and related to a daily 12-step recovery model. The wall of addiction stands out as one of my favorite challenge-course activities. It is front-loaded with each participant identifying a personal wall that is a barrier. Some examples of such personal walls are lack of trust, resentment, and anger. Metaphoric learning helps them imagine that getting over the wall with the help of the group simulates getting over personal walls with help. Awesome! It still gives me chills watching the participants and hearing them process it afterwards. An outpatient counselor once shared with me that a former participant had recounted her experience in the wall of addiction activity in a counseling session. The participant's personal wall was body image. She felt she was too heavy for the group to lift her over the wall. She made an analogy that she felt her problems were too heavy as well. During her aftercare counseling session, she identified that she continues to strive to get over her walls as she did with help that day on the challenge course.

One of the most exciting and rewarding parts of my job as a therapeutic recreation specialist is viewing the transition of an individual patient or group at the start of an activity compared to their positive, recovery-oriented outlook at the end. At first, many are unsure how recreation can have any bearing on their daily struggles in recovery from addiction. Yet, when they experience the value of teamwork, cooperation, group trust, and support, patients quickly realize how important these activities and lessons are in their new, healthy life of recovery. Most importantly, they experience clean and sober fun. The counseling staff, patients' families, and others see the value too. The following are anonymous quotes in response to the question "How did therapeutic recreation activities relate to your recovery?" They were taken directly from past participant discharge questionnaires, which we use to measure satisfaction and as a needs assessment tool.

> "Therapeutic recreation helped me to discover a part of myself that I thought had died."
> "It reminded me that I can have fun when I'm sober."
> "I learned to put trust in other people."
> "Pushed me to use teamwork, rely on others, patience, tolerance, and accepting the limitations of others."
> "It made me 'feel' how the program works."
> "I love the team-building and group activities, being able to laugh and learn how to work with others. Always left feeling better than when it started."
> "The way the recreation was integrated into the 12-step program was fantastic."

In addition to several participants who have touched my life, I have also had the privilege to work with several student interns. A recent intern came up with a conclusion at the end of her internship when she looked at the word "recovery" and stated, "You can't have *REC*overy without REC." Perhaps you can have recovery without recreation; however, healthy leisure can enhance overall recovery from addiction. It is my personal theory and belief that those who incorporate healthy recreation in their recovery post-discharge have a better chance at long-term sobriety. Leisure skills are relapse-prevention skills. And the participants and my colleagues at Marworth believe that, too!

Figure 14.7 Life Story: Advocating for Adventures in Sobriety: You Can't Have REcovery without REC

profession much easier. Earn and keep your national certification and, if applicable, state license. Taking skill development and maintenance of competency seriously demonstrates the professionalism of the field, and adds credibility to your advocacy efforts.

Continually add to your own skills, and extend yourself to new and important areas. You can gain increased expertise in areas that provide resources, such as grant writing or coding. Or, you may develop new skills, such as specialty certifications in areas such as aquatics, snow sports, or equine-assisted therapy. Perhaps you can broaden your role and pursue such things as case management, volunteer management, or Medicaid Service Coordination credentials.

Learn as much as you can about your agency. Look for new areas where therapeutic recreation services could be offered to improve the overall quality of the agency's services and address unmet or only partially met needs. Be ready to describe how therapeutic recreation can add to the agency's overall effectiveness in new and different areas.

Regular Communication with Decision-Makers

Maintain frequent communication with people in your agency, your community, and your professional networks that are in a position to make changes or create opportunities. Keep your immediate and higher-level supervisors abreast of all you are doing in therapeutic recreation. Collect and share stories, testimonials, and outcome data. Use internal and external media to share your message, whether it is an agency newsletter or a feature story in your local newspaper.

Celebrate and Share Successes

We help change lives on a routine basis. In therapeutic recreation, we bring joy and meaning to people's lives. When you have successes, share them broadly. Differentiate your message depending on your audience. Focus on economic impact, heart-warming stories, or statistics on positive outcomes, whichever message best strikes a chord. Always capture the joy and meaning that we bring to participants through recreation. Celebrate special times, like National Therapeutic Recreation Week, the International Day of Play, the National Turn Off the TV Day, or Take Back Your Time Day. Highlight the important role therapeutic recreation plays in improving recreation, well-being, and quality of life. Stage special events that bring attention to the services we provide and their impact on people's lives. For example, in one community, therapeutic recreation specialists sponsored an Annual Doll Clinic for children throughout the region that provided a wonderful community service, broadly educated the community about therapeutic recreation, and brought smiles to many children (see Figure 14.8, p. 406).

Network and Support

Build strong networks with fellow therapeutic recreation specialists in your community and through your professional associations, both locally and at the state and national levels. You can provide a stronger message about the importance and worth of therapeutic recreation with others than you can alone. Share what has worked with colleagues, and collect their best ideas for advocacy to try at your agency.

Network with other departments and professionals at your own agency (Volunteer Management Resource Center, 2009). Provide a clear and consistent message about what you do and the services you provide. Establish yourself as the expert on enhancing recreation experiences, building strengths, and improving well-being for participants. Share your knowledge, skills, and resources in recreation and the strengths approach. When others at your agency see a need to focus on any of these areas, if you have done your work, you will be the first person your colleagues call upon for help.

Get involved as a therapeutic recreation specialist in local initiatives, organizations, and boards. Attend important meetings about recreation and quality of life in your community, volunteer for community initiatives, get elected to commissions, or convene roundtable discussions. Represent your work as a therapeutic recreation specialist clearly, and educate others on the link between community initiatives, well-being, and your profession.

Be a Play Expert

It has never been easier to be an advocate for our profession! As a culture, we are realizing the importance of play, recreation, and leisure in quality of life, health, and well-being. To be a strong advocate, be well-versed in and ready to share the results of new and emerging research that clearly documents how important our work is for individuals and communities. In Figure 14.9, we provide some of the well-researched benefits of play and recreation. At the end of this chapter, we offer some newer resources that provide a layperson with an explanation of the large body of empirical research that documents how important it is to have play, recreation,

Life Story:

Advocating for the Profession through Community Service:
The Doll Clinic

Every year at a regional health facility, we provide the Annual Doll Clinic. This special event, organized by the therapeutic recreation specialists at the large medical center, is a cherished community event. Under our leadership, we provide a valued community service and educate people in the region about therapeutic recreation.

The Doll Clinic is a fun and educational event for children in our local communities. On this day, children bring their "sick" dolls, teddy bears, robots, and other such toys to have surgery! They experience what it is like to have their doll or toy admitted to the hospital, go through surgery, and come out happy and well. The goal of the event is to provide a medical play experience to children, to help them understand that going to the hospital is not too scary, and that loved ones leave the hospital better. The Doll Clinic's intent is to familiarize children with the hospitalization process, to help them understand it, and not fear it.

For the day, we set up a mock hospital in the lower level concourse of two adjoining medical facilities. The "hospital" includes an Admitting Department, a pre-op area, a triage area, a surgery area, a post-operative area, and a discharge area. We recruit volunteers from many departments: admissions, nursing, other allied health professionals like occupational therapists, physical therapists, social workers, dietitians, and the like. We also recruit the local quilting club to be our "surgeons." We provide a short pre-orientation to all the volunteers, so they know what role to play during the daylong Doll Clinic.

On the day of the Doll Clinic, the long line forms! Children come first to Admitting, where they and their dolls receive matching hospital bracelets. The child and doll are escorted to pre-op, where a "nurse" meets with them to explain what will happen in surgery, where the child can wait during surgery, and how they can rejoin their doll in the post-op area. The nurse then takes the doll's temperature and blood pressure, and lets the child listen to the heartbeat with a stethoscope. The doll is then wheeled into "surgery." The surgery area, which is behind closed "operating doors," is basically a large room full of volunteers patching holes, re-stuffing animals, gluing on parts, and the like! Meanwhile, the child is escorted to the waiting room off the surgery area, where a therapeutic recreation specialist provides educational color books about a visit to the hospital, and chats with the children about their questions as they wait. A nurse then comes and gets the child to reunite with their doll in post-op. Here the nurse provides discharge instructions and a take-home coloring sheet about what it was like to come to the hospital.

Therapeutic recreation specialists oversee the whole operation, and talk with parents as they wait for their children about the use of medical play in helping children prepare for a hospitalization. The event always receives a great deal of media attention, and in the process, nice exposure for therapeutic recreation. Using a community event, we are able to bring smiles to children, help children understand hospitalization, and put our profession in the spotlight of the public and other healthcare workers at our agency.

Figure 14.8 Life Story: Advocating for the Profession through Community Service: The Doll Clinic

- Play inspires you to think differently
- Play brings greater joy into your life
- Play reduces stress
- Play increases longevity
- Play reduces struggle, conflict, and worry
- Play unburdens you and increases your sense of lightness
- Play stimulates imagination, creativity, and curiosity
- Play softens the heart
- Play enhances your energy level
- Play provides you with opportunities to take risks
- Play increases your productivity with other life tasks
- Play helps you learn better
- Play engages you fully with others and with the world

Figure 14.9 The Benefits of Play! *(adapted from Brown, 2009; St. Clair, 2009)*

Primary Source Support:

Why We Advocate for Play

Johnson, K., & Klaas, S. (2007). The changing nature of play: Implications for pediatric spinal cord injury. *Journal of Spinal Cord Medicine, 30,* S71–S75.

Johnson, a therapeutic recreation specialist, and Klaas, a social worker, began their study by reviewing the literature on the critical importance of play in the lives of children and what typically developing children do for play. They then investigated the play of children with spinal cord injuries. Their results showed that children with spinal cord injury participated in activities that were sedentary in nature, involved little to no social interaction, and were conducted indoors. The large majority of children with spinal cord injury reported no organized activity such as sports, clubs, or youth centers, while their peers without disabilities were participating in these types of activities at an all-time high.

Johnson and Klaas recommended that every effort be made to increase the amount, quality, and nature of play and recreation experiences for children with spinal cord injuries. Not only are these children missing out on significant developmental opportunities, they are also being excluded from experiencing the powerful benefits of play in their lives and inclusion in their communities.

Figure 14.10 Primary Source Support: Why We Advocate for Play

and quality leisure in individual and community life. Read it and be ready to easily and quickly share it with others (see Figure 14.10).

Balancing Advocacy

Advocacy is a skill and philosophy that can have powerful outcomes that change not only the lives of individuals but services and systems as well. Advocacy has been used effectively by parents, self-advocates, and helping professionals to make changes that have improved quality of life and addressed social injustice when other approaches have failed (Pedlar et al., 1999). However, as a professional, you must continually weigh the costs and effort of advocacy and make sure they are worth the outcomes or benefits. Nisbett and Hagner (2000) share a lesson learned from their years of advocacy for people with disabilities; they tell a story of working aggressively with a student and family to help them gain inclusive versus segregated educational services from a school district. They lost the case, but more importantly, they lost their ability to work collaboratively with that school district as well as surrounding school districts for many years. According to Nisbett and Hagner:

> We did the right thing for this young man and his family but the wrong thing for the several hundred other students receiving separate services. . . . The school districts did not want to see us as part of the solution. In fact, they viewed us suspiciously . . . The immediate desire to help and to support inclusion must be fully assessed in terms of positive and negative impacts of involvement. (p. 5)

Taking a collaborative versus an adversarial approach in advocacy will help lessen negative impacts. By thoughtfully exploring how participants and agencies can mutually benefit by changes, you can avoid conflict and a "win-lose" situation. Searching for the collaborative or "win-win" outcome will help you be an effective advocate while maintaining important working relationships with community agencies.

If you feel your relationship with an agency or community entity would be threatened by a request for advocacy, it may be necessary to help the participant find an advocate who does not have this same need for an ongoing relationship and who can take on a more controversial advocacy role. Nisbett and Hagner (2000) recommend working with the participant to find an equally qualified advocate, or asking the participant to have the community agency itself invite you to help, instead of forcing yourself upon the agency. This can help create a more positive partnership between the participant, the agency, and you as an advocate.

Summary

Advocacy is working on behalf of yourself or others to make positive social change and reduce social injustice. In the ecological and strengths approach to helping others, advocacy is an invaluable skill and concept. Advocacy takes many forms: self-advocacy, individual

Self-Assessment of Learning

Using what you have learned about advocacy in this chapter, describe how you would approach each scenario provided here to bring about desired change.

Scenario #1 – Self-Advocacy and Helen

You are a therapeutic recreation specialist at the Hometown Hospital in the mental health unit. You and your team have been working with Helen for 2 weeks, as she has learned to manage her depression and begin to build the life she desires. She is being discharged back to her home in a nearby small town, where she lives with her parents and younger brother and works full-time at the local cafe. One of Helen's goals for discharge is to continue in the yoga class she started with you this past week at the YWCA. She loves the class, has begun to make friends there, and feels uplifted and relaxed after each session. Helen's family is very tight-knit, and they frown on activities outside the home; they see something like yoga as a silly, frivolous use of time. Helen wants your help in learning how she can advocate for her goal to keep doing yoga at the YWCA.

How will you help Helen learn self-advocacy skills? How will you support her in her efforts to achieve her goals for recreation?

___

Scenario #2 – Individual Advocacy and the Nelsons

You are a therapeutic recreation specialist at the Northstar Rehabilitation Center where you are helping John Nelson and his family prepare for discharge. John has reached the point in his rehabilitation after a spinal cord injury where he can live at home and attend outpatient therapy on a weekly basis. John is in 5th grade, and he and his family want him to attend the afterschool sports and recreation program at his elementary school. The school district has told the Nelsons that they are not equipped to have a child who uses a wheelchair at the program, and they do not have the staff to let John attend. The Nelsons have asked you to help them advocate for John to be in the program.

How will you help John and his family? How will you support them in their efforts to achieve John's goals for recreation?

___

Scenario #3 – Systems Advocacy and Equitable Seating

You are a therapeutic recreation specialist at the Hometown Independent Living Center. A theater in town is remodeling. A community member who uses a wheelchair contacts you to share what she learned about the remodeling plans and the lack of accessible seating. You follow up with the theater to verify that the theater is not putting integrated accessible seating in the theater but, instead, plans to leave the last row as open space where everyone using a wheelchair will park.

How will you advocate in this situation? What allies will you enlist? What is your plan to ensure an inclusive and equitable change at the theater?

___

Self-Assessment of Learning

Using what you have learned about advocacy in this chapter, describe how you would approach each scenario provided here to bring about desired change.

Scenario #4 – Advocating for the Strengths Approach

You are a therapeutic recreation specialist at the Rosewood Geriatric Center. During care-planning conferences, you have noticed an increasing level of negativity, cynicism, and even outright rude comments from other staff about the residents. Much of the care-planning conference focuses on the problem behaviors of residents and the "meddling" family members.

How will you advocate for a strengths approach in this situation? How will you influence the care-planning process?

_____
_____
_____
_____
_____
_____
_____

Scenario #5 – Advocating for the Profession

You are a therapeutic recreation specialist at the Hazel Treatment Center, an inpatient facility for chemical dependency treatment. You are in the elevator with a group of other staff, and one of them asks what you do. When you explain that you are a therapeutic recreation specialist, the staff member responds, "I wish I could get paid to goof around all day," and all the other staff on the elevator laugh.

How will you advocate in this situation? What will you say to the staff members?

_____
_____
_____
_____
_____
_____
_____

advocacy, and systems or community advocacy. All three share three requirements: a passionate desire to see positive change, a sound understanding of the change needed, and a willingness to "go public" to effect the change. In addition, all three share similar steps that include being clear on the need, having sound information, and a well-reasoned plan to effect change. In therapeutic recreation, we can teach self-advocacy skills to participants and support them in their advocacy efforts. We can also work with other professionals, organizations, or community entities to advocate for and with participants. Beyond advocacy for participants, we will find ourselves in a position to advocate for the strengths approach, for the profession of therapeutic recreation, and for the importance of play in people's lives.

Resources

Advocating Change Together (ACT)
http://www.selfadvocacy.org

Based in St. Paul, Minnesota, ACT is a non-profit disability rights organization "run by and for people with developmental disabilities." Their website describes what self-advocacy means, along with the roles that self-advocates, families, employers, service providers, political leaders, and community members can play to support self-advocacy.

American Association of People with Disabilities
http://www.aapd.com

This national organization organizes the disability community to be a powerful voice for political, economic, and social change. The website provides information and tools to join in national advocacy efforts for disability rights.

National Council on Independent Living (NCIL)
http://www.ncil.org

This national organization is the oldest cross-disability membership organization in the U.S. It represents Centers for Independent Living and Statewide Independent Living Councils, as well as individuals with disabilities and other organizations. The mission of NCIL is to advance independent living and the rights of people with disabilities through consumer-driven advocacy. On its website, it is possible to contact local and state independent living centers and councils located throughout the U.S.

Self-Advocacy Association of New York State (SANYS)
http://www.sanys.org

SANYS is a strong voice for and by people with developmental disabilities promoting independence, empowerment, leading by example, communicating, networking and encouraging each other. The SANYS website is rich with resources on self-advocacy, including inspiring stories, training materials, presentations, and links.

Self-Advocate Leadership Network (SALN)
http://www.theriotrocks.org

SALN is a partnership between the Human Services Research Institute and self-advocates across the country. Their mission is to "help people with developmental disabilities to become strong self-advocates" through a leadership training curriculum called *My Voice, My Choice*. The training provides information on how to become involved in systems related to self-determination, community integration, participant-driven supports, financial decisions related to services, and advocating for change. You can learn more about SALN and their curriculum at their website.

Self-Advocates Becoming Empowered (SABE)
http://www.sabeusa.org

SABE is a national self-advocacy organization with a board that includes representatives and members from every state. Newsletters, resources, a guide to People First Language, and more are available online.

National Advocacy Groups for Different Disability Areas

National groups representing the rights of different disability groups are an excellent resource for therapeutic recreation specialists. Here we list the primary advocacy groups in each disability area:

- Aging: *National Council on Aging*
  http://www.ncoa.org
- Developmental disabilities: *The ARC*
  http://www.thearc.org
- Developmental disabilities and self-advocacy: *People First*—every state has its own chapter. For an example, see *People First of California* at http://www.peoplefirstca.org
- Inclusion and significant disability: *TASH*
  http://www.tash.org
- Mental health: *National Alliance for Mental Illness (NAMI)*
  http://www.nami.org
- Physical and other disabilities: *ADAPT*
  http://www.adapt.org

Centers for Disease Control and Prevention (CDC) "Features"
http://www.cdc.gov/Features

The CDC's website is replete with information on health, wellness, disability, and more. One especially helpful section on the CDC website is called "Features." Monthly focus areas educate users on a vast array of topics on health, wellness, and disability in an easily understood format. Features are indexed alphabetically and by category for easy access to information you can use to educate yourself and thus improve your advocacy potential.

The Community Toolbox
http://ctb.ku.ed

The Community Toolbox, hosted at Kansas University, provides practical, step-by-step guidance in community-building skills. Over 45 training modules, from social action to needs assessment, are offered in the toolbox, with real examples supporting each.

Our Top Choices for Popular-Press Books on the Documented Importance of Play

(to assist in advocacy for the importance of recreation and leisure)

- *Play* by Stuart Brown
- *Flow: The Psychology of Optimal Experience* by Mihaly Csikszentmihalyi
- *The Science of Well-Being* by Ed Diener
- *Positivity* by Barbara Fredrickson
- *Last Child in the Woods* by Richard Louv
- *The How of Happiness* by Sonja Lyubomirsky
- *Spark!* by John Ratey
- *Authentic Happiness* by Martin Seligman

These books are available through most booksellers.

U.S. Play Coalition

http://usplaycoalition.clemson.edu

The U.S. Play Coalition is a partnership of universities, organizations, and individuals to promote the value of play throughout life. Through coalition building, communication, research, advocacy, and education, the Coalition encourages playfulness in daily life for a healthier in mind and body.

National Therapeutic Recreation Society (NTRS) Benefits of Therapeutic Recreation

http://www.nrpa.org

NTRS, under the leadership of Dr. Jane Kaufman Broida, developed a highly effective resource for professionals to advocate for the therapeutic recreation profession called *Therapeutic Recreation: The Benefits are Endless*. In the resource package, evidence on the beneficial outcomes of therapeutic recreation services are provided, as well as presentations and a video that can be used to share the benefits with others. The resource package is available from the National Recreation and Park Association website.

REFERENCES

Advocating Change Together (2009). *Definition of self-advocacy*. Retrieved from http://www.selfadvocacy.org

Bolte, B. (1993, March/April). Jerry's got to be kidding: Why people with disabilities aren't laughing. *The Utne Reader*, 103–104.

Brown, S. (2009). *Play: How it shapes the brain, opens the imagination, and invigorates the soul*. New York, NY: Penguin.

Ervin, M. (2009). *Jerry Lewis doesn't deserve a Humanitarian Award from the Oscars*. Retrieved from http://www.progressive.org/mag/mplewis021909.html

Harvard Project on Disability. (2008). *Change your life with human rights: A self-advocacy book for people with disabilities*. Boston, MA: The President and Fellows of Harvard College.

Hutchinson, P., & McGill, J. (1992). *Leisure, integration, and community*. Concord, ON, Canada: Leisurability.

Hutchinson, P., & Potschaske, C. (1998). Social change and institutions: Implications for recreationists. *Therapeutic Recreation Journal, 32*(2), 130–156.

Johnson, K., & Klaas, S. (2007). The changing nature of play: Implications for pediatric spinal cord injury. *Journal of Spinal Cord Medicine 30*, S71–S75.

Joint Commission. (2009). *Speak up: Know your rights*. Retrieved from http://www.jointcommission.org

Kansas University. (2010). *The community toolbox*. Retrieved from http://ctb.ku.edu

Kluth, P. (2006). Toward a social model of disability. Syracuse, NY: Center on Human Policy. Retrieved from http://www.disabilitystudiesforteachers.org

National Recreation and Park Association (NRPA). (2009). *Park advocate handbook*. Ashburn, VA: NRPA.

Nirje, B. (1992). The normalization principle papers. Uppsala, Sweden: Centre for Handicap Research, Uppsala University.

Nisbett, J., & Hagner, D. (2000). *Part of the community: Strategies for including everyone.* Baltimore, MD: Brookes.

Pedlar, A., Haworth, L., Hutchinson, P., Taylor, A., & Dunn, P. (1999). *A textured life: Empowerment and adults with developmental disabilities.* Waterloo, ON, Canada: Wilfrid Laurier University Press.

Russo, R. (1999). Applying a strengths-based practice approach in working with people with developmental disabilities and their families. *Families in Society: The Journal of Contemporary Human Services, 80,* 25–33.

St. Clair, M. (2009). The top ten benefits of play. Retrieved from http://ezinearticles.com/? Top-Ten-Benefits-of-Play&id=8101

Storey, K. (2004). The case against Special Olympics. *Journal of Disability Policy Studies, 15*(1), 35–42.

Szydlo, C., & Fisher, B. (2009). Advocating for nursing. *Advance, online version.* Retrieved from http://www.advanceweb.com

Teipel, K. (2001). The basic steps of advocacy and persuasion. University of Minnesota: National Adolescent Health Project. Retrieved from http://www.epi.umn.edu/mch/events/SummerInstitute/2004/advocacy1.pdf

Test, D., Fowler, C., Wood, W., Brewer, D., & Eddy, S. (2005). A conceptual framework for self-advocacy for students with disabilities. *Remedial and Special Education, 26*(1), 43–54.

Vance, S. (n.d.). *Legislative special.* Saratoga Springs, NY: NYSRPS.

Volunteer Management Resource Center. (2009). How to advocate for the profession. *The Idealist.* Retrieved from http://www.idealist.org

Chapter 15
BUILDING YOUR STRENGTHS AS A THERAPEUTIC RECREATION SPECIALIST

The hibiscus is bold and beautiful. It is highly therapeutic in many forms, but it requires care to grow well.

"Be the change you want to see in the world."
—*Mohandas Gandhi, Spiritual Leader and Activist*

OVERVIEW OF CHAPTER 15

- What is a "professional"?
- Aspects of a strengths-based professional
  - Being a strengths-based professional
  - Knowing and using ethics, the body of knowledge, and standards of practice
  - Assuring competence to others
  - Continuing to grow as a professional
  - Networking and professional support systems
- Limits to professionalization
- Giving back to the profession

FOCUS QUESTIONS

- What are the central attributes of a profession? What does it mean to be a member of a profession?
- "Professionalism" differs from *being* in a profession. What do we mean by that?
- In your practice in therapeutic recreation, how can the codes of ethics, standards of practice, research journals, professional associations, and other resources be helpful to you?
- How can you continue to grow and learn as a professional in therapeutic recreation? What can you do to further develop your practice wisdom and your ability to be an effective helper?
- Are there limits to what professions can accomplish? Can we ever do more harm than good?
- What is a strengths-based therapeutic recreation specialist?

AN INTRODUCTION TO PROFESSIONS AND PROFESSIONALISM

A definition of "profession":
A calling requiring specialized knowledge and often long and intensive academic preparation; a principal calling, vocation, or employment; the whole body of persons engaged in a calling

A definition of "professionalism":
The conduct, aims, or qualities that characterize or mark a profession or a professional person

A definition of "discipline":
A field of study; a branch of knowledge or learning

A definition of "field":
An area or division of an activity, subject, or profession; subject, or area of academic interest or specialization; profession, employment, or business

Throughout this book, we have used the term "profession" when we talk about therapeutic recreation. What do we mean by the word "profession"? What qualities or attributes does the field or discipline of therapeutic recreation possess that may qualify it as a profession? What can you do to be a strengths-based professional? Are there limits to professionalization? These are some of the questions we address in this chapter. Our larger purpose in this chapter is for you, as a developing strengths-based therapeutic recreation specialist, to identify areas where you can continue to learn and grow in the field in a reflective and thoughtful manner.

To begin our discussion, let's explore in more depth some common meanings of the words "profession" and "professionalism." In the beginning of the chapter, we provided dictionary definitions. If you approached people on the street and asked them to tell you what a profession is, many would say a doctor, lawyer, or even a college professor. Or they may mention sports and identify paid athletes as professionals (Winfield & Webster, 2004). These general perceptions, though seemingly very different, do share some commonalities. Professionals are thought of as highly skilled, like professional athletes. But they are also thought of as having high integrity, as being learned or knowledgeable, and as being needed for their knowledge, skills, and integrity for society to function. These common perceptions of what constitutes a profession are close to how sociologists and philosophers, within and outside of our field, have defined a profession.

According to scholars (Austin, Dattilo, & McCormick, 2002; Kestenbaum, 2005; Sylvester, 2002, 2005, 2009; Wilensky, 1964), the defining attributes of a **profession** include the following characteristics:

- Mastery of an organized body of knowledge built upon a sound philosophical and theoretical foundation
- A formal way of transmitting that knowledge to current and aspiring members of the profession
- Professional authority and assurance of competence to those who receive services
- Sanction of the community and a recognition of autonomy of the profession to regulate itself through its standards of practice
- Ethical beliefs and conduct monitored by the profession
- A service ideal; that is, service to society that is provided for more than professional gain and is a calling rather than a trade or occupation
- Virtuousness; an ethic of virtue

Professionalism, on the other hand, is often used to describe professional conduct and qualities exhibited by a professional (Austin, n.d.; Pellegrino, 2002). Pellegrino describes professionalism as loyalty to other members of the same profession, exclusivity based on credentials, and a concern for titles and self-interests of the group. He differentiates "profession," which has a moral heart, from "professionalism," which may have a self-serving heart. Sylvester (2002, 2009) has also differentiated between the "internal goods" of a profession and the "external goods" of professionalism. The internal goods of a profession put the people served above the needs of the professional. "Acting professional" is obviously a good thing to do; however, it does not make a profession. After all, even gangs exhibit professionalism (Moore, 2009), from having a body of knowledge to a code of ethics! Thus, a critical defining characteristic of a profession is virtue.

Sylvester (2009) has written extensively about virtuousness as the basis for the practice of therapeutic recreation. In essence, **virtue** is about the moral character of the therapeutic recreation specialist. Sylvester describes someone with excellent moral character as "a person who reflects on, feels strongly about, and consistently exhibits in his or her behavior such moral qualities as courage, fairness, honesty, and integrity" (p. 11). (Recall the detailed overview of these virtues from Chapter 5 *Strengths*). Sylvester asserts that a professional is one who has excellent character as much as one who has skills and knowledge and whose actions follow a code of ethics. He states, "While knowledge and skill are the pillars of a profession, virtue is its bedrock" (p. 23).

So, in sum, a profession has a specialized body of knowledge, a formal way of transmitting its knowledge, assurance of competence, autonomy, and—most importantly—ethics, a service ideal, and virtuousness in its members and its practice. Let's look more closely at each of the attributes of a profession and how you, as a therapeutic recreation specialist, can further develop each of them.

What Does it Mean to be a Strengths-Based Professional?

How can you focus on your development as a virtuous and ethical professional in therapeutic recreation? How can you nourish your own strengths and virtues and, in doing so, also nourish the field of therapeutic recreation? When you are a strengths-based professional, you have internalized and reflected on the attributes of your profession, and you conduct your daily practice using those attributes. We will focus the rest of this chapter on strategies you can use to develop as an authentic professional.

Strategy 1: Know and Use Your Strengths and Virtues in Practice

In Chapter 5 *Strengths* we introduced you to character strengths and virtues. Remember that character strengths and virtues are the positive traits that define who we are as human beings. Virtues are the six core characteristics valued across culture and time, which Peterson and Seligman (2004) identify as wisdom, courage, humanity, justice, temperance, and transcendence. Character strengths are the processes or pathways that define the broad virtues and allow people who exercise their strengths to live a life where virtues can be displayed. Table 15.1 lists these character strengths and virtues. Peterson and Seligman state that character strengths are the bedrock of the human condition and that strengths–congruent activity represents an important route to excellence and a good life.

Knowing your own strengths and virtues is an important aspect of practicing therapeutic recreation. When you put your strengths into action every day to help participants, you experience excellence in your work and build your moral character (see Figure 15.1). You can also target strengths you want to build further to improve your ability to practice therapeutic recreation more completely. Recall in Chapter 5 *Strengths* that you completed the VIA (Values in Action) strengths assessment. Review your results, and clarify those areas where you show strengths and virtues. Are your strengths and virtues important to your practice? Do you use them every day?

Professions like medicine have articulated virtues they feel are important to ethical and excellent practice (National Board of Medical Examiners, 2003; Pellegrino, 2002). These include virtues such as altruism, honor, integrity, respect, and humility (see Table 15.2). Sylvester (2009) asserts that, as a profession, therapeutic recreation needs to have the important dialogue about the virtues and strengths most important to our profession. He identifies fairness, honesty, courage, and justice as virtues common to all professions. But are there other strengths and virtues especially important to therapeutic recreation? Sylvester encourages our profession to explore and dialogue openly on what those other important virtues may be. For example, is creativity a key virtue for therapeutic recreation, or playfulness, zest, and vitality? Social intelligence and

Table 15.1 6 Core Virtues and 24 Character Strengths
(Peterson & Seligman, 2004)

Wisdom	Courage
• Curiosity	• Valor
• Love of learning	• Perseverance
• Judgment	• Integrity
• Ingenuity	• Zest and vitality
• Perspective	

Humanity	Justice
• Kindness	• Citizenship
• Loving	• Fairness
• Social intelligence	• Leadership

Temperance	Transcendence
• Self-control	• Appreciation of beauty
• Prudence	• Gratitude
• Humility	• Hope
• Forgiveness	• Spirituality
	• Humor

Life Story:

Discovering Our Strengths

I work with a group of talented, intelligent, and caring people. Though we work closely together, we are all very different. To help us understand and use our strengths so that each individual feels fulfilled and the group functions most effectively, we completed an assessment of our strengths and shared them. We used the Gallup Organization "Strengths Finder 2.0" assessment tool (Rath, 2007). Much like the Values in Action survey (VIA), it helps uncover and clarify your natural strengths and talents.

The Strengths Finder 2.0 is computerized, and each of us went to the website, completed the assessment, and reflected on our results. We then shared with each other our strengths, keeping a large matrix of who had what strengths in our work group. It was fun and affirming to share our strengths with each other. More importantly, it helps us as a team know more clearly who is really good at what. We can now easily help each other put our strengths into daily use. For example, one of us is really great at connectedness and social intelligence, while another has a strength in critical and analytic thinking. When considering who would most flourish planning the holiday party and who would most enjoy completing the department evaluation results, we had insight into whom to ask!

Using and building strengths in your work allows you to have the opportunity to do what you do best every day. It is one of the avenues to the good and flourishing life and helps each of us stay committed and passionate about our calling in the field.

Figure 15.1 Life Story: Discovering Our Strengths

Table 15.2 Professional Virtues Identified by the Medical Profession as Important to Practice (with example behaviors) *(National Board of Medical Examiners, 2003; Pellegrino, 2002)*

Altruism
- Promises to serve the patient's good
- Offers to help team members who are busy
- Contributes to the profession; active in local and national organizations

Honor and Integrity
- Forthcoming with information; does not withhold and/or use information for power
- Admits errors
- Deals with confidential information discreetly and appropriately

Caring and Compassion
- Treats the patient as an individual, taking into account lifestyle, beliefs, personal idiosyncrasies, and support system
- Communicates bad news with sincerity and compassion

Courage
- Advocates for the patient in a commercialized environment

Respect
- Respects patient rights/dignity (privacy/confidentiality, consent); knocks on door, introduces self, drapes patients appropriately, and shows respect for patient privacy needs
- Demonstrates tolerance to a range of behaviors and beliefs

Humility
- Uses power to heal and not for self-promotion
- Does not demean the patient

Responsibility and Accountability
- Demonstrates awareness of own limitations and identifies developmental needs and approaches for improvements
- Cares for self appropriately and presents self in a professional manner (i.e., demeanor, dress, hygiene)
- Recognizes and reports errors/poor behavior in peers
- Takes responsibility for appropriate share of team work
- Arrives on time
- Accountable for deadlines; completes assignments and responsibilities on time
- Answers letters, pages, e-mail, and phone calls in a timely manner

Excellence and Scholarship
- Masters techniques and technologies of learning
- Is self-critical and able to identify own areas for learning/practice improvement
- Has internal focus and direction, setting own goals
- Takes initiative in organizing, participating, and collaborating in peer study groups

Leadership
- Teaches others
- Helps build and maintain a culture that facilitates professionalism

friendship? Sylvester invites us, as a profession, to have a logical, coherent, and morally sound dialogue in order to develop an integrative narrative about the virtues we hold as important to therapeutic recreation practice (see Figure 15.2).

In addition to identifying his or her own strengths and virtues, a strengths-based therapeutic recreation specialist knows and uses the strengths and resources in her or his environment. Regardless of the delivery system in which you work (e.g., health care, social services, education, recreation), the people and places around you have resources to help you practice from a strengths approach. For example, in a healthcare setting, you have access to the expertise of transdisciplinary team members and can structure your practice to routinely include sharing of information and knowledge to better promote integrated and person-centered care. In a recreation setting, you have access to venues and people that can help build community and can structure your practice to include advocacy and systems change. In social services, you have access to resources with which you can structure individualized supports for participants, to help them have full and satisfying leisure in their lives. As a strengths-based therapeutic recreation specialist, developing the strengths in your practice environment is as important as developing your own strengths and virtues.

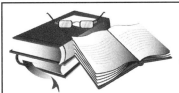

Primary Source Support:

A Therapeutic Recreation Ethic of Care

O'Keefe, C. (2005). Grounding the therapeutic recreation process in an ethic of care. In C. Sylvester (Ed.), *Philosophy of therapeutic recreation: Ideas and issues* (Vol. III). Ashburn, VA: National Therapeutic Recreation Society.

Scholars and philosophers in our field have repeatedly called for inquiry and discourse that illuminates and clarifies the conceptual and philosophical foundation of our field and helps us build our practice based on that foundation. This philosophic essay by Cathy O'Keefe provides exactly this type of discourse and is important primary source material to integrate into your work as a therapeutic recreation specialist.

O'Keefe first provides an overview of the ethics of care and a justification for its use in our field. An ethic of care "challenges us to approach the therapeutic process within a broader context that always sees the client as a growing person rather than as a diagnostic label hung on a disease . . . it treats the interaction between client and helper as relational rather than strictly clinical" (p. 73). O'Keefe provides strong justification for the use of an ethic of care to counterbalance the objectification of the prevalent medical model. She delineates the four phases of an ethic of care: caring about, caring for, caregiving, and care receiving.

O'Keefe then reinterprets the therapeutic recreation process couched in an ethic of care and from the participant's perspective. The first phase, assessment, is listening to the participant's story. Applying the philosophy of relational ethics, O'Keefe makes the case that superficial inquiry and selective data gathering cannot fully capture the lived experience of the participant. She then moves to the next phase, planning, which is more aptly about visioning, and truly reflecting the needs and wants of the participant. Intervention, or the implementation phase of the therapeutic recreation process, focuses on facilitating high-quality recreation or leisure experiences for participants. And lastly, evaluation is reflecting on efficacy with the participant. Was the participant able to make meaning from the experiences and own that meaning?

By using the philosophy of an ethic of care, O'Keefe helps us shift our thinking in a different way. It helps us stay focused on and true to person-centered care, "not measured by external standards but by the interior moral compass that matters most" (p. 82).

Figure 15.2 Primary Source Support: A Therapeutic Recreation Ethic of Care

In sum, an important attribute of being a professional in therapeutic recreation is being virtuous. This means knowing and using your own virtues and strengths in every aspect of your practice. It means reflecting on and consistently displaying moral behavior. And it means developing the strengths and resources in your practice environment for the benefit of participants and their goals for a better life. Sylvester (2009) put it eloquently, "A professional is not just a knower and a doer. He or she is also a *being*, more exactly, a *professional being*, referring to the kind of person one needs *to be* in order to achieve excellence as a professional" (p. 19). Being of sound moral character is aided by a code of ethics that can help guide you in your practice. In the next section, we explore professional ethics as another important attribute of a profession.

Strategy 2: Know and Use Professional Ethics

Ethics are theories of what is good or bad, right or wrong, in human conduct and affairs. Applied to a profession, ethics are the sets of rules or principles that guide moral professional behavior as we practice our craft. Ethics not only guide us in our actions, they alert us to what we should question and about what we should be vigilant.

A **code of ethics** is the written document developed by a profession that states the moral obligations of its members. A code of ethics provides guidelines but not absolute rules. Because ethics are applied to situations that may not have a clear direction, path, or answer, a code of ethics must provide guidance that is broad yet unambiguous enough to be helpful. A code of ethics, then, guides professional practice and protects participants by encouraging moral behavior on the part of professionals. A code of ethics also protects the profession from undue outside influences such as commercialization.

In therapeutic recreation, the codes of ethics of the American Therapeutic Recreation Association (ATRA), the Canadian Therapeutic Recreation Association (CTRA), and the National Therapeutic Recreation Society (NTRS) spell out the moral obligations of our profession. In Table 15.3, we offer the main elements of each of the codes. Though they differ in structure, the codes are similar in function and substance. Shank (1985), in a seminal article, clearly articulated the

Table 15.3 Comparison of the NTRS, ATRA, and CTRA Codes of Ethics *(ATRA, 2009; CTRA, 2005; NTRS, 2001)*

Code of Ethics Comparison		
NTRS Code of Ethics	**Comparable Principles in the ATRA Code of Ethics**	**Comparable Principles in the CTRA Code of Ethics**
Principle 1: Obligation of professional virtue • Integrity • Honesty • Fairness • Competence • Diligence • Awareness	Principle 4: Justice Principle 6: Veracity Principle 9: Competence	Principle 1: Professional Virtues • Integrity • Honesty • Fairness • Competence

Principle 2: Obligation of the professional to the individual
• Well-being
• Loyalty
• Respect
   - Freedom, autonomy, self-determination
   - Privacy
• Professional practices
	Principle 1: Beneficence
	Principle 2: Non-maleficence
	Principle 3: Autonomy
	Principle 5: Fidelity
	Principle 7: Informed consent
	Principle 8: Confidentiality and privacy
		Principle 2: Obligation of the professional to the individual and society
		• Well-being
		• Loyalty
		• Privacy and confidentiality
		Principle 3: Professional Practice

Principle 3: Obligation of the professional to other individuals and society • General welfare • Fairness	Principle 4: Justice	Principle 2: Obligation of the professional to the individual and society • Well-being • Loyalty • Privacy and confidentiality Principle 3: Professional Practice
Principle 4: Obligation of the professional to colleagues • Respect • Cooperation and support	Principle 5: Fidelity	Principle 4: Responsibilities to colleagues and the profession • Respect • Cooperation
Principle 5: Obligation of the professional to the profession • Knowledge • Respect • Reform	Principle 9: Competence	Principle 4: Responsibilities to colleagues and the profession • Respect • Knowledge
Principle 6: Obligation of the profession to society • Service • Equality • Advocacy	Principle 10: Compliance with laws and regulations	Principle 2: Obligation of the professional to the individual and society • Equal opportunity
Note: In 2010, NTRS became the Inclusion and Advocacy Network, still affiliated with the National Recreation and Park Association.		

ethical foundations, which are contained in the codes of ethics in therapeutic recreation. In Table 15.4, we provide the ethical principles and their meaning.

Ethical principles of autonomy, beneficence, non-maleficence, and justice are used to guide our moral reasoning in therapeutic recreation practice. Moral rules are derived from principles and provide further guidance to our decision-making as we work with participants. They include veracity, fidelity, confidentiality, and privacy. When we find ourselves in moral or ethical dilemmas, we draw on codes of ethics to help us choose our actions.

Ethical dilemmas are those situations where there appears to be a problem with no clear solution or when there are two equally unsatisfactory alternatives (Shank, 1985). In an ethical dilemma, you may need to choose to abide by one principle while violating another. Shank shares some examples of ethical dilemmas:

- A participant does not want to follow instructions that protect him from harm (a conflict between autonomy and non-maleficence).

- A professional does something that is good for the participant against her wishes

Table 15.4 Foundational Ethical Principles and Moral Rules in Therapeutic Recreation *(Shank, 1985)*

Ethical Principle	Explanation
Autonomy	Participants are given unconditional regard for their worthiness, their freedom to act on their own judgments and choose their own destinies, and their right to self-determination.
• Informed Consent	Participants have a right to make an informed choice about services based on complete information from the professional.
Beneficence	Professionals act in ways that benefit participants. They are actively kind and always have the interests of participants at heart.
Non-maleficence	Professionals cause no harm to participants. Harm is broadly conceptualized to mean any violation of participants' health, interests, privacy, or life.
Justice	Professionals provide services that are fair, just, and deserved. This principle also includes distributive justice, which means proper and fair distribution of resources and services.
Moral Rule	**Explanation**
Veracity	The duty of the professional to tell the truth and not deceive.
Fidelity	The professional is faithful and keeps promises (derived from the principles of beneficence and justice).
Confidentiality and Privacy	Participants have the right to govern their own affairs (derived from the principle of autonomy).
• Privacy	Participants have the right to control information about themselves.
• Confidentiality	Participants have the right to control others' access to information about themselves.

(paternalism, which is a conflict between beneficence and autonomy).

- A professional prevents a participant from doing something he wants to do that will infringe on the rights of others in the process (conflict between autonomy and justice).
- A professional with limited resources (time, staff, space) and high demand for service must decide who to work with first and who will have to wait (conflict between justice and beneficence).

These examples highlight the need for a clear and well-developed code of ethics to help us make difficult decisions in practice. And though there is often no right or wrong answer, if we use careful and deliberate reasoning, rely on the code of ethics and its principles and rules, and draw on our moral character, we will do the best we can. Shank (1985) stated, "Whatever decision is made, we must be clear about our reasoning" (p. 17). Sylvester (2002) stated, "Ethical conduct results from knowledge of principles, understanding of problem-solving methods, and sound character" (p. 328).

Therapeutic recreation, like any helping profession, abounds with situations where ethical decisions must be made. Here are a few possible situations where it is important to draw on ethics:

- Professional versus personal relationships with participants
- Public behavior as a professional, including confidentiality
- Dependency-producing services
- Research practices
- Divided loyalties, such as with your agency or your funding source

In Figure 15.3, Cathy O'Keefe shares additional ethical issues and reminds us of how important it is to make ethics a part of our everyday life as a professional. NTRS (2001) developed extensive interpretive guidelines to help you integrate ethics into your practice and assist you in developing the reasoning needed to effectively use ethical principles. As Sylvester, Voelkl, and Ellis (2001) stated, "The ability to think logically and rigorously about ethics, with attention to detail, nuance, and complexity, is paramount, as is the capacity to care deeply about the welfare of human beings" (p. 63).

Before ending this discussion in ethics, it is important to note that the National Council for Therapeutic

Life Story:

Doing Ethics Every Day
By Cathy O'Keefe, CTRS

I began my career in therapeutic recreation in 1972 on our city's inpatient psychiatric unit. I thought that ethical thinking and behavior were a given that every professional embraced simply as part of their commitment to work in health care. After all, the participants we work with are vulnerable, often children, elderly, and with cognitive impairments. I became a keen observer not only of the behavior of our participants but also of staff as I encountered situations that elicited responses ranging from the heroic, to the very appropriate, to the questionable, the unethical, and even the illegal.

Later, as an educator, I found that the clinical setting wasn't the only place where ethical difficulties can rise. I saw the potential for ethical problems in the university setting, in agencies where interns and graduates worked, in professional associations, and in the certification agency. For seven years, as the chair of the ethics committee for NTRS, I often was called by individuals from a variety of service settings to help sort out questions they had about ethics and look at the options they had for responding.

One thing is for sure—you will be challenged! I once received a call from a graduate who was working in a psychiatric setting. Her supervisor wanted to impose a quota of participants attending community outings after he learned that his agency could receive a sizable amount of money from insurance reimbursement for each participant's participation. The supervisor pressured her to take participants who she felt clearly weren't ready for the experience.

On another occasion, I received a call from a young professional working in a private, for-profit rehabilitation hospital. She was instructed by the head RN to charge for her services under OT because the amount of reimbursement was higher than that allowed for TR. When she objected, the RN insisted that if it wasn't acceptable to the insurance company, they would be informed and allowed to resubmit the charges. The young professional called me months later, in a panic, because she had signed off on many charge slips before learning that the entire hospital chain was under investigation for fraud. The RN quit before the investigators arrived, so the therapeutic recreation specialist had no one to explain or defend her actions. The health care organization, an HMO, was indicted for fraud, and it folded; their CEO was taken away in handcuffs. I don't know if the young professional who called me was individually charged; she never called me back to tell me what happened. I now tell all my students that it will be their signature, not a policy of a company, which defines where individual accountability lies.

"Doing ethics" is not like following a cookbook where we consult a formula for right behavior. Our field's three sets of ethical codes (CTRA, NTRS and ATRA) provide explanations of virtues and general statements of obligations for professional behavior. But real ethics is practiced as a way of living. It requires a foundational way of thinking that creates a solid base for understanding a bigger picture of what is right and good for individuals and society. If any part of our work requires life-long learning, it is ethics. I urge you to begin by taking courses in ethics now and build on that knowledge with reading in and outside our field. I want each of you, when you reach the end of your career, to look back and be proud of your ability to discern the best solution to the ethical issues you will face and know that you supported the integrity and virtuous contributions of a wonderful field.

Figure 15.3 Life Story: Doing Ethics Every Day

Recreation Certification (2008) also contains guidance to help you in your practice, focused on those who are Certified Therapeutic Recreation Specialists,® and sanctions that can be applied for violations of certification standards. In Table 15.5, we provide a few of the significant grounds for issuing sanctions, which can result in revocation or denial of professional certification.

In addition, the National Recreation and Park Association has developed a broad and inclusive code of ethics that you may find useful if you are working in a community parks and recreation agency. We provide the NRPA Code of Ethics in Table 15.6.

Lastly, in the *Self-Assessment of Learning* feature at the end of this chapter, we provide some ethical dilemmas for you to think through using the codes of ethics. Besides drawing heavily on ethics, you also must draw on your professional knowledge to be effective in your practice (also see Figure 15.4). Let's explore this important attribute of a profession next.

Strategy 3: Know and Use the Body of Knowledge

An important attribute of a profession is having a recognized body of knowledge and a formalized way to transmit that knowledge to the field. Knowledge is documented and transmitted through formal education programs at universities, through the peer-reviewed

My Cultural Lens:

"We-Self" and "I-Self" Cultures

Harold Coward is a cross-cultural philosopher and ethicist. In his book, *A Cross-Cultural Dialogue on Health Care Ethics*, co-written with Phinit Rattanakun, the authors explain how health care will need to develop a more family-centered and contextual approach to working with patients, paying attention to extended family and environmental contexts. This is especially true of cultures that are more collectivist and have a "we-self" versus an "I-self" orientation. Dr. Coward shares a story from his wife's practice as a nurse, where a young Aboriginal woman came in for a gynecological visit with her mother, grandmother, and several aunts. All the family members insisted on going into the exam room with the young woman, which was not designed for such a large group (instead it was designed for an "I-self" culture). During the exam, the grandmother did all the talking for the young woman, answering the most intimate questions about the young woman's gynecological health. "Everyone knew everything naturally, as they were a 'we-self.' And everyone expected to be involved in the treatment and any ethical decisions to be made" (p. 7). The authors shared this story to highlight the need for us to question some of our basic ethical principles. In this case, the principles of informed consent, privacy, and autonomy become key. Most of our codes of ethics are embedded in an "I-self" culture.

How would you reinterpret principles of confidentiality, privacy, autonomy, and informed consent in the context of collectivist cultures? or would you? Discuss these questions and issues with colleagues or fellow students.

Figure 15.4 My Cultural Lens: "We-Self" and "I-Self" Cultures *(Coward & Rattanakun, 1999)*

research journals in our field and related fields, and through the continual use of evidence-based practice.

Formal Education. In therapeutic recreation, the entry-level degree to work as a therapeutic recreation specialist is a Bachelor's degree. According to NCTRC (2009), the large majority of professionals working in the field (and who are certified) enter the field with a Bachelor's degree in therapeutic recreation (or recreation with a concentration in therapeutic recreation).

Some professionals enter the field through alternate paths. One path is to earn a Master's degree in therapeutic recreation after earning a Bachelor's degree in another field. Typically, these students must take prerequisite therapeutic recreation courses as a part of the course of study for the Master's degree, depending on university requirements. Another alternate path is to have a degree in another field, take additional courses in therapeutic recreation and support area courses, as well as work for 5 or more years in therapeutic recreation. However, according to the U.S. Department of Labor, most therapeutic recreation jobs require a college degree in therapeutic recreation (Bureau of Labor Statistics, 2012).

Table 15.5 A Sample of the Grounds for Issuing Sanctions from NCTRC *(adapted from NCTRC, 2008)*

National Council for Therapeutic Recreation Grounds for Issuing Sanctions

Below are some of the key violations that could result in revocation of professional certification or other sanctions. See the NCTRC website or standards publication for exact wording and a complete list.

- Deception of any sort to obtain certification or recertification for yourself or another

- Misrepresentation of certification

- Habitual use of alcohol or drugs, or a physical or mental condition which impairs competent and objective professional performance

- Gross or repeated negligence, malpractice, or misconduct as evidenced by a clear violation of the ethical guidelines of the profession (as referenced in NTRS and ATRA publications)

- Sanction by a healthcare organization, professional organization, or other body relating to therapeutic recreation practice, public health or safety or therapeutic recreation certification

- Conviction of, plea of guilty to, or plea of no contest to a felony or misdemeanor directly relating to therapeutic recreation practice and/or public health and safety. Felony convictions include rape, abuse of a patient or child, actual or threatened use of a weapon, violence, and prohibited sale, distribution, or possession of a controlled substance, among others

Table 15.6 NRPA Code of Ethics *(adapted from Clark, 1995)*

NRPA Professional Code of Ethics

- Assure that people of all ages and abilities have the opportunity to find the most satisfying use of their leisure time and improved quality of life

- Participate in continuing education, certification, and accreditation

- Adhere to the highest standards of integrity and honesty in all public and personal activities to inspire public confidence and trust

- Strive for personal and professional excellence and encourage professional development of associates and students

- Strive for the highest standards of professional competence, fairness, impartiality, efficiency, effectiveness, and fiscal responsibility

- Avoid any interest or activity that is in conflict with the performance of job responsibilities

- Promote the public interest and avoid personal gain or profit from the performance of job duties and responsibilities

- Support equal employment opportunities

The body of knowledge to practice in therapeutic recreation, then, is transmitted through a college education and an approved curriculum. To be an approved major at a university, the therapeutic recreation curriculum must meet the requirements of the university, the regional accrediting body for the university, and state education law. The regional accrediting body accredits the university as a whole, and all its majors and programs. For example, in the state of New York, the regional accrediting body for all colleges and universities is the Middle States Commission on Higher Education. In the state of Colorado, as another example, the regional accrediting body is the North Central Association of Colleges and Schools.

In addition to regional accreditation, university degree programs in recreation and therapeutic recreation are or can be accredited by a national external accreditation body to show that the discipline-specific curriculum meets standards set by the profession. In therapeutic recreation, the most established national accreditation body is the Council on Accreditation of Parks, Recreation, Tourism, and Related Professions (2009). Additionally, another accrediting body is the Committee on Accreditation of Recreational Therapy Education (2010). National accreditation is recognition that the body of knowledge of therapeutic recreation is transmitted to students in the Bachelor's degree program, has been scrutinized by peers, and has been judged as meeting the rigorous standards set by the profession.

In general, a Bachelor's degree in therapeutic recreation consists of general education and liberal arts and sciences courses, professional courses in recreation and therapeutic recreation, support courses in human development and functioning, and a capstone internship experience. A Master's degree, instead of having required general education and liberal arts and sciences courses, will have a strong core of research courses in addition to the therapeutic recreation, recreation, and support courses. Thus, by earning a Bachelor's or Master's degree in the field, you are demonstrating one of the attributes of a profession, learning the specialized body of knowledge.

Peer-Reviewed Journals. Another way the body of knowledge of a profession is transmitted is through its research community. Continually growing, learning, and adding to the body of knowledge is a hallmark of a profession. Research is the primary means of adding to and disseminating knowledge in therapeutic recreation and other professions. Research is published in peer-reviewed journals and disseminated to professionals in practice, whether through professional associations, journal databases, or research symposia proceedings. Peer-reviewed journals require that all articles published have undergone a rigorous blind review by a panel of peers with expertise in the research area. In Table 15.7, we offer a list of the most important journals in the field of therapeutic recreation, as well as related journals. Because no body of knowledge is fixed and stagnant, it is imperative to continue to read and learn in the field. In addition, reading and learning the peer-reviewed research literature helps you strengthen your evidence-based practice and shows your commitment as a professional in the field.

Evidence-Based Practice. One other way practicing professionals can add to and transmit the body of knowledge in therapeutic recreation is through conducting and sharing evidence-based practice. Recall

Table 15.7 Major Peer-Reviewed Journals in Therapeutic Recreation and Related Areas

JOURNAL	PUBLISHER
Specific to Therapeutic Recreation	
American Journal of Recreation Therapy	Weston Medical Publishing (USA)
Annual in Therapeutic Recreation	American Therapeutic Recreation Association (USA)
Journal of Leisurability	Leisurability Publications (published through 2000) (CAN)
Therapeutic Recreation Journal	National Recreation and Park Association (and Sagamore Publishing) (USA)
Recreation and Leisure (includes therapeutic recreation research)	
Annals of Leisure Research	Australia and New Zealand Association for Leisure Studies (AUS and NZ)
Journal of Experiential Education	Association of Experiential Education (USA)
Journal of Leisure Research	National Recreation and Parks Association (USA)
Journal of Park and Recreation Administration	American Academy for Park and Recreation Administration (USA)
Leisure Sciences	Taylor and Francis (USA)
Leisure Studies	Leisure Studies Association (UK)
Loisir/Leisure	Canadian Association of Leisure Studies (CAN)
Loisir et Société/Leisure & Society	Presses de l'Université du Quebec (CAN)
Managing Leisure	Institute of Sport, Parks and Leisure (UK)
Research in Outdoor Education	Coalition for Education in the Outdoors (USA)
Schole	Society for Parks and Recreation Educators/National Recreation and Parks Association (USA)
World Leisure Journal	World Leisure Organization
Related Journals in other Fields	
Activities, Adaptation and Aging	Routledge/Taylor and Francis (USA)
Adapted Physical Activity Quarterly	International Federation of Adapted Physical Activity
American Journal on Intellectual and Developmental Disabilities	American Association on Intellectual and Developmental Disabilities (USA)
Applied Psychology: Health and Well-Being	International Association of Applied Psychology
Disability and Health Journal	American Association on Health and Disability (USA)
Journal of Happiness Studies	Springerlink (Netherlands)
Journal of Positive Psychology	Routledge/Taylor Francis (International)
Quality of Life Research	International Society of Quality of Life Research
Research and Practice for Persons with Severe Disabilities (formerly JASH)	TASH (USA)
Research Quarterly for Exercise and Sport	American Alliance for Health, Physical Education, Recreation and Dance (USA)
Magazines (not peer-reviewed)	
Challenge	Disabled Sports USA
Journal of Physical Education, Recreation and Dance (JOPERD)	American Alliance for Health, Physical Education, Recreation and Dance (USA)
Palaestra	Adapted Physical Activity Council and U.S. Paralympics
Parks and Recreation	National Recreation and Parks Association (USA)

from Chapter 1 *Introduction* that we introduced you to the concept of evidence-based practice. Evidence-based practice is the integration of your individual practice experience with the best available external evidence and the body of knowledge in therapeutic recreation. Evidence-based practice is based on systematic research results, data collected by your own agency, and judgments made by the participant and you. A key part of evidence-based practice is reading research on an ongoing basis, and applying effective interventions from research into your own practice. Another key component of evidence-based practice is to conduct your own research studies. If you feel you do not have the skills and knowledge to do research on your own, you can partner with university researchers or other more experienced practitioners in your area or in one of your professional associations. Evidence-based practice is a competency you will need to be effective as a therapeutic recreation professional (O'Neil & PHPC, 1998; Shank & Coyle, 2002; Stumbo & Peterson, 2004).

Strategy 4: Know and Use Standards of Practice

An important attribute of a profession is autonomy—the ability to monitor and regulate its own practice based on its specialized body of knowledge. According to NTRS (2004):

> Standards of practice define a set of values and provide a means to evaluate the practice of therapeutic recreation. Professional standards of practice incorporate internal standards generated from within the profession (ethics codes, for example) and external standards generated by regulatory bodies outside of the profession. . . . while defining the scope and dimensions of a service. (p. 2)

When a profession sets and maintains standards, many benefits ensue. Standards affect the following outcomes:

- Consistently and rigorously place the focus of services on the participant
- Facilitate management of services by providing a framework for services and a means of accountability and evaluation
- Assist professionals in preparing for external accreditation from such regulatory bodies as JCAHO, CARF, or state boards of health
- Assist in planning services and programs both at the individual and agency level
- Assist in educating other disciplines about therapeutic recreation and our scope of service

Thus, standards of practice provide a framework on which to base your practice. Standards are an agreed-upon model of what correct practice is and what skills, knowledge, and dispositions are needed. Standards provide the minimum you should do in your practice in therapeutic recreation; in fact, if standards are not met, you would be found to be negligent.

In Table 15.8, we offer the main elements that are contained in the standards of practice from the National Therapeutic Recreation Society (2004), the American Therapeutic Recreation Association (2000), and the Canadian Therapeutic Recreation Association (2006). All three standards of practice provide guidance on how to conduct the therapeutic recreation process, documentation, evaluation, interventions, and work with a collaborative team. The standards of practice include the role of the participant, ethics, and sensitivity to diversity. The standards also include agency- or program-level standards, including outcome evaluation, research, and quality management. And all three contain standards related to professional competence and ongoing development as a professional through continuing education and other means. At the end of this chapter, we provide Web links for each of the standards of practice that we briefly summarize in Table 15.8. We invite you to read through the full sets of standards and learn them well enough to easily put them into practice every day.

As the profession evolves, so too do the standards of practice. Though the standards provided in Table 15.8 are current as of the publication of this book, it is imperative for you as a professional to stay informed on any new changes.

Strategy 5: Assure Your Competence to Others

Another important attribute of a profession is professional authority and assurance of competence to those who receive your services and to the public. **Credentialing** is the process for recognizing the competence or proficiency of individuals who practice in a specific profession. Credentialing can take the form of registration, certification, and licensure. In therapeutic recreation, the most common credentialing process is certification. However, depending on where you practice, you may also be registered or licensed. According to the National Council for Therapeutic Recreation (NCTRC, 2007):

Table 15.8 Standards of Practice for Therapeutic Recreation *(ATRA, 2000; CTRA, 2006; NTRS, 2004)*

Standards of Practice Comparison		
NTRS Standards	**Comparable Standards in the ATRA Standards**	**Comparable Standards in the CTRA Standards**
Standard 1: TR Process • Assessment • Planning • Implementation and operations • Evaluation	Standard 1: Assessment Standard 2: Treatment planning Standard 3: Plan implementation Standard 4: Re-assessment and evaluation Standard 5: Discharge and transition planning	Standard 1: Assessment Standard 2: Intervention plan development Standard 3: Intervention plan implementation Standard 5: Evaluation
Standard 2: Participant involvement		Standard 10: Sensitivity to diversity
Standard 3: Interventions and facilitation techniques	Standard 3: Plan implementation Standard 6: Recreation services	Standard 3: Intervention plan implementation Standard 6: Interdisciplinary collaboration
Standard 4: Documentation	Standards 1–5 cover documentation	Standard 4: Documentation
Standard 5: Outcomes	Standard 12: Program evaluation and research	Standard 8: Research
Standard 6: Professional staffing and credentials	Standard 9: Staff qualifications and competency assessment	Standard 7: Professional development
Standard 7: Ethics	Standard 7: Ethical conduct	Standard 9: Ethics
Standard 8: Quality management	Standard 8: Written plan of operation Standard 10: Quality management Standard 11: Resource management	Standard 11: Risk management

Note: Professional standards of practice are in constant revision as the profession evolves and grows. The standards provided throughout this book were the most current at the time of publication. In 2010, the National Therapeutic Recreation Society became the Inclusion and Accessibility Network, still affiliated with the National Recreation and Park Association.

A benchmark of any profession is its ability to routinely monitor its own practice through an on-going process of self-regulation. Paramount to this process is the establishment of a credentialing program which enables the profession to safeguard consumers by determining who is competent to practice. (p. 2)

Before we discuss each of the forms of credentialing, we want to clarify the difference between credentialing and accreditation. Accreditation happens at the organization level. We discussed professional accreditation for universities that offer therapeutic recreation degree programs earlier—that is an example of accreditation. Another example is the Joint Commission, which accredits hospitals and healthcare facilities. Credentialing such as licensure or certification, on the other hand, happens at the individual level. As a therapeutic recreation specialist, you become credentialed as an individual.

Certification is the most common form of credentialing in therapeutic recreation. It is a voluntary process where a non-governmental agency grants recognition of competence to individuals who meet the requirements set by the profession. In therapeutic recreation, we have a national certification program, which is managed by the National Council for Therapeutic Recreation Certification (NCTRC). To be granted certification, you must meet eligibility standards enforced by NCTRC to sit for a national certification examination. The eligibility standards include a college degree that demonstrates the body of knowledge in therapeutic recreation and an internship that meets specific criteria or work experience that meets certain conditions. If you meet the established eligibility requirements, you must then pass the certification examination.

NCTRC develops and manages the national certification exam. The exam is knowledge-based and is designed to reflect the current practice, or job duties and knowledge areas, of an entry level professional in therapeutic recreation. A job analysis, which is used to update the exam, is conducted every 10 years by surveying therapeutic recreation specialists about their work. In Table 15.9 we provide the job duties and knowledge areas of the 2007 job analysis conducted by NCTRC. The certification exam is given several times a year and is a computer-based multiple-choice exam. When a therapeutic recreation specialist passes the exam, he or she

Table 15.9 Professional Job Tasks and Knowledge Areas in Therapeutic Recreation *(NCTRC, 2007)*

Professional Job Task Domains	Professional Knowledge Areas
1. Professional roles and responsibilities 2. Assessment 3. Planning interventions and/or programs 4. Implementing interventions and/or programs 5. Evaluate outcomes of the interventions/ programs 6. Documenting intervention services 7. Working with treatment and/or service teams 8. Organizing programs 9. Managing TR/RT services 10. Public awareness and advocacy	1. Foundational knowledge 2. Practice of TR/RT 3. Organization of TR/RT services 4. Advancement of the profession
Each of the job-task and professional-knowledge domains listed above has multiple tasks and knowledge areas within it. A total of 58 job tasks and 73 professional knowledge areas are identified in the NCTRC 2007 Job Analysis. See the NCTRC website for specific tasks and knowledge areas (http://www.nctrc.org).	

becomes certified, and uses the designation "Certified Therapeutic Recreation Specialist"® or "CTRS."

Once you are certified in therapeutic recreation, you must maintain continued professional competence to maintain certification status. You do that through demonstrating continuing education and work experience in the field. We discuss continuing education later in this chapter, but here we want to direct you to the NCTRC website (http://www.nctrc.org/ctrsrenewal.htm) to learn the current and specific requirements for recertification.

In addition to national certification, some states in the U.S. require **licensure**. Licensure means there is a state law that requires you to have a license to practice therapeutic recreation in that state. The requirements for licensure vary by state, but most states have a practice board, made up of licensed professionals in the field, to oversee and enforce the licensure law. In 2012, the following states had licensure laws for therapeutic recreation practice: New Hampshire, North Carolina, Oklahoma, and Utah.

Registration is a record of those professionals who have met certain standards set by the field. A registry may be a record of those professionals who are licensed or certified. Or, it may be a record of those professionals who meet certain criteria approved by some organization, such as a professional association or even a governmental agency like a board of health. For example, in nursing, those who are licensed are Registered Nurses (RN). In occupational therapy, those who are nationally certified are then registered and use the designation OTR. In therapeutic recreation, some states require registration (e.g., Washington, California).

When you assure your competence in therapeutic recreation through a credential like the CTRS, it helps you fulfill your obligation to the public and to the participants you serve. It is an external verification of your qualifications and assures others that you have at least the minimum level of knowledge and experience to practice in the field. Credentialing also helps other professions understand the scope of therapeutic recreation practice, and so it facilitates collaborative practice.

An important final point we would like to make about credentialing, and in particular national certification, is that it is or should be shaped and controlled by the profession itself—this is a hallmark of a profession. It is imperative for therapeutic recreation specialists to be involved in the certification program, whether through volunteering on committees, running for board positions, or even just voting in board elections. It is crucial that the governing board of NCTRC, who is elected by Certified Therapeutic Recreation Specialists,® be representative of the whole field of therapeutic recreation. A hallmark of a profession is not just establishing a credentialing program but maintaining its validity by reflecting the breadth of the profession it represents. It takes participation from each of us to ensure therapeutic recreation has a credential that truly encompasses the profession.

Strategy 6: Continue to Grow as a Professional

You graduate from college with your degree in the field. You pass your national certification exam. You get your first job in the field of therapeutic recreation. Now what? Are you done learning and growing as a professional? Of course not, you say. There is so much to learn, and so much "practice wisdom" to develop. But how do you continue to grow and learn? What effective means do you have to continue your professional development? In this section, we want to share two primary approaches to building your strengths as a therapeutic recreation specialist: continuing education and clinical supervision (or formal mentoring). These two important paths for continuing your growth in the profession are accessible to you, but you may need to take a leadership role in making them happen.

Continuing Education

Continuing education is one way to increase your knowledge in the field and in related areas. It can take many forms, but it is typically a formalized educational experience of some sort. Most of us are familiar with college-sponsored courses or workshops for **college credit**. This is an excellent way to continue your learning, particularly by pursuing an advanced college degree in therapeutic recreation or a related field. College courses re-immerse you in the rich educational environment of the university setting, where learning is the central mission and focus.

Non-credit educational experiences are another avenue to gain continuing education. Non-credit experiences are highly varied and can include workshops, conferences, training institutes, online training, correspondence courses, webinars, and even reading research journals and being tested on what you read. Typically, non-credit educational experiences will be validated with **continuing education units** (CEUs), which document the learning experience. CEUs are needed for maintenance of certification and, if applicable, licensure. The most widely used standard for CEUs is 1 contact hour of a learning experience equals 0.1 CEU, or 10 hours equals 1.0 CEU. For an organization to offer CEUs for its educational experiences, it must meet certain standards, often set by the International Association for Continuing Education and Training (IACET, 2007). After successfully participating in an educational experience, you are issued a certificate or transcript that documents the number of CEUs earned.

The most common way that many therapeutic recreation specialists obtain continuing education is through the annual national, regional, and state conferences sponsored by our professional associations. Conferences provide a variety of educational sessions and often provide research symposia, guided discussions, book chats, off-site institutes, and other types of educational opportunities. Attending professional conferences not only helps you gain continuing education, it also supports your professional association, as these educational offerings often help to raise needed funds for the association to provide services to you the rest of the year.

Thus, building your knowledge and skills through continuing education helps you build your competence and exposes you to new and emerging practices. Continuing education tends to focus on the more technical knowledge aspects of your continuing growth as a professional. But, to truly develop as a whole professional, you must also focus on what has been called "tacit" knowledge or intuitive knowledge that is embedded in experience and expertise (Schon, 1983). This kind of knowledge, sometimes called practice wisdom, is developed through reflective practice. In the next section, we look at clinical supervision, or mentoring, an avenue to pursue reflective practice.

Clinical Supervision

As you gain experience in the field, and constantly compare that experience to the body of knowledge you have learned in your formal education, you slowly gain what is known as practice wisdom. **Practice wisdom** is a deep understanding of and appreciation for the helping process (Murray & Shank, 1994). It is knowing what to do in your practice as you integrate theoretical and practical knowledge, experience, and intuition. It is developed through what Schon (1983) called "reflection in action" and "reflection on action."

Reflection *in* action refers to our ability to "think on our feet" and to make decisions in new situations by drawing on metaphors and tacit knowledge. As we attain deeper and richer experiences in our practice of therapeutic recreation, we have more to draw on as we quickly and astutely respond to situations that present themselves. This is an important part of practice wisdom, and a sign of our developing expertise. Schon (1983) stated

> Competent practitioners usually know more than they can say. They exhibit a kind of knowing in practice, most of which is tacit . . . Indeed practitioners themselves often reveal a capacity for reflection on their intuitive knowing in the midst of action and sometimes use this capacity to cope with the unique, uncertain, and conflicted situations of practice. (p. 8)

Reflection in action can also be conceptualized as clinical reasoning, or the ability to make sound decisions in complex situations in practice. According to Higgs and colleagues (2008), the process of action-oriented critical thinking, or clinical reasoning, involves the following:

- A strong foundation of discipline-specific knowledge and discipline-specific philosophy

- Reflective inquiry—being able to compare the current situation to disciplinary knowledge and previous experience
- Self-awareness of the limits of one's knowledge, experience, and thinking skills to handle a situation
- Interactivity and mutual decision-making with the participant and his or her circle of support
- Interactivity with the environment and context
- Understanding of the impact of the task or activity at hand
- The ability to learn new knowledge through clinical reasoning, and to integrate the outcome of the current situation into future reflection in action
- Promotion of positive growth in not only the participant, but oneself as a practitioner

Reflection in action, or clinical reasoning, helps to develop expertise and practice wisdom (see Figure 15.5). Reflection in action is a daily and continuous approach to practice. It is an orientation toward your work that can be fostered by your professional peers and more experienced colleagues through reflection *on* action.

Reflection *on* action can occur in many ways, but one important avenue is through clinical supervision. **Clinical supervision** is an interaction between professionals to promote reflection on action. It occurs between more and less experienced professionals and its purpose is to enhance professional functioning and improve the quality of services to participants (Bernard & Goodyear, 2009). The focus of clinical supervision is on the helping relationship between the therapeutic recreation specialist and participants. Through reflection and an ongoing relationship with mentors during clinical supervision, the helping relationship with participants improves.

Clinical supervision is an important form of professional development. It is *not* managerial supervision, which is evaluative, concerned with organizational

Primary Source Support:

Traits of Experts in Clinical Reasoning

King, G., Currie, M., Bartlett, D., Gilpin, M., Willoughby, C., Tucker, M., Strachan, D., & Baxter, D. (2007). The development of expertise in pediatric rehabilitation therapists: Changes in approach, self-knowledge, and use of enabling and customizing strategies. *Developmental Neurorehabilitation, 10*(3), 223–240.

In this study, a team of researchers led by Dr. Gillian King studied the clinical reasoning of novice, intermediate, and expert pediatric rehabilitation therapists from various disciplines, including therapeutic recreation. A multifaceted battery of assessment tools was used to classify the therapists by level of clinical reasoning. The therapists were then asked to either respond to critical incident situations, and how they would handle them, or were asked to "think aloud" as they watched themselves work with participants on videotape.

The research team found three emerging themes from the interview results:
- First, they found that more experienced therapists showed a difference in their content knowledge. Experts were more holistic, supportive, functional, educational, and strengths-based in their approaches than novices or intermediates. Experts were less judgmental and more flexible.
- Second, they found that experts had more humility and more self-confidence than novices or intermediates. They engaged in self-evaluation at a higher level.
- Third, they found that experts were able to use strategies for change that were more meaningful to participants than novices or intermediate therapists. Experts were better able to help participants uncover their own goals, make the goals meaningful and relevant to participants, and make the achievement of goals more manageable. Experts were better able to enable participants to change using more customized strategies versus standardized interventions.

The researchers recommend that all helping professionals work toward the expert level through development of what they call "strategic meta-cognition knowledge." Much like "reflection in action," strategic meta-cognition knowledge is having the knowledge of available strategies and knowing when and where to apply them in the practice setting. It involves having a focus on strengths, on enabling strategies that allow optimal challenges and small steps, and on helping participants uncover their own strengths, goals, and skills. According to the researchers, this study helped make explicit the link between strengths-based practice, effectiveness, and the need for continuing development as a professional.

Figure 15.5 Primary Source Support: Traits of Experts in Clinical Reasoning

efficiency, and focused on whether a therapeutic recreation specialist meets the standards of the employer (Murray & Shank, 1994). It is *not* a continuing education experience, which tends to be short-term and not relationship-based. Clinical supervision is an ongoing relationship with a mentor or a group of mentors that facilitates the emotional competence and practice wisdom of the therapeutic recreation specialist. The central focus of clinical supervision is on the skills and strategies used in therapeutic recreation with participants.

There are three dominant models of clinical supervision: developmental, personal growth, and integrative (Bernard & Goodyear, 2009). The developmental approach emphasizes knowledge of professional roles and methods, and development of clinical skills. The personal growth approach emphasizes insight into self and affective sensitivity. The integrative model focuses on both personal growth and professional knowledge of the supervisee.

Clinical supervision has many benefits to practitioners. It helps improve competence and increase practice wisdom. It allows for open discussion among peers of ethical issues and problem situations. It provides a way to share information, learn and master therapeutic techniques, and gain exposure to other theoretical perspectives and ways of doing things. It counters "burn-out" and the "lone ranger" syndrome. And most importantly, it leads to improved services to participants.

Clinical supervision can be conducted individually (a supervisor and a supervisee), in a group (a supervisor to a group of supervisees), or through peer supervision (supervisees in a group rotate the leadership role). Group supervision can occur within an agency, between agencies, within one profession, or across professions.

In therapeutic recreation, many professionals work in departments or agencies where they are the only therapeutic recreation specialist (33%) or where there is one other therapeutic recreation specialist (14%) (NCTRC, 2009). This makes group supervision across agencies one of the only ways to pursue clinical supervision with other therapeutic recreation specialists. Though many agencies offer clinical supervision between differing disciplines (e.g., nursing, social work, occupational therapy), which can be very beneficial, you cannot work on integrating the theory, philosophy, and practice of your own discipline, therapeutic recreation, without having reflective dialogue with other therapeutic recreation specialists. Group supervision, and in particular peer supervision across agencies, is an ideal way to conduct this important reflection *on* action.

Group supervision has other benefits as well. It allows for more efficient use of time, money, and expertise. But efficiency is perhaps the least important benefit. Group supervision lessens dependency on a mentor and is less hierarchical. Group supervision, where therapeutic recreation specialists talk through situations as a group, provides opportunities for vicarious learning and allows novices to experts alike to share perspectives and a wider array of experiences and settings. During group supervision, there is greater quantity and diversity of feedback, as well as the potential for greater quality. During group supervision, there is greater opportunity to use action techniques, to mirror group processes that occur in practice, and to provide reassurance, validation, and a sense of community with other therapeutic recreation specialists.

Disadvantages to group supervision are the potential for individualized needs to not be met effectively in a group setting, breaches of confidentiality, and conflict as the group develops.

Like any group process, a functional, highly productive, and supportive supervision group tends to go through levels: forming (introductory phase), storming (conflict and role delineation phase), norming (goal clarification and development of group norms), and performing (working phase with shared vision) (Bonebright, 2010). In Figure 15.6 (p. 430), we present a model of the variables at work in the group supervision process. Quality supervision is characterized by a supportive and trusting environment where group members confront and challenge each other to try new behaviors and new ways of thinking. As you can see in the figure, when challenge and support are in balance, and quality supervision is in place, a group can move through typical phases of group development to the performance stage, where they can meet their goals for practice wisdom. If challenges are too high, and support is low, group development is slowed by competitiveness and feelings of being overwhelmed. If challenges are too low and support is high, group development is slowed by conveying low expectations, and even a message of disrespect and infantilization. Having a contract, ground rules, a structure for the group, and a screening process bringing members into the group will expedite group maturation to the performance stage. We will talk about each of these elements next.

Clinical supervision happens at a low rate in the field of therapeutic recreation (Jones & Anderson, 2004; NCTRC, 2009). In a national study, Jones and Anderson found that those therapeutic recreation specialists with the least experience in the field received no clinical supervision (see Figure 15.7, p. 431). A study

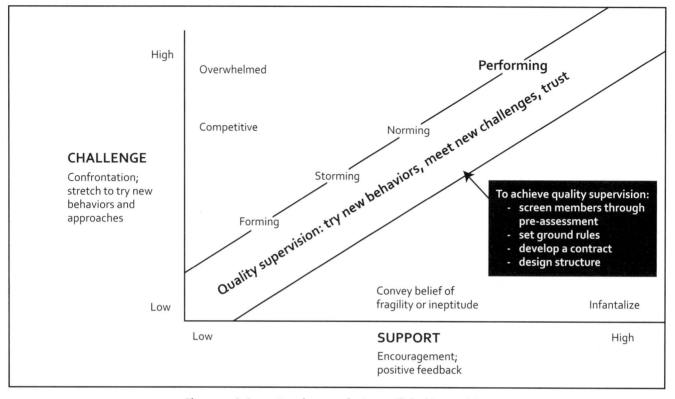

Figure 15.6 Group Development in Group Clinical Supervision

by NCTRC (2009) found that 44% of therapeutic recreation specialists received no clinical supervision. Because so few therapeutic recreation specialists are participating in clinical supervision and so many therapeutic recreation specialists are isolated "lone rangers" at their agencies, we want to offer some detailed information on how to develop a peer supervision group in your community.

Developing a Peer Supervision Group

Peer supervision is a form of group supervision where the leadership role is rotated and shared, where more and less experienced professionals participate as equals, and where each member of the group brings practice situations to the group to share and learn how to handle more effectively based on feedback from the group. In this section, we offer you the tools to develop a peer supervision group.

Figure 15.8 shows the steps to developing a peer supervision group. Because peer supervision is a collaborative approach that often involves therapeutic recreation specialists from different agencies, it is important to be very clear and structured in how the group is formed and how it functions. Let's talk through each step in developing and using a peer supervision group.

Pre-assessment. An important first step in forming a peer supervision group is for the group to develop criteria for inclusion in the group and make sure each member has a clear understanding of the purpose of the group. The criteria for inclusion would typically focus on a strong desire to improve helping skills and develop a broader repertoire of helping strategies.

Education about clinical supervision. It is important for all group members to have the same knowledge and understanding of what clinical supervision is, what its goals are, and how it is typically conducted. Local universities often have faculty who could assist in providing this education, if not in therapeutic recreation, then possibly in related fields such as social work or counseling.

Goal-setting. Each group member sets specific goals on what he or she wants to achieve as a result of peer supervision and shares those goals with the group at the first meetings. The group as a whole may set group goals as well.

Contract and ground rules development. The next important step is for the group to develop a contract and ground rules. A contract and ground rules help develop a sense of safety for group participation, help the group become productive more quickly, and help eliminate counterproductive group behavior. In Table 15.10, we offer a sample contract and ground rules from an actual peer supervision group.

Some logistics to include in the contract include the frequency of meetings, where meetings will be

Primary Source Support:

Status of Clinical Supervision in Therapeutic Recreation

Jones, D., & Anderson, L. (2004). The status of clinical supervision in therapeutic recreation: A national study. *Therapeutic Recreation Journal, 38*(4), 329–347.

In this study, we wanted to know "what was going on out there" in the field of therapeutic recreation in relation to clinical supervision. We surveyed 500 therapeutic recreation specialists across the United States.

We learned that the large majority (75%) of therapeutic recreation specialists were not receiving clinical supervision. Of those, most were therapeutic recreation specialists who had been in the field for less than 4 years. The areas of therapeutic recreation practice that respondents felt the most need for clinical supervision was advocacy and professional development.

We recommended that, as a profession, we develop education for clinical supervision (e.g., college courses, workshops, training modules) and structures for clinical supervision (e.g., local networks of professionals, professional associations). We concluded that we put our newer professionals at risk when they do not have access to the support and guidance of more experienced and wise professionals through ongoing clinical supervision. We challenge you to help us put these recommendations into practice!

Figure 15.7 Primary Source Support: Clinical Supervision in Therapeutic Recreation

Steps to Develop a Peer Supervision Group

- [ ] Pre-assessment; screen group members
- [ ] Educate group members on clinical supervision
- [ ] Develop and agree on a contract
- [ ] Develop and agree on ground rules
- [ ] Determine leader role
- [ ] Determine process commentator role
- [ ] Determine structure, i.e., Structured Group Supervision Model
- [ ] Choose method of capturing or recording practice situations where help is sought (action/reflection journal)
- [ ] Determine logistics:
  - [ ] How often to meet?
  - [ ] When?
  - [ ] Where?
  - [ ] Who arranges?

Figure 15.8 A Checklist for Peer Supervision

Table 15.10 A Sample Peer Supervision Group Contract and Ground Rules

Contract and Ground Rules
Therapeutic Recreation Peer Supervision Group

- We will meet for 1½ hours twice a month (currently the 2nd and 4th Monday of the month from 3:45–5:15pm). I agree to attend a MINIMUM of one time a month, but will try to attend both sessions.

- I will come to the first peer supervision meeting with goals that I want to achieve from the peer supervision group.

GROUND RULES OUR GROUP WILL USE:
- Above all, respect confidentiality; never use a participant's name.
- Keep discussion of participants and situations across agencies within the peer supervision group, and never talk about anything from the group outside our meeting times, even with coworkers also in the group.
- Use respectful communication.
- Come prepared with at least one situation for feedback each time we meet; have the situation recorded in your process journal.
- Pay attention to the emotional awareness of each group member as well as skill development.
- Everyone participates equally.
- Rotate responsibility of the leadership role (see role below).
- Rotate responsibility of the process commentator role (see role below).
- Start and end on time.
- Stick to participant-based situations and interactions to be addressed in group sessions.
- Take time at the end of each session to process and summarize issues and themes from the session.
- Start each session by reviewing the major issues and themes from the last session and updating any goals members may have.
- We can talk about any topic, as long as boundaries are respected (especially personal versus professional boundaries).
- Have a spirit of inquiry!

- Leadership/Facilitator Role:
    - Set up when and where the meeting will be.
    - Set up the meeting (any arrangements that need to be made).
    - Review the ground rules at the beginning of the session.
    - Facilitate goal identification from each member.
    - Keep the meeting flowing and focused.
    - Manage the group process (e.g., timekeeping).
    - Review past issues and facilitate review of issues at the end of the current session.

- Process Commentator Role:
    - Summarize the group process at the end of the session.
    - Possibly address inappropriate behavior and remind members of respectful communication.

I agree to the above contract. Signed: _____ Date: _____

---

held, expectations for attendance and preparedness, how situations will be documented and presented, and expectations for group norms.

Method of documentation and presentation of practice situations. Determine the manner in which group members will document the situations from their practice that they want to reflect on and bring to the peer supervision group for assistance and guidance. An ideal technique for documentation and reflection in the peer supervision settings is a process journal, or action/reflection journal. In the process journal, the therapeutic recreation specialist documents the interaction with the participant in a descriptive manner as objectively as possible in one column. In the second column, the therapeutic recreation specialist describes his or her thoughts, feelings, reactions, and concerns as the interaction progressed. After the peer supervision meeting where the journal entry is shared and discussed, the therapeutic recreation specialist again writes his or her interactions and reactions, this time in relation to the peer supervision feedback. In Table 15.11, we provide a sample journal page for process recordings that includes guiding questions to help you write about the interaction with a participant and to process feedback from a peer supervision session. The action/reflection or process journal forces critical reflection and provides an anonymous and convenient method to document practice scenarios to share in a peer supervision setting.

Structure. The peer supervision group members must determine what structure they will use during

Table 15.11 Sample Journal Page for Process Recordings *(adapted from Bernard & Goodyear, 2009)*

Interaction	Reaction
Entry #1: Participant Interaction/Session Describe the interaction (group or individual therapeutic recreation service) as objectively as you can. Here are some questions to help guide your entry: • What were the goals of the session? • Did anything happen during the session that caused you to reconsider your goals? How did you resolve this? • What was the major theme or activity of the session? • Describe the interpersonal dynamics between you and the participant(s) throughout the session. • How did individual differences (e.g., gender, ethnicity, race, developmental level) affect the session? • How successful was the interaction or session? Were the participant's goals achieved?	**Entry #2: Participant Interaction/Session** Describe your own feelings, thoughts, reactions, and concerns as the session progressed. Here are some questions to help guide your entry: • What was I feeling at various points during the interaction or session in relation to what was happening? • What was my personal reaction to the session? • What was I thinking as the session progressed? • How did I feel at the end of the interaction or session? • What did I learn about the helping process from this session or interaction? • What are my plans and goals for the next session? • What specific questions do I have for my peer supervisors regarding my work during this session?
Entry #3: Peer Supervision Session Describe the interaction during the peer supervision session as objectively as you can. Here are some questions to help guide your entry: • What specific feedback did I receive on my situation? • What group dynamics and group process occurred? • Which of my questions were answered? Which were not?	**Entry #4: Peer Supervision Session** Describe your feelings, thoughts, reactions, and concerns as the peer supervision session progressed. Here are some questions to help guide your entry: • What feeling did I experience as I listened to feedback and suggestions? • What were my thoughts during the peer supervision session? • Did I feel I benefited from the peer supervision session? In what way(s)?
IMPORTANT REMINDER: Do not use names or provide any identifying information about the participant(s) in your journal. The identity of participant(s) should remain completely anonymous.	

the supervision meeting to most effectively facilitate the sharing of process journals and give feedback. One effective structure is the Structured Group Supervision Model (SGSM) (Bernard & Goodyear, 2009; Wilbur, Roberts-Wilbur, Hart, Morris, & Betz, 1994). The group members will first decide who will start sharing their process journal. That person will then complete the first step in the process, the plea for help. In Table 15.12, we provide the steps involved in the SGSM. As you can see in the table, in this step, the supervisee (the group member receiving supervision) presents the information in her or his process journal. At the conclusion of presenting the information, the supervisee states, "I need help with . . ." and clearly asks the group what assistance is sought.

In the next step, the question period, the supervisors (the other group members giving clinical supervision) ask questions one at a time in an orderly manner until there are no more questions and everyone is clear on the situation. The supervisors do not give feedback at this time but only ask questions of the supervisee to get clear.

In the next step, step 3, supervisors give feedback to the supervisee. One at a time, supervisors share how they would handle the situation presented by the supervisee. Feedback continues until everyone has given all the feedback they have. The supervisee listens and takes notes but does not respond to feedback.

Before moving to step 4, the group takes a pause or break. This allows the supervisee time to reflect on the feedback given to him or her. After the break, the supervisee responds to the feedback. The supervisors remain silent and listen. The supervisee responds to all the feedback in round-robin fashion, explaining what was helpful and what was not.

The last step is a discussion phase. Supervisors and supervisee may summarize, react, and debrief. The process commentator summarizes the group process that was used throughout the session. Immediately after the session, the supervisee documents the supervision session in the action/reflection journal.

The structure of the SGSM provides for high-quality, thoughtful, and balanced interactions during the peer supervision meeting. By structuring feedback from every group member, all perspectives are shared, and this can lead to novel and new ways to handle situations that have become routinized for others. Whether you are the supervisee sharing your situation, or one of the supervisors, the session is rich with reflection on action.

Table 15.12 **Steps for the Structured Group Supervision Model**
(adapted from Wilber, Roberts-Wilbur, Hart, Morris, & Betz, 1994; Bernard & Goodyear, 2009)

Step One: Plea for Help   The supervisee states what assistance is needed from the supervision group. The supervisee shares the process journal. Following the presentation of information on the situation, the supervisee makes a plea for help by stating clearly, "I need help with…".
Step Two: Question Period   The supervisors ask the supervisee questions about the information presented to clarify, gain additional information, clear up misperceptions, and the like. The group members ask questions one at a time in an orderly manner (usually go around the room) until everyone is clear about the supervisee's situation and plea for help, and there are no more questions.
Step Three: Feedback   Supervisors respond to the information presented and the plea for help. They state how they would handle the supervisee's situation. The supervisee remains silent, listens carefully, and takes notes during the feedback. When all feedback has been given, the group takes a small pause or break.
Pause or Break   The supervisee uses this time to reflect on the feedback.
Step Four: Response   The supervisors remain silent as the supervisee responds to each group member's feedback. The supervisee tells the group members what was helpful and what was not.
Optional Step Five: Discussion   Group members summarize, react, and debrief the session.

Leadership roles. The group must decide on the role and function of the leader/facilitator and the process commentator. In the sample contract in Table 15.10, we provide one way the leader role could be structured. It is important to make a commitment to share this role so that the amount of work to sustain a peer supervision group does not fall to only one group member.

The process commentator pays careful attention to the group dynamics throughout the peer supervision meeting and shares his or her observations of the group process at the end of the session. The group members reflect on the feedback and set goals for the next session on things they want to improve in their group dynamics.

In summary, peer supervision is one way for practicing therapeutic recreation specialists to provide the support and feedback needed to foster reflection on action, which in turn improves reflection in action. Whether it is peer, group, or individual, clinical supervision is important to your professional growth and development. By thoughtfully and carefully attending to reflection, you will build your expertise and practice wisdom. You will be able to "think on your feet" in a way that is meaningful and helpful to participants. You will learn to critique habits and routines. As Schon (1983) stated:

> A practitioner's reflection can serve as a corrective to over-learning. Through reflection, he [sic] can surface and criticize the tacit understandings that have grown up around the repetitive experiences of a specialized practice, and can make new sense of the situations of uncertainty or uniqueness which he may allow himself to practice. (p. 67)

Clinical supervision and continuing education will help you become a competent and wise professional. Without them, you may be experienced, but not necessarily competent, as stated by Sechrest (as quoted in Bernard & Goodyear, 1998): "You are only young once, but it is possible to be immature forever. By analogy, you are only inexperienced once, but is it possible to be incompetent forever" (p. 2).

Strategy 7: Networking and Professional Support Systems

A hallmark of a profession is a culture or community that upholds the ethics and standards of the field, that advances knowledge in the field through research and continuing professional development, and that provides the vehicle to network, share, and dialogue about important trends, issues, and best practices. Professional associations are a primary vehicle for this type of professional networking. Professional associations form at the international, national, state/provincial, and local level.

In therapeutic recreation, we have several professional organizations we can join and become an active member. At the end of the chapter, in the *Resources* section, we provide the websites for several therapeutic recreation or related professional associations. There are many benefits from being a member of one of these groups:

- Advancement of public policy, through advocacy, online networking, e-mail alerts, legislative forums, and other ways to influence positive social change
- Professional education opportunities, such as national conferences, online learning, workshops, publications, research symposia, and research databases and statistics
- Partnerships, national initiatives, and grant opportunities
- Networking, through online social networking, listservs, special interest groups, committees, membership directories, meetings, and volunteer opportunities
- Awards and scholarships to recognize excellence in the profession
- Input into standards of practice, code of ethics, accreditation/higher education, and other important aspects of the profession
- Access to professional publications, trade magazines, books, professional liability insurance, volunteer management/screening tools, journal subscriptions, and more at membership rates

Being a member of professional organizations provides you with tools, support, networking, and most important, a voice in shaping the attributes of your own profession to serve the common good: ethics, standards, research, continuing education, advocacy, and a service ideal.

Limits of Professionalization

We have offered seven strategies that help you be a member of a profession. These seven strategies encompass the attributes of a profession. So, is therapeutic recreation a profession? Therapeutic recreation is one of a cluster of fields that are defined as "helping professions." Other fields include nursing, social work, counseling, other allied professions like occupational therapy or physical therapy, and the like. Some have argued that helping professions are not true professions, and others have argued that there are limits to professionalization (Hunnicut, 1980; Leahy, 1996). John McKnight, a professor at Northwestern University and a pioneer in community development, wrote an intriguing essay in 1992 that called into question how useful "professionals" were in helping people and communities, and what damage they can do as they try to help (see Figure 15.9). McKnight challenges professionals to avoid turning human need into a commodity. He asks us to nurture sustainable community strengths and connections and to always carefully evaluate if we are harming more than helping.

Other limiting forces to being a true professional are the irrational assumptions about professionalism that impede the helping process. In Figure 15.10, we ask you to compare and contrast the irrational assumptions that can hinder the relationship between participants and professionals. These assumptions can often operate on a subconscious level and can manifest themselves in unproductive ways as we practice therapeutic recreation. As a virtuous practitioner, it is important for you to pinpoint behaviors and attitudes that impede the helping relationship and openly work to change them.

Lastly, we want to take a step back and reflect on the differences between being a strengths-based professional versus one practicing from a deficits- or medical-model approach. In Figure 15.11, we invite you to think about these differences and how they might affect virtuous therapeutic recreation practice.

Giving Back to Society and the Profession

A part of being a true professional is supporting your calling through good work and authentic, moral actions. One way to exhibit a high level of professionalism is to give back to society with no expectation of personal gain. As a professional that has valued knowledge and skills, one way to do this is to offer "pro bono" work for individuals or organizations that need your help but cannot afford to pay for it ("pro bono" means "for the public good" in Latin). Pro bono differs from volunteerism in that you use your specific professional skills to provide service to others who cannot afford to pay for them. Many professions encourage their members to develop a pro bono ethic when they are students, and continue to do pro bono work throughout their careers (Hurst & Hartman, 2009). Our codes of ethics obligate us as professionals to be committed to pro bono work in our practice. Opportunities to do pro bono work abound in our communities, from supporting inclusion efforts at your local parks and recreation department, to

Primary Source Support:

Are We Helping or "Creating Deserts"?

McKnight, J. (1992). John Deere and the bereavement counselor. *Whole Community Catalog, 1*(1), 13–17.

Here we summarize a lecture given by Dr. McKnight to the Schumacher Society, an organization whose mission is to link people, land, and communities through education and social advocacy. In his lecture, Dr. McKnight tells a story to drive home his thesis, a story about the prairie settlers, a new technology, and the destruction of community.

According to McKnight, the Sauk Indians had lived in harmony with the bountiful, thriving prairie since recorded history. The settlers arriving from the East displaced the Sauk to a reservation, and moved into the fertile land with a new technology, the John Deere stainless steel plow. These settlers were largely poor farmers from Europe, who had farmed for centuries in harmony with the land in their native countries using sustainable practices handed down for generations. But this new technology was efficient, and busted the sod of the prairie quickly and expertly, so the settlers could plant crops at a rate never before experienced. They ignored the way of the Sauk and the way of their ancestors, slicing through the prairie ecosystem and changing it forever. Within one generation, the soil was depleted, and the natural root system that held it in place was gone, sliced away by the new technology, the stainless steel sod-busting plow. Soon, the flourishing prairie was a dust bowl of a desert, and all knowledge of how to restore it was forgotten. And so three deserts were created: the dust bowl, the Indian reservation, and the loss of the memories and knowledge of a people.

Dr. McKnight then creates a metaphor to help us understand how the new service professions, another kind of new technology, are like the John Deere plow, slicing away natural community connections and supports. He uses the "bereavement counselor" to represent the service professions, and tells another story. In this story, the bereavement counselor has a slick college degree, innovative techniques, and a certificate that displays his expertise and knowledge. The bereavement counselor knows better than family, friends, and neighbors how to help people grieve after the death of a loved one. Of course, people must pay for the service. And the bereavement counselor convinces the county board that taxes should pay for his services for those who are penniless and cannot pay on their own. So, several people begin using the bereavement counselor—after all, they are paying for it with their taxes. And more bereavement counselors and related helping professionals come to town and reinforce that people should see a counselor or they will have problems later in life. Family, friends, and neighbors stop coming by after a death in the family, as they don't have the title or certificate or expertise to help their loved one grieve. And they don't want to interrupt the work of the professionals. So the bereaved grieve alone, without the support of their community, with only the new technology and techniques of the bereavement counselor there to help them. And another desert is created. Natural connections severed between friends and neighbors, displaced by the service professional, just like the John Deere plow severed natural root systems.

Dr. McKnight's powerful metaphor begs us to step back and look critically at what it means to be a "helping professional" and what negative effects are caused by our interventions. He provides us with four tests of new service technologies, to determine whether we do more harm than good.

1. *Monetary cost*: Is the cost of the service worth the benefits to society? He gives the example of our healthcare system, which uses a significant portion of our national resources, yet ranks very low in quality among other nations.
2. *Specific counter-productivity*: Does the service actually create the inverse of its stated purpose? He gives examples of "sickening medicine" or "criminalizing juvenile correctional facilities."
3. *Loss of knowledge*: Does a service take away knowledge from others? For example, the La Leche League was formed by a small group of mothers who found a few older women who still remembered how to breastfeed their babies, after a few generations of women had been told by professional pediatricians that it was healthier to feed babies formula from bottles.
4. *Hidden curriculum*: Is the invisible message always there that says, "I am a professional—you will be better because I know better than you"?

Dr. McKnight cautions communities to be wary of the service professionals and the social deserts they can create. He challenges professionals to avoid making human need into a commodity. He asks us to nurture sustainable community strengths and connections and to always carefully evaluate if we are harming more than helping.

Figure 15.9 Primary Source Support: Are We Helping?

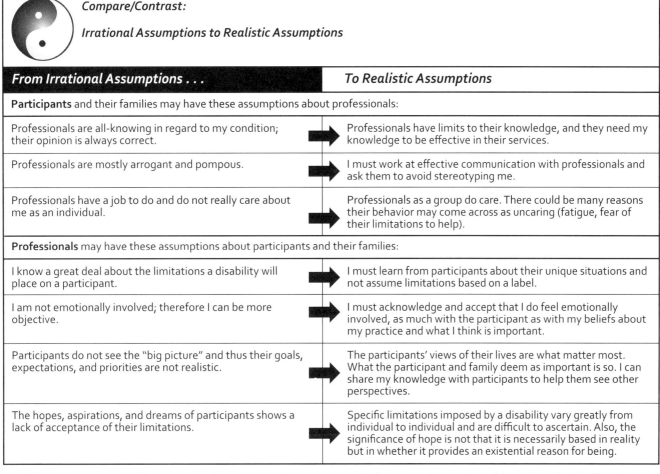

Figure 15.10 Compare/Contrast: Irrational Assumptions versus Realistic Assumptions *(adapted from Greer & Galtelli, 1985)*

assisting local athletes with disabilities organize leagues and practices, to teaching relaxation techniques at the local assisted-living facility. Providing pro bono work is a professional obligation that provides great intrinsic rewards and valuable community service.

BEING A STRENGTHS-BASED THERAPEUTIC RECREATION SPECIALIST

We would like to close this chapter on professionalism with a summary of the characteristics of a strengths-based therapeutic recreation specialist. A strengths-based therapeutic recreation specialist . . .

- Uses philosophy and ethics to guide practice.
- Focuses on the full range of ways to help participants, using strengths to build a life of meaning that includes high quality leisure and well-being.
- Embraces all aspects of the field, from helping participants build functional skills to exploring recreation passions to building community.
- Assumes that participants' dreams, goals, and aspirations are worthy of respect, support, and facilitation.
- Focuses on the participant *and* the participant's environment, being an advocate and community builder when needed.
- Recognizes when and where to help best, and when to nurture natural supports.
- Continues to build skills, knowledge, and competencies as well as deeper practice wisdom through continuing development, reflection, and supervision.
- Possesses skills and knowledge to help participants *and* communities, to strengthen functional ability *and* leisure well-being.
- Maintains the highest level of professionalism
- Has a continuing excitement to learn

Compare/Contrast:

Deficits-Based versus Strengths-Based Professionalism

From Deficits-Based Professionalism . . .	To Strengths-Based Professionalism
Professional is the expert concerning the participant's life	Participants, families, and communities are viewed as the experts
Expert professional interprets the person's story to arrive at a diagnosis	The professional knows the person through the person's interpretation of events and meanings—not through the professional's interpretation
Relationship marked by distance, power inequality, control, and manipulation	Relationship marked by collaboration, equality, mutual respect, and confidence in one's abilities
The skills of the professional are the primary resource for the work to be done	Help is focused on getting on with one's life, using the skills and resources of the person
Professional cynicism in relation to goals, dreams, and aspirations of the participant	Professional hopefulness
Expert-centered	Person-centered

Figure 15.11 Compare/Contrast: Deficits-Based versus Strengths-Based Professionalism

- Assures competence to the public through credentialing
- Gives back to the profession and society.
- Advocates for play, leisure, and recreation for participants even in the most inhospitable settings without apology or concern for status or reward.

Summary

Being a virtuous professional means having excellent character as well as skills and knowledge. It means ensuring that your actions follow a code of ethics. In this chapter, we provided you with seven strategies for being a strengths-based professional:

1. Knowing and using strengths and virtues in practice
2. Knowing and using ethics
3. Knowing and using the body of knowledge
4. Knowing and using standards of practice
5. Assuring competence to others
6. Continuing to grow as a professional, through continuing education and clinical supervision
7. Networking and developing professional support systems

Professions provide valuable and necessary services to society. But there are limits to professionalization, and it is important to continually reflect on your role with participants and your impact on communities, to ensure that you are helping more than harming others. Lastly, it is important to give back to society, through generous sharing of your professional expertise with no expectation of personal gain.

Resources

Codes of Ethics

The Code of Ethics for Therapeutic Recreation from the National Therapeutic Recreation Society
http://www.recreationtherapy.com/history/ntrs.htm

The Code of Ethics for Recreational Therapy from the American Therapeutic Recreation Association
http://www.atra-online.com/displaycommon.cfm?an=1&subarticlenbr=41

The Code of Ethics for Therapeutic Recreation from the Canadian Therapeutic Recreation Association
http://www.canadian-tr.org

Standards of Practice

The Standards of Practice for Therapeutic Recreation from the National Recreation and Park Association/National Therapeutic Recreation Society
These standards are presented in full in Table 15.13 as they are not readily available.

Table 15.13 NTRS Standards of Practice *(NTRS, 2004)*

NATIONAL THERAPEUTIC RECREATION SOCIETY STANDARDS OF PRACTICE FOR THERAPEUTIC RECREATION SERVICES

Introduction
The National Therapeutic Recreation Society (NTRS) Board of Directors approved the revised Standards of Practice for Therapeutic Recreation Services in September, 2004. What follows are the basic Standards of Practice, without criteria for each standard.

Standard I : Therapeutic Recreation Process
The therapeutic recreation specialist uses a systematic and purposeful process that consists of assessment, planning, implementation, and evaluation to create therapeutic recreation programs that benefit the participant's health, functional status, personal development and quality of life.

A. Assessment
The therapeutic recreation personnel (specialist) follow(s) a written plan for assessing and reassessing physical, emotional, cognitive, social, spiritual and leisure behaviors; functional abilities and skills; and lifestyle needs, strengths, preferences, and expectations of participants to ascertain relevant factors impacting the design of individual and comprehensive program plans.

B. Planning
The therapeutic recreation specialist uses assessment information to develop goals and objectives, content and processes, an evaluation plan and operational guidelines to manage and implement participant-oriented programs and services.

C. Implementation and Operations
The therapeutic recreation specialist establishes a therapeutic relationship, creates a safe environment and facilitates and supervises therapeutic recreation programs/services.

D. Evaluation
The therapeutic recreation specialist collects and analyzes summative data to make subsequent decisions about the individual participant's plan and specific therapeutic recreation programs and services according to agency evaluation and program protocols.

Standard II: Participant Involvement
The therapeutic recreation (specialist) personnel support(s) participant, caregiver, family, and significant other involvement in the therapeutic recreation process and create(s) opportunities to incorporate and empower the participant, caregiver, family and significant others during the therapeutic recreation process.

Standard III: Interventions and Facilitation Techniques
The therapeutic recreation (specialist) personnel use(s) interventions and facilitation techniques to promote changes that empower the individual toward improvement in his/her functional skills, leisure, health, personal development and quality of life.

Standard IV: Documentation
The therapeutic recreation specialist documents and records information; periodically reviews and updates documents; and maintains records on the management of programs and services to ensure accountability, effectiveness and compliance with regulations and standards.

Standard V: Outcomes
The therapeutic recreation specialist records data on the participant's response to the therapeutic recreation process in the behavioral areas, cognitive, physical, social, emotional, spiritual; leisure functioning; personal development; and, quality of life variables and uses these results to enhance the therapeutic recreation process.

Standard VI: Professional Staffing and Credentials
Qualified and properly credentialed personnel conduct and monitor the therapeutic recreation process and maintain their professional competence through appropriate professional development activities.

Standard VII: Ethics
Professionals and paraprofessionals are committed to advancing the use of therapeutic recreation services in order to ensure protection, quality, and promote the rights of persons receiving services.

Standard VIII: Quality Management
The therapeutic recreation specialist implements management policies and procedures in order to maintain the quality of therapeutic recreation programs and services. These protocols comply with governmental, accreditation, professional, and agency standards and regulations. Evaluation and research are conducted to enhance the therapeutic recreation process; and, management practices and research initiatives are compatible with agency protocols and professional standards.

The Standards of Practice for Therapeutic Recreation from the American Therapeutic Recreation Association (available for purchase)
http://www.atra-online.com/displaycommon.cfm?an=1&subarticlenbr=42

The Standards of Practice for Therapeutic Recreation from the Canadian Therapeutic Recreation Association
http://www.canadian-tr.org

National Council for Therapeutic Recreation Certification (NCTRC)

NCTRC provides complete information on how to apply for certification, prepare for the national exam, maintain certification, and more. One useful tool is the online verification database, where you can determine whether someone is actively certified. As standards for

Self-Assessment of Learning

Exercise #1: Professionalism and Being in a Profession

In this chapter, we have provided insight into what it means to be a member of a profession and to act in a professional way. Below is a two-part quiz. The first part is about "professionalism"—do you act like a professional? The second is about "being in a profession." Do you have virtues and morals that are needed by a member of a true profession? Do you endorse and participate in all aspects of your profession? Take both quizzes and see how you stand. Though it matters that you "act" professionally, it matters more that you "be" virtuous in a profession.

Part One: Professionalism Quiz

Do you act professionally on the job? Participants and others may judge us not on our technical skills and knowledge, but on how we look and act when we provide services. Take this quiz to see how you portray the image of professionalism at work on a daily basis with participants, colleagues, and others.

When meeting and interacting with participants and colleagues:
- ☐ Do you wear appropriate clothing for the situation or activity? Are you well-groomed and clean?
- ☐ Are you on time? Are you considerate of others' time?
- ☐ Do you shake hands firmly (not limp or bone-crushing)? Do you smile and make eye contact?
- ☐ Do you refrain from displaying dramatic emotions?

When in a meeting or activity:
- ☐ Do you come prepared? Have you done your homework?
- ☐ Do you respect the contributions of others and encourage their dialogue?
- ☐ Do you maintain your posture (not slouched with your feet up)?
- ☐ Do you focus on the group, and not on your PDA, cell phone, or laptop?
- ☐ Have you considered the various knowledge and skill levels of the group when interacting?
- ☐ Do you share the credit for successes with your team?

During verbal communication with participants and colleagues:
- ☐ Do you listen well and mirror back the information participants provide to ensure complete understanding of the message?
- ☐ Do you speak clearly, enunciating words clearly?
- ☐ Do you refrain from using slang or overusing words such as "like," "I went," or "umm"?
- ☐ Do you practice assertive communication?
- ☐ Are you able to articulate yourself clearly and succinctly?
- ☐ Do you explore and address the expectations of others?
- ☐ Are you truthful in all your interactions?

When communicating in writing:
- ☐ Do you spell-check and grammar-check your writing (including e-mail)?
- ☐ Do you show respect for the recipient of your e-mail by not discussing emotionally sensitive issues by e-mail?
- ☐ Do you keep e-mails focused and short while offering enough information to allow a course of action to be determined?

In the break room or lunchroom:
- ☐ Do you clean up after yourself?
- ☐ Do you eat only the food you've put in the fridge?
- ☐ Do you display good table manners when eating?

When speaking with your supervisors:
- ☐ Do you bring solutions to problems, not just problems?
- ☐ Do you reinforce the positives along with bringing up the negatives?
- ☐ Do you show your respect for their authority?
- ☐ Do you disclose information to them in a timely and relevant way?
- ☐ Are your expectations of them and the job reasonable for someone of your age and experience level?

When there is a problem with someone on your team:
- ☐ Do you speak to them directly to resolve the issue, refraining from gossip or "back-stabbing"?
- ☐ Do you have a smooth, calm approach to problem-solving?
- ☐ Do you demonstrate respect for the coworker and talk to their supervisors only if (a) you've tried to discuss the problem first directly with your coworker, or (b) you've been given permission to do so by the coworker?
- ☐ Do you report matters of unethical behavior to either your supervisor or your human resources representative?

In general:
- ☐ Do you act morally and ethically?
- ☐ Do you remain objective and open to the ideas and opinions of others?
- ☐ Do you invest time in others to build trust and rapport?
- ☐ Do you treat people like individuals and as you would like to be treated?
- ☐ Are you sensitive to people of different cultures, lifestyles, religions, and knowledge/experience levels?

Profession and Virtues Quiz

To integrate virtue ethics in your everyday practice:
- ☐ Do you know your own strengths and virtues and use them daily?
- ☐ Do you explore the meaningful virtues for therapeutic recreation with others in our field?
- ☐ Do you purposefully focus on building strengths and virtues in yourself and others?
- ☐ Do you explore and tap strengths and resources in your environment to further help participants?
- ☐ Do you take time to reflect on your moral qualities and how your daily behavior reflects those qualities?

To integrate the code of ethics in your practice:
- ☐ Do you have the code of ethics at your workplace in a conspicuous location?
- ☐ Do you know by memory the main ethical principles in the codes of ethics?
- ☐ Do you use the code of ethics to help you in decision-making during the moral dilemmas you may encounter in your everyday practice?
- ☐ Do you talk about the code of ethics with your colleagues and share insights into ways of handling challenging situations using the code of ethics?

To use and integrate the body of knowledge into your practice:
- ☐ Do you subscribe to and regularly read the research journals in therapeutic recreation?
- ☐ Do you read journals outside our field that have relevance to your practice?
- ☐ Do you talk about new research findings and evidence-based practice with your colleagues?
- ☐ Do you integrate what you learn from research and evaluation into your daily practice?
- ☐ Do you have the appropriate educational background for your job, and do you stay current with new developments in the field?

To exhibit autonomy and self-regulation:
- ☐ Do you have the standards of practice located in a conspicuous location at your workplace?
- ☐ Do you know by memory the main standards of practice for therapeutic recreation?
- ☐ Do you use the standards of practice to plan and implement your services?
- ☐ Do you make changes to your services and programs based on careful evaluation, using the standards of practice as a guide?
- ☐ Do you help colleagues understand and use the standards of practice in their work?

To assure your competence to others:
- ☐ Are you certified in therapeutic recreation?
- ☐ Do you maintain your certification, even if your employer does not require it?
- ☐ Do you display your certification in a conspicuous location at your workplace?
- ☐ Do you mentor and assist colleagues in obtaining and maintaining their certification?
- ☐ Do you seek out additional certifications for any other areas you need for practice?
- ☐ Do you explain your profession to participants with whom you work?

To truly meet the needs of participants and keep their well-being at the center of your practice:
- ☐ Do you diligently follow a person-centered, strengths-based process in assessing what is needed and planning how to most help the participant?
- ☐ Do you provide services participants need, not fit them into preexisting programs because that is what you have always offered?
- ☐ Is your approach individualized, ecological, and respectful?
- ☐ When participants ask for your help in advocating for positive social change, do you respond effectively?
- ☐ Do you look for ways to build natural supports, friendships, community, and social change that allow participants to reach their goals for leisure, well-being, and quality of life?
- ☐ Do you respect, validate, and support participants' goals, dreams, and aspirations for recreation and leisure?
- ☐ Do you do your best work for the good of participants and their families and not for your own status and advancement?
- ☐ Do you provide services in locations where participants can most benefit from them?

To continue to grow as a professional:
- ☐ Do you pursue continuing education, through conferences, workshops, webinars, college courses, or other means?
- ☐ Are you an active member of your state and national professional associations?
- ☐ Do you regularly participate in some form of mentoring or clinical supervision?
- ☐ Do you consistently work with colleagues to develop your critical thinking/clinical reasoning skills?
- ☐ Do you routinely take time to reflect on your involvement with participants, colleagues, and the profession?
- ☐ Do you give back to the profession? How?

Exercise #2: Applying the Codes of Ethics

Below are some ethical dilemmas you may encounter in your practice in therapeutic recreation. Some are actual incidents from the field. Use the codes of ethics, as well as virtue ethics, to make a decision on how you might respond to each dilemma.

Scenario #1
This is an actual request for advice from a local professional listserv:
"I am a volunteer at several nursing homes and one assisted living facility. Although I generally visit during the day accompanied by my certified therapy dog, on a number of occasions I have visited the assisted living facility on a Friday evening. I used to find six ladies playing Bingo on their own at a large round table and would join them during part of my visit. But in recent weeks they have sadly told me that they are no longer permitted to play Bingo. As a result, they do nothing. The director of the facility told me that Bingo was a 'non-approved activity' and thus the women would have to play some other game. (They do not play for money. They simply play for the fun of seeing how long it takes someone to complete a game.) I would like to inquire 1) whether Bingo is a 'non-approved activity' and, if so, what the consequences of such a designation are; and, 2) even if Bingo is a 'non-approved activity,' can administration/staff of this facility prohibit a group of residents from setting up a game of Bingo by themselves when no other activity is taking place? It should be noted that the women do not require professional assistance while playing; they set up and replace the materials themselves, and they are not disruptive while playing. Thank you for any input you can give me on this issue."
How would you respond to this request for advice on the listserv? What ethical principles can you use as guides in your response?

_____
_____
_____
_____

442 • Therapeutic Recreation Practice: A Strengths Approach

Scenario #2
You work in a psychosocial rehabilitation agency. An important part of your services is community adjustment and inclusion. While at the YMCA with a small group of participants, you run into some of your friends. "What are you up to? Who are you with?" are some of the questions they ask you when they come up to you to talk.
How would you handle this situation? What ethical principles can you use as guides in your response?

_____
_____
_____
_____

Scenario #3
During a team meeting (team includes you, physician, social worker, nurse, OT, dietitian, PT, psychologist), the participant being discussed becomes the butt of jokes and many disparaging comments by the team members. The participant has been frustrating to work with, but you feel very uncomfortable about the content and tone of the team meeting. You also have a strong desire to be a close part of the team.
How would you respond to this situation? What ethical principles can you use as guides in your response?

_____
_____
_____
_____

Scenario #4
You have worked for several days with an older woman who is recovering from a stroke. The other team members and the participant's adult children have determined the best choice for discharge is to have her placed in a long-term care facility. Some team members, based on assessments done near the beginning of the participant's rehabilitation stay and in an environment that was unfamiliar to her, have concluded she does not have the skills to live in her home. The participant wants very much to return to her own home. You have seen the participant in community re-entry and other therapeutic recreation activities function very well and show most skills needed for independent living.
How would you respond to this situation? What ethical principles can you use as guides in your response?

_____
_____
_____
_____

Exercise #3: Exploring New Knowledge

In Table 15.7, we provided a listing of some of the major journals in therapeutic recreation and related areas. We would like you to go on a scavenger hunt! Choose at least five peer-reviewed journals and one magazine from the list, head to the library or full-text databases and, for each journal, find one article that really excites you. List each article below:

1. Research Journal Name: _____
   Article Title: _____
   Why is it exciting to you? _____

2. Research Journal Name: _____
   Article Title: _____
   Why is it exciting to you? _____

3. Research Journal Name: _____
   Article Title: _____
   Why is it exciting to you? _____

4. Research Journal Name: _____
   Article Title: _____
   Why is it exciting to you? _____

5. Research Journal Name: _____
   Article Title: _____
   Why is it exciting to you? _____

6. Magazine Name: _____
   Article Title: _____
   Why is it exciting to you? _____

Exercise #4: Being a Strengths-Based Professional

Dr. Harlan "Gold" Metcalf, founder of the Recreation, Parks and Leisure Studies Department at SUNY Cortland, was fond of giving this advice to students and aspiring professionals:

> *"Stay consistently in the presence of the best in the sphere in which you seek attainment and make an honest response."*

How can you "stay consistently in the presence of the best" in your profession of therapeutic recreation?

_____
_____
_____
_____

certification and recertification continually change, you should check this site often.
http://www.nctrc.org

Professional Associations

You can be active in these professional organizations in therapeutic recreation:

- American Therapeutic Recreation Association
  http://www.atra-online.com

- Canadian Therapeutic Recreation Association
  http://www.canadian-tr.org

- Diversional Therapy Association of Australia
  http://www.diversionaltherapy.org.au

- National Recreation and Park Association (National Therapeutic Recreation Society became the Inclusion and Advocacy Network in 2010)
  http://www.nrpa.org

You can be active in these related professional organizations:

- American Association for Physical Activity and Recreation
  http://www.aahperd.org/aapar

- Association of Experiential Education
  http://www.aee.org

- Child Life Council
  http://www.childlife.org

- International Positive Psychology Association
  http://www.ippanetwork.org

- TASH
  http://www.tash.org

- World Leisure Organization
  http://www.worldleisure.org

REFERENCES

American Therapeutic Recreation Association (ATRA). (2000). *Standards for the practice of therapeutic recreation and self-assessment guide.* Hattiesburg, MS: American Therapeutic Recreation Association.

American Therapeutic Recreation Association (ATRA). (2009). *Code of ethics.* Hattiesburg, MS: American Therapeutic Recreation Association.

Austin, D. (n.d.). Professionalism: Exhibiting professional qualities. *ATRA Newsletter.* Hattiesburg, MS: American Therapeutic Recreation Association.

Austin, D., Dattilo, J., & McCormick, B. (2002). *Conceptual foundations for therapeutic recreation.* State College, PA: Venture Publishing, Inc.

Bernard, J., & Goodyear, R. (1998). *Fundamentals of clinical supervision* (2nd ed.). Boston, MA: Allyn & Bacon.

Bernard, J., & Goodyear, R. (2009). *Fundamentals of clinical supervision* (4th ed.). Boston, MA: Allyn & Bacon.

Bonebright, D. (2010). 40 years of storming: A historical review of Tuckman's Model of small group development. *Human Resource Development International, 13*(1), 111–120.

Bureau of Labor Statistics. (2012). Recreational therapists. *Occupational Outlook Handbook 2010–2011 Edition.* Retrieved from http://www.bls.gov/oco/ocos082.htm#emply

Canadian Therapeutic Recreation Association (CTRA). (2005). *Code of ethics.* Calgary, AB, Canada: CTRA. Retrieved from http://www.canadian-tr.org

Canadian Therapeutic Recreation Association (CTRA). (2006). *Standards of practice for recreation therapists and therapeutic recreation assistants.* Calgary, AB, Canada: Canadian Therapeutic Recreation Association.

Clark, D. (1995, August). A new code of ethics for NRPA. *Parks and Recreation*, 38–43.

Committee on Accreditation of Recreational Therapy Education. (2010). *Standards and guidelines.* Clearwater, FL: CAAHEP.

Council on Accreditation of Parks, Recreation, Tourism and Related Professions. (2009). *Learning outcomes standards and assessment.* Ashburn, VA: National Recreation and Park Association.

Coward, H., & Rattanakun, P. (1999). *A cross-cultural dialogue on health care ethics.* Waterloo, ON, Canada: Wilfrid Laurier University Press.

Greer, B., & Galtelli, B. (1985). Parents and professionals: Irrational assumptions in their communication. In R. Jones (Ed.), *Reflections on growing up disabled.* Washington, DC: Council for Exceptional Children.

Higgs, J., Jones, M., Loftus, S., & Christensen, N. (2008). *Clinical reasoning in the health professions* (3rd ed.). Oxford, UK: Elsevier.

Hunnicutt, B. (1980). To cope in autonomy: Therapeutic recreation and the limits of professionalism and intervention. *Journal of Expanding Horizons in Therapeutic Recreation, 3,* 122–134.

Hurst, A., & Hartman, J. (2009). *Pro bono: An emerging trend in America's professional schools.* San Francisco: Taproot Foundation. Retrieved from http://www.taprootfoundation.org/docs/Pro-Bono-An-Emerging-Trend-Professional-Schools.pdf

International Association of Continuing Education and Training. (2007). *ANSI/IACET 1-2007 standard.* Retrieved from http://www.iacet.org/content/iacet-standard.html

Jones, D., & Anderson, L. (2004). The status of clinical supervision in therapeutic recreation: A national study. *Therapeutic Recreation Journal, 38*(4), 329–347.

Kestenbaum, V. (2005). Professions, ethics, and unity. In C. Sylvester (Ed.), *Philosophy of therapeutic recreation: Ideas and issues,* (Vol. III). Asburn, VA: National Therapeutic Recreation Society.

King, G., Currie, M., Bartlett, D., Gilpin, M., Willoughby, C., Tucker, M., Strachan, D., & Baxter, D. (2007). The development of expertise in pediatric rehabilitation therapists: Changes in approach, self-knowledge, and use of enabling and customizing strategies. *Developmental Neurorehabilitation, 10*(3), 223–240.

Leahy, M. (1996). The commercial model and the future of therapeutic recreation. In C. Sylvester (Ed.), *Philosophy of therapeutic recreation: Ideas and issues,* (Vol. II). Ashburn, VA: National Therapeutic Recreation Society.

McKnight, J. (1992). John Deere and the bereavement counselor. *Whole Community Catalog, 1*(1), 13–17.

Moore, S. (2009). 147 gang members charged after inquiry in California. *New York Times,* May 21. Retrieved from http://www.nytimes.com/2009/05/22/us/22gangs.html

Murray, S., & Shank, J. (1994). Clinical supervision in therapeutic recreation: Contributing to competent practice. *Annual in Therapeutic Recreation, 5,* 83–93.

National Board of Medical Examiners. (2003). *Embedding professionalism in medical education.* Philadelphia, PA: National Board of Medical Examiners.

National Council for Therapeutic Recreation Certification (NCTRC). (2007). *Job analysis report.* New City, NY: NCTRC.

National Council for Therapeutic Recreation Certification (NCTRC). (2008). *Certification standards: Part IV NCTRC disciplinary process.* New City, NY: NCTRC. Retrieved from http://www.nctrc.org/documents/4Discipline.pdf

National Council for Therapeutic Recreation Certification (NCTRC). (2009). *CTRS profile: Current research on professionals in the field.* New City, NY: NCTRC. Retrieved from http://www.nctrc.org/standardsandpublications.htm

National Therapeutic Recreation Society (NTRS). (2001). *Code of ethics and interpretive guidelines.* Ashburn, VA: National Therapeutic Recreation Society.

National Therapeutic Recreation Society (NTRS). (2004). *Standards of practice for a continuum of care in therapeutic recreation.* Ashburn, VA: National Therapeutic Recreation Society.

O'Keefe, C. (2005). Grounding the therapeutic recreation process in an ethic of care. In C. Sylvester (Ed.), *Philosophy of therapeutic recreation: Ideas and issues* (Vol. III). Ashburn, VA: National Therapeutic Recreation Society.

O'Neil, E., & Pew Health Professions Commission (PHPC). (1998). *Recreating health professional practice for a new century*. San Francisco, CA: Pew Health Professions Commission.

Pellegrino, E. (2002). Professionalism, profession and the virtues of the good physician. *The Mount Sinai Journal of Medicine, 69*(6), 378–384.

Peterson, C., & Seligman, M. (2004). *Character strengths and virtues: A handbook and classification*. New York, NY: Oxford University Press.

Rath, T. (2007). *StrengthsFinder 2.0*. New York, NY: Gallup.

Schon, D. (1983). *The reflective practitioner: How professionals think in action*. New York, NY: Basic Books.

Shank, J. (1985). Bioethical principles and the practice of therapeutic recreation in clinical settings. *Therapeutic Recreation Journal, 19*(4), 31–40.

Shank, J., & Coyle, C. (2002). *Therapeutic recreation in health promotion and rehabilitation*. State College, PA: Venture Publishing, Inc.

Stumbo, N., & Peterson, C. (2004). *Therapeutic recreation program design: Principles and procedures* (4th ed.). San Francisco, CA: Pearson Education.

Sylvester, C. (2002). Ethics and the quest for professionalization. *Therapeutic Recreation Journal, 36*(4), 314–344.

Sylvester, C. (2005). Careers, callings, and the professionalization of therapeutic recreation. In C. Sylvester (Ed.), *Philosophy of therapeutic recreation: Ideas and issues,* (Vol. III). Asburn, VA: National Therapeutic Recreation Society.

Sylvester, C. (2009). A virtue-based approach to therapeutic recreation practice. *Therapeutic Recreation Journal, 43*(3), 9–25.

Sylvester, C., Voelkl, J., & Ellis, G. (2001). *Therapeutic recreation programming: Theory and practice*. State College, PA: Venture Publishing, Inc.

Wilbur, M., Roberts-Wilbur, J., Hart, G., Morris, R., & Betz, R. (1994). Structured group supervision: A pilot study. *Counselor Education and Supervision, 33*, 262–279.

Wilensky, H. (1964). The professionalization of everyone? *The American Journal of Sociology, 70*(2), 137–158.

Winfield, B., & Webster, B. (2004). *Communication in the public interest.* New Orleans: International Communication Association. Retrieved from http://www.allacademic.com/meta/p113428_index.html

Chapter 16
LOOKING AHEAD...

The poppy is bright, positive, sunny... so your journey as a strengths-based therapeutic recreation specialist begins.

"The future belongs to those who believe in the beauty of their dreams."
—*Eleanor Roosevelt*

"Simply by virtue of being human, you have within you the seeds of flourishing."
—*Barbara Fredrickson, scholar and psychologist*

OVERVIEW OF CHAPTER 16

- Reflecting upon your future as a therapeutic recreation specialist
- Final thoughts from the authors

FOCUS QUESTIONS

- What philosophy will guide you as you practice therapeutic recreation in the future?
- How do you define therapeutic recreation, and what model of practice will you follow?
- How does recreation serve as the foundation for what you do in therapeutic recreation?
- What personal strengths and resources do you bring to your practice?
- How will you collaborate and with whom?
- What approaches in the strengths-based therapeutic recreation process most appeal to you?
- How do you envision your work as a strengths-based advocate?
- Where will you look for inspiration to enhance your competence and professionalism?
- What resources from this book do you see yourself using in the future?
- What will your future as a therapeutic recreation professional look like 5 years from now?

AN OVERVIEW OF LOOKING AHEAD

A definition of "future":
A time that has not yet come; an expected or projected state

A definition of "journey":
A trip or expedition from one place to another; a gradual passing from one state to another regarded as more advanced, e.g., from innocence to mature awareness

Now that you have finished reading this book, how will you use these concepts and approaches in your practice as a therapeutic recreation specialist? What does this new knowledge mean to you? How will you draw upon strengths and resources in your everyday practice? How will you bring to life the spirit of strengths-based practice through your work?

In previous chapters, we offered you a wealth of definitions, perspectives, approaches, and stories related to strengths-based therapeutic recreation practice. This final chapter is one you will write yourself. As a kind of send-off, to encourage you to look ahead and reflect on your future work as a therapeutic recreation specialist, we offer you a series of worksheets to help you digest and debrief the content of this book. By completing these worksheets, we hope you can translate the information in this book to your own personal vision of what it means to be a therapeutic recreation specialist, keeping in mind the unique strengths, characteristics, and personality that you bring to your practice. There are, of course, no right or wrong answers. The only right answers are those that ring true for you.

Compare and Contrast: Deficits and Strengths

Throughout this book, we have compared and contrasted many themes related to the deficits approach and the strengths approach. Now is your turn to think through this paradigm shift in our field as you complete Worksheet 16.1. What comparisons can you draw related to perceptions, practices, orientation, language, and the like as you contemplate therapeutic recreation practice?

My Therapeutic Recreation Philosophy

It is important for you to have a clear understanding of your foundational beliefs about the field of therapeutic recreation and how those beliefs impact your practice. When your beliefs and your practice align, you will not only experience a sense of satisfaction and accomplishment in your work, you will be able to practice with conviction and passion. Complete Worksheet 16.2 to clarify your answers to questions related to your personal philosophy and vision of therapeutic recreation practice, the defining qualities of your future work, and your aspirations for your career.

My Definition of Therapeutic Recreation

In Chapter 3, we invited you to develop your own definition of therapeutic recreation. Recall that definition and, now that you have finished reading this book, think of how you might revise it. Read Rhonda Nelson's Life Story (see Figure 16.1) to help you think about the answers to the questions on Worksheet 16.3.

My Therapeutic Recreation Model of Practice

In Chapters 3 and 4, we presented the Flourishing through Leisure Model: An Ecological Extension of the Leisure and Well-Being Model and other therapeutic recreation models. Recall that a service model is a basically a graphic representation that captures the purpose and scope of practice. Take a look at the models in Chapter 3 and the Flourishing through Leisure Model presented in Chapter 4 and answer the questions on Worksheet 16.4 to reflect on the use of therapeutic recreation models in your future practice.

Recreation as the Foundation of My Work

Throughout this book, we have reiterated the centrality of recreation and strengths to therapeutic recreation practice—they are the heart of our practice. In order to help others develop meaningful recreation, it is important for you to be aware of your own recreation beliefs, values, behaviors, and activities. Complete Worksheet 16.5 to reflect on your own orientation to recreation.

Assessment of My Personal Strengths and Resources

Review Chapter 5 *Strengths* to refresh your memory of internal and external strengths and environmental resources. An essential part of your work in therapeutic recreation is helping people discover and build their strengths. To help others effectively find and use their strengths, one must recognize one's own strengths and resources and how they are expressed in one's life. Read Aimee Mullin's Life Story (see Figure 16.2), then complete Worksheet 16.6 to acknowledge your own strengths and consider how you can bring them to bear on your work in therapeutic recreation.

Myself as a Collaborator

A theme throughout this book is the importance of collaboration in the strengths-based approach. Collaboration brings together multiple perspectives, multiple resources, and multiple strengths to help people have the lives they want. Use Worksheet 16.7 to clarify your own strengths as a collaborator.

My View of the Therapeutic Recreation Process

We have presented the therapeutic recreation process in a slightly different way: discover, dream and design, deliver, and deliberate—in essence shifting the therapeutic recreation process to strengths-based language. Use the questions listed in Worksheet 16.8 to think through your orientation to the therapeutic recreation process in your practice.

My Life Story

In every chapter of this book, we have offered a variety of life stories to illustrate strengths-based practices in action. Now we invite you to ask yourself, "What have been my experiences in therapeutic recreation thus far? How have I applied strengths-based concepts in my work? How have my participants thrived through using these practices?" Reflect upon your experiences to develop your own "life story" using Worksheet 16.9.

Myself as a Strengths-Based Advocate

Advocacy is a central skill therapeutic recreation specialists use to help participants make meaningful change in themselves and their environments. As you

Life Story:

"What Do You Do?"
By Rhonda Nelson, Ph.D., CTRS

It's one of the most commonly asked questions of all time. "What do you do?" People often make this inquiry as soon as they have determined our name. The implication is clear; the work we have chosen to do makes a strong statement about our interests, values, knowledge, and skills. People naturally feel they have a better understanding of who we are by knowing something about our occupation. While others find themselves answering this question by explaining, "I'm a lawyer," "I'm a teacher," or "I'm a nurse," I often find myself replying, "I'm a recreation therapist." However, by responding this way, none of us are really answering the question asked. Instead, we are simply stating our job title or identifying our professional role.

This was brought to my attention while I was attending a party with a friend. I had casually noted on previous occasions that my friend, who works as an accountant, often responded in a non-traditional way to this common inquiry. I just assumed that she was trying to be quirky or comical by providing responses such as, "I try to make sense of other people's finances" or "I shuffle papers and crunch numbers all day." Yet, it was on the occasion when I heard her describe what I do that I finally understood her reason for replying in this manner. She was simply doing what others were not; she was answering the question.

It happened like this. We were standing with a group of people we had recently met. Everyone had introduced themselves by stating their name, and just as I took a bite of hors d'oeuvres, someone asked me the infamous question. "Rhonda, what do you do?" Seeing that I was unable to answer, my friend quickly chimed in. "She enriches people's lives."

Needless to say, the people we were talking to were very impressed! Yet, as I thought about it, I felt the description she gave was totally accurate. As a CTRS, that is what I do. In fact, that is what we all do. We enrich people's lives.

I felt proud of my professional role and the contributions I make through my work. I was honored that my friend perceived my job as having such a major impact on other people, and I realized that the full spectrum of what I do could never be accurately conveyed through a simple job title.

So, recently I got to thinking of how else I could answer the question of "What do you do?" Here are some answers I came up with:

- I cultivate creativity.
- I facilitate friendships.
- I help people to make positive changes in their life.
- I expand people's horizons.
- I inspire others to live their dreams.
- I educate, enlighten, and empower.
- I improve people's quality of life.
- I open doors to new experiences.
- I create a sense of community.
- I demonstrate alternative ways of doing things.
- I generate good times.
- I give people hope.

Those are a dozen things that I do. "What do YOU do?"

Figure 16.1 Life Story: What Do You Do? *(reprinted with permission)*

complete Worksheet 16.10, consider your own advocacy skills and how you will use them.

My Professional Growth and Inspiration

Learning is a lifelong process. In Chapter 15, we gave you many resources to continue your growth as a strengths-based therapeutic recreation specialist.

Reflect on how you will continue your development in the field as you complete Worksheet 16.11.

My Top Ten Resources

As authors, our goal has been to give you not only a new way of thinking, but to give you tools and resources to shift your practice to a strengths approach. Take inventory of the most useful resources you gleaned from the book. List them in Worksheet 16.12.

450 • THERAPEUTIC RECREATION PRACTICE: A STRENGTHS APPROACH

Life Story:

"Opportunity in Adversity—Using One's Strengths"

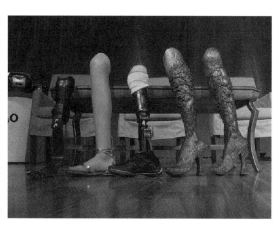

Though Aimee Mullins – world class athlete, model, actress, amputee—lost her legs as a young child, she went on to a life of adventure and accomplishments. She was one of the first athletes with a disability to compete (and consistently win) in Division I NCAA college athletics. Aimee challenged all notions of disability in her modeling career. Her "sexy" prostheses are seen on fashion runways throughout the world. Aimee embraces her life as a woman with a disability. She states, "Everyone has something rare and powerful to offer our society. The human ability to adapt is our greatest asset. All you really need is one person to show you the epiphany of your own power and you're off."
Aimee's strengths:
- Innovative thinker – she sees everything through the lens of consistent discovery
- Inclusive designer – she sees the complete picture
- Leader – she has learned to embrace change and challenge and helps others do so as well
- Positive body image – she celebrates her image as a vibrant, beautiful woman with a disability
- Advocate for equity in sports – she has made a difference in providing opportunity and access for all

Figure 16.2 Life Story: Opportunity in Adversity—Using One's Strengths

Life Story:

Hilary Lister Sails Solo around the British Isles

"When I'm sailing I go into a different world… it's like flying!"

In Chapter 2 *Paradigm Shifts* we introduced you to Hilary Lister, an Oxford-educated former scientist, who had a dream to sail solo around Great Britain (see Figure 2.6, p. 23).

Supported by a land and water crew, Hilary's journey took her past the east coasts of Ireland, Scotland, and England. Hilary trimmed the sails and controlled navigation by using a "sip" and "puff" method. Three pneumatic straws were connected to highly sensitive pressure switches on a computer, designed to respond to Hilary's breath commands.

The journey, sailed in a series of sections, took a total of 40 days. A low point was when the wind was still and Hilary couldn't set sail. The highlight was sailing alongside marine wildlife—in particular, seeing whales breached full-length out of the water!

Hilary completed the final leg of her journey on August 31, 2009, when she sailed into Dover harbor welcomed by a cheering crowd of well-wishers.

Celebrating her accomplishment, Hilary expressed, "I'm so relieved to be home—but looking forward to the next challenge. One thing I've learnt is that you can't predict the future—we couldn't even predict tomorrow's weather—so I'm not ruling anything out or anything in."

You may read more about Hillary's journey at www.hilarylister.com.

Figure 16.3 Life Story: Hilary Lister Sails Solo around the British Isles

My Letter from the Future

Write a letter to yourself that describes you as a therapeutic recreation specialist 5 years from now. Ask yourself: What would be my best possible future as a therapeutic recreation specialist? How did I get there, what does my future look like, what am I doing, what philosophy do I use in my practice? What other dreams do I have about being a therapeutic recreation professional? Use Worksheet 16.13 to write your letter.

FINAL THOUGHTS FROM THE AUTHORS

In writing this book, we have purposefully reinterpreted the way in which therapeutic recreation services have traditionally been approached. We have shifted the frame of reference from a problem-oriented, deficits approach to one centered around participants' strengths and aspirations. It has been our dream to see our field move in this direction, to reclaim its rootedness in recreation, and to see therapeutic recreation thrive and flourish in the breadth of settings in which we work.

Our intention is not to ignore problems and challenges which participants face. They are very real and have significant consequences in their lives. However, as we have repeatedly shown throughout this book, a focus on problems really doesn't support the aspirations and dreams of participants. Therapeutic recreation is a profession built around hope because the substance of our work revolves around leisure, well-being, and quality of life. By focusing on the strengths of our field, we are highly effective at building the strengths of participants.

When we started writing this book, Hilary Lister, who we featured in Chapter 2 *Paradigm Shifts* (see Figure 2.6, p. 23), embarked upon her dream to sail solo around the British Isles. It seemed then like an impossible task, yet, as we finished this book, she completed her journey at sea! Read about her inspiring adventure in Figure 16.3. As we have been writing this book, we have drawn strength and inspiration from Hilary's story. Our task of writing has often felt insurmountable too, yet our conviction to bring a strengths approach to our field—to see participants flourish and thrive through this positive orientation—has carried us through to these final pages. We hope this book will also inspire you, as Hilary's journey has inspired us and many others to follow their dreams and aspirations.

"One evening an old Cherokee told his grandson about a battle that goes on inside people. He said, 'My son, the battle is between two wolves inside us all. One is Negativity. It's anger, sadness, stress, contempt, disgust, fear, embarrassment, guilt, shame and hate. The other is Positivity. It's joy, gratitude, serenity, interest, hope, pride, amusement, inspiration, awe, and above all, love.' The grandson thought about it for a minute and then asked his grandfather: 'Which wolf wins?' The old Cherokee simply replied, 'The one you feed.'"

—as cited in Fredrickson, 2009, p. 179

REFERENCES

Fredrickson, B. (2009). *Positivity*. New York, NY: Crown.

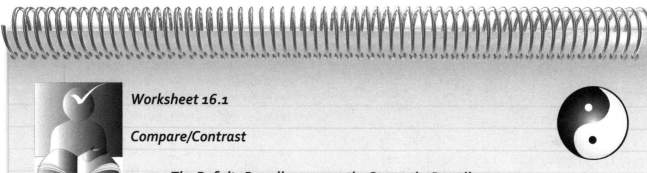

Worksheet 16.1

Compare/Contrast

The Deficits Paradigm versus the Strengths Paradigm

What comparisons can you draw related to perceptions, practices, orientation, language, and the like, which are and can be used in therapeutic recreation practice?

From a Deficits Approach . . .	To a Strengths Approach

Worksheet 16.2

My Therapeutic Recreation Philosophy

- What is my personal philosophy of therapeutic recreation practice?
- What vision do I have for my practice?
- What will be the defining qualities of my work as a therapeutic recreation specialist?
- What are my aspirations as a therapeutic recreation specialist?

Worksheet 16.3

My Definition of Therapeutic Recreation

- What was my definition of therapeutic recreation when I wrote it for Chapter 3?
- Now that I have read this book, how would I refine my definition?
- What would I tell a stranger who asked about my line of work as we both stepped onto an elevator?

Chapter 16—Looking Ahead... • 455

Worksheet 16.4

My Model of Therapeutic Recreation Practice

- How will I use the Flourishing through Leisure Model or other models to help guide me in my future strengths-based practice?
- How well does the Flourishing through Leisure Model align with my own perspective of therapeutic recreation? What about other therapeutic recreation models?

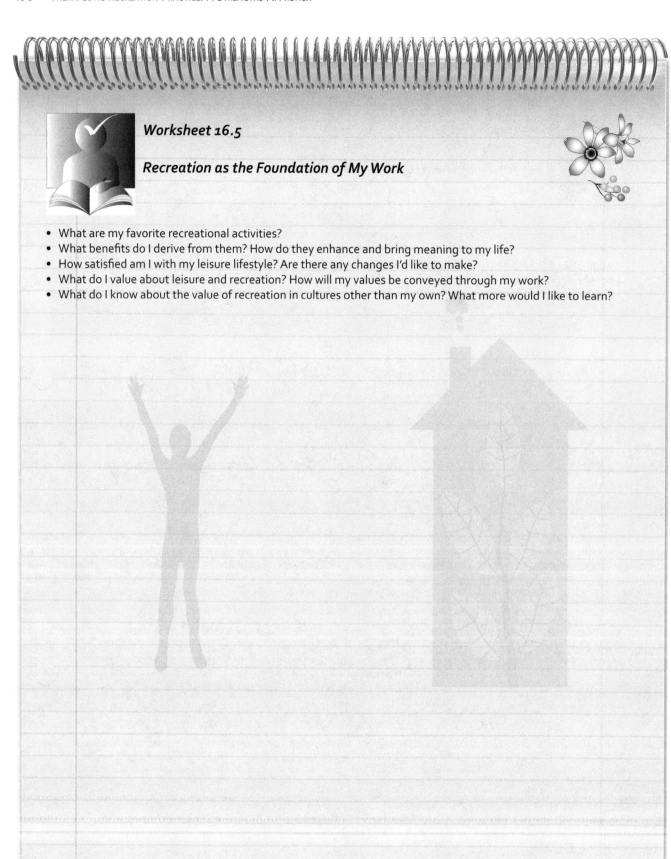

Worksheet 16.5

Recreation as the Foundation of My Work

- What are my favorite recreational activities?
- What benefits do I derive from them? How do they enhance and bring meaning to my life?
- How satisfied am I with my leisure lifestyle? Are there any changes I'd like to make?
- What do I value about leisure and recreation? How will my values be conveyed through my work?
- What do I know about the value of recreation in cultures other than my own? What more would I like to learn?

Worksheet 16.6

My Personal Strengths and Resources

- What are my internal character strengths and virtues?
- What are my internal strengths related to assets, gifts, passions, and talents?
- How will these strengths enhance my practice of therapeutic recreation?
- What external strengths and resources can I draw on for support of my work?
- How do my strengths support my cultural competence? What strengths in this area would I like to develop further?

Worksheet 16.7

Myself as a Collaborator

- What strengths in collaboration do I bring to the table?
- What collaborative skills and approaches would I like to develop further?
- Which team members do I especially look forward to working with, and why?
- How does my cultural background influence the way I approach collaboration? How can I be respectful and inclusive of team members from diverse cultural backgrounds, especially those with backgrounds that differ from my own?

Worksheet 16.8

My View of the Therapeutic Recreation Process

- What strengths-based assessment principles are most meaningful to me?
- Which assessment instruments and methods would I especially like to try?
- Which planning approaches can I see myself using?
- Which implementation processes appeal to me the most?
- How will I plan for transition supports and inclusion in my practice?
- Which documentation/evaluation tools and procedures do I see as particularly relevant?
- What are some aspects related to cultural competence that I need to keep in mind throughout the therapeutic recreation process?
- Where can I find research that will keep me current in best practices in therapeutic recreation?

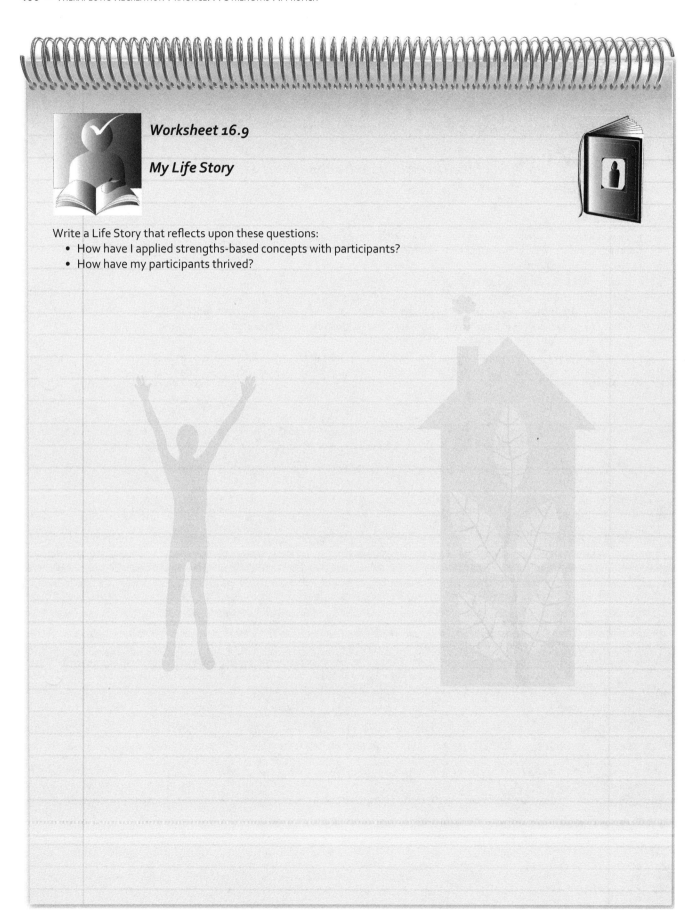

Worksheet 16.9

My Life Story

Write a Life Story that reflects upon these questions:
- How have I applied strengths-based concepts with participants?
- How have my participants thrived?

Worksheet 16.10

Myself as a Strengths-Based Advocate

- How will I encourage the participants with whom I work to be self-advocates?
- What advocacy skills and strengths do I possess that will help me advocate for strengths-based practices in my places of current or future employment?
- How will I put my skills and strengths into action?
- How can I be an advocate for the profession of therapeutic recreation?

Worksheet 16.11

My Personal Growth and Inspiration

- How will I continue to learn and grow in the field of therapeutic recreation? Where will I look for inspiration?
- What areas of practice would I like to study further? How would I like to engage in further study?
- What organizations in therapeutic recreation or related organizations would I like to join?
- What conferences would I like to attend?
- Who will be in my community of therapeutic recreation specialists? Who will be my mentors?
- How can I enhance my cultural competence?
- What books and journals will I read to keep abreast of new developments in the field of therapeutic recreation?

Worksheet 16.12

Top Ten Resources

- What are the top ten resources from this book that I can see myself using in therapeutic recreation?

1
2
3
4
5
6
7
8
9
10

- How might I use these resources in my current or future practice?

Worksheet 16.13

My Letter from the Future

Write a letter to yourself that describes *you* as a therapeutic recreation specialist 5 years from now. Ask yourself: What would be my best possible future as a therapeutic recreation specialist? What does my future look like? What am I doing? What philosophy do I use in my practice? What other dreams do I have about being a therapeutic recreation professional?

Date:

Dear (your name),

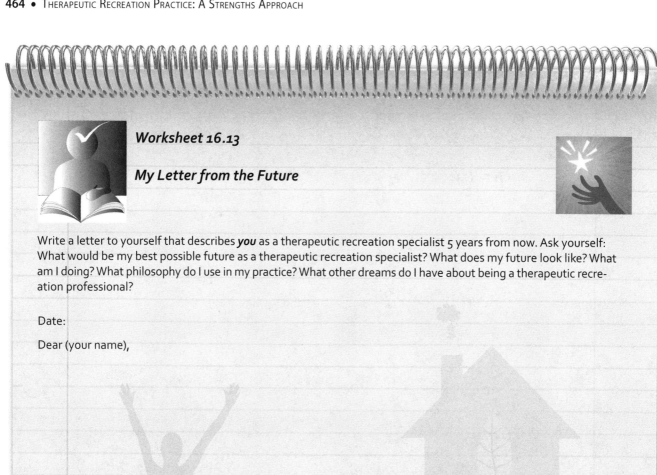

Sincerely,

(your signature)

Index

"A Credo for Support" 147, 150, 155
abilities
    functional 36, 47, 49
accessibility
    administrative 401
    physical 401
    programmatic, and service 402
acting happy 296
activity
    adaptation 279, 281, 284
    analysis 258–259, 279–282
    analysis domains 280, 282
    and equipment adaptations 71
    goals 250
advocacy
    balancing 407
    definition of 391
    for a strengths approach on the team 172–173
    for changes in environment 400–401
    for the profession of therapeutic recreation 403, 405
    individual level 398
    legislative checklist 399–401
    persuasive 398
    system or community level 399
aging in place 279, 281, 322
alternate forms of communication 294
anticipation dialogues 265, 267
Aristotle 31, 110
Aspiration 87
Aspirations Index 221–222
assessment
    advantages and disadvantages 200–201
    arena 203
    battery 201
    checklist 191–193
    components of 183
    criterion-referenced 190–191
    cultural relevance 190
    example of an assessment report 195, 230
    fairness 190
    functional 218
    norm-referenced 190–191
    of cognitive strengths 219
    of functional resources 222–224
    of global outcomes 224
    of leisure interests, preferences, and passions 216–217
    of leisure resources 222
    of physical strengths 219, 221
    of psychological and emotional strengths 218–219
    rationale 181–182
    report format 194–195
    sample initial assessment 193–194
    selection questions 226, 228
    standardized 201–203
    team-based 205
    techniques or approaches 195
    usability 190
Assessment Tools for Recreational Therapy and Related Fields (Red Book) 213–214
Assets 222–223
attitudes
    building positive accepting 298
authentic
    assessment 186–187
    environment 186
    goals 249–250
    learning 278–279
    leisure 285
avoiding overthinking 300

beauty and aesthetics in the environment 325–326
behavior
    ABC Model 304–305
    antecedent 304
    challenging 302–305
    consequence 304
    conditioning 307
    describing 304–305
    identifying 304–305
    positive reinforcement 306–308
    principles and terminology 304
    specific positive feedback 308
Behavioral and Emotional Rating Scale (BERS) 218
Best Friends Approach (in Alzheimer's care) 18
Borg Rating of Perceived Exertion Scale 219–220
Brief Happiness Questionnaire 225
Broaden-and-Build theory of positive emotions 99–100, 110, 114–116

cognitive strengths and resources 298, 301
capabilities
    approach 16, 31
certification 424–427
character strengths and virtues
    definition of 87–88
    use of 297–298
charity
    definition of 391–392
    charity-based versus advocacy-based helping 393
circle of courage 135–136
circle of friends 18, 222–223
circle of support 18, 160–161, 245–246
clinical pathways 259
clinical reasoning 239, 258, 427–428
clinical supervision
    definition of 428
    peer supervision 429–434
    sample contract 430, 432
    sample ground rules 430, 432
    steps to develop peer supervision group 430–431
    structured group supervision model 433–434
code of ethics 417–420
collaboration
    and networking 169, 172
    behavior on a team 169
    interpersonal skills for 172–173
Collaboration and Transdisciplinary Rating Scale 177–178
community
    and environmental resources for recreation and leisure development (asset-based) 82
    coaching (in community development) 19
    community-building theory 130
    creating livable communities 134–135
    definition of 131
    of worship/meditation 314
    parks and recreation agency 165, 420
    resources and supports 68, 70–71
competency
    definition of 85
continuing education
    definition of 427
    continuing education units (CEUs) 427
coping
    four stages of 116–117
    methods of 117, 297
    strategies 116–117, 297
    strengthening 297
credentialing 424–426
cultural competence 5–6

culture
    of hope, support, and encouragement 75
    normative patterns 125
    shifting 315, 317
Culture-Free Self-Esteem Inventory 219

deficits-based approach 12, 209, 402
developmental assets 17
dignity of risk 147, 155
disability as a variation in the human condition 19–20
discharge
    planning 338–341
    summary 340, 372–373, 385
documentation
    the "C"s of 372–374
    charting by exception 370–371
    checklist 374–377
    DARP notes 370–371
    elements of 368–371, 376–377
    focus charting 370–371
    importance of 362, 368, 385
    narrative progress notes 369, 371, 377
    of the plan 259, 368–372
    organization 372
    PIE charting 370–371
    SOAP notes 370–371
    Streamlining 374–375
    transition discharge plan 368–369, 372
    writing guidelines 372, 377, 385
domains
    affective 252–253
    behavioral and learning performance 252
    cognitive 86–87, 252
    leisure 68–75
    psychological or emotional 68–69, 225, 327
    physical or psychomotor 252
    social 71–72
    spiritual 74
dreaming
    definition of 237

ecological assessment
    broad 201–202, 222, 355
    focused 202, 355
    tool 222, 228–229
ecological perspective 19, 31, 36, 50, 55, 62, 95, 202, 298
Education for All Handicapped Children Act 338, 341
electronic records 375, 377
empowerment
    definition of 361, 365–366
ethic of care 417

ethics
    ethical dilemmas 418, 420
    ethical principles 418–419
eudaimonia
    definition of 31
evaluation
    definition of 362
    empowerment evaluation 365–367
    formative 362–365, 368
    of individual participant 362, 380–382, 385
    of services of agency 380–381, 385, 402, 424
    process versus outcome 365
    summative 362–365, 368, 380
evidence-based practice 7–8, 422, 424
exclusion
    negative outcomes of 350
existential
    dimension to practice 154
    outcomes 154–155

facilitation
    of cognitive strengths in the person 70
    of environmental cues and prompts 71
    of environmental resources to build physical
        strengths 73
    of environmental resources to build psychological
        and emotional strengths 69–70
    of environmental resources to build social strengths
        71–72
    of physical strengths in the person 72
    of positive behavioral supports 69
    of proximity to nature 74
    of psychological and emotional strengths in the
        person 69
    of real choices for leisure 68
    of safe environments 73
    of social strengths in the person 71
    of social supports 68
    of spiritual resources in the environment 74
    of spiritual strengths in the person 74
    of typical lifestyle rhythms 68
family
    development principles 313
    empowering 312
    empowerment skills 316–317
    support and involvement 93–96, 312
Family Development Credential Program 313
flow
    channel 113–114
    conditions of 113, 287
    cultivating 115
    cultivating with people with dementia 115

forgiveness 91, 324
friendship
    adult 301, 310
    building friendships 310, 398
    children 129–130, 310–313
Functional Independence Measure (FIM) 207

Global Assessment of Functioning (GAF) 209
goals
    approach 250
    appropriate 250
    authentic 249–250
    flexible 250
    harmonious 250
    intrinsic 249
    linking to actions and strategies 255–257
    reducing to behavioral terms 256
    strengthening commitment 300–301
gratitude
    expressing 324
    journal 324

happiness
    and well-being 31–33, 110–111, 225
healthcare
    participant rights 396
Healthy People 2020
    goals 123
    leading health indicators 123–124
hedonic 32, 250
helping
    relationships 276–278
high expectations and positive attitudes
    as an external strength 98–99
    communication of 70
hope 91–92, 325
hopefulness 151–152

implementation
    principles 276
    strengths versus deficits approach 274
inclusion
    and the therapeutic recreation process 352–357
    and transition 337, 341–357
    as a therapeutic intervention 349
    definition of 341
    facilitating inclusive environments 275
    fostering inclusivity and diversity 71
    inclusion process 352–357
    NTRS Position Statement on Inclusion 342
    positive outcomes 351–352
    quality indicators 357

rationale 346–347
training staff 354–355, 401
Inclusion U 222, 292
Inclusivity Assessment Tool 222
Individuals with Disabilities Education Act (IDEA) 338, 341
Individualized Education Plan (IEP) 259–261
instructional cue hierarchy 305–306
integration 341, 344
interdisciplinary approach 165–166
interests 66–68, 84–85
International Classification of Functional, Disability and Health
    body function and structure 121–122, 205
    ICF definition of recreation and leisure 123
    ICF checklist 122, 205–206
    participation 122, 205
    role of recreation and leisure 122
interviews
    advantages and disadvantages 196–197
    basic interviewing skills 198
    content, wording, and sequencing 199
    conversational 196–197, 216
    interview guide approach 202–203, 205
    standardized closed-ended 196
    standardized open-ended 196
    strengths-based 209, 211
    typical phases 196–197
interventions
    commonly used in therapeutic recreation 70–72, 326

job titles of a therapeutic recreation specialist 56–57
journals in therapeutic recreation and related areas 226, 421–423

kindness 90, 301

language
    in the strengths approach 22, 172
    person-first 21
    teams' use of 172, 174
    use of "participant" 22
    use of term "therapeutic recreation" 172, 174
learned helplessness 112–113
learned optimism 111–113, 293
Learning Styles Inventory 219
leisure
    assessments 213–218
    asset mapping 222–223
    awareness 215–216
    coaching 291, 293
    coping 116–118
    discovery of aspirations for 67
    education 285
    gratifications 53, 66, 285, 287
    interests 216–218, 290
    key characteristics 30
    knowledge 290–291
    leisure-related knowledge areas 86–88, 290
    performance 86
    rationale 37
    role in strengths versus deficits approach 37–38
    savoring 285
    skills 65, 86–87,
    strengths and resources 203–205, 213, 285
    virtuous 66, 288
Leisure Competence Measure 213, 215–216
Leisure Diagnostic Battery
    areas measured 213, 215
Leisurescope Plus 218
licensure 424–426
lobbying
    definition of 391–392
logic model
    example of 382–383
    inputs 381–384
    outputs 381–384
    processes 381–382, 384
    use of 381–386

mainstreaming 341, 344
MAPS 18, 215–216, 259
meditation 74, 324–325
mindful leisure
    how to facilitate 66, 288
    use of 66
Minimum Data Set (MDS) 209
Miracle Question 211–212, 221
multidisciplinary approach 165–166, 174
multiple intelligences 85–86

natural cues
    and consequences 47, 69
    enhancing 298
nature
    benefits of 325–326
    nature-based activities 325
    strategies for connecting with 325–326
networking 172, 174, 434–435
neuroscience 15–16, 325
normalization
    and social role valorization 124, 127–129
    implications of 124, 129

objectives
    behavior 251-256
    condition 254-255
    criterion or standard 253-255
    measurable 251-255
    SMART 251
observation
    common errors in 199
    how to reduce errors 198-199
    structured 197, 200
    techniques 198-200
opportunities
    for contribution 93, 96
    for participation 93, 96
    to engage in meaningful social roles 71-72
optimism
    cultivating 293
    how to facilitate 69, 296
    learned optimism 111-113, 293
    positive thinking 16, 113
    versus pessimism 112
outcomes
    cognitive 353
    functional 35, 37-39
    health 160
    in the Flourishing through Leisure Model 63, 76, 203
    inclusive recreation 351-353
    leisure 353
    physical 353
    psychological and emotional 353
    social 353
    spiritual 353
Oxford Happiness Questionnaire 190-191, 225

parent-professional partnerships 312
passion
    definition of 85
    Passion Interview 217
    Passion Scale 217
PATH (Planning for Alternative Tomorrows with Hope) 18, 259, 262
Perceived Wellness Survey 225
Person-Activity Fit Diagnostic 218
person-centered movement 160
person-first language 21
Personal Futures Planning 259-260, 262
physical activity 54, 72-73, 219, 319-320
plan
    comprehensive team-based 246
    discipline-specific 247
    types of 246, 259-260

planning
    definition of 237
    link between assessment and planning 239
    principles that guide 240-241
    process 241, 243-244
    rationale 238, 259
play expert 405
positive behavioral supports
    assumptions of 302-303
positive emotions
    portfolios of 295
positive psychology
    resources 25
    theories 109-110
positive reinforcement 306-308
positivity ratio 116, 218
Positivity Self-Test 218
practice wisdom 226
preferences 84-85
principles defined 145
pro bono work 435, 437
profession
    attributes of 414, 422, 435
    definition of 413-414
professional
    organizations 435
    virtues 414-418
professionalism
    definition of 413-414
    limits of 435
progress notes
    content 370-371
    reports 368-369
protective factors
    youth 82, 136, 148

quality assurance and performance improvement 382, 384-385
quality improvement (QI) 382, 384-385
quality of life
    a flourishing life 225
    health-related 35
Quality of Life Model 33-34
Quality of Life Research Unit 33-34
Quality of Life Scale 226-227
quiet spaces 298

record review 195-196
recovery model 17-18
recreation
    as a context in which to build strengths 36-38
    as a strength 81-82

benefits of 102, 348
community resources 68, 73, 92, 95–96, 298, 337
home resources 92, 95–96
interests
    forms of 84–85
preferences
    forms of 84–85
Recreation Inventory for Inclusive Participation 222
referral 369–370
rehabilitation
    community-based 19
reinforcement
    primary 308
    secondary 308
reliability
    coefficient 189
    Cronbach's alpha 189
    definition of 189
    dependability 189–190
    inter-rater 189
    internal consistency 189
    split-half 189
    test-retest 189
reminiscing positive events 298, 301
resiliency
    definition of 138
    in adolescents 137
    in adults 137–138
    in children 137
roles in transdisciplinary approach
    enrichment 170
    exchange 170
    expansion 170
    extension 170
    role release 170
    role support 170

Satisfaction with Life Scale 188, 225
savoring in leisure 53, 65, 285
sea change 11, 19
self-advocacy
    building 393
    conceptual framework 395
    ten concrete steps 397
self-determination
    enhancing through recreation process 48
self-efficacy
    definition of 119–120
    pathways to 119
skills 85–86
SOAP notes 370–371

social capital defined 131–132
social interaction patterns, 280, 283
social model of disability 19, 36, 44, 62–63
social role valorization 127–129
social skills training 301–302
social support
    and friendships 93–95
    identifying supportive individuals and groups 298
    lack of 129
spirituality
    community of worship and meditation 74–75
    meditation 324–325
    practicing 324
standards of practice 182, 238, 424
stigma and social identity 128
strengths
    and virtues 87–89, 297–298, 414–417
    character strengths 87–89, 297–298, 325
    cognitive strengths and resources 298, 300–301
    definition of 81
    external 92–93, 203
    internal 82–83, 203
    physical strengths and resources 203, 222, 319–320
    play, recreation, and leisure 99–100
    psychological and emotional strengths and resources 69, 298
    social strengths and resources 301
    spiritual strengths and resources 325

strengths approach
    biological support for 13–14
    psychological support for 15–16
    social support for 15–16
    theory 108
    versus deficits-based approach 12, 154
supports
    natural 72, 223, 291
    peer 72
Supports Intensity Scale 223–224

talents 85
task analysis 202, 258, 281, 355
taxonomy
    of the affective domain 252–253
    of the cognitive domain 254
    of the psychomotor 252–253
team approaches or models 165
teams
    composition of 160, 164–165
    definition of 159
    in a long-term care agency 209

in a mental health agency 164–165
in a physical rehabilitation agency 164
in an education agency 165
interdisciplinary 166
key members 160, 164, 174
multidisciplinary 164–165, 174
role of circle of support 160–161, 174
role of participant 160–161, 164, 245
role of team members 160–161, 164–165, 168–170, 174
transdisciplinary 167–169, 174

theory
definition of 108

therapeutic recreation
academic definitions 40
definition of 37–42
professional association definitions 39

therapeutic recreation process
deliberate 361, 448
deliver 238–239, 259, 348, 368, 448
discover 186, 448
documentation 367–369, 432
dream and design 265–266, 448
evaluation 50, 355–356, 361–368, 380–385
implementation 273–274, 353, 355
in-depth assessment 194–195, 205
initial assessment 193–196, 239
initial contact 183, 193, 195
planning 237–241, 244, 255, 258–260, 265
referral 193, 352–355, 368–369

therapeutic recreation service models
Aristotelian Good Life Model 46–47
continuum approach 42–47
pitfalls 47–48
The Ecological Model 50
The Flourishing through Leisure Model 63–77
The Health Protection/Health Promotion Model 44–45
integrated models 48–50
The Leisure Ability Model 43–44
The Leisure and Well-Being Model 50–55
The Optimizing Lifelong Health through Therapeutic Recreation Model 49–50
The Self-Determination and Enjoyment Enhancement Model 48–49
Therapeutic Recreation Service Delivery and Outcome Models 45–46

Toronto Quality of Life Profile 226
transdisciplinary
strengths assessment worksheet 213
team approach 165–171

team interview questions 212
teams in rehabilitation 171

transition
and inclusion 341–357
definition of 338
planning 355
planning process 340

United Nations Convention on the Rights of Persons with Disabilities 394, 396
universal design
examples of 323
principles of 321–322

validity
concurrent 187
construct 188
content 187
convergent 188
credibility 189–190
criterion-related 187–188
discriminant 188
face 187
predictive 187–188
social 189

values clarification 325
Values in Action Strengths Assessment 221
virtues
courage 88–90
humanity 90
justice 90–91
temperance 91
transcendence 91–92
wisdom 89

well-being
definition of 31
the "good life" 47
objective 35
six dimensions of 32
subjective 32

WHO Quality of Life Scale 226
World Health Organization
Redefinition of disability 121–123
wraparound services 278–279

OTHER BOOKS FROM VENTURE PUBLISHING, INC.

21st Century Leisure: Current Issues, Second Edition
    by Valeria J. Freysinger and John R. Kelly

Active Living in Older Adulthood: Principles and Practices of Activity Programs
    by Barbara A. Hawkins

Activity Experiences and Programming within Long-Term Care
    by Ted Tedrick and Elaine R. Green

Adventure Programming
    edited by John C. Miles and Simon Priest

Assessment: The Cornerstone of Activity Programs
    by Ruth Perschbacher

Beyond Baskets and Beads: Activities for Older Adults with Functional Impairments
    by Mary Hart, Karen Primm, and Kathy Cranisky

Boredom Busters: Themed Special Events to Dazzle and Delight Your Group
    by Annette C. Moore

Brain Fitness
    by Suzanne Fitzsimmons

Client Assessment in Therapeutic Recreation Services
    by Norma J. Stumbo

Client Outcomes in Therapeutic Recreation Services
    by Norma J. Stumbo

Conceptual Foundations for Therapeutic Recreation
    edited by David R. Austin, John Dattilo, and Bryan P. McCormick

Constraints to Leisure
    edited by Edgar L. Jackson

Dementia Care Programming: An Identity-Focused Approach
    by Rosemary Dunne

Dimensions of Choice: Qualitative Approaches to Parks, Recreation, Tourism, Sport, and Leisure Research, Second Edition
    by Karla A. Henderson

Diversity and the Recreation Profession: Organizational Perspectives, Revised Edition
    edited by Maria T. Allison and Ingrid E. Schneider

Effective Management in Therapeutic Recreation Service, Second Edition
    by Marcia Jean Carter and Gerald S. O'Morrow

Evaluating Leisure Services: Making Enlightened Decisions, Third Edition
    by Karla A. Henderson and M. Deborah Bialeschki

Everything from A to Y: The Zest Is up to You! Older Adult Activities for Every Day of the Year
    by Nancy R. Cheshire and Martha L. Kenney

Experience Marketing: Strategies for the New Millennium
    by Ellen L. O'Sullivan and Kathy J. Spangler

Facilitation of Therapeutic Recreation Services: An Evidence-Based and Best Practice Approach to Techniques and Processes
    edited by Norma J. Stumbo and Brad Wardlaw

Facilitation Techniques in Therapeutic Recreation, Second Edition
    by John Dattilo and Alexis McKenney

File o' Fun: A Recreation Planner for Games & Activities, Third Edition
    by Jane Harris Ericson and Diane Ruth Albright

Getting People Involved in Life and Activities: Effective Motivating Techniques
    by Jeanne Adams

Health Promotion for Mind, Body, and Spirit
    by Suzanne Fitzsimmons and Linda L. Buettner

Human Resource Management in Recreation, Sport, and Leisure Services
    by Margaret Arnold, Regina Glover, and Cheryl Beeler

Inclusion: Including People With Disabilities in Parks and Recreation Opportunities
  by Lynn Anderson and Carla Brown Kress

Inclusive Leisure Services, Third Edition
  by John Dattilo

Internships in Recreation and Leisure Services: A Practical Guide for Students, Fifth Edition
  by Edward E. Seagle, Jr., Ralph W. Smith, and Tammy B. Smith

Interpretation of Cultural and Natural Resources, Second Edition
  by Douglas M. Knudson, Ted T. Cable, and Larry Beck

Intervention Activities for At-Risk Youth
  by Norma J. Stumbo

Introduction to Outdoor Recreation: Providing and Managing Resource Based Opportunities
  by Roger L. Moore and B.L. Driver

Introduction to Recreation and Leisure Services, Eighth Edition
  by Karla A. Henderson, M. Deborah Bialeschki, John L. Hemingway, Jan S. Hodges, Beth D. Kivel, and H. Douglas Sessoms

Introduction to Therapeutic Recreation: U.S. and Canadian Perspectives
  by Kenneth Mobily and Lisa Ostiguy

An Introduction to Tourism
  by Robert W. Wyllie

Introduction to Writing Goals and Objectives: A Manual for Recreation Therapy Students and Entry-Level Professionals
  by Suzanne Melcher

Leadership and Administration of Outdoor Pursuits, Third Edition
  by James Blanchard, Michael Strong, and Phyllis Ford

Leadership in Leisure Services: Making a Difference, Third Edition
  by Debra J. Jordan

Leisure and Leisure Services in the 21st Century: Toward Mid Century
  by Geoffrey Godbey

The Leisure Diagnostic Battery Computer Software (CD)
  by Peter A. Witt, Gary Ellis, and Mark A. Widmer

Leisure Education I: A Manual of Activities and Resources, Second Edition
  by Norma J. Stumbo

Leisure Education II: More Activities and Resources, Second Edition
  by Norma J. Stumbo

Leisure Education III: More Goal-Oriented Activities
  by Norma J. Stumbo

Leisure Education IV: Activities for Individuals with Substance Addictions
  by Norma J. Stumbo

Leisure Education Program Planning: A Systematic Approach, Third Edition
  by John Dattilo

Leisure for Canadians
  edited by Ron McCarville and Kelly MacKay

Leisure, Health, and Wellness: Making the Connections
  edited by Laura Payne, Barbara Ainsworth, and Geoffrey Godbey

Leisure Studies: Prospects for the Twenty-First Century
  edited by Edgar L. Jackson and Thomas L. Burton

Leisure in Your Life: New Perspectives
  by Geoffrey Godbey

Making a Difference in Academic Life: A Handbook for Park, Recreation, and Tourism Educators and Graduate Students
  edited by Dan Dustin and Tom Goodale

Managing to Optimize the Beneficial Outcomes of Leisure
  edited by B. L. Driver

Marketing in Leisure and Tourism: Reaching New Heights
  by Patricia Click Janes

More Than a Game: A New Focus on Senior Activity Services
    by Brenda Corbett

The Multiple Values of Wilderness
    by H. Ken Cordell, John C. Bergstrom, and J. M. Bowker

N.E.S.T. Approach: Dementia Practice Guidelines for Disturbing Behaviors
    by Linda L. Buettner and Suzanne Fitzsimmons

The Organizational Basis of Leisure Participation: A Motivational Exploration
    by Robert A. Stebbins

Outdoor Recreation for 21st Century America
    by H. Ken Cordell

Parks for Life: Moving the Goal Posts, Changing the Rules, and Expanding the Field
    by Will LaPage

The Pivotal Role of Leisure Education: Finding Personal Fulfillment in This Century
    edited by Elie Cohen-Gewerc and Robert A. Stebbins

Planning and Organizing Group Activities in Social Recreation
    by John V. Valentine

Planning Areas and Facilities for Sport and Recreation: Predesign Process, Principles, and Strategies
    by Jack A. Harper

Planning Parks for People, Second Edition
    by John Hultsman, Richard L. Cottrell, and Wendy Z. Hultsman

Programming for Parks, Recreation, and Leisure Services: A Servant Leadership Approach, Third Edition
    by Donald G. DeGraaf, Debra J. Jordan, and Kathy H. DeGraaf

Puttin' on the Skits: Plays for Adults in Managed Care
    by Jean Vetter

Recreation and Leisure: Issues in an Era of Change, Third Edition
    edited by Thomas Goodale and Peter A. Witt

Recreation and Youth Development
    by Peter A. Witt and Linda L. Caldwell

Recreation for Older Adults: Individual and Group Activities
    by Judith A. Elliott and Jerold E. Elliott

Recreation Program Planning Manual for Older Adults
    by Karen Kindrachuk

Recreation Programming and Activities for Older Adults
    by Jerold E. Elliott and Judith A. Sorg-Elliott

Reference Manual for Writing Rehabilitation Therapy Treatment Plans
    by Penny Hogberg and Mary Johnson

Service Living: Building Community through Public Parks and Recreation
    by Doug Wellman, Dan Dustin, Karla Henderson, and Roger Moore

Simple Expressions: Creative and Therapeutic Arts for the Elderly in Long-Term Care Facilities
    by Vicki Parsons

A Social Psychology of Leisure, Second Edition
    by Douglas A. Kleiber, Gordon J. Walker, and Roger C. Mannell

Special Events and Festivals: How to Organize, Plan, and Implement
    by Angie Prosser and Ashli Rutledge

The Sportsman's Voice: Hunting and Fishing in America
    by Mark Damian Duda, Martin F. Jones, and Andrea Criscione

Survey Research and Analysis: Applications in Parks, Recreation, and Human Dimensions
    by Jerry Vaske

Taking the Initiative: Activities to Enhance Effectiveness and Promote Fun
    by J. P. Witman

Therapeutic Recreation and the Nature of Disabilities
    by Kenneth E. Mobily and Richard D. MacNeil

Therapeutic Recreation: Cases and Exercises, Second Edition
  by Barbara C. Wilhite and M. Jean Keller

Therapeutic Recreation in Health Promotion and Rehabilitation
  by John Shank and Catherine Coyle

Therapeutic Recreation in the Nursing Home
  by Linda Buettner and Shelley L. Martin

Therapeutic Recreation Programming: Theory and Practice
  by Charles Sylvester, Judith E. Voelkl, and Gary D. Ellis

Therapeutic Recreation Protocol for Treatment of Substance Addictions
  by Rozanne W. Faulkner

The Therapeutic Recreation Stress Management Primer
  by Cynthia Mascott

Traditions: Improving Quality of Life in Caregiving
  by Janelle Sellick

Trivia by the Dozen: Encouraging Interaction and Reminiscence in Managed Care
  by Jean Vetter